McDougal Littell

BRIDGES TO
LITERATURE

Teacher's Edition
Level III

McDougal Littell
A HOUGHTON MIFFLIN COMPANY
Evanston, Illinois • Boston • Dallas

INCLUDES SKILLBUILDER COPYMASTERS FOR
READING • LITERATURE • VOCABULARY

Author

Jane Greene Literacy Intervention Specialist; Reading, Writing, Language, Evaluation Consultant to schools nationwide; author of *LANGUAGE! A Literacy Intervention Curriculum.* Dr. Greene established the underlying goals and philosophy, advised on the tables of contents, reviewed prototypes, and supervised the development of the assessment strand.

English Language Advisor

Judy Lewis Director, State and Federal Programs for reading proficiency and high-risk populations, Folsom, California; Editor, *Context,* a newsletter for teachers with English learners in their classes. Ms. Lewis reviewed selections for the program and provided special guidance on the development of EL notes.

Consultant

Olga Bautista Reading Facilitator, Will C. Wood Middle School, Sacramento, California. Ms. Bautista provided advice on reading, pacing, and EL instruction during the development phase and reviewed final prototypes of both the Pupil Edition and Teacher's Edition.

ISBN 0-618-11888-8

2 3 4 5 6 7 8 9 – BMW – 05 04 03 02

Teacher Panel

Katherine S. Barg, Teacher
Central Middle School
San Carlos, California

Claudette Burk, English Department Chairperson
Tetzlaff Middle School
Cerritos, California

Susan Busenius, Core Teacher
Valley View School
Pleasanthill, California

Deborah Dei Rossi, Teacher
Cunha Intermediate School
Half Moon Bay, California

Lana Fenech, Teacher, Technology Coordinator
Borel Middle School
San Mateo, California

Joy Martineau, Language Arts Teacher
Warner Middle School
Westminster, California

Annie Muchnick, Literacy Coach
Garvey School
Rosemead, California

Joanne Nash, English Teacher
Sunnyvale Middle School
Sunnyvale, California

Patricia Radotich, Teacher
Woodbridge Middle School
Woodbridge, California

Frances Rubin, English Teacher
Emerson Middle School
Los Angeles, California

Sue Sermeno, Grade Level Coordinator
North Park Middle School
Pico Rivera, California

Margaret Williams, English Language Arts Chairperson
Carmenita Middle School
Cerritos, California

Teacher Reviewers

Lillie Alfred, Teacher
Altgeld School
Chicago, Illinois

Tracy Arrington, Teacher
George W. Curtis School
Chicago, Illinois

Stephanie Gates, Teacher
Miriam G. Canter Middle School
Chicago, Illinois

Regina Gooden-Hampton, Teacher
Kipling Elementary School
Chicago, Illinois

Student Reviewers

Aunyetta Crosby, Detroit, Michigan

Phimy Danh, Long Beach, California

Julie Daniels, Sacramento, California

Maria Fraga, Sacramento, California

Eduardo Obeso, Detroit, Michigan

Erik Quirk, Encinitas, California

Michael Roett, Tallahassee, Florida

Michelle Schmitt, Tallahassee, Florida

Barbara Schwenk, Weston, Massachusetts

Renee Sevier, Long Beach, California

Shane, Lincoln, Massachusetts

Dr. Jane F. Greene

BUILDING BRIDGES: CLOSING THE READING GAP

THE PROBLEM

Current literacy statistics tell a sad tale: according to the most recent report of the National Assessment of Educational Progress (NAEP), 38 percent of fourth-grade students and 26 percent of eighth-grade students are reading at a "below basic" level of achievement. That is, they have little or no mastery of the skills necessary to perform work at each grade level.

The problem continues, of course, as students move into the upper grades. Significant numbers of high school students are reading well below grade level, and legions are unable to access their textbooks or to learn independently by reading. In other words, many students are in real danger of never being able to fully access all the information that will be crucial to their success in school and in the workplace.

CONFUSING LITERACY WITH LITERATURE

There are many reasons for the growing numbers of struggling readers. But one development seems to have had a very strong impact on reading skills: During the last quarter of the twentieth century, reading instruction in the United States gradually shifted in focus from literacy to literature. And therein lies the problem: literature and literacy are two very different things.

Literature Isn't Literacy. Literature is a subject that students can study as they are becoming more and more literate. Literacy, on the other hand, requires a lengthy developmental process of maturing and seasoning facility with the written word. Literacy comprises a synergistic array of abilities in many areas, including the following:

1. development of phonological awareness

2. decoding and encoding at the level of automaticity

3. accessing a broad and rich vocabulary

4. understanding basic premises of nonfiction and fiction

5. thinking beyond the words of the text itself, through more and more sophisticated higher level thinking skills

6. developing sensitivity to and comprehension of levels of language, tone, voice, and a wide array of literary devices employed by myriad writers

In recent decades, however, teachers have been directed not to focus on some of these skills directly. Instead, they were told that the skills would come "naturally" to children immersed in literature.

But students who have not learned the times tables cannot do fractions, and students who have not mastered basic decoding, vocabulary, and comprehension skills cannot read Baldwin, Shakespeare, Poe, or Soto. So, as a result of the methodologies employed during the last quarter-century, many students never developed the abilities they needed to access increasingly difficult materials. And as they moved up in grade level, these students fell farther and farther behind—until they became the "nonreaders" many middle school and high school teachers now encounter in their English classrooms.

The point is this: no matter how much a teacher wants them to read grade-level textbooks, these students simply can't. And even though we have tried to provide alternative means for some of these students to gain credit—watch and discuss a video, participate in a play, create a diorama or a poster—we also know that these tasks do not result in an improvement in reading or writing or spelling; they do nothing to increase literacy. So what do we do?

HELPING DELAYED READERS

The challenge of how to help delayed readers may seem daunting. After all, most middle school and high school teachers were not trained to teach reading. They were trained to teach literature, language, and composition, but never to initiate the reading process. Our students, however, through their frustration and their lack of success, are pleading with us to rethink these assumptions and help them. And this is not as difficult as it may seem.

The first step we need to take is to become clear about what delayed readers need. There really are no surprises here. Delayed readers need

- abundant practice in reading materials at their own instructional levels
- direct instruction in fundamental reading skills
- direct teaching of vocabulary, morphology, and comprehension
- reading materials that move them along the developmental reading continuum, based on the difficulty level of the selections

Time is also a critical factor in helping delayed readers. Students who are delayed by more than two years in reading development cannot make up that difference in one year. In fact, these students typically regress on each year's standardized tests if they are not given the opportunity to participate in accelerated reading intervention: direct instruction in skills basic to development in reading. In other words, if we fail to provide them with some kind of intervention, students who are significantly behind are guaranteed to remain behind.

Finally, students who are significantly delayed need abundant time on task in an accelerated intervention setting. Accelerated intervention does not, however, mean a return to the days of tracking. Tracking meant isolating struggling readers in separate classrooms and feeding them a diet of watered-down curricula and low expectations. Instead, accelerated intervention means identifying the students' achievement levels and providing the students with the right materials to facilitate their growth.

THE ROLE OF *BRIDGES TO LITERATURE*

Many high-interest, low-vocabulary reading materials are available to the teacher who is attempting to address the needs of delayed readers. However, these materials are far from adequate for the purpose. In order to actively help their students make the transition from decoding text to reading literature and other on-level texts, to truly prepare students to transition into the traditional literature classroom, teachers need more than the simplistic, easily decodable stories that hi-lo materials provide. Teachers need

- student-appropriate selections accompanied by the development of vocabulary and comprehension skills
- a rich array of literature and nonfiction genres that provide the way to introduce students to the academic language and concepts of literature
- a means of exposing students to the authors, stories, and themes that lead to cultural literacy
- tools to measure their students' gains in reading

This series, *Bridges to Literature,* was created to meet all these needs. The section on pages vii–xiv will tell you how it accomplishes its goals.

REFERENCES

Adams, M.J. (1990). *Beginning to Read: Thinking and Learning About Print.* Cambridge, MA: MIT Press.

Beck, I.L., Perfett, C.A., & McKeown, M.B. (1982). Effects of long-term vocabulary instruction on lexical access and reading comprehension. *Journal of Educational Psychology,* 74(4), 506–521.

Chall, J. (1983). *Stages of Reading Development.* New York: McGraw-Hill.

Glenn, C.L. (1997). A review of the National Research Council study *Improving Schooling for Language Minority Children: A Research Agenda. READ Abstracts.* Amherst, MA: The Institute for Research in English Acquisition and Development.

Kaméenui, E., Carnine, D., & Freschi, R. (1982). Effects of text construction and instructional procedures for teaching word meanings on comprehension and recall. *Reading Research Quarterly,* 17(3), 367–388.

Lyon, G.R. (1998). Why reading is not a natural process. *Educational Leadership,* 55(6), 14–18.

Moats, L. (1995). The missing foundation in teacher education. *American Educator,* 19(2), 9+43–51.

United States Department of Education (1995). National Assessment of Educational Progress.

WHAT IS BRIDGES?

Bridges to Literature can actually be considered three programs in one:

- **a leveled reading series,**
- **a course in reading comprehension and vocabulary building,**
- **an introduction to literature.**

It is designed to meet the needs of delayed readers—students who cannot access the traditional language arts curriculum. By providing them with on-level instruction and accessible, high-interest selections, *Bridges* allows these students to make a smooth, comfortable transition from basic reading instruction to on-level literature study.

A LEVELED READING SERIES.

BRIDGES comprises three volumes that include selections at the following readability levels:

Level I	3rd grade to low 4th grade
Level II	4th grade to low 5th grade
Level III	5th grade to low 6th grade

EACH VOLUME CONTAINS

- Twelve units organized by genre, theme, or both
- Readable, high interest selections that gradually increase in difficulty
- A mix of classic tales, contemporary stories, and rich nonfiction
- Bridges to History: Selections tied to the social studies curriculum
- Reader's Choice: Longer selections for independent reading

1 FICTION **Not According to Plan**

2 NONFICTION **Courage Counts**

3 MIXED GENRES **We Are Family**

4 DRAMA **Who's in Charge?**

5 POETRY **Special Places**

6 MIXED GENRES **The Battle Is On!**

7 FICTION **Decisions Don't Come Easily**

8 NONFICTION **Hard to Believe**

9 MIXED GENRES **Making Adjustments**

10 POETRY **Appearances Can Fool You**

11 MIXED GENRES **Bridges to History**

12 READER'S CHOICE **Longer Selections for Independent Reading**

A COURSE IN READING COMPREHENSION, VOCABULARY BUILDING, AND LITERATURE

Developing readers need to learn a variety of key concepts, skills, and strategies if they are to grow as readers and learn to manage more complex literature. *Bridges to Literature* includes the following support to help them achieve this goal.

- Prereading activities that help students connect to the literature
- Instruction in on-level literature concepts and skills
- A preview of key vocabulary terms

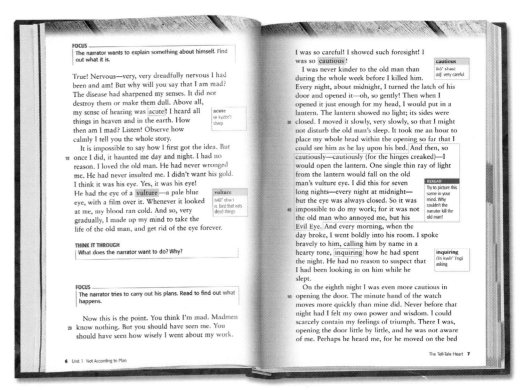

- Purpose-setting guides
- Selections broken into manageable "chunks"
- Reading and Comprehension guides—*Focus, Reread,* and *Think It Through*—help students apply the strategies of a good reader.
- Point-of-use vocabulary help

HOW DO I KNOW WHAT TO DO?
The Teacher's Edition will guide you. . .

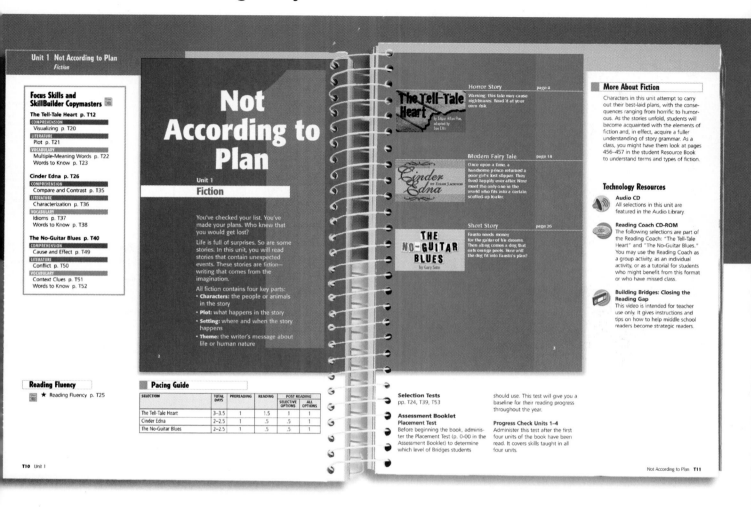

UNIT OPENER

This concise overview provides you with the information you need to begin planning each unit of study.

Focus Skills

Here you will find a list of the focus skills for each selection, along with corresponding copymasters.

Pacing Guide

Use this chart to get a sense of the time needed to cover each selection.

More About. . .

This information will help you introduce the genre or theme to your students.

Technology

Use the technology pieces listed here to ensure that you make the most of every lesson. See page xiv for a detailed description of these components.

Assessment

These assessment tools will help you monitor student progress and adjust instruction.

More support for each selection!

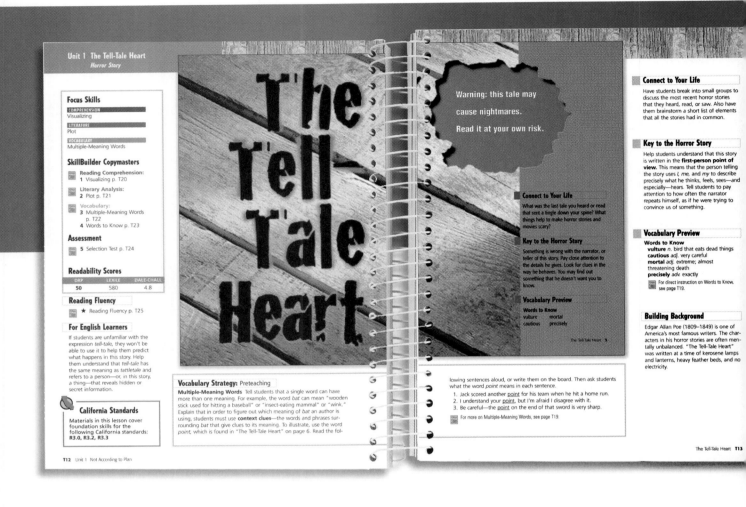

LESSON OPENER

Use this page to plan specific lessons. Take advantage of these lesson objectives, teaching tips, and ideas for introducing the selection to your students.

Focus Skills

Specific focus skills are presented in three strands: Comprehension, Literature, and Vocabulary. Use the accompanying copymasters to enhance instruction of each skill.

Readability Scores

Scores are provided for three readability formulas. Selections are arranged in order of increasing difficulty, as indicated by their DRP® (Degrees of Reading Power) scores.

Reading Fluency

Use this copymaster to help students improve fluency, and for use in informal assessment.

For English Learners

Use these specific tips to help English learners understand unfamiliar words, phrases, and cultural references.

Prereading Activities

The following features help you introduce and preteach the selection:
- Connect to Your Life
- Key to the Short Story
- Building Background
- Vocabulary Strategy

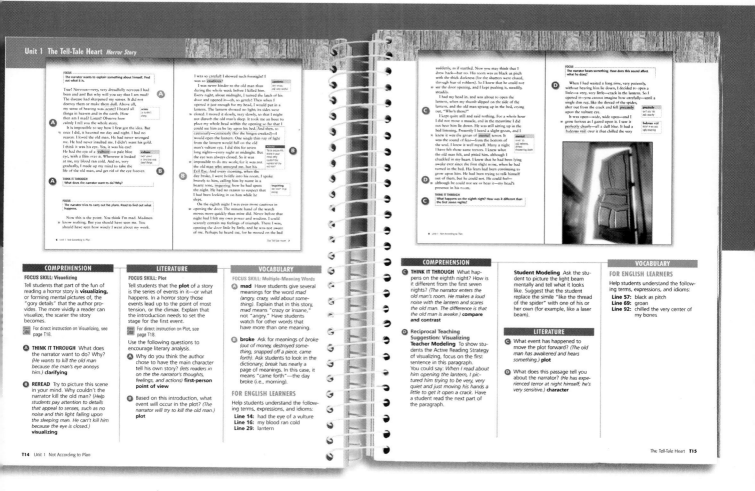

GUIDED READING

The teacher notes on these pages help you guide your students through the selection and introduce them to important skills. Color-coding clearly indicates the following three skill strands

- ● **Comprehension**
- ● **Literature**
- ● Vocabulary

These teacher notes provide you with

- explicit instruction for focus skills
- answers to embedded reading questions
- optional speaking and listening activities
- tips for modeling and reciprocal teaching
- help for English learners

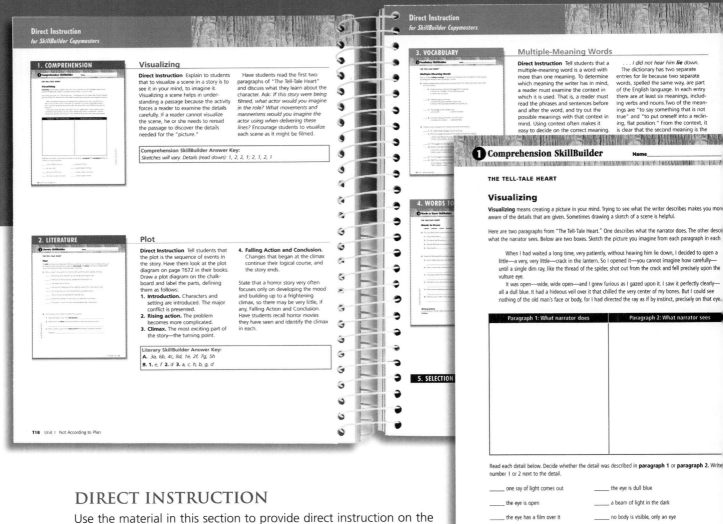

DIRECT INSTRUCTION

Use the material in this section to provide direct instruction on the focus skills introduced in the selection.

- Teaching guides to help you explain skills and concepts clearly to students.

- Copymasters for student practice of each skill
  Comprehension Skills
  Literature Skills
  Vocabulary Skills
  Words to Know

- Answer Key for each copymaster

HOW DO I MONITOR PROGRESS?
A variety of assessment options give you the right tools.

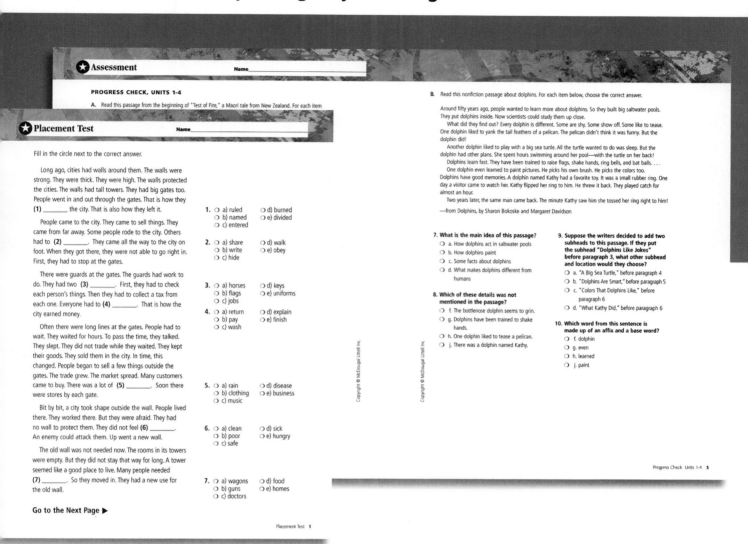

ASSESSMENT

The Assessment Booklet offers many tools that you can use to place students in correct materials, monitor their growth as readers, and assess their understanding of skills and concepts. Use these tools throughout the year to help you evaluate student progress and adjust instruction as needed.

In addition, the Teacher's Edition offers both fluency checks and selection tests to allow ongoing assessment as students move through the selections.

Included in the Assessment Booklet
Reading Tests: The following tests allow you to determine your students' approximate reading level and then check their growth throughout the year.
- Placement Test
- Mid-Year Reading Test
- End-of-Year Reading Test

Concept and Skill Assessment: Three *Progress Checks,* which offer students new selections to read and respond to, are included for use after Units 4, 8, and 12. These tests will help you determine how well students have understood the skills and concepts that have been introduced in the book.

WHAT TECHNOLOGY CAN I USE?

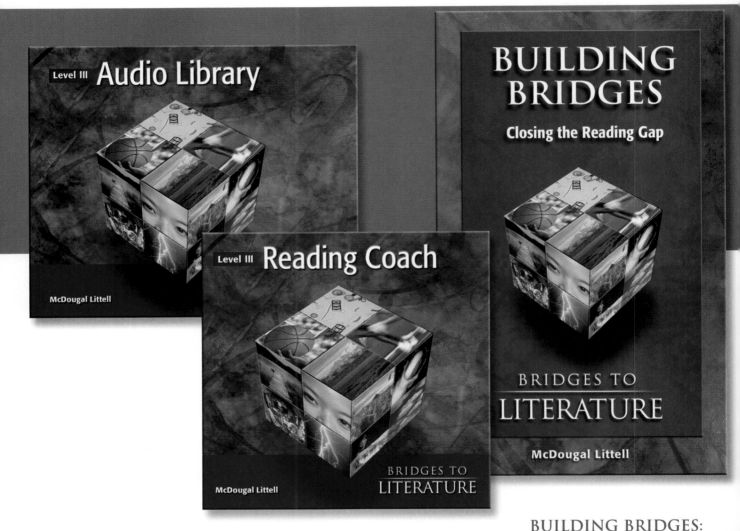

AUDIO CD

Selections from *Bridges to Literature* are available on audio CDs and allow your students to

- hear pronunciation, phrasing, and interpretation
- access the text more easily
- catch up if they have missed reading and discussion in class

READING COACH

This interactive CD-ROM is an electronic version of *Bridges to Literature.* Your students can use this exciting tool to

- read selections online, chunked as in the text
- respond to questions using electronic sticky notes
- highlight text electronically
- record their responses in an electronic notebook
- hear vocabulary words pronounced in English and in Spanish
- see and hear vocabulary definitions

BUILDING BRIDGES: CLOSING THE READING GAP

This 25-minute professional development video shows specific ways you as a teacher can help struggling reade It provides solutions to problems and shows, rather than tells, how you can improve reading comprehension in a heterogeneous classroom.

TABLE OF CONTENTS
Teacher's Edition Table of Contents
with Correlation to Pupil Edition and Technology

BRIDGES TO
LITERATURE

McDougal Littell
A HOUGHTON MIFFLIN COMPANY
Evanston, Illinois • Boston • Dallas

READING • LITERATURE • VOCABULARY

Author

Jane Greene Literacy Intervention Specialist; Reading, Writing, Language, Evaluation Consultant to schools nationwide; author of *LANGUAGE! A Literacy Intervention Curriculum.* Dr. Greene established the underlying goals and philosophy, advised on the tables of contents, reviewed prototypes, and supervised the development of the assessment strand.

English Language Advisor

Judy Lewis Director, State and Federal Programs for reading proficiency and high-risk populations, Folsom, California; Editor, *Context,* a newsletter for teachers with English learners in their classes. Ms. Lewis reviewed selections for the program and provided special guidance on the development of EL notes.

Consultant

Olga Bautista Reading Facilitator, Will C. Wood Middle School, Sacramento, California. Ms. Bautista provided advice on reading, pacing, and EL instruction during the development phase and reviewed final prototypes of both the Pupil Edition and Teacher's Edition.

ISBN 0-618–08735-4

Teacher Panel

Katherine S. Barg, Teacher
Central Middle School
San Carlos, California

Claudette Burk, English Department Chairperson
Tetzlaff Middle School
Cerritos, California

Susan Busenius, Core Teacher
Valley View School
Pleasanthill, California

Deborah Dei Rossi, Teacher
Cunha Intermediate School
Half Moon Bay, California

Lana Fenech, Teacher, Technology Coordinator
Borel Middle School
San Mateo, California

Joy Martineau, Language Arts Teacher
Warner Middle School
Westminster, California

Annie Muchnick, Literacy Coach
Garvey School
Rosemead, California

Joanne Nash, English Teacher
Sunnyvale Middle School
Sunnyvale, California

Patricia Radotich, Teacher
Woodbridge Middle School
Woodbridge, California

Frances Rubin, English Teacher
Emerson Middle School
Los Angeles, California

Sue Sermeno, Grade Level Coordinator
North Park Middle School
Pico Rivera, California

Margaret Williams, English Language Arts
  Chairperson
Carmenita Middle School
Cerritos, California

Teacher Reviewers

Lillie Alfred, Teacher
Altgeld School
Chicago, Illinois

Tracy Arrington, Teacher
George W. Curtis School
Chicago, Illinois

Stephanie Gates, Teacher
Miriam G. Canter Middle School
Chicago, Illinois

Regina Gooden-Hampton, Teacher
Kipling Elementary School
Chicago, Illinois

Student Reviewers

Aunyetta Crosby, Detroit, Michigan

Phimy Danh, Long Beach, California

Julie Daniels, Sacramento, California

Maria Fraga, Sacramento, California

Eduardo Obeso, Detroit, Michigan

Erik Quirk, Encinitas, California

Michael Roett, Tallahassee, Florida

Michelle Schmitt, Tallahassee, Florida

Barbara Schwenk, Weston, Massachusetts

Renee Sevier, Long Beach, California

Shane, Lincoln, Massachusetts

BRIDGES TO
LITERATURE
Level III

Reader's Choice LONGER SELECTIONS FOR INDEPENDENT READING

Student Resources

Some selections available on the Reading Coach CD-ROM

Focus Skills and SkillBuilder Copymasters

The Tell-Tale Heart p. T12

COMPREHENSION
Visualizing p. T20

LITERATURE
Plot p. T21

VOCABULARY
Multiple-Meaning Words p. T22
Words to Know p. T23

Cinder Edna p. T26

COMPREHENSION
Compare and Contrast p. T35

LITERATURE
Characterization p. T36

VOCABULARY
Idioms p. T37
Words to Know p. T38

The No-Guitar Blues p. T40

COMPREHENSION
Cause and Effect p. T49

LITERATURE
Conflict p. T50

VOCABULARY
Context Clues p. T51
Words to Know p. T52

Reading Fluency

 ★ Reading Fluency p. T25

Not According to Plan

Unit 1

Fiction

You've checked your list. You've made your plans. Who knew that you would get lost?

Life is full of surprises. So are some stories. In this unit, you will read stories that contain unexpected events. These stories are fiction— writing that comes from the imagination.

All fiction contains four key parts:
- **Characters:** the people or animals in the story
- **Plot:** what happens in the story
- **Setting:** where and when the story happens
- **Theme:** the writer's message about life or human nature

2

Pacing Guide

SELECTION	TOTAL DAYS	PREREADING	READING	POST READING	
				SELECTIVE OPTIONS	ALL OPTIONS
The Tell-Tale Heart	3–3.5	1	1.5	1	1
Cinder Edna	2–2.5	1	.5	.5	1
The No-Guitar Blues	2–2.5	1	.5	.5	1

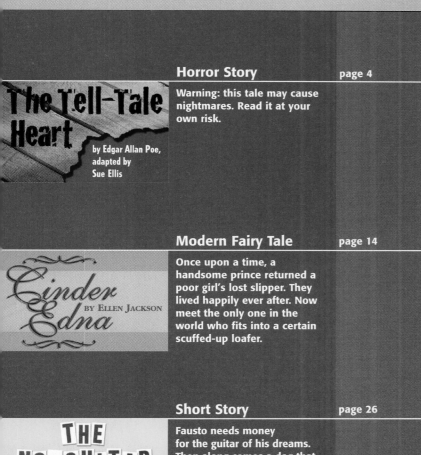

3

More About Fiction

Characters in this unit attempt to carry out their best-laid plans, with the consequences ranging from horrific to humorous. As the stories unfold, students will become acquainted with the elements of fiction and, in effect, acquire a fuller understanding of story grammar. You might have them look, as a class, at pages 456–457 in the Student Resources section to understand terms and types of fiction.

Technology Resources

Audio CD
All selections in this unit are featured in the Audio Library.

Reading Coach CD-ROM
The following selections are part of the Reading Coach: "The Tell-Tale Heart" and "The No-Guitar Blues." You may use Reading Coach selections as a group activity, as an individual activity, or as a tutorial for students who might benefit from this format or who have missed class.

Building Bridges: Closing the Reading Gap
This video is intended for teacher use only. It gives instructions and tips on how to help middle school readers become strategic readers.

Assessment

Selection Tests
pp. T24, T39, T53

Assessment Booklet
Placement Test
Before beginning the book, administer the Placement Test (pp. 5–12 in the Assessment Booklet) to determine which level of Bridges students should use. This test will give you a baseline for their reading progress throughout the year.

Progress Check Units 1–4
Administer this test after the first four units of the book have been read. It covers skills taught in all four units.

Focus Skills

COMPREHENSION
Visualizing

LITERATURE
Plot

VOCABULARY
Multiple-Meaning Words

SkillBuilder Copymasters

 Reading Comprehension:
1 Visualizing p. T20

 Literary Analysis:
2 Plot p. T21

 Vocabulary:
3 Multiple-Meaning Words p. T22
4 Words to Know p. T23

Assessment

 5 Selection Test p. T24

Readability Scores

DRP	LEXILE	DALE-CHALL
50	580	4.8

Reading Fluency

 ★ Reading Fluency p. T25

For English Learners

If students are unfamiliar with the expression *tell-tale,* they won't be able to use it to help them predict what happens in this story. Help them understand that *tell-tale* has the same meaning as *tattletale* and refers to a person—or, in this story, a thing—that reveals hidden or secret information.

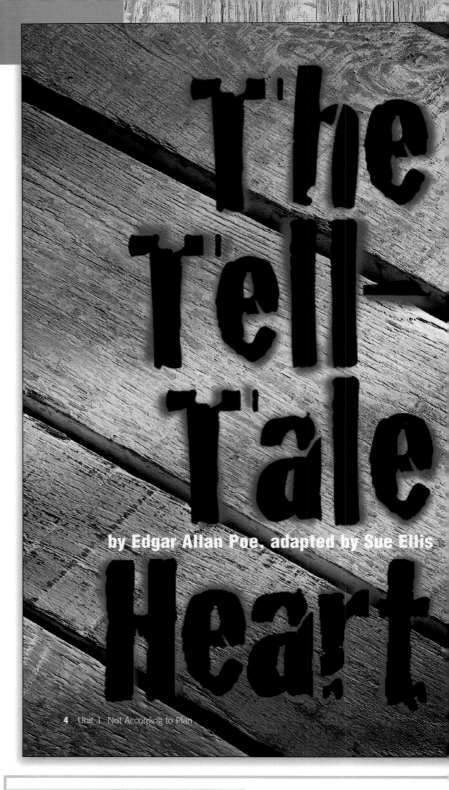

by Edgar Allan Poe, adapted by Sue Ellis

4 Unit 1 Not According to Plan

Vocabulary Strategy: Preteaching

Multiple-Meaning Words Tell students that a single word can have more than one meaning. For example, the word *bat* can mean "wooden stick used for hitting a baseball" or "insect-eating mammal" or "wink." Explain that in order to figure out which meaning of *bat* an author is using, students must use **context clues**—the words and phrases surrounding *bat* that give clues to its meaning. To illustrate, use the word *point,* which is found in "The Tell-Tale Heart" on page 6. Read the fol-

Warning: This tale may cause nightmares. Read it at your own risk.

Connect to Your Life

What was the last tale you heard or read that sent a tingle down your spine? What things help to make horror stories and movies scary?

Key to the Horror Story

Something is wrong with the narrator, or teller of this story. Pay close attention to the details he gives. Look for clues in the way he behaves. You may find out something that he doesn't want you to know.

Vocabulary Preview

Words to Know

vulture   mortal
cautious   precisely

 Reading Coach CD-ROM selection

Connect to Your Life

Have students break into small groups to discuss the most recent horror stories that they heard, read, or saw. Also have them brainstorm a short list of elements that all the stories had in common.

Key to the Horror Story

Help students understand that this story is written in the **first-person point of view.** This means that the person telling the story uses *I, me,* and *my* to describe precisely what he thinks, feels, sees—and especially—hears. Tell students to pay attention to how often the narrator repeats himself, as if he were trying to convince us of something.

Vocabulary Preview

Words to Know
vulture *n.* bird that eats dead things
cautious *adj.* very careful
mortal *adj.* extreme; almost threatening death
precisely *adv.* exactly

For direct instruction on Words to Know, see page T19.

Building Background

Edgar Allan Poe (1809–1849) is one of America's most famous writers. The characters in his horror stories are often mentally unbalanced. "The Tell-Tale Heart" was written at a time of kerosene lamps and lanterns, heavy feather beds, and no electricity.

lowing sentences aloud, or write them on the board. Then ask students what the word *point* means in each sentence.

1. Jack scored another <u>point</u> for his team when he hit a home run.
2. I understand your <u>point</u>, but I'm afraid I disagree with it.
3. Be careful—the <u>point</u> on the end of that sword is very sharp.

 For more on Multiple-Meaning Words, see page T19.

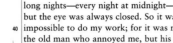

FOCUS
The narrator wants to explain something about himself. Find out what it is.

True! Nervous—very, very dreadfully nervous I had been and am! But why will you say that I am mad? The disease had sharpened my senses. It did not destroy them or make them dull. Above all, my sense of hearing was acute! I heard all things in heaven and in the earth. How then am I mad? Listen! Observe how calmly I tell you the whole story.

> **acute**
> (ə kyōōt')
> sharp

10   It is impossible to say how I first got the idea. But once I did, it haunted me day and night. I had no reason. I loved the old man. He had never wronged me. He had never insulted me. I didn't want his gold. I think it was his eye. Yes, it was his eye! He had the eye of a vulture—a pale blue eye, with a film over it. Whenever it looked at me, my blood ran cold. And so, very gradually, I made up my mind to take the life of the old man, and get rid of the eye forever.

> **vulture**
> (vŭl' chər)
> *n.* bird that eats dead things

THINK IT THROUGH
What does the narrator want to do? Why?

FOCUS
The narrator tries to carry out his plans. Read to find out what happens.

Now this is the point. You think I'm mad. Madmen 20 know nothing. But you should have seen me. You should have seen how wisely I went about my work.

6   Unit 1   Not According to Plan

I was so careful! I showed such foresight! I was so cautious!

> **cautious**
> (kô' shəs)
> *adj.* very careful

    I was never kinder to the old man than during the whole week before I killed him. Every night, about midnight, I turned the latch of his door and opened it—oh, so gently! Then when I opened it just enough for my head, I would put in a lantern. The lantern showed no light; its sides were 30 closed. I moved it slowly, very slowly, so that I might not disturb the old man's sleep. It took me an hour to place my whole head within the opening so far that I could see him as he lay upon his bed. And then, so cautiously—cautiously (for the hinges creaked)—I would open the lantern. One single thin ray of light from the lantern would fall on the old man's vulture eye. I did this for seven long nights—every night at midnight— but the eye was always closed. So it was 40 impossible to do my work; for it was not the old man who annoyed me, but his Evil Eye. And every morning, when the day broke, I went boldly into his room. I spoke bravely to him, calling him by name in a hearty tone, inquiring how he had spent the night. He had no reason to suspect that I had been looking in on him while he slept.

> **REREAD**
> Try to picture this scene in your mind. Why couldn't the narrator kill the old man?

> **inquiring**
> (ĭn kwīr' ĭng)
> asking

    On the eighth night I was even more cautious in 50 opening the door. The minute hand of the watch moves more quickly than mine did. Never before that night had I felt my own power and wisdom. I could scarcely contain my feelings of triumph. There I was, opening the door little by little, and he was not aware of me. Perhaps he heard me, for he moved on the bed

The Tell-Tale Heart   7

COMPREHENSION

FOCUS SKILL: Visualizing

Tell students that part of the fun of reading a horror story is **visualizing,** or forming mental pictures of, the "gory details" that the author provides. The more vividly a reader can visualize, the scarier the story becomes.

 For direct instruction on Visualizing, see page T18.

Ⓐ THINK IT THROUGH What does the narrator want to do? Why? *(He wants to kill the old man because the man's eye annoys him.)* **clarifying**

Ⓑ REREAD Try to picture this scene in your mind. Why couldn't the narrator kill the old man? *(Help students pay attention to details that appeal to senses, such as no noise and thin light falling upon the sleeping man. He can't kill him because the eye is closed.)* **visualizing**

LITERATURE

FOCUS SKILL: Plot

Tell students that the **plot** of a story is the series of events in it—or what happens. In a horror story those events lead up to the point of most tension, or the climax. Explain that the introduction needs to set the stage for the first event.

 For direct instruction on Plot, see page T18.

Use the following questions to encourage literary analysis.

Ⓐ Why do you think the author chose to have the main character tell his own story? *(lets readers in on the the narrator's thoughts, feelings, and actions)* **first-person point of view**

Ⓑ Based on this introduction, what event will occur in the plot? *(The narrator will try to kill the old man.)* **plot**

VOCABULARY

FOCUS SKILL: Multiple-Meaning Words

Ⓐ mad Have students give several meanings for the word *mad (angry, crazy, wild about something).* Explain that in this story, *mad* means "crazy or insane," not "angry." Have students watch for other words that have more than one meaning.

Ⓑ broke Ask for meanings of *broke (out of money, destroyed something, snapped off a piece, came forth).* Ask students to look in the dictionary; *break* has nearly a page of meanings. In this case, it means "came forth"—the day broke (i.e., morning).

FOR ENGLISH LEARNERS

Help students understand the following terms, expressions, and idioms:

Line 14: had the eye of a vulture
Line 16: my blood ran cold
Line 29: lantern

suddenly, as if startled. Now you may think that I drew back—but no. His room was as black as pitch with the thick darkness (for the shutters were closed, through fear of robbers). So I knew that he could not
60 see the door opening, and I kept pushing it, steadily, steadily.

I had my head in, and was about to open the lantern, when my thumb slipped on the side of the lantern, and the old man sprang up in the bed, crying out, "Who's there?"

C

I kept quite still and said nothing. For a whole hour I did not move a muscle, and in the meantime I did not hear him lie down. He was still sitting up in the bed listening. Presently I heard a slight groan, and I
70 knew it was the groan of mortal terror. It was the sound of fear—from the bottom of the soul. I knew it well myself. Many a night I have felt those same terrors. I knew what the old man felt, and pitied him, although I chuckled in my heart. I knew that he had been lying awake ever since the first slight noise, when he had turned in the bed. His fears had been continuing to grow upon him. He had been trying to talk himself out of them, but he could not. He could
80 feel—although he could not see or hear it—my head's presence in his room.

> **mortal**
> (môr′ tl)
> *adj.* extreme;
> almost
> threatening death

D

THINK IT THROUGH
What happens on the eighth night? How is it different from the first seven nights?

C

8 Unit 1 Not According to Plan

FOCUS
The narrator hears something. How does this sound affect what he does?

D When I had waited a long time, very patiently, without hearing him lie down, I decided to open a little—a very, very little—crack in the lantern. So I opened it—you cannot imagine how carefully—until a single dim ray, like the thread of the spider, shot out from the crack and fell precisely upon the vulture eye.

It was open—wide, wide open—and I
90 grew furious as I gazed upon it. I saw it perfectly clearly—all a dull blue. It had a hideous veil over it that chilled the very

> **precisely**
> (prĭ sīs′ lē)
> *adv.* exactly

> **hideous veil**
> (hĭd′ ē əs vāl′)
> ugly covering

C **THINK IT THROUGH** What happens on the eighth night? How is it different from the first seven nights? *(The narrator enters the old man's room. He makes a loud noise with the lantern and scares the old man. The difference is that the old man is awake.)* **compare and contrast**

D **Reciprocal Teaching Suggestion: Visualizing Teacher Modeling** To show students the Active Reading Strategy of visualizing, focus on the first sentence in this paragraph. You could say: *When I read about him opening the lantern, I pictured him trying to be very, very quiet and just moving his hands a little to get it open a crack.* Have a student read the next part of the paragraph.

Student Modeling Ask the student to picture the light beam mentally and tell what it looks like. Suggest that the student replace the simile "like the thread of the spider" with one of his or her own (for example, like a laser beam).

LITERATURE

C What event has happened to move the plot forward? *(The old man has awakened and hears something.)* **plot**

D What does this passage tell you about the narrator? *(He has experienced terror at night himself; he's very sensitive.)* **character**

FOR ENGLISH LEARNERS

Help students understand the following terms, expressions, and idioms:

Line 57: black as pitch
Line 69: groan
Line 92: chilled the very center of my bones

center of my bones. But I could see nothing of the old man's face or body, for I had directed the ray as if by instinct, precisely on that eye.

And now have I not told you that what you mistake for madness is only the extreme sharpness of my senses? Now, I say, there came to my ears a low, dull, quick sound, such as a ticking clock makes when covered in cotton. I knew that sound too well too. It was the beating of the old man's heart.

> **REREAD**
> How is the sound of the clock like the sound of the old man's heart?

E

C

But even yet I kept still. I scarcely breathed. I held the lantern motionless. I tried to see how steadily I could keep the ray upon the eye. Meanwhile the awful drumming of the heart increased. It grew quicker and quicker, and louder and louder every instant. The old man's terror must have been extreme! It grew louder, I say, louder every moment!—do you hear me well? I have told you that I am nervous: so I am. And now at the dead hour of night, amid the awful silence of that old house, this strange noise began to terrify me. Yet, for some minutes longer I stood still. But the beating grew louder, louder! I thought the heart must burst. And now a new fear seized me—the sound would be heard by a neighbor! The old man's hour had come! With a loud yell, I threw open the lantern and leaped into the room. He shrieked once—once only. In an instant I dragged him to the floor, and pulled the heavy bed over him.

> **REREAD**
> What causes the narrator to carry out his deed?

F

G

But for many minutes, the heart beat on with a muffled sound. This, however, did not worry me; it would not be heard through the wall. Finally it stopped. The old man was dead. I removed the bed and looked at the corpse. Yes, he was stone,

10 Unit 1 Not According to Plan

stone dead. I placed my hand upon the heart and held it there many minutes. There was no beating. He was stone dead. His eye would trouble me no more.

If you still think me mad, you will think so no longer when I describe how I hid the body. The night was ending, and I worked fast but in silence. First I cut up the corpse. I cut off the head and the arms and the legs. I then took up three boards from the floor of the room and hid the body parts. Then I replaced the boards so cleverly and carefully that no human eye—not even *his*—could have noticed anything wrong. There was nothing to wash out—no stain of any kind, not even blood. I had been too cautious for that. A tub had caught all—ha, ha!

H

THINK IT THROUGH
What does the narrator do? How does he feel about it?

FOCUS
The police arrive. Read to find out how the narrator covers up his crime.

When I ended my work, it was four o'clock—still dark as midnight. As the bell sounded the hour, there came a knocking at the street door. I went down to open it with a light heart—for what had I now to fear? Three men entered who introduced themselves as police officers. A shriek had been heard by a neighbor during the night. The neighbor had called the police, and they had come to search the house.

I smiled—for what had I to fear? I welcomed the gentlemen. The shriek, I said, was my own in a dream. The old man, I mentioned, had gone to the

D

The Tell-Tale Heart 11

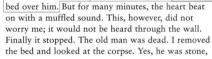

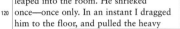

COMPREHENSION

E **REREAD** How is the sound of the clock like the sound of the old man's heart? *(regular ticking; low, dull, quick sound)* **compare and contrast**

F **REREAD** What causes the narrator to carry out his deed? *(He thinks the neighbors will hear the old man's heart.)* **cause and effect**

G Ask: How exactly did he kill the old man? *(The bed in those days was a big feather mattress. He probably dumped the man off and dropped the mattress on him.)* **clarifying**

H **THINK IT THROUGH** What does the narrator do? How does he feel about it? *(He kills the old man, chops up his body, and hides the parts under the floorboards. He feels very proud of his deed.)* **summarizing**

VOCABULARY

C **beating** Based on the phrase *of the old man's heart,* students should easily be able to tell that, in this context, the word *beating* means "pulsating or throbbing." **multiple meanings**

D **light** Have students discuss several meanings of *light.* They should conclude that, in this context, it means "not heavy, cheerful."

FOR ENGLISH LEARNERS

Help students understand the following expression:
Line 127: stone dead

country. I took my visitors all over the house. I told them to search—search well. I led them, finally, to his room. I felt so confident that I brought chairs into the room and told them to rest here. I myself boldly put my chair upon the very spot under which I'd buried the corpse of the victim.

THINK IT THROUGH

How does the narrator react when the police arrive? How do you explain this reaction?

FOCUS

Something unexpected happens. Read to discover what the narrator reveals.

The officers were satisfied. My manner had convinced them. I was totally at ease. They sat, and
160 while I answered cheerily, they chatted. But soon, I felt myself getting pale and wished they were gone. My head ached, and I heard a ringing in my ears: but still they sat and still chatted. The ringing became more distinct; it continued and became more distinct. I talked more freely to get rid of the feeling, but it continued and got clearer—until, finally, I found that the noise was not within my ears.

distinct
(dĭ stĭngkt')
clear

I now grew very pale; but I talked faster and
170 louder. Yet the sound increased—and what could I do? It was *a low, dull, quick sound—much like a ticking clock sounds when covered in cotton.*

REREAD
Where has the narrator used these words before?

I gasped for breath—and yet the officers didn't hear it. I talked more quickly, more emotionally; but the noise steadily increased. Why wouldn't they leave? I paced the floor, as if excited by

12 Unit 1 Not According to Plan

the conversation—but the noise kept increasing. What could I do? I foamed—I raged—I swore. I swung my
180 chair and scraped it on the boards, but the noise arose again and continually increased. It grew louder—louder! And still the men chatted pleasantly and smiled. Was it possible that they didn't hear it? No, no! they heard!—they suspected—they knew! They were laughing at my horror! This I thought and this I think. But anything was better than this agony. I could not bear those smiles any longer! I felt that I must scream or die—and now—again—listen! louder! louder!—
190 "Villains!" I shrieked. "Pretend no more! I admit the deed!—Tear up the planks—here, here! It is the beating of his hideous heart!"

THINK IT THROUGH

1. What does the narrator end up telling the police?
2. What may have caused him to tell them this? Explain.
3. Do you think the heart was really beating at the end? Explain your answer.
4. How does the narrator show that he's mad? Use details from the story to support your answer.

The Tell-Tale Heart 13

COMPREHENSION

ⓘ **THINK IT THROUGH** How does the narrator react when the police arrive? How do you explain this reaction? *(polite, helpful, and hospitable; wants to show nothing is wrong)* **character**

ⓙ **REREAD** Where has the narrator used these words before? *(page 10, lines 100–101, describing the ticking sound)* **details**

ⓚ **THINK IT THROUGH**

1. What does the narrator end up telling the police? *(where he buried the old man)* **details**

2. What may have caused him to tell them this? Explain. *(his insanity; he thought he heard the dead man's heart beating louder and louder)* **making inferences**

3. Do you think the heart was really beating at the end? Explain your answer. *(Most will say no, it was in the narrator's imagination. The narrator's guilt causes him to hear the heart.)* **making inferences**

4. How does the narrator show that he's mad? Use details from the story to support your answer. *(his constant denial of his insanity, his obsession with the eye, his killing the man because of his eye, his hearing the dead heart beat, his behavior with the police)* **character** **LITERATURE**

LITERATURE

ⓔ Point out how the short phrases build tension. Ask students to describe the narrator's state of mind. *(He's going crazy.)* Explain that the suspense is building to the climax. **plot**

ⓕ This is the climax of the story, or the turning point. All the suspense has built up to this moment. The narrator finally loses his control. Point out that in a horror story, the climax is often the end of the story. **climax**

VOCABULARY

FOR ENGLISH LEARNERS

Help students understand the following expressions and idioms:

Line 161: getting pale
Line 179: foamed, raged, swore

1. COMPREHENSION

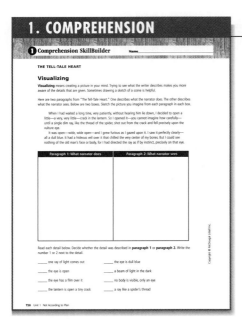

Visualizing

Direct Instruction Explain to students that to visualize a scene in a story is to see it in your mind, to imagine it. Visualizing a scene helps in understanding a passage because the activity forces a reader to examine the details carefully. If a reader cannot visualize the scene, he or she needs to reread the passage to discover the details needed for the "picture."

Have students read the first two paragraphs of "The Tell-Tale Heart" and discuss what they learn about the character. Ask: *If this story were being filmed, what actor would you imagine in the role? What movements and mannerisms would you imagine the actor using when delivering these lines?* Encourage students to visualize each scene as it might be filmed.

> **Comprehension SkillBuilder Answer Key:**
> *Sketches will vary. Details (read down): 1, 2, 2, 1; 2, 1, 2, 1*

2. LITERATURE

Plot

Direct Instruction Tell students that the plot is the sequence of events in the story. Give them copies of the plot diagram on page T672. Draw a plot diagram on the chalkboard and label the parts, defining them as follows:
1. **Introduction.** Characters and setting are introduced. The major conflict is presented.
2. **Rising action.** The problem becomes more complicated.
3. **Climax.** The most exciting part of the story—the turning point.

4. **Falling Action and Conclusion.** Changes that began at the climax continue their logical course, and the story ends.

State that a horror story very often focuses only on developing the mood and building up to a frightening climax, so there may be very little, if any, Falling Action and Conclusion. Have students recall horror movies they have seen and identify the climax in each.

> **Literary SkillBuilder Answer Key:**
> **A.** *3a, 6b, 4c, 8d, 1e, 2f, 7g, 5h*
> **B. 1.** *e, f* **2.** *d* **3.** *a, c, h, b, g*

3. VOCABULARY

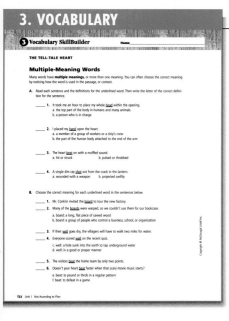

Multiple-Meaning Words

Direct Instruction Tell students that a multiple-meaning word is a word with more than one meaning. To determine which meaning the writer has in mind, a reader must examine the context in which it is used. That is, a reader must read the phrases and sentences before and after the word and try out the possible meanings with that context in mind. Using context often makes it easy to decide on the correct meaning.

Discuss this example from "The Tell-Tale Heart":

*. . . I did not hear him **lie** down.*

The dictionary has two separate entries for *lie* because two separate words, spelled the same way, are part of the English language. In each entry there are at least six meanings, including verbs and nouns. Two of the meanings are "to say something that is not true" and "to put oneself into a reclining, flat position." From the context, it is clear that the second meaning is the one that fits best.

Vocabulary SkillBuilder Answer Key:
A. 1. *a* **2.** *b* **3.** *b* **4.** *b*   **B. 1.** *b* **2.** *a* **3.** *c* **4.** *d* **5.** *f* **6.** *e*

---

4. WORDS TO KNOW

Words to Know

Direct Instruction When presenting the **Words to Know,** you might include the following information about the words.

- **Vultures** are large, ugly birds that feed on the dead. Many people find them frightening.
- **Cautious** comes from the Latin word *cautiō,* "care." Other words in the same family are *caution, precaution, cautiously.*
- **Mortal** comes from the Latin word *mors,* meaning "death." Anything that is mortal can die. Immortals cannot die. A mortal wound is fatal—the receiver will die. A mortal disease will cause death.
- **Precisely** means "exactly, strictly, and distinctly." Other words in the same family are *precise* and *precision.*

Writing Activity Encourage students to be as descriptive as they are able. Have volunteers read aloud their completed paragraphs.

Words to Know SkillBuilder Answer Key:
A. 1. *cautious* **2.** *precisely* **3.** *vulture* **4.** *mortal*
B. 1. *No. A cautious person is careful.*
   2. *No. It's a wild bird.*
   3. *Yes. You could die.*
   4. *A surgeon. If he/she errs, someone might die.*
   5. *No. The enemy wants his or her death.*
   6. *No. Vultures eat dead animals.*

---

5. SELECTION TEST

Selection Test Answer Key:
A. 1. *c* **2.** *c* **3.** *a* **4.** *b*
B. *He thought they could hear the beating heart; he went crazy.*

THE TELL-TALE HEART

Visualizing

Visualizing means creating a picture in your mind. Trying to see what the writer describes makes you more aware of the details that are given. Sometimes drawing a sketch of a scene is helpful.

Here are two paragraphs from "The Tell-Tale Heart." One describes what the narrator does. The other describes what the narrator sees. Below are two boxes. Sketch the picture you imagine from each paragraph in each box.

> When I had waited a long time, very patiently, without hearing him lie down, I decided to open a little—a very, very little—crack in the lantern. So I opened it—you cannot imagine how carefully— until a single dim ray, like the thread of the spider, shot out from the crack and fell precisely upon the vulture eye.
>
> It was open—wide, wide open—and I grew furious as I gazed upon it. I saw it perfectly clearly— all a dull blue. It had a hideous veil over it that chilled the very center of my bones. But I could see nothing of the old man's face or body, for I had directed the ray as if by instinct, precisely on that eye.

Paragraph 1: What narrator does	Paragraph 2: What narrator sees

Read each detail below. Decide whether the detail was described in **paragraph 1** or **paragraph 2.** Write the number 1 or 2 next to the detail.

_____ one ray of light comes out   _____ the eye is dull blue

_____ the eye is open   _____ a beam of light in the dark

_____ the eye has a film over it   _____ no body is visible, only an eye

_____ the lantern is open a tiny crack   _____ a ray like a spider's thread

THE TELL-TALE HEART

Plot

The **plot** of a story is the series of events that make up the story. In a horror story, most of the plot builds up to the climax. The events that build up are called the **rising action.** The **climax** is the most exciting part of the story, or the turning point. Often a horror story ends at the climax.

A. Write a number, 1–8, on each line to show the order in which the events happened in the story.

_____ a. The narrator opens the lantern and sees that the old man's eye is open.

_____ b. Police come to the door because neighbors heard the old man's cry.

_____ c. The narrator kills the old man.

_____ d. The noise of the beating heart finally makes the narrator tell the police what he's done.

_____ e. The narrator claims he is not mad and will prove it by telling his story.

_____ f. The narrator becomes frightened by the old man's eye.

_____ g. The narrator welcomes the police officers and invites them to sit and talk.

_____ h. The narrator cuts up the old man's body and hides the parts under the floor.

B. Use the letters a–h from above to complete these questions.

1. Which two events are part of the **introduction?**_____

2. Which event is the **climax**—the most exciting part or the turning point of the story?

_____

3. Which five events are part of the **rising action?** Write the letters in the order that the events

happened. _____

THE TELL-TALE HEART

Multiple-Meaning Words

Many words have **multiple meanings,** or more than one meaning. You can often choose the correct meaning by noticing how the word is used in the passage, or context.

A.   Read each sentence and the definitions for the underlined word. Then write the letter of the correct definition for the sentence.

_____ **1.** It took me an hour to place my whole <u>head</u> within the opening.
          a. the top part of the body in humans and many animals
          b. a person who is in charge

_____ **2.** I placed my <u>hand</u> upon the heart.
          a. a member of a group of workers or a ship's crew
          b. the part of the human body attached to the end of the arm

_____ **3.** The heart <u>beat</u> on with a muffled sound.
          a. hit or struck   b. pulsed or throbbed

_____ **4.** A single dim ray <u>shot</u> out from the crack in the lantern.
          a. wounded with a weapon   b. projected swiftly

B.   Choose the correct meaning for each underlined word in the sentences below.

_____ **1.** Mr. Conklin invited the <u>board</u> to tour the new factory.

_____ **2.** Many of the <u>boards</u> were warped, so we couldn't use them for our bookcase.

          a. board: a long, flat piece of sawed wood
          b. board: a group of people who control a business, school, or organization

_____ **3.** If their <u>well</u> goes dry, the villagers will have to walk two miles for water.

_____ **4.** Everyone scored <u>well</u> on the recent quiz.

          c. well: a hole sunk into the earth to tap underground water
          d. well: in a good or proper manner

_____ **5.** The visitors <u>beat</u> the home team by only two points.

_____ **6.** Doesn't your heart <u>beat</u> faster when that scary movie music starts?

          e. beat: to pound or throb in a regular pattern
          f. beat: to defeat in a game

THE TELL-TALE HEART

Words to Know

vulture   cautious   mortal   precisely

A. Fill in each blank with the correct word from the list above.

1. A very careful person is _____ and tries to avoid danger.

2. The beam of light fell exactly, or _____, where he aimed it.

3. One kind of bird eats dead animals. It is a _____.

4. A person with a _____ illness is facing death.

B. Answer the following questions and give a reason for each.

1. Does a cautious person take a lot of chances? _____ Why or why not?

   _____

2. Would a vulture make a good house pet? _____ Why or why not?

   _____

3. If you have a mortal illness, is it serious? _____ Why or why not?

   _____

4. Who needs to work more precisely: a surgeon or a person mowing a lawn? _____ Why?

   _____

5. Does someone's mortal enemy want him or her to have good health? _____ Why or why not?

   _____

6. Would you want a vulture to be looking at you in a hungry manner? _____ Why or why not?

   _____

Writing Activity
In a few sentences, describe a nightmare you've had or one you imagine. Use at least one of the **Words to Know.**

THE TELL-TALE HEART

A. Fill in the circle beside the letter of the correct answer.

1. Why does the narrator want to kill the old man?
  ○ a. because he hates the old man
  ○ b. because he wants the old man's gold
  ○ c. because he fears the old man's eye

2. After he kills the old man, what does the narrator do with his body?
  ○ a. He buries him outside.
  ○ b. He hits him with a lantern.
  ○ c. He cuts the body into pieces and hides them under the floor.

3. According to the narrator, what does the old man's beating heart sound like?
  ○ a. a ticking clock
  ○ b. a vulture's wings flapping
  ○ c. someone pounding on a door

4. Why do three policemen go to the narrator's house?
  ○ a. They are investigating a murder in the town.
  ○ b. A neighbor heard a cry and notified the police.
  ○ c. They see the narrator's lights on at four in the morning.

B. In your own words, explain why the narrator tells the police where he buried the old man.

_____

_____

_____

Name_____

Reader directions:

Cut this paper in half. Practice reading the passage aloud until you don't make any mistakes. Then have someone listen to you read. Try to sound the way you think the narrator sounds.

from The Tell-Tale Heart

True! Nervous—very, very dreadfully nervous I had been and am! But why will you say that I am mad? The disease had sharpened my senses. It did not destroy them or make them dull. Above all, my sense of hearing was acute! I heard all things in heaven and in the earth. How then am I mad? Listen! Observe how calmly I tell you the whole story.

It is impossible to say how I first got the idea. But once I did, it haunted me day and night. I had no reason. I loved the old man. He had never wronged me. He had never insulted me. I didn't want his gold. I think it was his eye. Yes, it was his eye!

✂ **cut along dotted line**
- -

Checker directions:

Follow along as the passage is read. Make a dot under each word the reader misses.
Show the reader the missed words. Erase the dots and repeat for each reading.

from The Tell-Tale Heart

True! Nervous—very, very dreadfully nervous I had been and am! But why will you say that I am mad? The disease had sharpened my senses. It did not destroy them or make them dull. Above all, my sense of hearing was acute! I heard all things in heaven and in the earth. How then am I mad? Listen! Observe how calmly I tell you the whole story.

It is impossible to say how I first got the idea. But once I did, it haunted me day and night. I had no reason. I loved the old man. He had never wronged me. He had never insulted me. I didn't want his gold. I think it was his eye. Yes, it was his eye!

Use this chart for Timed Readings and Repeated Readings.

Reading	1	2	3	4	5
Time (minutes/seconds)					
Words Missed					

Focus Skills

COMPREHENSION
Compare and Contrast

LITERATURE
Characterization

VOCABULARY
Idioms

SkillBuilder Copymasters

 Reading Comprehension:
1 Compare and Contrast
p. T35

 Literary Analysis:
2 Characterization p. T36

 Vocabulary:
3 Idioms p. T37
4 Words to Know p. T38

Assessment

 5 Selection Test p. T39

Readability Scores

DRP	LEXILE	DALE-CHALL
54	690	4.8

For English Learners

To students who didn't grow up hearing fairy tales in English, the phrase *Once upon a time* may be unfamiliar. Explain that many English fairy tales begin with this phrase, and that it serves to let listeners or readers know that the story is a make-believe tale.

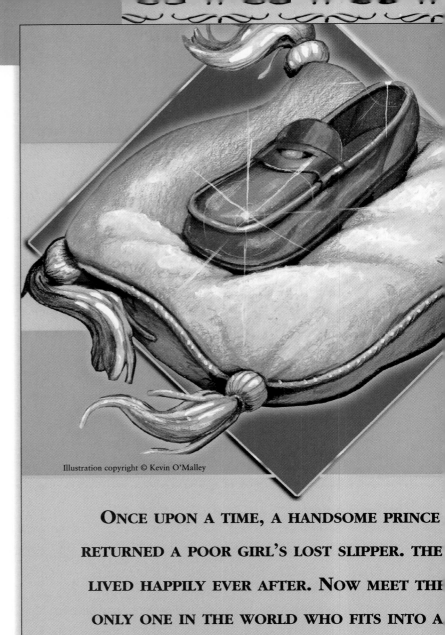

Illustration copyright © Kevin O'Malley

ONCE UPON A TIME, A HANDSOME PRINCE
RETURNED A POOR GIRL'S LOST SLIPPER. THE
LIVED HAPPILY EVER AFTER. NOW MEET THE
ONLY ONE IN THE WORLD WHO FITS INTO A
CERTAIN SCUFFED-UP LOAFER.

14   Unit 1 Not According to Plan

Vocabulary Strategy: Preteaching

Idioms Explain to students that an **idiom** is a phrase or an expression that cannot be understood from the meaning of its individual words. Copy the two columns shown on the facing page on the board. See how many of the boldfaced idioms students can match with their meanings. If you think individual students will need help, have them work in pairs or small groups.

Cinder Edna

BY ELLEN JACKSON

Connect to Your Life

Is there really such a thing as living happily ever after? Share your opinion with a partner.

Key to the Modern Fairy Tale

The first Cinderella tale was told long ago. There are hundreds of versions of Cinderella tales. "Cinder Edna" was written only a few years ago. It mixes old things with new. As you read about Cinder Edna, think about how well she fits your ideas about the original Cinderella.

Vocabulary Preview

Words to Know

cinders	dainty	profile
spunky	elegant	

Cinder Edna **15**

walking on air	feel embarrassed
pulling your leg	joking with you
on pins and needles	ill
lose face	feeling very happy
under the weather	feeling very nervous

 For more on Idioms, see page T34.

Connect to Your Life

Once students have established their opinions, organize a debate having both sides of the question, affirmative and negative, represented. Encourage students to use facts to support their opinions.

Key to the Modern Fairy Tale

Help students understand that tales told in the oral tradition often "change with the times" as they are told and retold. Although "Cinder Edna" closely resembles the original "Cinderella" in many ways, the characters in "Cinder Edna" speak and act in ways that reflect modern American society.

Vocabulary Preview

Words to Know
cinders *n.* ashes
spunky *adj.* having spirit or courage
dainty *adj.* beautiful in a delicate way
elegant *adj.* classy
profile *n.* side view of a face

For direct instruction on Words to Know, see page T34.

Building Background

Explain to students that modern fairy tales are usually based on well-known traditional tales but are set in today's world. This means that although the characters and events are the same or similar in both tales, the speech, thoughts, and actions of the modern characters are usually quite different from those of the traditional characters. Have students tell everything they know about the traditional tale of "Cinderella"—characters, plot, ending— as you record the features on the chalkboard. Leave the list in view as students read "Cinder Edna."

Once upon a time there were two girls who lived next door to each other. You may have heard of the first one. Her name was Cinderella. Poor Cinderella was forced to work from morning till night, cooking and scrubbing pots and pans and picking up after her cruel stepmother and wicked stepsisters. When her work was done, she sat among the cinders to keep warm, thinking about all her troubles.

> **cinders**
> (sĭn′ dərz)
> *n.* ashes

10　Cinder Edna, the other girl, was also forced to work for her wicked stepmother and stepsisters. But she sang and whistled while she worked. Moreover, she had learned a thing or two from doing all that housework—such as how to make a tuna casserole sixteen different ways and how to get spots off everything from rugs to ladybugs.

Edna had tried sitting in the cinders a few times. But it seemed like a silly way to spend time. Besides, it just made her clothes black and sooty. Instead when the housework was done, she kept warm by mowing
20　the lawn and cleaning parrot cages for the neighbors at $1.50 an hour. She also taught herself to play the accordion.

Even with her ragged, sooty clothing Cinderella was quite beautiful.

 Edna, on the other hand, wasn't much to look at. But she was strong and spunky and knew some good jokes—including an especially funny one about an anteater from Afghanistan.

> **spunky**
> (spŭng′ kē)
> *adj.* having spirit or courage

THINK IT THROUGH
What is the biggest difference between the two girls?

Illustration copyright © Kevin O'Malley

30　Now, one day the king announced that he would give a ball and that all the ladies of the land were invited. Cinderella's stepsisters set about choosing what they would wear. All day they ordered Cinderella around as they made their preparations.

Cinder Edna's stepsisters were excited, too. On the evening of the ball they trimmed their toenails and flossed their teeth. They put on their most beautiful

---

COMPREHENSION

FOCUS SKILL: Compare and Contrast

Explain to students that **compare** means "to look for ways two people or things are alike." **Contrast** means "to look for ways in which two people or things are different."

For direct instruction on Compare and Contrast, see page T33.

 THINK IT THROUGH What is the biggest difference between the two girls? *(Cinderella is beautiful. She sits among the cinders to think about her troubles. Cinder Edna is not beautiful. She uses hard work and a sense of humor to help her deal with her hardships.)* **compare and contrast**

LITERATURE

FOCUS SKILL: Characterization

Tell students that **characters** are the people who take part in the action of a story. Readers learn about characters in the following ways:
- what the character says, does, and thinks
- what other characters say about him or her
- what the narrator says about the character

For direct instruction on Characterization, see page T33.

Use the following questions to encourage literary analysis.

 How does the narrator describe Cinder Edna? *(strong and spunky)* **characterization**

VOCABULARY

FOCUS SKILL: Idioms

Remind students that an **idiom** has little or nothing to do with the individual meanings of the words it contains.

A **on the other hand** Help students understand that this idiom has nothing to do with hands. Rather, it means "from the opposite point of view."

FOR ENGLISH LEARNERS

Help students understand the following:

Line 12: moreover
Line 25: wasn't much to look at
Line 32: set about

gowns and drove away, leaving Edna behind to clean up after them.

40 Cinderella sat among the cinders and sighed. "Oh how I wish I had a fairy godmother who could change these rags into a beautiful gown so that I, too, could go to the ball."

No sooner said than done. Cinderella *did* have a fairy godmother, and she just happened to be passing by. With a wave of her magic wand, she changed Cinderella's rags into a beautiful gown. On Cinderella's incredibly tiny feet appeared a pair of dainty glass slippers.

B
50 Cinder Edna didn't believe in fairy godmothers. Instead she had used her cage-cleaning money to put a dress on layaway for just these kinds of occasions.

B

dainty
(dān' tē) *adj.* beautiful in a delicate way

"And my comfortable loafers will be perfect for dancing," she said as she slipped them onto her feet.

Meanwhile Cinderella's big, bright eyes brimmed with tears. "But, Fairy Godmother, how will I get to the ball?"

60 The fairy godmother was surprised that her goddaughter couldn't seem to figure anything out for herself. However, with another wave of the wand, she changed a pumpkin into a carriage, six white mice into horses, and a stray rat into a coachman.

"Be sure to leave before midnight," she warned Cinderella as she helped her into the elegant carriage.

B
Cinder Edna took the bus.

elegant
(ĕl' ĭ gənt) *adj.* classy

THINK IT THROUGH

C The girls have different personalities. How does this show in how they handle problems?

18 Unit 1 Not According to Plan

FOCUS
Find out what effect Cinderella and Cinder Edna have on those they meet.

When Cinderella arrived at the ball, everyone thought she was a princess. The king's son Randolph
70 was taken with her great beauty. He asked her to dance, but Cinderella could only sway a bit to the music. She was afraid of mussing her hair, and she knew those fragile glass slippers would break if she danced too hard.

D

REREAD
What do you learn about Cinderella from these details?

Just then Cinder Edna entered the room. She made straight for the refreshment table and poured herself some punch. It was Randolph's princely duty to greet everyone, so he came over to say hello.

80 "What's it like, being a prince?" Edna asked, to make conversation.

"Quite fantastic," said the prince. "Mostly I review the troops and sit around on the throne looking brave and wise." He turned his head so that Edna could see how handsome his chin looked from the right side.

C
"Borrring," thought Edna.

"Excuse me, but we recycle plastic around here," said a little man with glasses and a warm smile.

"Just ignore him," said Randolph. "He's only my
90 younger brother, Rupert. He lives in a cottage in the back and runs the recycling plant and a home for orphaned kittens."

REREAD
How are the princes different?

E

Cinder Edna immediately handed Rupert her cup. "Would you like to dance?" asked Rupert.

Cinder Edna and Rupert danced and danced. They did the Storybook Stomp and the Cinnamon Twist.

Cinder Edna 19

COMPREHENSION

B Ask: What do the girls think of fairy godmothers? *(Cinderella believes in fairy godmothers, but Cinder Edna doesn't.)* **compare and contrast**

C **THINK IT THROUGH** The girls have different personalities. How does this show in how they handle problems? *(Cinderella relies on her fairy godmother for everything she needs, but Cinder Edna gets what she needs by paying for it. She also takes the bus to the ball. Cinder Edna is self-sufficient, but Cinderella is not.)* **compare and contrast**

D **REREAD** What do you learn about Cinderella from these details? *(She's very careful about her appearance. She doesn't want to do anything that might ruin her looks.)* **characterization**
LITERATURE

E **REREAD** How are the princes different? *(Rupert runs the recycling plant and a home for orphaned kittens, but Randolph sits around on his throne looking brave and wise—and handsome.)* **compare and contrast**

LITERATURE

B What details does the author provide to let you know that this story is a modern fairy tale? *(Cinder Edna puts a dress on layaway; she takes the bus to the ball.)* **modern fairy tale**

C Which character lets you know what kind of person Randolph is? How does the character describe him? *(Cinder Edna calls Randolph boring.)* **characterization**

VOCABULARY

B **put a dress on layaway** Tell students that *layaway* is a method of purchasing something and making small payments over time until it is paid for in full. Then the purchaser takes the item home.

FOR ENGLISH LEARNERS

Help students understand the following expressions and idioms:

Line 44: no sooner said than done
Line 70: taken with
Line 76: made straight for

They did the Worm and the Fish. They boogied and woogied. At last they stopped for a round of punch.
100 Edna learned that Rupert (1) loved tuna casserole, (2) played the concertina, (3) knew some good jokes.

concertina
(kŏn' sər tē' nə)
small accordion

She told him the one about the anteater from Afghanistan and he told her the one about the banana from Barbados.

D

20 Unit 1 Not According to Plan

Illustration copyright © Kevin O'Malley

They were deep in a conversation about gum wrappers and rusty tin cans when the clock began to strike twelve.

"Oh," cried Cinderella, running for the door. "The
110 magic spell disappears at midnight."

"Oh, oh," cried Cinder Edna, running for the door. "The buses stop running at midnight!"

C

Randolph and Rupert ran after the two girls.

"Wait! Wait!" they called. But it was too late.

As the girls vanished into the night, the two princes ran smack-dab into each other on the palace steps.

Whap! They landed with a thud. Rupert's glasses went flying and broke into a million pieces on the cement.

F

120 "Look what you made me do!" said Randolph. "Now she's gone—the only girl I ever loved."

"Well, didn't you get her name?" asked Rupert impatiently. "The one I love is named Edna."

"Gee, I forgot to ask," said Randolph, scratching his head.

G

H THINK IT THROUGH
How does each prince react to the girl he has met?

FOCUS
The future begins to unfold for the two couples. Read to find out what happens to each couple.

As Rupert got up he stumbled over something. When he leaned close to look, he saw two shoes lying side by side on the steps. One was a scuffed-up loafer. The other was a dainty glass slipper. "These definitely
130 should be recycled," he said.

E

Cinder Edna 21

COMPREHENSION

F What keeps Randolph and Rupert from catching up with Cinderella and Cinder Edna? *(They run into each other, causing Rupert to break his glasses.)* **details**

G Based on Randolph's last statement, who do you think is the brighter brother? *(Rupert, who at least learned the name of the girl he loves)* **evaluating**

H THINK IT THROUGH How does each prince react to the girl he has met? *(Rupert falls in love with Cinder Edna, and Randolph falls in love with Cinderella.)* **compare and contrast**

LITERATURE

D Why do you think Cinder Edna and Rupert are attracted to each other? *(Both work hard, like to tell jokes, and play musical instruments.)* **characterization**

E Rupert finds a glass slipper and a scuffed-up loafer. Reread his remark. What doesn't he understand about what he's found? *(He doesn't understand that he's found shoes that belong to Cinderella and Cinder Edna.)* **character**

VOCABULARY

C **the buses stop running** Help students understand that this idiom doesn't mean that buses have legs. Rather, it means that the bus company closes and stops giving people bus rides at midnight.

FOR ENGLISH LEARNERS

Help students understand the following:

Line 98: a round of punch
Line 115: smack-dab

"No! No!" said Randolph. "This is how we'll find them. We'll try these shoes on all the women in the kingdom. When we find the feet that fit these shoes, we'll have found our brides-to-be!"

Rupert looked at his brother with disbelief. "That is positively amazing," he said, "the most amazingly dumb idea I've ever heard. You could end up married to a midget. I have a much better idea." But Randolph wouldn't listen. He ran to his room to get
140 his beauty sleep.

The next day he put his plan into action. He went to every house in the kingdom, trying to cram women's feet into the glass slipper.

Rupert, too, put his plan into action. First he looked up all the Ednas in the palace directory. Then he visited them and asked each one this question: "How many recipes do you know for tuna casserole?"

Randolph soon became discouraged. All the feet he saw were either too large, too wide, too long,
150 or adorned with electric pink toenail polish.

adorned
(ə dôrnd')
decorated

Rupert, too, was discouraged. While some Ednas could name tuna casserole with pecan sauce, and others could name tuna casserole with sour cream and rice, no one could name more than seven kinds of tuna casserole.

Finally Randolph got to Cinderella's house. The cruel stepsisters were eager to try on the glass slipper, but, of course, it didn't fit either of them.
160 Suddenly Randolph noticed a woman in rags, sitting forlornly among the cinders in the corner. Something about her seemed familiar.

forlornly
(fər lôrn' lē)
sadly

"Oh, Miss. Why don't you try this on?" he suggested. With trembling hands, Cinderella tried on the glass slipper. It fit perfectly!

Randolph swept her up in his arms and carried her away to the palace so that they could be married.

Meanwhile Rupert reached Cinder Edna's house.
170 Her wicked stepsisters wanted to try on the loafer, but Rupert wouldn't let them because they weren't named Edna.

At that moment, Cinder Edna came in from mowing the lawn. Her heart almost stopped when she saw Rupert. He blinked nearsightedly at her.

Without his glasses Cinder Edna looked something like a large plate of mashed potatoes.

nearsightedly
(nîr' sī' tīd lē)
in a way showing that he is unable to see objects clearly

"Are you, let's see . . . Ashes Edna?" he
180 asked, peering closely at his list of names. "No, I already talked to her." He wasn't sure these Ednas with an extra name counted, but he had already tried the just plain Ednas.

"*Cinder.* Cinder Edna," she said.

"Oh. Well, can you name sixteen different kinds of tuna casserole?"

"Of course," she said, and she began to name them. She rattled off fifteen different kinds, including tuna casserole with pickled pigs feet, and then she stopped.
190 What was the last one anyway?

"Only fifteen," said Rupert, turning to go.

"Well, maybe I can't name sixteen kinds of tuna casserole," said Edna. "But I *do* know a great joke about a kangaroo from Kalamazoo."

Rupert stopped in his tracks.

"My love!" he said. He gave her a kiss. "Will you marry me?"

REREAD
Why does Rupert realize she's the right Edna?

COMPREHENSION

I Compare the brothers' plans to find the girls. Which plan would you choose? Why? (*Randolph tries the glass slipper on every woman in the kingdom, while Rupert visits all the Ednas in the palace directory and asks them how many tuna casserole recipes they know. Most students probably would choose Rupert's plan because it's more efficient.*) **compare and contrast**

J **Reciprocal Teaching Suggestion: Predicting Teacher Modeling** To demonstrate the Active Reading Strategy of predicting, focus on three paragraphs, starting with the one at the bottom of page 22. You could say: *This seems to be a good point to predict that Randolph will get together with Cinderella. She looks familiar to him. I also think she's actually Cinderella because she's described as sitting forlornly—or sadly—among the cinders. In the old versions of the tale, that's what she does. As I continue reading, I see that her foot does fit the slipper. The information shows me that this time my prediction is on target.*

Student Modeling Have a volunteer model predicting what will happen in Rupert's search for Cinder Edna. Remind the student to use evidence from the text. Then have the student read the next few paragraphs to verify the prediction.

K **REREAD** Why does Rupert realize she's the right Edna? (*When she can't name all sixteen tuna casserole recipes, she tells Rupert a joke instead.*) **making inferences**

LITERATURE

F What object does Rupert use to find Edna in this modern fairy tale that the prince in the original tale didn't have? (*a palace phone book*) **details**

VOCABULARY

D **swept her up** Help students understand that this idiom has nothing to do with sweeping or cleaning with a broom. Rather, it means "picked her up with a swift brushing motion."

E **stopped in his tracks** Help students understand that this idiom means that he stopped right where he was.

FOR ENGLISH LEARNERS

Help students understand the following:

Line 133: brides-to-be
Line 136: end up
Line 139: beauty sleep

Illustration copyright © Kevin O'Malley

Soon after that, Randolph and Ella (she dropped the cinder part) and Rupert and Edna (she did the same) were married in a grand double ceremony.

So the girl who had once been known as Cinderella ended up in a big palace. During the day she went to endless ceremonies and listened to dozens of speeches by His Highness the Grand Archduke of Lethargia and the Second Deputy Underassistant of

200

G

24   Unit 1 Not According to Plan

---

nothing to look at but her husband's perfect profile while he talked endlessly of troops, parade formations, and uniform buttons.

210   And the girl who had been known as Cinder Edna ended up in a small cottage with solar heating. During the day she studied waste disposal engineering and cared for orphaned kittens. And at night she and her husband laughed and joked, tried new recipes together, and played duets on the accordion and concertina.

Guess who lived happily ever after.

L

profile
(prō′ fīl′)
n. side view of a face

M

H

N

THINK IT THROUGH

1. What happens to Cinderella and Randolph? What happens to Cinder Edna and Rupert?
2. Which couple do you think lives happily ever after? Explain your opinion.
3. Which character in this tale is your favorite? Why?

Cinder Edna   25

COMPREHENSION

L In your opinion, what is life like for Cinderella? *(Most students will agree that she's bored by her royal duties and by her husband's descriptions of his responsibilities.)* **evaluating**

M How is Cinder Edna's life different from Cinderella's? *(Cinder Edna has no royal duties. She's involved in activities that matter to her. She and her husband laugh together and share activities.)* **compare and contrast**

N **THINK IT THROUGH**

1. What happens to Cinderella and Randolph? What happens to Cinder Edna and Rupert? *(The couples get married in a double ceremony.)* **details**

2. Which couple do you think lives happily ever after? Explain your opinion. *(Most students will say that Edna and Rupert live happily ever after because they have fun sharing their favorite activities.)* **making inferences**

3. Which character in this tale is your favorite? Why? *(Students' opinions will vary but probably will be based on the character with whom they can identify most closely.)* **evaluating**

Option for Speaking and Listening
Use questions 2 and 3 on page 25 to allow students to have a debate. Be sure students use examples from the text to explain and support their opinions.

RETEACHING

If students need more help understanding **Compare and Contrast,** use pages T647–T649.

LITERATURE

G *Lethargia* means "tiredness," so the Grand Archduke of Lethargia is in charge of being tired. Look at the names of the speechmakers and how the writer describes what they do. Are they as important as they seem? *(Students will*

probably answer that these royal positions seem useless and even funny but not important.)* **character**

H Which version do you like better—the traditional "Cinderella" or the more modern "Cinder Edna"? Explain your choice. *(Some students will prefer the traditional tale because it is the one they grew up hearing, while others will prefer the modern tale because they can identify with it more.)* **literary analysis**

VOCABULARY

FOR ENGLISH LEARNERS

Help students understand the following:

Line 211: solar heating
Line 211: waste disposal engineering
Line 216: ever after

1. COMPREHENSION

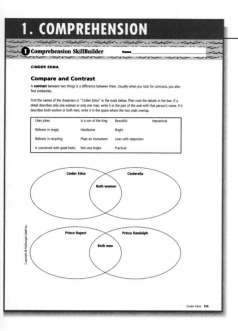

Compare and Contrast

Direct Instruction Tell students that one way to understand a story better is to compare and contrast the people and things in the story. **Comparing** is looking for what two people or things have in common. **Contrasting** is looking for differences.

Point out that the tale of "Cinder Edna" is funny because of its contrasts with the familiar story of "Cinderella." Have students discuss the end of "Cinder Edna" and contrast the activities of the two heroines after their marriages.

> **Comprehension SkillBuilder Answer Key:**
> **Cinder Edna:** *Likes jokes, Practical, Believes in recycling, Plays an instrument*
> **Both women:** *Lives with stepsisters* **Cinderella:** *Beautiful, Believes in magic, Is concerned with good looks, Impractical* **Prince Rupert:** *Likes jokes, Bright, Believes in recycling, Plays an instrument* **Both men:** *Is a son of the king* **Prince Randolph:** *Handsome, Is concerned with good looks, Not very bright*

2. LITERATURE

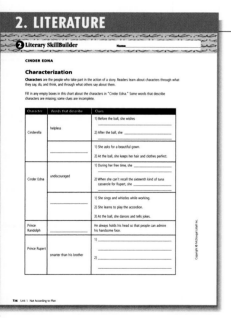

Characterization

Direct Instruction Tell students that the **characters** in a story are the people, and sometimes the animals, who take part in the story's events. Explain that writers often describe characters directly, but more often the reader must figure out what sort of person the character is from what he or she says, does, or is reported to think. Another source of information is what the other characters say about the character, and how they act when they are near the character. All of

these clues that the author provides are called **characterization.**

Have students read the three paragraphs that describe the reactions of the two princes to the discovery of the shoes left behind by the two heroines (beginning with "As Rupert got up" and ending with "to get his beauty sleep"). Ask: *What do you learn about each prince from what he does? from what he says? from what the other prince says to or about him?*

> **Literary SkillBuilder Answer Key:**
> **Cinderella—1)** *(Before the ball, she wishes)* for a fairy godmother to help her.
> **2)** *(After the ball, she)* waits for the prince to bring the shoe to her.
>
> *Descriptive terms may vary. Possible terms: concerned about appearances, proud*
>
> **Cinder Edna—1)** *(During her free time, she)* earns money / learns new skills / plans for the future. **2)** *(When she can't recall the sixteenth kind of tuna casserole for Rupert, she)* offers to tell a joke instead.
>
> *Descriptive terms may vary. Possible terms: cheerful, good-humored, easy-going*
>
> **Prince Randolph—***Descriptive terms may vary. Possible terms: proud, vain*
>
> **Prince Rupert—***Proofs of intelligence may vary. Possible proofs: He runs the recycling plant; he knows how to play the concertina; he thinks of a good plan to find Edna; he recognizes Edna by her jokes instead of her shoe; he marries Edna.*

Direct Instruction
for SkillBuilder Copymasters

3. VOCABULARY

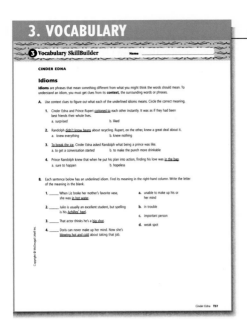

Idioms

Direct Instruction Tell students that an **idiom** is a phrase or expression that means something different from the normal meanings of the separate words in the phrase. Explain that when they read an idiom, they will have to make sense of the whole phrase rather than the individual words.

Have students tell the meanings of the following underlined idioms from the context—surrounding words or phrases—of the paragraphs:

Because my cold made me grouchy and my cold medicine made me sleepy, I was a <u>wet blanket</u> at the victory party after the game. I finally went home so everyone else could have a good time.

Don't tell Allen about the surprise party for Lecia. Otherwise, he's sure to <u>spill the beans</u> to Lecia herself, and the surprise will be ruined.

Make sure students see that neither a blanket nor beans are being discussed in these sentences. Instead, the phrases *wet blanket* and *spill the beans* have meanings that have nothing to do with blankets and beans. A *wet blanket* is "a person who keeps others from having a good time." *Spill the beans* means "tell a secret."

Vocabulary SkillBuilder Answer Key:

A.
1. *b* **2.** *b* **3.** *a* **4.** *a*

B.
1. *b* **2.** *d* **3.** *c* **4.** *a*

4. WORDS TO KNOW

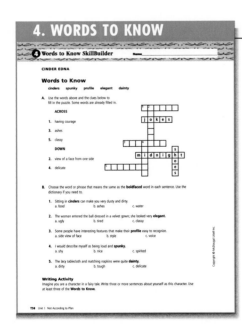

Words to Know

Direct Instruction Briefly explain to students how a crossword puzzle works. Review the process of finding the number of a clue (*e.g.,* 3 across) and filling in one of the **Words to Know,** beginning with the box that contains the number 3. The same applies to the "down" words. Inform them that there are words from "Cinder Edna" already placed in the puzzle that are *not* **Words To Know.** These filled-in words can give clues to the missing words.

Writing Activity Encourage students to be as descriptive as they are able. Have volunteers read aloud their completed paragraphs.

Words to Know SkillBuilder Answer Key:

A.
1. *across: spunky*
2. *down: profile*
3. *across: cinders*
4. *down: dainty*
5. *across: elegant*

B.
1. *b*
2. *c*
3. *a*
4. *c*
5. *c*

5. SELECTION TEST

Selection Test Answer Key:

A. 1. *b* **2.** *a* **3.** *c* **4.** *c*
B. *Cinder Edna buys a dress on layaway, takes a bus to the ball, makes money on the side.*

CINDER EDNA

Compare and Contrast

A **contrast** between two things is a difference between them. Usually when you look for contrasts, you also find similarities.

Find the names of the characters in "Cinder Edna" in the ovals below. Then read the details in the box. If a detail describes only one woman or only one man, write it in the part of the oval with that person's name. If it describes both women or both men, write it in the space where the two ovals overlap.

Likes jokes	Is a son of the king	Beautiful	Impractical
Believes in magic	Handsome	Bright	
Believes in recycling	Plays an instrument	Lives with stepsisters	
Is concerned with good looks	Not very bright	Practical	

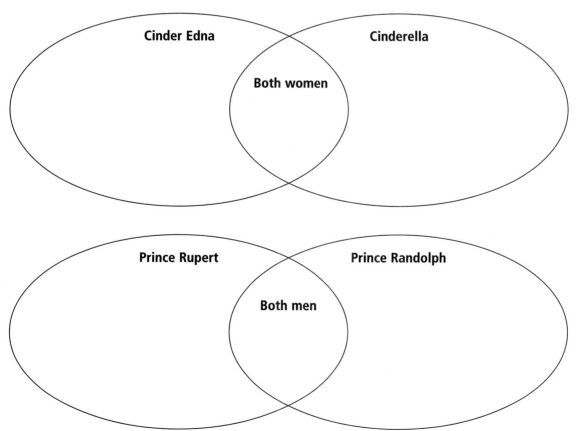

CINDER EDNA

Characterization

Characters are the people who take part in the action of a story. Readers learn about characters through what they say, do, and think, and through what others say about them.

Fill in any empty boxes in this chart about the characters in "Cinder Edna." Some words that describe characters are missing; some clues are incomplete.

Character	Words that describe	Clues
Cinderella	helpless	1) Before the ball, she wishes _____ 2) After the ball, she _____
	_____	1) She asks for a beautiful gown. 2) At the ball, she keeps her hair and clothes perfect.
Cinder Edna	undiscouraged	1) During her free time, she _____ 2) When she can't recall the sixteenth kind of tuna casserole for Rupert, she _____
	_____	1) She sings and whistles while working. 2) She learns to play the accordion. 3) At the ball, she dances and tells jokes.
Prince Randolph	_____	He always holds his head so that people can admire his handsome face.
Prince Rupert	smarter than his brother	1) _____ 2) _____

CINDER EDNA

Idioms

Idioms are phrases that mean something different from what you might think the words should mean. To understand an idiom, you must get clues from its **context,** the surrounding words or phrases.

A. Use context clues to figure out what each of the underlined idioms means. Circle the correct meaning.

1. Cinder Edna and Prince Rupert <u>cottoned to</u> each other instantly. It was as if they had been best friends their whole lives.
   a. surprised   b. liked

2. Randolph <u>didn't know beans</u> about recycling. Rupert, on the other, knew a great deal about it.
   a. knew everything   b. knew nothing

3. <u>To break the ice</u>, Cinder Edna asked Randolph what being a prince was like.
   a. to get a conversation started   b. to make the punch more drinkable

4. Prince Randolph knew that when he put his plan into action, finding his love was <u>in the bag</u>.
   a. sure to happen   b. hopeless

B. Each sentence below has an underlined idiom. Find its meaning in the right-hand column. Write the letter of the meaning in the blank.

1. _____ When Liz broke her mother's favorite vase, she was <u>in hot water</u>.

       a. unable to make up his or her mind

2. _____ Julio is usually an excellent student, but spelling is his <u>Achilles' heel</u>.

       b. in trouble

3. _____ That actor thinks he's a <u>big shot</u>.

       c. important person

4. _____ Doris can never make up her mind. Now she's <u>blowing hot and cold</u> about taking that job.

       d. weak spot

CINDER EDNA

Words to Know

cinders   spunky   profile   elegant   dainty

A. Use the words above and the clues below to
fill in the puzzle. Some words are already filled in.

ACROSS

1. having courage

3. ashes

5. classy

DOWN

2. view of a face from one side

4. delicate

B. Choose the word or phrase that means the same as the **boldfaced** word in each sentence. Use the
dictionary if you need to.

1. Sitting in **cinders** can make you very dusty and dirty.
   a. food   b. ashes   c. water

2. The woman entered the ball dressed in a velvet gown; she looked very **elegant.**
   a. ugly   b. tired   c. classy

3. Some people have interesting features that make their **profile** easy to recognize.
   a. side view of face   b. style   c. voice

4. I would describe myself as being loud and **spunky.**
   a. shy   b. nice   c. spirited

5. The lacy tablecloth and matching napkins were quite **dainty.**
   a. dirty   b. tough   c. delicate

Writing Activity

Imagine you are a character in a fairy tale. Write three or more sentences about yourself as this character. Use
at least three of the **Words to Know.**

CINDER EDNA

A. Fill in the circle beside the letter of the correct answer.

1. What does Cinderella do to stay warm when she isn't working for her stepmother and stepsisters?
- ○ a. She mows the lawn.
- ○ b. She sits among the cinders.
- ○ c. She cleans parrot cages.

2. What does Cinder Edna think of Prince Randolph?
- ○ a. She thinks he is very boring.
- ○ b. She thinks he is very funny.
- ○ c. She thinks he is very smart.

3. Why does Cinder Edna get upset when the clock strikes twelve?
- ○ a. The magic spell disappears at midnight.
- ○ b. The ball is over, and she doesn't want to leave.
- ○ c. The buses stop running at midnight.

4. How does Prince Randolph plan to find Cinderella?
- ○ a. by placing an ad in the classified section of the paper
- ○ b. by looking for all the Ellas in the palace directory
- ○ c. by trying the glass slipper on all the women in the kingdom

B. How do you know that Cinder Edna is better able to take care of herself than Cinderella? Write two reasons.

_____

_____

_____

_____

Focus Skills

COMPREHENSION
Cause and Effect

LITERATURE
Conflict: External and Internal

VOCABULARY
Context Clues: General

SkillBuilder Copymasters

 Reading Comprehension:
1 Cause and Effect p. T49

 Literary Analysis:
2 Conflict p. T50

 Vocabulary:
3 Context Clues p. T51
4 Words to Know p. T52

Assessment

 5 Selection Test p. T53

Readability Scores

DRP	LEXILE	DALE-CHALL
53	670	4.4

For English Learners

Students who didn't grow up in the United States may not understand the relationship in this story between Roger the dog and his owners. If necessary, explain that many people treat and talk to their pets as if they were children. Some people even dress and groom their pets, feed them gourmet food, and give them beds that look like miniature versions of humans' beds.

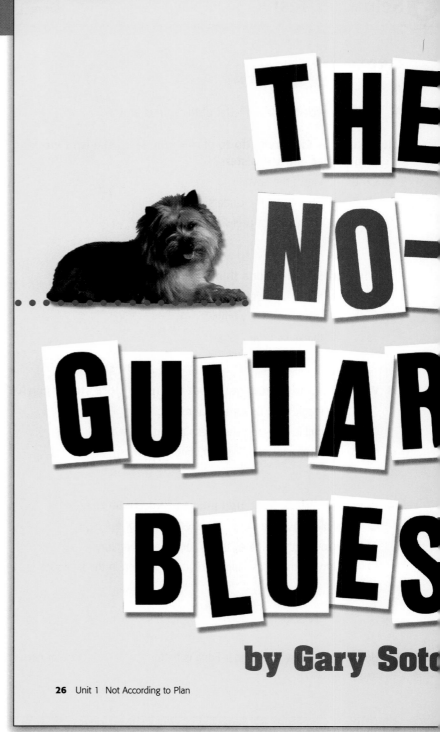

26 Unit 1 Not According to Plan

More About Los Lobos

The Grammy-award-winning musical group Los Lobos ("The Wolves") is mentioned in the beginning of this story. The group was started in the early 1970s by four high school students in East Los Angeles. They gained steady recognition and success over the years with their distinct musical styles, including rock and roll, blues, funk, and traditional Mexican music. Los Lobos is perhaps best known for their chart-topping version of "La Bamba," which they recorded in 1987 as part of their soundtrack for a movie about Ritchie Valens, the first Hispanic rock-and-roll star.

Connect to Your Life

Have you ever tried to convince your parent that you really need extra money? What was the answer? If he or she said no, what did you do?

Key to the Short Story

This story takes place in Fresno, California. The time is probably the 1980s, when the TV show *American Bandstand* was very popular. This show inspired many teenagers to form rock bands and to dream about becoming famous.

Vocabulary Preview

Words to Know

mission	turnover	secondhand
distracted	deceitful	

 Reading Coach CD-ROM selection

austo needs money
r the guitar of his
reams. Then along
omes a dog that eats
range peels. How
ill the dog fit into
austo's plan?

The No-Guitar Blues **27**

Connect to Your Life

Engage students in a group discussion about their reasons for needing extra money. To facilitate discussion, use a web graphic like the one on page T668. Are there any reasons that come up more than others? If so, what are they and why? What are the most common ways that students have tried to make extra money?

Key to the Short Story

Inform students that the TV show *American Bandstand* launched the careers of countless early musical stars. Its host, Dick Clark, went on to create the American Music Awards, a show that is broadcast once a year.

Ask students if there are any shows on TV today that inspire teenagers to become musicians. If so, what are they, and in what ways do they influence today's teens? Invite students to discuss each show's appeal.

Vocabulary Preview

Words to Know
mission *n.* special duty
distracted *adj.* not paying attention
turnover *n.* fruit-filled pastry
deceitful *adj.* full of lies
secondhand *adj.* used; not new

 For direct instruction on Words to Know, see page T48.

Building Background

Tell students that they will see a number of Spanish words in "The No-Guitar Blues." The pronunciations and definitions appear beside these words.

Vocabulary Strategy: Preteaching

Context Clues Remind students that the words and phrases surrounding a word that provide hints about its meaning are called **context clues.** Then write the following sentences on the board, and help students identify the words or phrases that help them figure out each underlined word.

1. Fausto received a <u>grimy</u>, dirt-caked quarter in exchange for doing a job.
2. Fausto saw that Roger was a sort of fancy dog, a <u>terrier</u> or something.

 For more on Context Clues, see page T48.

FOCUS
Fausto makes his first attempt to get money for a guitar. Find out what happens.

A The moment Fausto saw the group Los Lobos on "American Bandstand," he knew exactly what he wanted to do with his life—play guitar. His eyes grew large with excitement as Los Lobos ground out a song while teenagers bounced off each other on the crowded dance floor.

He had watched "American Bandstand" for years and had heard Ray Camacho and the Teardrops at Romain Playground, but it had never occurred to him
10 that he too might become a musician. That afternoon Fausto knew his ~~mission~~ in life: to play guitar in his own band; to sweat out his songs and prance around the stage; to make money and dress weird.

mission
(mĭsh′ ən)
n. special duty

A Fausto turned off the television set and walked outside, wondering how he could get enough money to buy a guitar. He couldn't ask his parents because they would just say, "Money doesn't grow on trees" or "What do you think we are,
20 bankers?" And besides, they hated rock music. They were into the ~~conjunto~~ music of Lydia Mendoza, Flaco Jimenez, and Little Joe and La Familia. And, as Fausto recalled, the last album they bought was *The Chipmunks Sing Christmas Favorites.*

conjunto
(kŏn hōōn′ tō)
old-fashioned style of Mexican music

REREAD
Why will Fausto have a problem getting a guitar?B

But what the heck, he'd give it a try.
A He returned inside and watched his mother make tortillas. He leaned against the kitchen counter, trying to work up the nerve to ask her for a guitar. Finally,
30 he couldn't hold back any longer.

"Mom," he said, "I want a guitar for Christmas."

28 Unit 1 Not According to Plan

She looked up from rolling tortillas. "Honey, a guitar costs a lot of money."

"How 'bout for my birthday next year," he tried again.

"I can't promise," she said, turning back to her tortillas, "but we'll see."

Fausto walked back outside with a buttered tortilla. He knew his mother was right. His father was a
40 warehouseman at Berven Rugs, where he made good money but not enough to buy everything his children wanted. B Fausto decided to mow lawns to earn money, and was pushing the mower down the street before he realized it was winter and no one would hire him. He returned the mower and picked up a rake. He hopped onto his sister's bike (his had two flat tires) and rode north to the nicer section of Fresno in search of work. He went door-to-door, but after three hours he managed to get only one job, and not to rake leaves. He was
50 asked to hurry down to the store to buy a loaf of bread, for which he received a grimy, dirt-caked quarter.

THINK IT THROUGH
C Whom does Fausto ask for a guitar? What is the result?

FOCUS
Read to find out how a dog gives Fausto a new idea.

He also got an orange, which he ate sitting at the curb. While he was eating, a dog walked up and sniffed his leg. Fausto pushed him away and threw an orange peel skyward. The dog caught it and ate it in one gulp. The

COMPREHENSION	LITERATURE	VOCABULARY

COMPREHENSION

FOCUS SKILL: Cause and Effect

Explain that a **cause** tells why something happened, and an **effect** tells what happened. The cause comes before the effect, or result. As you discuss common examples of cause-and-effect relationships, you might write each cause on the board and connect the cause to an effect, using an arrow.

📖 For direct instruction on Cause and Effect, see page T47.

A Ask: What suddenly causes Fausto to want a guitar? *(Seeing Los Lobos on* American Bandstand *makes him want to be a musician.)* **cause and effect**

B **REREAD** Why will Fausto have a problem getting a guitar? *(He doesn't have enough money; his parents hate rock music.)* **details**

C **THINK IT THROUGH** Whom does Fausto ask for a guitar? What is the result? *(His mother; she refuses, explaining that a guitar is too expensive.)* **cause and effect**

LITERATURE

FOCUS SKILL: Conflict

Tell students that a **conflict** is a struggle between two opposing forces. An **external conflict** can be a struggle between a character and another person or group, or between a character and nature. In an **internal conflict,** the struggle goes on in a character's own mind.

📖 For direct instruction on Conflict, see page T47.

Use the following questions to encourage literary analysis.

A Why does Fausto struggle with asking his mother for a guitar? *(He knows that his parents don't have a lot of money and that they hate rock music.)* **internal conflict**

B What things stand in the way of Fausto's getting what he wants? *(His mother refuses because the family doesn't have the money; since it's winter, Fausto can't earn money mowing lawns.)* **external conflict**

VOCABULARY

FOCUS SKILL: Context Clues

A **tortillas** Help students use context clues to understand the meaning of *tortillas.* In lines 27–28, Fausto's mother makes them. In line 32, she is rolling them. In line 38, he has a buttered tortilla. A *tortilla* must be a rolled food that can be buttered and eaten.

FOR ENGLISH LEARNERS

Help students understand the following expressions and idioms:

Line 4: ground out
Line 12: sweat out
Line 29: work up the nerve
Line 40: made good money

dog looked at Fausto and wagged his tail for more. Fausto tossed him a slice of orange, and the dog
60 snapped it up and licked his lips.

"How come you like oranges, dog?"

The dog blinked a pair of sad eyes and whined.

"What's the matter? Cat got your tongue?" Fausto laughed at his joke and offered the dog another slice.

At that moment a dim light came on inside Fausto's head. He saw that it was sort of a fancy dog, a terrier or something, with dog tags and a shiny collar. And it looked well fed and healthy. In his neighborhood, the dogs were never licensed, and if they got sick they
70 were placed near the water heater until they got well.

This dog looked like he belonged to rich people. Fausto cleaned his juice-sticky hands on his pants and got to his feet. The light in his head grew brighter. It just might work. He called the dog, patted its muscular back, and bent down to check the license.

REREAD
What do you think Fausto plans to do?

D

"Great," he said. "There's an address."

The dog's name was Roger, which struck Fausto as weird
80 because he'd never heard of a dog with a human name. Dogs should have names like Bomber, Freckles, Queenie, Killer, and Zero.

Fausto planned to take the dog home and collect a reward. He would say he had found Roger
90 near the freeway. That would

scare the daylights out of the owners, who would be so happy that they would probably give him a reward. He felt bad about lying, but the dog *was* loose. And it might even really be lost, because the address was six blocks away.

THINK IT THROUGH

E

What does Fausto decide to do? How does he seem to feel about his plan?

FOCUS

Read to find out what happens when Fausto meets Roger's owners.

B

Fausto stashed the rake and his sister's bike behind a bush, and, tossing an orange peel every time Roger became distracted, walked the
100 dog to his house. He hesitated on the porch until Roger began to scratch the door with a muddy paw. Fausto had come this far, so he figured he might as well go through with it. He knocked softly. When no one answered, he rang the doorbell. A man in a silky bathrobe and slippers opened the door and seemed confused by the sight of his dog and the boy.

distracted
(dĭ străk' tĭd) *adj.* not paying attention

C

"Sir," Fausto said, gripping Roger by the collar. "I found your dog by the freeway. His dog license says
110 he lives here." Fausto looked down at the dog, then up to the man. "He does, doesn't he?"

The man stared at Fausto a long time before saying in a pleasant voice, "That's right." He pulled his robe tighter around him because of the cold and asked Fausto to come in. "So he was by the freeway?"

COMPREHENSION

D **REREAD** What do you think Fausto plans to do? *(He's probably thinking about returning the lost dog for a reward.)* **predicting**

E **THINK IT THROUGH** What does Fausto decide to do? How does he seem to feel about his plan? *(He decides to take Roger back to his owners and collect a reward; he feels bad about lying, but the dog was loose, if not actually lost.)* **details**

LITERATURE

C Why do you think Fausto goes through with the plan anyway? *(He really wants the money for a guitar, so he justifies his lying by saying that the dog was loose.)* **motive**

VOCABULARY

B **stashed** Help students use the words *behind a bush* to understand that in the context of this story, to "stash" something means to hide it. Ask why Fausto would want to hide his rake and his sister's bike before taking Roger home. *(Fausto doesn't want anyone to find the rake and bike.)*

FOR ENGLISH LEARNERS

Help students understand the following expressions and idioms:

Line 61: How come?
Line 63: Cat got your tongue?
Line 65: light came on
Line 73: light in his head
Line 103: go through with it

"Uh-huh."

"You bad, snoopy dog," said the man, wagging his finger. "You probably knocked over some trash cans, too, didn't you?"

D Fausto didn't say anything. He looked around, amazed by this house with its shiny furniture and a television as large as the front window at home. Warm bread smells filled the air and music full of soft tinkling floated in from another room.

"Helen," the man called to the kitchen. "We have a visitor." His wife came into the living room wiping her hands on a dish towel and smiling. "And who have we here?" she asked in one of the softest voices Fausto had ever heard.

> **REREAD**
> How do the husband and wife greet Fausto? **F**

"This young man said he found Roger near the freeway."

Fausto repeated his story to her while staring at a perpetual clock with a bell-shaped glass, the kind his aunt got when she celebrated her twenty-fifth anniversary. The lady frowned and said, wagging a finger at Roger, "Oh, you're a bad boy."

> **perpetual clock**
> (pər pĕch′ ōō əl klŏk′)
> clock that runs without stopping

"It was very nice of you to bring Roger home," the man said. "Where do you live?"

"By that vacant lot on Olive," he said. "You know, by Brownie's Flower Place."

The wife looked at her husband, then Fausto. Her eyes twinkled triangles of light as she said, "Well, young man, you're probably hungry. How about a turnover?"

"What do I have to turn over?" Fausto asked, thinking she was talking about yard work or something like turning trays of dried raisins.

> **turnover**
> (tûrn′ ō′ vər)
> *n.* fruit-filled pastry

"No, no, dear, it's a pastry." She took him by the elbow and guided him to a kitchen that sparkled with copper pans and bright yellow wallpaper. She guided him to the kitchen table and gave him a tall glass of milk and something that looked like an empanada. Steamy waves of heat escaped when he tore it in two. He ate with both eyes on the man and woman who stood arm-in-arm smiling at him. They were strange, he thought. But nice.

> **empanada**
> (ĕm′ pä nä′ dä)
> meat-filled Mexican pastry

C

"That was good," he said after he finished the turnover. "Did you make it, ma'am?"

"Yes, I did. Would you like another?"

"No, thank you. I have to go home now."

As Fausto walked to the door, the man opened his wallet and took out a bill. "This is for you," he said. "Roger is special to us, almost like a son."

G

Fausto looked at the bill and knew he was in trouble. Not with these nice folks or with his parents but with himself. How could he have been so deceitful? The dog wasn't lost. It was just having a fun Saturday walking around.

> **deceitful**
> (dĭ sēt′ fəl)
> *adj.* full of lies

E

"I can't take that."

"You have to. You deserve it, believe me," the man said.

"No, I don't."

"Now don't be silly," said the lady. She took the bill from her husband and stuffed it into Fausto's shirt pocket. "You're a lovely child. Your

F

COMPREHENSION

F **REREAD** How do the husband and wife greet Fausto? *(They welcome him and are quite friendly.)* **details**

G Ask: How well does Fausto's plan work? *(It works well: Roger's owners give Fausto money for returning Roger safely.)* **cause and effect**

LITERATURE

D Why is this place so amazing to Fausto? *(With its shiny furniture, large TV, and soft music, it's nothing like his house. He's probably never seen anything like it.)* **setting**

E Why does Fausto say that he can't take the money? *(He's feeling guilty now for having lied to get it.)* **internal conflict**

F Earlier in the story, Fausto didn't mind lying. What do you think makes him change his mind? *(After he meets the people and they are so kind to him, he feels bad for lying and taking their money.)* **internal conflict**

VOCABULARY

C **both eyes on the man and woman** Make sure that students understand that this expression means Fausto is watching the couple very closely.

FOR ENGLISH LEARNERS

Help students understand the following:

Line 136: twenty-fifth anniversary

parents are lucky to have you. Be good. And come see us again, please."

H
THINK IT THROUGH
How does Fausto react to Roger's owners?

FOCUS
Read to see how the reward makes Fausto feel.

Fausto went out, and the lady closed the door. Fausto clutched the bill through his shirt pocket. He felt like ringing the doorbell and begging them to please take the money back, but he knew they would
190 refuse. He hurried away, and at the end of the block, pulled the bill from his shirt pocket: it was a crisp twenty-dollar bill.

"Oh, man, I shouldn't have lied," he said under his breath as he started up the street like a zombie. He wanted to run to church for Saturday confession, but it was past four-thirty, when confession stopped.

He returned to the bush where he had hidden the rake and his sister's bike and rode home
200 slowly, not daring to touch the money in his pocket. At home, in the privacy of his room, he examined the twenty-dollar bill. He had never had so much money. It was probably enough to buy a secondhand guitar. But he felt bad, like the time he stole a dollar from the secret fold inside his older brother's wallet.

Fausto went outside and sat on the fence. "Yeah," he said. "I can probably get a guitar for twenty. Maybe at a yard sale—things are cheaper."
210 His mother called him to dinner.

zombie
(zŏm' bē)
one who is almost lifeless

secondhand
(sĕk' ənd händ')
adj. used; not new

34 Unit 1 Not According to Plan

The next day he dressed for church without anyone telling him. He was going to go to eight o'clock mass.
G
"I'm going to church, Mom," he said. His mother was in the kitchen cooking papas and chorizo con huevos. A pile of tortillas lay warm under a dishtowel.

"Oh, I'm so proud of you, Son." She beamed, turning over the crackling papas.

D
His older brother, Lawrence, who was at the table reading the funnies, mimicked, "Oh, I'm so proud of you, my son," under his breath.

At Saint Theresa's he sat near the front. When Father Jerry began by saying that we are all sinners, Fausto thought he looked right at him. Could he know? Fausto fidgeted with guilt. No, he thought. I only did it yesterday.

H
Fausto knelt, prayed, and sang. But he couldn't forget the man and the lady, whose names he didn't even know, and the empanada they had given him. It
230 had a strange name but tasted really good. He wondered how they got rich. And how that dome clock worked. He had asked his mother once how his aunt's clock worked. She said it just worked, the way the refrigerator works. It just did.

Fausto caught his mind wandering and tried to concentrate on his sins. He said a Hail Mary and sang, and when the wicker basket came his way, he stuck a hand reluctantly in his pocket and pulled out the twenty-dollar bill. He ironed it between his palms,
240 and dropped it into the basket. The grown-ups stared. Here was a kid dropping twenty dollars in the basket while they gave just three or four dollars.

papas
(pä' päs)
potatoes

chorizo con huevos
(chō rē' zō kŏn wä' vōs)
Mexican dish of sausage and eggs

I
THINK IT THROUGH
What does Fausto do with the money? Why?

The No-Guitar Blues 35

H **COMPREHENSION**

THINK IT THROUGH How does Fausto react to Roger's owners? *(He thinks they're nice; their friendliness makes him feel guilty for taking the reward money.)* **cause and effect**

I **THINK IT THROUGH** What does Fausto do with the money? Why? *(He puts it in the offering basket at church because he feels guilty about lying.)* **cause and effect**

LITERATURE

G Why does Fausto go to eight o'clock mass without anyone telling him to go? *(Students probably will say that he wants to correct his wrongdoing, or make up for lying and taking the money.)* **motive**

H What conflict is Fausto having? *(He wants to use the twenty dollars to buy a guitar, but he can't stop thinking about the people he lied to.)* **internal conflict**

VOCABULARY

D **mimicked** Help students understand that when Lawrence says under his breath, "Oh, I'm so proud of you, my son," he is repeating his mother's words. Therefore, *mimicked* must mean "repeated" or "imitated."

FOR ENGLISH LEARNERS

Help students understand the following expressions and idioms:

Line 196: confession
Line 209: yard sale
Line 220: funnies

FOCUS

Is Fausto's dream of a guitar over? Read on to see what happens.

There would be a second collection for Saint Vincent de Paul, the lector announced. The wicker baskets again floated in the pews, and this time the adults around him, given a second chance to show their charity, dug deep into their wallets and purses and dropped in fives and tens. This time Fausto tossed in the grimy quarter.

I 250   Fausto felt better after church. He went home and played football in the front yard with his brother and some neighbor kids. He felt cleared of wrongdoing and was so happy that he played one of his best games of football ever. On one play, he tore his good pants, which he knew he shouldn't have been wearing. For a second, while he examined the hole, he wished he hadn't given the twenty dollars away.

    Man, I coulda bought me some Levi's, he thought. He pictured his twenty dollars being spent to buy

J 260 church candles. He pictured a priest buying an armful of flowers with *his* money.

    Fausto had to forget about getting a guitar. He spent the next day playing soccer in his good pants, which were now his old pants. But that night during dinner, his mother said she remembered seeing an old bass guitarron the last time she cleaned out her father's garage.

> **guitarron**
> (gē tä rōn′)
> Mexican guitar

"It's a little dusty," his mom said, serving his favorite enchiladas, "But I think it works. Grandpa
270 says it works."

    Fausto's ears perked up. That was the same kind the guy in Los Lobos played. Instead of asking for the guitar, he waited for his mother to offer it to him. And she did, while gathering the dishes from the table.

    "No, Mom, I'll do it," he said, hugging her. "I'll do the dishes forever if you want."

E   It was the happiest day of his life. No, it was the second-happiest day of his life. The happiest was when his grandfather Lupe placed the guitarron,
280 which was nearly as huge as a washtub, in his arms. Fausto ran a thumb down the strings, which vibrated in his throat and chest. It sounded beautiful, deep and eerie. A pumpkin smile widened on his face.

    "OK, *hijo*, now you put your fingers like this," said his grandfather, smelling of tobacco and aftershave. He took Fausto's fingers and placed them on the strings. Fausto strummed a chord on the guitarron, and the bass resounded in their chests.

> **hijo**
> (ē′ hō)
> son

290   The guitarron was more complicated than Fausto imagined. But he was confident that after a few more lessons he could start a band that would someday play on "American Bandstand" for the dancing crowds.

K **THINK IT THROUGH**

1. How does Fausto get a guitar?
2. Do you think Fausto was right to give the money to the church? Why or why not?
3. How do you think Fausto is feeling when he offers to wash the dishes forever? Explain.

36   The No-Guitar Blues **37**

COMPREHENSION

J **Reciprocal Teaching**
Suggestion: Connecting
Teacher Modeling To demonstrate the Active Reading Strategy of connecting, you could say: *At this point, Fausto briefly regrets giving away the money, even though he'd first felt very relieved. I had an experience like this recently. I was looking for a sweater and then I remembered I'd donated it to charity, along with some other old clothing. Even though it seemed like a very good thing at the time to contribute to a good cause, I suddenly found myself missing that sweater. Still, like Fausto, I got over it quickly. Reading about him, I can understand how he has second thoughts.*

Student Modeling Have a volunteer connect to the preceding paragraph, in which Fausto ruins his good pants. Ask the student to tell his or her thoughts aloud.

K **THINK IT THROUGH**

1. How does Fausto get a guitar? *(His grandfather gives him a bass guitarron that he had in his garage.)* **details**

2. Do you think Fausto was right to give the money to the church? Why or why not? *(Some students might say that Fausto was right because it made up for his lying. Others might say that he was wrong and should have given the money back to Roger's owners.)* **evaluating**

3. How do you think Fausto is feeling when he offers to wash the dishes forever? Explain. *(He is extremely happy and grateful to his mother for offering him the guitarron. He also might be feeling that he did the right thing by giving his money to the church.)* **making inferences**

Option for Speaking and Listening
Use question 2 on page 37 for a debate. Encourage students to state their arguments and then support them with at least three reasons.

RETEACHING

If students need more help understanding **Cause and Effect**, use pages T642–T646.

LITERATURE

I How do you know that Fausto has solved his internal conflict? *(He feels better after church.)* **internal conflict**

How else might Fausto have solved his conflict? *(Some students may say that he never should have lied and taken the money in the first place. Others may say that he should have returned the money to Roger's owners.)* **evaluating**

VOCABULARY

E **bass guitarron** Help students use context clues to figure out what a bass guitarron looks and sounds like.

1. COMPREHENSION

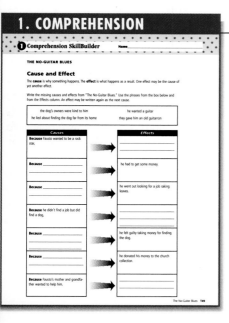

Cause and Effect

Direct Instruction Tell students that many events in stories are connected by cause-and-effect relationships. The **cause** is the reason why something happens. The **effect** is what happens as a result of the cause. The cause happens before the effect. Explain, also, that the effect may become a cause of yet another effect. There can be a long chain of causes and effects. To provide an example, discuss a familiar story such as "The Three Bears." The story begins with the problem of too-hot porridge. Say: *Because the porridge needs time to cool, the bears go for a walk. Because the bears are out on their walk, their house is empty. Because the house is empty, Goldilocks enters without supervision. Because she is not watched, . . .* Challenge the students to carry the chain of cause and effect to the end of the story.

> **Comprehension SkillBuilder Answer Key:**
> *(Because Fausto wanted to be a rock star,) he wanted a guitar.*
> *(Because) he wanted a guitar, (he had to get some money.)*
> *(Because) he had to get some money, (he went out looking for a job raking leaves.)*
> *(Because he didn't find a job but did find a dog,) he lied about finding the dog far from its home.*
> *(Because) he lied about finding the dog far from its home, (he felt guilty taking money for finding the dog.)*
> *(Because) he felt guilty taking money for finding the dog, (he donated his money to the church collection.)*
> *(Because Fausto's mother and grandfather wanted to help him,) they gave him an old guitarron.*

2. LITERATURE

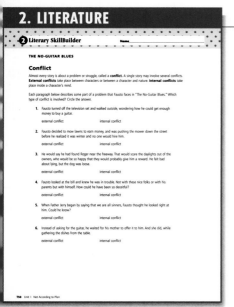

Conflict: External and Internal

Direct Instruction Tell students that some kind of struggle takes place in almost every story. This struggle is called a **conflict**. Conflicts may be external or internal:

- An **external conflict** can be a struggle between a character and another individual or a group, or between a character and nature. For example, a character may struggle against a blizzard or a hurricane.
- An **internal conflict** is a struggle within a character. This struggle is usually about a difficult decision the character must make. The character often has to struggle with his or her own feelings.

Point out that in many stories there may be more than one conflict. Also, both external and internal conflicts are sometimes found in the same story.

Discuss the conflicts in "The No-Guitar Blues." Ask: *What is Fausto's biggest problem as the story begins? What does he need that others can give him?* Explain that Fausto's wish to get this thing is the external conflict. Then ask: *About midway through the story, something happens that makes Fausto feel angry toward himself. What is it? How does he stop feeling bad about himself?* Explain that Fausto's guilt over lying and his efforts to get rid of the guilt make up the internal conflict.

> **Literary SkillBuilder Answer Key:**
> **1.** *internal conflict*
> **2.** *external conflict*
> **3.** *internal conflict*
> **4.** *internal conflict*
> **5.** *internal conflict*
> **6.** *external conflict*

3. VOCABULARY

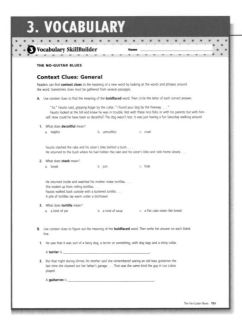

Context Clues: General

Direct Instruction Tell students that clues in the text called **context clues** help readers figure out the meaning of many unfamiliar words. Context clues are usually found in the same sentence or paragraph as the unfamiliar word, but if the word is used more than once, there may be clues in each of the several passages. Explain that sometimes context clues only hint at what the word means. Give students these steps to follow when trying to figure out a word's meaning.

- Use context clues to decide what part of speech the word is.

- If the word is a noun, look for clues about what the thing looks like, how it sounds, or what it does.
- If the word is a verb, look for clues about how the action affects events.
- If the word is an adjective or adverb, imagine how the word fits together with the thing it is describing.
- Once you think you know what the word means, replace the word in the text with that definition and read the sentence again. The sentence should make sense. As you continue, make sure the word continues to make sense with that meaning.

Vocabulary SkillBuilder Answer Key:	
A. 1. *b* **2.** *c* **3.** *c*	**B.** *Wording may vary.* **1.** *a kind of fancy dog* **2.** *a kind of guitar*

4. WORDS TO KNOW

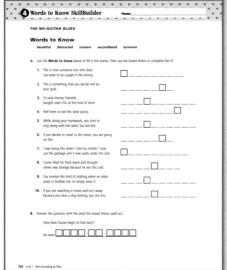

Words to Know

Direct Instruction As you present the **Words to Know,** here are some points you might want to cover. Help students identify the parts of the vocabulary words. Stress the importance of finding the base of each word. Help students remove prefixes and suffixes first.

- **deceit** + ful = *deceitful*
- **distract** + ed = *distracted*
- **turnover** and **secondhand** are compound words

Tell students to fill in the blanks by reading the clues and finding the words in the Words to Know list. There are two clues for each word. If students have difficulty determining a word from the clue alone, they can count the blanks and fill in the corresponding word with the same number of letters. Students may also begin placing the boxed letters from questions 1–10 into the boxes at the bottom of the page as they move down the list. Point out to students that the boxed letters are in order and they need not unscramble or rearrange letters to spell out the last answer.

Words to Know SkillBuilder Answer Key:

A.
1. *deceitful*
2. *mission*
3. *secondhand*
4. *turnover*
5. *distracted*
6. *mission*
7. *deceitful*
8. *turnover*
9. *secondhand*
10. *distracted*

B. *door-to-door*

5. SELECTION TEST

Selection Test Answer Key:
A. 1. *b* **2.** *c* **3.** *a* **4.** *c*
B. *Fausto receives a guitarron from his grandfather.*

THE NO-GUITAR BLUES

Cause and Effect

The **cause** is why something happens. The **effect** is what happens as a result. One effect may be the cause of yet another effect.

Write the missing causes and effects from "The No-Guitar Blues." Use the phrases from the box below and from the Effects column. An effect may be written again as the next cause.

| the dog's owners were kind to him | he wanted a guitar |
| he lied about finding the dog far from its home | they gave him an old guitarron |

Causes	**Effects**
Because Fausto wanted to be a rock star,	_____ _____
Because _____ _____	he had to get some money.
Because _____ _____	he went out looking for a job raking leaves.
Because he didn't find a job but did find a dog,	_____ _____ _____
Because _____ _____ _____	he felt guilty taking money for finding the dog.
Because _____ _____	he donated his money to the church collection.
Because Fausto's mother and grandfather wanted to help him,	_____ _____

Copyright © McDougal Littell Inc.

THE NO-GUITAR BLUES

Conflict

Almost every story is about a problem or struggle, called a **conflict.** A single story may involve several conflicts. **External conflicts** take place between characters or between a character and nature. **Internal conflicts** take place inside a character's mind.

Each paragraph below describes some part of a problem that Fausto faces in "The No-Guitar Blues." Which type of conflict is involved? Circle the answer.

1. Fausto turned off the television set and walked outside, wondering how he could get enough money to buy a guitar.

    external conflict   internal conflict

2. Fausto decided to mow lawns to earn money, and was pushing the mower down the street before he realized it was winter and no one would hire him.

    external conflict   internal conflict

3. He would say he had found Roger near the freeway. That would scare the daylights out of the owners, who would be so happy that they would probably give him a reward. He felt bad about lying, but the dog was loose.

    external conflict   internal conflict

4. Fausto looked at the bill and knew he was in trouble. Not with these nice folks or with his parents but with himself. How could he have been so deceitful?

    external conflict   internal conflict

5. When Father Jerry began by saying that we are all sinners, Fausto thought he looked right at him. Could he know?

    external conflict   internal conflict

6. Instead of asking for the guitar, he waited for his mother to offer it to him. And she did, while gathering the dishes from the table.

    external conflict   internal conflict

THE NO-GUITAR BLUES

Context Clues: General

Readers can find **context clues** to the meaning of a new word by looking at the words and phrases around the word. Sometimes clues must be gathered from several passages.

A. Use context clues to find the meaning of the **boldfaced** word. Then circle the letter of each correct answer.

> "Sir," Fausto said, gripping Roger by the collar. "I found your dog by the freeway. . . . "
> Fausto looked at the bill and knew he was in trouble. Not with these nice folks or with his parents but with himself. How could he have been so deceitful? The dog wasn't lost. It was just having a fun Saturday walking around.

1. What does **deceitful** mean?
   a. helpful   b. untruthful   c. cruel

> Fausto stashed the rake and his sister's bike behind a bush. . . .
> He returned to the bush where he had hidden the rake and his sister's bike and rode home slowly. . . .

2. What does **stash** mean?
   a. break   b. join   c. hide

> He returned inside and watched his mother make tortillas. . . .
> She looked up from rolling tortillas. . . .
> Fausto walked back outside with a buttered tortilla. . . .
> A pile of tortillas lay warm under a dishtowel.

3. What does **tortilla** mean?
   a. a kind of pie   b. a kind of soup   c. a flat bread

B. Use context clues to figure out the meaning of the **boldfaced** word. Then write the answer on each blank line.

1. He saw that it was sort of a fancy dog, a terrier or something, with dog tags and a shiny collar.

   A **terrier** is _____.

2. But that night during dinner, his mother said she remembered seeing an old bass guitarron the last time she cleaned out her father's garage. . . . That was the same kind the guy in Los Lobos played.

   A **guitarron** is _____.

THE NO-GUITAR BLUES

Words to Know

deceitful   distracted   mission   secondhand   turnover

A. Use the **Words to Know** above to fill in the blanks. Then use the boxed letters to complete Part B.

1. This is how someone acts who does not want to be caught in the wrong.

2. This is something that you decide will be your goal.

3. To save money, Danielle bought used CDs at this kind of store.

4. Neil loves to eat this tasty pastry.

5. While doing your homework, you start to sing along with the radio. You are this.

6. If you decide to travel to the moon, you are going on this.

7. I was being this when I told my mother I took out the garbage and it was really under the sink.

8. Carlos liked his food warm and thought James was strange because he ate this cold.

9. You receive this kind of clothing when an older sister or brother can no longer wear it.

10. If you are watching a movie and turn away because you hear a dog barking, you are this.

B. Answer the question with the word the boxed letters spell out.

How does Fausto begin to find work?

He went ☐☐☐☐ - ☐☐ - ☐☐☐☐ .

THE NO-GUITAR BLUES

A. Fill in the circle beside the letter of the correct answer.

1. What does Fausto want to do with his life?

○ a. start a lawn-mowing service

○ b. play the guitar in his own band

○ c. be a television announcer

2. What causes Fausto to make that decision?

○ a. He has always wanted to be on television.

○ b. His school counselor tells him it's a good idea.

○ c. He sees Los Lobos on *American Bandstand.*

3. What does Fausto plan to do with Roger the dog?

○ a. take Roger to his owners and collect a reward

○ b. take him along on his lawn-mowing jobs

○ c. walk him every day to make money for a guitar

4. Why doesn't Fausto want to take the money from Roger's owners?

○ a. He already makes enough money from mowing lawns.

○ b. He knows they need the money much more than he does.

○ c. He feels he doesn't deserve it because he has lied to them.

B. In your own words, tell what musical instrument Fausto receives and from whom.

_____

_____

Focus Skills and SkillBuilder Copymasters

A Slave p. T56
COMPREHENSION
Chronological Order p. T63
LITERATURE
Literary Nonfiction p. T64
VOCABULARY
Prefixes p. T65
Words to Know p. T66

Wilma Mankiller p. T68
COMPREHENSION
Making Judgments p. T77
Details p. T78
VOCABULARY
Idioms p. T79
Words to Know p. T80

Cesar Chavez: Civil-Rights Champion p. T82
COMPREHENSION
Fact and Opinion p. T89
LITERATURE
Biography p. T90
VOCABULARY
Context Clues p. T91
Words to Know p. T92

Roberto Clemente: Hero and Friend p. T94
COMPREHENSION
Chronological Order p. T102
Reading for Details p. T103
VOCABULARY
Specialized Vocabulary p. T104
Words to Know p. T105

Reading Fluency

 ★ Reading Fluency p. T107

Courage Counts

Unit 2
Nonfiction

Once someone ran from slavery when there was no clear way out. Once a woman became the first female chief of her tribe. Once someone took chances so that others could have better lives. What did these people have in common? Courage.

Nonfiction is writing about real people, places, and events.

• **Biography:** This is an account of a person's life written by another person.

• **True Account:** This is a real-life incident in someone's life that reads like a story.

38

Pacing Guide

SELECTION	TOTAL DAYS	PREREADING	READING	POST READING	
				SELECTIVE OPTIONS	ALL OPTIONS
A Slave	2.5–3	1	1	.5	1
Wilma Mankiller	2–2.5	1	.5	.5	1
Cesar Chavez: Civil-Rights Champion	2–2.5	1	.5	.5	1
Roberto Clemente: Hero and Friend	2.5–3	1	1	.5	1

True Account — page 40

A SLAVE

BY VIRGINIA HAMILTON

Slaves had heard of secret places along the way to freedom. Discover how one man finds his way to the Underground Railroad.

Biography — page 48

Wilma Mankiller

by Linda Lowery

An old saying states, "You can't go home again." Wilma Mankiller proved the saying wrong. She returned to her home and became its chief.

Biography — page 60

Cesar Chavez: Civil-Rights Champion

by Nancy Lobb

How can the powerless become powerful? Cesar Chavez spent his life finding the answers.

Biography — page 68

Roberto Clemente: Hero and Friend

by Irma Zepeda

What makes a hero? Perhaps it is courage and the desire to help others. Find out about the life of a hero.

39

More About Nonfiction

Three biographies and a true account describe significant moments in the lives of four real-life individuals in this unit. The lives depicted here are colorful. Each figure reaches a dramatic turning point that not only changes his or her life but in some way improves the lives of others. You might have students look at pages 458–459 in the Student Resources section to understand terms and types of nonfiction.

Technology Resources

Audio CD
All selections in this unit are featured in the Audio Library.

Reading Coach CD-ROM
The following selections are part of the Reading Coach: "Wilma Mankiller" and "Roberto Clemente: Hero and Friend." You may use Reading Coach selections as a group activity, as an individual activity, or as a tutorial for students who might benefit from this format or who have missed class.

Building Bridges: Closing the Reading Gap
This video is intended for teacher use only. It gives instructions and tips on how to help middle school readers become strategic readers.

Assessment

Selection Tests
pp. T67, T81, T93, T106

Assessment Booklet
Progress Check Units 1–4
Administer this test after the first four units of the book have been read. It covers skills taught in all four units.

Focus Skills

COMPREHENSION
Chronological Order

LITERATURE
Literary Nonfiction

VOCABULARY
Prefixes

SkillBuilder Copymasters

Reading Comprehension:
1 Chronological Order p. T63

Literary Analysis:
2 Literary Nonfiction p. T64

Vocabulary:
3 Prefixes p. T65
4 Words to Know p. T66

Assessment

5 Selection Test p. T67

Readability Scores

DRP	LEXILE	DALE-CHALL
50	670	3.8

For English Learners

You might spend time discussing slavery and the Civil War, including division between the North and South, with students unfamiliar with American history.

A SLAVE

BY VIRGINIA HAMILTON

Into Bondage (1936), Aaron Douglas. Oil on canvas 60 3/8" x 60 1/2". In the collection of the Corcoran Gallery of Art, Washington, DC. Museum Purchase and partial gift from Thurlow Evans Tibbs. The Evans-Tibbs Collection.

40 Unit 2 Courage Counts

More About Those Who Helped

Known officially as the members of the Religious Society of Friends, the Quakers became established in England in the 1600s. They settled a colony in Pennsylvania early in America's history. Quakers have a history of working for humanitarian causes. Make sure students understand that in the United States, although slavery was practiced primarily in the South, many people there objected to it and sacrificed their safety by acting against it. For example, Sarah and Angelina Grimké grew up on a slave plantation. However, after becoming Quakers, they rejected slavery and gave lectures about its evils.

Detail of *Into Bondage* (1936), Aaron Douglas.

SLAVES HAD
HEARD OF
SECRET PLACES
ALONG THE WAY
TO FREEDOM.
DISCOVER HOW
ONE MAN FINDS
HIS WAY TO THE
UNDERGROUND
RAILROAD.

Connect to Your Life

What do you know about slavery in America's past? What did freedom mean to slaves? Have a partner make a word web for either the word *slavery* or *freedom*. Make and fill in your own web for the other word. Then compare and contrast your webs.

Key to the True Account

"The Underground Railroad" got its name because of the actions of a runaway slave. His name was Tice Davids. As you read his true story, notice that in some parts, the type is italic. Think of these words as "voices" from the past that Tice Davids is remembering.

Vocabulary Preview

Words to Know

plantation   settlement
revived   rails

A Slave **41**

Connect to Your Life

If partners need help getting started on their word or concept webs, you may want to suggest the following categories: *Meaning; Synonyms; Antonyms; People, Places, Things, or Events I Connect with the Word.* For an example of a concept web, see page T668.

Key to the True Account

This nonfictional account is written in the style of a fictional story. The italicized dialogue throughout serves to illustrate how Tice Davids and others spoke in 1831, which adds to the authenticity of Davids's story.

Vocabulary Preview

Words to Know
  plantation *n.* large farm in the South where workers raised crops
  revived *v.* refreshed
  settlement *n.* small community
  rails *n.* two steel bars that form train tracks

 For direct instruction on Words to Know, see page T62.

Building Background

The Underground Railroad was a network of escape routes that slaves used from about 1830 to 1860. The busiest routes ran though Ohio, Indiana, and Pennsylvania. Many slaves followed these routes to the Great Lakes and then sailed on to Canada, especially after Congress enforced the strict Fugitive Slave Act of 1850. Two of the most famous "conductors" on the Railroad were Harriet Tubman, an escaped slave who helped about 300 slaves, and Levi Coffin, a Quaker who helped more than 3,000 slaves. Coffin's home, in what is now Fountain City, Indiana, was on three major escape routes.

Vocabulary Strategy: Preteaching

Prefixes Explain that an **affix** is a word part that can be attached to a root word to make a new word. An affix added to the beginning of a word is called a **prefix.** Copy the following chart, and have students add at least one more word to each row in the last column.

Prefix	Meaning	Examples
dis-	not; the absence of	dislike, disbelief, _____
un-	not; the opposite of	unreal, unable, _____
under-	below; beneath	underpass, underarm, _____

 For more on Prefixes, see page T62.

FOCUS

Tice Davids has reached a life-changing moment. Read about the action he takes.

 The underground road was named for the deed of an actual man born a slave who one day ran away from slavery. It became the name given to all the secret trails that led north, and to the system of human helpers against slavery—black, white, and red—who braved prison and even death to lead the running-aways to freedom.

> **running-aways**
> runaway slaves

 Tice Davids inspired the first use of the
10 term "underground road." On a day in 1831
that seemed ordinary, full of pain and hard
work for him, Davids discovered that he had changed.
He wondered how it had happened that on this day he
could not bear to be a slave a moment longer.

It was time for him to make his way
north. And so he ran.

Tice knew where he was going. There
were Friends across the Ohio River,
waiting. North would be somewhere there,
and on and on. Word of that had come to
20 him on the plantation. Whispers about
liberty had made their way through the
servants' quarters and on to the fields.
They spread on the wind down to the
riverbank. Tice had an idea of what it was
to be free. It meant that he might rest
without fear covering him like a blanket as he slept. It
meant that nobody could buy or sell him.

Not all those who were slaves had the daring to
escape. It wasn't that Tice was without fear. But, like
30 others before him, given the chance, he'd take it.

> **Friends**
> Quakers, members of a religious group that was against slavery

> **plantation**
> (plăn tā′ shən)
> *n.* large farm in the South where workers raised crops

There were those, black and free, who combed the riverbank, looking to help the running-aways. And there were certain Presbyterian ministers from the South who had formed a new church and had settled in the counties of
40 southern Ohio. They were known to be friends of slaves. Like ever-present eagles with fierce, keen eyes, they too watched the great river for the running-aways.

Trusted to be a good servant, Tice had taken his life into his own hands and had run. And now he
50 hurried, running.

Detail of *Into Bondage* (1936), Aaron Douglas.

THINK IT THROUGH

 Where is Tice going? Who did he think might help him?

FOCUS

Tice's journey has begun. Find out how Tice deals with the problems he faces.

"Look for the lantern!" That had been the urgent message passed along the slave quarters for those who would run at night.

"Listen for the bell!" Word was that the lone, distant sound of a bell clanging could be heard from across the wide river—when the wind was right. Other

---

COMPREHENSION

FOCUS SKILL: Chronological Order

Explain that **chronological order** is the order in which events happened. Words and phrases called **signal words,** such as *first, then,* and dates, often help make the order of events clearer.

For direct instruction on Chronological Order, see page T61.

 Ask students what signal words tell them when Tice Davids decides to escape. *(On a day in 1831)* **chronological order**

 THINK IT THROUGH Where is Tice going? Who did he think might help him? *(across the Ohio River to the North; friends of slaves would help him, such as free blacks and ministers)* **main idea**

LITERATURE

FOCUS SKILL: Literary Nonfiction

Explain that **literary nonfiction** tells about actual people, places, and events, but it does so by telling a story. Literary nonfiction includes literary elements such as characters, setting, plot, and dialogue.

For direct instruction on Literary Nonfiction, see page T61.

Use the following questions to encourage literary analysis.

 How are the lantern and the bell important to the setting? *(They let running-aways know that they are getting close to a safe house.)* **setting**

VOCABULARY

FOCUS SKILL: Prefixes

An **affix,** or word part, added to the beginning of a word is called a **prefix.** Remind students that knowing the meanings of different affixes can help them understand unfamiliar words.

 underground Students can use the prefix *under-* to help them figure out what this word means.

 discovered Explain to students that the meaning of *dis-* in this case is "remove." Something discovered is something that is new knowledge—knowledge that is removed from being covered.

FOR ENGLISH LEARNERS

Help students understand the following expressions and idioms:

Line 8: inspired the first use
Line 13: could not bear
Line 14: make his way
Line 19: word of that
Line 28: had the daring
Line 32: combed the riverbank
Line 47: taken his life into his own hands
Line 52: slave quarters

times, the bell seemed to clang up and down the shore. The river might be covered in fog. And hidden deep in the mist on the shore, a running-away could clearly
60 hear the bell. He could follow its ringing all the way over and to a safe house.

safe house
secret place used to hide escaped slaves

Tice Davids would have to find a way across the great water if he was ever to be free. With luck he might find a usable boat or raft along the shore. What would he do if there was nothing to ride across on?

C Capture for him was unthinkable, and he kept on running.

70 *"Heard tell that on the other side, a slave is no longer such. They say that on the other side of the wide water, a slave is a free man."*

That was the word and the truth that all Kentucky slaves believed. He kept that in mind as he ran. He looked back, knowing what he would see. There were the planter and his
80 men, coming after him. The slave owner. Some called him master; Tice wouldn't when he could avoid it.

C Friends, waiting across the river, was the word he could count on. If only he could get to the Friends!

Detail of *Into Bondage* (1936), Aaron Douglas.

44 Unit 2 Courage Counts

He had been running for some time. Almost as
90 though he were dreaming, he lifted one leg and then the other. Whatever had possessed him to try to break out?

Now he was at the Kentucky shore and it was empty. There was no boat to row, no raft to pole. The distant Ohio shore seemed farther than far. There was nothing for it but to swim.

Tice waded into the water, tired out before he began. The cold wet of the river shocked him, revived him. He knew to calm himself down and soon got his mind in hand. He
100 began moving his arms, swimming in clean, long strokes.

E About halfway across, Tice thought he heard a bell. The sound gave him strength and he swam gamely on.

revived
(rĭ vĭvd')
v. refreshed; past tense of *revive*

REREAD
How does Tice show courage in crossing the river?

D

D It took the slave owner time to locate a skiff, but a small boat was found at last. He and his men shoved off and gave chase. The slave owner never let his slave out of his sight. Even when Tice staggered from the water onto the Ohio shore, the
110 owner glared through the mist and pinpointed the dark, exhausted figure.

"Think we have him now," he said. He blinked to get the wet from his eyes. It was one blink too many. Tice Davids was gone. Disappeared!

"It's not believable," the owner said. "I saw him before my eyes and now he's gone. Vanished! It's not possible, but there it is."

F **THINK IT THROUGH**
What does Tice do that is so surprising to the slave owner?

A Slave 45

COMPREHENSION

C **Reciprocal Teaching**
Suggestion: Clarifying
Teacher Modeling To demonstrate the Active Reading Strategy of clarifying, focus on the fifth paragraph, beginning at line 85. You could say: *When I got to this point of the account, I had to ask myself, "Now, who are the Friends again?" So what I needed to do was to turn back to the beginning of "A Slave" to find the spot where I'd first seen the term. I found it on page 42, line 17. There's a note there that gives information about this group. When I flipped back to Tice's escape, I had no problem understanding what sort of friends he was trying to reach.*

Student Modeling Ask a student to read lines 103–105 and clarify why the sound of the bell gave Tice strength. The student should say that he or she remembers reading about a bell earlier

in the story, then should reread lines 51–61, and finally should explain why the sound of the bell gave Tice strength.

D **REREAD** How does Tice show courage in crossing the river? *(When he finds no boat or raft, he decides to swim across.)* **making inferences**

E Ask: When Tice is in the river, at what point does he think he hears a bell? How do you know? *(The signal words* About halfway across *make it clear.)* **chronological order**

F **THINK IT THROUGH** What does Tice do that is so surprising to the slave owner? *(He vanishes.)* **cause and effect**

VOCABULARY

C **unthinkable** Students can use the meanings of the prefix *un- to* help them figure out what this word means.

D **skiff** Ask students what words in the same sentence tell what *skiff* means. *(a small boat)* **context clues**

FOR ENGLISH LEARNERS

Help students understand the following expressions and idioms:

Line 69: heard tell
Line 69: no longer such
Line 91: whatever had possessed him
Line 99: got his mind in hand
Line 104: swam gamely on
Line 107: shoved off and gave chase
Line 113: one blink too many

A Slave PE 44–45 • **T59**

FOCUS
What happens to Tice? Read to find out how the search ends.

The slave owner searched the shore every which
way. He looked into ditches. He and his men beat
120 the bushes and crept into caves and gazed up into
trees. They poked the haystacks in the fields. They
talked to people in the slavery-hating
settlement at Ripley, Ohio, and they had
their suspicions. But not one of the
townsfolk would admit to having seen
anybody running away. The Kentucky slave
owner never again saw Tice Davids.

> **settlement**
> (sĕt' l mənt)
> *n.* small
> community

"Well, I'm going home," he said finally. He and his
men crossed the river again and returned to Kentucky.
130 "Only one way to look at it," he told everyone at
home, shaking his head in disbelief. "Tice must've
gone on an underground road!"

Tice Davids made his way north through all of
Ohio, all the way to Sandusky, on Lake Erie. There,
at last, he settled, a free man—and the first to travel
the underground road.

Later, the underground road took on an inspiring
new name in honor of the amazing steam
trains on parallel rails then coming into
140 their own in America: *the Underground
Railroad!*

> **rails**
> (rālz)
> *n.* two steel bars
> that form train
> tracks

Those who guided the running-aways
along the highly secret system of the
Underground Railroad had the cleverness to call
themselves "conductors," the name used on the steam
railway trains. The safe houses and secret hiding
places known to the conductors were called
"stations" and "depots," after railway stations and

46 Unit 2 Courage Counts

railway depots. Eventually, Tice Davids became a
150 conductor on the Underground Railroad, helping
other running-aways escape.

THINK IT THROUGH

1. Why was Tice Davids able to escape? Use evidence
   from the selection to support your answer.
2. When Tice reached freedom, he could have left
   danger behind. Why do you think he chose to
   become a conductor on the Underground Railroad?
3. What advice would Tice have given to a slave who
   had not yet decided to run?

Detail of *Into Bondage* (1936),
Aaron Douglas.

A Slave **47**

COMPREHENSION

G Ask students what clue words help them know that it takes Tice a long time to reach Sandusky. *(at last)* **chronological order**

H THINK IT THROUGH

1. Why was Tice Davids able to escape? Use evidence from the selection to support your answer. *(Freedom meant so much to him that he was willing to chance escaping; he kept the idea of freedom firmly in his mind at all times; he was clever, strong-willed, and physically strong.)* **making inferences**

2. When Tice reached freedom, he could have left danger behind. Why do you think he chose to become a conductor on the Underground Railroad? *(He valued freedom so much that he was willing to risk his life to help others have it too.)* **drawing conclusions**

3. What advice would Tice have given to a slave who had not yet decided to run? *(Possible answer:*

As long as you're a slave, your life and your soul are not your own. If you don't have freedom, you might as well be dead.) **theme** LITERATURE

RETEACHING

If students need more help understanding **Chronological Order,** use pages T639–T641.

LITERATURE

B What does the author use to help explain how Tice inspired the term "underground road"? Why do you think she didn't just explain it in the narration? *(dialogue; it makes the explanation more believable and exciting to have the slave owner say it)* **literary nonfiction**

Character Profile

Students can work in pairs or small groups to create a **Character Profile** for Tice Davids. See page T673 for the copymaster.

VOCABULARY

E **disbelief** In this case, the prefix *dis-* means "the opposite of." Students can use the meaning of the prefix to help them figure out the meaning of the word.

FOR ENGLISH LEARNERS

Help students understand the following expressions and idioms:

Line 118: every which way
Line 119: beat the bushes
Line 138: in honor of
Line 139: coming into their own

RETEACHING

If students need more help understanding **Prefixes,** use pages T612–T613.

1. COMPREHENSION

① Comprehension SkillBuilder Name

A SLAVE

Chronological Order

Usually events in a story are told in **chronological order,** or the order they happened. In "A Slave," some of the events are described out of sequence. That is, their order in the story does not match the order in which they happened.

When did each event listed below happen? Write each event in the correct square on the chart. The first one has been done for you.

Tice Davids runs away from the plantation.
News of friends who will help running-aways reaches the slaves.
The slave owner talks to people in Ripley, Ohio.
Ministers from the south move to Ohio.
Tice Davids swims across the Ohio River.
Tice settles in Sandusky, Ohio.
Tice disappears on the shore.
Tice is told to look for the lantern and listen for the bell.

Before Tice's escape	During Tice's escape	After Tice's escape
Ministers from the south move to Ohio.		
		The system of helping slaves is named the Underground Railroad.

A Slave **T63**

Chronological Order

Direct Instruction Tell students that in most stories, events are described in **chronological order,** or the order they happened. Writers describe the first event in the story first, the second event second, and so on. Explain that sometimes a writer describes events out of order. As an example, point out that in "A Slave," the action begins with Tice Davids's decision to escape.

The writer then explains, by going back in time, how Tice knows where to run. The writer tells that long before the day of the escape, the knowledge of friends waiting across the river had come to the plantation. Remind students that although the events are not told in chronological order, it is important to understand the order of events to make sense of the story.

Comprehension SkillBuilder Answer Key:

Before Tice's escape
News of friends who will help running-aways reaches the slaves.
Tice is told to look for the lantern and listen for the bell.

During Tice's escape
Tice Davids runs away from the plantation.

Tice Davids swims across the Ohio River.
Tice disappears on the shore.

After Tice's escape
The slave owner talks to people in Ripley, Ohio.
Tice settles in Sandusky, Ohio.

---

2. LITERATURE

② Literary SkillBuilder Name

A SLAVE

Literary Nonfiction

Literary **nonfiction** tells about real people and events. It is based on fact but includes some words and scenes that are made up by the writer.

A. Read each sentence below that describes a scene in "A Slave." Decide if it tells something that can probably be found in records or something made up by the writer. Put a check in the correct column.

	Fact from records	Made up by writer
1. Tice Davids escapes to freedom by crossing the Ohio River.		
2. Some people wait at the riverbank, looking for runaway slaves that needed help.		
3. As Tice ran to freedom, he repeated the words, "Look for the lantern! Listen for the bell!"		
4. The slave owner says, "I saw him before my eyes and now he's gone."		
5. Tice Davids makes his way to Sandusky, Ohio, and lives there as a free man.		
6. The road for runaway slaves became known as the Underground Railroad.		

B. In each pair of sentences below, only one sentence is true of literary nonfiction. Put a check mark (✔) in front of that sentence. Then cross out the words literary nonfiction in the incorrect sentence. Above the crossed-out words, write another kind of writing that will make the sentence true.

1. _____ Literary nonfiction is based on fact.
   _____ Literary nonfiction is based on make-believe.

2. _____ To write literary nonfiction a writer must use a lot of imagination.
   _____ To write literary nonfiction a writer must do a lot of research.

T64 Unit 2 Courage Counts

Literary Nonfiction

Direct Instruction Tell students that **literary nonfiction** is writing that tells about a historical event in the form of a story. Literary nonfiction has the elements of a story; that is, it has characters, setting, and a plot. However, it is based on real events rather than the imagination of the writer. Writers of literary nonfiction must do a great deal of research to discover the facts about their subject. When writers are unable to uncover details, such as conversations or a character's thoughts, they may make them up. Stress that the important events of a nonfiction selec-

tion—such as dates and what a famous person did—are not made up.

Discuss these two events from "A Slave." Ask: Which of these events are facts? Was anything about these events made up?

A man named Tice Davids was a slave in Kentucky.

The slave owner gave up looking for Tice and announced, "Well, I'm going home."

Both events are facts; however, the slave owner's comment was probably made up and added by the writer.

Literary SkillBuilder Answer Key:

A.

1. *fact*	**4.** *made up*
2. *fact*	**5.** *fact*
3. *made up*	**6.** *fact*

B.
1. *Check—before first sentence. Replacement words above second sentence—either* fiction *or a particular type of fiction, such as* short story, mystery, *or* folk tale

2. *Check—before second sentence. Replacement words above first sentence—either* fiction *or a particular type of fiction, such as* short story, mystery, *or* folk tale

---

3. VOCABULARY

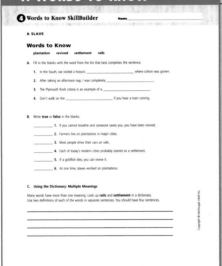

Prefixes

Direct Instruction Tell students that a **prefix** is a word part added to the beginning of a base word. Explain that every prefix has a meaning. When you add a prefix to a base word, the resulting word has a meaning different from that of the base word alone.

Tell students that the prefix *un-* means "not." Read these words aloud and ask students what they mean: *unafraid, ungrateful, unsafe,* and *unexciting.*

Tell students that the prefix *re-* means "again." Read these words aloud and ask students what they mean: *recolor, relearn,* and *repack.*

Tell students that the prefix *dis-* means "not" or "the opposite of." Read these words aloud and ask students what they mean: *discourteous, disadvantage,* and *disagree.*

Vocabulary SkillBuilder Answer Key:

A.
1. *unsuccessful; not successful*
2. *recapture; capture again*
3. *disappear; the opposite of appear*
4. *renamed; named again*
5. *unable; not able*
6. *disbelief; the opposite of belief* or *not believing*

B.
1. *unable*   4. *disappear*
2. *unsuccessful*   5. *disbelief*
3. *recapture*   6. *renamed*

---

4. WORDS TO KNOW

Words to Know

Direct Instruction As you present the **Words to Know,** here are some points you might want to cover.

Help students to identify the parts of the vocabulary words. Stress the importance of finding the base of each word. Help students remove prefixes and suffixes first.

- **settle** + -ment = *settlement*
  -ment: suffix meaning "action or process" or "result of an action or process"
- **plant** + -ation = *plantation*
  -ation: suffix meaning "something connected with an action or process"
- re- + **vive** + -ed = *revived*
  re-: prefix meaning "again"; **viv:** Latin root meaning "live"

Other words that contain the root *viv* include *vivacious* and *vivid. Viva* is a term used in Spanish and Italian, meaning "long live." Point out that all of these words are communicating a kind of energy or a force of life.

Instruct students to provide evidence for their conclusions in the true-and-false section (B), particularly if they believe a statement to be false.

Words to Know SkillBuilder Answer Key:

A. 1. *plantation* **2.** *revived* **3.** *settlement* **4.** *rails*

B. 1. *true* **2.** *false* **3.** *false* **4.** *true* **5.** *false* **6.** *true*

C. Using the Dictionary: Multiple meanings *Pair students or have them work in small groups to complete the sentences. Note that in most dictionaries,* rail *will have two or three separate listings, while* settlement *will have two definitions under one listing. Help struggling students understand the context of each definition so that they may use the word correctly in the sentence.*

---

5. SELECTION TEST

Selection Test Answer Key:

A. 1. *true* **2.** *false* **3.** *true* **4.** *true* **5.** *false* **6.** *true* **7.** *true* **8.** *false* **9.** *true*

B. *other running-aways to escape to the North.*

A SLAVE

Chronological Order

Usually events in a story are told in **chronological order,** or the order they happened. In "A Slave," some of the events are described out of sequence. That is, their order in the story does not match the order in which they happened.

When did each event listed below happen? Write each event in the correct square on the chart. The first one has been done for you.

Tice Davids runs away from the plantation.

News of friends who will help running-aways reaches the slaves.

The slave owner talks to people in Ripley, Ohio.

Ministers from the south move to Ohio.

Tice Davids swims across the Ohio River.

Tice settles in Sandusky, Ohio.

Tice disappears on the shore.

Tice is told to look for the lantern and listen for the bell.

Before Tice's escape	During Tice's escape	After Tice's escape
Ministers from the south move to Ohio.		
		The system of helping slaves is named the Underground Railroad.

A SLAVE

Literary Nonfiction

Literary nonfiction tells about real people and events. It is based on fact but includes some words and scenes that are made up by the writer.

A. Each sentence below describes a scene in "A Slave." Decide if it tells something that can probably be found in records or something made up by the writer. Put a check in the correct column.

	Fact from records	Made up by writer
1. Tice Davids escapes to freedom by crossing the Ohio River.	_____	_____
2. Some people wait at the riverbank, looking for runaway slaves that need help.	_____	_____
3. As Tice runs to freedom, he repeats the words "Look for the lantern! Listen for the bell!"	_____	_____
4. The slave owner says, "I saw him before my eyes and now he's gone."	_____	_____
5. Tice Davids makes his way to Sandusky, Ohio, and lives there as a free man.	_____	_____
6. The road for runaway slaves becomes known as the Underground Railroad.	_____	_____

B. In each pair of sentences below, only one sentence is true of literary nonfiction. Put a check mark [✔] in front of that sentence. Then cross out the words *literary nonfiction* in the incorrect sentence. Above the crossed-out words, write another kind of writing that will make the sentence true.

1. _____ Literary nonfiction is based on fact.

_____ Literary nonfiction is based on make-believe.

2. _____ To write literary nonfiction a writer must use a lot of imagination.

_____ To write literary nonfiction a writer must do a lot of research.

A SLAVE

Prefixes

A **prefix** is a word part added to the beginning of a base word. Some common prefixes are *un-*, which means "not," *re-*, which means "again," and *dis-*, which means "not" or "the opposite of."

A. Add the prefix to the base word. Write the new word on the line. Then write its meaning.

1. un- + successful = _____

   Meaning: _____

2. re- + capture = _____

   Meaning: _____

3. dis- + appear = _____

   Meaning: _____

4. re- + named = _____

   Meaning: _____

5. un- + able = _____

   Meaning: _____

6. dis- + belief = _____

   Meaning: _____

B. Choose the correct word from Exercise A to complete each sentence.

1. Tice Davids realized he was _____ to bear being a slave any longer.

2. Tice was afraid that he would be caught and his escape attempt would be

   _____.

3. He knew the slave owner would chase him and try to _____ him.

4. The slave owner was amazed to see Tice _____ after the slave had staggered onto the shore.

5. Shaking his head in _____, the slave owner said Tice must have taken an underground road.

6. Later, the underground road was _____ the Underground Railroad.

A SLAVE

Words to Know

plantation   revived   settlement   rails

A. Fill in the blanks with the word from the list that best completes the sentence.

1. In the South, we visited a historic _____ where cotton was grown.

2. After taking an afternoon nap, I was completely _____.

3. The Plymouth Rock colony is an example of a _____.

4. Don't walk on the _____ if you hear a train coming.

B. Write **true** or **false** in the blanks.

_____ **1.** If you cannot breathe and someone saves you, you have been revived.

_____ **2.** Farmers live on plantations in major cities.

_____ **3.** Most people drive their cars on rails.

_____ **4.** Each of today's modern cities probably started as a settlement.

_____ **5.** If a goldfish dies, you can revive it.

_____ **6.** At one time, slaves worked on plantations.

C. Using the Dictionary: Multiple Meanings

Many words have more than one meaning. Look up **rails** and **settlement** in a dictionary.
Use two definitions of each of the words in separate sentences. You should have four sentences.

_____

_____

_____

_____

A SLAVE

A. Write **true** or **false** on the line next to each statement.

_____ **1.** Tice Davids was a real person who lived during the 1800s.

_____ **2.** He was born a slave in the state of Ohio.

_____ **3.** One day in 1831, Tice decided to escape to the North.

_____ **4.** He took off running and headed for the Ohio River.

_____ **5.** When he got to the river, he took a raft across.

_____ **6.** Before the slave owner could catch him, Tice disappeared from sight.

_____ **7.** The slave owner said that Tice must have gone on an underground road.

_____ **8.** Tice walked underground for the rest of his trip.

_____ **9.** He made it to Sandusky, Ohio, and became a free man.

B. Fill in the blank to complete the second sentence.

Tice Davids became a "conductor" on the Underground Railroad. He did this by helping _____

_____

Focus Skills

COMPREHENSION
Making Judgments
Details

LITERATURE
Informative Nonfiction

VOCABULARY
Idioms

SkillBuilder Copymasters

 Reading Comprehension:
1 Making Judgments p. T77
2 Details p. T78

 Vocabulary:
3 Idioms p. T79
4 Words to Know p. T80

Assessment

 5 Selection Test p. T81

Readability Scores

DRP	LEXILE	DALE-CHALL
56	470	5.8

For English Learners

When Wilma Mankiller moved to San Francisco from Oklahoma, she was teased about her name, her race, the way she talked, and the way she dressed. Can any of your students relate to Wilma's experiences? Invite them to explain.

Wilma Mankiller

by Linda Lowery

48   Unit 2 Courage Counts

More About the Cherokee

In the early 1800s—especially after gold was discovered in Georgia in 1828—the U.S. government began demanding that all Indians in the Southeast be relocated west of the Mississippi River. In 1835, some Cherokees signed a treaty and moved on their own. Most, however, were forced to march the Trail of Tears. About 1,000 Cherokees hid out in the Great Smoky Mountains. In time they were allowed to stay, and they became known as the Eastern Band of Cherokees.

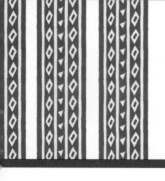

An old saying states, "You can't go home again." Wilma Mankiller proved the saying wrong. She returned to her home and became its chief.

Connect to Your Life

Recall the last time you found yourself in a strange place. How long did it take you to get used to it? Make a list of what made the place different. With a partner, talk about the kinds of adjustments you had to make.

Key to the Biography

This biography describes major happenings in the life of Wilma Mankiller. She belongs to the Cherokee Nation of Oklahoma. The Cherokee once lived happily in the southeastern sections of the country. Then came the winter of 1838–1839. U.S. soldiers forced more than 17,000 Cherokee people to leave their homeland. This event became known as the Trail of Tears. As you read, pay close attention to the details about this event. Although Wilma wasn't born until more than a century later, notice the effects the event has on her life.

Vocabulary Preview

Words to Know

coyotes   council
bugles   swirling

 Reading Coach CD-ROM selection

Connect to Your Life

As partners talk about the strange places they found themselves in, be sure they describe which adjustments were easier and which ones were more difficult, and why.

Key to the Biography

Since this selection discusses events that happened both before and during Wilma's life, tell students to pay special attention to the signal words that the author uses. They will help students keep the events in the proper sequence, or time order.

Vocabulary Preview

Words to Know
coyotes *n.* small animals that are similar to wolves
bugles *n.* horns that are shorter than a trumpet
council *n.* a body of people elected to plan, discuss, or give advice
swirling *v.* moving with a twisting motion

 For direct instruction on Words to Know, see page T76.

Building Background

In 1985, Wilma Mankiller (born 1945) became the first woman chief of the Cherokee Nation. Under her leadership the tribe grew from 55,000 to 156,000 members. Today the Cherokee tribe is one of the largest in the United States. Some of Mankiller's other achievements include her induction into the Oklahoma Women's Hall of Fame in 1986, her re-election as chief in 1987 (which she won by a landslide 82 percent), and her election to the presidency of the Inter-Tribal Council of Oklahoma. In 1995, Mankiller chose not to seek reelection as chief of the Cherokee Nation.

Vocabulary Strategy: Preteaching

Idioms Remind students that an **idiom** is an expression whose total meaning is different from the meaning of its individual words. To illustrate, see how many of the boldfaced idioms students can match with their meanings.

keep a stiff upper lip   hurry
fly off the handle   tell a secret
shake a leg   get very angry
let the cat out of the bag   be very brave

For more on Idioms, see page T76.

A view of the Oklahoma plains

FOCUS

Young Wilma Mankiller finds herself in a new place. Read to find out how the differences there affect her.

San Francisco, 1956

Wilma Mankiller dove under the covers. It was warm and safe under the handmade quilt. Outside, screams of wild animals echoed off the walls. This was Wilma's first night in San Francisco, California, and she was afraid.

She knew the sound of wolves. The sound outside was not wolves. She knew the sound of coyotes. It was not coyotes.

When she woke up the next morning,
10 still yawning from too little sleep, Wilma found out what had made the animal screams. It was something she had never heard back home in Oklahoma. It was the sound of police sirens.

San Francisco was full of things Wilma had never seen or heard of before. People disappeared from her hallway in boxes called elevators.

coyotes
(kī ō' tēz)
n. small animals that are similar to wolves

All night long, flashy lights blinked on and off outside her window. Everything seemed strange and
20 frightening, so different from home.

In her mind, Wilma traveled back to her grandfather's land on Mankiller Flats, in Oklahoma. Her family was happy there, living close to other Cherokee families. They had springwater to drink, woods full of deer and foxes, and a home her father had built.

But Wilma's father, Charley Mankiller, often worried about money. Money never went very far when there were nine children to raise. He wanted to
30 give them the best schools, the best home, the best life he could.

When Wilma was ten, the United States government came up with a plan for Indian families. They promised houses and jobs to families who would move to cities. At night, in their house on Mankiller Flats, Wilma and her brothers and sisters pressed their ears against the bedroom door, listening. Their parents talked about moving. They talked about cities

A view of the city of San Francisco

FOCUS SKILL 1: Making Judgments

Tell students that when they read, they must use clues from the selection as well as their own knowledge and opinions in order to **make judgments,** or decisions, about whether something is accurate or inaccurate, true or false, or right or wrong.

 For direct instruction on Making Judgments, see page T75.

FOCUS SKILL 2: Details

Explain that paying attention to the facts and **details** in this selection will make it easier for students to make judgments as they read.

 For direct instruction on Details, see page T75.

Ⓐ Ask: What unfamiliar sound does Wilma hear that makes it difficult for her to sleep? What are the "boxes" that she sees in her hallway? *(police sirens; elevators)* **details**

Ⓑ Have students describe Wilma's home in Mankiller Flats. *(She lived close to other Cherokee families, she had springwater to drink, there were foxes and deer in the woods, her father had built their home.)* **details**

LITERATURE

FOCUS SKILL: Informative Nonfiction

Explain that **informative nonfiction** gives facts and details about real people, places, and events.

VOCABULARY

FOCUS SKILL: Idioms

Remind students that an **idiom** is an expression that means something other than the surface or literal meaning of the words.

Ⓐ **money never went very far**
Help students understand that this idiom doesn't mean that the money never got up and went somewhere far. Rather, it means that Charley Mankiller didn't have enough money.

FOR ENGLISH LEARNERS

Help students understand the following expressions and idioms:

Line 1: dove under the covers
Line 10: too little sleep
Line 30: give them the best . . . he could
Line 33: came up with a plan

like Chicago, New York, and Detroit. Would the
40 schools be better in the city? Would life there be
happier for their children?

Moving sounded awful to Wilma. Her parents,
however, decided it was a good idea. In October
1956, the family moved away from Mankiller Flats.

As they left, Wilma watched very hard out the car
window. She wanted to remember everything about
the home she loved: the colors of the birds, the shapes
of the trees, the sounds of the animals.

THINK IT THROUGH

Why is moving to San Francisco such a major change for
Wilma?

FOCUS

Read to discover what helps Wilma get used to her new
surroundings.

In her new home, colors and shapes and sounds
50 were scary—and mean too. When Wilma's new
teacher called her name in school, the class laughed.
To Cherokees, "Mankiller" was a special title, given
to someone who protected the tribe. To the kids in
school, it was a joke. They teased her about how she
talked. They thought she dressed strangely.

When Wilma walked home from school,	**REREAD**
she saw signs in shop windows. They	What does a sign
said, "NO DOGS, NO INDIANS."	like this say
Wilma felt as if she had moved to the far	about some
	people in
	Wilma's new
	city?
60 side of the moon.

To comfort herself, Wilma thought about home: the
hawks soaring in the sky, the whispers of the wind in
the treetops.

52 Unit 2 Courage Counts

She also thought of other Cherokees who had
struggled through hard times. About 150 years ago,
many Cherokee people were forced to move far from
home. It was a terrible journey. It is called the Trail of
Tears. Wilma remembered the story the way she had
heard it many times from her father and her relatives.

The Trail of Tears, 1838

70 Years ago, Wilma's family told her, no Cherokees
lived in Oklahoma. Their home was the southeast.
How they loved that land! Soft rain fell on the hills.
Apples, plums, and peaches grew on the trees.

But white settlers wanted the green land of the
southeast. President Andrew Jackson decided that
white settlers were more important than the Indians
who lived there. In 1830, the president signed the
Indian Removal Act.

It was a law. It said that all Cherokees had to leave
80 Georgia and Alabama, North Carolina and South

Cherokee Movement to Oklahoma, 1838–1840

Wilma Mankiller 53

C Ask: When does Wilma's family move to San Francisco? What clue words help you know this? *(The heading* **San Francisco, 1956** *on page 50 and the signal words* In October 1956 *tell when they move.)* **chronological order**

D **THINK IT THROUGH** Why is moving to San Francisco such a major change for Wilma? *(Compared to Oklahoma, it is noisy and crowded and full of things she's never seen or heard before.)* **cause and effect**

E **REREAD** What does a sign like this say about some people in Wilma's new city? *(They don't like Indians, and they treat them no better than they treat dogs.)* **making inferences**

F Ask: When did the U.S. army begin marching the Cherokees on the Trail of Tears? About how many years later does Wilma move to San Francisco? *(1838; about 120 years later)* **chronological order**

G Have students begin at the right and trace with their finger the movement of the Cherokees to Oklahoma. In what state did the movement begin? *(Georgia)* **understanding visuals**

FOR ENGLISH LEARNERS

Help students understand the following expressions and idioms:

Line 59: the far side of the moon
Line 62: whispers of the wind in the treetops

Carolina, Tennessee and Virginia. The Cherokees refused. They loved their home.

So, in 1838, President Van Buren sent in the army. Soldiers dragged Cherokees from their log cabins. Soldiers loaded Cherokees onto wagons. Soldiers shot **H** Cherokees who tried to get away.

The bugles sounded. The wagons began rolling away. Children stood up and waved good-bye to their mountain homes. The
90 Cherokees traveled 1,200 miles west, through rain, sleet, and snow. When wagons broke down, some people had to walk.

> **bugles**
> (byōō' gəlz)
> *n.* horns that are shorter than a trumpet

In the next two years, about 17,000 Cherokees were sent west. Four thousand died on the way. The army left the Cherokees on land that later became Oklahoma. There were no houses, no churches, and no schools.

Many mothers and fathers, children and grandparents, were sick from the
100 trip. They had nothing left but the spirit within them. Because of that spirit, they survived.

> **REREAD**
> How do you think this move affected the people who lived through it?

I

B Wilma had always kept the story of the Trail of Tears in her heart. She was the great-great-great-granddaughter of the people who had cried on that trail. In San Francisco, Wilma cried too. There, she felt lucky about only one thing. The Cherokee people who had been shipped to Oklahoma never got to go back home. Wilma knew that one day, she would go
110 home again.

J **THINK IT THROUGH**
How does Wilma compare her move to the Trail of Tears?

FOCUS
Wilma does return to Mankiller Flats. Read to see what new challenges she finds there.

Home Again in Oklahoma, 1977

It took her over twenty years, but Wilma did go home. By then, in 1977, she had two daughters, Gina and Felicia. She packed them up and moved back to Mankiller Flats.

It felt wonderful to be near Cherokee friends again. She was happy to watch the robins and bluebirds from her porch. She heard the coyotes howl in the moonlight, and she wasn't afraid.

K

Wilma soon got a job with the Cherokee Nation.
120 Cherokees are people of two nations: the United States and the Cherokee Nation. The government in Washington, D.C., makes all the big decisions in the United States. The government in Tahlequah, Oklahoma, makes all the big decisions in the Western Cherokee Nation.

Wilma's job was to visit Cherokee people all over eastern Oklahoma. Many were poor. They had no lights in their houses and no water. Wilma helped them make their homes safer and better. One day in
130 1983, Wilma was on her way to work. She drove down a dirt road, thinking. The chief of the Cherokee Nation had offered her a job yesterday. He wanted her to be his assistant and run for deputy chief. What an honor to be asked! This was the second highest job in the Cherokee Nation.

> **honor**
> (ŏn' ər)
> sign of great respect

But Wilma was a quiet person. To become deputy chief, she would have to win an election. She did not like talking to crowds. She didn't
140 want to be on television. "No," she had told the

COMPREHENSION

H Ask: What seems unjust about this period in history? *(For years before the white settlers arrived, the Cherokees had lived in the Southeast. Now they are being cruelly forced off their land to go and live in a cold, barren, undeveloped place. For no reason, thousands are killed.)* **making judgments**

I **REREAD** How do you think this move affected the people who lived through it? *(Possible responses: It was heartbreaking, not only because of the loss of their homes, but also because as they moved, they lost members of the tribe and suffered many injuries.)* **making judgments**

J **THINK IT THROUGH** How does Wilma compare her move to the Trail of Tears? *(Against her will, she has moved from a place she loves to one she dislikes. This makes her cry many tears.)* **details**

K Ask: What does Wilma enjoy upon her return to Mankiller Flats? *(being near Cherokee friends, watching robins and blue-birds, hearing coyotes howl)* **details**

VOCABULARY

B **kept the story . . . in her heart**
Help students understand that this idiom doesn't mean that Wilma literally had a story in her heart. Rather, it means that she always remembered the story of the Trail of Tears.

FOR ENGLISH LEARNERS

Help students understand the following expressions and idioms:

Line 87: the bugles sounded
Line 89: mountain homes
Line 100: the spirit within them
Line 113: she packed them up
Line 133: run for deputy chief

chief. Chief Swimmer had been disappointed. "Think about it," he said. Now, as she drove along, she wondered if she had made the right decision.

Suddenly, she saw something through the oak trees. She stopped her station wagon and stared out the window. There sat an old, broken-down bus. Curtains hung in the windows. Laundry sagged on the line. Was this really someone's home?

> **REREAD**
> Try to picture this scene in your mind. What kind of life do you think the people who live here lead?

L

150 Wilma got out of her car and walked closer. She could see that a family lived inside.

The bus had no roof. What happens when it rains? she wondered.

C Deep inside her, something tugged at Wilma. When she was a girl, the United States government had promised a better life for Indians in San Francisco. They broke their promise. If Wilma were deputy chief, she would have power to help change the lives of Cherokee people. She knew she would keep her
160 promises.

Stones flew as Wilma drove to Chief Swimmer's house. She had something to tell him. Her time to be a leader had come. She would run for deputy chief.

THINK IT THROUGH

M Why doesn't Wilma want the job of deputy chief? What changes her mind?

FOCUS

New problems come from an unexpected place. Read to find out how Wilma tries to solve them.

Wilma got right to work. She swallowed her shyness and talked to crowds of people. She asked them to vote for her. The Cherokee people had always

Cherokee dancers at Chehaw National Indian Festival

been grateful for Wilma's work. They had given her warm welcomes when she visited.

But suddenly people were unfriendly, even angry.
170 Something was very wrong. Wilma could feel it. Soon the truth came out. People were talking behind Wilma's back.

D

"We Cherokees never had a woman as deputy chief," they said. "It's a job for a man," they said. Wilma was shocked. What a strange idea! In history, Cherokee women had always been treated the same as men.

N

Women were medicine healers. Women were warriors. Women were council
180 members. How could anyone say only men make good leaders? Had the Cherokees picked up this idea from white people? Wilma thought so.

> **council**
> (koun′ səl)
> n. body of people elected to plan, discuss, or give advice

L **REREAD** Try to picture this scene in your mind. What kind of life do you think the people who live here lead? *(extremely harsh and depressing, with no hope of improvement without outside help)* **making judgments**

Teacher Modeling: Visualizing
Use the Reread near the top of page 56 to demonstrate the Active Reading Strategy of visualizing.

You could say: *This passage about what Wilma sees is brief, but it does paint a clear picture in my mind of the living conditions of many Cherokees in Mankiller Flats. I can see the laundry hanging on a line that goes from tree to tree. I can see a broken-down bus. It looks like a rusted, yellow school bus that has no tires. I can "see" this scene that Wilma Mankiller saw. It helps me to understand better why she wants to take an even closer look.*

M **THINK IT THROUGH** Why doesn't Wilma want the job of deputy chief? What changes her mind? *(She is a quiet and private person, and the office would force her to talk to crowds and be on TV; but she wants to help people like the family who live in the bus.)* **details**

N Ask: Why is Wilma so shocked that the Cherokees don't want a woman deputy chief? *(Throughout history, Cherokee women had always been treated the same as men.)* **cause and effect**

C **something tugged at Wilma** Help students understand that this means that Wilma was having a strong feeling about something.

D **talking behind Wilma's back** Help students understand that this idiom means that people were gossiping about Wilma, not that they were standing behind her and talking.

FOR ENGLISH LEARNERS

Help students understand the following expressions and idioms:

Line 157: broke their promise
Line 164: swallowed her shyness

When white settlers came to America, they brought new ideas with them. Some of their ideas were good. Some were not. One idea was that men were more important than women. Wilma set out to prove that this idea was wrong. In her speeches, she never talked about being a woman. She only talked about her hopes and dreams for the Cherokee people. She promised to get money for houses, hospitals, and children's centers. She promised to help her people make their towns better.

The trouble did not stop. Neither did Wilma. Someone slashed the tires on Wilma's car. Strangers shouted mean words on the phone. Someone threatened to kill her. Everything around her was **swirling** like a whirlwind. But inside, Wilma kept still. She reached deep down for strength. Long ago, her people had survived the Trail of Tears. When she was young, Wilma had survived San Francisco. Wilma and the people who cried on the trail had survived because they knew the Cherokee Way.

You do not think about the bad things. You think about the good. Even if you feel you will never make it, you move ahead. It is called "being of good mind." If she practiced the Cherokee Way, Wilma knew she could survive—and win—this election. Finally, the Cherokee people went to

swirling
(swûr' lĭng)
v. moving with a twisting motion

Wilma Mankiller standing before the seal of the Cherokee Nation

the **polls** to vote. They voted for Chief Swimmer and Wilma Mankiller. On August 14, 1983, Wilma became the first Cherokee woman ever to be deputy chief. But that was only the beginning.

polls
(pōlz)
places where votes are cast

When Chief Swimmer was given a job in Washington, D.C., Wilma became chief.

It was 1985 when Wilma sat down at the chief's desk for the first time. "You look very natural sitting there," someone said. People hugged Wilma. They cried tears of happiness for her.

Wilma knew her job as chief would be hard work. But she was not frightened. She felt as if all the Cherokee people who had walked the Trail of Tears were with her. Their strength was her strength, just as it had been when she was a girl in San Francisco. Wilma had come home to Oklahoma. Now she was Chief Mankiller, the first woman chief in Cherokee history.

THINK IT THROUGH

1. Before she got the job, Wilma Mankiller faced both inner and outer conflicts, or problems. List both the inner and outer problems she overcame.
2. Review the different hardships Wilma Mankiller faced. Why did she succeed?
3. What qualities helped Wilma become a good leader? Use details from the text to support your choices.

COMPREHENSION

O Ask: How and when does Wilma become chief of the Cherokee Nation? *(She gets the job in 1985 when Chief Swimmer takes a job in Washington, D.C.)* **details**

P **THINK IT THROUGH**

1. Before she got the job, Wilma Mankiller faced both inner and outer conflicts, or problems. List both the inner and outer problems she overcame. *(inner—shyness and modesty; outer—bias against women, vandalism, death threat)* **conflict** LITERATURE

2. Review the different hardships Wilma Mankiller faced. Why did she succeed? *(She learned to draw comfort and strength from the past struggles of her people.)* **drawing conclusions**

3. What qualities helped Wilma become a good leader? Use details from the text to support your choices. *(determination—to return to Oklahoma and, later, to help her people; willingness—to push herself and grow as a person; drive—to do what it took to get elected; courage—to keep going even after vandalism and a death threat)* **making judgments**

Option for Writing In a sentence or two, explain which conflict you think was the hardest for Wilma to overcome, and why.

VOCABULARY

E **she reached deep down for strength** Help students understand that this idiom doesn't mean that Wilma literally reached down into something and picked up or pulled out strength. Rather, it means that she convinced herself to be strong.

FOR ENGLISH LEARNERS

Help students understand the following expressions and idioms:

Line 197: Everything around her was swirling like a whirlwind.
Line 205: the Cherokee Way
Line 209: never make it
Line 216: went to the polls

RETEACHING

If students need more help understanding **Idioms,** use pages T618–T619.

1. COMPREHENSION

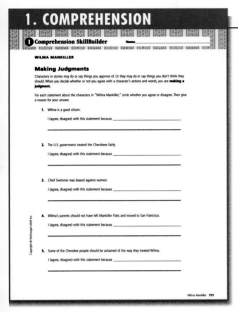

Making Judgments

Direct Instruction Point out that everyone has standards, or rules to live by. Explain that when readers see what characters in stories say and do, they should compare these words and actions with their own standards. This process is called **making judgments.** Tell students that when readers make judgments, they decide whether they agree or disagree, approve or disapprove of characters' words and actions.

Point out that since people's standards are not always alike, neither are their judgments. Explain that judgments are personal and can vary with each reader's experiences and beliefs. Emphasize, however, that judgments must be supported by details from the selection.

> **Comprehension SkillBuilder Answer Key:**
>
> *Opinions and reasons will vary. Possible answers:*
>
> **1.** *agree—because Wilma worked hard for the good of her people*
> **2.** *disagree—because government officials told the Cherokee people lies and made them move from their homes*
> **3.** *disagree—because he asked Wilma to be his deputy chief*
> **4.** *agree—because Wilma always missed her Oklahoma home; disagree—because moving to San Francisco gave Wilma opportunities she wouldn't have had living in Mankiller Flats*
> **5.** *agree—because some of them prejudged Wilma and decided that just because she was a woman she shouldn't run for office*

2. COMPREHENSION

Details

Direct Instruction Tell students that **details** are small pieces of information. Explain that details tell more about the main ideas in a story or article and help to describe a person, place, or thing more completely than a main idea alone can.

Show students how details can paint a complete picture by helping them create a concept map about your classroom. First, draw a circle on the board and label it "Our Classroom."

Next, have students look around and identify details about the classroom that would help readers picture the room. Record their suggestions in circles that connect to the central circle to form a concept map. When they are finished, ask a volunteer to read the details aloud. Finally, ask students to think of a sentence that states a main idea that can connect all these details, and record that topic sentence on the board too.

> **Comprehension SkillBuilder Answer Key:**
>
> *close to other Cherokee families; springwater to drink; woods filled with deer and foxes; a home built by Wilma's father*
>
> *Details about students' own homes will vary.*

3. VOCABULARY

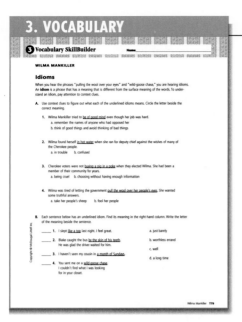

Idioms

Direct Instruction Tell students that an **idiom** is an expression that means something other than the surface meaning of the words. Ask students if they have ever heard the idiom "getting the hang of it." Then read this sentence aloud: *I could never make a basket before, but after many days of practice, I think I'm getting the hang of it.* (becoming skillful) Point out that they can understand an idiom easily by using context clues.

Read aloud these sentences containing idioms. Ask students to use context clues to figure out what the underlined idiom in each sentence means.

• Jerry <u>has an itchy foot</u> and loves to read travel brochures. *(can't stay still; wants to travel)*
• Let's not <u>put the cart before the horse</u>. First win the lottery and then decide what to do with the money. *(do things out of order)*

Vocabulary SkillBuilder Answer Key:

A.
1. *b*
2. *a*
3. *b*
4. *b*

B.
1. *c*
2. *a*
3. *d*
4. *b*

4. WORDS TO KNOW

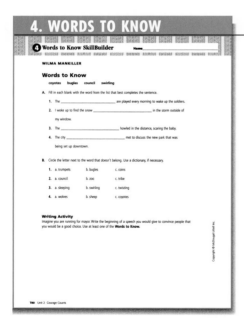

Words to Know

Direct Instruction As you present the **Words to Know,** here are some points you might want to cover.
• **council** is from the Latin *concilium*. Its homophone is *counsel*.
• **bugles** is from the Latin *būculus*. Other definitions of *bugle* are "a tubular glass or plastic bead used to trim clothing" and "an herb in the mint family (also called *bugleweed*)."

• **coyotes** is an American Spanish word taken from the Nahuatl Indian language; coyotes are native to western North America.
• **swirl** + -ing = *swirling*

Writing Activity Pair students or have them work in small groups to complete the exercise. Have volunteers read their creations aloud.

Words to Know SkillBuilder Answer Key:

A.
1. *bugles*
2. *swirling*
3. *coyotes*
4. *council*

B.
1. *c*
2. *b*
3. *a*
4. *b*

5. SELECTION TEST

Selection Test Answer Key:

A. 1. *Mankiller Flats* 2. *scary* 3. *dressed* 4. *Trail of Tears* 5. *twenty* 6. *Cherokee Nation* 7. *bus* 8. *woman* 9. *of good mind*

B. *the first woman chief in Cherokee history.*

Name_____

WILMA MANKILLER

Making Judgments

Characters in stories may do or say things you approve of. Or they may do or say things you don't think they should. When you decide whether or not you agree with a character's actions and words, you are **making a judgment.**

For each statement about the characters in "Wilma Mankiller," circle whether you agree or disagree. Then give a reason for your answer.

1. Wilma is a good citizen.

I (agree, disagree) with this statement because _____

_____

2. The U.S. government treated the Cherokees fairly.

I (agree, disagree) with this statement because _____

_____

3. Chief Swimmer was biased against women.

I (agree, disagree) with this statement because _____

_____

4. Wilma's parents should not have left Mankiller Flats and moved to San Francisco.

I (agree, disagree) with this statement because _____

_____

5. Some of the Cherokee people should be ashamed of the way they treated Wilma.

I (agree, disagree) with this statement because _____

_____

WILMA MANKILLER

Details

Details are small bits of information. By combining details, writers can give a complete picture of a person, place, thing, event, or idea.

Fill in the following concept map with details from this paragraph from "Wilma Mankiller."

> In her mind, Wilma traveled back to her grandfather's land on Mankiller Flats, in Oklahoma. Her family was happy there, living close to other Cherokee families. They had springwater to drink, woods full of deer and foxes, and a home her father had built.

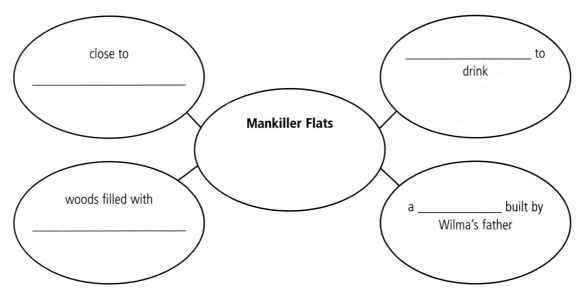

Now make a concept map with four details that tell what you like about your own home.

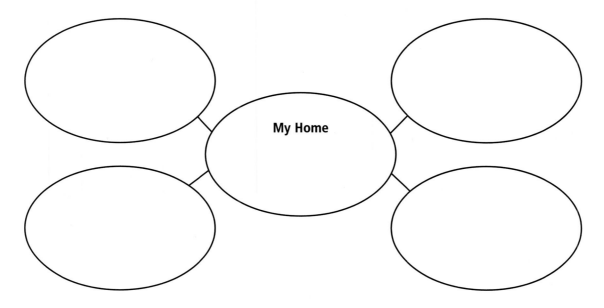

WILMA MANKILLER

Idioms

When you hear the phrases "pulling the wool over your eyes" and "wild-goose chase," you are hearing idioms. An **idiom** is a phrase that has a meaning that is different from the surface meaning of the words. To understand an idiom, pay attention to context clues.

A. Use context clues to figure out what each of the underlined idioms means. Circle the letter beside the correct meaning.

1. Wilma Mankiller tried to <u>be of good mind</u> even though her job was hard.
    a. remember the names of anyone who had opposed her
    b. think of good things and avoid thinking of bad things

2. Wilma found herself <u>in hot water</u> when she ran for deputy chief against the wishes of many of the Cherokee people.
    a. in trouble   b. confused

3. Cherokee voters were not <u>buying a pig in a poke</u> when they elected Wilma. She had been a member of their community for years.
    a. being cruel   b. choosing without having enough information

4. Wilma was tired of letting the government <u>pull the wool over her people's eyes</u>. She wanted some truthful answers.
    a. take her people's sheep   b. fool her people

B. Each sentence below has an underlined idiom. Find its meaning in the right-hand column. Write the letter of the meaning beside the sentence.

_____ **1.** I slept <u>like a top</u> last night. I feel great.

_____ **2.** Blake caught the bus <u>by the skin of his teeth</u>. He was glad the driver waited for him.

_____ **3.** I haven't seen my cousin in <u>a month of Sundays</u>.

_____ **4.** You sent me on a <u>wild-goose chase</u>. I couldn't find what I was looking for in your closet.

a. just barely

b. worthless errand

c. well

d. a long time

WILMA MANKILLER

Words to Know

coyotes   bugles   council   swirling

A. Fill in each blank with the word from the list that best completes the sentence.

1. The _____ are played every morning to wake up the soldiers.

2. I woke up to find the snow _____ in the storm outside of

    my window.

3. The _____ howled in the distance, scaring the baby.

4. The city _____ met to discuss the new park that was

    being set up downtown.

B. Circle the letter next to the word that doesn't belong. Use a dictionary, if necessary.

1. a. trumpets   b. bugles   c. coins

2. a. council   b. zoo   c. tribe

3. a. sleeping   b. swirling   c. twisting

4. a. wolves   b. sheep   c. coyotes

Writing Activity
Imagine you are running for mayor. Write the beginning of a speech you would give to convince people that you would be a good choice. Use at least one of the **Words to Know.**

WILMA MANKILLER

A. Fill in each numbered blank in the following paragraph with a word or phrase from the list.

woman   Cherokee Nation   scary
dressed   bus   twenty
of good mind   Mankiller Flats   Trail of Tears

When Wilma Mankiller was ten years old, her family moved from

(1) _____, Oklahoma, to San Francisco, California. Wilma disliked

San Francisco and found it noisy and **(2)** _____. In school, Wilma's

classmates made fun of the way she talked and **(3)** _____. To

comfort herself, Wilma thought about the Cherokee people and their journey called the

(4) _____. More than **(5)** _____

years later, in 1977, Wilma finally made it back to Oklahoma. In 1983, she was offered a job as

deputy chief of the **(6)** _____. At first she turned it down, but

seeing a family living in a **(7)** _____ made her change

her mind. Many people didn't want Wilma to win the election because she was a

(8) _____. But Wilma stayed **(9)** "_____"

and won the election.

B. Fill in the blank to complete the sentence.

In 1985, after Chief Swimmer took a job in Washington, D.C., Wilma became _____

_____

Focus Skills

COMPREHENSION
Fact and Opinion

LITERATURE
Biography

VOCABULARY
Context Clues: Definition

SkillBuilder Copymasters

 Reading Comprehension:
1 Fact and Opinion p. T89

 Literary Analysis:
2 Biography p. T90

 Vocabulary:
3 Context Clues p. T91
4 Words to Know p. T92

Assessment

 5 Selection Test p. T93

Readability Scores

DRP	LEXILE	DALE-CHALL
53	530	4.6

For English Learners

Students will probably be unaware of this country's labor movement and of the era of protest in the 1960s. This biography of a history-making union leader presents a number of terms, such as *farm-workers, migrant workers, nonviolent protest, union, fasts,* and *boycott.* Most of the terms are defined at the point of use.

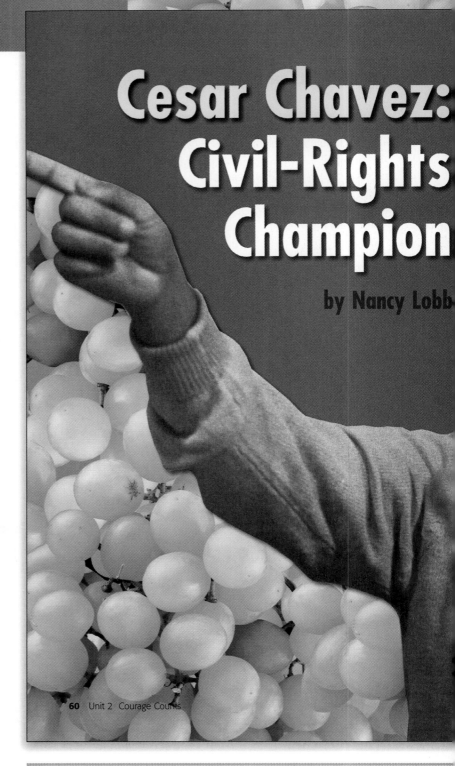

Cesar Chavez: Civil-Rights Champion

by Nancy Lobb

60 Unit 2 Courage Counts

Vocabulary Strategy: Preteaching

Context Clues Tell students that several of the words in this selection are surrounded by **context clues,** words or sentences that provide definitions of the words. Write the following examples on the board. Then have students point out or circle the definition of each underlined word.

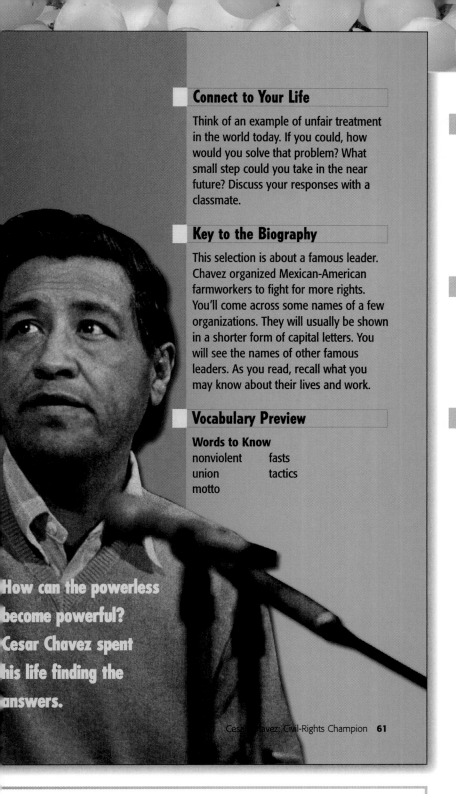

Connect to Your Life

Think of an example of unfair treatment in the world today. If you could, how would you solve that problem? What small step could you take in the near future? Discuss your responses with a classmate.

Key to the Biography

This selection is about a famous leader. Chavez organized Mexican-American farmworkers to fight for more rights. You'll come across some names of a few organizations. They will usually be shown in a shorter form of capital letters. You will see the names of other famous leaders. As you read, recall what you may know about their lives and work.

Vocabulary Preview

Words to Know

nonviolent	fasts
union	tactics
motto	

How can the powerless become powerful? Cesar Chavez spent his life finding the answers.

Cesar Chavez: Civil-Rights Champion **61**

Connect to Your Life

You might help students start this discussion by saying, "One thing that really bothers me is . . . " Suggest that they fill in the statement with a current issue, such as school dress codes. Then have pairs of students share their examples of unfair treatment.

Key to the Biography

To set a purpose for reading, you may want to have the class work together to begin a **K-W-L chart** on Cesar Chavez. See page T664 for instructions and page T666 for copymaster.

Vocabulary Preview

Words to Know
nonviolent *adj.* not using force as a way of getting results
union *n.* organized group of workers
motto *n.* sentence that expresses a group's goals
fasts *n.* periods of time without food
tactics *n.* methods used to get results

 For direct instruction on Words to Know, see page T88.

Building Background

Cesar Chavez's practices of nonviolent protest and fasting were greatly influenced by Mohandas Gandhi, whom followers called Mahatma, "Great Soul." Gandhi lived in search of truth and tolerance. To that end he began a method of direct social action called Satyagraha, which is based on courage, truth, and nonviolence. He chose to protest by fasting rather than fighting. Martin Luther King, Jr., also believed in nonviolence and won the Nobel Peace Prize in 1964. Ironically, both men were assassinated for their beliefs.

---

1. Most of the work was "stoop labor." That meant that (pickers had) (to bend over all day to pick the crops).
2. Chavez led a boycott of California grapes. This meant that (no one) (would buy grapes unless farmers met some of the workers') (demands).

 For more on Context Clues, see page T88.

FOCUS

Find out about the hardships Cesar Chavez faced during his early years.

 A saint. A hero. The Mexican-American Dr. Martin Luther King, Jr. All these things have been said about Cesar Chavez.

Chavez was a civil-rights leader. He led *La Causa,* the farmworkers' fight for their rights. Chavez won great gains for farmworkers.

 Cesar Chavez was born in 1927 near Yuma, Arizona. In 1938 his family could not pay their taxes. So, they lost their farm. With many others, they left
10 for California, where they had heard there was work.

The Chavez family became migrant workers. They traveled from farm to farm, picking crops. They lived in labor camps. Home might be a tent, or it might be a one-room shack. For sure there would be no running water and no bathroom.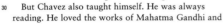

The life of the migrant workers was hard. Most of the work was "stoop labor." That meant the pickers had to bend over all day to pick the crops. They were paid very little.

20 Some farmers even cheated the workers out of the little they earned. The workers could not speak English. So there was little they could do to fight back. They also feared being sent back to Mexico. Life there was even harder.

The Chavez children went to school when they could. Chavez later said he went to over sixty-five grade schools "for a day, a week or a few months." Chavez finished eighth grade. This was far more education than most migrant children got.

30 But Chavez also taught himself. He was always reading. He loved the works of Mahatma Gandhi and

62   Unit 2 Courage Counts

Dr. Martin Luther King, Jr. From these men he learned the idea of nonviolent protest.

> **nonviolent**
> (nŏn vī′ ə lənt)
> *adj.* not using force as a way of getting results

THINK IT THROUGH

How was Cesar like the other children of migrant workers? How was he different?

FOCUS

As a young man, Cesar began to tackle the problems of farmworkers. Learn how he first attracted attention.

During World War II, Chavez served in the Navy. When he returned, he married his girlfriend, Helen. They began working on a farm near San Jose with seven other family members. Later Chavez figured out that the nine workers put together were making twenty-three cents an hour!

40 Chavez joined the Community Service Organization (CSO). This group was working to help Mexican Americans better themselves.

Chavez worked in the fields by day. At night he worked to get Mexican Americans to register to vote. In just two months he signed up 4,000 workers.

The farm owners found out what Chavez was doing. They were afraid he would make trouble. So they fired him. Chavez began working full time for the CSO. He held meetings
50 to talk with workers. More workers joined the CSO.

> **REREAD**
> Find two events that led to changes in Cesar's life.

Chavez worked ten years for the CSO. Then in 1962 he left the group. Chavez wanted to form a farmworkers union. The CSO did not. So Chavez went out on his own.

> **union**
> (yōon′ yən)
> *n.* organized group of workers

Cesar Chavez: Civil-Rights Champion   63

COMPREHENSION

FOCUS SKILL: Fact and Opinion

Tell students that a **fact** is a statement that can be proved and is not debatable. An **opinion,** however, is a statement that can't be proved. Therefore, it can be debated.

For direct instruction on Fact and Opinion, see page T87.

 Ask: What clues in the first two paragraphs tell you that the author admires Chavez? *(uses* saint *and* hero *to describe him; compares him to Martin Luther King, Jr.; says he won great gains for farmworkers.)* **author's perspective**

B Ask if the statement "Cesar Chavez was born in 1927 near Yuma, Arizona" is a fact or an opinion. How do you know? *(It is a fact; it can be proved.)* **fact and opinion**

C **THINK IT THROUGH** How was Cesar like other children of migrant workers? How was he different? *(Alike: traveled and*

picked crops, lived in a labor camp, went to school when he could. Different: finished eighth grade, taught himself, was always reading.)* **compare and contrast**

D **REREAD** Find two events that led to changes in Cesar's life. *(He was fired as a farmworker when he got 4,000 workers registered to vote. As a worker for the CSO, he led other workers to join.)* **details**

LITERATURE

FOCUS SKILL: Biography

Explain to students that a **biography** is an account of a person's life that's written by another person. The writer of a biography, called a biographer, often researches his or her subject in order to provide accurate information.

For direct instruction on Biography, see page T87.

Use the following questions to encourage literary analysis.

 How do you think the biographer

got this information about Chavez? *(Possible answer: through an interview with Chavez or researching articles about Chavez)* **biography**

VOCABULARY

FOCUS SKILL: Context Clues

Remind students to use **context clues**—particularly those that provide **definitions**—to figure out any words they don't know.

A **migrant workers** Students should find the definition in the next sentence.

FOR ENGLISH LEARNERS

Help students understand the following expressions and idioms:

Line 5: the farmworkers' fight for their rights
Line 6: great gains
Line 9: lost their farm
Line 20: cheated the workers out of
Line 34: served in the Navy
Line 55: went out on his own

Chavez, his wife, and eight children moved to Delano, California. Using their life savings of $1,200, they formed the National Farm Workers
60 Association (NFWA). This group later became the United Farm Workers (UFW).

Workers were glad to sign up. Their motto was the phrase "¡Sí, se puede!" ("Yes, it can be done!") This was the beginning of Chavez's life work.

Only three years later, the NFWA gained the world's attention. It joined a strike, or *huelga*, against grape growers in the Delano area. It was this
70 *huelga* that brought fame to Chavez.

Strikes, fasts, and marches. With these tools, Chavez proved that farmworkers had power. Together they could bargain with farmers for better wages and working conditions.

motto
(mŏt′ ō)
n. sentence that expresses the group's goals

REREAD
Do you think this is a good motto? Explain.

fasts
(făsts)
n. periods of time without food

THINK IT THROUGH
Why do you think the farmworkers followed Cesar?

FOCUS
Read to find out what kind of leader Cesar became.

It all began when Filipino grape pickers struck for higher wages. The NFWA joined in. The strike was to go on for five years.

The story of Chavez and the migrant workers soon
80 reached the ears of all America. Newspapers and TV spread the story of *La Causa*. In 1966 ten thousand people from all over the United States marched on the

Cesar Chavez appearing at a rally for the United Farm Workers

state capital in Sacramento. Still the grape growers would not give in.

Chavez knew the public supported the farmworkers. So he announced a boycott of California grapes. This meant that no one would buy grapes unless farmers met some of the workers' demands.

Chavez sent workers to different cities all around
90 the United States. They asked store owners not to sell grapes. They asked the public not to buy grapes. Many truck drivers agreed not to haul grapes. The boycott spread. Many grape growers went out of business. But still the strike went on.

REREAD
Why do you think Cesar tried a boycott?

After a few years, some of the strikers began to get tired. They wanted to use more violent methods of getting what they wanted. Riots, dynamite, and shooting were suggested. But Chavez
100 insisted on using only nonviolent tactics. To bring attention to this point, he began a twenty-five-day hunger strike.

tactics
(tăk′ tĭks)
n. methods used to get results

COMPREHENSION

E **REREAD** Do you think this is a good motto? Explain. *(Most students will say yes, it's positive and motivating.)* **making judgments**

F **THINK IT THROUGH** Why do you think the farmworkers followed Cesar? *(He had dedicated his life and savings to help them; he was influential and fair; he was one of them.)* **drawing conclusions**

G Ask: Is the statement "The story of Chavez and the migrant workers soon reached the ears of all America" a fact? How do you know? *(No, it can't be proved and can be debated; it's unlikely that every person in America heard the story.)* **fact and opinion**

H **REREAD** Why do you think Cesar tried a boycott? *(It would hurt the farmers in their pocketbooks, yet was nonviolent and got the public involved.)* **cause and effect**

LITERATURE

B Why do you think the biographer chose to include this particular fact about Chavez's work? *(It is the event that made Chavez famous.)* **biography**

C Have students review the biography to find a fact that shows why Cesar took such a strong stand against violence. *(Early in the biography, the writer mentions Chavez's love for the works of Mahatma Gandhi and Dr. Martin Luther King, Jr.)* **biography**

VOCABULARY

B **boycott** Students can use the next sentence to figure out the meaning of this word.

FOR ENGLISH LEARNERS

Help students understand the following expressions and idioms:

Line 76: struck for higher wages
Line 82: marched on the state capital
Line 101: to bring attention to this point

Chavez won the support of civil rights groups and churches. Many famous Americans joined *La Causa*. Robert Kennedy was a close friend of Chavez. Dr. Martin Luther King, Jr., supported Chavez. Union leaders and even the pope supported *La Causa*. Money to help the striking workers came too. At last, the grape growers gave in. After five years, the grape
110 boycott was over. So was the strike. Chavez and the farmworkers had won.

THINK IT THROUGH

Why was Cesar's firm position on nonviolence a wise choice in this strike?

FOCUS

Cesar's work continued. Read to find out what other sacrifices he made.

Over the next twenty years, *La Causa* went on. Chavez kept working to help the farmworkers. He demanded an end to the use of dangerous pesticides on crops. He won rest periods for pickers. And the hated short hoe was banned.

> **pesticides**
> (pĕs' tĭ sīdz')
> chemicals used
> to kill insects

In the 1970's Chavez led a lettuce boycott and another grape boycott. In a 1972 protest
120 over right-to-work laws he went on a twenty-four-day fast. In 1988 he went on a thirty-six-day fast to protest the use of pesticides in fields. This fast caused much damage to his kidneys.

In 1993 Chavez died at the age of sixty-six. Doctors said his death was caused by fasting and his life of hardship.

Cesar Chavez had devoted his life to *La Causa*. All his life he chose to live penniless. He never owned a

A student at a holiday celebration holds a sign that reads "Long Live Cesar!"

house or a car. He never took enough money to live
130 on, earning only $6,000 his last year. The rest of the money he raised he poured back into the UFW. Although his health was failing in his later years, he never quit working for the union.

Cesar Chavez was one of the truly heroic figures of the twentieth century. He gave dignity and hope not only to farmworkers, but to all Mexican Americans. Cesar Chavez was a giant in the civil-rights movement of the United States.

> **REREAD**
> Notice that the writer expresses opinions about Chavez at the end.

THINK IT THROUGH

1. What sacrifices did Cesar make for the cause of the farmworkers?
2. What did Cesar achieve for the workers? What methods did he use to achieve them?
3. The author says Cesar Chavez was one of the truly heroic figures. Has she proved her statement? How?

COMPREHENSION

I **THINK IT THROUGH** Why was Cesar's firm position on non-violence a wise choice in this strike? *(He gained the support of civil-rights groups, churches, and many famous people; he finally won the strike; he avoided possible bloodshed.)* **cause and effect**

J **REREAD** Notice that the writer expresses opinions about Cesar at the end. *(You might wish to draw students' attention to such words and phrases as* truly heroic *and* giant, *which suggest the writer's personal view of her subject.)* **fact and opinion**

K **THINK IT THROUGH**

1. What sacrifices did Cesar make for the cause of the farmworkers? *(He used his life savings to form the NFWA; he went on several fasts, which damaged his kidneys and eventually caused his death; he lived penniless.)* **fact and opinion**

2. What did Cesar achieve for the workers? What methods did he use to achieve them? *(Using nonviolent methods, he got the short hoe banned and won rest periods, better wages, and better working conditions.)* **fact and opinion**

3. The author says Cesar Chavez was one of the truly heroic figures. Has she proved her statement? How? *(Most will say yes, she gave several factual examples of how Chavez acted heroically.)* **author's perspective**

K-W-L Chart

Have the class complete the **K-W-L chart** that they began earlier in this lesson. See page T664 for instructions and page T666 for copymaster.

RETEACHING

If students need more help understanding **Fact and Opinion,** use pages T656–T658.

LITERATURE

D Ask: How much of Chavez's life did the biographer cover? *(from his birth in 1927 up through his death in 1993)* **biography**

VOCABULARY

FOR ENGLISH LEARNERS

Help students understand the following expressions and idioms:

Line 116: the hated short hoe was banned

Line 131: poured back into

Line 135: gave dignity and hope not only . . .

Line 138: a giant in the civil-rights movement

RETEACHING

If students need more help understanding **Context Clues,** use pages T608–T611.

1. COMPREHENSION

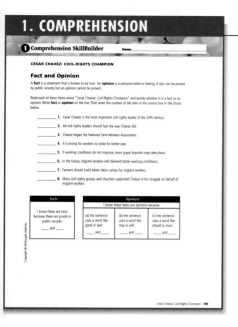

Fact and Opinion

Direct Instruction Write this statement on the chalkboard or say it to the students: *Cesar Chavez was a Mexican-American civil-rights leader.* Note that this statement is called a fact. Define a **fact** as a thing or event known to be true or to have really happened. Next write or say this statement: *Chavez was the greatest Mexican American in history.* Stress that this statement is an opinion. Define an **opinion** as a personal belief, feeling, or judgment about a thing or event. Stress that facts can be proved, but opinions cannot.

Tell the students that certain words may help them to understand the difference between a fact and an opinion.

- *Must, should, ought to* are words that explain what the writer wishes or how he or she feels about something, but not how it actually is.
- *Good, bad, best, most, worst* are judgment words.
- *Will* or *may* make a prediction, that is, tell what the writer thinks may happen in the future. This is a kind of opinion too.

Comprehension SkillBuilder Answer Key:

1. *opinion*
2. *opinion*
3. *fact*
4. *opinion*
5. *opinion*
6. *opinion*
7. *opinion*
8. *fact*

Chart
Facts: *3 and 8*
Opinions: *(a) 1 and 4; (b) 5 and 6; (c) 2 and 7*

2. LITERATURE

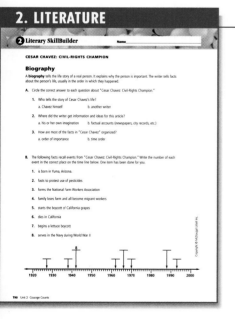

Biography

Direct Instruction Explain to the students that a **biography** tells the factual story of a real person's life. The writer, called a biographer, gathers a great deal of information about the person and then decides which facts to include in the story. Usually the information is in chronological order, that is, events are told in the order in which they happened. Most biographies include the following facts:

- Date and place of birth
- Information about important events in the subject's life
- Facts on how and why the subject chose a certain job or career
- Personal qualities that make the person unique
- Date and place of death

Literary SkillBuilder Answer Key:

A.
1. *b*
2. *b*
3. *b*

B.
Time line –left to right: 1, 4, 8, 3, 5, 7, 2, 6

3. VOCABULARY

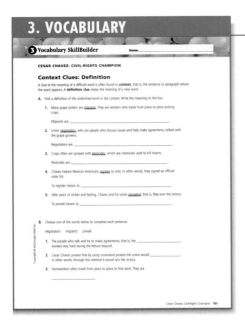

Context Clues: Definition

Direct Instruction Recall that writers use **context clues,** or hints in the passage in which a word appears, to help a reader understand a new or unfamiliar word. Note that one type of context clue is called a **definition clue.** A definition clue actually tells the meaning of the new word.

Tell the students that the following words and phrases often signal definition clues:

is or *are* Some farmers hire **crop dusters.** Crop dusters <u>are</u> pilots who spray chemicals on the crops.

who is An **agronomist,** <u>who is</u> a farm manager, chooses the best crops for each farm area.

which is **Endive,** <u>which is</u> a type of plant used in salads, grows in California.

in other words Many civil-rights leaders **endorsed** the grape boycott. <u>In other words,</u> they approved it.

that is One successful protest against the grape growers included a **huelga,** <u>that is</u>, a strike.

Vocabulary SkillBuilder Answer Key:

A.
1. *workers who travel from place to place picking crops*
2. *people who discuss issues and help make agreements*
3. *chemicals used to kill insects*
4. *sign an official voter list.*
5. *win the victory*

B.
1. *negotiators*
2. *prevail*
3. *migrants*

---

4. WORDS TO KNOW

Words to Know

Direct Instruction As you present the **Words to Know,** here are some points you might want to cover. The word *union* is a derivative of the Latin word *ūnus,* meaning "one." Other words in the same family are *unite, uniform,* and *unit.* Point out to students that the prefix *uni-* is a clue that a word's definition has to do with the concept of "one."

The word *fast* has multiple meanings. Most students are most likely familiar with the primary definition—"marked by great speed." There is an abundance of differences in the use of the word, however. For instance, someone can be "fast asleep" or have a "fast grip" on something. Some students may have difficulty understanding the use of this word in these contexts. A study of such idioms can help students gain facility with language.

Verify that students are familiar with word searches. In this particular search, words are spelled only horizontally and vertically. This can be an engaging preliminary to the main exercise—matching the word to its definition.

Writing Activity Pair students or have them work in small groups to complete the exercise. Have volunteers read their creations aloud.

Words to Know SkillBuilder Answer Key:

A. 1. *tactics* 2. *union* 3. *nonviolent* 4. *motto* 5. *fasts*
B. 1. *nonviolent* 2. *fasts* 3. *tactics* 4. *union* 5. *motto*

---

5. SELECTION TEST

Selection Test Answer Key:

A. 1. *a* 2. *c* 3. *c* 4. *c* 5. *a* 6. *b* 7. *b* 8. *c* 9. *a*
B. *personal wealth; his health, time, and energy; his life*

CESAR CHAVEZ: CIVIL-RIGHTS CHAMPION

Fact and Opinion

A **fact** is a statement that is known to be true. An **opinion** is a personal belief or feeling. A fact can be proved by public records, but an opinion cannot be proved.

Read each of these items about "Cesar Chavez: Civil-Rights Champion" and decide whether it is a fact or an opinion. Write **fact** or **opinion** on the line. Then write the number of the item in the correct box in the charts below.

_____ 1. Cesar Chavez is the most important civil-rights leader of the 20th century.

_____ 2. All civil-rights leaders should fast the way Chavez did.

_____ 3. Chavez began the National Farm Workers Association.

_____ 4. It is wrong for workers to strike for better pay.

_____ 5. If working conditions do not improve, more grape boycotts may take place.

_____ 6. In the future, migrant workers will demand better working conditions.

_____ 7. Farmers should build better labor camps for migrant workers.

_____ 8. Many civil-rights groups and churches supported Chavez in his struggle on behalf of migrant workers.

Facts
I know these are facts because there are proofs in public records: _____ and _____

Opinions		
I know these items are opinions because		
(a) the sentence uses a word like *good* or *bad:* _____ and _____	(b) the sentence uses a word like *may* or *will:* _____ and _____	(c) the sentence uses a word like *should* or *must:* _____ and _____

CESAR CHAVEZ: CIVIL-RIGHTS CHAMPION

Biography

A **biography** tells the life story of a real person. It explains why the person is important. The writer tells facts about the person's life, usually in the order in which they happened.

A. Circle the correct answer to each question about "Cesar Chavez: Civil-Rights Champion."

   1. Who tells the story of Cesar Chavez's life?

   a. Chavez himself   b. another writer

   2. Where did the writer get information and ideas for this article?

   a. his or her own imagination   b. factual accounts (newspapers, city records, etc.)

   3. How are most of the facts in "Cesar Chavez" organized?

   a. order of importance   b. time order

B. The following facts recall events from "Cesar Chavez: Civil-Rights Champion." Write the number of each event in the correct place on the time line below. One item has been done for you.

   1. is born in Yuma, Arizona.

   2. fasts to protest use of pesticides

   3. forms the National Farm Workers Association

   4. family loses farm and all become migrant workers

   5. Ten thousand people march on the state capital in Sacramento in support of the grape pickers' strike.

   6. dies in California

   7. fasts to protest right-to-work laws

   8. serves in the Navy during World War II

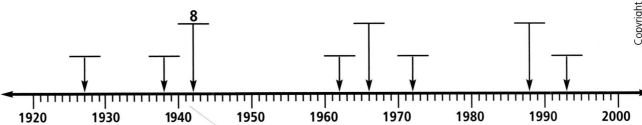

CESAR CHAVEZ: CIVIL-RIGHTS CHAMPION

Context Clues: Definition

A clue to the meaning of a difficult word is often found in **context,** that is, the sentence or paragraph where the word appears. A **definition clue** states the meaning of a new word.

A. Find a definition of the underlined word in the context. Write the meaning on the line.

1. Many grape pickers are <u>migrants</u>. They are workers who travel from place to place picking crops.

    Migrants are _____.

2. Union <u>negotiators</u>, who are people who discuss issues and help make agreements, talked with the grape growers.

    Negotiators are _____.

3. Crops often are sprayed with <u>pesticides</u>, which are chemicals used to kill insects.

    Pesticides are _____.

4. Chavez helped Mexican Americans <u>register</u> to vote. In other words, they signed an official voter list.

    To register means to _____.

5. After years of strikes and fasting, Chavez and his union <u>prevailed</u>, that is, they won the victory.

    To prevail means to _____.

B. Choose one of the words below to complete each sentence.

negotiators   migrants   prevail

1. The people who talk and try to make agreements, that is, the _____, worked very hard during the lettuce boycott.

2. Cesar Chavez proved that by using nonviolent protest the union would _____. In other words, through this method it would win the victory.

3. Farmworkers often travel from place to place to find work. They are

    _____.

CESAR CHAVEZ: CIVIL-RIGHTS CHAMPION

Words to Know

nonviolent   union   motto   tactics   fasts

A. Fill in the blanks with the word from the list that best completes the sentence.

1. Each of the men running for president had some plans, or
    _____, to get votes.

2. A _____ protects the rights of workers.

3. I believe in peaceful change, and therefore I'm _____.

4. "Work hard, play hard" is our _____.

5. To protest unfair laws the workers refused to eat and went on _____.

B. Locate the **Words to Know** in the Word Search below. Then match each with its definition.

q	n	x	j	y	h	d	g	b	m	m	p
m	k	h	u	z	e	x	a	w	p	o	n
a	n	o	n	v	i	o	l	e	n	t	a
l	b	s	i	i	f	c	f	a	s	t	s
r	c	i	o	w	o	u	j	v	v	o	f
t	b	s	n	t	y	d	o	k	u	q	e
r	t	n	c	g	t	a	c	t	i	c	s

1. not using force _____

2. periods of time without food _____

3. methods used to get results _____

4. organized group of workers _____

5. sentence that states group goals _____

Writing Activity

Work with a group of students to create a motto that fits your group. Read it aloud to the rest of the class. Use at least one of the **Words to Know.**

CESAR CHAVEZ: CIVIL-RIGHTS CHAMPION

A. Complete each statement by filling in the circle beside the correct answer.

1. Cesar Chavez is best remembered for his work as a
   ○ a. civil-rights leader.   ○ b. migrant worker.   ○ c. grape grower.

2. Chavez and his wife used their life savings to form the
   ○ a. National Boycotters Association.
   ○ b. National Grape Growers Association.
   ○ c. National Farm Workers Association.

3. The group's motto, "¡Sí, se puede!," meant
   ○ a. "See, it can be boycotted!"
   ○ b. "Yes, it can be grown!"
   ○ c. "Yes, it can be done!"

4. The group led its first famous strike against the
   ○ a. California pesticide manufacturers.
   ○ b. California lettuce growers.
   ○ c. California grape growers.

5. This strike went on for
   ○ a. five years.   ○ b. five months.   ○ c. five days.

6. During the strike, Chavez used only
   ○ a. violent forms of protest.
   ○ b. nonviolent forms of protest.
   ○ c. riots, dynamite, and shooting.

7. He first learned these ideas from Mahatma Gandhi and
   ○ a. the pope of the Roman Catholic church.
   ○ b. Dr. Martin Luther King, Jr.
   ○ c. Robert Kennedy.

8. After the strike, Chavez helped the farmworkers for
   ○ a. ten more years.   ○ b. fifteen more years.   ○ c. twenty more years.

9. In 1988, he went on a thirty-six-day fast that damaged his
   ○ a. kidneys.   ○ b. heart.   ○ c. stomach.

B. In your own words, explain what Cesar Chavez gave up for his union.

_____

_____

Focus Skills

COMPREHENSION
Chronological Order
Reading for Details (SQ3R)

LITERATURE
Biography

VOCABULARY
Specialized Vocabulary

SkillBuilder Copymasters

 Reading Comprehension:
1 Chronological Order p. T102
2 Reading for Details p. T103

 Vocabulary:
3 Specialized Vocabulary p. T104
4 Words to Know p. T105

Assessment

 5 Selection Test p. T106

Readability Scores

DRP	LEXILE	DALE-CHALL
52	640	4.2

Reading Fluency

 ★ Reading Fluency p. T107

For English Learners

Amateur and professional athletes are viewed differently throughout the world. In some countries, such as the United States and Puerto Rico, many athletes are regarded as national heroes. Invite students from other countries to discuss the status of athletes in their countries. Do students feel that athletes make good heroes and role models?

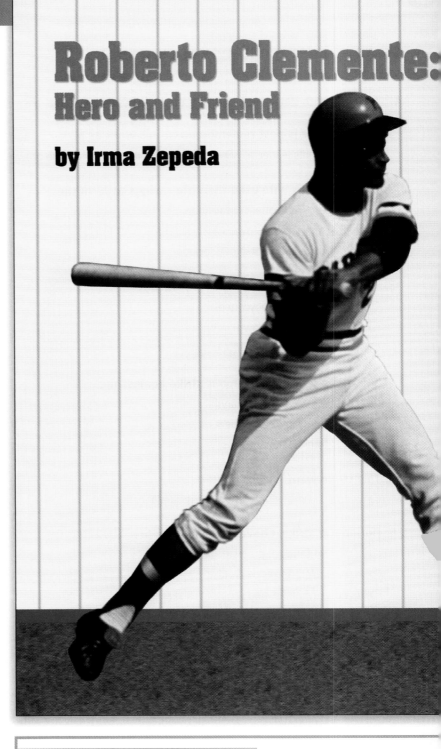

Roberto Clemente:
Hero and Friend
by Irma Zepeda

Vocabulary Strategy: Preteaching

Specialized Vocabulary Tell students that when they read, they often come across words that are related to the topic of the selection. For example, in this biography there are many words related to the topic of baseball. The words shown on the next page are called **specialized vocabulary.** Before students read the selection, have them match these baseball terms to their definitions. Write the terms and definitions on the board and read students the definitions.

What makes a hero? Perhaps it is courage and the desire to help others. Find out about the life of a hero.

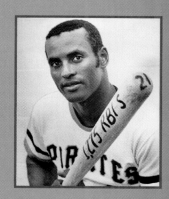

Connect to Your Life

Who are your heroes? What stories about heroes have your parents shared? With a partner, make a list of heroes. Talk about their qualities and actions.

Key to the Biography

This true account of Clemente's life includes terms and figures about baseball. If necessary, reread those sections to make sure you understand them. Roberto Clemente started out on a team in the *minor leagues* of baseball. There, players develop their skills. If their abilities impress others, they move up to the *major leagues.*

Vocabulary Preview

Words to Know
determined   prejudice
prospects   potential

 Reading Coach CD-ROM selection

Roberto Clemente: Hero and Friend **69**

World Series	hits ÷ times at bat
outfield	games between major-league champs
scout	person who throws the baseball
pitcher	area beyond the bases
batting average	person looking for talented players

 For more on Specialized Vocabulary, see page T101.

Connect to Your Life

As partners talk about the heroes on their list, are they noticing similarities among them? If so, what are they? Do students think it is possible that all heroes share certain characteristics? Why or why not?

Key to the Biography

Context clues and students' prior knowledge will help them understand most of the baseball terms in this selection. If they need more help, however, have them use an encyclopedia or other reference source.

Vocabulary Preview

Words to Know
determined *adj.* not willing to change one's mind
prospects *n.* people with possibilities
prejudice *n.* unfair treatment, usually based on race or religion
potential *n.* ability

For direct instruction on Words to Know, see page T101.

Building Background

Roberto Clemente wasn't always considered a hero. Five years after he joined the last-place Pittsburgh Pirates, his team won the 1960 World Series. Though Clemente played exceptionally well that season, he felt he was passed over for the Most Valuable Player (MVP) award because of his unpopularity among sportswriters—the very people who choose the winner. Reporters disliked Clemente because he often spoke out against their racial prejudices. As a result, they rarely mentioned Clemente in their articles, even when he played brilliantly. Clemente was so bitter over his MVP slight that he refused to wear his 1960 World Series ring.

Anytime you have an opportunity to make things better and you don't, then you are wasting your time on this Earth.
—Roberto Clemente

FOCUS

Learn about the goal Roberto Clemente sets early in his life.

Roberto Clemente was born on August 18, 1934. He was born on the island of Puerto Rico. Roberto's family lived in a small house in the town of Carolina. Like most families there, the Clementes worked hard to earn a living. Roberto's father worked long days cutting sugar cane. In his spare time, he also sold meat and other foods to earn a few extra dollars. To help the family, the Clemente children held odd jobs. Roberto delivered milk for a
10 few pennies a day.

The Clementes could not buy any luxuries—not even a baseball for Roberto. Instead, Roberto and his friends used sticks to practice batting cans. They had no gloves, pads, or even a real bat. They simply loved the game. To Roberto, baseball players were heroes. He dreamed of becoming a great player someday. Roberto was determined to work hard to make his dream come true.

> **determined**
> (dĭ tûr′ mĭnd)
> *adj.* not willing to change one's mind

70 Unit 2 Courage Counts

In high school, Roberto joined the baseball team.
20 Roberto was a top runner, but he knew that speed was not enough. Baseball players needed strong arms to throw the ball fast and hit it hard. To strengthen his arms and legs, Roberto joined the track team. He threw the javelin and ran in races. The javelin is a light spear with a pointed edge. It is used in distance-throwing contests. Roberto once threw the javelin 195 feet. For a high school student, that was an amazing act. Whenever Roberto had a chance, he squeezed a rubber ball. This would help strengthen his arm
30 muscles. In time, Roberto became one of the best players on the team.

THINK IT THROUGH

 What steps does Roberto take to become a great baseball player?

FOCUS

Read to find out how Roberto performs in the minor leagues.

One day as Roberto was playing ball, Pedrín Zorilla watched him closely. Zorilla was the owner of a local baseball team. He was also a scout for the Brooklyn Dodgers. A scout is a person who looks for talented players. Zorilla asked Roberto to join his team. This was Roberto's first professional contract. He made little money, but he knew it would be enough to help his family. There was one problem. Roberto's
40 parents were unhappy with his decision to become a baseball player. They wanted him

---

COMPREHENSION

FOCUS SKILL 1: Chronological Order

Remind students that **chronological order** is the order in which events happen in time. Writers often use signal words, such as time words, to show the order of those events more clearly.

 For direct instruction on Chronological Order, see page T100.

FOCUS SKILL 2: Reading for Details

Tell students that **reading for details** and following the chronological order of this selection will help them understand what happened to Roberto Clemente, when it happened, and why.

 For direct instruction on Reading for Details, see page T100.

A THINK IT THROUGH What steps does Roberto take to become a great baseball player? *(He joins his school's baseball and track teams, and he squeezes a rubber ball to strengthen his arms.)* **details**

B Ask: Which signal words tell you when Roberto is spotted by the owner of a baseball team? *(One day)* **chronological order**

VOCABULARY

FOCUS SKILL: Specialized Vocabulary

Remind students to use context clues, their prior knowledge of baseball, and any reference sources necessary to figure out the **specialized vocabulary** in this selection.

A scout Have students find the definition of *scout* in the next sentence. Let them discuss what a *professional contract* means.

FOR ENGLISH LEARNERS

Help students understand the following expressions and idioms:

Line 9: held odd jobs
Line 18: dream come true
Line 27: amazing act

C to go to college. After Roberto pleaded with them, they finally gave in.

The next season, the Dodgers held a clinic in San Juan. A clinic is a group session in which baseball prospects are asked to try out. Al Campanis, the chief scout, did not have high hopes for the prospects. He did not think any player would be good enough for
50 the majors.

However, Roberto proved to be different. Campanis watched Roberto fire fast balls at the catcher. Then Campanis had the boys run the 60-yard dash. Roberto's record was 6.4 seconds. The world record was 6.1 seconds. The final test was batting the ball. So far, Roberto was a terrific discovery. Campanis knew he should not build false hope. Roberto had to hit the ball against one of the Dodgers' minor league pitchers. To everyone's surprise, line drives rocketed off
60 Roberto's bat. He was amazing!

Campanis wanted to sign Roberto at once. However, major league rules did not allow a prospect to be signed before he graduated from high school. In 1954, after his high school graduation, Roberto joined the Dodgers' farm team in Montreal, Canada. Farm teams help young players get ready for the major leagues. At the time, scouts from other teams could watch young players. If the scouts wanted, they could sign a
70 contract with a player.

Even though the Dodgers wanted to sign Roberto, there was still some prejudice in the major leagues. Behind the scenes, major league teams avoided having more than four black players. The Dodgers already

prospects
(prŏs′ pĕkts′)
n. people with possibilities

B
line drives
hits that move low and fast, usually in a straight line

D

prejudice
(prĕj′ ə dĭs)
n. unfair treatment, usually based on race or religion

72 Unit 2 Courage Counts

had four black players. They did not want to lose Roberto, so they sent him to Montreal.

The Dodgers kept quiet
80 about Roberto. They did not play him often so that scouts would not notice him. However, their plan failed. Scouts from the Pittsburgh Pirates thought Roberto had the potential to become a great player. They quickly signed a contract with him. At the time, Pittsburgh was last in the National League.
90 When Roberto joined the team in 1955, they had lost more than 100 games. The team had placed last for three years in a row. They needed a powerful player like Roberto.

Roberto Clemente in uniform as a Pittsburgh Pirate

potential
(pə tĕn′ shəl)
n. ability

THINK IT THROUGH
What sets Roberto above the rest of the players?

FOCUS
Roberto's career as a Pittsburgh Pirate soars. Read to find out what he achieves.

E

F

Roberto played hard that first year. As a right fielder, he caught balls in midair to block home runs. Many times he threw his body against walls or fences to catch the ball. Pain mattered little to him.

C

Roberto Clemente: Hero and Friend 73

C Ask: Do you think his parents make the right decision? Explain. *(Most students will say yes, because his parents allow Roberto to follow his dream; others might think a college education would help him better in the long run.)* **making judgments**

D Ask: Which two phrases help you know when Roberto joins the Dodgers' farm team? *(In 1954 and after his high school graduation)* **chronological order**

E Ask: When does Roberto join the Pittsburgh Pirates? *(in 1955)* **chronological order**

F **THINK IT THROUGH** What sets Roberto above the rest of the players? *(He can pitch, run incredibly fast, and hit line drives.)* **details**

B **minor league, major league** (lines 58, 62) Explain that the opposite nature of *minor* and *major* is a key to the importance of the leagues. Ask which is better. *(major leagues)*

C **midair** Have students separate this word into a prefix and a base word to facilitate understanding. *(mid- + air)*

FOR ENGLISH LEARNERS

Help students understand the following expressions and idioms:

Line 42: they finally gave in
Line 44: held a clinic
Line 47: did not have high hopes
Line 52: fire fast balls
Line 53: 60-yard dash
Line 57: build false hope
Line 57: hit the ball against
Line 59: rocketed off Roberto's bat
Line 73: behind the scenes

As a batter, he swung at almost every ball. This is
100 usually the sign of a young, inexperienced player. Most
players learn to control their swing as they gain
experience. At the end of the year, Roberto's batting
average was .255. A batting average of .300 is better
than most. By the end of his second year, Roberto was
batting at .311.

G

When Roberto was not playing for the Pirates, he
would return to Puerto Rico. While he was there he
played in the Winter Leagues. Most ball players rest
during the off-season. Roberto continued to play no
110 matter how tired he was. He knew that his people
might never see him play in person. He wanted his
fans to enjoy watching him. In 1966, an article in
Sporting News reported, "Every Puerto Rican is a
Roberto Clemente fan."

Clemente catching a ball in midair

74 Unit 2 Courage Counts

Roberto was a hero. His fans knew Roberto had
worked to become a professional baseball player.
They also knew how much he cared about them.

In 1960 and 1971, Roberto led the Pirates to the
World Series. The Pirates won both times, although
120 the odds were against them. Roberto was chosen the
MVP (Most Valuable Player) in the 1971 World Series.
He batted .414, hit 2 home runs, and had 12 hits and
4 RBIs. On September 30, 1972, Roberto
had his 3000th career hit. At the time, only
ten men had achieved this goal.

> **RBIs**
> runs batted in;
> a rating of a
> player's batting
> ability

THINK IT THROUGH
H What are Roberto's achievements as a player?

FOCUS
With all Roberto's success, he was still setting goals. Discover
how Roberto wished to help others.

He was finally the baseball player he had dreamed
of becoming. But Roberto had one more dream. It was
perhaps his most important dream. With money from
governments, businesses, and many other people, he
130 had plans to build Ciudad Deportiva (Sports City). He
wanted to give the children of Puerto Rico a place
where they could learn about sports. Roberto believed
that young children could learn the value of hard work
through sports. He wanted to give children something
that would be rewarding and helpful. But his dream
would have to wait.

I On December 23, 1972, an earthquake struck
Managua, Nicaragua. Roberto had visited Managua
the year before. While he was there, Roberto met a

Roberto Clemente: Hero and Friend 75

COMPREHENSION

G Have students describe, in their own words, Roberto's talent as a player. *(His batting average is high, and he catches balls in midair.)* **summarizing**

Reciprocal Teaching Suggestion: Evaluating
Teacher Modeling To demonstrate the Active Reading Strategy of evaluating, direct students' attention to lines 102–105.
You could say: *I don't know much about baseball statistics. When I read these three sentences, it was the second sentence, the one starting on line 103, that helped me to understand Roberto Clemente's ability. Since I understand that a batting average of .300 is better than average, I could draw a conclusion that Clemente, with an average of .311, was a quite remarkable player. Also, he seemed to improve with experience.*

Student Modeling Direct students to read lines 118–125 on page 75, focusing on line 122. Have a volun-

teer model how he or she would evaluate Roberto Clemente's performance during the World Series. *(Possible response: Clemente's batting average of .414 indicates that he performed brilliantly.)*

H **THINK IT THROUGH** What are Roberto's achievements as a player? *(two World Series victories, MVP in 1971 World Series, 3000th hit in 1972)* **details**

I Ask: What important event happens on December 23, 1972? *(An earthquake strikes Managua, Nicaragua.)* **chronological order**

VOCABULARY

FOR ENGLISH LEARNERS

Help students understand the following:

Line 120: the odds were against them

young orphan boy, Julio Parrales. The boy had lost both his legs in a car accident. Thanks to Roberto, Julio would soon have a pair of artificial legs.

When Roberto heard the news of the earthquake, he began to worry about Julio. Right away he signed up to help the victims. He collected money, food, clothes, and medicine. Roberto would not rest until he had enough supplies to fill an airplane. He wanted to make sure that the supplies reached the poorest people.

On December 31, 1972, Roberto and four others filled an old plane with the supplies. Before takeoff, the plane had engine problems. Roberto's family and friends begged him not to go. But he insisted that he would deliver the supplies himself. Shortly after takeoff, the plane began to lose speed. It crashed into the sea after going only about a mile.

When news of the accident spread, thousands of people searched the sea for days. They found the remains of the pilot, a sock, and a small suitcase that belonged to Roberto. The searchers finally gave up. They believed that Roberto and the others had drowned. Five days after the crash, Manny Sanguillen, Roberto's old friend and teammate, led his own search. To his disappointment, only fish and sharks roamed the sea. Roberto's body was never found. That New Year's Eve, the country lost a hero.

REREAD
All these people searched. How does that show their love for Roberto?

Today, Roberto is remembered as one of the greatest athletes. In 1973, he was the first Hispanic voted into the Hall of Fame. The Hall of Fame is the highest honor a baseball player can receive. Many schools and parks across the United States and in Puerto Rico are named after Roberto

Clemente. In Carolina, Puerto Rico, visitors are greeted with a twelve-foot statue of Roberto as they enter the Roberto Clemente Sports City—his final dream come true.

THINK IT THROUGH

1. Which of Roberto Clemente's goals was reached after his death?
2. Becoming a Baseball Hall of Fame member shows that Roberto was an outstanding player. Find evidence from the selection that shows him as an outstanding human being.
3. Look over the details about Roberto's disappearance. Use the information to make a time line of the events.

COMPREHENSION

J Ask: How many days after the earthquake does Roberto die in a plane crash? How do you know? *(From the signal words "On December 31, 1972," students can figure out that he dies eight days later.)* **chronological order**

K REREAD *All* these people searched. How does that show their love for Roberto? *(They loved him so much that they didn't want to stop looking for him.)* **making inferences**

L THINK IT THROUGH

1. Which of Roberto Clemente's goals was reached after his death? *(His Sports City was finally built.)* **details**

2. Becoming a Baseball Hall of Fame member shows that Roberto was an outstanding player. Find evidence from the selection that shows him as an outstanding human being. *(played ball in Puerto Rico during off-season so his fans* could see him, planned a Sports City for poor children, helped Julio Parrales get artificial legs, died while delivering supplies to Nicaraguan earthquake victims) **details**

3. Look over the details about Roberto's disappearance. Use the information to make a time line of the events. *(December 31: plane has problems, takes off, crashes after one mile; January 5: Manny Sanguillen searches)* **chronological order**

Option for Writing Students can work alone or with a partner to write a brief tribute to Roberto Clemente, explaining why he was considered a hero both on and off the baseball field.

RETEACHING

If students need more help understanding **Chronological Order,** use pages T639–T641.

VOCABULARY

FOR ENGLISH LEARNERS

Help students understand the following:

Line 140: lost both his legs
Line 171: the highest honor
Line 179: his final dream come true

1. COMPREHENSION

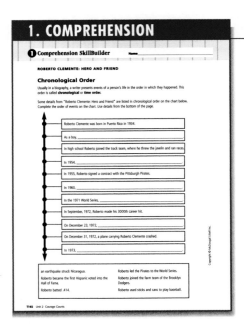

Chronological Order

Direct Instruction Tell students that in most stories, events are described in **chronological order,** or the order they happened. Writers describe the first event in the story first, the second event second, and so on. Point out that "Roberto Clemente" begins with Clemente's birth and ends with an event or two following his fatal accident.

Explain that a writer may tell about an event out of time order if it helps the reader understand the meaning or importance of an earlier or later event. Have students identify at least four separate events in this statement, put them in time order, and then compare that order of events with the order in the sentence:

I missed the bus because when I was halfway to the bus stop, I remembered that I hadn't put my homework into my backpack and I had to go back for it. (didn't put homework into backpack and left home without it; remembered homework on way to bus stop; went back for homework; missed bus)

Comprehension SkillBuilder Answer Key:

As a boy, <u>Roberto used sticks and cans to play baseball</u>; In 1954, <u>Roberto joined the farm team of the Brooklyn Dodgers</u>; In 1960, <u>Roberto led the Pirates to the World Series</u>; In the 1971 World Series, <u>Roberto batted .414</u>; On December 23, 1972, <u>an earthquake struck Nicaragua</u>; In 1973, <u>Roberto became the first Hispanic voted into the Hall of Fame</u>.

2. COMPREHENSION

Reading for Details (SQ3R)

Direct Instruction Remind students that nonfiction includes all factual writing, including the content of textbooks. It's important to understand and recall correctly the details in such nonfiction writing; for most people, reading an account a single time is not enough to become aware of and memorize all the important facts. Explain that one of the most effective ways of studying is the **SQ3R** method. Write the words represented by SQ3R on the chalkboard and briefly discuss each one.

Survey—Get an overview of the material. Look for subheads, charts, illustrations, or anything else that suggests what the article will tell about.

Question—Ask questions about what you might learn in the article. Start with words like *who, what, when, where, why,* and *how.*

Read—Read carefully, looking for answers to your prereading questions and adding any new questions that come up.

Record—Without looking at the article, write answers to all your questions. Also note any other facts or ideas that seem important to you.

Review—Check your answers against the article. If there is anything you cannot answer or understand, re-read the article.

Comprehension SkillBuilder Answer Key:
Survey: *b*
Question: *Answers will vary. Possible answers: Who was Roberto Clemente? Why is he worth reading about?*
Record/Review: 1. *Puerto Rico (or Carolina, Puerto Rico)* **2.** *Pittsburgh*
3. *(Choice of facts will vary, but facts must appear in the article.)*

3. VOCABULARY

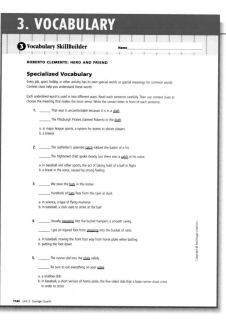

Specialized Vocabulary

Direct Instruction Tell students that many fields of work or activity have their own special words. People who are not in those fields must often use context clues or the dictionary to find out what such words mean.

Explain that some words have only one meaning and that that meaning is used only in a particular field. For example, the word *teleprompter* is used only to name a device that helps a speaker in presenting a prepared speech before an audience, often a television audience.

At other times, a familiar word may have several meanings, and only one of those meanings is used in a particular field. For example, have students compare different meanings of the word *strike* in the fields of baseball, union organizing, clock making, and military action.

> **Vocabulary SkillBuilder Answer Key:**
> **1.** *b, a*
> **2.** *a, b*
> **3.** *b, a*
> **4.** *a, b*
> **5.** *b, a*

4. WORDS TO KNOW

Words to Know

Direct Instruction As you present the **Words to Know,** here are some points you might want to cover.

Point out to students that there is a general rule for forming the past tense of words ending in a consonant: Double the final consonant in a word of more than one syllable if the word is accented on the last syllable. Examples of this include these words: *transferring, admitted, allotting,* *permitting.*

- **determined** is the past tense of *determine*
- **prejudice** is related to the word *prejudge*

Writing Activity Encourage students to be creative. Have volunteers read their creations aloud.

> **Words to Know SkillBuilder Answer Key:**
>
> **A.**
> **1.** *a*
> **2.** *b*
> **3.** *b*
> **4.** *c*
>
> **B.**
> **1.** *prospects*
> **2.** *determined*
> **3.** *potential*
> **4.** *prejudice*

5. SELECTION TEST

> **Selection Test Answer Key:**
> **A.** **1.** *Puerto Rico* **2.** *childhood* **3.** *rubber ball* **4.** *javelin* **5.** *farm team*
> **6.** *high school* **7.** *Pittsburgh Pirates* **8.** *World Series* **9.** *earthquake*
> **B.** *The plane crashed, leaving no survivors.*

ROBERTO CLEMENTE: HERO AND FRIEND

Chronological Order

Usually in a biography, a writer presents events of a person's life in the order in which they happened. This order is called **chronological** or **time order.**

Some details from "Roberto Clemente: Hero and Friend" are listed in chronological order on the chart below. Complete the order of events on the chart. Use details from the bottom of the page.

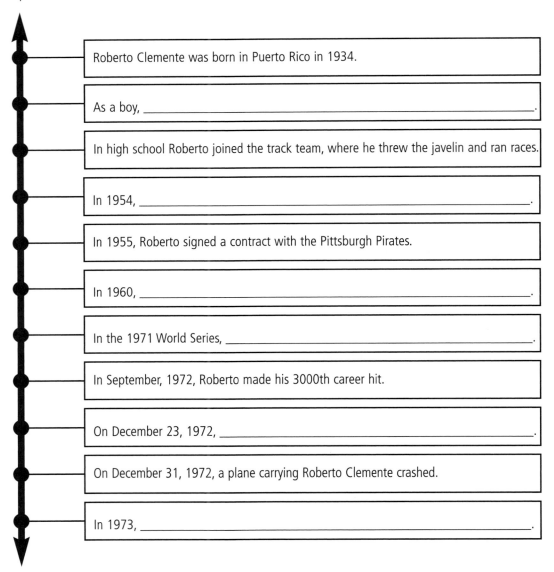

Roberto Clemente was born in Puerto Rico in 1934.

As a boy, _____.

In high school Roberto joined the track team, where he threw the javelin and ran races.

In 1954, _____.

In 1955, Roberto signed a contract with the Pittsburgh Pirates.

In 1960, _____.

In the 1971 World Series, _____.

In September, 1972, Roberto made his 3000th career hit.

On December 23, 1972, _____.

On December 31, 1972, a plane carrying Roberto Clemente crashed.

In 1973, _____.

---

an earthquake struck Nicaragua.

Roberto became the first Hispanic voted into the Hall of Fame.

Roberto batted .414.

Roberto led the Pirates to the World Series.

Roberto joined the farm team of the Brooklyn Dodgers.

Roberto used sticks and cans to play baseball.

ROBERTO CLEMENTE: HERO AND FRIEND

Reading for Details (SQ3R)

Often you read nonfiction to learn and remember facts. A way to study and remember what you read is the SQ3R method. **SQ3R** stands for **Survey** (look over), **Question** (ask what you want to learn from the nonfiction), **Read, Record** (take notes), and **Review.**

Use the SQ3R method to study "Roberto Clemente: Hero and Friend." Follow these directions.

Survey Take a brief look at the selection. Which one of the following features do you see? Circle that choice.

    a. charts and graphs

    b. photographs

    c. headings

    d. subheadings

Question Write two questions that most people would have about Roberto Clemente.

_____

_____

Read Read (or reread) "Roberto Clemente: Hero and Friend." Before you start, write your beginning time here:

_____. When you finish, write your ending time here: _____.

Record Without looking back at the story, answer these questions.

    1. Where was Roberto born? _____

    2. For which city did he play as a major league ball player? _____

    3. What is one other fact in the article? _____

Review Find answers to the questions in the article. Place a check mark next to each fact you remembered correctly.

ROBERTO CLEMENTE: HERO AND FRIEND

Specialized Vocabulary

Every job, sport, hobby, or other activity has its own special words or special meanings for common words. Context clues help you understand these words.

Each underlined word is used in two different ways. Read each sentence carefully. Then use context clues to choose the meaning that makes the most sense. Write the correct letter in front of each sentence.

1. _____ That seat is uncomfortable because it is in a <u>draft</u>.

   _____ The Pittsburgh Pirates claimed Roberto in the <u>draft</u>.

   a. in major league sports, a system for teams to obtain players
   b. a breeze

2. _____ The outfielder's splendid <u>catch</u> robbed the batter of a hit.

   _____ The frightened child spoke clearly, but there was a <u>catch</u> in his voice.

   a. in baseball and other sports, the act of taking hold of a ball in flight
   b. a break in the voice, caused by strong feeling

3. _____ We store the <u>bats</u> in this locker.

   _____ Hundreds of <u>bats</u> flew from the cave at dusk.

   a. in science, a type of flying mammal
   b. in baseball, a club used to strike at the ball

4. _____ Usually, <u>stepping</u> into the bucket hampers a smooth swing.

   _____ I got an injured foot from <u>stepping</u> into the bucket of nails.

   a. in baseball, moving the front foot way from home plate when batting
   b. putting the foot down

5. _____ The runner slid into the <u>plate</u> safely.

   _____ Be sure to eat everything on your <u>plate</u>.

   a. a shallow dish
   b. in baseball, a short version of home plate, the five-sided slab that a base runner must cross
      in order to score

ROBERTO CLEMENTE: HERO AND FRIEND

Words to Know

determined   **prospects**   **prejudice**   **potential**

A. Circle the letter of the word or phrase that is most similar to the **boldfaced** word. Use the dictionary, if you need to.

1. Jan knew many other **prospects** were interviewing for the job.

a. people with possibilities   b. young mothers   c. lawyers

2. Lawrence got involved with groups that tried to get rid of **prejudice.**

a. insects   b. unfair treatment   c. pollution

3. I am **determined** to win this leg of the race.

a. very scared   b. firmly decided   c. against

4. My chorus instructor said I had the **potential** to become an amazing singer.

a. vocal cords   b. grades   c. ability

B. Answer each question by filling in a word from the list at the top.

1. What could you call a group of possible friends? _____

2. If someone tries as hard as she can to get something, what is she? _____

3. If you don't do your best, you aren't living up to your what? _____

4. What word describes an attitude against people of color? _____

Writing Activity

Imagine that you are a sports star. What is your sport? What position do you play? Write at least three sentences about your life as a famous figure, using at least one of the **Words to Know.**

ROBERTO CLEMENTE: HERO AND FRIEND

A. Complete each statement with a word or phrase from the list.

rubber ball	high school	javelin
earthquake	Pittsburgh Pirates	Puerto Rico
childhood	farm team	World Series

1. Roberto Clemente was born in _____ in 1934.

2. Ever since his _____ he dreamed of becoming a baseball

   player.

3. To prepare himself, he squeezed a _____ to strengthen his

   arm muscles.

4. Roberto also ran races and threw a _____.

5. When Al Campanis saw Roberto play, he wanted to sign him for the Dodgers'

   _____.

6. However, Roberto could not sign until he finished _____.

7. In 1955, Roberto signed with the _____.

8. With that team, Roberto won the 1960 and 1971 _____.

9. After an _____ struck Nicaragua in 1972, Roberto decided to

   take some supplies there.

B. In your own words, explain what probably happened to Roberto Clemente's plane.

_____

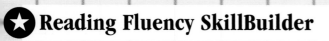
Reading Fluency SkillBuilder

Name_____

Reader directions:

Cut this paper in half. Practice reading the passage aloud until you don't make any mistakes. Then have someone listen to you read. Try to sound as if you're reading a magazine article.

from Roberto Clemente: Hero and Friend

The Clementes could not buy any luxuries—not even a baseball for Roberto. Instead, Roberto and his friends used sticks to practice batting cans. They had no gloves, pads, or even a real bat. They simply loved the game. To Roberto, baseball players were heroes. He dreamed of becoming a great player someday. Roberto was determined to work hard to make his dream come true.

In high school, Roberto joined the baseball team. Roberto was a top runner, but he knew that speed was not enough. Baseball players needed strong arms to throw the ball fast and hit it hard.

✂ **cut along dotted line**

- -

Checker directions:

Follow along as the passage is read. Make a dot under each word the reader misses. Show the reader the missed words. Erase the dots and repeat for each reading.

from Roberto Clemente: Hero and Friend

The Clementes could not buy any luxuries—not even a baseball for Roberto. Instead, Roberto and his friends used sticks to practice batting cans. They had no gloves, pads, or even a real bat. They simply loved the game. To Roberto, baseball players were heroes. He dreamed of becoming a great player someday. Roberto was determined to work hard to make his dream come true.

In high school, Roberto joined the baseball team. Roberto was a top runner, but he knew that speed was not enough. Baseball players needed strong arms to throw the ball fast and hit it hard.

Use this chart for Timed Readings and Repeated Readings.

Reading	1	2	3	4	5
Time (minutes/seconds)					
Words Missed					

Focus Skills and SkillBuilder Copymasters

We Are Family

Unit 3
Mixed Genres

When it comes to families, closeness is what matters. Families can tackle anything.

This unit contains different **genres,** or kinds of literature. You will be reading four types.

- **Novel Excerpt:** A novel is a long work of fiction that takes time to read. An excerpt is a part of a novel.

- **Poem:** a short piece of writing that expresses an idea or feeling

- **Informative Article:** nonfiction that gives readers facts about a certain topic

- **Short Story:** a work of fiction that can be read in one sitting

78

Pacing Guide

SELECTION	TOTAL DAYS	PREREADING	READING	POST READING	
				SELECTIVE OPTIONS	ALL OPTIONS
Trombones and Colleges	2–2.5	1	.5	.5	1
In a Neighborhood in Los Angeles	2	1	.5	.5	1
Mudslinging	2–2.5	1	.5	.5	1
Another April	3–3.5	1	1.5	.5	1

More About Mixed Genres

The selections in this unit present different views of and insights into family interaction. Character portrayals range from young people to older adults, and all the issues ultimately center around the wisdom gained through togetherness. Students will also explore a variety of genres, including a novel excerpt, two poems, an informative article, and a short story.

Technology Resources

Audio CD
All selections in this unit are featured in the Audio Library.

Reading Coach CD-ROM
All of the selections in this unit are part of the Reading Coach. You may use Reading Coach selections as a group activity, as an individual activity, or as a tutorial for students who might benefit from this format or who have missed class.

Building Bridges: Closing the Reading Gap
This video is intended for teacher use only. It gives instructions and tips on how to help middle school readers become strategic readers.

Assessment

Selection Tests
pp. T122, T129, T139, T155

Assessment Booklet
Progress Check Units 1–4
Administer this test after the first four units of the book have been read. It covers skills taught in all four units.

TROMBONES AND COLLEGES

by Walter Dean Myers

Focus Skills

COMPREHENSION
Making Inferences

LITERATURE
Theme

VOCABULARY
Context Clues

SkillBuilder Copymasters

 Reading Comprehension:
1 Making Inferences p. T118

 Literary Analysis:
2 Theme p. T119

 Vocabulary:
3 Context Clues p. T120
4 Words to Know p. T121

Assessment

 5 Selection Test p. T122

Readability Scores

DRP	LEXILE	DALE-CHALL
50	770	5.4

For English Learners

Students may have trouble with the idioms in this selection. Help them understand that the expressions are not necessarily a combination of literal meanings of words. You might let other students explain the meanings of the expressions sometimes.

More About the Novel

Fast Sam, Cool Clyde, and Stuff is a book about friendship. A group of young neighborhood adolescents headed up by Clyde, Sam, and "Stuff" (a.k.a. Francis) decide to form a club dedicated to helping and protecting one another.

They support one another through report-card days, a basketball championship, the threat of drugs and violence, and even death. An ALA Notable Book in 1975, this novel has timeless appeal.

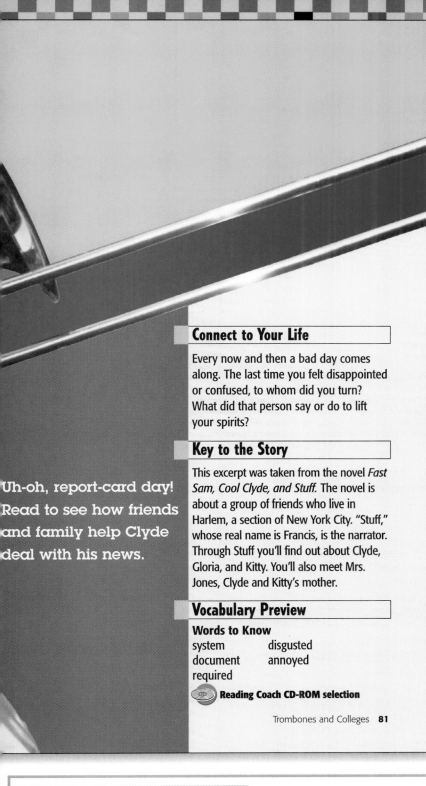

Connect to Your Life

Every now and then a bad day comes along. The last time you felt disappointed or confused, to whom did you turn? What did that person say or do to lift your spirits?

Key to the Story

This excerpt was taken from the novel *Fast Sam, Cool Clyde, and Stuff.* The novel is about a group of friends who live in Harlem, a section of New York City. "Stuff," whose real name is Francis, is the narrator. Through Stuff you'll find out about Clyde, Gloria, and Kitty. You'll also meet Mrs. Jones, Clyde and Kitty's mother.

Vocabulary Preview

Words to Know

system	disgusted
document	annoyed
required	

 Reading Coach CD-ROM selection

Trombones and Colleges **81**

Uh-oh, report-card day! Read to see how friends and family help Clyde deal with his news.

Connect to Your Life

After they read Connect to Your Life, have students reread the teaser on the same page and predict what Clyde's bad day is probably about *(report card)*. Then lead a class discussion about their own recent bad days, and who helped them.

Key to the Story

A story told in the first-person point of view is narrated by one of its main characters. In this novel, that character is nicknamed Stuff. Through Stuff's eyes, students will meet the other characters and will learn what happens on report-card day.

Vocabulary Preview

Words to Know
system *n.* set way of doing things
document *n.* official report
required *adj.* needed
disgusted *adj.* irritated and impatient
annoyed *adj.* bothered

For direct instruction on Words to Know, see page T117.

Building Background

Earlier in the novel, Clyde's father is killed in a work accident, and Clyde decides to honor him by switching from his high school's commercial program to its academic program in order to prepare for college. "Trombones and Colleges" tells what happens when Clyde receives his first report card after switching programs.

Vocabulary Strategy: Preteaching

Context Clues Explain to students that **context clues** are words and phrases near a word that give hints to its meaning. Write these sentences on the board and have students circle words and phrases that help them figure out the meaning of the underlined word.

1. Clyde's (report card) was on the table and we sat around it like it was some kind of (big important) document.
2. She (poured some rice) into a colander (to wash it off.)

 For more on Context Clues, see page T117.

FOCUS

See what situation Clyde faces because of his poor grades.

FOCUS

See what situation Clyde faces because of his poor grades.

It was a dark day when we got our report cards. The sky was full of gray clouds and it was sprinkling rain. I was over to Clyde's house and Gloria and Kitty were there. Sam probably would have been there too, only he had got a two-week job in the afternoons helping out at Freddie's. Actually he only did it so that his mother would let him be on the track team again. Sam and his mother had this little **system**
10 going. He would do something good-doing and she'd let him do something that he wanted to.

> **system**
> (sĭs′ təm)
> *n.* set way of doing things

Clyde's report card was on the kitchen table and we all sat around it like it was some kind of a big important **document**. I had got a pretty good report card and had wanted to show it off but I knew it wasn't the time. Clyde pushed the card toward me and I read it. He had all satisfactory remarks on the side labeled Personal Traits and Behavior. He had also
20 received B's in music and art appreciation. But everything else was either a C or a D except mathematics. His mathematics mark was a big red F that had been circled. I don't know why they had to circle the F when it was the only red mark on the card. In the Teacher's Comments section someone had written that Clyde had "little ability to handle an **academic program**."

> **document**
> (dŏk′ yə mənt)
> *n.* official report

 "A little ability is better than none," I said. No one said anything so I figured it
30 probably wasn't the right time to try to cheer Clyde up.

> **academic program**
> classes in subjects that lead to college

I knew all about his switching from a **commercial program** to an academic program, but I really hadn't thought he'd have any trouble.

> **commercial program**
> classes in subjects that lead directly to a job

"I saw the grade adviser today. He said I should switch back to the commercial program." Clyde looked like he'd start crying any minute. His eyes were red and his voice was shaky.
40 "He said that I had to take mathematics over and if I failed again or failed another **required** subject I couldn't graduate. The way it is now I'm going to have to finish up in the summer because I switched over."

> **required**
> (rĭ kwīrd′)
> *adj.* needed

THINK IT THROUGH

What does Clyde have to do in order to stay in an academic program?

FOCUS

Clyde's mother comes home. Read to find out what Clyde decides.

"I think you can pass it if you really want to," Kitty said. Clyde's sister was so pretty I couldn't even look at her. If I did I started feeling funny and couldn't talk right. Sometimes I daydreamed about marrying her.
50 Just then Clyde's mother came in and he gave a quick look at Kitty.

"Hi, young ladies and young gentlemen." Mrs. Jones was a kind of heavy woman but she was pretty, too. You could tell she was Kitty's mother if you looked close. She put her package down and started

---

COMPREHENSION

FOCUS SKILL: Making Inferences

Explain to students that **inferences** are logical guesses they make about what the author did not say but meant. They "read between the lines" and use their own experience to figure out what is meant.

For direct instruction on Making Inferences, see page T116.

A **Teacher Modeling: Making Inferences** *I can already spot two clues about Clyde's poor grades. At the beginning of the second paragraph, the narrator describes how everyone is sitting around, very aware of the report card on the table. The narrator would like to share his good news about his own grades but decides against it. The information in these sentences leads me to guess, or infer, that Clyde's grades aren't good and that his friends are all very sympathetic.*

B **THINK IT THROUGH** What does Clyde have to do in order to stay in an academic program? *(take mathematics over—and pass it—and finish school in the summer)* **details**

LITERATURE

FOCUS SKILL: Theme

Tell students that a **theme** is a message about life or human nature that an author is trying to convey. Sometimes a theme is stated outright. At other times, however, readers must infer the theme based on things that the characters do and say. Questions throughout the Literature strand will help students discover the main theme of this selection.

For direct instruction on Theme, see page T116.

Use the following questions to encourage literary analysis.

A On the basis of what you've read so far, how would you describe Stuff, the narrator? *(He is sensitive to the other characters' feelings, and he's positive and supportive.)* **characterization**

What details from the text support your opinions? *(He knows it's not the right time to show off his report card, and he says that a little ability is better than none.)* **details**

VOCABULARY

FOCUS SKILL: Context Clues

A **satisfactory** Have students look for **context clues** in the sentences after *satisfactory*. Point out that B's, C's, and D's are mentioned next; they are in contrast with the F Clyde received in mathematics. This is a contrast clue; *satisfactory* is contrasted with an F. *Satisfactory* must mean "all right."

FOR ENGLISH LEARNERS

Help students understand the following:

Line 9: good-doing
Line 16: show it off
Line 36: grade adviser
Line 48: daydreamed

taking things out. "I heard you people talking when I first came in. By the way you hushed up I guess you don't want me to hear what you were talking about. I'll be out of your way in a minute, soon as I put the
60 frozen foods in the refrigerator."

"I got my report card today," Clyde said. His mother stopped taking the food out and turned toward us. Clyde pushed the report card about two inches toward her. She really didn't even have to look at the card to know that it was bad. She could have told that just by looking at Clyde. But she picked it up and looked at it a long time. First she looked at one side and then the other and then back at the first side again.

REREAD
What do you think Clyde's mother will say?

C

70 "What they say around the school?" she asked, still looking at the card.

"They said I should drop the academic course and go back to the other one." I could hardly hear Clyde, he spoke so low.

"Well, what you going to do, young man?" She looked up at Clyde and Clyde looked up at her and there were tears in his eyes and I almost started crying. I can't stand to see my friends cry. "What are you going to do, Mr. Jones?"

B

80 "I'm—I'm going to keep the academic course," Clyde said.

"You think it's going to be any easier this time?" Mrs. Jones asked.

"No."

THINK IT THROUGH
Which program does Clyde choose? Is this the choice you expected him to make? Give reasons for your answer.

D

COMPREHENSION

C **REREAD** What do you think Clyde's mother will say? *(Some might predict that she'll get mad or call him stupid; others might say she'll feel sorry for him.)* **predicting**

Reciprocal Teaching Suggestion: Predicting
Teacher Modeling To show students the Active Reading Strategy of predicting, focus on lines 70–79. You could say: *When Clyde's mom came in, I was wondering how she was going to react to the report card. Since Clyde was already upset, I figured Mrs. Jones would be upset too. Then I read on, and I saw that her action didn't fit my prediction. She was taking a more positive approach. Mrs. Jones doesn't criticize him or make any decisions for him. She asks him what he plans to do.*
Student Modeling Stop at this point. Choose a student to demonstrate how to make a prediction about Clyde's decision. Have him or her make guesses about the charac-

ter's actions and then continue reading to confirm them.

D **THINK IT THROUGH** Which program does Clyde choose? Is this the choice you expected him to make? Give reasons for your answer. *(the academic course; Possible reason: Clyde is upset about having to switch back to a commercial program. He doesn't want to do what "they" told him.)* **details**

LITERATURE

B How does Stuff, the narrator, show his sensitivity here? *(He sees Clyde crying and feels ready to cry himself.)* **characterization**

VOCABULARY

FOR ENGLISH LEARNERS

Help students understand the following:

Line 57: hushed up
Line 73: hardly hear
Line 78: can't stand

FOCUS

Clyde's problem triggers a memory. Read to find out the memory Mrs. Jones shares.

"Things ain't always easy. Lord knows that things ain't always easy." For a minute there was a faraway look in her eyes, but then her face turned into a big smile. "You're just like your father, boy. That man never would give up on anything he really wanted.
90 Did I ever tell you the time he was trying to learn to play the trombone?"

"No." Clyde still had tears in his eyes but he was smiling, too. Suddenly everybody was happy. It was like seeing a rainbow when it was still raining.

REREAD
Why do you think everyone reacts this way?

"Well, we were living over across from St. Nicholas Park in this little rooming house. Your father was working on a job down on Varick Street that made transformers or some such nonsense—anyway, he
100 comes home one day with this long package all wrapped up in brown paper. He walks in and sits it in the corner and doesn't say boo about what's in the bag. So at first I don't say anything either, and then I finally asks him what he's got in the bag, and he says, 'What bag?' Now this thing is about four feet long if it's an inch and he's asking *what* bag." Mrs. Jones wiped the crumbs from Gloria's end of the table with a quick swipe of the dish cloth, leaving a swirling pattern of tiny bubbles. Gloria tore off a paper towel
110 and wiped the area dry.

"Now I look over at him and he's trying to be nonchalant. Sitting there, a grown man, and big as he wants to be and looking for all the world like somebody's misplaced son. So I says, 'The bag in the corner.' And

nonchalant
(nŏn' shə länt')
not seeming to care

86 Unit 3 We Are Family

he says, 'Oh, that's a trombone I'm taking back to the pawn shop tomorrow.' Well, I naturally ask him what he's doing with it in the first place, and he says he got
120 carried away and bought it but he realized that we really didn't have the thirty-five dollars to spend on foolishness and so he'd take it back the next day. And all the time he's sitting there scratching his chin and rubbing his nose and trying to peek over at me to see how I felt about it. I just told him that I guess he knew what was best. Only the next day he forgot to take it back, and the next day he forgot to take it back, and finally I broke down and told him why didn't he keep it. He said he would if I thought he should.

130 "So he unwraps this thing and he was just as happy with it as he could be until he tried to get a tune out of it. He couldn't get a sound out of it at first, but then he started oomping and woomping with the thing as best he could. He worked at it and worked at it and you could see he was getting disgusted. I think he was just about to give it up when the lady who lived under us came upstairs and started complaining about the noise. It kept her Napoleon awake, she said. Napoleon was a dog.
140 Little ugly thing, too. She said your father couldn't play, anyway.

disgusted
(dĭ's gŭs' tĭd)
adj. irritated and impatient

"Well, what did she say that for? That man played that thing day and night. He worked so hard at that thing that his lips were too sore for him to talk right sometime. But he got the hang of it."

"I never remembered Pop playing a trombone," said Clyde.

"Well, your father had a streak in him that made him stick to a thing," she said, pouring some rice into

Trombones and Colleges 87

COMPREHENSION

E **REREAD** Why do you think everyone reacts this way? *(They probably are relieved that Clyde's mother isn't upset with him, and they are anticipating a humorous story about Clyde's father.)* **making inferences**

F Ask: Why does Clyde's father feel guilty about buying the trombone? *(He knows the trombone cost more money than he should have spent, and he didn't really need it.)* **details**

G Ask: What do you think Clyde's father wants his wife to do? *(He wants her to tell him to keep it.)* **making judgments**

LITERATURE

C Why did Clyde's father play his trombone day and night? *(When the lady downstairs told him he couldn't play the trombone, it made him want to try even harder.)* **motive**

VOCABULARY

B **had a streak in him . . . stick to a thing** Help students understand that Clyde's father didn't have some sort of stripe in his body that made him literally stick to things. Instead, these idioms mean that Clyde's father possessed a certain quality or characteristic that made him keep doing a thing and not give up.

FOR ENGLISH LEARNERS

Help students understand the following expressions and idioms:

Line 127: broke down
Line 133: oomping and woomping

150 a colander to wash it off, "but every year his goals got bigger and bigger and he had to put some things down so that he could get to others. That old trombone is still around here some place. Probably in one of them boxes under Kitty's bed. Now, you children, excuse me, young ladies and gentlemen, get on out of here and let me finish supper."

H THINK IT THROUGH
Why do you think Mrs. Jones shares this memory about Clyde's father?

88 Unit 3 We Are Family

FOCUS
Discover how Clyde reacts to what his mom has shared.

We all went into Clyde's living room.

"That was my mom's good-doing speech," Clyde said. "She gets into talking about what a great guy 160 my father was and how I was like him and whatnot."

"You supposed to be like your father," Sam said. "He was the one that raised you, right?"

"She wants me to be like him, and I want to be like him, too, I guess. She wants me to keep on trying with the academic thing."

"What do you want to do," Sam asked, "give it up?"

"No. Not really. I guess I want people like my mother to keep on telling me that I ought to do it, really. Especially when somebody tells me I can't do it."

170 "Boy," Sam said, sticking his thumbs in his belt and leaning back in the big stuffed chair, "you are just like your father."

Then we all went into Clyde's room and just sat around and talked for a while. Mostly about school and stuff like that, and I wanted to tell Clyde that I thought I could help him if he wanted me to. I was really getting good grades in school, but I thought that **C** Clyde might get annoyed if I mentioned it. But then Gloria said that we could study 180 together sometime and that was cool too.

annoyed
(ə noid')
adj. bothered

I THINK IT THROUGH

1. From Clyde's viewpoint, why does his mother share the memory about his father?
2. Mrs. Jones might have reacted differently to Clyde's report card. Why do you think she reacts as she does?
3. How does Clyde feel about his mom's desire that he keep on trying?

Trombones and Colleges **89**

COMPREHENSION

H **THINK IT THROUGH** Why do you think Mrs. Jones shares this memory about Clyde's father? *(She's trying to give Clyde a sense of hope.)* **making inferences**

I **THINK IT THROUGH**

1. From Clyde's viewpoint, why does his mother share the memory about his father? *(He thinks his mother is trying to encourage him to be like his father and not give up on the academic course.)* **theme** LITERATURE

2. Mrs. Jones might have reacted differently to Clyde's report card. Why do you think she reacts as she does? *(Students probably will say that she knows that switching courses has been difficult for Clyde, and she wants to encourage him to keep trying, rather than discourage him so that he quits.)* **making inferences**

3. How does Clyde feel about his mom's desire that he keep on trying? *(He likes it. He wants her to keep encouraging him.)* **details**

Option for Drama: Suggest that interested students act out the trombone scene between Clyde's mother and father on pages 86 and 87.

RETEACHING

If students need more help understanding **Making Inferences,** use pages T650–T652.

LITERATURE

Teacher Modeling: Theme *I'm beginning to see a theme running through this selection. First Kitty tells Clyde that he can pass the academic program if he really wants to. Next, Clyde's mother tells a story about how her husband stuck with things even when they were hard. Then Clyde says that he's going to*

continue the academic course even though it's going to be hard. I guess the main theme, or message, that the author is trying to share in this selection is to never give up on anything you really want to do—even when people tell you that you can't do it.

VOCABULARY

If students need more help understanding context clues, use pages T117 and T120.

C **mentioned** Have students look at the whole paragraph for context clues. Point out that the friends are talking casually. Synonyms for *mentioned* are in the paragraph: *talked, tell,* and *said.*

FOR ENGLISH LEARNERS

Help students understand the following:
Line 160: whatnot

1. COMPREHENSION

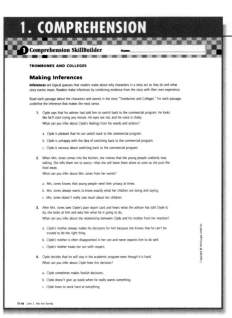

Comprehension SkillBuilder Name _____

TROMBONES AND COLLEGES

Making Inferences

Inferences are logical guesses that readers make about why characters in a story act as they do and what story events mean. Readers make inferences by combining evidence from the story with their own experience.

Read each passage about the characters and events in the story "Trombones and Colleges." For each passage, underline the inference that makes the most sense.

1. Clyde says that his adviser had told him to switch back to the commercial program. He looks like he'll start crying any minute. His eyes are red, and his voice is shaky.
   What can you infer about Clyde's feelings from his words and actions?
   a. Clyde is pleased that he can switch back to the commercial program.
   b. Clyde is unhappy with the idea of switching back to the commercial program.
   c. Clyde is nervous about switching back to the commercial program.

2. When Mrs. Jones comes into the kitchen, she notices that the young people suddenly stop talking. She tells them not to worry—that she will leave them alone as soon as she puts the food away.
   What can you infer about Mrs. Jones from her words?
   a. Mrs. Jones knows that young people need their privacy at times.
   b. Mrs. Jones always wants to know exactly what her children are doing and saying.
   c. Mrs. Jones doesn't really care much about her children.

3. After Mrs. Jones sees Clyde's poor report card and hears what the adviser has told Clyde to do, she looks at him and asks him what he is going to do.
   What can you infer about the relationship between Clyde and his mother from her reaction?
   a. Clyde's mother always makes his decisions for him because she knows that he can't be trusted to do the right thing.
   b. Clyde's mother is often disappointed in her son and never expects him to do well.
   c. Clyde's mother treats her son with respect.

4. Clyde decides that he will stay in the academic program even though it is hard.
   What can you infer about Clyde from this decision?
   a. Clyde sometimes makes foolish decisions.
   b. Clyde doesn't give up easily when he really wants something.
   c. Clyde loves to work hard at everything.

T116 Unit 3 We Are Family

Making Inferences

Direct Instruction Tell students that an **inference** is a logical guess a reader makes, based on evidence in the text. It is like reading between the lines, figuring out what the author means but doesn't state. Point out that minor details can help them make an inference. Have students make an inference using the clues in the following example:

- **Clue:** With a worried look, Clyde silently places his report card on the kitchen table.
  Ask: *What clues tell you how Clyde feels?* (worried look, silently) *In your experience, what would make you feel worried if you had just brought home your report card?* (You might worry about the reaction to a bad report card.)
- **Inference:** The report card shows that Clyde is not doing well in school.

Point out that more than one inference can often be made from story evidence. Explain that good readers try to verify their guesses as they continue to read.

> **Comprehension SkillBuilder Answer Key:**
>
> **1.** *b* **2.** *a* **3.** *c* **4.** *b*

2. LITERATURE

Literary SkillBuilder Name _____

TROMBONES AND COLLEGES

Theme

The **theme** of a story is the lesson about life or human nature that it teaches.

Read this list of themes. For each event from "Trombones and Colleges," choose a theme that the event teaches or reminds you of. Write it in the box. Make up a theme to match the last event.

Themes
If you work hard, you can do almost anything you want to do.
Love and support from your family can make you feel better when times are hard.
Good friends don't hurt each other's feelings.

Story Event	Theme or Lesson Taught
The narrator is careful not to tell Clyde that his own report card was good when he sees how bad Clyde feels.	
Clyde's father always set his goals high and never stopped trying, even when people said he wasn't good enough.	
Clyde feels better when his mother lets him know that she is glad that he will keep trying the academic program.	
Clyde and his friends decide that they will all study together sometimes.	

Trombones and Colleges **T119**

Theme

Direct Instruction Tell students that the **theme** of a piece of writing is the message about life or about human nature that the work reveals. Explain that story writers usually communicate their themes through the events of the stories and through the words and actions of the characters. Point out that even simple stories may have more than one theme.

Suggest that one way of identifying the theme or themes of a story is to ask yourself, What lessons about life did the characters in the story learn? What lessons about life and human behavior did I learn by reading this story?

Emphasize that although many themes may be possible, a theme is valid only when the text supports it. For example, since the story "Trombones and Colleges" centers on temporary setbacks, memories of a father who never quit, and support from family and friends, themes about these topics are logical and acceptable.

> **Literary SkillBuilder Answer Key:**
>
> *Good friends don't hurt each other's feelings; If you work hard, you can do almost anything you want to do; Love and support from your family can make you feel better when times are hard.*
>
> *Possible themes: Everyone needs help sometimes; Doing jobs together makes them easier.*

3. VOCABULARY

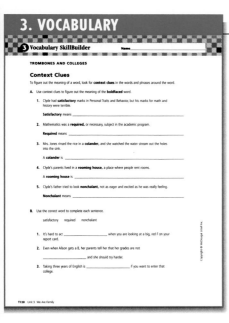

Context Clues

Direct Instruction Explain that **context clues** are words and phrases that surround a word. Tell students to use context clues when trying to figure out the meaning of a new word.

Some context clues give the definition of the unfamiliar word, as in this example:

- The countryside was dotted with <u>hillocks</u>, which are little hills.

Some context clues restate the unfamiliar word in a different way.

- This bus takes you to the <u>commercial</u>, or business, district of the city.

Some context clues give an antonym, or opposite, of the unfamiliar word.

- Clyde's father was <u>disgusted</u>, not pleased, with the way he played the trombone at first.

Sometimes context clues explain the unfamiliar word by giving general clues.

- The cook beat the eggs with a <u>whisk</u> and then let the beaten egg drip off its thin metal wires.

Vocabulary SkillBuilder Answer Key:
Wording of answers will vary. Possible answers:

A.
   1. *all right* **2.** *necessary* **3.** *a bowl or pot with holes for rinsing foods*
   4. *a place where people rent rooms* **5.** *unconcerned, casual*

B.
   1. *nonchalant* **2.** *satisfactory* **3.** *required*

---

4. WORDS TO KNOW

Words to Know

Direct Instruction As you present the **Words to Know,** here are some points you might want to cover.

For the words *required, annoyed,* and *disgusted,* help students to identify the base of each word and note the *-ed* suffix:

   require + -ed = *required*
   annoy + -ed = *annoyed*
   disgust + -ed = *disgusted*

Point out that *disgust* is defined as both a noun and a verb, but that *dis-*

gusted can be an adjective also. In this story, *disgusted* is characterized by impatience, but it can also mean "sickened" or "offended." Both *annoyed* and *disgusted* have similar meanings in this story; they are practically synonyms.

Writing Activity Pair students or have them work in small groups to complete the exercise. Have volunteers read their excuses aloud.

Words to Know SkillBuilder Answer Key:
A.
   1. *system* **2.** *document* **3.** *annoyed* **4.** *disgusted* **5.** *required*
B.
   1. *c* **2.** *e* **3.** *a* **4.** *b* **5.** *d*

---

5. SELECTION TEST

Selection Test Answer Key:
A. 1. *report card* **2.** *mathematics* **3.** *grade adviser* **4.** *mother*
   5. *academic program* **6.** *easy* **7.** *father* **8.** *trombone* **9.** *give up*
B. *Possible answers: He wants to be like his father and stick to it; His mother wants him to stay in it; He wants to stay in it himself.*

TROMBONES AND COLLEGES

Making Inferences

Inferences are logical guesses that readers make about why characters in a story act as they do and what story events mean. Readers make inferences by combining evidence from the story with their own experience.

Read each passage about the characters and events in the story "Trombones and Colleges." For each passage, underline the inference that makes the most sense.

1. Clyde says that his adviser had told him to switch back to the commercial program. He looks like he'll start crying any minute. His eyes are red, and his voice is shaky.
   What can you infer about Clyde's feelings from his words and actions?

   a. Clyde is pleased that he can switch back to the commercial program.

   b. Clyde is unhappy with the idea of switching back to the commercial program.

   c. Clyde is nervous about switching back to the commercial program.

2. When Mrs. Jones comes into the kitchen, she notices that the young people suddenly stop talking. She tells them not to worry—that she will leave them alone as soon as she puts the food away.
   What can you infer about Mrs. Jones from her words?

   a. Mrs. Jones knows that young people need their privacy at times.

   b. Mrs. Jones always wants to know exactly what her children are doing and saying.

   c. Mrs. Jones doesn't really care much about her children.

3. After Mrs. Jones sees Clyde's poor report card and hears what the adviser has told Clyde to do, she looks at him and asks him what he is going to do.
   What can you infer about the relationship between Clyde and his mother from her reaction?

   a. Clyde's mother always makes his decisions for him because she knows that he can't be trusted to do the right thing.

   b. Clyde's mother is often disappointed in her son and never expects him to do well.

   c. Clyde's mother treats her son with respect.

4. Clyde decides that he will stay in the academic program even though it is hard.
   What can you infer about Clyde from this decision?

   a. Clyde sometimes makes foolish decisions.

   b. Clyde doesn't give up easily when he really wants something.

   c. Clyde loves to work hard at everything.

TROMBONES AND COLLEGES

Theme

The **theme** of a story is the lesson about life or human nature that it teaches.

Read this list of themes. For each event from "Trombones and Colleges," choose a theme that the event teaches or reminds you of. Write it in the box. Make up a theme to match the last event.

Themes

If you work hard, you can do almost anything you want to do.

Love and support from your family can make you feel better when times are hard.

Good friends don't hurt each other's feelings.

Story Event	Theme or Lesson Taught
The narrator is careful not to tell Clyde that his own report card was good when he sees how bad Clyde feels.	_____ _____ _____ _____
Clyde's father always set his goals high and never stopped trying, even when people said he wasn't good enough.	_____ _____ _____ _____
Clyde feels better when his mother lets him know that she is glad that he will keep trying the academic program.	_____ _____ _____ _____
Clyde and his friends decide that they will all study together sometimes.	_____ _____ _____ _____

TROMBONES AND COLLEGES

Context Clues

To figure out the meaning of a word, look for **context clues** in the words and phrases around the word.

A. Use context clues to figure out the meaning of the **boldfaced** word.

1. Clyde had **satisfactory** marks in Personal Traits and Behavior, but his marks for math and history were terrible.

   Satisfactory means _____

2. Mathematics was a **required,** or necessary, subject in the academic program.

   Required means _____

3. Mrs. Jones rinsed the rice in a **colander,** and she watched the water stream out the holes into the sink.

   A **colander** is _____

4. Clyde's parents lived in a **rooming house,** a place where people rent rooms.

   A **rooming house** is _____

5. Clyde's father tried to look **nonchalant,** not as eager and excited as he was really feeling.

   Nonchalant means _____

B. Use the correct word to complete each sentence.

   satisfactory   required   nonchalant

1. It's hard to act _____ when you are looking at a big, red F on your report card.

2. Even when Alison gets a B, her parents tell her that her grades are not

   _____ and she should try harder.

3. Taking three years of English is _____ if you want to enter that college.

TROMBONES AND COLLEGES

Words to Know

system   required   annoyed   document   disgusted

A. Fill in each blank with one of the **Words to Know.**

1. Sam and his mother had a _____ for doing laundry.

2. Clyde's report card looked like a very important _____.

3. Clyde became _____ when his sister continued to bother him.

4. When Clyde's father couldn't play the trombone, he became irritated and impatient, or

_____.

5. Some classes are _____, or needed, to graduate.

B. Match each word with a definition. Write the letter of the correct definition on the blank.

_____ **1.** system   a. needed

_____ **2.** document   b. irritated and impatient

_____ **3.** required   c. set way of doing things

_____ **4.** disgusted   d. bothered

_____ **5.** annoyed   e. official report

Writing Activity

Suppose your friend received a bad report card. Write three sentences to make excuses for him or her. Use at least two of the **Words to Know.**

TROMBONES AND COLLEGES

A. Fill in each blank with a word or a phrase. Choose from the list below.

trombone	easy	mathematics
grade adviser	give up	report card
father	mother	academic program

1. In "Trombones and Colleges," Clyde has just gotten his _____ and is very upset.

2. He has received an F in _____.

3. Clyde's _____ has told him that he should switch back to the commercial program.

4. After Clyde's _____ reads his report card, she asks him what he wants to do.

5. Clyde tells her that he wants to stay in the _____.

6. Clyde's mother tells him that things aren't always _____.

7. She also tells Clyde that he is just like his _____.

8. Then she tells him and his friends a story about Mr. Jones and his

    _____.

9. Through her story, she is trying to tell Clyde not to _____.

B. In your own words, write two reasons why Clyde decides to stay in the academic program.

_____

_____

Focus Skill

LITERATURE
Speaker

SkillBuilder Copymaster

 Literary Analysis:
1 Speaker p. T128

Assessment

 2 Selection Test p. T129

In a Neighborhood in Los Angeles

by Francisco X. Alarcón

What puts the grand in grandmother? This poem has some answers.

Connect to Your Life

You may have grandparents in your life. Or you may only know of grandparents through old photographs or your parents' stories. Recall what you know.

90 Unit 3 We Are Family

Key to the Poem

Reading Coach CD-ROM selectio

In a poem, the **speaker** is the voice that talks to the reader. The speaker may even use the word I to express a thought or a feeling. In this poem, the speaker is probably the poet himself talking abou his own grandmother. In many other poems, the speaker and the poet may not be the same. A po sometimes speaks through a character.

Connect to Your Life

Guide students in a discussion of their favorite memories about a grandparent. Be sure they discuss why they chose a particular memory and why their grandparent is or was so special.

Key to the Poem

Be sure students understand that even though a poem may contain the words *I, me,* and *my,* the speaker of the poem is not necessarily the person who wrote the poem. Can students think of some reasons why a poet might choose someone else to tell the message in a poem?

Presenting the Poem

Read the poem aloud to the students one or two times. Ask students to listen for the meaning: What point is the poet trying to make? Suggest that students read the poem aloud to each other and then tell each other what they think the point is.

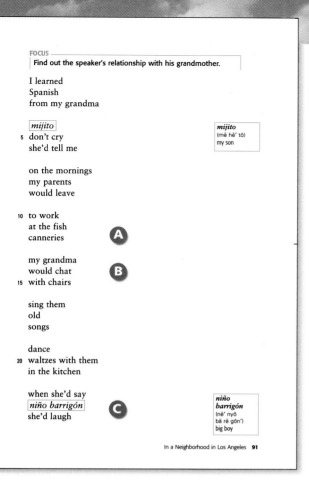

Find out the speaker's relationship with his grandmother.

I learned
Spanish
from my grandma

mijito
5 don't cry
she'd tell me

on the mornings
my parents
would leave

10 to work
at the fish
canneries **A**

my grandma
would chat **B**
15 with chairs

sing them
old
songs

dance
20 waltzes with them
in the kitchen

when she'd say
niño barrigón **C**
she'd laugh

mijito
(mē hē′ tō)
my son

niño
barrigón
(nē′ nyō
bä rē gōn′)
big boy

In a Neighborhood in Los Angeles **91**

For English Learners

In some cultures it is common for a grandparent or older relative to babysit for the children while their parents go off to work. In other cultures the children are cared for by a paid babysitter, or they are placed in daycare while their parents are working. Invite students to discuss the perceived benefits and drawbacks of each situation.

LITERATURE

FOCUS SKILL: Speaker

Remind students that the **speaker** of a poem may or may not be the person who wrote the poem, even when the poem uses *I* and *me*. This lesson will help students understand the speaker in this poem and his relationship with his grandmother.

 For direct instruction on Speaker, see page T127.

Use these questions to encourage literary analysis.

A What do you know about the speaker? *(has a Hispanic grandmother; as a boy, lived in Los Angeles.)* What clues tell you these things? *(Spanish words and translation, title, the fact that he needs to be watched while his parents work)* **speaker**

B Explain to students that **alliteration** is the repeating of sounds at the beginnings of words, such as **C**athy's **c**luttered **k**itchen. Have them find alliteration in lines 14–15 *(chat with chairs)* and 16–18 *(sing songs)*. Suggest that the alliteration helps give a light or happy feeling to this poem. Its effect in other poems might be different. **alliteration**

C What do lines 19–24 tell you about the grandmother's personality? *(She's cheerful, happy, and creative and likes to have fun.)* **characterization**

VOCABULARY

FOR ENGLISH LEARNERS

Help students understand the following terms:

Line 11: fish canneries
Line 14: chat

25 with my grandma
I learned
to count clouds **D**

to point out
in flowerpots
30 mint leaves

my grandma
wore moons
on her dress

Mexico's mountains **E**
35 deserts
ocean

in her eyes
I'd see them
in her braids

40 I'd touch them
in her voice **F**
smell them

one day
I was told: **G**
45 she went far away

but still
I feel her
with me

whispering
50 in my ear
mijito

H **THINK IT THROUGH**

1. How does the speaker feel about his grandmother?
   Find lines in the poem to support your answer.
2. What details from the poem show the
   grandmother's special qualities?
3. In what way do you think the speaker's
   grandmother remains with him?

LITERATURE

D **count clouds, Mexico's mountains** (lines 27 and 34) Help students reread these phrases and emphasize the beginning sounds in each one. Remind them that this repetition of beginning sounds is called **alliteration.**

E In lines 34–42, how did the speaker use his senses through his grandmother to appreciate Mexico's mountains, deserts, and ocean? *(seeing: in her eyes; touch: in her braids; smell: in her voice)* What seems odd about the last image? *(Smell from voice is an unusual combination.)* **sensory imagery**

F **Teacher Modeling: Form** *Hmm, the poet has done something interesting here. I actually had to read these lines a few times over before I could figure out what they meant. At first I read the lines just as they are grouped, and they just weren't making any sense. But when I read them again, I grouped them like this, and then they made perfect sense: "in her eyes / I'd see them," "in her braids / I'd touch them," "in her voice / I smell them." When I read the lines that way, they gave me a beautiful picture of the speaker's impression of his grandmother.*

G What has happened to her? *(She has died.)* **making inferences**
COMPREHENSION

H **THINK IT THROUGH**

1. How does the speaker feel about his grandmother? Find lines in the poem to support your answer. *(He loves and misses her. He has good memories of her. She loved life and taught him many things. Lines might include 19–30, 37–42, 49–51.)* **speaker**

2. What details from the poem show the grandmother's special qualities? *(Possible answers: Her singing and dancing with chairs show that she loved life. She taught the speaker to count clouds and appreciate the outdoor world.)* **characterization**

3. In what way do you think the speaker's grandmother remains with him? *(in his memory and when he looks at the world)* **drawing conclusions**
COMPREHENSION

1. LITERATURE

Speaker

Direct Instruction Tell students that the **speaker** in a poem or a story is the character speaking to the reader. Explain that sometimes the speaker is the writer himself or herself. At other times, the speaker is another person, an animal, or even an object. Tell students that the identity of the speaker may not always be obvious immediately. Explain that readers must pay attention to clues the writer leaves to understand who is speaking.

Tell students that because writers can speak with a variety of voices, they are free to be anyone or anything in their work. They are not restricted to their own lives for subject matter.

Discuss the identity of the speaker of "In a Neighborhood in Los Angeles." Ask students which clues helped them understand that the speaker is someone, probably an adult, remembering his grandmother. Point out that the speaker uses words that an adult might use, but he is recalling details that would be important to a child.

Literary SkillBuilder Answer Key:

A.
   1. *a grandparent*
   2. *a turtle*
   3. *a park bench*
   4. *a child in bed*

B. *Answers will vary.*

---

2. SELECTION TEST

Selection Test Answer Key:
A. 1. *b* **2.** *a* **3.** *c* **4.** *b*
B. *He felt as if she were still with him.*

IN A NEIGHBORHOOD IN LOS ANGELES

Speaker

The **speaker** in a poem or a story is the voice who is speaking to the reader. The writer uses that character's voice.

A. Read each passage. Identify the character who is speaking.

1. I remember the day Anna was born like it was yesterday. I went to the hospital with a toy for the baby. My daughter lay in bed looking happy and proud. My son-in-law took me to the nursery to see Anna. I loved her from the moment I saw her.

   The speaker is _____.

2. I have a great life. Every day, I sit on a rock in the pond and warm myself in the sun. When I get hungry, I slide into the water and look for a snack. Whenever I feel afraid, I pull my head, arms, and legs into my shell.

   The speaker is _____.

3. It's a sunny day, so I know people will visit me. I'll just sit here and wait in the park by the footpath. Mothers will sit on me while they watch their children play. Bird lovers will rest on me while they feed the birds. I'm starting to look a little rundown. I wonder if I will get painted today.

   The speaker is _____.

4. I'm afraid when Mommy turns the lights off. I hope there are no monsters under my bed. What is that sound? Is it coming from my closet? I'm glad that Mommy came back and turned that little light on.

   The speaker is _____.

B. Try to remember what it was like to be a young child in your home on a holiday. Write two or three sentences in which the speaker is you when you were about seven years old. Be sure to use the word *I* in your sentences.

_____

_____

_____

IN A NEIGHBORHOOD IN LOS ANGELES

A. Fill in the circle beside the letter of the correct answer.

1. Who babysat for the speaker?
- ○ a. his mother
- ○ b. his grandmother
- ○ c. a child-care center

2. What words best describe the grandmother's personality?
- ○ a. joyful, fun-loving
- ○ b. proper, formal
- ○ c. sad, depressed

3. What did his grandmother teach the boy to do?
- ○ a. ride a bike
- ○ b. fix her hair
- ○ c. love nature

4. What happened to the grandmother?
- ○ a. She moved back to Mexico.
- ○ b. She died.
- ○ c. She went to work in the fish canneries.

B. In your own words, tell how the speaker felt about his grandmother after she was gone.

_____

_____

Focus Skills

COMPREHENSION
Summarizing
Author's Purpose

LITERATURE
Informative Nonfiction

VOCABULARY
Synonyms

SkillBuilder Copymasters

 Reading Comprehension:
1 Summarizing p. T135
2 Author's Purpose p. T136

 Vocabulary:
3 Synonyms p. T137
4 Words to Know p. T138

Assessment

 5 Selection Test p. T139

Readability Scores

DRP	LEXILE	DALE-CHALL
52	610	5.2

Mudslinging

by Jennifer Owings Dewey

Some families stick together like glue. Others use mud. This information about one Native American group will give you a new view of marriage.

Connect to Your Life

When you think of the word *wedding,* what pictures come to your mind? Jot down a description or make a quick sketch.

Key to the Article

A **ritual** is an action or a ceremony. People perform a ritual to celebrate or to recognize a special event. This informative article tells about mudslinging, a ritual of the Hopi people.

Vocabulary Preview

Words to Know
custom   hilarity
sacred   disputes
wistful

 Reading Coach CD-ROM selec

94 Unit 3 We Are Family

Connect to Your Life

Students can work individually on their description or sketch, or they can form small groups and brainstorm a description. If students work in groups, have one person in each group volunteer to be the recorder or the sketch artist.

Key to the Article

Have students read the title and the first paragraph on page 95 to find out what Mudslinging is. Can students find a word in this paragraph that means the same thing as *ritual? (custom)*

Vocabulary Preview

Words to Know
custom *n.* something done regularly by a group
sacred *adj.* holy
wistful *adj.* dreamy
hilarity *n.* fun and laughter
disputes *n.* arguments

 For direct instruction on Words to Know, see page T134.

FOCUS

Read to discover what happens during the first part of the Mudslinging ritual.

"Here is something hard to believe," a Hopi friend named Dan once told me. "Adult people throwing mud at each other for a reason. It's a Hopi custom we call Mudslinging."

 custom
(kŭs' təm)
n. something done regularly by a group

"Tell me," I urged. I'd never heard of Mudslinging. It sounded like fun to have a reason to throw mud at somebody.

"Marriage is a solemn passage among the Hopi," Dan said. "In our villages the wedding

solemn passage
serious event

10 ceremonies go on for a week. The day before the wedding, the groom's father visits the bride's house. He knocks on the door and insists on being let in. With him are other members of the groom's family: aunts and uncles, sisters and brothers.

"Those inside the house open the door just a crack and say, 'Who are you? What do you want?' They act like they don't know him. 'War is declared!' the groom's father announces loudly. He pushes the door open, and then the craziness begins."

20 Dan pauses before going on with his story. He grins, his dark eyes shiny with humor.

"The groom and his family have secretly prepared buckets of mud, which they have brought with them. The mud is four different colors, one for each of the four directions: north, south, east, and west. It is sacred mud. These people rush into the bride's house and grab everyone, including the bride, and drag them out into the yard. The groom's family dig into the buckets of

sacred
(sā' krĭd)
adj. holy

30 mud and begin throwing it, smearing it on every person they can catch. The bride's family dip into the

Mudslinging **95**

COMPREHENSION

FOCUS SKILL 1: Summarizing

Tell students that to **summarize** a piece of writing is to restate, in your own words, the main ideas and important details of the piece. Use the suggestions that follow to help students summarize "Mudslinging."

 For direct instruction on Summarizing, see page T133.

FOCUS SKILL 2: Author's Purpose

Tell students that authors write for several different purposes or reasons. They write to entertain, to inform, to express opinions or feelings, and to persuade. Point out that a written work usually has only one important purpose behind it. However, there may be more than one purpose involved.

For direct instruction on Author's Purpose, see page T133.

A Ask: How long does a Hopi wedding ceremony last? *(a week)* **details**

B Teacher Modeling: Summarizing *If I wanted to briefly describe the events leading up to the actual mud throwing, I might summarize them like this: On the day before the wedding, the groom's father and other family members go to the bride's house and knock on the door. The bride's family act as though they don't know their visitors and ask who they are and what they want. The groom's father then pushes the door open and yells, "War is declared!" He and his family drag the bride's family outside, and the mud throwing begins.*

Tell students that a **synonym** is a word that means the same, or nearly the same, as another word. Writers use synonyms to avoid repetition. Read aloud these examples: *answer, respond; call, shout; go, leave.* Then write the boldfaced words on the board. Elicit from volunteers one synonym for each word.

plan *(arrange)*   **add** *(increase)*

For direct instruction on Synonyms, see page T134.

Building Background

Mudslinging is not the only sacred ceremony that the Hopi perform. They also have a ritual called the snake dance, which they perform for nine days every August. The snake dance is one of the ceremonies that the Hopi perform to ask for peace, rain, health, and good harvests.

VOCABULARY

FOCUS SKILL: Synonyms

Synonyms Tell students that when they are reading and come to a word they don't know, they can look in the surrounding context to see if they can find a synonym of the unknown word.

A Mudslinging Help students skim this page and the next page to find the two phrases that are synonyms of *Mudslinging: throwing mud* (line 2) and *flinging mud* (line 34).

FOR ENGLISH LEARNERS

Help students understand the following expressions and idioms:

Line 10: go on
Line 15: just a crack
Line 21: eyes shiny with humor

mud, too. Before long the yard is swarming with people of all ages, from babies to old grandmothers and grandfathers, flinging mud at each other as if they've lost their minds.

"While this goes on, some of the mud throwers yell insults back and forth at each other. It is the aunties of the groom who do this. They say how ugly the bride is, what a terrible cook her mother is, things
40 like that."

C THINK IT THROUGH
What happens to the bride's side of the family?

FOCUS
The description of Mudslinging continues. Find out what Dan sees as a possible reason for Mudslinging.

I laughed to hear this. "What happens next?" I asked. Dan was eager to continue his description of the Mudslinging.

"If the bride's people are able to catch the groom's father, they hold him down and give him a haircut. This makes him feel foolish. It's an insult." Dan's grin widened. "The Mudslinging ends peacefully. Once the buckets are emptied and everyone is coated with mud, the participants shake hands and make
50 peace. Food is shared, a feast of corn and mutton, a lot of food."

REREAD
Retell what happens here. **D**

"And the wedding takes place the next day?" I asked.

"Yes," Dan said, a wistful expression appearing on his handsome face. "This is how it was for me when I got married.

wistful
(wĭst′ fəl)
adj. dreamy

96 Unit 3 We Are Family

There was much hilarity, and sacred rituals, too, and then I became a husband, no longer a single man."

hilarity
(hĭ lăr′ ĭ tē)
n. fun and laughter

60   "Why do they do the Mudslinging? Was it fun when it happened to you? Or was it horrible?"

"It was a lot of fun. Maybe the reason for it is to get troubles over with in a happy way before the marriage, the mother-in-law problems, the father-in-law problems."

I nodded. It made sense.

B "When two families come together and become joined, there are always disputes. It's expected. Mudslinging gets everyone's energy
70 for arguing out of the way, at least for a while," Dan added. A thoughtful smile came to his face when he was finished with his storytelling.

disputes
(dĭ spyōōts′)
n. arguments

E

F THINK IT THROUGH
1. What does Dan think is the reason for Mudslinging?
2. How does Dan feel about Mudslinging? How do you know?
3. If you could, would you participate in a Mudslinging? Why or why not?

COMPREHENSION

C **THINK IT THROUGH** What happens to the bride's side of the family? *(They are visited by the groom's family, and a Mudslinging takes place. During the Mudslinging the families throw four colors of sacred mud at each other, and the groom's aunts insult the bride's family.)* **summarizing**

D **REREAD** Retell what happens here. *(If the bride's family can catch the groom's father, they insult him by cutting his hair. When all the mud is gone, everyone makes peace and sits down to a feast.)* **summarizing**

E Ask: What do you think the author's purpose or purposes were for writing this article? *(to inform and entertain)* **author's purpose**

F **THINK IT THROUGH**

1. What does Dan think is the reason for Mudslinging? *(It avoids problems before the marriage occurs.)* **details**

2. How does Dan feel about Mudslinging? How do you know? *(He says that the Mudslinging before his wedding was a lot of fun, and he smiles a lot while he explains the event.)* **making inferences**

3. If you could, would you participate in a Mudslinging? Why or why not? *(Have students support their answers with at least three reasons.)* **drawing conclusions**

VOCABULARY

B **Teacher Modeling: Synonyms**
When I first read the word disputes, I wasn't sure what it meant. So I kept reading. When I read "Mudslinging gets everyone's energy for arguing out of the way," I figured that the word arguments must be a synonym of disputes.

FOR ENGLISH LEARNERS

Help students understand the following expressions and idioms:

Line 32: swarming
Line 34: as if they've lost their minds
Line 49: make peace
Line 59: a single man

1. COMPREHENSION

Comprehension SkillBuilder   Name_____

MUDSLINGING

Summarizing

In a **summary**, you write the important ideas from a text in a shortened form and in your own words.

Read each passage from "Mudslinging." Then circle the letter of the better summary.

1. The day before the wedding, the groom's father visits the bride's house. He knocks on the door and insists on being let in. With him are other members of the groom's family: aunts and uncles, sisters and brothers.
   Those inside the house open the door just a crack and say, "Who are you? What do you want?" They act like they don't know him. "War is declared!" the groom's father announces loudly. He pushes the door open, and then the craziness begins.

   a. The groom's father, along with the rest of the groom's family—aunts, uncles, sisters, and brothers—visit the bride's house, and the craziness begins.

   b. When the groom's father visits the bride's house, he demands to be let in. The bride's family act like they don't know him, and the war begins.

2. The groom and his family have secretly prepared buckets of mud, which they have brought with them. The mud is four different colors, one for each of the four directions: north, south, east, and west. It is sacred mud. These people rush into the bride's house and grab everyone, including the bride, and drag them out into the yard. The groom's family dig into the buckets of mud and begin throwing it, smearing it on every person they can catch. The bride's family dip into the mud, too. Before long the yard is swarming with people of all ages, from babies to old grandmothers and grandfathers, flinging mud at each other as if they've lost their minds.

   a. The groom and his family bring buckets of mud. After they pull everyone from the bride's house outside, they begin to throw mud at the bride and their family. The bride's family starts throwing mud from the buckets at the groom's family. Soon everyone is throwing mud.

   b. The groom's family brings pails of mud. The mud is sacred. It is four different colors for the four directions: the north, the south, the east, and the west.

3. The Mudslinging ends peacefully. Once the buckets are emptied and everyone is coated with mud, the participants shake hands and make peace. Food is shared, a feast of corn and mutton, a lot of food.

   a. The Mudslinging ends peacefully. The participants shake hands and make peace.

   b. After the Mudslinging ends, everyone makes peace and shares a feast.

Mudslinging   T135

Summarizing

Direct Instruction Tell students that a **summary** includes all the important ideas from a passage, but in a shortened form. Emphasize that when students write summaries, they should use their own words, not just repeat the words from the text being summarized.

Read aloud this passage from "Mudslinging." Then read aloud the summary. Point out that the summary includes only the major ideas of the passage and ignores minor details.

"While this [the Mudslinging] goes on, some of the mud throwers yell insults back and forth at each other. It is the aunties of the groom who do this. They say how ugly the bride is, what a terrible cook her mother is, things like that."
Summary: The mud throwers trade insults. The groom's aunts insult the bride and her family.

Comprehension SkillBuilder Answer Key:

1. *b*

2. *a*

3. *b*

2. COMPREHENSION

Comprehension SkillBuilder   Name_____

MUDSLINGING

Author's Purpose

The reason why an author writes is called the **author's purpose**.

Read each passage below. Then fill in the chart with the author's purpose. Choose from these purposes:

to teach or inform
to entertain
to persuade the reader to think or act in a certain way
to share thoughts and feelings

Passage	Author's Purpose
1. Be sure to come to our beautiful city on your next trip. While you are here, you can see works of art in our museums. You can see a play or visit the world-famous zoo. If you want to know more about the fun you can have here, look at our Web site today. Don't wait. Act now!	
2. Riddle: What do you give an alligator that demands dinner? Answer: Anything it wants	
3. The Mudslinging ends peacefully. Once the buckets are emptied and everyone is coated with mud, the participants shake hands and make peace. Food is shared, a feast of corn and mutton, a lot of food.	
4. I love the country after a snowstorm. To me, the tree branches covered with snow look like something from a fairy tale. The sunlight on the new snow almost blinds me with its clean whiteness. If I ever moved away from my snowy home, I'd make sure that, at least once every winter, I could visit it just after a big snowfall.	

T136   Unit 3 We Are Family

Author's Purpose

Direct Instruction Tell students that the author's purpose is the reason why an author writes. **Authors' purposes** include the following:

- to entertain readers
- to teach or inform readers about a topic or event
- to share thoughts or feelings
- to persuade readers to think, feel, or act in a certain way

Point out that there may be more than one purpose for a single work. Read these passages from "Mudslinging" and discuss the author's purpose for each:

"Marriage is a solemn passage among the Hopi," Dan said. "In our villages the wedding ceremonies go on for a week. The day before the wedding, the groom's father visits the bride's house." *(Purpose: to inform or teach)*

"It was a lot of fun. Maybe the reason for it is to get troubles over with in a happy way before the marriage, the mother-in-law problems, the father-in-law problems." *(Purpose: to share thoughts and feelings)*

Comprehension SkillBuilder Answer Key:

1. *to persuade the reader to think or act in a certain way*

2. *to entertain*

3. *to teach or inform*

4. *to share thoughts and feelings*

Direct Instruction
for SkillBuilder Copymasters

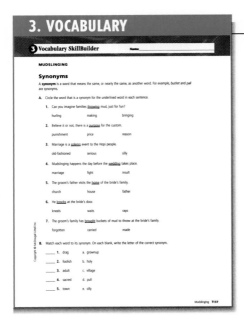

Synonyms

Direct Instruction Tell students that a **synonym** is a word that means the same, or nearly the same, as another word. Read aloud these pairs of synonyms as examples: *say, tell; brave, courageous;* and *chef, cook.* Explain that writers usually try to avoid using the same word over and over. Instead they may substitute a synonym. Point out that even though the synonym might not have exactly the same meaning as the first word, the meanings are very close.

You may wish to show students a thesaurus and go through the process of looking up a word such as *party* and finding its list of synonyms.

Read these sentences aloud and ask students to suggest synonyms for each underlined word.

He pushes the door open and then everyone starts acting <u>crazy</u>. *(silly, wild, foolish)*

These people <u>rush</u> into the bride's house. *(hurry, run, speed, race)*

Vocabulary SkillBuilder Answer Key:

A.

1. *hurling*	**3.** *serious*	**5.** *house*	**7.** *carried*
2. *reason*	**4.** *marriage*	**6.** *raps*	

B. 1. *d* **2.** *e* **3.** *a* **4.** *b* **5.** *c*

Words to Know

Direct Instruction As you present the **Words to Know,** here are some points you might want to cover. Help students to identify the parts of the vocabulary words. Stress the importance of finding the base of each word. Help students remove prefixes and suffixes first.

- **custom** is also an adjective meaning "made to order"
- **sacred** can also be defined as "devoted specifically to a single use, purpose, or person"
- **wist** + -ful = *wistful*
- **dispute** can be either a noun or a verb

- **hilarity** is from the Latin *hilaritās*

Writing Activity Help students to understand how acrostics work. Here is a sample acrostic:

Marriage will unite us
Until we met we were lonely
Do you remember our first date?

Pair students or have them work in small groups to complete the exercise. Have volunteers read their creations aloud.

Words to Know Skillbuilder Answer Key:

A.

1. *custom* **2.** *wistful* **3.** *disputes* **4.** *hilarity* **5.** *sacred*

B.

1. *false* **2.** *true* **3.** *true* **4.** *false* **5.** *true*

Selection Test Answer Key:
A. 1. *true* **2.** *true* **3.** *false* **4.** *true*
B. Possible answer: *is on his or her mind about the bride's or groom's side of the family.*

MUDSLINGING

Summarizing

In a **summary,** you write the important ideas from a text in a shortened form and in your own words.

Read each passage from "Mudslinging." Then circle the letter of the better summary.

1. The day before the wedding, the groom's father visits the bride's house. He knocks on the door and insists on being let in. With him are other members of the groom's family: aunts and uncles, sisters and brothers.

    Those inside the house open the door just a crack and say, "Who are you? What do you want?" They act like they don't know him. "War is declared!" the groom's father announces loudly. He pushes the door open, and then the craziness begins.

    a. The groom's father, along with the rest of the groom's family—aunts, uncles, sisters, and brothers—visits the bride's house, and the craziness begins.

    b. The groom's father visits the bride's house and demands to be let in. The bride's family pretend they don't know him, and the war begins.

2. The groom and his family have secretly prepared buckets of mud, which they have brought with them. The mud is four different colors, one for each of the four directions: north, south, east, and west. It is sacred mud. These people rush into the bride's house and grab everyone, including the bride, and drag them out into the yard. The groom's family dig into the buckets of mud and begin throwing it, smearing it on every person they can catch. The bride's family dip into the mud, too. Before long the yard is swarming with people of all ages, from babies to old grandmothers and grandfathers, flinging mud at each other as if they've lost their minds.

    a. The groom and his family bring buckets of mud. After they pull everyone from the bride's house outside, they begin to throw mud at the bride and her family. The bride's family starts throwing mud from the buckets at the groom's family. Soon everyone is throwing mud.

    b. The groom's family brings pails of mud. The mud is sacred. It is four different colors for the four directions: the north, the south, the east, and the west.

3. The Mudslinging ends peacefully. Once the buckets are emptied and everyone is coated with mud, the participants shake hands and make peace. Food is shared, a feast of corn and mutton, a lot of food.

    a. The Mudslinging ends peacefully. The participants shake hands and make peace.

    b. After the Mudslinging ends, everyone makes peace and shares a feast.

MUDSLINGING

Author's Purpose

The reason why an author writes is called the **author's purpose.**

Read each passage below. Then fill in the chart with the author's purpose. Choose from these purposes:

- to teach or inform
- to entertain
- to persuade the reader to think or act in a certain way
- to share thoughts and feelings

Passage	Author's Purpose
1. Be sure to come to our beautiful city on your next trip. While you are here, you can see works of art in our museums. You can see a play or visit the world-famous zoo. If you want to know more about the fun you can have here, look at our Web site today. Don't wait. Act now!	_____ _____ _____
2. Riddle: What do you give an alligator that demands dinner? Answer: Anything it wants	_____ _____ _____
3. The Mudslinging ends peacefully. Once the buckets are emptied and everyone is coated with mud, the participants shake hands and make peace. Food is shared, a feast of corn and mutton, a lot of food.	_____ _____ _____
4. I love the country after a snowstorm. To me, the tree branches covered with snow look like something from a fairy tale. The sunlight on the new snow almost blinds me with its clean whiteness. If I ever moved away from my snowy home, I'd make sure that, at least once every winter, I could visit it just after a big snowfall.	_____ _____ _____

Name_____

MUDSLINGING

Synonyms

A **synonym** is a word that means the same, or nearly the same, as another word. For example, *bucket* and *pail* are synonyms.

A. Circle the word that is a synonym for the underlined word in each sentence.

1. Can you imagine families <u>throwing</u> mud, just for fun?

   hurling   making   bringing

2. Believe it or not, there is a <u>purpose</u> for the custom.

   punishment   price   reason

3. Marriage is a <u>solemn</u> event to the Hopi people.

   old-fashioned   serious   silly

4. Mudslinging happens the day before the <u>wedding</u> takes place.

   marriage   fight   insult

5. The groom's father visits the <u>home</u> of the bride's family.

   church   house   father

6. He <u>knocks</u> at the bride's door.

   kneels   waits   raps

7. The groom's family has <u>brought</u> buckets of mud to throw at the bride's family.

   forgotten   carried   made

B. Match each word to its synonym. On each blank, write the letter of the correct synonym.

_____ **1.** drag   a. grownup

_____ **2.** foolish   b. holy

_____ **3.** adult   c. village

_____ **4.** sacred   d. pull

_____ **5.** town   e. silly

MUDSLINGING

Words to Know

custom   sacred   wistful   disputes   hilarity

A. Fill in each blank with the word from the list that best completes the sentence.

1. Mudslinging is a Hopi _____ that is done when people get married.

2. Dan's face became _____ as he remembered his wedding day.

3. Sometimes family members have arguments, or _____.

4. Mudslinging is a time of much fun and _____.

5. The Hopi use four kinds of _____ mud for the Mudslinging.

B. Write **true** or **false** in each blank.

_____ 1. A **custom** is a bucket filled with mud.

_____ 2. Something that is **sacred** is the same as something that is holy.

_____ 3. A **wistful** expression is dreamy.

_____ 4. **Hilarity** means names people call each other.

_____ 5. Saying mean things to someone can cause **disputes.**

Writing Activity

An **acrostic** is a poem or series of lines in which the beginning letters form a message or name. Look at the word "mud" as shown below. Next to each letter, use the **Words to Know** to write a sentence about the Hopi marriage ritual.

M _____

U _____

D _____

MUDSLINGING

A. Write **true** or **false** next to each statement.

_____ **1.** Mudslinging is a favorite ceremony performed by the Hopi people.

_____ **2.** In Hopi villages, wedding ceremonies go on for a week.

_____ **3.** To begin a Mudslinging, the groom's father yells, "Let the games begin!"

_____ **4.** The mud used in a Mudslinging is four different colors.

B. Fill in the blank to complete the second sentence.

Mudslinging helps to use up everyone's energy for arguing. Everyone can say whatever

_____

_____

Focus Skills

COMPREHENSION
Details

LITERATURE
Setting

VOCABULARY
Compound Words

SkillBuilder Copymasters

 Reading Comprehension:
1 Details p. T151

 Literary Analysis:
2 Setting p. T152

 Vocabulary:
3 Compound Words p. T153
4 Words to Know p. T154

Assessment

 5 Selection Test p. T155

Readability Scores

DRP	LEXILE	DALE-CHALL
50	760	4.2

For English Learners

Different cultures have different views about older adults and how they should be treated. Invite students to discuss what they know about their family's or culture's feelings toward and treatment of older adults.

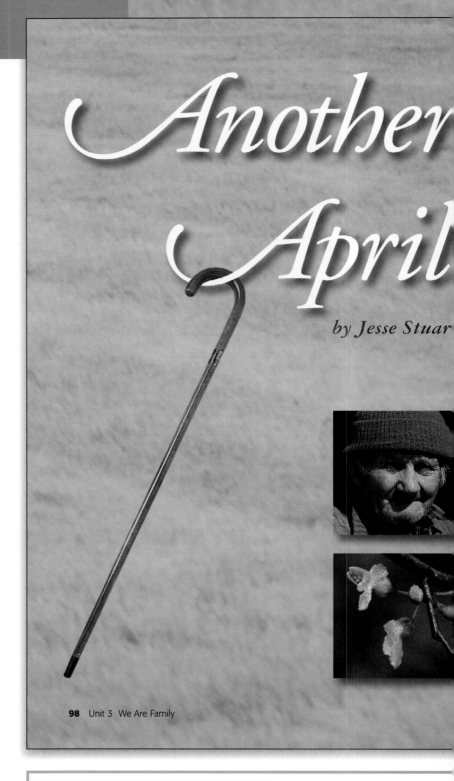

Another April

by Jesse Stuart

98 Unit 3 We Are Family

Vocabulary Strategy: Preteaching

Tell students that a **compound word** is a word made up of two smaller words put together. As students read "Another April," remind them that they can figure out what the compound words mean by taking them apart and thinking about the meaning of each of their smaller words.

On the board, write the compound words that appear at the end of this lesson. Have students draw a line between each compound's two smaller words and then write a definition of the compound that uses its two smaller words.

It's finally spring. Grandpa is free to go outdoors. As he enjoys some of his favorite things, discover what matters to his family.

Connect to Your Life

Do you know an elderly person whose health is failing? Do you know how to act toward this person? What feelings have you had when you've been around someone very old? Discuss your feelings with classmates.

Key to the Story

In this short story, the narrator tells about a grandfather who is very old. Grandpa is being watched by his daughter and grandson. Watch for the ways these three family members treat one another.

Vocabulary Preview

Words to Know

coarse   bundled
timber   terrapin

 Reading Coach CD-ROM selection

Another April **99**

Connect to Your Life

Guide students in a discussion of how they feel and act when they are around people who are very old. Why do they feel and act as they do?

Key to the Story

As students compare the two characters' behavior toward Grandpa, encourage them to discuss the possible reasons for each character's behavior.

Vocabulary Preview

Words to Know
coarse *adj.* rough
timber *n.* tree
bundled *adj.* wrapped up
terrapin *n.* turtle

 For direct instruction on Words to Know, see page T150.

---

over/coat *coat* that is worn *over* other clothing

snow/drift *drift,* or pile, of *snow* that has been blown there by the wind

basket/ball *ball* that is put through a *basket* of netting

 For more on Compound Words, see page T150.

FOCUS

Grandpa is eager to get outdoors again. Read to find out what he wants to do.

"Now, Pap, you won't get cold," Mom said as she put a heavy wool cap over his head.

"Huh, what did ye say?" Grandpa asked, holding his big hand cupped over his ear to catch the sound.

"Wait until I get your gloves," Mom said, hollering real loud in Grandpa's ear. Mom had forgotten about his gloves until he raised his big bare hand above his ear to catch the sound of Mom's voice.

"Don't get 'em," Grandpa said, "I won't ketch cold."

10   Mom didn't pay any attention to what Grandpa said. She went on to get the gloves anyway. Grandpa turned toward me. He saw that I was looking at him.

"Yer Ma's a-puttin' enough clothes on me to kill a man," Grandpa said; then he laughed a coarse laugh like March wind among the pine tops at his own words. I started laughing but not at Grandpa's words. He thought I was laughing at them and we both laughed together. It pleased

20   Grandpa to think that I had laughed with him over

> coarse
> (kôrs)
> *adj.* rough

something funny that he had said. But I was laughing at the way he was dressed. He looked like a picture of Santa Claus. But Grandpa's cheeks were not cherry-red like Santa Claus's cheeks. They were covered with white thin beard—and above his eyes were long white eyebrows almost as white as percoon petals and very much longer.

REREAD
Is the grandson laughing with or at Grandpa?

A

30   Grandpa was wearing a heavy wool suit that hung loosely about his big body but fitted him tightly round the waist where he was as big and as round as a flour barrel. His pant legs were as big 'round his pipestem legs as emptied meal sacks. And his big shoes, with his heavy wool socks dropping down over their tops, looked like sled runners. Grandpa wore a heavy wool shirt and over his wool shirt he wore a heavy wool sweater and then his coat over the

40   top of all this. Over his coat he wore a heavy overcoat and about his neck he wore a wool scarf.

A

B

> pipestem
> (pīp' stĕm')
> thin, like the thin end of a pipe

B

The way Mom had dressed Grandpa you'd think there was a heavy snow on the ground but there wasn't. April was here instead, and the sun was shining on the green hills where the wild plums and the wild crab apples were in bloom enough to make you think there were big snowdrifts sprinkled over the green hills. When I looked at Grandpa and then looked out at the window at the sunshine and the green grass, I laughed

50   more. Grandpa laughed with me.

A

"I'm a-goin' to see my old friend," Grandpa said just as Mom came down the stairs with his gloves.

"Who is he, Grandpa?" I asked, but Grandpa just looked at my mouth working. He didn't know what I was saying. And he hated to ask me the second time.

Another April **101**

COMPREHENSION

FOCUS SKILL: Details

Explain to students that when they are reading for **details,** they are looking for clues that the author has provided. Sometimes the details describe characters, places, or objects. At other times the details describe how characters speak, think, and act—and why.

For direct instruction on Details, see page T149.

A REREAD Is the grandson laughing with or at Grandpa? *(He's laughing at him.)* **details**

B Ask: Name some details that help you picture Grandpa's physical appearance. *(Possible answers: He has big hands and a big body, his cheeks are covered with a white thin beard, his eyebrows are white, his waist is big, and his legs are like pipestems.)* **details**

LITERATURE

FOCUS SKILL: Setting

Tell students that the **setting** is where and when the action of the story takes place. Poems and plays also have settings. Types of settings may include a particular location, historical period (past, present, or future), season of the year, time of day, and so on. The importance of the setting can vary from work to work.

For direct instruction on Setting, see page T149.

Use the questions that follow to encourage literary analysis.

A At what time of year is this story taking place? *(in April, in the spring; the weather is warm enough to allow Grandpa to go outdoors)* **setting**

VOCABULARY

FOCUS SKILL: Compound Words

A pipestem Help students break this compound apart and then use its smaller words to figure out the compound's meaning.

B Teacher Modeling: Compound Words *Well, here's a good example of how to figure out a compound word. The story says* Over his coat he wore a heavy overcoat. *That phrase itself shows me how to break the compound word* overcoat *into the words* over *and* coat. *Then it helps me understand that an overcoat is a coat that you wear* over *other clothing.*

FOR ENGLISH LEARNERS

Help students understand the following expressions, idioms, and dialect:

Line 9: ketch cold
Line 13: Yer Ma's a-puttin'
Line 37: sled runners

Mom put the big wool gloves on Grandpa's hands. He stood there just like I had to do years ago, and let Mom put his gloves on. If Mom didn't get his fingers back in the glove-fingers exactly right, Grandpa
60 quarreled at Mom. And when Mom fixed his fingers exactly right in his gloves the way he wanted them, Grandpa was pleased.

REREAD Describe how you think Mom is treating Grandpa. **C**

"I'll be a-goin' to see 'im," Grandpa said to Mom. "I know he'll still be there."

THINK IT THROUGH **D**
Where is Grandpa going? Why does getting ready take so long?

FOCUS
Read to discover why Mom is so careful about Grandpa.

Mom opened our front door for Grandpa and he stepped out slowly, supporting himself with his big cane in one hand. With the other hand he held to the door facing. Mom let him out
70 of the house just like she used to let me out in the spring. And when Grandpa left the house, I wanted to go with him, but Mom wouldn't let me go. I wondered if he would get away from the house—get out of Mom's sight—and pull off his shoes and go barefooted and wade the creeks like I used to do when Mom let me out. Since Mom wouldn't let me go with Grandpa, I watched him as he walked slowly down the path in front of our house. Mom stood there watching Grandpa too. I think she was
80 afraid that he would fall. But Mom was fooled;

C

facing
frame

102 Unit 3 We Are Family

Grandpa toddled along the path better than my baby brother could.

"He used to be a powerful man," Mom said more to herself than she did to me. "He was a timber cutter. No man could cut more timber than my father; no man in the timber woods could sink an ax deeper into a log than my father. And no man could lift the end of a bigger saw log
90 than Pop could."

timber
(tĭm' bər)
n. tree

REREAD How does this description of Grandpa compare to how he is now? **E**

"Who is Grandpa goin' to see, Mom?" I asked.

"He's not goin' to see anybody," Mom said.

"I heard 'im say that he was goin' to see an old friend," I told her.

"Oh, he was just a-talkin'," Mom said.

I watched Grandpa stop under the pine tree in our front yard. He set his cane against the pine tree trunk, pulled off his gloves and put them in his pocket. Then
100 Grandpa stooped over slowly, as slowly as the wind bends down a sapling, and picked up a pine cone in his big soft fingers. Grandpa stood fondling the pine cone in his hand. Then, one by one, he pulled the little chips from the pine cone—tearing it to pieces like he was hunting for something in it—and after he had torn it to pieces he threw the pine-cone stem on the ground. Then he pulled pine needles from a low-hanging pine bough, and
110 he felt of each pine needle between his fingers. **B**

bough
(bou)
tree branch

Another April 103

He played with them a long time before he started down the path.

"What's Grandpa doin'?" I asked Mom.

But Mom didn't answer me.

"How long has Grandpa been with us?" I asked Mom.

"Before you's born," she said. "Pap has been with us eleven years. He was eighty when he quit cuttin' 120 timber and farmin'; now he's ninety-one."

I had heard her say that when she was a girl he'd walk out on the snow and ice barefooted and carry wood in the house and put it on the fire. He had shoes but he wouldn't bother to put them on. And I heard her say that he would cut timber on the coldest days without socks on his feet but with his feet stuck down in cold brogan shoes, and he worked stripped above the waist so his arms would have freedom 130 when he swung his double-bitted ax. I had heard her tell how he'd sweat and how the sweat in his beard would be icicles by the time he got home from work on the cold winter days. Now Mom wouldn't let him get out of the house, for she wanted him to live a long time.

REREAD Why do you think Mom shared these memories about Grandpa? **F**

G **THINK IT THROUGH**
How does Mom feel about the changes in her father?

FOCUS
Grandpa's walk continues. Read to find out a change the narrator notices about his grandfather.

As I watched Grandpa go down the path toward the hog pen, he stopped to examine every little thing

along his path. Once he waved his cane at a 140 butterfly as it zigzagged over his head, its polka-dot wings fanning the blue April air. Grandpa would stand when a puff of wind came along, and hold his face against the wind and let the wind play with his white whiskers. I thought maybe his face was hot under his beard and he was letting the wind cool his face. When he reached the hog pen, he called the hogs down to the fence. They came running and grunting to 150 Grandpa just like they were talking to him. I knew that Grandpa couldn't hear them trying to talk to him, but he could see their mouths working and he knew they were trying to say something. He leaned his cane against the hog pen, reached over the fence, and patted the hogs' heads. Grandpa didn't miss patting one of our seven hogs.

D

H

REREAD Picture this scene in your mind. **I**

As he toddled up the little path alongside the hog pen, he stopped under a blooming 160 dogwood. He pulled a white blossom from a bough that swayed over the path above his head, and he leaned his big bundled body against the dogwood while he tore each petal from the blossom and examined it carefully. There wasn't anything his dim blue eyes missed. He stopped under a redbud tree before he reached the garden to break a tiny spray of redbud blossoms. He took each blossom from the spray and examined it carefully.

E

bundled
(bŭn' dĭd)
adj. wrapped up

F

C

COMPREHENSION

F **REREAD** Why do you think Mom shared these memories about Grandpa? *(Possible answers: She wants her son to see that the bundled-up old man he sees now was once able to thrive in cold weather. Mom is simply thinking out loud as she remembers her father when he was younger.)* **making inferences**

G **THINK IT THROUGH** How does Mom feel about the changes in her father? *(She feels she has to protect him, since he's now very old and no longer strong enough to deal with the harshness of the outdoors.)* **making inferences**

H Why is Grandpa behaving like this? *(Students probably will say it's because he wants to observe, feel, and enjoy everything as thoroughly as possible.)* **making inferences**

I **REREAD** Picture this scene in your mind. *(See the Teacher Modeling suggestion that follows.)* **visualizing**

Teacher Modeling: Visualizing
To show students the Active Reading Strategy of visualizing, focus on the Reread for lines 149–157.
You could say: *Reading this paragraph makes me realize how details can help readers "see" what is happening in a story. I can see all those hogs running toward Grandpa. I can imagine their mouths opening and him patting their heads, even though he can't hear them. They're acting like dogs.*

LITERATURE

C Earlier in the story, Grandpa did the same thing with a pine cone. What effect do you think this setting is having on Grandpa? *(He's studying certain things in nature very closely. It seems as if he's trying to memorize the things he sees and feels.)* **setting**

VOCABULARY

D **butterfly** Explain that *butterfly* is an example of a compound word that doesn't have the meaning of the two words that form it. The word *fly* suggests an insect. However, the literal meaning of *butter* does not add to the meaning of the compound word.

polka-dot Point out that this word is a compound word that is hyphenated.

E **alongside** Students should be able to figure out the meaning by looking at the meanings of the two joined words.

dogwood Explain that *dogwood* is a compound word made up of two words whose literal meanings do not fit together neatly.

F **redbud** Help students use the smaller words to figure out the compound's meaning.

170 "Gee, it's funny to watch Grandpa," I said to Mom; then I laughed.

"Poor Pap," Mom said. "He's seen a lot of Aprils come and go. He's seen more Aprils than he will ever see again."

I don't think Grandpa missed a thing on the little circle he took before he reached the house. He played with a bumblebee that was bending a windflower 180 blossom that grew near our corncrib beside a big bluff. But Grandpa didn't try to catch the bumblebee in his big bare hand. I wondered if he would and if the bumblebee would sting him, and if he would holler. Grandpa even pulled a butterfly cocoon from a blackberry briar that grew beside his path. I saw him try to tear it into shreds but he couldn't. There wasn't any butterfly in it, for I'd seen it before. I wondered if the butterfly with the polka-dot wings, that Grandpa waved his cane at when he first left the house, had 190 come from this cocoon. I laughed when Grandpa couldn't tear the cocoon apart.

"I'll bet I can tear that cocoon apart for Grandpa if you'd let me go help him," I said to Mom.

> **REREAD** Why doesn't the boy seem to take Grandpa's walk seriously?

"You leave your Grandpa alone," Mom said. "Let 'im enjoy April."

Then I knew that this was the first time Mom had let Grandpa out of the house all winter. I knew that Grandpa loved the sunshine and the fresh 200 April air that blew from the redbud and dogwood blossoms. He loved the bumblebees, the hogs, the pine cones, and pine needles. Grandpa didn't miss a thing along his walk. And every day from now on

until just before frost Grandpa would take this little walk. He'd stop along and look at everything as he had done summers before. But each year he didn't take as long a walk as he had taken the year before. Now this spring he didn't go down to the lower end of the hog pen as he had done last year. And when I 210 could first remember Grandpa going on his walks, he used to go out of sight. He'd go all over the farm. And he'd come to the house and take me on his knee and tell me about all what he had seen. Now Grandpa wasn't getting out of sight. I could see him from the window along all of his walk.

> **THINK IT THROUGH** How is the grandson's view of Grandpa changing as he watches him and listens to Mom?

> **FOCUS** Find out whom Grandpa finally meets.

Grandpa didn't come back into the house at the front door. He toddled around back of the house toward the smokehouse, and I ran through the living room to the dining room so I could 220 look out the window and watch him.

> smokehouse place where meat is kept

"Where's Grandpa goin'?" I asked Mom.

"Now never mind," Mom said. "Leave Grandpa alone. Don't go out there and disturb him."

"I won't bother 'im, Mom," I said. "I just want to watch 'im."

"All right," Mom said.

> **REREAD** Do you believe the boy is taking Grandpa's walk more seriously now? Explain.

COMPREHENSION

J **REREAD** Why doesn't the boy seem to take Grandpa's walk seriously? *(He's too young to understand how important the walk is to Grandpa. He's watching Grandpa's actions without thinking about his feelings.)* **making inferences**

K Ask: This time, how is Grandpa's walk different from those he took last year? *(He doesn't go down to the lower end of the hog pen, and he doesn't go far enough to get out of the narrator's sight.)* **compare and contrast**

L **THINK IT THROUGH** How is the grandson's view of Grandpa changing as he watches him and listens to Mom? *(He remembers how much his grandpa loves the outdoors and what it means to be out on this day. He's realizing how Grandpa's walk has changed, even from the previous spring.)* **compare and contrast**

M **REREAD** Do you believe the boy is taking Grandpa's walk more seriously now? Explain. *(Possible answers: No, he's still behaving as if he's waiting for Grandpa to do something funny. Yes, the boy now seems to be genuinely interested in the old man's purpose for the walk. His mother seems slightly more convinced that her son doesn't simply want to make fun of Grandpa.)* **drawing conclusions**

LITERATURE

D Name at least three of the things that Grandpa pays attention to as he walks up the path. *(Possible answers: a butterfly cocoon, the wind, the hogs, a dogwood blossom, a spray of redbud blossoms)* **setting**

VOCABULARY

G See how many examples of compound words students can spot in the third paragraph. *(bumblebee, corncrib, windflower, butterfly, blackberry, and polka-dot)* Have them notice how these words are very visually descriptive.

H **smokehouse** Have a student identify the words that make up this compound word.

FOR ENGLISH LEARNERS

Help students understand the following:
Line 177: missed a thing
Line 217: toddled around

But Mom wanted to be sure that I didn't bother him so she followed me into the dining room. Maybe
230 she wanted to see what Grandpa was going to do. She stood by the window, and we watched Grandpa as he walked down beside our smokehouse where a tall sassafras tree's thin leaves fluttered in the blue April wind. Above the smokehouse and the tall sassafras was a blue April sky—so high you couldn't see the sky-roof. It was just blue space and little white clouds floated upon this blue.

When Grandpa reached the smokehouse he leaned his cane against the sassafras tree. He let himself
240 down slowly to his knees as he looked carefully at the ground. Grandpa was looking at something and I wondered what it was. I just didn't think or I would have known.

"There you are, my good old friend," Grandpa said.

"Who is his friend, Mom?" I asked.

Mom didn't say anything. Then I saw.

"He's playin' with that old terrapin, Mom," I said.

terrapin
(tĕr′ ə pĭn)
n. turtle

"I know he is," Mom said.
250 "The terrapin doesn't mind if Grandpa strokes his head with his hand," I said.

"I know it," Mom said.

"But the old terrapin won't let me do it," I said. "Why does he let Grandpa?"

"The terrapin knows your Grandpa."

"He ought to know me," I said, "but when I try to stroke his head with my hand, he closes up in his shell."

Mom didn't say anything. She stood by the window watching Grandpa and listening to Grandpa talk to
260 the terrapin.

"My old friend, how do you like the sunshine?" Grandpa asked the terrapin.

The terrapin turned his fleshless face to one side like a hen does when she looks at you in the sunlight. He was trying to talk to Grandpa; maybe the terrapin could understand what Grandpa was saying.

"Old fellow, it's been a hard winter," Grandpa said. "How have you fared under the smokehouse floor?"

fared
(fârd)
been doing

270 "Does the terrapin know what Grandpa is sayin'?" I asked Mom.

"I don't know," she said.

"I'm awfully glad to see you, old fellow," Grandpa said.

He didn't offer to bite Grandpa's big soft hand as he stroked his head.

"Looks like the terrapin would bite Grandpa," I said.

"That terrapin has spent the winters under that smokehouse for fifteen years," Mom said. "Pap has
280 been acquainted with him for eleven years. He's been talkin' to that terrapin every spring."

Another April **109**

COMPREHENSION

N Ask: What exactly is Grandpa's friend? *(a terrapin turtle)* **details**

O Ask: How do you think the narrator feels about the fact that the turtle is Grandpa's friend and doesn't bite him? *(Some students may say that the narrator is a bit jealous. Others may say that he is happy for Grandpa. Still others may say he feels a combination of both feelings.)* **drawing conclusions**

LITERATURE

E The author keeps repeating the words *blue* and *blue April* in this paragraph. How do these words help you picture the setting? *(The repetition of these words helps readers see the sky and feel and smell the air as they can only look, feel, and smell on a bright, crisp day in April.)* **setting**

F What can you tell about Grandpa from the way he treats the terrapin? *(Students may say that Grandpa really cares for the terrapin and is very happy to see him. He is also concerned about how the terrapin is doing after the hard winter.)* **characterization**

VOCABULARY

I **Teacher Modeling: Compound Words** Sky-roof. *Now that's an interesting compound word. If I take it apart, I have the words sky and roof. I know what both of those words mean, but I also know that the sky doesn't have a roof. I think the author actually made this word up for the narrator to use because the narrator is young and maybe thinks that the sky has a roof, or top.*

"How does Grandpa know the terrapin is old?" I asked Mom.

"It's got 1847 cut on its shell," Mom said. "We know he's ninety-five years old. He's older than that. We don't know how old he was when that date was cut on his back."

"Who cut 1847 on his back, Mom?"

290 "I don't know, child," she said, "but I'd say whoever cut that date on his back has long been under the ground."

THINK IT THROUGH
In what way does the terrapin respond to Grandpa? How is it different from the way it has behaved with the boy?

FOCUS
As you read, notice all the things the terrapin makes the boy think about.

Then I wondered how a terrapin could get that old and what kind of a looking person he was who cut the date on the terrapin's back. I wondered where it happened—if it happened near where our house stood. I wondered who lived here on this land then, what kind of a house they lived in, and if they had a sassafras with tiny thin April leaves on its top growing in their yard, and if the person that cut that 300 date on the terrapin's back was buried at Plum Grove, if he had farmed these hills where we lived today and cut timber like Grandpa had—and if he had seen the Aprils pass like Grandpa had seen them and if he enjoyed them like Grandpa was enjoying this April. I wondered if he had looked at the dogwood blossoms, the redbud blossoms, and talked to this same terrapin.

110 Unit 3 We Are Family

"Are you well, old fellow?" Grandpa asked the terrapin.

The terrapin just looked at Grandpa.

310 "I'm well as common for a man of my age," Grandpa said.

"Did the terrapin ask Grandpa if he was well?" I asked Mom.

"I don't know," Mom said. "I can't talk to a terrapin."

"But Grandpa can."

"Yes."

"Wait until tomatoes get ripe and we'll go to the garden together," Grandpa said.

320 "Does the terrapin eat tomatoes?" I asked Mom.

"Yes, that terrapin has been eatin' tomatoes from our garden for fifteen years," Mom said. "When Mick was tossin' the terrapins out of the tomato patch, he picked up this one and found the date cut on his back. He put him back in the patch and told him to help himself. He lives from our garden every year. We don't bother him and don't allow anybody else to bother him. He spends his winters under our smokehouse floor buried in the dry ground."

330 "Gee, Grandpa looks like the terrapin," I said. Mom didn't say anything; tears came to her eyes. She wiped them from her eyes with the corner of her apron.

REREAD
Why does Mom cry?

"I'll be back to see you," Grandpa said. "I'm a-gettin' a little chilly; I'll be gettin' back to the house."

The terrapin twisted his wrinkled neck without moving his big body, poking his head deeper into the April wind as Grandpa pulled his bundled body up by 340 holding to the sassafras tree trunk.

Another April 111

COMPREHENSION

P **THINK IT THROUGH** In what way does the terrapin respond to Grandpa? How is it different from the way it has behaved with the boy? *(The terrapin seems friendly to Grandpa. It allows Grandpa to stroke its head. When the boy has tried to pet it, it has drawn its head into its shell.)* **compare and contrast**

Q **REREAD** Why does Mom cry? *(Watching her father, she thinks about how he has aged. When her son compares him to an old turtle, she fully realizes how old her father has gotten.)* **drawing conclusions**

Teacher Modeling: Clarifying
To show students the Active Reading Strategy of clarifying, focus on the paragraph that begins at line 292. You could say: *When I read the boy's thoughts in this paragraph on page 110, I realized the boy himself was realizing something. The boy starts wondering about whoever might've*

lived on this same land at the time the date was carved into the terrapin's back. He wonders if that person's connection to farming and to nature was like his grandpa's connection. I concluded that the boy has finally come to understand that his grandfather is more than someone to be amused by. The word April is repeated several times in the paragraph, almost as if the boy, in his thinking, is adding up years. He finally seems to appreciate the many springs that have come and gone in the life of a person who has had a strong connection to the land.

VOCABULARY

FOR ENGLISH LEARNERS

Help students understand the following expressions and idioms:

Line 290: long been under the ground

Line 293: what kind of a looking person he was

Line 310: as common for a man of my age

Line 326: help himself

Line 331: tears came to her eyes

"Good-by, old friend!"

The terrapin poked his head deeper into the wind, holding one eye on Grandpa, for I could see his eye shining in the sinking sunlight.

Grandpa got his cane that was leaned against the sassafras tree trunk and hobbled slowly toward the house. The terrapin looked at him with first one eye and then the other.

THINK IT THROUGH

1. What is the terrapin doing as Grandpa leaves?
2. Grandpa calls the terrapin his "old friend." What do you think he and the terrapin have in common?
3. Has the boy's attitude toward his grandfather changed? Support your opinion with examples.

On Aging
by Maya Angelou

When you see me sitting quietly,
Like a sack left on the shelf,
Don't think I need your chattering,
I'm listening to myself.
5 Hold! Stop! Don't pity me!
Hold! Stop your sympathy!
Understanding if you got it,
Otherwise I'll do without it!

When my bones are stiff and aching
10 And my feet won't climb the stair,
I will only ask one favor:
Don't bring me no rocking chair.

When you see me walking, stumbling,
Don't study and get it wrong.
15 'Cause tired don't mean lazy
And every goodbye ain't gone.
I'm the same person I was back then,
A little less hair, a little less chin,
A lot less lungs and much less wind,
20 But ain't I lucky I can still breathe in.

COMPREHENSION

THINK IT THROUGH

1. What is the terrapin doing as Grandpa leaves? *(He is poking his head into the air and looking at Grandpa.)* **details**

2. Grandpa calls the terrapin his "old friend." What do you think he and the terrapin have in common? *(Possible answers: They are both in their 90s, they both move slowly, they both have wrinkled skin, and they both like to visit the garden.)* **compare and contrast**

3. Has the boy's attitude toward his grandfather changed? Support your opinion with examples. *(At the beginning of the story, the boy seems to think his grandpa's behavior is funny. As Grandpa's walk progresses, the boy becomes more curious about the old man's actions. By the time Grandpa makes contact with his "old friend," a terrapin, the boy realizes the close connection his grandfather has always had with nature.)* **drawing conclusions**

Option for Writing Use question 2 on page 112 to have students fill out a Venn diagram that compares and contrasts Grandpa and the terrapin.

RELATED READING

Background Information People have different ways of treating and viewing older adults. In "Another April," the narrator views his 91-year-old grandpa as amusing and curious, while his mother views Grandpa as childlike and helpless. In the poem "On Aging," the speaker, who is an older adult, views the older adults differently.

1. What message do you think the speaker is trying to convey in this poem? *(Possible answer: Even though the speaker's body has changed, he or she is still the same person inside.)* **theme**

2. If Grandpa from "Another April" were to read this poem, do you think he would agree or disagree with the speaker? *(Students probably will say that Grandpa would agree with the speaker. They might cite the fact that Grandpa tells his daughter not to get his gloves and then tells the narrator, "Yer Ma's a-puttin' enough clothes on me to kill a man.")* **making inferences**

Direct Instruction
for SkillBuilder Copymasters

1. COMPREHENSION

Details

Direct Instruction Tell students that **details** support, or tell more about, the main idea of a paragraph. Point out that paying attention to details helps readers understand and respond to what they read.

Read aloud this description of Grandpa from "Another April." After you are finished reading, ask students to repeat the details they remember.

Grandpa was wearing a heavy wool suit that hung loosely about his big body but fitted him tightly round the waist where he was as big and as round as a flour barrel. His pant legs were as big 'round his pipestem legs as emptied meal sacks. And his big shoes, with his heavy wool socks dropping down over their tops, looked like sled runners. Grandpa wore a heavy wool shirt and over his wool shirt he wore a heavy wool sweater and then his coat over the top of all this. Over his coat he wore a heavy overcoat and about his neck he wore a wool scarf.

Comprehension SkillBuilder Answer Key:
1. *timber cutter*
2. *Possible answers: cut timber, sunk an ax into a log, lifted a big saw log*
3. *butterfly*
4. *calls the hogs to the fence*
5. *pats each hog's head*
6. *the lower end of the hog pen*
7. *out of sight; all over the farm*
8. *take the child on his knee and tell what he saw on his walk*

---

2. LITERATURE

Setting

Direct Instruction Tell students that the **setting** of a story tells when and where the story takes place. Point out that in "Another April," the writer describes the setting in detail. Explain that the writer wants to re-create a time and place as perfectly as possible in this story so that readers can feel as if they are there with the story's characters. Point out that in addition to painting a picture of a time and a place in a description, the words the writer chooses can often create a particular mood.

Read aloud this passage from "Another April." Have each student draw the scene on a sheet of paper. Then ask students to describe the story. Is it frightening, comical, or peaceful? *(peaceful)*

April was here instead, and the sun was shining on the green hills where the wild plums and the wild crab apples were in bloom enough to make you think there were big snowdrifts sprinkled over the green hills.

Literary SkillBuilder Answer Key:
Student drawings should show as many of these details as possible: pine tree in the front yard, a fenced hog pen with a blooming tree nearby, and behind the house a smokehouse and a tall tree with few leaves.

3. VOCABULARY

Vocabulary SkillBuilder — Name_____

ANOTHER APRIL

Compound Words

A **compound word** is made by putting two words together. Sometimes the words are written as one word. Other times, the words are combined with a hyphen (-). Sometimes the two words are written as separate words but used together:

A. Combine each word in Row 1 with a word in Row 2 to make a compound word. Complete the sentences with the compound words you make.

Row 1: bare over bumble dining polka-
Row 2: bee footed room coat dot

1. Grandpa watched the _____ buzz near the windflower.
2. Mom made Grandpa wear his _____ to go outside.
3. The child took off his shoes and ran _____ through the creek.
4. Grandpa waved his cane at a butterfly with _____ wings.
5. The child could see Grandpa through the window in the _____.

B. Circle the compound words in these sentences about the story "Another April." Then, under each sentence, write the words that go together to make each compound word.

1. The old man had long white eyebrows above his eyes.
   _____ + _____

2. The blossoms of the trees looked like big snowdrifts sprinkled over the green hills.
   _____ + _____

3. Above the smokehouse and the tall sassafras was a blue April sky—so high you couldn't see the sky-roof.
   _____ + _____
   _____ + _____

4. He even pulled a butterfly cocoon from a blackberry briar that grew beside his path.
   _____ + _____
   _____ + _____

Another April **T153**

Compound Words

Direct Instruction Tell students that **compound words** are words made by joining two shorter words. Explain that readers can often discover the meaning of unfamiliar compound words by separating them into their parts.
- Some compound words are written as one word: *blueberry*
- Some compound words are written with a hyphen: *baby sitter*
- Some compound words are written as two words that are used together: *ice cream*

Explain that when students are in doubt about how to write a particular compound word—that is, whether to write it as one word, as a hyphenated word or as two words—they should look the word up in the dictionary.

Vocabulary SkillBuilder Answer Key:

A.
1. *bumblebee*
2. *overcoat*
3. *barefooted*
4. *polka-dot*
5. *dining room*

B.
1. *eye + brows*
2. *snow + drifts*
3. *smoke + house, sky + roof*
4. *butter + fly, black + berry*

---

4. WORDS TO KNOW

Words to Know SkillBuilder — Name_____

ANOTHER APRIL

Words to Know

coarse timber bundled terrapin

A. Circle the letter next to the word or phrase that is most similar to the **boldfaced** word.

1. Grandpa's hands were **coarse**—like the bark of a tree.
   a. gentle   b. soft   c. rough

2. When it is cold, Grandpa is **bundled** in a heavy wool coat.
   a. hidden   b. wrapped up   c. sweating

3. The old **terrapin** lives in the pond.
   a. rock   b. fish   c. turtle

4. We used **timber** from the forest to build the fire.
   a. wood   b. leaves   c. flowers

B. Fill in each blank with the word from the list that best completes the sentence.

1. The _____ walked slowly on its four legs.
2. The boy's mother _____ him in two sweaters and a coat.
3. Settlers cut _____ to make houses.
4. The rough sandpaper is _____.

Writing Activity
Write three sentences about springtime. Use at least three **Words to Know.**

T154 Unit 3 We Are Family

Words to Know

Direct Instruction As you present the **Words to Know,** here are some points you might want to cover.
- The words *coarse* and *course* are homophones, words that sound alike but have different meanings and spellings.
- The words *timber* and *timbre* are homophones. *Timber* is defined as "trees or wooded land considered as a source of wood." *Timbre* is defined as "the combination of qualities of a sound that distinguishes it from other sounds of the same pitch and volume."
- **bundle** + -ed = *bundled*

Writing Activity This is an activity that encourages descriptive writing. Encourage students to be as creative as they can in describing spring.

Words to Know SkillBuilder Answer Key:

A.
1. *c*
2. *b*
3. *c*
4. *a*

B.
1. *terrapin*
2. *bundled*
3. *timber*
4. *coarse*

---

5. SELECTION TEST

Selection Test Answer Key:
A. **1.** *spring* **2.** *farm* **3.** *Santa Claus* **4.** *hearing* **5.** *timber cutter* **6.** *walk*
7. *inside* **8.** *leave him alone* **9.** *a turtle*
B. *The terrapin has a date carved into its back.*

ANOTHER APRIL

Details

Details tell more about the main ideas in a paragraph.

Answer the questions below, using details from the following paragraphs.

"He used to be a powerful man," Mom said more to herself than she did to me. "He was a timber cutter. No man could cut more timber than my father; no man in the timber woods could sink an ax deeper into a log than my father. And no man could lift the end of a bigger saw log than Pop could."

1. What had been Pop's job? _____

2. Name two tasks Pop had done well on the job. _____

_____

As I watched Grandpa go down the path toward the hog pen, he stopped to examine every little thing along his path. Once he waved his cane at a butterfly as it zigzagged over his head, its polka-dot wings fanning the blue April air. . . . When he reached the hog pen, he called the hogs down to the fence. . . . He leaned his cane against the hog pen, reached over the fence, and patted the hogs' heads. Grandpa didn't miss patting one of our seven hogs.

3. At what does Grandpa wave his cane? _____

4. What does Grandpa do first when he reaches the hog pen? _____

5. How does Grandpa show that he likes the hogs? _____

_____

But each year he didn't take as long a walk as he had taken the year before. Now this spring he didn't go down to the lower end of the hog pen as he had done last year. And when I could first remember Grandpa going on his walks, he used to go out of sight. He'd go all over the farm. And he'd come to the house and take me on his knee and tell me about all what he had seen. Now Grandpa wasn't getting out of sight. I could see him from the window along all of his walk.

6. Where did Grandpa go last year that he doesn't go now? _____

_____

7. Where did Grandpa used to go on his walks? _____

8. What did Grandpa used to do when he came back from his walks? _____

_____

ANOTHER APRIL

Setting

The **setting** of a story is when and where it takes place. In some stories, the setting is described in detail.

Read each passage from "Another April." On the sketch below, draw in the objects that Grandpa saw on his walk. Include as many details as you can.

1. Since Mom wouldn't let me go with Grandpa, I watched him as he walked slowly down the path in front of our house.

2. I watched Grandpa stop under the pine tree in our front yard.

3. As I watched Grandpa go down the path toward the hog pen, he stopped to examine every little thing along his path.

4. When he reached the hog pen, he called the hogs down to the fence.

5. As he toddled up the little path alongside the hog pen, he stopped under a blooming tree.

6. Grandpa didn't come back into the house at the front door. He toddled around back of the house toward the smokehouse.

7. We watched Grandpa as he walked down beside our smokehouse where a tall sassafras tree's thin leaves fluttered in the blue April wind.

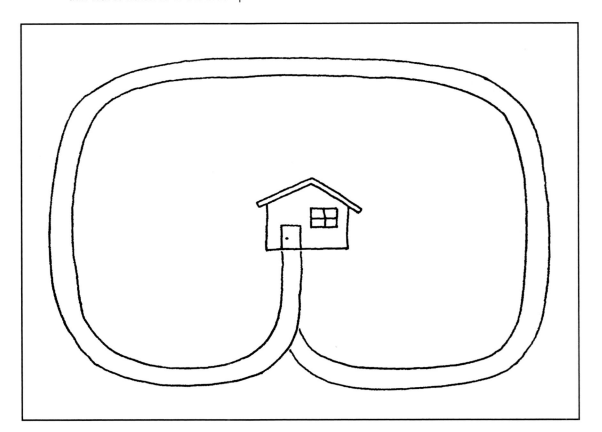

ANOTHER APRIL

Compound Words

A **compound word** is made by putting two words together. Sometimes the words are written as one word. Other times, the words are combined with a hyphen [-]. Sometimes the two words are written as separate words but used together.

A. Combine each word in Row 1 with a word in Row 2 to make a compound word. Complete the sentences with the compound words you make.

> Row 1:   bare   over   bumble   dining   polka-
> Row 2:   bee   footed   room   coat   dot

1. Grandpa watched the _____ buzz near the windflower.

2. Mom made Grandpa wear his _____ to go outside.

3. The child took off his shoes and ran _____ through the creek.

4. Grandpa waved his cane at a butterfly with _____ wings.

5. The child could see Grandpa through the window in the _____.

B. Circle the compound words in these sentences about the story "Another April." Then, under each sentence, write the words that go together to make each compound word.

1. The old man had long white eyebrows above his eyes.

    _____ + _____

2. The blossoms of the trees looked like big snowdrifts sprinkled over the green hills.

    _____ + _____

3. Above the smokehouse and the tall sassafras was a blue April sky—so high you couldn't see the sky-roof.

    _____ + _____

    _____ + _____

4. He even pulled a butterfly cocoon from a blackberry briar that grew beside his path.

    _____ + _____

    _____ + _____

ANOTHER APRIL

Words to Know

coarse   timber   bundled   terrapin

A. Circle the letter next to the word or phrase that is most similar to the **boldfaced** word.

1. Grandpa's hands were **coarse**—like the bark of a tree.

    a. gentle   b. soft   c. rough

2. When it is cold, Grandpa is **bundled** in a heavy wool coat.

    a. hidden   b. wrapped up   c. sweating

3. The old **terrapin** lives in the pond.

    a. rock   b. fish   c. turtle

4. We used **timber** from the forest to build the fire.

    a. wood   b. leaves   c. flowers

B. Fill in each blank with the word from the list that best completes the sentence.

1. The _____ walked slowly on its four legs.

2. The boy's mother _____ him in two sweaters and a coat.

3. Settlers cut _____ to make houses.

4. The rough sandpaper is _____.

Writing Activity
Write three sentences about springtime. Use at least three **Words to Know.**

ANOTHER APRIL

A. Answer each question by circling the correct answer in the sentence.

1. Does this story take place in the winter or the spring?

2. Is the setting of this story a big city or a farm?

3. When Grandpa is all bundled up, does the narrator say he looks like Santa Claus
or the Great Pumpkin?

4. Does Grandpa have trouble seeing or hearing?

5. Did Grandpa use to be a timber cutter or a haircutter?

6. Does Grandpa walk or drive to see his old friend?

7. Does the narrator watch Grandpa from the inside of the house or the outside?

8. When Grandpa can't tear apart the cocoon, does the narrator's mom tell him to help
Grandpa or leave him alone?

9. Does Grandpa's old friend turn out to be a turtle or a butterfly?

B. In your own words, tell why everyone knows the terrapin is very old.

_____

_____

Who's in Charge?

Unit 4
Drama

Can you control everything that happens to you? Good or bad, some things are beyond our control. The characters in this unit would probably agree. Events often leave them wondering, "Who's in charge?"

When you read the plays, or **dramas,** pay attention to what the characters say to each other. The characters tell the story in a play. You will be reading the **script,** or written form, of each play. Imagine how the actors would say the words you are reading. In fact, the best way to enjoy a play is to see it acted on the stage. Maybe you will act out parts of the play yourself.

114

Reading Fluency

 ★ Reading Fluency p. T195

Pacing Guide

SELECTION	TOTAL DAYS	PREREADING	READING	POST READING	
				SELECTIVE OPTIONS	ALL OPTIONS
The Telephone	4–4.5	.5	3	.5	1
The Prince and the Pauper	8–8.5	1	6	1	1.5

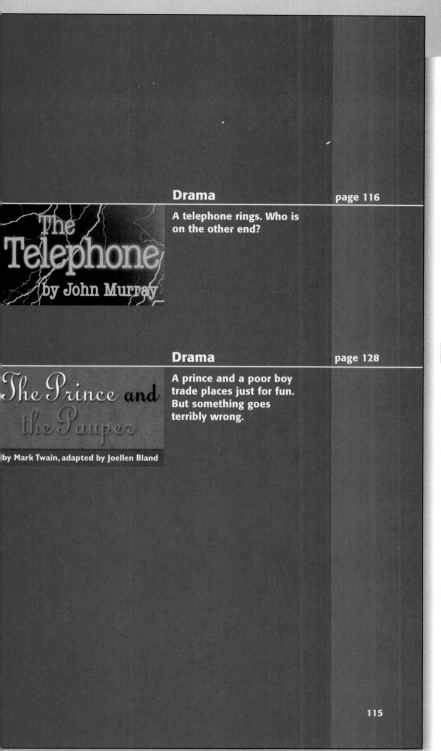

115

More About Drama

This unit introduces students to the genre
of drama. They will learn about dramatic
form—the conventions of drama—in the
first play, a mystery. In the second play,
the much longer classic *The Prince and
the Pauper,* students will learn how to follow a plot. Help students understand
how to read drama by letting them read
at least parts of these plays aloud. Refer
them to pages 460–461 in the Student
Resources section to familiarize them with
dramatic terms and staging.

Technology Resources

Audio CD
The two selections in this unit are
featured in the Audio Library.

Reading Coach CD-ROM
The two selections in this unit are
part of the Reading Coach. You
may use Reading Coach selections
as a group activity, as an individual
activity, or as a tutorial for students
who might benefit from this format
or who have missed class.

**Building Bridges: Closing the
Reading Gap**
This video is intended for teacher
use only. It gives instructions and
tips on how to help middle school
readers become strategic readers.

Assessment

Selection Tests
pp. T171, T194

**Assessment Booklet
Progress Check Units 1–4**
Administer this test after the first
four units of the book have been
read. It covers skills taught in all
four units.

Focus Skills

COMPREHENSION
Making Inferences

LITERATURE
Dramatic Form

VOCABULARY
Suffixes

SkillBuilder Copymasters

 Reading Comprehension:
1 Making Inferences p. T167

 Literary Analysis:
2 Dramatic Form p. T168

 Vocabulary:
3 Suffixes p. T169
4 Words to Know p. T170

Assessment

 5 Selection Test p. T171

Readability Scores

DRP	LEXILE	DALE-CHALL
50	NA	3.2

For English Learners

Many of the sentences in the stage directions lack the articles *a, an,* and *the.* Help students understand such sentences by inserting the articles. For example: *Victor enters, carrying* **a** *tray with* **a** *teapot and cups. He puts* **the** *tray on* **the** *coffee table.*

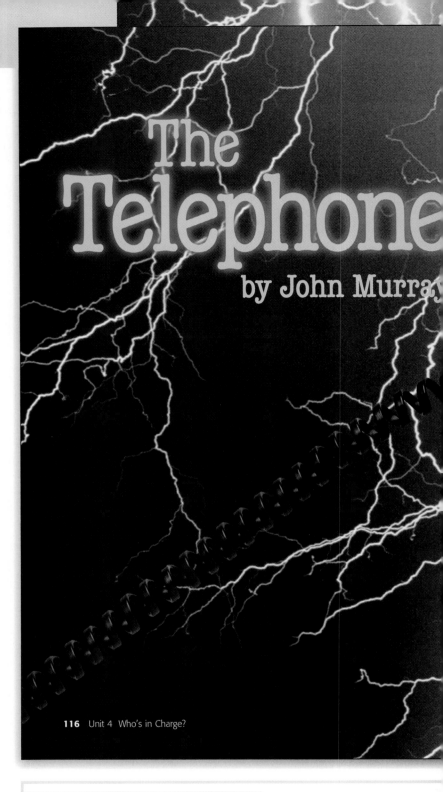

The Telephone
by John Murray

116 Unit 4 Who's in Charge?

Vocabulary Strategy: Preteaching

Suffixes Remind students that when they run across words that seem long, one strategy is to look for base words and suffixes. The suffixes have meanings that will help them unlock the meaning of the words. Write the following words on the board. Have students break the words into their parts. Review the meaning of the suffixes with students, and have them explain the meaning of the longer words.

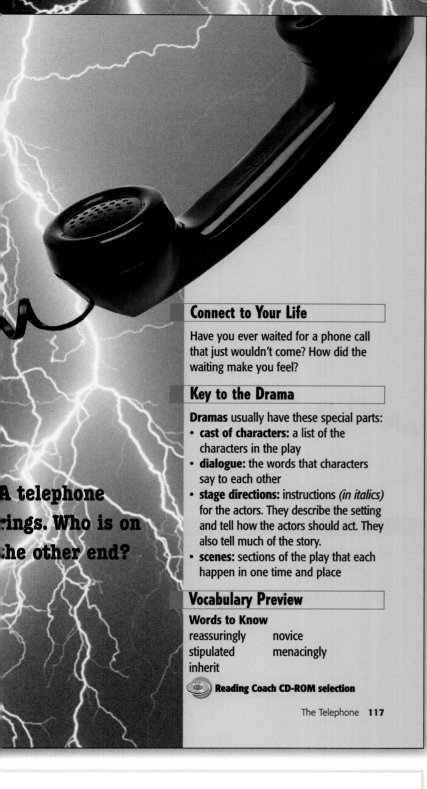

Connect to Your Life

Have you ever waited for a phone call that just wouldn't come? How did the waiting make you feel?

Key to the Drama

Dramas usually have these special parts:
- **cast of characters:** a list of the characters in the play
- **dialogue:** the words that characters say to each other
- **stage directions:** instructions *(in italics)* for the actors. They describe the setting and tell how the actors should act. They also tell much of the story.
- **scenes:** sections of the play that each happen in one time and place

Vocabulary Preview

Words to Know

reassuringly   novice
stipulated   menacingly
inherit

 Reading Coach CD-ROM selection

The Telephone   **117**

A telephone rings. Who is on the other end?

Connect to Your Life

Discuss the tension that can build when people are waiting for something to happen, especially if it is something potentially unpleasant. Ask why it is sometimes so hard to wait for something.

Key to the Drama

Explain to students that in a drama, the plot of the story is revealed mostly through the dialogue that is spoken between the characters. Be sure that students understand that the stage directions often tell part of the story that is not told through the dialogue. Emphasize the importance of reading all stage directions.

Vocabulary Preview

Words to Know
  reassuringly *adv.* in a way that makes one trust
  stipulated *v.* ordered
  inherit *v.* receive from one who has died
  novice *n.* beginner
  menacingly *adv.* in a threatening way

For direct instruction on Words to Know, see page T166.

Building Background

Before students begin reading, it may help them to understand how everyone in this play is related. Aunt Elizabeth is the widow of the late Jonathan Hathaway. Victor Hathaway is their nephew. He is married to Mildred, and he has a brother named Spencer. Now that Uncle Jonathan is believed to be dead, his millions belong to Aunt Elizabeth. In the event of her death, however, Victor and Spencer will inherit the money.

Word	Base Word	Suffix	Meaning of Suffix	Meaning of Word
restless	rest	-less	= without	without rest
helpful	help	-ful	= full of, having	full of help
nervous	nerve	-ous	= full of, having	having nerves
bitterly	bitter	-ly	= in a certain way; like	in a bitter way

 For more on Suffixes, see page T166.

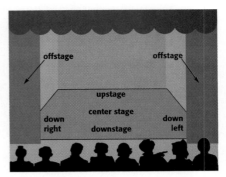

FOCUS
Read the cast of characters, the narrator's words, and all the stage directions. Find out what you need to know in order to understand this play.

Cast of Characters

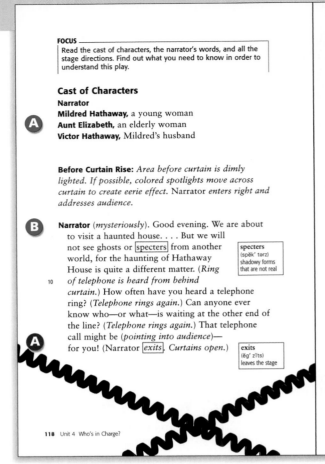

(A) Narrator
Mildred Hathaway, a young woman
Aunt Elizabeth, an elderly woman
Victor Hathaway, Mildred's husband

Before Curtain Rise: *Area before curtain is dimly lighted. If possible, colored spotlights move across curtain to create eerie effect. Narrator enters right and addresses audience.*

(B) **Narrator** (*mysteriously*). Good evening. We are about to visit a haunted house. . . . But we will not see ghosts or specters from another world, for the haunting of Hathaway House is quite a different matter. (*Ring*
10 *of telephone is heard from behind curtain.*) How often have you heard a telephone ring? (*Telephone rings again.*) Can anyone ever know who—or what—is waiting at the other end of the line? (*Telephone rings again.*) That telephone call might be (*pointing into audience*)— for you! (*Narrator exits. Curtains open.*)

specters
(spĕk' tərz) shadowy forms that are not real

exits
(ĕg' zĭts) leaves the stage

(A)

118 Unit 4 Who's in Charge?

Time: *Late evening.*
Setting: Drawing room *of Hathaway House. Through* French window *, upstage,*
20 *we see occasional flashes of lightning. Sounds of thunder are heard from offstage. There is a sofa down left, and a telephone on a table beside it.*

drawing room
room used for guests

French window
window that goes all the way to the floor

At Curtain Rise: Mildred Hathaway *stands near French window, pulling back drapes and staring out at storm.* Aunt Elizabeth, *wearing black shawl, sits on sofa. She touches telephone, then nods to herself. There is a flash of lightning.* Mildred *jumps, then crosses hurriedly to sit beside* Elizabeth.

(A) **(C)**

(B) **THINK IT THROUGH**
Where does this play take place? Who are the characters?

The Telephone **119**

COMPREHENSION

FOCUS SKILL: Making Inferences

Remind students that **inferences** are logical guesses based on evidence. Readers make inferences by combining information in the text with what they know from their own experience.

For direct instruction on Making Inferences, see page T165.

(A) Ask: Who do you think is calling on the phone? Why might that person be calling? *(Accept all predictions at this point. Tell students to remember their predictions so they can check them later.)*
predicting

(B) **THINK IT THROUGH** Where does this play take place? Who are the characters? *(in the drawing room of the haunted Hathaway House; Narrator, Mildred and Victor Hathaway, Aunt Elizabeth)*
dramatic form LITERATURE

LITERATURE

FOCUS SKILL: Dramatic Form

Remind students that the features of **dramatic form** are a play's cast of characters, stage directions, and dialogue.

For direct instruction on Dramatic Form, see page T165.

Use the following questions to encourage literary analysis.

(A) Why do you think the playwright had this play take place during a storm? *(The thunder and lightning add to the scary mood.)* **mood**

VOCABULARY

FOCUS SKILL: Suffixes

As students read this drama, remind them to break words into base words and suffixes in order to figure out their meaning.

(A) **elderly** Have students break the word into its parts to explain it. *(elder + -ly = like an elder)*

(B) **mysteriously** Have students break the word into its parts to explain it. *(mystery + -ous + -ly = in a way full of mystery)*

(C) **hurriedly** Have students break the word into its parts to explain it. *(hurry + -ed + -ly = in a rushed way)*

FOR ENGLISH LEARNERS

Help students understand the following expressions:

Line 1: area before curtain
Line 4: addresses audience

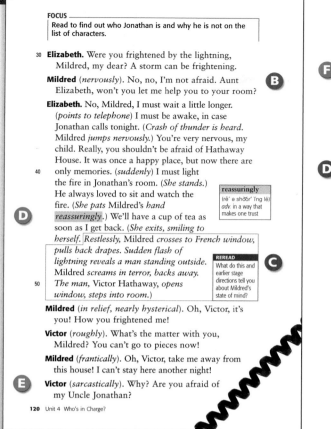

Read to find out who Jonathan is and why he is not on the list of characters.

30 **Elizabeth.** Were you frightened by the lightning, Mildred, my dear? A storm can be frightening.

Mildred (*nervously*). No, no, I'm not afraid. Aunt Elizabeth, won't you let me help you to your room? **B**

Elizabeth. No, Mildred, I must wait a little longer. (*points to telephone*) I must be awake, in case Jonathan calls tonight. (*Crash of thunder is heard. Mildred jumps nervously.*) You're very nervous, my child. Really, you shouldn't be afraid of Hathaway House. It was once a happy place, but now there are

40 only memories. (*suddenly*) I must light the fire in Jonathan's room. (*She stands.*) He always loved to sit and watch the fire. (*She pats Mildred's hand reassuringly.*) We'll have a cup of tea as soon as I get back. (*She exits, smiling to herself. Restlessly, Mildred crosses to French window, pulls back drapes. Sudden flash of lightning reveals a man standing outside. Mildred screams in terror, backs away.*

50 *The man, Victor Hathaway, opens window, steps into room.*) **C**

Mildred (*in relief, nearly hysterical*). Oh, Victor, it's you! How you frightened me!

Victor (*roughly*). What's the matter with you, Mildred? You can't go to pieces now!

Mildred (*frantically*). Oh, Victor, take me away from this house! I can't stay here another night!

Victor (*sarcastically*). Why? Are you afraid of my Uncle Jonathan? **E**

> reassuringly
> (rē′ ə shŏŏr′ ĭng lē)
> *adv.* in a way that makes one trust

REREAD
What do this and earlier stage directions tell you about Mildred's state of mind?

---

60 **Mildred.** Yes, I am! This house belongs to your Aunt Elizabeth, not to us. Why did you ever bring me here?

Victor (*laughing bitterly*). You're a silly fool! **F**

Mildred (*hysterically*). But, you don't understand! Elizabeth still waits every day for Jonathan to telephone her—and he's been dead for six weeks! (*Sudden crash of thunder is heard. She points to French window. She continues in frenzied tones.*) We all know he's out there in the family

70 vault. We went to the funeral and saw them seal the door of his tomb!

> vault
> (vôlt)
> place for burials

THINK IT THROUGH **D**
Who is Jonathan and where is he?

Read on to discover why Victor is so bitter.

Victor. My dear wife, *we* know that Uncle Jonathan is dead, but Aunt Elizabeth can't seem to accept it. You know Uncle Jonathan was always afraid of being buried alive. He stipulated in his will that a telephone should be installed in the vault. So here we have it—a direct line to Jonathan Hathaway's vault. (*points to telephone*)

80 **Mildred** (*wringing her hands*). I know all that, but—

Victor (*interrupting*). Jonathan was a wealthy man. When Aunt Elizabeth is gone, my brother Spencer

> **REREAD** **E**
> Why did Jonathan want a telephone in the vault?

> stipulated **F**
> (stĭp′ yə lā′ tĭd)
> *v.* ordered; past tense of *stipulate*

COMPREHENSION

C **REREAD** What do this and earlier stage directions tell you about Mildred's state of mind? (*She's edgy, nervous, frightened.*) **stage directions** LITERATURE

D **THINK IT THROUGH** Who is Jonathan and where is he? (*Aunt Elizabeth's late husband; buried in the family vault*) **making inferences**

E **REREAD** Why did Jonathan want a telephone in the vault? (*so he could call someone in case he got buried alive*) **making inferences**

F Have students think back to their earlier prediction and ask if they still think the same person was calling. Why or why not? (*Accept all predictions with evidence. Possible answer: Jonathan was calling from his vault. Evidence: had phone put in, was afraid of being buried alive*) **predicting**

LITERATURE

B How can you tell that Mildred is lying when she tells Aunt Elizabeth that she is not afraid? (*The stage directions say that she speaks nervously.*) **stage directions**

VOCABULARY

D **reassuringly, restlessly** (lines 44 and 46) Have students separate these words into their parts to understand them. (*re- + assure + -ing + -ly = in a way that brings trust again; rest + -less + -ly = in a way without rest*)

E **sarcastically** Have students break apart the word to explain it. (*sarcastic + -al + -ly = in a way filled with sarcasm*)

F **hysterically** Have students break apart the word to explain it. (*hysteric + -al + -ly = in a way marked by hysteria*)

FOR ENGLISH LEARNERS

Help students understand the following expressions and idioms:

Line 35: in case
Line 46: crosses to French window
Line 53: how you frightened me
Line 55: go to pieces
Line 78: direct line

C and I will inherit the millions of dollars he left to her. Think of it, Mildred—millions of dollars!

> **inherit**
> (ĭn hĕr´ ĭt)
> *v.* receive from one who has died

Mildred (*drawing away, frightened*). I don't want the money, Victor. Please take me away from here!

G 90 **Victor** (*soothingly*). All in good time, my dear. When Aunt Elizabeth is no longer with us.

Mildred. Don't say such things!

Victor (*abruptly*). Where is Aunt Elizabeth?

Mildred (*pointing to door*). Upstairs—preparing Jonathan's room.

Victor. Good. Nothing must happen to Aunt Elizabeth—not yet. I have other plans for her! I'm going upstairs for a moment myself. (*He exits. From* 100 *offstage, clock is heard chiming eleven times. As it chimes,* Mildred *paces floor.*)

> **REREAD**
> What do you think Victor's "plans" are? **G**

THINK IT THROUGH
What is keeping Victor from getting his uncle's money? **H**

FOCUS
Read on to find out *exactly* what Victor plans to do to Aunt Elizabeth.

Mildred. Eleven o'clock. Uncle Jonathan died at eleven o'clock. (*She sits on sofa, stares at phone. Suddenly phone rings.* Mildred *screams, jumps to her feet. Phone rings*

again. Slowly, her hand trembling, she 110 *picks up receiver, speaks into phone.*) Yes? Yes? . . . who's there? (*shrilly*) Why don't you answer? Please, answer me! (*Slowly she hangs up receiver.*) There was no one on the line! (*Behind her, drapes at French window move. She turns and begins to walk toward window as if sleepwalking, her hand outstretched, trembling. Suddenly drape is thrown aside and* Victor *strides into room.* Mildred *gasps and collapses onto sofa.*) Victor, what were you 120 doing out there?

> **REREAD**
> Who do you think called? **I**

Victor. Just conducting a little experiment.

Mildred (*suddenly remembering*). The telephone! The telephone rang from Jonathan's vault!

Victor. Relax, my dear. Have you forgotten that I'm not a novice at working with telephones? After all, I am an electrical engineer.

> **novice**
> (nŏv´ ĭs)
> *n.* beginner

Mildred (*horrified*). Did *you* make that phone ring, Victor?

J 130 **Victor** (*nodding*). Yes. I spliced the wire and connected it to a buzzer outside. (*menacingly*) I don't intend to wait any longer to inherit the Hathaway fortune.

> **menacingly**
> (mĕn´ ĭ sĭng lē)
> *adv.* in a threatening way

D

Mildred. Don't talk like that, Victor!

Victor. Quiet! When Aunt Elizabeth returns, I'll make some excuse to leave the room. Then the telephone will ring again. . . . Perhaps the shock will be too much for Aunt Elizabeth's heart.

Mildred. I won't let you do this! I'm going to tell her 140 what you're planning!

COMPREHENSION

G **REREAD** What do you think Victor's "plans" are? *(Accept responses that can be supported by evidence. Possible answer: Something bad will happen to Elizabeth. Evidence: He says "not yet" after saying that nothing must happen to her.)* **making inferences**

H **THINK IT THROUGH** What is keeping Victor from getting his uncle's money? *(He can't inherit it until Aunt Elizabeth dies.)* **problem and solution**

I **REREAD** Who do you think called? *(Accept any reasonable answer that students can support.)* **making inferences**

J Have students think back to earlier predictions. Ask: Now who do you think was calling? Why? *(Possible answer: Victor. Evidence: He's an electrical engineer; he admitted he called.)* **predicting**

LITERATURE

C What is Victor's goal, or motive? *(to get Aunt Elizabeth's fortune)* **motive**

D Aside from what is revealed in the dialogue, how else do you know that Victor is not a nice person? *(The stage directions say that he speaks abruptly and menacingly.)* **stage directions**

VOCABULARY

G **soothingly** Have students break apart this word to explain it. *(soothe + -ing + -ly = in a way that calms)*

FOR ENGLISH LEARNERS

Help students understand the following expressions and idioms:

Line 90: all in good time
Line 91: no longer with us
Line 114: on the line
Line 117: drape is thrown aside
Line 125: not a novice (double negative)

Victor (*menacingly*). No, I don't think you'll do that. (*She backs away from him, frightened.*) Cooperate with me, Mildred, and in a little while you'll have the luxuries you've always wanted. (*Aunt Elizabeth enters.*)

(K) THINK IT THROUGH
What is Victor planning to do?

FOCUS
Read on to find out if Mildred goes along with Victor's plan.

Elizabeth. It's so nice and warm in Jonathan's room. Such a bright fire! I know he'll be delighted.

(E) **Victor.** How about a cup of tea, Aunt Elizabeth?

Mildred (*quickly*). I'll fix it.

150 **Victor.** No, Mildred. (*smiles*) I'll attend to the tea. I'll attend to everything. (*He exits right.*)

(H) **Mildred** (*desperately*). Wouldn't you like to lie down, Auntie? I'll bring the tea to your room.

Elizabeth (*sadly*). No, I'll wait here a little while longer. The telephone call, you know. (*She sits on sofa.*)

Mildred. But it's so cold in here.

Elizabeth. I don't mind the cold, my dear. You know, I feel so close to Jonathan tonight. Oh, how he loved to sit in this room with me! He never

160 liked being alone. (*gestures to phone*) That's why he wanted the telephone. He was afraid of being left there—alone—in the dark.

> gestures
> (jĕs′ chərz)
> points with a hand

Mildred (*nervously*). Please don't talk like that, Aunt Elizabeth.

124 Unit 4 Who's in Charge?

Elizabeth (*taking her hand*). Don't worry, dear. Someday Jonathan will come back, and I'll never be alone again. (*Telephone rings. Mildred jumps and*

REREAD
What does this tell you about Elizabeth? **(L)**

170 *stares at* Aunt Elizabeth *in terror. Aunt Elizabeth smiles happily.*) It's Jonathan! I knew he'd call. (*She reaches for telephone. Mildred grabs her hand.*) **(F)**

Mildred (*desperately*). Don't answer that phone! Don't you understand? Jonathan is dead! (*Phone rings again.*)

Elizabeth (*with quiet dignity*). Please, Mildred, I must answer. (*Mildred releases her hand, and Elizabeth picks up receiver and speaks into it.*) Hello? Hello? Is that you, Jonathan? . . . I can't

180 hear anything. . . . Jonathan? (*Slowly she replaces receiver; to* Mildred) There was no one on the line. Jonathan needed me, and you kept me away from the telephone. (*Victor enters, carrying tray with teapot and cups. He puts tray on coffee table.*) **(M)**

(N) THINK IT THROUGH
How does Mildred try to protect Aunt Elizabeth from Victor?

The Telephone 125

COMPREHENSION

(K) **THINK IT THROUGH** What is Victor planning to do? (*do away with his aunt—possibly by scaring her to death—so he can inherit her money*) **making inferences**

(L) **REREAD** What does this tell you about Elizabeth? (*Possible answers: that she is not rational; that she believes her husband will come back from being dead*) **making inferences**

(M) Ask students: Who does Elizabeth think is calling? (*Jonathan*) Who does Mildred think is calling? (*Victor*) How does Elizabeth feel toward Mildred? (*angry*) **clarifying**

(N) **THINK IT THROUGH** How does Mildred try to protect Aunt Elizabeth from Victor? (*by keeping Elizabeth away from the phone so she won't hear whatever Victor is planning to say to shock her*) **drawing conclusions**

LITERATURE

(E) What kind of person do you think Mildred is? Give evidence. (*Possible answer: caring; evidence: She tries to keep Elizabeth away from Victor, who plans to harm her.*) **characters**

(F) What actions are described in the stage directions? (*Elizabeth reaches for the phone; Mildred stops her.*) **stage directions**

VOCABULARY

(H) **desperately** Have students analyze this word by breaking it into parts. (*desperate + -ly = in a desperate way*)

FOR ENGLISH LEARNERS

Help students understand the following expressions:

Line 150: attend to
Line 157: mind the cold

The Telephone PE 124–125 • **T163**

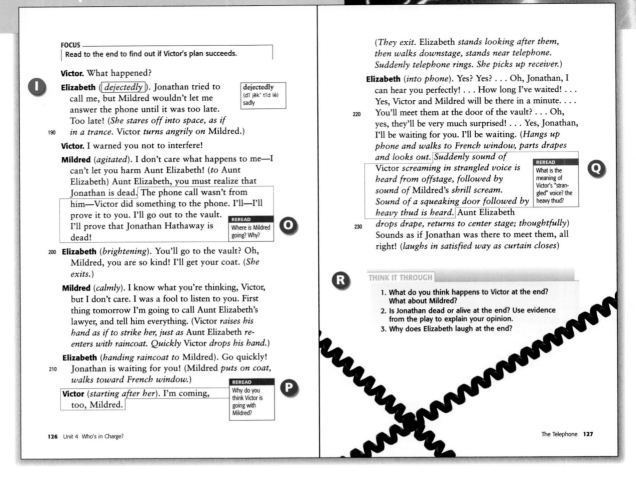

FOCUS
Read to the end to find out if Victor's plan succeeds.

Victor. What happened?

Elizabeth (*dejectedly*). Jonathan tried to call me, but Mildred wouldn't let me answer the phone until it was too late. Too late! (*She stares off into space, as if in a trance.* Victor *turns angrily on* Mildred.)

190

> **dejectedly**
> (dĭ jĕk′ tĭd lē)
> sadly

Victor. I warned you not to interfere!

Mildred (*agitated*). I don't care what happens to me—I can't let you harm Aunt Elizabeth! (*to Aunt Elizabeth*) Aunt Elizabeth, you must realize that Jonathan is dead. The phone call wasn't from him—Victor did something to the phone. I'll—I'll prove it to you. I'll go out to the vault. I'll prove that Jonathan Hathaway is dead!

> **REREAD**
> Where is Mildred going? Why?

O

Elizabeth (*brightening*). You'll go to the vault? Oh, Mildred, you are so kind! I'll get your coat. (*She exits.*)

200

Mildred (*calmly*). I know what you're thinking, Victor, but I don't care. I was a fool to listen to you. First thing tomorrow I'm going to call Aunt Elizabeth's lawyer, and tell him everything. (*Victor raises his hand as if to strike her, just as Aunt Elizabeth re-enters with raincoat. Quickly Victor drops his hand.*)

Elizabeth (*handing raincoat to* Mildred). Go quickly! Jonathan is waiting for you! (*Mildred puts on coat, walks toward French window.*)

210

Victor (*starting after her*). I'm coming, too, Mildred.

> **REREAD**
> Why do you think Victor is going with Mildred?

P

(*They exit.* Elizabeth *stands looking after them, then walks downstage, stands near telephone. Suddenly telephone rings. She picks up receiver.*)

Elizabeth (*into phone*). Yes? Yes? . . . Oh, Jonathan, I can hear you perfectly! . . . How long I've waited! . . . Yes, Victor and Mildred will be there in a minute. . . . You'll meet them at the door of the vault? . . . Oh, yes, they'll be very much surprised! . . . Yes, Jonathan, I'll be waiting for you. (*Hangs up phone and walks to French window, parts drapes and looks out. Suddenly sound of* Victor *screaming in strangled voice is heard from offstage, followed by sound of* Mildred's *shrill scream. Sound of a squeaking door followed by heavy thud is heard.* Aunt Elizabeth *drops drape, returns to center stage; thoughtfully*) Sounds as if Jonathan was there to meet them, all right! (*laughs in satisfied way as curtain closes*)

220

230

> **REREAD**
> What is the meaning of Victor's "strangled" voice? the heavy thud?

Q

THINK IT THROUGH

R

1. What do you think happens to Victor at the end? What about Mildred?
2. Is Jonathan dead or alive at the end? Use evidence from the play to explain your opinion.
3. Why does Elizabeth laugh at the end?

126 Unit 4 Who's in Charge?

The Telephone **127**

COMPREHENSION

O REREAD Where is Mildred going? Why? *(to the vault; to prove to Elizabeth that Jonathan is really dead)* **clarifying**

P REREAD Why do you think Victor is going with Mildred? *(to stop her)* **drawing conclusions**

Q REREAD What is the meaning of Victor's "strangled" voice? the heavy thud? *(Possible answers abound: Uncle Jonathan is strangling Victor; the door makes a thud as he closes Victor in the vault; something frightens Victor, and Mildred closes him in the vault.)* **making inferences**

R THINK IT THROUGH

1. What do you think happens to Victor at the end? What about Mildred? *(Possible answers may include that Victor dies, Mildred lives, or they both die.)* **making inferences**

2. Is Jonathan dead or alive at the end? Use evidence from the play to explain your opinion. *(Some may say he's alive. He and Elizabeth have outsmarted Victor to keep him from getting their money. Others may have a different explanation.)* **drawing conclusions**

3. Why does Elizabeth laugh at the end? *(She's happy that their plan has worked.)* **making inferences**

Option for Speaking and Listening
Have students act out the last page, choosing a student to portray Aunt Elizabeth talking on the phone with Jonathan and another student to read the stage directions. Let several pairs of students act out the scene. Encourage them to read with the intonation that they think Elizabeth would use when telling Jonathan that Mildred and Victor would be surprised and when she laughs at the end.

RETEACHING

If students need more help understanding **Making Inferences,** use pages T650–T652.

VOCABULARY

I dejectedly Have students analyze this word by breaking it into parts. *(deject + -ed + -ly = in a dejected way, sad)*

FOR ENGLISH LEARNERS

Help students understand the following expressions and idioms:

Line 207: as if to strike her
Line 208: drops his hand
Line 212: starting after her
Line 214: looking after them

1. COMPREHENSION

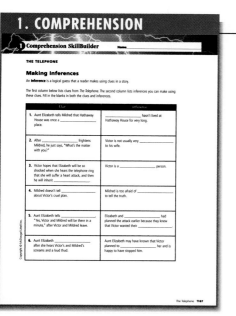

Making Inferences

Direct Instruction Tell students that an **inference** is a logical guess a reader makes, using clues in the text. Explain that writers usually expect readers to make inferences about characters, setting, and plot. Readers need to read "between the lines" to understand what is meant and not said. Point out that to make a logical inference, readers need to pay close attention to clues in the text and then combine them with their own experiences and common sense.

Have students figure out what inferences can be made using the clues in the following examples:

- **Clue:** Fans in the stands are smiling, clapping, and shouting.
  Inference: Their team has just scored.
- **Clue:** People in a cemetery are dressed in black and are crying.
  Inference: They have just buried a friend or relative.

Comprehension SkillBuilder Answer Key:

Clue	Inference
1. happy	Mildred
2. Victor	kind
3. her fortune	cruel, greedy
4. Aunt Elizabeth	Victor
5. Jonathan	Jonathan, fortune
6. laughs	kill

2. LITERATURE

Dramatic Form

Direct Instruction Explain that plays are intended to be presented by actors to an audience, so they are written in a way that makes that process easy. Discuss **dramatic form** by pointing out the following in *The Telephone*:

- The list (or cast) of characters tells the names of the characters in the play. It may tell something about each character too.
- General stage directions are usually given before the story begins. *Time* tells when the play takes place. *Setting* describes the scenery and the objects that should be on the stage. *At Rise* or *At Curtain Rise* tells what the audience should see when the curtain rises.
- Each character's words follow his or her name, making it easy for actors to spot their own lines.
- Information in parentheses (and usually italics) tells actors how they should say their lines or where they should move onstage.
- The stage directions describe sounds that are important to the plot and tell when they should be heard.

Literary SkillBuilder Answer Key:
1. *Aunt Elizabeth; Victor; Mildred*
2. *c, a and b, a*
3. *raincoat; telephone*
4. *a telephone ringing; a woman screaming; thunder*
5. *b, c, a*

3. VOCABULARY

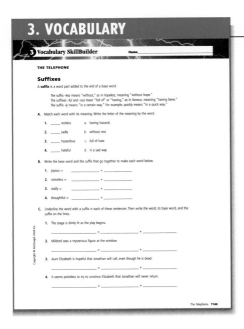

Suffixes

Direct Instruction Tell students that a **suffix** is a word part added to the end of a base word. Explain that the resulting new word has a meaning different from that of the base word alone. Write the following on the board:

Suffix	Meaning	Example
-less	without	helpless
-ful and -ous	full of; having	frightful, marvelous
-ly	in a certain way	calmly

Explain that knowing the meanings of suffixes can help readers understand meanings of unfamiliar words. Remind them especially of negative suffixes, such as -less. Breaking words down into parts makes them easier to read and understand.

Vocabulary SkillBuilder Answer Key:

A.
1. b
2. d
3. a
4. c

B.
1. joy + -ous
2. noise + -less
3. real + -ly
4. thought + -ful

C.
1. dimly = dim + -ly
2. mysterious = mystery + -ous
3. hopeful = hope + -ful
4. pointless = point + -less

4. WORDS TO KNOW

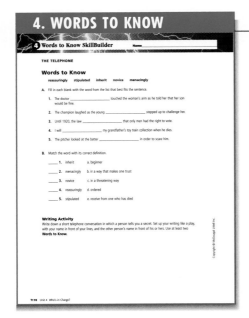

Words to Know

Direct Instruction As you present the **Words to Know,** here are some points you might want to cover. Help students identify the parts of the vocabulary words. Stress the importance of finding the base of each word. Help students remove prefixes and suffixes first.

- re- + **assure** + -ing + -ly = reassuringly
- **stipulate** + -ed = stipulated
  stipulate: from the Latin word stipulārī, "to bargain"
- **inherit:** in the same family of words as heir
- **novice:** from the Latin word novus, meaning "new"
- **menace** + -ing + -ly = menacingly
  menace: traces back to the Latin word minae, meaning "threats"

Writing Activity This activity can help students become comfortable with the play's format. Pair students or have them work in small groups to complete the exercise. Have volunteers read their creations aloud.

Words to Know SkillBuilder Answer Key:

A. 1. reassuringly **2.** novice **3.** stipulated **4.** inherit **5.** menacingly

B. 1. e **2.** c **3.** a **4.** b **5.** d

5. SELECTION TEST

Selection Test Answer Key:

A. 1. c **2.** c **3.** b **4.** a
B. Possible answer: Jonathan strangles him and locks him in the vault.

THE TELEPHONE

Making Inferences

An **inference** is a logical guess that a reader makes using clues in a story.

The first column below lists clues from *The Telephone*. The second column lists inferences you can make using these clues. Fill in the blanks in both the clues and inferences.

Clue	Inference
1. Aunt Elizabeth tells Mildred that Hathaway House was once a _____ place.	_____ hasn't lived at Hathaway House for very long.
2. After _____ frightens Mildred, he just says, "What's the matter with you?"	Victor is not usually very _____ to his wife.
3. Victor hopes that Elizabeth will be so shocked when she hears the telephone ring that she will suffer a heart attack, and then he will inherit _____.	Victor is a _____ person.
4. Mildred doesn't tell _____ about Victor's cruel plan.	Mildred is too afraid of _____ to tell the truth.
5. Aunt Elizabeth tells _____, "Yes, Victor and Mildred will be there in a minute," after Victor and Mildred leave.	Elizabeth and _____ had planned the attack earlier because they knew that Victor wanted their _____.
6. Aunt Elizabeth _____ after she hears Victor's and Mildred's screams and a loud thud.	Aunt Elizabeth may have known that Victor planned to _____ her and is happy to have stopped him.

THE TELEPHONE

Dramatic Form

Plays are meant to be acted out. So playwrights write them in a special way so that actors and directors know exactly what to do.

Answer these questions about the play *The Telephone*.

1. Circle the names of the characters for which the director needs to find actors.

    Aunt Elizabeth   Victor   Jonathan   Mildred

2. On the line next to the character's name, write the letter of the stage directions that character needs to follow.

    _____ Mildred   _____ Aunt Elizabeth   _____ Victor

    a. (. . . *raises hand as if to strike her, just as* Aunt Elizabeth *re-enters with raincoat. Quickly . . . drops hand.*)
    b. (*Laughs in satisfied way as curtain closes.*)
    c. (*She sits on sofa, stares at phone. Suddenly phone rings. . . . screams, jumps to her feet. Phone rings again. Slowly, her hand trembling, she picks up receiver, speaks into phone.*)

3. Which of these objects, or props, are needed for the play? Circle your answers.

    raincoat   telephone   large key

4. Which of these sounds should the audience hear? Circle your answers.

    a telephone ringing   a dog barking   a woman screaming   thunder

5. Match these stage directions from *The Telephone* with their labels. Write the letter of the matching stage direction on the line.

    _____ Setting   _____ Time   _____ At Curtain Rise

    a. Mildred Hathaway *stands near French window, pulling back drapes and staring out at storm.* Aunt Elizabeth, *wearing black shawl, sits on sofa. She touches telephone, then nods to herself. There is a flash of lightning.* Mildred *jumps, then crosses hurriedly to sit beside* Elizabeth.
    b. *Drawing room of Hathaway House. Through French window, upstage, we see occasional flashes of lightning. Sounds of thunder are heard from offstage. There is a sofa down left, and a telephone on a table beside it.*
    c. *Late evening.*

THE TELEPHONE

Suffixes

A **suffix** is a word part added to the end of a base word.

> The suffix -*less* means "without," as in *hopeless,* meaning "without hope."
> The suffixes -*ful* and -*ous* mean "full of" or "having," as in *famous,* meaning "having fame."
> The suffix -*ly* means "in a certain way." For example, *quickly* means "in a quick way."

A. Match each word with its meaning. Write the letter of the meaning by the word.

1. _____ restless   a. having hazards

2. _____ sadly   b. without rest

3. _____ hazardous   c. full of hate

4. _____ hateful   d. in a sad way

B. Write the base word and the suffix that go together to make each word below.

1. joyous =   _____ + _____

2. noiseless =   _____ + _____

3. really =   _____ + _____

4. thoughtful =   _____ + _____

C. Underline the word with a suffix in each of these sentences. Then write the word, its base word, and the suffix on the lines.

1. The stage is dimly lit as the play begins.

    _____ = _____ + _____

2. Mildred sees a mysterious figure at the window.

    _____ = _____ + _____

3. Aunt Elizabeth is hopeful that Jonathan will call, even though he is dead.

    _____ = _____ + _____

4. It seems pointless to try to convince Elizabeth that Jonathan will never return.

    _____ = _____ + _____

Name_____

THE TELEPHONE

Words to Know

reassuringly   stipulated   inherit   novice   menacingly

A. Fill in each blank with the word from the list that best fits the sentence.

1. The doctor _____ touched the woman's arm as he told her that her son would be fine.

2. The champion laughed as the young _____ stepped up to challenge her.

3. Until 1920, the law _____ that only men had the right to vote.

4. I will _____ my grandfather's toy train collection when he dies.

5. The pitcher looked at the batter _____ in order to scare him.

B. Match the word with its correct definition.

_____ **1.** inherit   a. beginner

_____ **2.** menacingly   b. in a way that makes one trust

_____ **3.** novice   c. in a threatening way

_____ **4.** reassuringly   d. ordered

_____ **5.** stipulated   e. receive from one who has died

Writing Activity
Write down a short telephone conversation in which a person tells you a secret. Set up your writing like a play, with your name in front of your lines, and the other person's name in front of his or hers. Use at least two **Words to Know.**

THE TELEPHONE

A. Fill in the circle beside the correct answer.

1. Why are Victor and Mildred visiting Aunt Elizabeth?
- ○ a. Aunt Elizabeth is ill and needs their help.
- ○ b. They are paying their respects to her late husband.
- ○ c. Victor wants to kill her so he can inherit her money.

2. From whom is Aunt Elizabeth expecting a phone call?
- ○ a. the funeral home
- ○ b. her dead husband's lawyer
- ○ c. her dead husband

3. Why does Mildred try to keep Aunt Elizabeth from answering the phone?
- ○ a. She doesn't want Aunt Elizabeth to tie up the line.
- ○ b. She doesn't want Aunt Elizabeth to be frightened.
- ○ c. She knows it's going to be a wrong number.

4. Who calls Aunt Elizabeth from the vault at the end of the play?
- ○ a. Uncle Jonathan
- ○ b. Victor
- ○ c. Mildred

B. In your own words, tell what happens to Victor when he gets to the vault.

_____

_____

_____

_____

Focus Skills

COMPREHENSION
Sequence

LITERATURE
Plot

VOCABULARY
Context Clues

SkillBuilder Copymasters

 Reading Comprehension:
1 Sequence p. T190

 Literary Analysis:
2 Plot p. T191

 Vocabulary:
3 Context Clues p. T192
4 Words to Know p. T193

Assessment

 5 Selection Test p. T194

Assessment Booklet
Progress Check Units 1–4

Readability Scores

DRP	LEXILE	DALE-CHALL
50	NA	3.6

Reading Fluency

 ★ Reading Fluency p. T195

For English Learners

Since a good portion of this play takes place in a British palace in 1547, the language reflects that setting. If necessary, help students understand such expressions as *if it please you; indeed, my lord; I salute your Gracious Highness; be off;* and *by your favor, sir.*

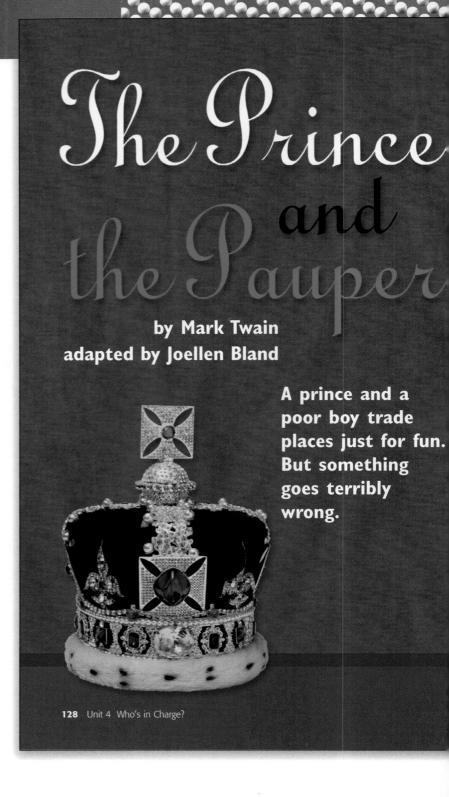

The Prince and the Pauper

by Mark Twain
adapted by Joellen Bland

A prince and a poor boy trade places just for fun. But something goes terribly wrong.

128 Unit 4 Who's in Charge?

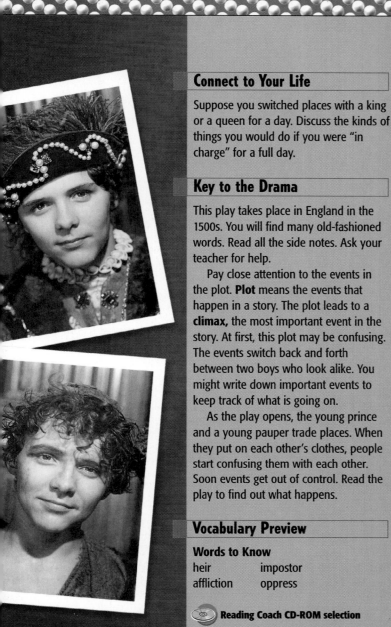

Connect to Your Life

Suppose you switched places with a king or a queen for a day. Discuss the kinds of things you would do if you were "in charge" for a full day.

Key to the Drama

This play takes place in England in the 1500s. You will find many old-fashioned words. Read all the side notes. Ask your teacher for help.

Pay close attention to the events in the plot. **Plot** means the events that happen in a story. The plot leads to a **climax,** the most important event in the story. At first, this plot may be confusing. The events switch back and forth between two boys who look alike. You might write down important events to keep track of what is going on.

As the play opens, the young prince and a young pauper trade places. When they put on each other's clothes, people start confusing them with each other. Soon events get out of control. Read the play to find out what happens.

Vocabulary Preview

Words to Know
heir   impostor
affliction   oppress

 Reading Coach CD-ROM selection

The Prince and the Pauper **129**

■ Connect to Your Life

Guide students with questions such as these: Would they lie around and "get the royal treatment"? Would they work on improving conditions for their people? Would they promote a pet project?

■ Key to the Drama

Tell students to pay particular attention to the stage directions in order to keep track of what's happening to each main character: the prince and the pauper. Help students use a two-column chart like the one on page T657 to list the plot events under each character's name.

■ Vocabulary Preview

Words to Know
heir *n.* one who gets a person's money or title after the person dies
affliction *n.* cause of pain
impostor *n.* person who pretends to be someone else
oppress *v.* rule harshly

 For direct instruction on Words to Know, see page T189.

■ Building Background

The novel *The Prince and the Pauper* was written by Mark Twain, whose given name was Samuel Langhorne Clemens. Although the book is considered a classic today, it received mixed reviews when it was published in 1881. A group of refined New England readers appreciated Twain's depiction of old London, which he captured after spending months studying old British manuscripts. Others, however, criticized anachronisms in Twain's language.

The pictures in this version of the play come from the movie *The Prince and the Pauper* produced in 1937, starring Errol Flynn as Miles Hendon, befriender of the Prince, and twins Bobby and Billy Mauch as the prince and the pauper.

Vocabulary Strategy: Preteaching

Context Clues Explain that readers can often figure out the meaning of an unfamiliar word by looking for **context clues,** words and phrases near the word that give hints to its meaning. Have students circle the context clues for the underlined words in the following sentences.

1. This <u>impostor</u> has been (pretending to be the Prince).

2. I have always dreamed of (seeing) a real prince, if (only for a moment). I hope to <u>glimpse</u> him today.

 For more on Context Clues, see page T189.

Five hundred years ago, England was not an easy place to live, especially if you were poor. The pauper in the title of this play was very poor—a **pauper** is a person who has nothing at all. Paupers made their living by begging in the streets. Even children were sent out to the streets to beg. Keep this in mind as you read *The Prince and the Pauper*.

FOCUS

Try to visualize the setting and the stage directions to figure out what is going on at the beginning of the play.

Cast of Characters
Edward, Prince of Wales
Tom Canty, the Pauper
Lord Hertford
Lord St. John
King Henry VIII
Herald
Miles Hendon
John Canty, Tom's father
Hugo, a young thief
Two Women
Justice
Constable (policeman)
Jailer
Sir Hugh Hendon
Two Prisoners
Two Guards
Three Pages
Lords and Ladies
Villagers

All photographs of characters are from the movie version of *The Prince and the Pauper*.

 Scene 1
Time: 1547.
Setting: *Westminster Palace, England. Gates leading to courtyard are right. Slightly to left, off courtyard and inside gates, interior of palace* anteroom *is visible. There is couch with rich robe draped on it, screen at rear, bellcord, mirror, chairs, and table holding bowl of nuts and large golden seal. Piece of armor hangs on one wall. Exits rear*
10 *and downstage.*

> anteroom
> (ăn' tē rŏŏm')
> waiting room

 At Curtain Rise: Two Guards *stand left and right of gates. Several* Villagers *hover nearby, straining to see into courtyard where* Prince *is playing.* Two Women *enter right.*

COMPREHENSION

FOCUS SKILL: Sequence

Explain that **sequence** is the order in which things happen in time. Paying attention to **signal words**—such as *first, before, next*—in the stage directions will help students follow the sequence.

 For direct instruction on Sequence, see page T188.

LITERATURE

FOCUS SKILL: Plot

Remind students that the **plot** is the sequence of events in a story. Explain that the plot is about a problem that a character or characters must solve. Review the idea that the **climax** is the most important event, one that is the turning point of a story. The climax brings a change to the main character.

For direct instruction on Plot, see page T188.

Use the questions that follow to encourage literary analysis.

A When and where does this play begin? *(in 1547; outside Westminster Palace, England)* **setting**

B What kind of characters do you think will be involved in this play? *(royalty and common people)* **plot**

VOCABULARY

FOCUS SKILL: Context Clues

Remind students to try to use **context clues** to figure out any words they don't know.

A **courtyard** Students can use context clues to figure out that a *courtyard* is a space enclosed by gates or the walls of a building.

FOR ENGLISH LEARNERS

Help students understand the following expressions and idioms:

Line 6: draped on it
Line 6: screen at rear

1st Woman. I have walked all morning just to have a glimpse of Westminster Palace.

2nd Woman. Maybe if we can get near enough to the gates, we can see the young prince. (*Tom Canty, dirty and ragged, comes out of crowd and steps close to gates.*)

20

Tom. I have always dreamed of seeing a real prince! (*Excited, he presses his nose against the gates.*)

1st Guard. Mind your manners, you young beggar! (*Seizes Tom by collar and sends him sprawling into crowd. Villagers laugh as Tom slowly gets to his feet.*)

(A)

(B)

Prince (*rushing to gates*). How dare you treat a poor subject of the King in such a manner! Open the gates and let him in!

30

(*As Villagers see Prince, they remove hats, and bow low.*)

> **subject**
> (sŭb′ jĭkt)
> person under the
> king's control

Villagers (*shouting together*). Long live the Prince of Wales! (*Guards open gates and Tom slowly passes through, as if in a dream.*)

Prince (*to Tom*). You look tired, and you have been treated cruelly. I am Edward, Prince of Wales. What is your name?

Tom (*in awe*). Tom Canty, Your Highness.

(B)

THINK IT THROUGH
How did Tom Canty get into the palace?

How does the boy named Tom inspire the Prince to do something risky?

40

Prince. Come into the palace with me, Tom. (*Prince leads Tom into anteroom. Villagers pantomime conversation, and all but a few exit.*) Where do you live, Tom?

> **pantomime**
> (păn′ tə mīm′)
> pretend to talk,
> but make no
> sound

(C)

Tom. In Offal Court, Your Highness.

Prince. Offal Court? That's an odd name. Do you have parents?

Tom. Yes, Your Highness.

Prince. How does your father treat you?

Tom. If it please you, Your Highness, when I am not able to beg for a penny for our supper, he treats me to beatings.

50

> **REREAD**
> What kind of life
> does Tom have?

(C)

Prince (*shocked*). What! My father is not a calm man, but he does not beat me. (*looks at Tom thoughtfully*) You speak well and have an easy grace. Have you been schooled?

Tom. Very little, Your Highness. A good priest who shares our house has taught me from his books.

Prince. Do you have a pleasant life in Offal Court?

Tom. Pleasant enough, Your Highness, save when I am hungry. We have Punch and Judy shows, and sometimes we lads have fights in the street.

60

(C)

Prince (*eagerly*). I should like that. Tell me more.

Tom. In summer, we run races and swim in the river, and we love to wallow in the mud.

(D)

COMPREHENSION

(A) Ask students why they think the guard tosses Tom into the crowd and tells him to mind his manners. (*The guard doesn't want Tom to bother the Prince.*) **making inferences**

(B) THINK IT THROUGH How did Tom Canty get into the palace? (*The Prince invited him in.*) **clarifying**

(C) REREAD What kind of life does Tom have? (*a hard one: begs for food and father beats him*) **clarifying**

LITERATURE

(C) Have a volunteer look up *offal* in a dictionary (waste parts of butchered animals). Point out that it is pronounced like *awful*. Twain made a play on words here, using a homonym that describes the place Tom lived. **humor**

VOCABULARY

(B) sprawling Help students see that the context clues *by collar, sends him into the crowd,* and *gets to his feet* help explain *sprawling*.

(C) Punch and Judy shows Explain that these were puppet shows in old England.

(D) wallow Ask what "in the mud" suggests about the meaning of *wallow*. (*play, slosh*)

FOR ENGLISH LEARNERS

Help students understand the following expressions:

Line 22: presses his nose against the gates
Line 23: Mind your manners
Line 41: all but a few exit
Line 50: treats me to beatings
Line 54: an easy grace
Line 59: save when I am hungry

Prince (*wistfully*). If I could wear your clothes and
play in the mud just once, with no one to forbid
me, I think I could give up the crown!

Tom (*shaking his head*). And if I could wear your fine
clothes just once, Your Highness. . .

70 **Prince.** Would you like that? Come then. We shall
change places. You can take off your rags and put
on my clothes—and I will put on
yours. (*He leads* Tom *behind screen,
and they return shortly, each wearing
the other's clothes.*) Let's look in this
mirror. (*leads* Tom *to mirror*)

> **REREAD**
> Describe the
> Prince now.
> Describe Tom.

D

Tom (*in the* Prince's *clothes*). Oh, Your Highness, it is
not proper for me to wear such clothes.

E
80
Prince (*in* Tom's *rags, excitedly*). Heavens,
do you not see it? We look like brothers!
We have the same features and bearing.
If we went about together, dressed alike,
there is no one who could say which is the
Prince of Wales and which is Tom Canty.

D

> **bearing**
> (bâr' ĭng)
> the way a person
> stands, sits, walks,
> or behaves

F
THINK IT THROUGH
Why are the Prince and Tom envious of each other's lives?

FOCUS
Read on to find out how the Prince gets into trouble.

Tom (*drawing back, rubbing hand*). Your Highness, I
am frightened. . . .

Prince. Do not worry. (*seeing* Tom *rub hand*) Is that a
bruise on your hand?

Tom. Yes, but it is a slight thing, Your Highness.

90 **Prince** (*angrily*). It was shameful and cruel of that
guard to strike you. Do not stir a step until I come
back. I command you! (*He picks up
golden seal and carefully puts it into
piece of armor. He then dashes out to
gates.*) Open! Unbar the gates at once!
(2nd Guard *opens gates, and as* Prince
runs out, 1st Guard *seizes him,* boxes *him
on the ear, and knocks him to ground.*)

> **REREAD**
> Watch for this
> seal later.

G

E

> **boxes**
> (bŏk' sĭz)
> hits

1st Guard. Take that, you little beggar, for
100 the trouble you have made for me with the Prince.
(*Villagers roar with laughter.*)

Prince (*picking himself up, turning on* Guard
furiously). I am Prince of Wales! You shall hang for
laying your hand on me!

E

COMPREHENSION

D **REREAD** Describe the Prince now.
Describe Tom. *(The Prince is in
rags; Tom is in royal clothing.)*
visualizing

E At what point does the Prince
notice that he and Tom look like
brothers? *(after they change into
each other's clothes)* **sequence**

F **THINK IT THROUGH** Why are the
Prince and Tom envious of each
other's lives? *(The Prince never
plays in the mud; Tom never wears
fine clothes.)* **making inferences**

G **REREAD** Watch for this seal later.
*(Explain that a seal is a device with
a design or words on it, used to
stamp official documents. Ask students to predict how it might be
important in the plot.)* **plot**
LITERATURE

LITERATURE

D Ask students to notice that the
conflict has been introduced
here. What might happen? *(Since
the boys look like twins, they could
switch places.)* **conflict**

E What mistake has the Prince
made here? *(He assumed the
guard knew he was the Prince.)*
plot

VOCABULARY

E **unbar** Students can use context
clues to figure out that when the
Prince tells the guards to *unbar*
the gates, he is saying to unlock,
or open, them.

FOR ENGLISH LEARNERS

Help students understand the following expressions and idioms:

Line 81: the same features and
bearing
Line 82: went about together
Line 85: drawing back
Line 91: stir a step
Line 101: roar with laughter

1st Guard (*presenting arms; mockingly*). I salute Your Gracious Highness!
F (*then, angrily shoving* Prince *aside*) Be off, you mad bag of rags! (Prince *is surrounded by* Villagers, *who hustle him off.*)

> REREAD
> Why does the guard treat the Prince this way?

H

110 **Villagers** (*ad lib, as they exit, shouting*). Make way for His Royal Highness! Make way for the Prince of Wales! Hail to the Prince! (*etc.*)

I **THINK IT THROUGH**
What has happened to the Prince?

FOCUS
What is happening at the same time to Tom, the beggar dressed as the Prince?

Tom (*admiring himself in mirror*). If only the boys in Offal Court could see me! They will not believe me when I tell them about this. (*looks around anxiously*) But where is the Prince? (*looks cautiously into courtyard. Two Guards immediately snap to attention and salute. He quickly ducks back into anteroom as Lords St. John and Hertford enter at rear.*)

F 120

G **Hertford** (*going toward* Tom, *then stopping and bowing low*). My Lord, you look distressed. What is wrong?

> REREAD
> Who does Hertford think he's talking to?

J

Tom (*trembling*). Oh, I beg of you, be merciful. I am no prince, but poor Tom Canty of Offal Court. Please let me see the Prince, and he will give my rags back to me and let me go unhurt.
130 (*kneeling*) Please, be merciful and spare me!

> merciful
> (mûr′ sĭ fəl)
> showing great kindness

G

136 Unit 4 Who's in Charge?

Hertford (*disturbed*). Your Highness, on your knees? To me? (*bows quickly, then, aside to* St. John) The Prince has gone mad! We must inform the King. (*to* Tom) A moment, Your Highness. (Hertford *and* St. John *exit rear.*)

Tom. Oh, there is no hope for me now. They will hang me for certain! (Hertford *and* St. John *reenter, supporting* King. Tom *watches in awe as they help him to couch, where he sinks down wearily.*)

140 **King** (*beckoning* Tom *close to him*). Now, my son, Edward, my prince. What is this? Do you mean to deceive me, the King, your father, who loves you and treats you so kindly?

Tom (*dropping to his knees*). You are the King? Then I have no hope!

> REREAD
> Why do you think Tom is scared?

K

H

King. (*stunned*). My child, you are not well. Do not break your father's old heart. Say you know me.

Tom. Yes, you are my lord the King, whom God
150 preserve.

King. True, that is right. Now, you will not deny that you are Prince of Wales, as they say you did just a while ago?

Tom. Your Grace, believe me, I am the lowest of your subjects, being born a pauper, and it is by great mistake that I am here. I am too young to die. Oh, please, spare me, sire!

King (*amazed*). Die? Do not talk so, my child. You shall not die.

160 **Tom** (*gratefully*). God save you, my king! And now, may I go?

King. Go? Where would you go?

The Prince and the Pauper 137

Tom. Back to the alley where I was born and bred to misery.

King. My poor child, rest your head here. (*He holds Tom's head and pats his shoulder, then turns to Hertford and St. John.*) Alas, I am old and ill, and my son is mad. But this shall pass. Mad or sane, he is my heir and shall rule England. Tomorrow he shall be installed and confirmed in his princely dignity! Bring the Great Seal!

heir
(âr)
n. one who gets a person's money or title after the person dies

Hertford (*bowing low*). Please, Your Majesty, you took the Great Seal from the Chancellor two days ago to give to His Highness the Prince.

King. So I did. (*to Tom*) My child, tell me, where is the Great Seal?

Tom (*trembling*). Indeed, my lord, I do not know.

REREAD
Why doesn't Tom know where the seal is?

King. Ah, your affliction hangs heavily upon you. 'Tis no matter. You will remember later. Listen, carefully! (*gently, but firmly*) I command you to hide your affliction in all ways that be within your power. You shall deny to no one that you are the true prince, and if your memory should fail you upon any occasion of state, you shall be advised by your uncle, the Lord Hertford.

affliction
(ə flĭk' shən)
n. cause of pain

Tom (*resigned*). The King has spoken. The King shall be obeyed.

THINK IT THROUGH
Why does the King think his son is mad?

FOCUS
Will Tom convince anyone that he is not the Prince?

King. And now, my child, I go to rest. (*He stands weakly, and Hertford leads him off, rear.*)

Tom (*wearily, to St. John*). May it please your lordship to let me rest now?

St. John. So it please Your Highness, it is for you to command and us to obey. But it is wise that you rest, for this evening you must attend the Lord Mayor's banquet in your honor. (*He pulls bellcord, and Three Pages enter and kneel before Tom.*)

Tom. Banquet? (*Terrified, he sits on couch and reaches for cup of water, but 1st Page instantly seizes cup, drops to one knee, and serves it to him. Tom starts to take off boots, but 2nd Page stops him and does it for him. He tries to remove cape and gloves, and 3rd Page does it for him.*) I wonder that you do not try to breathe for me also! (*Lies down cautiously. Pages cover him with robe, then back away and exit.*)

St. John (*to Hertford, as he enters*). Plainly, what do you think?

plainly
(plān' lē)
honestly

Hertford. Plainly, this. The King is near death, my nephew the Prince of Wales is clearly mad and will mount the throne mad. God protect England, for she will need it!

St. John. Does it not seem strange that madness could so change his manner from what it used to be? It troubles me, his saying he is not the Prince.

COMPREHENSION

L Follow up on predictions made earlier. Ask: Why do you think the King wants the Great Seal? *(probably for documents for tomorrow's installation of the Prince)* **predicting**

M **REREAD** Why doesn't Tom know where the seal is? *(because he doesn't know what it is)* **making inferences**

N **THINK IT THROUGH** Why does the King think his son is mad? *(He doesn't know that Tom is not his son, so what Tom is saying doesn't make sense.)* **cause and effect**

LITERATURE

I If you were playing Tom's part in this play, how would you read lines 190–191? Why? *(as if he's given up trying to convince the King who he is and will go along with the King's command; because the stage direction says he is resigned)* **dialogue**

J What do others think about Tom? *(Hertford and the King think he's crazy.)* **characterization**

VOCABULARY

FOR ENGLISH LEARNERS

Help students understand the following expressions and idioms:

Line 181: your affliction hangs heavily upon you
Line 182: 'Tis no matter
Line 186: deny to no one
Line 187: if your memory should fail you upon any occasion of state

Hertford. Peace, my lord! If he were an
impostor and called himself the Prince,
that would be natural. But was there ever
an impostor, who being called Prince by
the King and court, denied it? Never!
This is the true Prince gone mad. And tonight all
(K) London shall honor him. (*Hertford and St. John
exit. Tom sits up, looks around helplessly, then gets
up.*)

impostor
(ĭm pŏs′ tər)
n. person who
pretends to be
someone else

230 **Tom.** I should have thought to order something to eat.
(*sees bowl of nuts on table*) Ah! Here are some
(L) nuts! (*Looks around, sees Great Seal in armor,
takes it out, looks at it curiously.*) This will make a
good nutcracker. (*He takes bowl of nuts, sits on
couch and begins to crack nuts with Great Seal and
eat them, as curtain falls.*)

* * * * *

THINK IT THROUGH
(O) Why do people believe that Tom is the Prince, even though
he keeps saying that he is not?

FOCUS
Now read on to discover what's happening to the real Prince
out on the streets.

Scene 2

Time: *Later that night.*

Setting: *A street in London, near Offal Court. Played
before curtain.*

240 **At Curtain Rise:** Prince *limps in, dirty and
tousled. He looks around wearily.
Several* Villagers *pass by, pushing against
him.*

tousled
(tou′ zəld)
made untidy

Prince (*dressed in rags*). I have never seen this poor
section of London. I must be near Offal Court. If
(M) only I can find it before I drop! (*John
Canty steps out of crowd, seizes* Prince
roughly.)

250 **Canty.** Out at this time of night, and I
warrant you haven't brought a farthing
home! If that is the case and I do not
break all the bones in your miserable
body, then I am not John Canty.

warrant
(wôr′ ənt)
declare

farthing
(fär′ thĭng)
old British coin

Prince (*eagerly*). Oh, are you his father?

Canty. *His* father? I am *your* father, and—

(P) REREAD
Who is John
Canty and who
does he think
the Prince is?

Prince. Take me to the palace at once,
and your son will be returned to you.
The King, my father, will make you rich beyond
your wildest dreams. Oh, save me, for I am indeed
260 the Prince of Wales.

Canty (*staring in amazement*). Gone stark mad! But
mad or not, I'll soon find where the soft places lie
in your bones. Come home! (*starts to drag* Prince
off)

Prince (*struggling*). Let me go! I am the Prince of
Wales, and the King shall have your life for this!

Canty (*angrily*). I'll take no more of your madness!
(*Raises stick to strike, but* Prince *struggles free and
runs off.* Canty *runs after him.*)

* * * * *

THINK IT THROUGH
(Q) Why does Tom's father think the Prince is mad?

COMPREHENSION

(O) **THINK IT THROUGH** Why do people believe that Tom is the Prince, even though he keeps saying that he is not? (*They believe an impostor would never admit it.*) **cause and effect**

(P) **REREAD** Who is John Canty and who does he think the Prince is? (*Tom Canty's father; his son Tom*) **making inferences**

(Q) **THINK IT THROUGH** Why does Tom's father think the Prince is mad? (*He thinks his son is claiming to be the Prince of Wales.*) **making inferences** How is the Prince's situation like Tom's? (*Others think the boys are mad and don't believe them.*) **compare and contrast**

LITERATURE

(K) What complications have happened in the plot on Tom's side? (*They think he's the Prince and crazy; he can't convince them that he's not; tonight he has to attend a banquet and pretend he's the Prince.*) **plot**

(L) What do the stage directions reveal in lines 232–236? (*that Tom uses the Great Seal as a nutcracker*) What do they remind us about? (*where the seal is*) **stage directions**

(M) Whom does the Prince meet near Offal Court? (*Tom's father, John Canty*) **plot**

VOCABULARY

FOR ENGLISH LEARNERS

Help students understand the following expressions:

Line 226: This is the true Prince gone mad

Line 236: as curtain falls

Line 262: where the soft places lie in your bones

R FOCUS
Now read to find out what's happening back at the Palace. Will Tom really be crowned King?

Scene 3

S 270 **Setting:** *Same as Scene 1 (inside Palace), with addition of dining table, set with dishes and goblets, on raised platform. Throne-like chair is at head of table.*

At Curtain Rise: *A banquet is in progress. Tom, in royal robes, sits at head of table, with Hertford at his right and St. John at his left. Lords and Ladies sit around table, eating and talking softly.*

Tom (*dressed as Prince; to Hertford*). What is this, my Lord? (*holds up plate*)

280 **Hertford.** Lettuce and turnips, Your Highness.

Tom. Lettuce and turnips? I have never seen them before. Am I to eat them?

N **Hertford** (*discreetly*). Yes, Your Highness, if you so desire. (*Tom begins to eat food with his fingers. Fanfare of trumpets is heard, and Herald enters, carrying scroll. All turn to look.*)

> **discreetly**
> (dĭ skrēt′ lē)
> in a wisely cautious way

Herald (*reading from scroll*). His Majesty, King Henry VIII, is dead! The King is dead! (*All rise and turn to Tom, who sits, stunned.*)

H 290

All (*together*). The King is dead. Long live the King! Long live Edward, the King of England! (*All bow to Tom. Herald bows and exits.*)

O

Hertford (*to Tom*). Your Majesty, we must call the council. Come, St. John.

> **council**
> (koun′ səl)
> group that makes decisions

> **REREAD**
> Why are they calling Tom the King?

T

(*Hertford and St. John lead Tom off at rear. Lords and Ladies follow, talking among themselves. At gates, down right, Villagers enter and mill about.*
300 *Prince enters right, pounds on gates and shouts.*)

Prince (*still in rags*). Open the gates! I am the Prince of Wales! Open, I say! And though I am friendless with no one to help me, I will not be driven from my ground.

Miles Hendon (*entering through crowd*). Though you be Prince or not, you are indeed a gallant lad and not friendless. Here I stand to prove it, and you might have a worse friend than Miles Hendon.

> **gallant**
> (găl′ ənt)
> brave

310 **1st Villager.** 'Tis another prince in disguise. Take the lad and dunk him in the pond! (*He seizes Prince, but Miles strikes him with flat of his sword. Crowd, now angry, presses forward threateningly, when fanfare of trumpets is heard offstage. Herald, carrying scroll, enters up left at gates.*)

Herald. Make way for the King's messenger! (*reading from scroll*) His Majesty, King Henry VIII is dead! The King is dead! (*He exits right, repeating*
320 *message, and Villagers stand in stunned silence.*)

Prince (*stunned*). The King is dead!

1st Villager (*shouting*). Long live Edward, King of England!

Villagers (*together*). Long live the King! (*shouting, ad lib*) Long live King Edward! Heaven protect Edward, King of England!

Miles (*taking Prince by arm*). Come, lad, before the crowd remembers us. I have a room at the inn, and

---

COMPREHENSION

R **FOCUS** Have students predict whether Tom will become king, and check their predictions later. **predicting**

S Over how much time do Scenes 1–3 take place? How do you know? *(an afternoon and evening; The time for Scene 2 says "Later that night." The introduction to Scene 3 tells readers to find out what's happening back at the Palace.)* **sequence**

T **REREAD** Why are they calling Tom the King? *(When a king dies, his son becomes king. Since they think Tom is the Prince, they think he is the new King.)* **making inferences**

LITERATURE

N Why does Hertford speak discreetly in lines 283–284? How might you read Hertford's line? *(He doesn't want others to know that he's advising the mad Prince on what to eat; in a quiet voice or a whisper.)* **dialogue**

O What major event has complicated the plot? *(The King has died.)* **plot**

VOCABULARY

H **stunned** Students should be able to use context clues to figure out that the word *stunned* means "shocked and confused."

FOR ENGLISH LEARNERS

Help students understand the following expressions:

Line 283: if you so desire
Line 285: Fanfare of trumpets
Line 303: I will not be driven from my ground
Line 305: Though you be Prince or not
Line 310: 'Tis
Line 312: flat of his sword

330 you can stay there. (*He hurries off with stunned Prince. Tom, led by Hertford, enters courtyard up rear. Villagers see them.*)

Villagers (*together*). Long live the King! (*They fall to their knees as curtains close.*)

* * * * *

REREAD
Why might you call this a "near miss"?

THINK IT THROUGH
How has the King's death affected both Tom and the Prince?

FOCUS
Read Scene 4 to learn what happens when Miles falls asleep.

Scene 4

Setting: Miles's *room at inn. At right is table set with dishes and bowls of food, a chair at each side. At left is bed, with table and chair next to it, and a window. Candle is on table.*

At Curtain Rise: Miles *and* Prince *approach table.*

340 **Miles.** I have had a hot supper prepared. I'll bet you're hungry, lad.

Prince (*dressed in rags*). Yes, I am. It's kind of you to let me stay with you, Miles. I am truly Edward, King of England, and you shall not go unrewarded. (*sits at table*)

Miles (*to himself*). First he called himself Prince, and now King. Well, I will humor him. (*starts to sit*)

Prince (*angrily*). Stop! Would you sit in the presence of the King?

350 **Miles** (*surprised, standing up quickly*). I beg your pardon, Your Majesty. I was not thinking. (*Stares*

uncertainly at Prince, *who sits at table, expectantly.* Miles *starts to uncover dishes of food, serves* Prince *and fills glasses.*)

Prince. Miles, you have a gallant way about you. Are you nobly born?

Miles. My father is a baronet, Your Majesty.

baronet
(băr′ ə nĭt)
British nobleman

Prince. Then you also must be a baronet.

360 **Miles** (*shaking his head*). My father banished me from home seven years ago, so I fought in the wars. I was taken prisoner, and I have spent the past seven years in prison. Now I am free, and I am returning home.

banished
(băn′ ĭsht)
forced to leave

Prince. You must have been shamefully wronged! But I will make things right for you. You have saved me

144 Unit 4 Who's in Charge?

The Prince and the Pauper **145**

COMPREHENSION

U REREAD Why might you call this a "near miss"? *(The two boys were almost in the same place at the same time.)* **plot** LITERATURE

V THINK IT THROUGH How has the King's death affected both Tom and the Prince? *(Tom is now being mistaken for the King instead of the Prince; the real Prince is so stunned he goes off with a stranger who promises to help him.)* **cause and effect**

LITERATURE

P Why does the Prince call himself King now? How does this show the conflict? *(He should be king because his father has died, but he's stuck in his role as a beggar.)* **conflict**

VOCABULARY

FOR ENGLISH LEARNERS

Help students understand the following expressions:

Line 347: I will humor him
Line 355: a gallant way about you
Line 356: nobly born

from injury and possible death. Name your reward and if it be within the compass of my royal power, it is yours.

370

Miles (*pausing briefly, then dropping to his knee*). Since Your Majesty is pleased to hold my simple duty worthy of reward, I ask that I and my successors may hold the privilege of sitting in the presence of the King.

> REREAD
> Why is Miles acting like this?

W

I

Prince (*taking* Miles's *sword, tapping him lightly on each shoulder*). Rise and seat yourself. (*returns sword to* Miles, *then rises and goes over to bed*)

Miles (*rising*). He should have been born a king. He plays the part to a marvel! If I had not thought of this favor, I might have had to stand for weeks. (*sits down and begins to eat*)

380

146 Unit 4 Who's in Charge?

Prince. Sir Miles, you will stand guard while I sleep. (*lies down and instantly falls asleep*)

Miles. Yes, Your Majesty. (*With a* **rueful** *look at his uneaten supper, he stands up.*) Poor little chap. I suppose his mind has been disordered with ill usages. (*covers* Prince *with his cape*) Well, I will be his friend and watch over him. (*Blows out candle, then yawns and sits on chair next to bed, and falls asleep.* John Canty *and* Hugo *appear at window, peer around room, then enter cautiously through window. They lift the sleeping* Prince, *staring nervously at* Miles.)

> **rueful**
> (roo′ fəl)
> unhappy

390

> REREAD
> Does Miles believe the Prince? How do you know?

X

Q

Canty (*in a loud whisper*). I swore the day he was born he would be a thief and a beggar, and I won't lose him now. Lead the way to the camp, Hugo! (Canty *and* Hugo *carry* Prince *off right, as* Miles *sleeps on and curtain falls.*)

400

* * * * *

Y

THINK IT THROUGH
Why do John Canty and Hugo carry off the Prince?

FOCUS
What will the Prince's life be like with John Canty?

Z

Scene 5
Time: *Two weeks later.*
Setting: *Country village street. May be played before curtain.*
Before Curtain Rise: Villagers *walk about.* Canty, Hugo, *and* Prince *enter.*

The Prince and the Pauper 147

COMPREHENSION

W **REREAD** Why is Miles acting like this? (*He's humoring the Prince because he feels sorry for him.*) **making inferences**

X **REREAD** Does Miles believe the Prince? How do you know? (*No; he says the boy's mind is disordered.*) **making inferences**

Y **THINK IT THROUGH** Why do John Canty and Hugo carry off the Prince? (*They think he is Tom, and they want him to return to begging.*) **motive** LITERATURE

Z Which signal words tell you how much time has passed between Scenes 4 and 5? (*"Two weeks later"*) **sequence**

LITERATURE

Q In the stage directions, in lines 392–401, what important actions further the plot? (*Miles falls asleep; John Canty and Hugo carry the Prince away.*) **plot**

VOCABULARY

I **privilege** Help students use the context clues (*reward, sitting in the presence of a king, favor*) to understand that privilege means "special advantage."

FOR ENGLISH LEARNERS

Help students understand the following expressions and idioms:

Line 369: within the compass of my royal power

Line 380: plays the part to a marvel

Line 389: disordered with ill usages

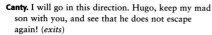

Canty. I will go in this direction. Hugo, keep my mad son with you, and see that he does not escape again! (*exits*)

410 **Hugo** (*seizing* Prince *by the arm*). He won't escape! I'll see that he earns his bread today, or else!

Prince (*dressed in rags; pulling away*). I will not beg with you, and I will not steal! I have suffered enough in this miserable company of thieves!

Hugo. You shall suffer more if you do not do as I tell you! (*raises clenched fist at* Prince) Refuse if you dare! (Woman *enters, carrying wrapped bundle in a basket on her arm.*) Wait here until I come back.

420 (Hugo *sneaks along after* Woman, *then snatches her bundle, runs back to* Prince, *and thrusts it into his arms.*) Run after me and call, "Stop, thief!" Be sure you lead her astray! (*Runs off.* Prince *throws down bundle in disgust.*)

> **REREAD**
> What does Hugo do to try to trick the woman?

(AA)

Woman. Help! Thief! Stop, thief! (*rushes at* Prince *and seizes him, just as several* Villagers *enter*) You little thief! What do you mean by robbing a poor woman? Somebody bring the constable! (Miles *enters and watches.*)

430 **1st Villager** (*grabbing* Prince). I'll teach him a lesson, the little villain!

Prince (*struggling*). Unhand me! I did not rob this woman!

Miles (*stepping forth and pushing man back with the flat of his sword*). Let us proceed gently, my friends. This is a matter for the law.

Prince (*springing to* Miles's *side*). You have come just in time, Sir Miles. Carve this rabble to rags!

148　Unit 4　Who's in Charge?

Miles. Speak softly. Trust in me and all shall go well.
440 (Constable *enters*)

Constable (*reaching for* Prince). Come along, young rascal!

Miles. Gently, good friend. He shall go peaceably to the Justice.

(BB)

Prince. I will not go before a Justice! I did not do this thing!

Miles (*taking him aside*). Sire, will you reject the laws of the ⟨realm⟩, yet demand that your subjects respect them?

> realm
> (rēlm)
> kingdom

450 **Prince** (*after a pause; calmly*). You are right, Sir Miles. Whatever the King requires a subject to suffer under the law, he will suffer himself while he holds the station of a subject.

> **REREAD**
> How do Miles and the Prince feel about obeying the law?

(CC)

(Constable *leads them off right.* Villagers *follow.*)

* * *

Setting: *Office of the* Justice. *A high bench is at center.*

At Curtain Rise: Justice *sits behind bench.* Constable
460 *enters with* Miles *and* Prince, *followed by* Villagers. Woman *carries wrapped bundle.*

Constable (*to* Justice). A young thief, your worship, is accused of stealing a dressed pig from this poor woman.

Justice (*looking down at* Prince, *then* Woman). My good woman, are you absolutely certain this lad stole your pig?

Woman. It was none other than he, your worship.

The Prince and the Pauper　149

COMPREHENSION

(AA) **REREAD** What does Hugo do to try to trick the woman? *(He steals her bundle and gives it to the Prince. Then he tells the Prince to make it look like he has retrieved the bundle from Hugo and is chasing him—only he wants the Prince to run the wrong way so that they won't get caught.)* **sequence**

(BB) Why has the Prince been arrested? *(for robbing a woman)* **clarifying**

(CC) **REREAD** How do Miles and the Prince feel about obeying the law? *(They both feel that the law should be obeyed; however, the Prince says he will obey it only while he is in the position of a subject.)* **making inferences**

VOCABULARY

FOR ENGLISH LEARNERS

Help students understand the following expressions and idioms:

Line 432: Unhand me
Line 438: Carve this rabble to rags
Line 463: dressed pig

Justice. Are there no witnesses to the contrary? (*All shake their heads.*) Then the lad stands convicted. (*to* Woman) What do you hold this property to be worth?

> **REREAD**
> What does this tell about how the law treats common people?

DD

Woman. Three shillings and eight pence, your worship.

> shillings, pence
> British coins

Justice (*leaning down to* Woman). Good woman, do you know that when one steals a thing above the value of thirteen pence, the law says he shall hang for it?

480 **Woman** (*upset*). Oh, what have I done? I would not hang the poor boy for the whole world! Save me from this, your worship. What can I do?

J

Justice (*gravely*). You may revise the value, since it is not yet written in the record.

Woman. Then call the pig eight pence, your worship.

Justice. So be it. You may take your property and go. (*Woman starts off, and is followed by* Constable. Miles *follows them cautiously down right.*)

490 **Constable** (*stopping* Woman). Good woman, I will buy your pig from you. (*Takes coins from his pocket.*) Here is eight pence.

Woman. Eight pence! It cost me three shillings and eight pence.

Constable. Indeed! Then come back before his worship and answer for this. The lad must hang!

> **REREAD**
> Why does the woman let the constable pay so little for the pig?

EE

Woman. No! No! Say no more. Give me the eight pence and hold your peace.

500 (Constable *hands her coins and takes pig.* Woman *exits, angrily.* Miles *returns to bench.*)

Justice. The boy is sentenced to a fortnight in the common jail. Take him away, Constable! (Justice *exits.* Prince *gives* Miles *a nervous glance.*)

> fortnight
> (fôrt′ nīt)
> two weeks

Miles (*following* Constable). Good sir, turn your back a moment and let the poor lad escape. He is innocent.

Constable (*outraged*). What? You say this to me? Sir, I

510 arrest you in—

Miles. Do not be so hasty! (*slyly*) The pig you have purchased for eight pence may cost you your neck, man.

Constable (*laughing nervously*). Ah, but I was merely jesting with the woman, sir.

> jesting
> (jĕs′ tĭng)
> joking

R

Miles. Would the Justice think it a jest?

Constable. Good sir! The Justice has no more sympathy with a jest than a dead corpse! (*perplexed*) Very well, I will turn my back and see

520 nothing! But go quickly! (*exits*)

Miles (*to* Prince). Come, my liege. We are free to go. And that band of thieves shall not set hands on you again. I swear it!

> liege
> (lēj)
> lord or king

Prince (*wearily*). Can you believe, Sir Miles, that in the last fortnight, I, the King of England, have escaped from thieves and begged for food on the road? I have slept in a barn with a calf! I have washed dishes

530 in a peasant's kitchen, and narrowly escaped death. And not once in all my

> **REREAD**
> Compare the Prince's experience with Tom's.

FF

COMPREHENSION

DD **REREAD** What does this tell about how the law treats common people? (*The law doesn't treat them very fairly.*) **making inferences**

EE **REREAD** Why does the woman let the constable pay so little for the pig? (*If she says the pig is worth more, the boy will have to hang.*) **cause and effect**

FF **REREAD** Compare the Prince's experience with Tom's. (*The Prince has lived like a pauper, while Tom has lived like a prince.*) **compare and contrast**

LITERATURE

R How does Miles keep the Prince out of jail? (*He threatens to turn the constable in, so the constable lets the Prince escape.*) **plot**

VOCABULARY

J **revise** Students should be able to use context clues to figure out that the word *revise* means "change or fix."

FOR ENGLISH LEARNERS

Help students understand the following expressions and idioms:

Line 469: no witnesses to the contrary
Line 471: the lad stands convicted
Line 496: answer for this
Line 499: hold your peace
Line 512: may cost you your neck
Line 519: turn my back and see nothing

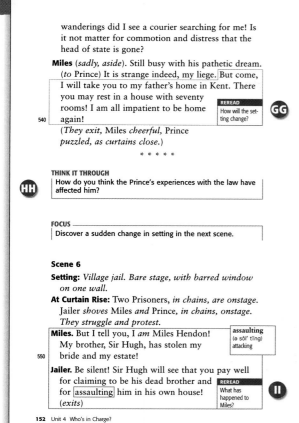

wanderings did I see a courier searching for me! Is it not matter for commotion and distress that the head of state is gone?

Miles (*sadly, aside*). Still busy with his pathetic dream. (*to* Prince) It is strange indeed, my liege. But come, I will take you to my father's home in Kent. There you may rest in a house with seventy rooms! I am all impatient to be home again!

540

(*They exit,* Miles *cheerful,* Prince *puzzled, as curtains close.*)

> **REREAD** How will the setting change? **GG**

* * * * *

THINK IT THROUGH

HH How do you think the Prince's experiences with the law have affected him?

FOCUS

Discover a sudden change in setting in the next scene.

Scene 6

Setting: *Village jail. Bare stage, with barred window on one wall.*

At Curtain Rise: *Two Prisoners,* in chains, *are onstage.* Jailer *shoves* Miles *and* Prince, in chains, *onstage. They struggle and protest.*

Miles. But I tell you, I *am* Miles Hendon! My brother, Sir Hugh, has stolen my bride and my estate!

550

Jailer. Be silent! Sir Hugh will see that you pay well for claiming to be his dead brother and for assaulting him in his own house! (*exits*)

> **assaulting**
> (ə sôl′ tĭng)
> attacking

> **REREAD** What has happened to Miles? **II**

152 Unit 4 Who's in Charge?

Miles (*sitting with head in hands*). Oh, my dear Edith . . . now wife to my brother Hugh, against her will, and my poor father . . . dead!

1st Prisoner. At least you have your life, sir. I am to be hanged for killing a deer in the King's park.

560

2nd Prisoner. And I must hang for stealing a yard of cloth to dress my children.

S **Prince** (*moved; to* Prisoners). When I mount the throne, you shall be free. And the laws that have dishonored you shall be swept from the books. (*turning away*) Kings should go to school to learn their own laws and be merciful.

K **1st Prisoner.** What does the lad mean? I have heard that the King is mad, but merciful.

2nd Prisoner. He is to be crowned at Westminster

570

tomorrow.

Prince (*violently*). King? What King, good sir?

1st Prisoner. Why, we have only one, his most sacred majesty, King Edward the Sixth.

2nd Prisoner. Whether he be mad or not, his praises are on all men's lips. He has saved many innocent lives, and plans to destroy the cruelest laws that oppress people.

> **oppress**
> (ə prĕs′)
> v. rule harshly

Prince (*turning away, shaking his head*). How can this be? Surely it is not that

580

little beggar boy! (Sir Hugh *enters with* Jailer.)

> **REREAD** What has the Prince just realized? **JJ**

Sir Hugh. Seize the impostor! (Jailer *pulls* Miles *to his feet.*)

Miles. Hugh, this has gone far enough!

The Prince and the Pauper 153

Sir Hugh. You will sit in the public stocks, and the boy would join you if he were not so young. See to it, jailer, and after two hours, you may release them. Meanwhile, I ride to London for the coronation! *(Sir Hugh exits and Miles is hustled out by Jailer.)*

Prince. Coronation! There can be no coronation without me! *(curtain)*

* * * * *

stocks
(stŏks)
wooden frame
with holes for
feet and hands,
used to punish

coronation
(kôr′ə nā′ shən)
ceremony for
crowning a king

KK **THINK IT THROUGH**
What has the Prince learned while in jail?

FOCUS
Learn whether the Prince makes it to the coronation.

Scene 7
Time: Coronation Day.
Setting: *Outside gates of Westminster Abbey, played before curtain. Painted screen or flat at rear represents Abbey. Throne is center. Bench is near it.*
At Curtain Rise: Lords *and* Ladies *crowd Abbey. Outside gates,* Guards *drive back cheering* Villagers, *among them* Miles.
Miles *(distraught).* I've lost him! Poor little chap! He has been swallowed up in the crowd! *(Fanfare of trumpets is heard, then* Hertford, St. John, Lords *and* Ladies *enter slowly, followed by* Pages, *one of whom carries crown on small cushion.* Tom *follows*

procession, looking about nervously. Suddenly, Prince, *in rags, steps from crowd, his hand raised.)*

Prince. I forbid you to set the crown of England upon that head. I am the King! **T**

Hertford. Seize the vagabond!

Tom. I forbid it! He *is* the King! *(kneeling before* Prince*)* Oh, my lord the King, let poor Tom Canty be the first to say, "Put on your crown and enter into your own right again." *(Hertford and several Lords look closely at both boys.)* **LL**

REREAD
Read this passage aloud. Take turns acting out the parts.

Hertford. This is strange indeed. *(to* Tom*)* By your favor, sir, I wish to ask certain questions of this lad.

Prince. I will answer truly whatever you may ask, my lord.

Hertford. But if you have been well trained, you may answer my questions as well as our lord the King. I need definite proof. *(thinks a moment)* Ah! Where lies the Great Seal of England? It has been missing for weeks, and only the true Prince of Wales can say where it lies. **MM**

REREAD
Where did the Prince carefully put the seal at the beginning of the play?

Tom. Wait! Was the seal round and thick, with letters engraved on it? *(Hertford nods.)* I know where it is, but it was not I who put it there. The rightful King shall tell you. *(to* Prince*)* Think, my King, it was the very last thing you did that day before you rushed out of the palace wearing my rags. **NN**

Prince *(pausing).* I recall how we exchanged clothes, but have no recollection of hiding the Great Seal. **L**

154 Unit 4 Who's in Charge?

The Prince and the Pauper 155

COMPREHENSION

KK **THINK IT THROUGH** What has the Prince learned while in jail? *(that the law is unfair, that Tom will be crowned king tomorrow, that the people love Tom)* **details**

LL **REREAD** Read this passage aloud. Take turns acting out the parts. *(Tell students to use the stage directions to help them act out what is happening.)* **stage directions** LITERATURE

MM **REREAD** Where did the Prince carefully put the seal at the beginning of the play? *(into a piece of armor)* **recall**

NN Follow up on predictions made earlier. Ask: How does knowing where the seal is help the Prince regain his position? *(proves who he is)* Does this agree with your earlier prediction about the importance of the seal to the plot? *(Accept all answers.)* **predicting**

LITERATURE

T What has been the main problem of the play? *(The real Prince needs to get back and become king.)* Point out that this scene is the climax of the play: the Prince and Tom get back together in their rightful spots before Tom is crowned king. **climax**

VOCABULARY

L **recollection** Students should figure out this word from the context clue of remembering where the seal is and from the context clue *recall.*

FOR ENGLISH LEARNERS

Help students understand the following expressions and idioms:

Line 596: flat at rear
Line 599: Guards drive back cheering Villagers

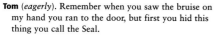

Tom (*eagerly*). Remember when you saw the bruise on my hand you ran to the door, but first you hid this thing you call the Seal.

640 **Prince** (*suddenly*). Ah! I remember! (*to St. John*) My good St. John, you shall find the Great Seal in the armor that hangs on the wall in my [chamber]. (St. John *hesitates, but at a nod from* Tom *hurries off.*)

chamber
(chăm' bər) room

 Tom (*pleased*). Right, my King! Now the [scepter] of England is yours again. (St. John *returns in a moment with Great Seal, holds it up for all to see.*)

scepter
(sĕp' tər) special stick that is a symbol of power

All (*shouting*). Long live Edward, King of
650 England! (Tom *takes off cape and throws it over* Prince's *rags. Trumpet fanfare is heard. St. John takes crown and places it on* Prince. *All kneel.*)

Hertford. Let the small impostor be flung into the Tower!

Prince (*firmly*). I will not have it so. But for him, I would not have my crown. (*to* Tom) My poor boy, how was it you could remember where I hid the Seal?

660 **Tom** (*embarrassed*). I did not know what it was, my King, and I used it to. . . crack nuts. (*All laugh.* Miles *steps forward, staring in amazement.*)

Miles. Is he really the King, the [sovereign] of England, and not the poor and friendless Tom o' Bedlam I thought he was? (*sinks down on bench*) I wish I had a bag to hide my head in!

sovereign
(sŏv' ər ĭn) ruler

156 Unit 4 Who's in Charge?

1st Guard (*rushing up to him*). Stand up, you mannerless clown! How dare you sit in the presence
670 of the King!

Prince. Do not touch him! He is my trusty servant, Miles Hendon, who saved me from shame and possible death. For his service, he owns the right to sit in my presence.

Miles (*bowing, then kneeling*). Your Majesty!

Prince. Rise, Sir Miles. I command that Sir Hugh Hendon, who sits within this hall, be seized and put under lock and key until I have need of him. (*beckons to* Tom) From what I have heard, Tom
680 Canty, you have governed the realm with royal gentleness and mercy in my absence. Henceforth, you shall hold the honorable title of King's Ward! (Tom *kneels and kisses* Prince's *hand.*) And because I have suffered with the poorest of my subjects and felt the cruel force of unjust laws, I pledge myself to a reign of mercy for all! (*All bow low, then rise.*)

All (*shouting*). Long live the King! Long live Edward, King of England!

PP **THINK IT THROUGH**

1. Why did the confusion between the Prince and Tom continue throughout the play?
2. How was Miles rewarded for his friendship and loyalty? How was Tom rewarded for his actions?
3. Why did the Prince promise to rule with mercy for all?

The Prince and the Pauper **157**

COMPREHENSION

OO Follow up on this prediction made earlier: Did Tom become king? (*no*) **predicting**

PP **THINK IT THROUGH**

1. Why did the confusion between the Prince and Tom continue throughout the play? (*They were dressed like each other; Prince was unaware of Tom; they never saw each other.*) **cause and effect**

2. How was Miles rewarded for his friendship and loyalty? How was Tom rewarded for his actions? (*King gave Miles the right to sit in his presence and jailed his brother; gave Tom title of King's Ward*) **details**

3. Why did the Prince promise to rule with mercy for all? (*He had experienced the unjust laws of his kingdom, so he vowed to change them.*) **cause and effect**

Option for Speaking and listening
Have students act out the last two

pages, starting with line 645. To involve the whole class, include the nonspeaking actors (Lords, Ladies, Guards, cheering Villagers, Sir Hugh) as well as those with speeches (Tom, Hertford, Prince, 1st Guard, Miles).

RETEACHING

If students need more help understanding **Sequence,** use pages T639–T641.

LITERATURE

U Point out that after Tom and the Prince's real identities are known, the rest of the play finishes the story and ties up loose ends. This is called **falling action and conclusion. plot**

VOCABULARY

M **henceforth** Students should be able to figure out that *henceforth* means "from now on" or "from today forward."

FOR ENGLISH LEARNERS

Help students understand the following expressions and idioms:

Line 654: flung into the Tower
Line 656: but for him
Line 665: Tom o' Bedlam
Line 678: under lock and key

RETEACHING

If students need more help understanding **Context Clues,** use pages T609–T611.

1. COMPREHENSION

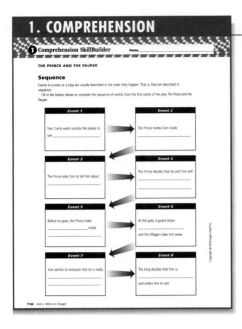

Sequence

Direct Instruction Tell students that writers usually tell about story events in the order in which they happen. The events are described in **sequence.**

Point out that in plays, events are organized by scenes. Readers should understand that time has passed between the end of one scene and the beginning of the next. Point out the way the time is specified at the beginning of Scene 2 (Time: *Later that night*) and the beginning of Scene 5 (Time: *Two weeks later*).

Explain that one event leads logically to the next in *The Prince and the Pauper.* For that reason, it is important to pay attention to the sequence of events within scenes. Read aloud these story events and have students number their sequence. Discuss how the events are connected.
- Miles Hendon takes the Prince away while the crowd is distracted. (3)
- The Prince demands to be let into the castle, and people threaten him. (1)
- A herald announces the King's death. (2)

Comprehension SkillBuilder Answer Key:

1. *the Prince*
2. *the palace*
3. *his life*
4. *switch clothes and change places*

5. *a golden seal, a piece of armor*
6. *the Prince*
7. *a poor boy, not the Prince*
8. *mad*

---

2. LITERATURE

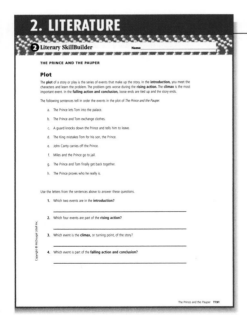

Plot

Direct Instruction Remind students that the **plot** is the sequence of events in a story or play. Draw a plot diagram on the board.

Explain each category in relation to *The Prince and the Pauper:*

Introduction: You meet the main characters and learn what problem they have to solve. (*Prince and Tom; people confuse them with each other*)

Rising Action: The problem gets more complicated. (*Prince gets in trouble; Tom fears punishment*)

Climax: The most important event changes the course of the story. (*Prince and Tom meet and establish true identities*)

Falling Action and Conclusion: The problem is solved: loose ends are tied up. (*Prince proves who he is, becomes king, and rewards people*)

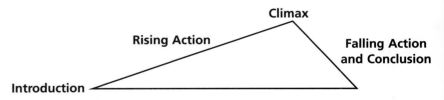

Literary SkillBuilder Answer Key:
1. *a, b* **2.** *c, d, e, f* **3.** *g* **4.** *h*

---

3. VOCABULARY

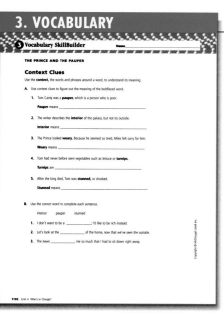

Context Clues

Direct Instruction Tell students that writers often leave clues in the text that help readers understand new or unfamiliar words. Explain that such clues are called **context clues.** Give students these hints on how to recognize and use context clues:

- Words and phrases such as *is, which is, who is, that is,* and *in other words* often signal definition clues. **Example:** *The Prince led Tom into the <u>anteroom</u>. In other words, they went into the waiting room.*
- The word *or* is sometimes a signal that a synonym for a new word will be given. **Example:** *Tom was <u>flabbergasted</u>, or greatly surprised, by the Prince's offer to change places.*
- Words that mean the opposite of the new word can be clues. **Example:** *Tom was fed a <u>sumptuous</u> feast, but he usually had simple food.*
- Writers sometimes provide hints about how a thing looks, sounds, feels, or tastes, or about what it does. **Example:** *A <u>fanfare</u> of trumpets is heard, and Herald enters, carrying scroll.*

Vocabulary SkillBuilder Answer Key:

A.
1. *a person who is poor*
2. *inside*
3. *tired*
4. *vegetables*
5. *shocked*

B.
1. *pauper*
2. *interior*
3. *stunned*

---

4. WORDS TO KNOW

Words to Know

Direct Instruction As you present the **Words to Know,** here are some points you might want to cover. Tell students:

- The base word of *affliction* is *afflict.* The word *afflict* is a verb. By adding suffixes to the base word, you can change the parts of speech (for example, *afflict* + *-ion* = *affliction,* which is a noun).
- The word *impostor* can also be spelled *imposter.* The first spelling in a dictionary is preferred.
- The word *oppress* can also mean "to cause to feel burdened in spirit." **Example:** *Too much grief can <u>oppress</u> a person.* The word *oppress* originated from the Latin word *opprimere,* which means "to press against."

Writing Activity Encourage students to be as creative as they want. Have volunteers read their creations aloud to the class.

Words to Know SkillBuilder Answer Key:

A. 1. *affliction* **2.** *impostor* **3.** *heir* **4.** *oppress* **5.** *affliction* **6.** *heir*
     7. *impostor* **8.** *oppress*
B. 1. *air* **2.** *heir*

---

5. SELECTION TEST

Selection Test Answer Key:

A. 1. *c* **2.** *b* **3.** *c* **4.** *b*
B. *The Prince told everyone where he had hidden the seal.*

THE PRINCE AND THE PAUPER

Sequence

Events in a story or a play are usually described in the order they happen. That is, they are described in sequence.

    Fill in the blanks below to complete the sequence of events from the first scene of the play *The Prince and the Pauper.*

Event 1	*Event 2*
Tom Canty waits outside the palace to see _____.	The Prince invites Tom inside _____.

Event 3	*Event 4*
The Prince asks Tom to tell him about _____.	The Prince decides that he and Tom will _____ _____.

Event 5	*Event 6*
Before he goes, the Prince hides _____ inside _____.	At the gate, a guard seizes _____, and the Villagers take him away.

Event 7	*Event 8*
Tom admits to everyone that he is really _____ _____.	The King decides that Tom is _____ and orders him to rest.

THE PRINCE AND THE PAUPER

Plot

The **plot** of a story or play is the series of events that make up the story. In the **introduction,** you meet the characters and learn the problem. The problem gets worse during the **rising action.** The **climax** is the most important event. In the **falling action and conclusion,** loose ends are tied up and the story ends.

The following sentences tell in order the events in the plot of *The Prince and the Pauper.*

    a.   The Prince lets Tom into the palace.

    b.   The Prince and Tom exchange clothes.

    c.   A guard knocks down the Prince and tells him to leave.

    d.   The King mistakes Tom for his son, the Prince.

    e.   John Canty carries off the Prince.

    f.   Miles and the Prince go to jail.

    g.   The Prince and Tom finally get back together.

    h.   The Prince proves who he really is.

Use the letters from the sentences above to answer these questions.

    1. Which two events are in the **introduction?**

    _____

    2. Which four events are part of the **rising action?**

    _____

    3. Which event is the **climax,** or turning point, of the story?

    _____

    4. Which event is part of the **falling action and conclusion?**

    _____

THE PRINCE AND THE PAUPER

Context Clues

Use the **context,** the words and phrases around a word, to understand its meaning.

A. Use context clues to figure out the meaning of the boldfaced word.

1. Tom Canty was a **pauper,** which is a person who is poor.

   Pauper means _____

2. The writer describes the **interior** of the palace, but not its outside.

   Interior means _____

3. The Prince looked **weary.** Because he seemed so tired, Miles felt sorry for him.

   Weary means _____

4. Tom had never before seen vegetables such as lettuce or **turnips.**

   Turnips are _____

5. After the king died, Tom was **stunned,** or shocked.

   Stunned means _____

B. Use the correct word to complete each sentence.

   interior   pauper   stunned

1. I don't want to be a _____; I'd like to be rich instead.

2. Let's look at the _____ of the home, now that we've seen the outside.

3. The news _____ me so much that I had to sit down right away.

THE PRINCE AND THE PAUPER

Words to Know

heir   affliction   impostor   oppress

A. Fill in each blank with the word from the list that best completes the sentence.

1. The death of Jessica's dog caused her more pain and _____ than we imagined.

2. The man pretending to be the president is an _____.

3. Jaime is an only child and the _____ to the family fortune.

4. The cruel ruler chose to _____ the people and treat them harshly.

5. Kevin's knee injury was an _____ for many years.

6. When a king dies, he leaves his title to his _____.

7. She tried to deceive everyone, but we knew that she was an _____.

8. Some laws treat people fairly, while others _____ people.

B. **Homophones** are words that sound alike but have different spellings and definitions. For example:

heir (n.) someone who gets a person's money or title after the person dies

air (n.) the invisible mixture of odorless, tasteless gases surrounding the earth

Place the correct homophone in the following sentences.

1. The _____ felt warm on my skin.

2. Sonia is the _____ to her parents' property.

Writing Activity

If you could switch places with anyone for a day, who would it be? Why? Write one or two sentences. Use at least one of the **Words to Know.**

THE PRINCE AND THE PAUPER

A. Fill in the circle beside the letter of the correct answer.

1. After Tom tells the Prince what his life is like,
- ○ a. the Prince gives Tom a new pair of clothes.
- ○ b. the Prince decides to run away and live like Tom.
- ○ c. the two boys change into each other's clothes.

2. When the Prince goes out to yell at the guard for mistreating Tom,
- ○ a. he locks the guard out of the palace and tells him to get a new job.
- ○ b. he gets locked out of the palace because everyone thinks he's Tom.
- ○ c. the guard apologizes, and the Prince spares his life.

3. For weeks, the two boys
- ○ a. enjoy pretending they are each other.
- ○ b. run around the village together.
- ○ c. are mistaken for each other.

4. But the real Prince is finally revealed on the day
- ○ a. he is supposed to be hanged.
- ○ b. he is supposed to become king.
- ○ c. Tom is supposed to be hanged.

B. In your own words, explain how the Prince finally proved who he really was.

_____

_____

_____

_____

Reader directions:

Cut this paper in half. Practice reading the passage aloud until you don't make any mistakes.
Then have someone listen to you read. Try to sound the way you think the murderer sounds.

from "The Tell-Tale Heart"

Now this is the point. You think I'm mad. Madmen know nothing. But you should have
seen me. You should have seen how wisely I went about my work. I was so careful! I
showed such foresight! I was so cautious!

I was never kinder to the old man than during the whole week before I killed him. Every
night, about midnight, I turned the latch of his door and opened it—oh, so gently! Then
when I opened it just enough for my head, I would put in a lantern. The lantern showed
no light; its sides were closed.

✁ **cut along dotted line**

- -

Checker directions:

Follow along as the passage is read. Make a dot under each word the reader misses.
Show the reader the missed words. Erase the dots and repeat for each reading.

from "The Tell-Tale Heart"

Now this is the point. You think I'm mad. Madmen know nothing. But you should have
seen me. You should have seen how wisely I went about my work. I was so careful! I
showed such foresight! I was so cautious!

I was never kinder to the old man than during the whole week before I killed him. Every
night, about midnight, I turned the latch of his door and opened it—oh, so gently! Then
when I opened it just enough for my head, I would put in a lantern. The lantern showed
no light; its sides were closed.

Use this chart for Timed Readings and Repeated Readings.

Reading	1	2	3	4	5
Time (minutes/seconds)					
Words Missed					

Copyright © McDougal Littell Inc.

Focus Skills and SkillBuilder Copymasters 📋

Dust of Snow p. T198

LITERATURE
Rhyme p. T201

Elevator p. T202

LITERATURE
Form p. T205

Haiku p. T206

LITERATURE
Haiku p. T209

Happy Thought p. T210

LITERATURE
Mood p. T213

Daybreak in Alabama p. T214

LITERATURE
Imagery p. T217

Graffiti p. T218

LITERATURE
Speaker p. T222

VOCABULARY
Unit 5 Vocabulary SkillBuilder
p. T223

Special Places

Unit 5
Poetry

Poets use ideas, images, and feelings. Poets choose words for their sounds and meanings. Some poems create a **mood**, or feeling. Others may have a special **form**, or shape, such as the haiku you will read. The poems in this unit will show you special places.

Poets use many tools to create their poems. Sometimes they use **rhyme**, words that end in the same sound. **Sensory imagery**—words that appeal to the five senses—is also important in poetry. All poems have a **speaker**, the voice that talks to the reader. As you read, let the speakers take you to special places.

158

▮ Pacing Guide

The suggested Post Reading time varies, depending on how you use it. For example, you might have the class complete each SkillBuilder after reading the corresponding poem, or you might have them complete all the SkillBuilders in one session at the end of this unit.

SELECTION	TOTAL DAYS	PREREADING	READING	POST READING
Special Places (all poems)	3.5–4	1	2	.5–1

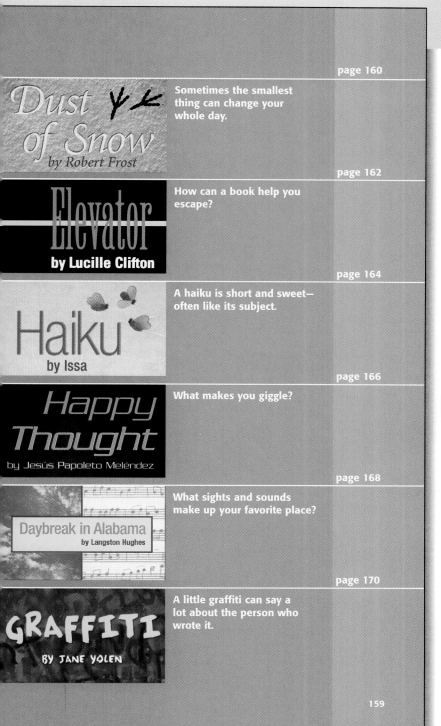

159

More About Poetry

Students are introduced to the genre of poetry in this unit. They will learn poetic elements of form, rhythm and rhyme, imagery, and mood, as well as speaker and theme. They will also learn that poetry can rhyme but does not have to (free verse). You might teach these elements as a group or with the poems that contain particular elements. When reading each poem, be sure to use suggestions in Presenting the Poem to help students enjoy and appreciate the sounds of the poems. Refer students to pages 462–463 in the Student Resources section to familiarize them with poetry terms.

Technology Resources

Audio CD
All poetry selections in this unit are featured in the Audio Library.

Reading Coach CD-ROM
All poetry selections in this unit are part of the Reading Coach. You may use Reading Coach selections as a group activity, as an individual activity, or as a tutorial for students who might benefit from this format or who have missed class.

Building Bridges: Closing the Reading Gap
This video is intended for teacher use only. It gives instructions and tips on how to help middle school readers become strategic readers.

Assessment

Unit Test
Unit 5 poetry is assessed on pages T224–T225.

Assessment Booklet
Progress Check Units 5–8
Administer this test after units 5 through 8 of the book have been read. It covers skills taught in all four units.

Focus Skill

LITERATURE
Rhyme

SkillBuilder Copymaster

Literary Analysis:
1 Rhyme p. T201

Assessment

2 All Unit 5 poetry is assessed on pages T224–T225.

Dust of Snow

by Robert Frost

Sometimes the smalles[t] thing can change your whole day.

Connect to Your Life

Have you ever had a bad day? Was *everything* about that day bad? Did the sun shine? Was your lunch okay? Think of one small thing that went *right* on your bad day.

Key to the Poem

Reading Coach CD-ROM selectio[n]

Words **rhyme** when the sounds at the ends are repeated. In this poem, *crow* and *snow* end in the same sound. Read the poem aloud; listen fo[r] the rhyming words. Also listen for the **speaker**, the voice talking to you.

Vocabulary In line 8, **rued** means "felt sorry about."

160 Unit 5 Special Places

Connect to Your Life

Explain that this poet, Robert Frost, had a way of focusing on one little thing and revealing a whole world. Help students understand that little things might really be very important events. Help each student thoroughly explore his or her "small event" in order to understand its impact on his or her life.

Key to the Poem

You may want to try having the class read this poem aloud in unison so they can hear the rhyming words as clearly as possible.

Presenting the Poem

Read the poem aloud to the class several times. First ask the students to close their eyes and visualize the scene. On successive readings, ask students to focus on what is happening and how the speaker feels at the beginning and at the end.

Let students take turns reading aloud. Help them become aware of how this little poem "expands" each time they hear it.

Dust of Snow
by Robert Frost

A

The way a crow
Shook down on me
The dust of snow
From a hemlock tree

B

5 Has given my heart
A change of mood
And saved some part
Of a day I had rued.

C

THINK IT THROUGH

1. The speaker is the voice talking to you in every poem. What happens in lines 1–4 that makes the speaker feel better?
2. Do you think the speaker is expecting anything to happen? Why or why not?
3. Which words rhyme in the first half of the poem? In the second half?

Dust of Snow **161**

LITERATURE

FOCUS SKILL: Rhyme

Explain that the most common form of rhyme in poetry is **end rhyme,** in which the rhyming words fall at the ends of lines.

For direct instruction on Rhyme, see page T200.

Use the following questions to encourage literary analysis.

A Tell students that the pattern of end rhyme helps create a rhythm throughout this poem. Read the poem aloud again and have students clap out the rhythm. **rhythm, rhyme**

B Help students understand the message, or theme, of this poem. Ask why they think the poet bothered to write about such a small incident as a bird shaking snow onto a person. *(the incident had meaning to the poet; it made him feel better)* **theme**

C **THINK IT THROUGH**

1. The speaker is the voice talking to you in every poem. What happens in lines 1–4 that makes the speaker feel better? *(A crow moving in a hemlock tree shakes snow down upon the speaker.)* **cause and effect** COMPREHENSION

2. Do you think the speaker is expecting anything to happen? Why or why not? *(Probably not; the speaker probably is concentrating on his or her bad day. The sudden dusting of snow probably takes the speaker's mind off things, which lightens his or her mood.)* **making inferences** COMPREHENSION

3. Which words rhyme in the first half of the poem? In the second half? *(First half: crow/snow, me/tree. Second half: heart/part, mood/rued.)* **rhyme**

1. LITERATURE

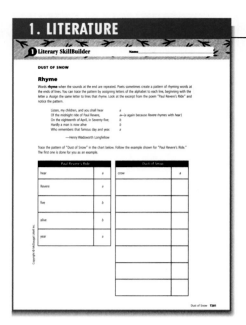

Rhyme

Direct Instruction Tell students that **rhyme** is the repetition of sound at the end of words. For example, the words *plain* and *gain* rhyme. Point out that traditional poems use rhyming words at the ends of lines. This use of rhyme can form a pattern. Explain to students that one way to trace a pattern of rhyme is to assign letters of the alphabet to the word at the end of each line. Assign the same letter to lines that end in words that rhyme. Write the following example on the board, and ask students to pay attention to the rhyming words at the end of each line.

The cat that lives in my **house**	a
Is afraid of the big, fat **mouse.**	a
Whenever my cat hears a **sound,**	b
He leaps to escape the thing with a **bound.**	b

Literary SkillBuilder Answer Key:

crow	*a*		*heart*	*c*
me	*b*		*mood*	*d*
snow	*a*		*part*	*c*
tree	*b*		*rued*	*d*

DUST OF SNOW

Rhyme

Words **rhyme** when the sounds at the end are repeated. Poets sometimes create a pattern of rhyming words at the ends of lines. You can trace the pattern by assigning letters of the alphabet to each line, beginning with the letter *a*. Assign the same letter to lines that rhyme. Look at the excerpt from the poem "Paul Revere's Ride" and notice the pattern.

Listen, my children, and you shall hear	*a*
Of the midnight ride of Paul Revere,	*a*←(*a* again because *Revere* rhymes with *hear*)
On the eighteenth of April, in Seventy-five;	*b*
Hardly a man is now alive	*b*
Who remembers that famous day and year.	*a*

—Henry Wadsworth Longfellow

Trace the pattern of "Dust of Snow" in the chart below. Follow the example shown for "Paul Revere's Ride." The first one is done for you as an example.

Paul Revere's Ride	
hear	*a*
Revere	*a*
five	*b*
alive	*b*
year	*a*

Dust of Snow	
crow	*a*

Focus Skill

Form

SkillBuilder Copymaster

 Literary Analysis:
1 Form p. T205

Assessment

 2 All Unit 5 poetry is assessed on pages T224–T225.

Elevator
by Lucille Clifton

How can a book help you escape?

Connect to Your Life

When do you feel that you want to escape or get away? What makes you feel better?

Key to the Poem

The **form** of a poem is the way the words and lines are arranged on the page. Sometimes a poem can look like what it is about. This tall, narrow poem should remind you of an elevator. What is the speaker doing there?

Vocabulary In line 5, **project** means "public housing."

Reading Coach CD-ROM selection

162 Unit 5 Special Places

Connect to Your Life

You may need to model some "starter ideas" such as "when I have too much homework to finish" or "when my baby brother or sister cries."

Key to the Poem

Point out that this poem is written in free verse, another aspect of its form. The lines do not rhyme or have traditional rhythm.

Presenting the Poem

Read the poem aloud to the class twice. Then ask the students to follow along while you read it again. Point out that their eyes will move fairly quickly down the poem as they read—like an elevator moving down. Give students opportunities to read the poem aloud to each other or to the class.

Elevator

by Lucille Clifton

A

down
in the corner
my book and i
traveling
5 over the project
walls
so the world
is more than this
elevator
10 stuck between
floors again
and home
is a corner
where i crouch
15 safe
reading waiting
to start moving
up

B

THINK IT THROUGH

1. What is the speaker doing in the elevator? How does this activity make the speaker feel?
2. What do you think the speaker means in lines 7–9: "so the world is more than this elevator"?
3. What do you think this poet is trying to tell you about life?

Elevator **163**

LITERATURE

FOCUS SKILL: Form

Remind students that a poem's **form** includes its overall shape as well as its arrangement of words and lines on a page.

For direct instruction on Form, see page T204.

Use the following questions to encourage literary analysis.

A Why do you think the poet started this poem with the word *down* and ended it with the word *up*? *(Some might say that the form suggests movement: from the top of a building you go down in an elevator, and from the bottom you go up.)* **form**

B **THINK IT THROUGH**

1. What is the speaker doing in the elevator? How does this activity make the speaker feel? *(sitting and reading a book; safe, hopeful)* **speaker**

2. What do you think the speaker means in lines 7–9: "so the world is more than this elevator"? *(Some might say that the book takes the speaker's mind out of the closed box of the elevator. Others might say that books can even take the speaker out of the projects.)* **form**

3. What do you think this poet is trying to tell you about life? *(Students might say that you can always "go up" or get better, or that books or education can enlarge your world.)* **theme**

1. LITERATURE

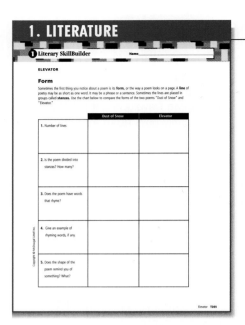

Form

Direct Instruction Tell students that the **form** of a poem is the shape the words and lines make on the page. Poets arrange words into lines. The lines may or may not be sentences. Explain that much traditional poetry typically has a formal structure in which lines are grouped together in stanzas. However, many poems do not have a formal structure, such as free verse. The lines vary from one to the next, and sometimes there is no specific pattern. Tell students that the term *form* can refer to a number of poetic elements, including the following:

line: the words that fit on one line of a poem

stanza: a group of lines in a poem

rhyme: repetition of the same sound at the ends of words that are often at the ends of lines (*book* and *look*)

rhythm: the beat of the poem

Literary SkillBuilder Answer Key:

"Dust of Snow": **1.** *8* **2.** *yes, 2* **3.** *yes*
4. *crow/snow, me/tree, heart/part, or mood/rued* **5.** *no*

"Elevator": **1.** *18* **2.** *no* **3.** *no* **4.** *none* **5.** *yes, an elevator*

ELEVATOR

Form

Sometimes the first thing you notice about a poem is its **form,** or the way a poem looks on a page. A **line** of poetry may be as short as one word. It may be a phrase or a sentence. Sometimes the lines are placed in groups called **stanzas.** Use the chart below to compare the forms of the two poems "Dust of Snow" and "Elevator."

	Dust of Snow	Elevator
1. Number of lines		
2. Is the poem divided into stanzas? How many?		
3. Does the poem have words that rhyme?		
4. Give an example of rhyming words, if any.		
5. Does the shape of the poem remind you of something? What?		

Focus Skill

LITERATURE

Haiku

SkillBuilder Copymaster

 Literary Analysis:
1 Haiku p. T209

Assessment

 2 All Unit 5 poetry is assessed
on pages T224–T225.

Haiku

by Issa

A haiku is short and sweet—
often like its subject.

Connect to Your Life

Do you ever stop to watch
one tiny insect? Or do you
ever look at just one petal
on a flower? What is the
smallest, simplest thing
you have ever stopped
to study?

Key to the Poem

A **haiku** is a short Japanese poem. It usually has
only three lines. Haiku poets often write about
details in nature. In only three lines, the poet
must create a clear picture for the reader. Let
each of these haiku put a picture in your mind.

**Reading Coach
CD-ROM selectio**

164 Unit 5 Special Places

Connect to Your Life

Suggest that students write their
thoughts about the simplest thing they
have ever studied. Have them write the
name of the object and all that they
remember about it. This process will
help them clarify their thoughts about
the subject and focus on the most
important aspect.

Key to the Poem

Help students understand that in
addition to describing one small thing in
nature, a **haiku** can describe a
single moment or a single feeling.

Presenting the Poem

Read all three haiku aloud to the class.
Then encourage volunteers to take turns
reading their favorite one aloud. When
they are listening, encourage the students to visualize the tiny scene that
each poem describes.

Haiku

by Issa

(A)
Don't worry, spiders,
I keep house
    casually.

(B)
            Don't kill that fly!
    Look—it's wringing its hands,
        wringing its feet.

(C)
        Under the evening moon
the snail
        is stripped to the waist.

(D)
THINK IT THROUGH

1. What small subject does each haiku describe?
2. How are the subjects of these haiku like the subject of "Dust of Snow" on page 161?
3. Make a simple drawing to illustrate one of these haiku.

Haiku **165**

Building Background

In a traditional haiku, the three lines contain five, seven, and five syllables respectively. Since the haiku on this page were originally written in Japanese, their English translations do not follow this exact pattern of syllables. Kobayashi Nobuyuki (1763–1827) was considered a master of the haiku. His pen name, Issa, means "cup of tea."

LITERATURE

FOCUS SKILL: Haiku

For direct instruction on Haiku, see page T208.

Use the following questions to encourage analysis of the haiku.

(A) In the first haiku, what is the speaker saying to spiders? *(that they shouldn't worry because the speaker won't clean up their webs)* **making inferences** COMPREHENSION

(B) In the second haiku, why might the speaker be telling someone not to kill the fly? *(Possible answers: because the speaker is compassionate; because the fly is begging the person not to kill it)* **making inferences** COMPREHENSION

(C) In the third haiku, what does the poet mean by the lines "the snail is stripped to the waist"? *(that the snail is halfway out of its shell)* **imagery**

(D) **THINK IT THROUGH**

1. What small subject does each haiku describe? *(spiders, a fly, a snail)* **haiku**

2. How are the subjects of these haiku like the subject of "Dust of Snow" on page 161? *(All are one small thing or moment in nature.)* **compare and contrast** COMPREHENSION

3. Make a simple drawing to illustrate one of these haiku. *(Drawings should focus on the subject of the poem and should not contain a lot of superfluous detail.)* **imagery**

VOCABULARY

FOR ENGLISH LEARNERS

Help students understand the following idiom:

Line 2: keep house

1. LITERATURE

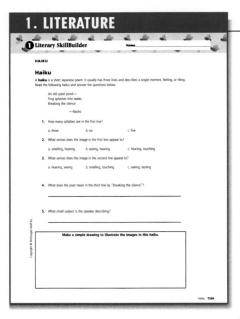

Haiku

Direct Instruction Tell students that a **haiku** is a short Japanese poem. Explain that a traditional haiku has three lines—the first and third lines contain five syllables each, and the second contains seven syllables. Then tell the students that most modern haiku keep the basic three-line format but do not follow the seventeen-syllable count. Further explain that many haiku of the old masters do not have the traditional syllable count in their English translations.

Tell students that traditional haiku deal with short observations of nature or feelings and moments that may be overlooked. Often, a haiku focuses on an image that stays with the reader. Explain that these images appeal to our senses: sight, hearing, smell, taste, and touch.

Write the following haiku on the board and have a volunteer read it aloud. Ask students to pay attention to the image the poem conveys. Also point out the number of syllables in each line. Mention that this haiku follows the traditional five-seven-five-syllable format.

When the wind passes	5
The sparrows in the branches	7
They cling so tightly.	5

Literary SkillBuilder Answer Key:

1. *c*

2. *b*

3. *a*

4. *There is no more silence.*

5. *a frog*

HAIKU

Haiku

A **haiku** is a short Japanese poem. It usually has three lines and describes a single moment, feeling, or thing. Read the following haiku and answer the questions below.

> An old quiet pond—
> Frog splashes into water,
> Breaking the silence
>
>   —Basho

1. How many syllables are in the first line?

   a. three   b. six   c. five

2. What senses does the image in the first line appeal to?

   a. smelling, hearing   b. seeing, hearing   c. hearing, touching

3. What senses does the image in the second line appeal to?

   a. hearing, seeing   b. smelling, touching   c. seeing, tasting

4. What does the poet mean in the third line by "Breaking the silence"?

_____

5. What small subject is the speaker describing?

_____

Make a simple drawing to illustrate the images in this haiku.

Focus Skill

LITERATURE
Mood

SkillBuilder Copymaster

Literary Analysis:
1 Mood p. T213

Assessment

2 All Unit 5 poetry is assessed on pages T224–T225.

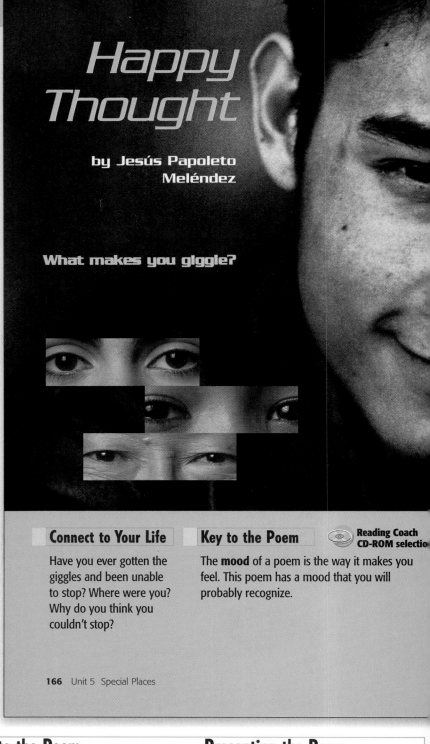

Happy Thought

by Jesús Papoleto Meléndez

What makes you giggle?

Connect to Your Life

Have you ever gotten the giggles and been unable to stop? Where were you? Why do you think you couldn't stop?

Key to the Poem

The **mood** of a poem is the way it makes you feel. This poem has a mood that you will probably recognize.

Reading Coach CD-ROM selectio

166 Unit 5 Special Places

Connect to Your Life

If you feel brave, guide the students in a "giggle experiment." Ask them to try not to giggle while staring at each other. After just a few minutes, students either will be giggling or struggling to suppress giggles. Help them understand that the cause of their giggles is both the act of suppressing a giggle and the knowledge that others are watching.

Key to the Poem

Explain that poets create different **moods** to help readers feel what they are describing. As students read "Happy Thought" aloud a few times, discuss what the poet does to create the mood.

Presenting the Poem

After reading the poem aloud to the class, suggest that students read it aloud by taking turns reading the lines. Assign sequential lines to students in a row or scatter assigned lines around the room. Let students enjoy the effect of listening to the lines slip from student to student. Point out that this effect imitates the content of the poem.

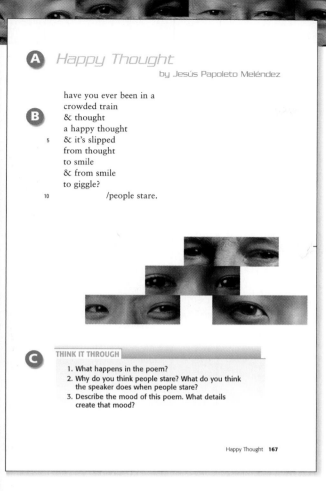

A Happy Thought
by Jesús Papoleto Meléndez

B

have you ever been in a
crowded train
& thought
a happy thought
5   & it's slipped
from thought
to smile
& from smile
to giggle?
10   /people stare.

C **THINK IT THROUGH**

1. What happens in the poem?
2. Why do you think people stare? What do you think
   the speaker does when people stare?
3. Describe the mood of this poem. What details
   create that mood?

Happy Thought **167**

LITERATURE

FOCUS SKILL: Mood

 For direct instruction on Mood, see page T212.

Use the following questions to encourage literary analysis of mood.

A Explain that the title alone can set the mood of this poem by letting the reader know it's about something happy. Ask students to identify evidence of the happy mood within the poem itself. *(happy thought, smile, giggle)* **mood**

B Guide students to understand how the poet used repetition. Ask where he repeated amper-sands—*and* signs. *(lines 3, 5, and 8)* Then ask students to find how the poet repeated the words *from* and *to* in every-other-line fashion. *(from thought, to smile, from smile, to giggle)* **repetition**

C THINK IT THROUGH

1. What happens in the poem? *(The speaker gets the giggles on a train, and people stare.)* **summarizing** COMPREHENSION

2. Why do you think people stare? What do you think the speaker does when people stare? *(People probably stare because they are wondering what the speaker is giggling about. The speaker probably starts giggling even more.)* **making inferences** COMPREHENSION

3. Describe the mood of this poem. What details create that mood? *(happy and lighthearted; details include the words* happy thought, smile, *and* giggle.*)* **mood**

Direct Instruction
for SkillBuilder Copymaster

1. LITERATURE

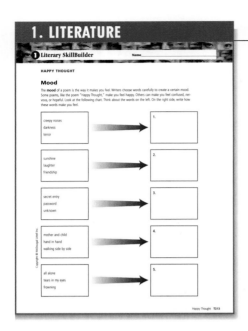

Mood

Direct Instruction Tell students that **mood** is the feeling a reader gets from reading a poem. The mood in a poem is often created through the writer's choice of words. Explain that writers choose words carefully and purposefully to create an emotion in the reader. Imagery, metaphor, rhyme, and rhythm can also contribute to the mood of the poem. Write the following poem on the board and ask a volunteer to read it aloud.

Giddy, my eyes danced with the clouds,
Chasing a riot of balloons
Escaped from their earthbound vendor—
I laughed aloud.

Ask students the following questions: What images does the writer use to create a mood? *(clouds, balloons, laughter)* Which of the following words describe the mood of the poem: *joyous, mysterious,* or *depressing? (joyous)*

Literary SkillBuilder Answer Key:
Possible responses:
1. *scared, afraid, nervous, jumpy*
2. *happy, lucky, glad, hopeful*
3. *mysterious, secretive, puzzled*
4. *loving, warm, caring, peaceful, happy*
5. *sad, unhappy, gloomy, mournful, unlucky*

HAPPY THOUGHT

Mood

The **mood** of a poem is the way it makes you feel. Writers choose words carefully to create a certain mood. Some poems, like the poem "Happy Thought," make you feel happy. Others can make you feel confused, nervous, or hopeful. Look at the following chart. Think about the words on the left. On the right side, write how these words make you feel.

creepy noises darkness terror	**1.**

sunshine laughter friendship	**2.**

secret entry password unknown	**3.**

mother and child hand in hand walking side by side	**4.**

all alone tears in my eyes frowning	**5.**

Focus Skill

LITERATURE

Imagery

SkillBuilder Copymaster

 Literary Analysis:
1 Imagery p. T217

Assessment

 2 All Unit 5 poetry is assessed
on pages T224–T225.

Daybreak in Alabama

by Langston Hughes

What sights and sounds make up your favorite place?

Connect to Your Life

Think of a place that you like. Draw a picture of three things you like about that place. What colors are they? How do they sound? smell? taste? feel to the touch?

Key to the Poem

Some poems contain **sensory imagery,** or words that help you make pictures in your mind. The words make you use your senses. You can almost see, smell, hear, taste, or touch something. What images in this poem help you imagine daybreak in Alabama?

Reading Coach CD-ROM selection

168 Unit 5 Special Places

Connect to Your Life

When students have finished drawing, have them break into pairs to explain and share their pictures. Encourage them to use as many descriptive words as possible as they explain how their three favorite things sound, smell, taste, and/or feel.

Key to the Poem

As students read the poem, have them match the images in the poem with the five senses. Use a concept web like the one on page T668. Label the large circles with the senses, and add circles for the images that match each sense.

Presenting the Poem

Read this poem aloud to students. Then try a "tandem reading" with different students assigned to read each line (image). Let students choose which image they want to read aloud. Choose a narrator to read the first four lines and the last four lines.

Daybreak in Alabama
by Langston Hughes

When I get to be a composer
I'm gonna write me some music about
Daybreak in Alabama
And I'm gonna put the purtiest songs in it
5 Rising out of the ground like a swamp mist
And falling out of heaven like soft dew.
I'm gonna put some tall tall trees in it
And the scent of pine needles
And the smell of red clay after rain
10 And long red necks
And poppy colored faces
And big brown arms
And the field daisy eyes
Of black and white black white black people
15 And I'm gonna put white hands
And black hands and brown and yellow hands
And red clay earth hands in it
Touching everybody with kind fingers
And touching each other natural as dew
20 In that dawn of music when I
Get to be a composer
And write about daybreak
In Alabama.

THINK IT THROUGH

1. Find an image in the poem that tells how something looks. What colors are mentioned?
2. Now find images that tell how something smells and how something feels to the touch.
3. How do those images make you feel about Alabama? How does the speaker feel about Alabama?

Daybreak in Alabama **169**

Building Background

Langston Hughes (1902–1967) spent many years living and working in Harlem, a section of New York City. Hughes's love of music greatly influenced the style and content of his writing. He wrote his poems in both free verse and rhyme, and his words often captured the rhythm of jazz and blues, his favorite styles of music.

For English Learners

Since this poem contains dialect, you may want to read it to students a few times and discuss any words or phrases that they might have trouble understanding.

LITERATURE

FOCUS SKILL: Imagery

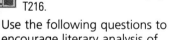
For direct instruction on Imagery, see page T216.

Use the following questions to encourage literary analysis of imagery.

A Read the poem again. What is your favorite image, and why? To which sense or senses does it appeal? *(Accept reasonable responses.)* **imagery**

B If the poet used musical instruments to represent the images in this poem, which one might he use for the "black and white black white black people" and the "white hands and black hands"? Why? *(Students might say a piano or an organ because they have black and white keys.)* **imagery**

C **THINK IT THROUGH**

1. Find an image in the poem that tells how something looks. What colors are mentioned? *(Possible answers: a rising swamp mist, dew falling from heaven, tall tall trees, long red necks, poppy colored faces, big brown arms, field daisy eyes, black and white people and hands, brown and yellow hands, red clay earth hands)* **imagery**

2. Now find images that tell how something smells and how something feels to the touch. *(Smells: pine needles, red clay after rain; Feels: red clay earth hands touching with kind fingers, touching each other as natural as dew.)* **imagery**

3. How do those images make you feel about Alabama? How does the speaker feel about Alabama? *(Students probably will say that the images make Alabama sound like a beautiful and inviting place. The speaker loves and is proud of Alabama.)* **mood**

VOCABULARY

FOR ENGLISH LEARNERS

Help students understand the following expressions:

Line 1: get to be
Line 2: gonna write me
Line 4: purtiest

1. LITERATURE

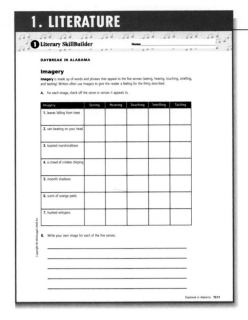

Imagery

Direct Instruction Tell students that **imagery** is a word or phrase that appeals to the five senses. Explain that sensory images draw readers into a poem and allow readers to share the experience of the speaker. Images can help the reader see a place, a person, or a scene. Sometimes images can help us hear a noise, smell an odor, feel something rough or soft, and taste something bitter or sweet. Write the following examples of imagery on the board or read them aloud. Ask students to explain which sense each image appeals to.

> Cold, wet morning *(feeling)*
> trail of sunflowers *(seeing/ smelling)*
> scorching tea *(feeling/tasting)*
> rumbling thunder *(hearing)*
> sweet perfume *(smelling)*

Literary SkillBuilder Answer Key:

A. *Answers may vary.*
   1. *seeing*
   2. *hearing/touching*
   3. *seeing/tasting/touching/smelling*
   4. *seeing/hearing*
   5. *seeing*
   6. *smelling*
   7. *hearing*

B. *Accept all reasonable responses.*

DAYBREAK IN ALABAMA

Imagery

Imagery is made up of words and phrases that appeal to the five senses (seeing, hearing, touching, smelling, and tasting). Writers often use imagery to give the reader a feeling for the thing described.

A. For each image, check off the sense or senses it appeals to.

Imagery	Seeing	Hearing	Touching	Smelling	Tasting
1. leaves falling from trees					
2. rain beating on your head					
3. toasted marshmallows					
4. a crowd of crickets chirping					
5. moonlit shadows					
6. scent of orange peels					
7. hushed whispers					

B. Write your own image for each of the five senses.

_____

_____

_____

_____

_____

Focus Skill

LITERATURE
Speaker

SkillBuilder Copymasters

 Literary Analysis:
1 Speaker p. T222

 Vocabulary:
2 All Unit 5 vocabulary is covered on page T223.

Assessment

 3 All Unit 5 poetry is assessed on pages T224–T225.

GRAFFITI

BY JANE YOLEN

A LITTLE GRAFFITI CAN SAY
A LOT ABOUT THE PERSON
WHO WROTE IT.

170 Unit 5 Special Places

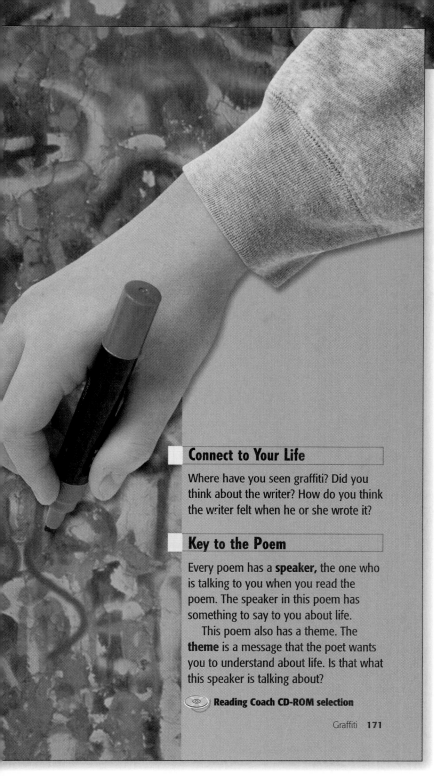

Connect to Your Life

Where have you seen graffiti? Did you think about the writer? How do you think the writer felt when he or she wrote it?

Key to the Poem

Every poem has a **speaker,** the one who is talking to you when you read the poem. The speaker in this poem has something to say to you about life.

This poem also has a theme. The **theme** is a message that the poet wants you to understand about life. Is that what this speaker is talking about?

Reading Coach CD-ROM selection

Graffiti **171**

Connect to Your Life

Before you have students break into discussion groups, make sure they understand that graffiti (which is the plural of *graffito*) are symbols or words drawn on walls, sidewalks, and other surfaces, usually public. Point out that most cities have laws against writing on public surfaces.

Key to the Poem

Remind students that even though a poem contains the words *I, me,* and *my,* the **speaker** of the poem is not necessarily the person who wrote it. Help students understand that a poet sometimes chooses to tell his or her poem through someone else in order to present a different or unique point of view.

Presenting the Poem

Read this poem aloud to the class. Explain that it is written in free verse, which is written like conversation, not in rhyme. Explain that the lines are not complete thoughts but are just breaking points within sentences. Tell the class that you are reading it by sentences, not by lines. Encourage students to read along so they can see where the lines break while hearing the sentences spoken. Explain that it can be hard to understand a poem written in free verse because the lines do not rhyme and do not always contain meaningful units of speech.

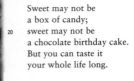

GRAFFITI

BY JANE YOLEN

I read a sad poem
on the wall
on my way to school:

SOME DAY SUGAR
5 YOU GONNA FIND
NO ONE IN THE WORLD
GONNA GIVE YOU SWEET

But I thought of Mama
ironing my skirt
10 this morning,
Daddy giving me
a brand new box of crayons,
and all my aunts and uncles
lining up for hugs
15 yesterday,
a whole day
before my birthday.

Sweet may not be
a box of candy;
20 sweet may not be
a chocolate birthday cake.
But you can taste it
your whole life long.

Anyway—
25 what does someone know
who has to use a wall
to write a poem?

THINK IT THROUGH

1. What does the message on the wall mean to you?
2. Does the speaker agree or disagree with the message on the wall? How do you know?
3. What is the theme of this poem, or its message about life?

172   Unit 5 Special Places

Graffiti **173**

LITERATURE

FOCUS SKILL: Speaker

Remind students that the **speaker** of a poem is not necessarily the person who wrote it. For example, the poet who wrote "Graffiti" is a grown woman who wrote the poem from the perspective of a young girl.

 For direct instruction on Speaker, see page T221.

Use the following questions to encourage literary analysis.

A Think back to the poem "Elevator" in this unit. How are the forms of both poems alike? *(Both poems are written in free verse and sound like conversation.)* **free verse**

B THINK IT THROUGH

1. What does the message on the wall mean to you? *(Possible answers: There are going to be times in life when no one is nice or helpful, when life is hard, and/or when things don't turn out the way you want them to.)* **theme**

2. Does the speaker agree or disagree with the message on the wall? How do you know? *(She disagrees. She says that the sweet things people do for her now will stay with her all her life, and she asks what a person who writes poems on walls knows.)* **making inferences** COMPREHENSION

3. What is the theme of this poem, or its message about life? *(Possible answers: You can find joy—or sweet—in small things; appreciate what you have.)* **theme**

VOCABULARY

FOR ENGLISH LEARNERS

Help students understand the following expressions and idioms:

Line 5: you gonna find
Line 7: gonna give you sweet

Direct Instruction
for SkillBuilder Copymasters

1. LITERATURE

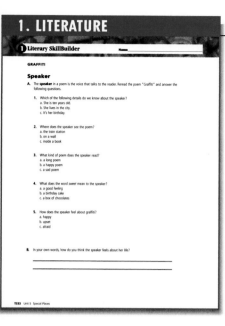

Speaker

Direct Instruction Tell students that the **speaker** is the voice that talks to the reader. Point out that the speaker in a poem is like the narrator in a story. Often, the speaker expresses the poet's own feelings; however, the speaker can be anyone—man or woman, child or adult, an animal, or even an object.

Explain that the identity of the speaker is not apparent immediately. Readers must gather clues that the writer leaves to understand who is speaking. From these clues, readers can learn more details about the speaker. For example, readers can learn the age of the speaker, where the speaker lives, what the speaker does for a living, and how the speaker feels about a certain subject. Ask students to choose a poem in this unit and see what details they can learn about the speaker.

> **Literary SkillBuilder Answer Key:**
> **A. 1.** c **2.** b **3.** c **4.** a **5.** b
> **B.** *The speaker enjoys her life and feels hopeful.*

2. VOCABULARY

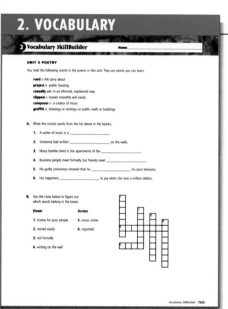

Vocabulary

Direct Instruction Poems from which vocabulary words come: *rued:* "Dust of Snow"; *project:* "Elevator"; *casually:* "Haiku"; *slipped:* "Happy Thought"; *composer:* "Daybreak in Alabama"; *graffiti:* "Graffiti"

When presenting the vocabulary, you might break four words into their base words and suffixes:

- **compose** + -er = *composer* (one who composes).
- **casual** + -ly = *casually* (in a casual way). Note two *l*'s in *casual**ly***.
- **slip** + -ed = *slipped* (past tense of slip). Note that when *-ed* is added the ending consonant of the base word is doubled if it is preceded by a short vowel.
- **rue** + -ed = *rued* (felt sorry). Note that only a *d* is added to show the past tense of a word that ends in *e*.
- **Graffiti** is an old word that started in Rome when people defaced public buildings.
- **Project** has many meanings. Suggest that students look up the meanings in a dictionary.

> **Vocabulary SkillBuilder Answer Key:**
> **A. 1.** *composer* **2.** *graffiti* **3.** *project* **4.** *casually* **5.** *rued* **6.** *slipped*
> **B. Down: 1.** *project* **2.** *slipped* **3.** *casually* **4.** *graffiti*
> **Across: 5.** *composer* **6.** *rued*

3. UNIT TEST

Unit Test

Direct instruction Students will need to look at the poems while answering these questions.

> **Unit Test Answer Key:**
> **A. 1.** b **2.** a **3.** a **4.** b **5.** c **6.** b **7.** b **8.** a **9.** c
> **B.** *Possible answer: Most are happy or feel hopeful.*

GRAFFITI

Speaker

A. The **speaker** in a poem is the voice that talks to the reader. Reread the poem "Graffiti" and answer the following questions.

1. Which of the following details do we know about the speaker?
   a. She is ten years old.
   b. She lives in the city.
   c. It's her birthday.

2. Where does the speaker see the poem?
   a. the train station
   b. on a wall
   c. inside a book

3. What kind of poem does the speaker read?
   a. a long poem
   b. a happy poem
   c. a sad poem

4. What does the word *sweet* mean to the speaker?
   a. a good feeling
   b. a birthday cake
   c. a box of chocolates

5. How does the speaker feel about graffiti?
   a. happy
   b. upset
   c. afraid

B. In your own words, how do you think the speaker feels about her life?

_____

_____

UNIT 5 POETRY

You read the following words in the poems in this unit. They are words you can learn.

rued *v.* felt sorry about

project *n.* public housing

casually *adv.* in an informal, unplanned way

slipped *v.* moved smoothly and easily

composer *n.* a creator of music

graffiti *n.* drawings or writings on public walls or buildings

A. Write the correct words from the list above in the blanks.

1. A writer of music is a _____.

2. Someone had written _____ on the walls.

3. Many families lived in the apartments of the _____.

4. Business people meet formally, but friends meet _____.

5. His guilty conscience showed that he _____ his poor behavior.

6. Her happiness _____ to joy when she won a million dollars.

B. Use the clues below to figure out which words belong in the boxes.

Down

1. homes for poor people

2. moved easily

3. not formally

4. writing on the wall

Across

5. music writer

6. regretted

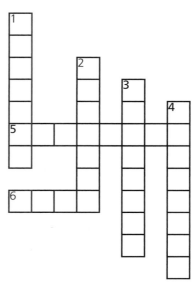

UNIT 5 SPECIAL PLACES

A. You will need to look back at the poems in this unit in order to answer some of these questions. Fill in the circle beside the correct answer.

1. Look back at "Dust of Snow." Which lines from the poem rhyme?
○ a. lines 1 and 2, lines 3 and 4
○ b. lines 1 and 3, lines 2 and 4
○ c. lines 2 and 3, lines 4 and 5

2. How does the speaker's mood change in "Dust of Snow"?
○ a. The speaker feels better.
○ b. The speaker feels worse.
○ c. The speaker gets angry.

3. Look back at "Elevator." What is the speaker doing in the elevator?
○ a. reading
○ b. talking to a friend
○ c. daydreaming

4. Which is the best subject for a haiku?
○ a. history of the world
○ b. a sleeping animal
○ c. a person's birthday party

5. In "Happy Thought," what is the mood?
○ a. worried
○ b. serious
○ c. happy

6. Look back at "Daybreak in Alabama." Which lines from the poem appeal to the sense of sight?

◯ a. lines 8 and 9

◯ b. lines 11 and 12

◯ c. lines 18 and 19

7. In "Daybreak in Alabama," how do the first six lines in the poem make you feel?

◯ a. gloomy

◯ b. hopeful

◯ c. excited

8. In "Graffiti," what does the speaker disagree with?

◯ a. the sad writing on a wall

◯ b. the need to iron a skirt

◯ c. the hugs from aunts and uncles

9. What kind of poetry is "Graffiti"?

◯ a. rhyming

◯ b. haiku

◯ c. free verse

B. Think about the speakers in the poems in this unit. In your own words, explain what kind of feeling most of the speakers have in common.

_____

_____

Focus Skills and SkillBuilder Copymasters

High as Han Hsin p. T228
COMPREHENSION
Sequence p. T238
LITERATURE
Style p. T239
VOCABULARY
Context Clues p. T240
Words to Know p. T241

For Want of a Horseshoe Nail p. T244
COMPREHENSION
Summarizing p. T249
LITERATURE
Historical Fiction p. T250
VOCABULARY
Multiple-Meaning Words p. T251
Words to Know p. T252

Shot Down Behind Enemy Lines p. T254
COMPREHENSION
Visualizing p. T262
LITERATURE
Descriptive Details p. T263
VOCABULARY
Prefixes and Suffixes p. T264
Words to Know p. T265

Fa Mulan p. T268
COMPREHENSION
Problem and Solution p. T276
LITERATURE
Climax p. T277
VOCABULARY
Context Clues p. T278
Words to Know p. T279

Reading Fluency

 ★ Reading Fluency pp. T267, T281

The Battle Is On!

Unit 6
Mixed Genres

In a war, a battle is a kind of test. A battle can be a test of strength. It can be a test of courage or of wisdom. A fighter must be ready for all that a battle might be. Even then, there's no promise of survival.

In this unit, you'll read a **folk tale, historical fiction,** a **true account,** and a **legend.** You'll meet fighters from across time and learn their fighting ways. You'll read about what it's like to win or to lose.

174

Pacing Guide

SELECTION	TOTAL DAYS	PREREADING	READING	POST READING	
				SELECTIVE OPTIONS	ALL OPTIONS
High as Han Hsin	3.5–4	1	2	.5	1
For Want of a Horseshoe Nail	2–2.5	1	.5	5	1
Shot Down Behind Enemy Lines	2.5–3	1	1	.5	1
Fa Mulan	3–3.5	1	1.5	.5	1

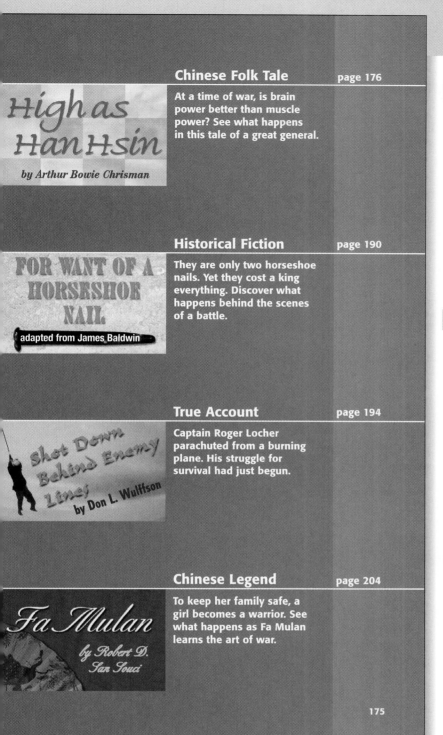
More About Mixed Genres

Conflict in the extreme is the thread connecting the experiences in this unit. The deadly nature of war is depicted in a tale, legend, and true account, with warriors who span ancient to fairly recent times. Readers will come to understand that it takes certain qualities—keen perception, decisiveness, and shrewdness—to bring the most extreme form of conflict to resolution.

Technology Resources

Audio CD
All selections in this unit are featured in the Audio Library.

Reading Coach CD-ROM
All four selections in this unit are part of the Reading Coach. You may use Reading Coach selections as a group activity, as an individual activity, or as a tutorial for students who might benefit from this format or who have missed class.

Building Bridges: Closing the Reading Gap
This video is intended for teacher use only. It gives instructions and tips on how to help middle school readers become strategic readers.

Assessment

Selection Tests
pp. T242, T253, T266, T280

Assessment Booklet
Midyear Reading Test
Administer the Midyear Reading Test (pp. 13–20 in the Assessment Booklet) to determine student gains in reading progress since the Placement Test.

Progress Check Units 5–8
Administer this test after the units 5 through 8 of the book have been read. It covers skills taught in all four units.

Focus Skills

COMPREHENSION
Sequence

LITERATURE
Style

VOCABULARY
Context Clues

SkillBuilder Copymasters

Reading Comprehension:
1 Sequence p. T238

Literary Analysis:
2 Style p. T239

Vocabulary:
3 Context Clues p. T240
4 Words to Know p. T241

Assessment

5 Selection Test p. T242

Readability Scores

DRP	LEXILE	DALE-CHALL
51	630	5.6

For English Learners

Because the inverted syntax and unusual language in this selection may be difficult for many students, you may want to have the class follow along silently while you read the tale aloud. Pause when necessary to check students' understanding or to explain the author's meaning.

High as Han Hsin

At a time of war, is brain power better than muscle power? See what happens in this tale of a great general.

translated by
Arthur Bowie Chrisman

176 Unit 6 The Battle Is On!

More About Style

Style involves *how* something is said rather than what is said. The style of "High as Han Hsin" is somewhat humorous and playful, especially in the word choices. Tell students to watch for the humorous way the narrator tells what happens. Point out that the writer probably chose certain words or phrases to give the tale a grand, storyteller-like tone.

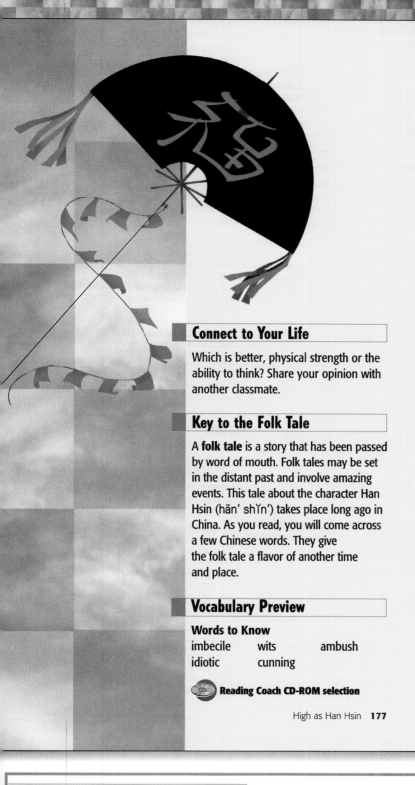

Connect to Your Life

Which is better, physical strength or the ability to think? Share your opinion with another classmate.

Key to the Folk Tale

A **folk tale** is a story that has been passed by word of mouth. Folk tales may be set in the distant past and involve amazing events. This tale about the character Han Hsin (hän' shǐn') takes place long ago in China. As you read, you will come across a few Chinese words. They give the folk tale a flavor of another time and place.

Vocabulary Preview

Words to Know

imbecile	wits	ambush
idiotic	cunning	

 Reading Coach CD-ROM selection

High as Han Hsin **177**

Connect to Your Life

As partners discuss physical strength versus mental ability, tell them to use as many examples as possible to support their opinions. (You may want to remind them that it's their "thinking ability" that is helping them discuss this topic.)

Key to the Folk Tale

Since this tale takes place long ago, the author writes in a style that is different from the way people talk today. Explain that as students get used to the author's unusual sentence construction, repetition, and subtle humor, they will have an easier time understanding the story.

Vocabulary Preview

Words to Know
  imbecile *n.* silly or stupid person
  idiotic *adj.* stupid
  wits *n.* ability to think fast
  cunning *n.* skill in fooling others
  ambush *n.* hiding place for a surprise attack

📖 For direct instruction on Words to Know, see page T237.

Building Background

"High as Han Hsin" is from a book of Chinese stories for children called *Shen of the Sea.* Since several shens come up in this story—such as the shen who places the stars in the sky, the shen who watches over imbeciles, the Shen of Storms, and the Shen of the Sky—you may want to tell students before they begin reading that a shen is a Chinese supreme being, or god, and that the Chinese had many shens.

Vocabulary Strategy: Preteaching

Context Clues Remind students that the **context clues** surrounding an unknown word can help them understand what the word means. Have students tell whether the context surrounding each underlined word restates the word's meaning or gives the opposite meaning.

1. One large star <u>mounted</u> higher and higher the while its companions fell. *(opposite)*
2. Wise men, <u>astrologers</u>, they who scan the heavens, said: "The stars that fall are mighty men who die." *(restatement)*

📖 For more on Context Clues, see page T237.

Unit 6 High as Han Hsin *Chinese Folk Tale*

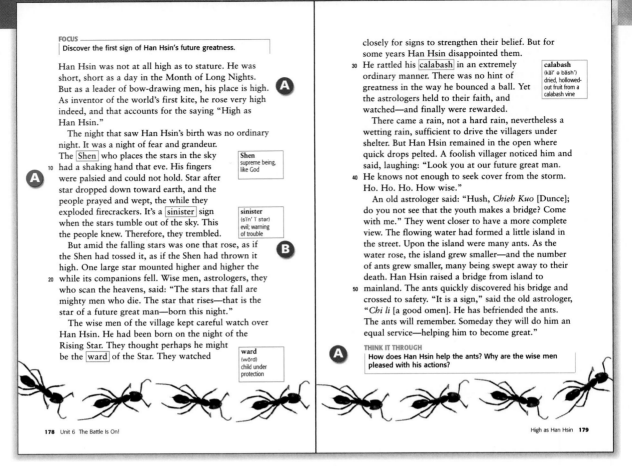

COMPREHENSION

FOCUS SKILL: Sequence

Remind students that **sequence** is the order in which things happen in time.

📖 For direct instruction on Sequence, see page T236.

🅐 **THINK IT THROUGH** How does Han Hsin help the ants? Why are the wise men pleased with his actions? *(He builds them a bridge to escape their flooding island. The wise men are pleased that Han Hsin has built a bridge for the ants. His helping the ants shows the wise men that the signs they had seen at his birth are accurate after all. Han Hsin does seem destined for greatness with help from the ants.)* **problem and solution**

LITERATURE

FOCUS SKILL: Style

Explain that in this folk tale the style of writing is a bit different from what students are used to.

📖 For direct instruction on Style, see page T236.

Use the following questions to encourage literary analysis.

🅐 Ask students what the subjects of the third and fourth sentences are (*place* and *he*). Point out that they are not at the beginning of the sentences. Many sentences in this story have subjects hidden in the middle of the sentence. **style**

🅑 Point out in lines 17–18 the words " . . . as if the Shen had tossed it." Then ask students how the end of the sentence is like the phrase you pointed out. *(It is a different way of saying the same thing.)* **style**

VOCABULARY

FOCUS SKILL: Context Clues

As students read this folk tale, remind them to look for **context clues** that restate an unfamiliar word's meaning or give its opposite meaning.

🅐 **palsied** Help students find the restatement context clues. *(shaking hand)*

FOR ENGLISH LEARNERS

Help students understand the following expressions and idioms:

Line 3: bow-drawing men
Line 5: accounts for the saying
Line 17: amid the falling stars
Line 30: rattled his calabash
Line 53: do him an equal service

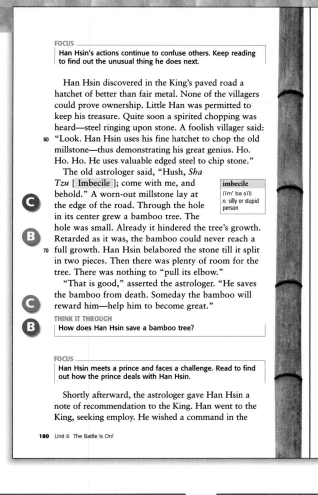

FOCUS

Han Hsin's actions continue to confuse others. Keep reading to find out the unusual thing he does next.

Han Hsin discovered in the King's paved road a hatchet of better than fair metal. None of the villagers could prove ownership. Little Han was permitted to keep his treasure. Quite soon a spirited chopping was heard—steel ringing upon stone. A foolish villager said: 60 "Look. Han Hsin uses his fine hatchet to chop the old millstone—thus demonstrating his great genius. Ho. Ho. Ho. He uses valuable edged steel to chip stone."

The old astrologer said, "Hush, *Sha Tzu* [Imbecile]; come with me, and behold." A worn-out millstone lay at the edge of the road. Through the hole in its center grew a bamboo tree. The hole was small. Already it hindered the tree's growth. Retarded as it was, the bamboo could never reach a 70 full growth. Han Hsin belabored the stone till it split in two pieces. Then there was plenty of room for the tree. There was nothing to "pull its elbow."

"That is good," asserted the astrologer. "He saves the bamboo from death. Someday the bamboo will reward him—help him to become great."

imbecile
(ĭm′ bə sīl)
n. silly or stupid person

THINK IT THROUGH
How does Han Hsin save a bamboo tree?

FOCUS

Han Hsin meets a prince and faces a challenge. Read to find out how the prince deals with Han Hsin.

Shortly afterward, the astrologer gave Han Hsin a note of recommendation to the King. Han went to the King, seeking employ. He wished a command in the

army. But His Majesty was in a sulky mood and would 80 not see the boy. Therefore, Han continued his journey into Chin Chou, a neighboring country. He went to the ruler, Prince Chin, and exhibited his note. The prince read—and laughed. "You are too small to serve in my army. My soldiers are giants, all—very strong. You—are *Ko Tsao* [Little hopping insect]. No." Han solemnly declared that his strength was that of a river in flood, and begged for a trial. "Well, if you are determined," said the prince, "take my spear and raise it above your head." The prince's spear was 90 solid iron from point to heel, and longer than the mast of a sea-venturing junk. Furthermore, it had been greased with tiger fat to prevent rust. Han grasped the spear to raise it. His fingers slipped. Down crashed the heavy weapon. "Take whips and lash him out of the city—clumsy knave that he is!" Prince Chin roared in a great voice—angrily. The spear had missed His Royal Person by the merest mite.

junk
(jŭngk)
Chinese ship

REREAD
Why does Prince Chin give Han this impossible test?

An old councilor spoke: "Your Highness, surely it 100 cannot be that you intend to let the rogue live? He will someday return with an army to take revenge."

"Nonsense," said the prince. "He is no more than an ant—and idiotic besides. How could such a fellow secure an army?"

"Nevertheless, I fear the ant will work your downfall. He must be killed." The councilor insisted. He argued so strongly for Han's death that, rather than hear more, the prince consented. "It is useless. But do as you wish. Send a squad of 110 horses to overtake him and fetch back his head."

idiotic
(ĭd′ ē ŏt′ ĭk)
adj. stupid

THINK IT THROUGH
Why does the prince give Han Hsin a death sentence?

COMPREHENSION

B **THINK IT THROUGH** How does Han Hsin save a bamboo tree? *(He splits the millstone that the bamboo is growing through so it can grow without something in the way.)* **problem and solution**

C Ask students to paraphrase, or restate in their own words, lines 95–98. *(Possible paraphrase: The heavy weapon crashed down. "He is such a clumsy knave!" roared Prince Chin angrily. "Take whips and lash him out of the city.")* **paraphrasing**

D **THINK IT THROUGH** Why does the prince give Han Hsin a death sentence? *(The councilor persuades the prince with the fear that in the future, Han Hsin will somehow cause the prince's downfall.)* **cause and effect**

LITERATURE

C Ask students why they think the writer reversed the order of words in some of the sentences in lines 63–71. *(Since this story took place long ago, the author might have done this to imitate the style of an ancient storyteller.)* **style**

VOCABULARY

B **retarded** Have students find the restatement clues. *(hindered the tree's growth)*

C **reward** Have students find the restatement clues. *(help him to become great)*

D **insisted** Ask for restatement clues. *(argued so strongly)*

FOR ENGLISH LEARNERS

Help students understand the following expressions and idioms:

Line 70: belabored the stone
Line 78: wished a command in the army
Line 98: His Royal Person
Line 104: secure an army
Line 110: overtake him and fetch back his head

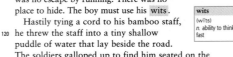

FOCUS

Find out how a stick of bamboo helps Han Hsin.

E   When Han Hsin beheld the soldiers approaching at top speed, there was no doubt in his mind as to what harsh errand brought them. He knew they intended to have his head. But Han, having lived so long with his head, had become fond of it, and preferred to keep it on his shoulders. But how? How could it be saved? There was no escape by running. There was no place to hide. The boy must use his wits.

D

    Hastily tying a cord to his bamboo staff,
120 he threw the staff into a tiny shallow puddle of water that lay beside the road. The soldiers galloped up to find him seated on the bank—fishing—and weeping. "And what ails you, simpleton?" a soldier asked. "Have you lost your nurse?" Between sobs Han answered, "I am hungry and I can't catch any fish." "What a booby!" said another soldier. "He fishes in a puddle no larger than a copper cash." "Look," said yet another, "he throws in the pole, and holds the hook in his hand. What a
130 *chieh kuo;* as foolish as Nu Wa, who melted stones to mend a hole in the sky. Do you suppose this is the creature we were told to kill?" He was answered: "Nonsense. Prince Chin doesn't send his cavalry to kill an ant. Spur your horses."

E

> **wits**
> (wĭts)
> *n.* ability to think fast

    When the troops returned and reported their lack of success, there was much talk. The councilor raged, offering to resign. He was positive that so long as Han Hsin lived, the government would be in danger. He was bitter because the troops had
140 mistaken Han's cunning for imbecility.

F

> **cunning**
> (kŭn' ĭng)
> *n.* skill in fooling others

182   Unit 6 The Battle Is On!

    Merely to humor the councilor, Prince Chin mounted a horse and galloped away with his troops.

F

THINK IT THROUGH

Why do the soldiers leave Han Hsin alone?

FOCUS

Prince Chin and Han Hsin meet again. Find out how Han Hsin deals with him.

    Han Hsin put his best foot foremost, hurrying toward the border. He longed to trudge the turf of his own country once more. It was not that homesickness urged his steps. Han felt reasonably sure that his friends, the soldiers, would shortly take the road again. The next time they might not be so easily deluded. Therefore, he hastened. But
150 it was useless. His own country was still miles distant when he beheld the dust of men who whipped their horses.

> **deluded**
> (dĭ lōō' dĭd)
> fooled

E

    It is not pleasant to have one's head lopped off. At times it is almost annoying. Han thought quickly. Near by was a melon patch. The melons were large in their ripeness. Upon a huge striped *hsi kua* the boy sat him down and wept. The tears coursed down his cheeks, and his body shook with sobbing. Undoubtedly, his sorrow was great.
160   Prince Chin stopped his steed with a jerk. "*Ai chi*— such grief. Are you trying to drown yourself with tears?" "I—I—I am hungry," stammered Han Hsin. "Hungry? Then why don't you eat a melon?" "I would, sire, but I've lost my knife. So I must s-s-starve." The prince was well assured that he had met with the most foolish person in the world. "What?

High as Han Hsin   **183**

COMPREHENSION

E **Reciprocal Teaching**

Suggestion: Predicting

Teacher Modeling To demonstrate the Active Reading Strategy of predicting, focusing on the first and second paragraphs, you could say: *Reading lines 111–116, at the beginning of the first paragraph, I started thinking, Uh-oh, they're coming after Han Hsin. What can he do? Then I recalled how almost from the beginning of the tale, most people criticize Han Hsin because they think he's an idiot. Except for the wise men and the councilor, they don't look beyond his appearance. That led me to predict that since he's really smart, he'll use what people think of him to his advantage. Then I read on and, sure enough, that's what he does when the soldiers come along. He pretends not to know how to fish.*

Student Modeling Ask a student to read lines 131–134 and make a prediction, based on the story so far, about what might

happen when the army returns. Encourage the student to cite information from the story to support the prediction. Then have the student read lines 135–142 and tell how his or her prediction was similar to or different from what actually happened.

F **THINK IT THROUGH** Why do the soldiers leave Han Hsin alone? *(They think he is too stupid to do anyone any harm and that he can't be the one Prince Chin wants them to kill.)* **cause and effect**

LITERATURE

D What is humorous about lines 113–116? *(In spite of the serious danger that Han Hsin is in, the author has him make a joke about keeping his head on his shoulders.)* **humor**

E Tell students that understatement is a kind of humor. The author states a fact in a way that is less

than truthful or without as much emphasis as it should have. Give a couple of examples. Then have students read lines 153–156 to find examples of understatement. *("It is not pleasant to have one's head lopped off. At times it is almost annoying.")* **humor**

VOCABULARY

E **booby** Have students find a restatement of *booby*. *(foolish, line 130)*

F **cunning** Have students find a contrast clue to the meaning of *cunning*. *(imbecility)*

FOR ENGLISH LEARNERS

Help students understand the following expressions and idioms:

Line 134: Spur your horses
Line 141: to humor the councilor
Line 143: put his best foot foremost
Line 147: take the road again
Line 160: stopped his steed with a jerk

Starve because you have no knife? . . . Strike the
melon with a stone. . . . Such a dunce. It would never
do for me to behead this fellow. The Shen who
170 watches over imbeciles would be made angry." A
trooper slashed a dozen melons with his sword. Surely
a dozen would save the idiot from starvation. Oh,
what an idiot!

F Han Hsin sat on the ground, obscuring
his features in the red heart of a melon as
the prince and his men departed. His lips
moved—but not in eating. His lips moved
in silent laughter.

> obscuring
> (ŏb skyŏŏr' ĭng)
> hiding

THINK IT THROUGH

G How does Han Hsin escape punishment from Prince Chin? How
are his actions similar to when he escapes the soldiers?

FOCUS

Find out what steps Han Hsin takes to win an important job.

Han Hsin bothered no more Kings with notes
180 setting forth the argument that he had been born
under a lucky star, and so deserved well. Quite

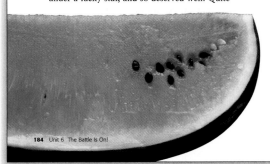

184 Unit 6 The Battle Is On!

casually, he fell in with King Kao Lin's army. He
received no pay. His name was not on the
muster. He hobnobbed with all the
soldiers and soon became a favorite. The
boy had a remarkable memory. He learned
the name of every soldier in the army.
Further, he learned the good and bad traits of each
soldier, knew who could be depended upon and who
G 190 was unreliable. He knew from what village each man
came, and he could describe the village with
exactness. All from hearing the soldiers talk.

> muster
> (mŭs' tər)
> list of troops

A fire destroyed the army muster roll. Han Hsin
quickly wrote a new list, giving the name of each
man, his age, his qualities, his parents, and his village.
King Kao Lin marveled. Shortly afterward, he added
Han's name to the list—a general.

G

THINK IT THROUGH

H How does Han Hsin win the position of general?

FOCUS

Han Hsin is now a general. Find out the surprises he has for
two of Prince Chin's armies.

Prince Chin made war upon King Kao Lin. He
marched three armies through the kingdom, and where
200 the armies had passed there was desolation,
and no two stalks of grain remained in any
field. Han Hsin moved against the smallest
of the three armies. The enemy waited, well hidden
above a mountain pass through which Han
must march. It was an excellent ambush—
there was no other passage. The mountain
was so steep no man could climb it.

> desolation
> (dĕs' ə lā' shən)
> destruction

> ambush
> (ăm' bŏŏsh)
> n. hiding place
> for a surprise
> attack

High as Han Hsin 185

COMPREHENSION

G **THINK IT THROUGH** How does
Han Hsin escape punishment
from Prince Chin? How are his
actions similar to when he
escapes the soldiers? *(Han Hsin
hides his face in a melon that he
tricks the prince into having a
trooper provide. As with the soldiers, Han Hsin disguises himself
by pretending that he is stupid.)*
compare and contrast

H **THINK IT THROUGH** How does
Han Hsin win the position of general? *(When a fire destroys the
muster roll, Han Hsin writes a new
detailed list from memory.)* **cause
and effect**

LITERATURE

F What does Han Hsin's encounter
with Prince Chin tell you about
him? *(that he's a clever and imaginative person who solves problems
quickly and convincingly—and
humorously)* **character**

G How can you tell that Han Hsin is
a very good listener with an
excellent memory? *(Just by listening to the soldiers talk, he is able to
make a new muster that includes
not only each soldier's name but
his age, qualities, parents, and village.)* **character**

VOCABULARY

G **unreliable** Have students
find a contrast clue to the meaning of *unreliable*. *("could be
depended upon")*

FOR ENGLISH LEARNERS

Help students understand the following expressions and idioms:

Line 168: It would never do
Line 182: fell in with
Line 184: hobnobbed

210 Han caused his soldiers to remove their jackets and fill them with sand, afterward tying bottom and top securely. The sandbags were placed against a cliff, to form a stairway. Up went Han and his men, to come upon the enemy from behind and capture the whole army—cook and general.

> **REREAD**
> How does Han Hsin avoid the ambush?

The second hostile army retreated to the river Lan Shui. It crossed the river, then burned all boats and bridges. So safe from pursuit felt the hostile general, he neglected to post sentries. Instead, he ordered all the men to feast and
220 make pleasure. Han Hsin ordered his men to remove the iron points from their spears. The hollow bamboo shafts of the spears were lashed together, forming rafts. Armed only with light bows, the men quickly crossed Lan Shui River and pounced upon their unready enemy. The feast was eaten by soldiers other than those for whom it had been intended.

> **sentries**
> (sĕn′ trēz)
> watchmen

THINK IT THROUGH
How does Han Hsin defeat the two armies?

FOCUS
Han Hsin now plans against Prince Chin's largest army. See what idea he discovers along the way.

Prince Chin led the third and largest army. He had far more braves than Han commanded. There could be no whipping him in open battle. In strategy lay the
230 only hope. Han Hsin clothed many thousand scarecrows and placed them in the battle line—a scarecrow, a soldier—another scarecrow, another

> **scarecrows**
> (skâr′ krōz′)
> fake figures made to look like people

soldier. In that manner, to all appearance, he doubled his army. Forthwith, he wrote a letter demanding surrender—pointing out that since his army was so much larger than Chin Pa's, to fight would be a useless sacrifice.

Prince Chin took long to decide upon his course. So
240 long it took him that Han grew impatient and sat down to write again. While he wrote, a strong wind broke upon the camp. The papers on Han's table were lifted high in air. Higher and higher they swirled, higher than an eagle—for the Shen of Storms to read. Han's golden knife, resting on a paper, was lifted by the wind, transported far over the foeman's camp.

Immediately an idea seethed in the leader's mind. If a small piece of paper could carry a knife, might not a large piece carry the knife's owner?
250 Especially when that owner happened to be not much more weighty than a three-day bean cake? It seemed reasonable.

> **REREAD**
> What idea is Han Hsin getting?

Again the little general took spears from his soldiers. The iron points were removed and the long bamboo shafts were bound together in a frame. Over the frame was fastened tough bamboo paper in many sheets. Away from prying enemy eyes, the queer contrivance was sent into the air. It
260 proved skyworthy, lifting its maker to a fearsome height. Thus was the *feng cheng* invented. Thus was the kite, little brother of the airplane, invented by Han Hsin.

> **contrivance**
> (kən trī′ vəns)
> invention

THINK IT THROUGH
Summarize the two parts of Han Hsin's plan.

COMPREHENSION

Ⓘ REREAD How does Han Hsin avoid the ambush? *(He has his men climb the other side of the mountain rather than go through the ambush pass.)* **clarifying**

Ⓙ THINK IT THROUGH How does Han Hsin defeat the two armies? *(While the first army waits to ambush Han Hsin, he has his men capture the enemy from behind. To defeat the second army, Han Hsin has his men make rafts, cross the river, and pounce upon the unprepared enemy.)* **problem and solution**

Ⓚ REREAD What idea is Han Hsin getting? *(He's getting the idea to lift himself into the air on a large piece of paper—which will turn out to be the first kite.)* **making inferences**

Ⓛ THINK IT THROUGH Summarize the two parts of Han Hsin's plan. *(He uses scarecrows to give the appearance of having an army twice its actual size. He invents the kite, which he plans to use as a way to transport himself.)* **summarizing**

LITERATURE

Ⓗ In what instances does bamboo come in handy to Han Hsin? What earlier event is a clue to these instances? *(He uses his bamboo staff as a fishing rod, and he uses his men's spear shafts to make rafts and a kite frame. He also uses bamboo paper for the kite. His breaking the stone so the bamboo could grow unhindered foreshadowed these instances.)* **foreshadowing**

VOCABULARY

Ⓗ feng cheng Have students skim to find a restatement clue to the meaning of this word. *(kite)*

FOR ENGLISH LEARNERS

Help students understand the following expressions and idioms:

Line 218: post sentries
Line 235: Forthwith
Line 246: foeman's camp
Line 247: an idea seethed in the leader's mind
Line 251: three-day bean cake
Line 257: prying enemy eyes
Line 259: proved skyworthy

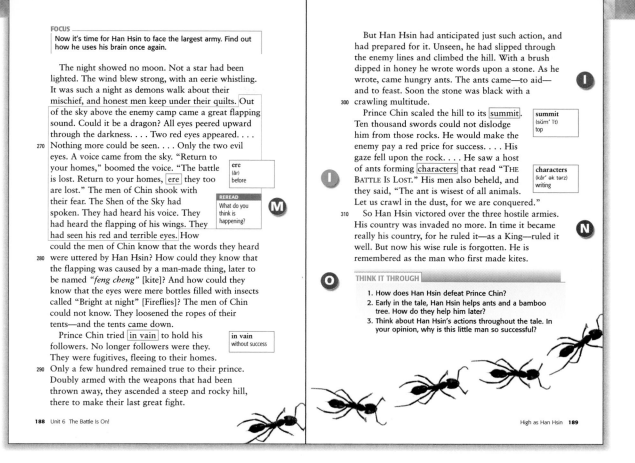

Now it's time for Han Hsin to face the largest army. Find out how he uses his brain once again.

The night showed no moon. Not a star had been lighted. The wind blew strong, with an eerie whistling. It was such a night as demons walk about their mischief, and honest men keep under their quilts. Out of the sky above the enemy camp came a great flapping sound. Could it be a dragon? All eyes peered upward through the darkness. . . . Two red eyes appeared. . . .
270 Nothing more could be seen. . . . Only the two evil eyes. A voice came from the sky. "Return to your homes," boomed the voice. "The battle is lost. Return to your homes, **ere** they too are lost." The men of Chin shook with their fear. The Shen of the Sky had spoken. They had heard his voice. They had heard the flapping of his wings. They had seen his red and terrible eyes. How could the men of Chin know that the words they heard
280 were uttered by Han Hsin? How could they know that the flapping was caused by a man-made thing, later to be named *"feng cheng"* [kite]? And how could they know that the eyes were mere bottles filled with insects called "Bright at night" [Fireflies]? The men of Chin could not know. They loosened the ropes of their tents—and the tents came down.

Prince Chin tried **in vain** to hold his followers. No longer followers were they. They were fugitives, fleeing to their homes.
290 Only a few hundred remained true to their prince. Doubly armed with the weapons that had been thrown away, they ascended a steep and rocky hill, there to make their last great fight.

ere
(âr)
before

REREAD
What do you think is happening? **M**

in vain
without success

188 Unit 6 The Battle Is On!

But Han Hsin had anticipated just such action, and had prepared for it. Unseen, he had slipped through the enemy lines and climbed the hill. With a brush dipped in honey he wrote words upon a stone. As he wrote, came hungry ants. The ants came—to aid—and to feast. Soon the stone was black with a
300 crawling multitude.

Prince Chin scaled the hill to its **summit**. Ten thousand swords could not dislodge him from those rocks. He would make the enemy pay a red price for success. . . . His gaze fell upon the rock. . . . He saw a host of ants forming **characters** that read "THE BATTLE IS LOST." His men also beheld, and they said, "The ant is wisest of all animals. Let us crawl in the dust, for we are conquered."
310 So Han Hsin victored over the three hostile armies. His country was invaded no more. In time it became really his country, for he ruled it—as a King—ruled it well. But now his wise rule is forgotten. He is remembered as the man who first made kites.

I

summit
(sŭm' ĭt)
top

I

characters
(kăr' ək tərz)
writing

N

THINK IT THROUGH

1. How does Han Hsin defeat Prince Chin?
2. Early in the tale, Han Hsin helps ants and a bamboo tree. How do they help him later?
3. Think about Han Hsin's actions throughout the tale. In your opinion, why is this little man so successful?

O

High as Han Hsin 189

COMPREHENSION

M **REREAD** What do you think is happening? *(Han Hsin, being carried by the kite, is hovering over Chin's camp and telling the men to go home because the battle is lost.)* **making inferences**

N Ask students to paraphrase the last paragraph of this tale. *(Possible paraphrase: Han Hsin defeated the three armies, and his country was never invaded again. He became King and ruled his country well. But that rule is forgotten. People remember him as the man who made the first kites.)* **paraphrasing**

O **THINK IT THROUGH**

1. How does Han Hsin defeat Prince Chin? *(First he puts scarecrows in the battle line to make it look as if he has twice as many men. Then he writes a letter demanding Chin surrender. Next he makes a kite from spear shafts and bamboo paper, and he puts fireflies in a bottle to make them look like glowing eyes. He*

uses the kite to hover over Chin's camp and tells him to surrender because the battle is lost. In one last move, he writes "The Battle Is Lost" in honey, and ants begin eating the honey and filling in the words. This scares Chin's men, and they surrender.) **sequence**

2. Early in the tale, Han Hsin helps ants and a bamboo tree. How do they help him later? *(Han Hsin makes bamboo rafts and a kite. The rafts help him win a battle. The kite frightens the enemy. The ants fill in the message written in honey. This message frightens the enemy soldiers and causes them to flee.)* **cause and effect**

3. Think about Han Hsin's actions throughout the tale. In your opinion, why is this little man so successful? *(because he's extremely intelligent and creative)* **drawing conclusions**

Option for Speaking Using question 3 on page 189, have pairs or small groups choose and briefly act

out scenes from the tale that show Han Hsin's ability to think quickly.

RETEACHING

If students need more help understanding **Sequence,** use pages T639–T641.

LITERATURE

I What earlier event is a clue that the ants might aid Han Hsin? *(his building them a bridge in the rain, and a wise man saying the ants will help Han in return)* **foreshadowing**

VOCABULARY

I **beheld** Students can skim to find the context clues that restate the meaning of *beheld. (saw)*

FOR ENGLISH LEARNERS

Help students understand the following expressions and idioms:

Line 301: scaled the hill
Line 304: pay a red price

1. COMPREHENSION

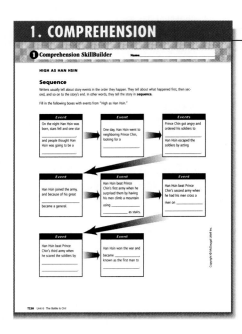

Sequence

Direct Instruction Tell students that in most stories, writers tell about events in the order they happen. The events are described in **sequence**. The first event leads to the second, the second to the third, and so on.

Explain that writers often use signal words to make the order of events clear. Words, phrases, and clauses such as *then, next, the following day*, and *when he returned* help the reader put events in order. Read these sentences from "High as Han Hsin" aloud and have students identify the words and phrases that signal that one event follows the other.

Shortly afterward, the astrologer gave Han Hsin a note of recommendation to the King.

When Han Hsin beheld the soldiers approaching at top speed, there was no doubt in his mind as to what harsh errand brought them.

When the troops returned and reported their lack of success, there was much talk. The councilor raged, offering to resign.

Comprehension SkillBuilder Answer Key:

On the night Han Hsin was born, stars fell and one star <u>rose</u>, and people thought Han Hsin was going to be a <u>great man</u>.; One day, Han Hsin went to neighboring Prince Chin, looking for a <u>job</u>.; Prince Chin got angry and ordered his soldiers to <u>kill Han Hsin</u>. Han Hsin escaped the soldiers by acting <u>foolish</u>.; Han Hsin joined the army, and because of his great <u>memory</u> became a general.; Han Hsin beat Prince Chin's first army when he surprised them by having his men climb a mountain using <u>jackets filled with sand</u> as stairs.; Han Hsin beat Prince Chin's second army when he had his men cross a river on <u>rafts of bamboo spears</u>.; Han Hsin beat Prince Chin's third army when he scared the soldiers by <u>flying above them on a kite and telling them that the war was lost</u>.; Han Hsin won the war and became <u>king</u>, known as the first man to <u>make kites</u>.

---

2. LITERATURE

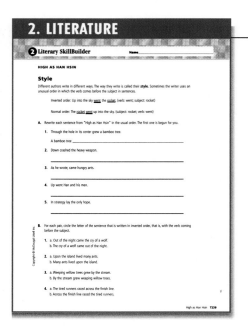

Style

Direct Instruction Tell students that every author writes a little differently. The way they write is called their **style**. List these ways in which one author's style can differ from another: length of sentences, complexity of sentences, use of descriptive details, vocabulary used, tone, and mood.

Tell students that the author of "High as Han Hsin" uses **inverted order** in some of his sentences, with the verb coming before the subject—

just the opposite of the more usual order of subject before verb.

Write the following sentence on the board. Help students see that it was written in inverted order by locating the subject and the verb.

Out of the sky above the enemy camp <u>came</u> a great flapping <u>sound</u>.

Now rewrite the sentence in the more normal order of subject before verb.

A great flapping <u>sound</u> <u>came</u> out of the sky above the enemy camp.

Literary SkillBuilder Answer Key:

A.
1. *A bamboo tree grew through the hole in its center.*
2. *The heavy weapon crashed down.*
3. *As he wrote, hungry ants came.*
4. *Han and his men went up.*
5. *The only hope lay in strategy.*

B. 1. *a* **2.** *a* **3.** *b* **4.** *b*

Direct Instruction
for SkillBuilder Copymasters

3. VOCABULARY

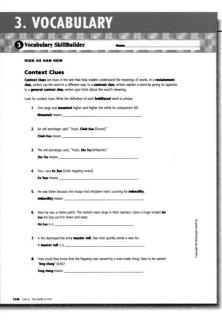

Context Clues

Direct Instruction Remind students that **context clues** are clues within the text that help readers understand new or unfamiliar words. Tell them that there are several types of context clues.

- A **restatement clue** says the word again in a different way. These clues are often set apart from the rest of the sentence by the word *or*, commas, dashes, parentheses, or, occasionally, brackets.
  Example: "*Ai chi*—such grief."

- A **contrast clue** provides a word or phrase that means the opposite of the new word. If you know the word's opposite, you can guess its meaning.
  Example: The soldiers thought that Han Hsin was a simpleton, but instead he was a clever person.

- A **general clue** is a hint about the meaning of a new word.
  Example: "I - I - I am hungry," stammered Han Hsin.

Vocabulary SkillBuilder Answer Key:

1. *climbed* or *rose*
2. *Dunce*
3. *Imbecile*
4. *Little hopping insect*
5. *stupidity*
6. *melon*
7. *list*
8. *kite*

4. WORDS TO KNOW

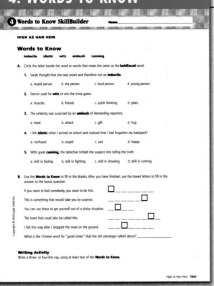

Words to Know

Direct Instruction As you present the **Words to Know,** here are some points you might want to cover. Instruct students to complete the first exercise by using the context clues.

Tell students to fill in the blanks in Section B by reading the clues and finding the word from the Words to Know list. If they have difficulty placing the word from the clue alone, they may count the blanks and fill in the corresponding word with the same number of letters. The students may also begin placing the boxed letters from questions 6–10 into the boxes at the bottom of the page as they move down the list. Point out to the students that the boxed letters are in order and they need not unscramble or rearrange letters to spell out the bonus question answer.

Writing Activity Pair students or group them together to work on the exercise. Have them read their creations aloud.

Words to Know SkillBuilder Answer Key:

A.
1. *a*
2. *c*
3. *b*
4. *b*
5. *a*

B.
cunning
ambush
wits
imbecile
idiotic

Bonus Question: chi li

5. SELECTION TEST

Selection Test Answer Key:
A. 1. *a* **2.** *c* **3.** *a* **4.** *b* **5.** *c* **6.** *b* **7.** *c* **8.** *b* **9.** *a*
B. *He used his intelligence.*

High as Han Hsin **T237**

HIGH AS HAN HSIN

Sequence

Writers usually tell about story events in the order they happen. They tell about what happened first, then second, and so on to the story's end. In other words, they tell the story in **sequence.**

Fill in the following boxes with events from "High as Han Hsin."

Event

On the night Han Hsin was born, stars fell and one star

_____,

and people thought Han Hsin was going to be a

_____.

Event

One day, Han Hsin went to neighboring Prince Chin, looking for a

_____.

Events

Prince Chin got angry and ordered his soldiers to

_____.

Han Hsin escaped the soldiers by acting

_____.

Event

Han Hsin joined the army, and because of his great

_____

became a general.

Event

Han Hsin beat Prince Chin's first army when he surprised them by having his men climb a mountain

using _____

_____ as stairs.

Event

Han Hsin beat Prince Chin's second army when he had his men cross a

river on _____

_____

Event

Han Hsin beat Prince Chin's third army when he scared the soldiers by

_____

_____.

Event

Han Hsin won the war and

became _____,

known as the first man to

_____.

HIGH AS HAN HSIN

Style

Different authors write in different ways. The way they write is called their **style.** Sometimes the writer uses an unusual order in which the verb comes before the subject in sentences.

> Inverted order: Up into the sky <u>went</u> the <u>rocket</u>. (verb: went; subject: rocket)

> Normal order: The <u>rocket</u> <u>went</u> up into the sky. (subject: rocket; verb: went)

A. Rewrite each sentence from "High as Han Hsin" in the usual order. The first one is begun for you.

1. Through the hole in its center grew a bamboo tree.

A bamboo tree _____

2. Down crashed the heavy weapon.

_____

3. As he wrote, came hungry ants.

_____

4. Up went Han and his men.

_____

5. In strategy lay the only hope.

_____

B. For each pair, circle the letter of the sentence that is written in inverted order, that is, with the verb coming before the subject.

1. a. Out of the night came the cry of a wolf.
    b. The cry of a wolf came out of the night.

2. a. Upon the island lived many ants.
    b. Many ants lived upon the island.

3. a. Weeping willow trees grew by the stream.
    b. By the stream grew weeping willow trees.

4. a. The tired runners raced across the finish line.
    b. Across the finish line raced the tired runners.

HIGH AS HAN HSIN

Context Clues

Context clues are clues in the text that help readers understand the meanings of words. In a **restatement clue,** writers say the word in a different way. In a **contrast clue,** writers explain a word by giving its opposite. In a **general context clue,** writers give hints about the word's meaning.

Look for context clues. Write the definition of each **boldfaced** word or phrase.

1. One large star **mounted** higher and higher the while its companions fell.

   Mounted means _____.

2. An old astrologer said: "Hush, **Chieh Kuo** [Dunce]."

   Chieh Kuo means _____.

3. The old astrologer said, "Hush, **Sha Tzu** [Imbecile]."

   Sha Tzu means _____.

4. You—are **Ko Tsao** [Little hopping insect].

   Ko Tsao means _____.

5. He was bitter because the troops had mistaken Han's cunning for **imbecility**.

   Imbecility means _____.

6. Near by was a melon patch. The melons were large in their ripeness. Upon a huge striped **hsi kua** the boy sat him down and wept.

   Hsi kua is a _____.

7. A fire destroyed the army **muster roll.** Han Hsin quickly wrote a new list.

   A **muster roll** is a _____.

8. How could they know that the flapping was caused by a man-made thing, later to be named "**feng cheng**" [kite]?

   Feng cheng means _____.

HIGH AS HAN HSIN

Words to Know

imbecile   idiotic   wits   ambush   cunning

A. Circle the letter beside the word or words that mean the same as the **boldfaced** word.

1. Sarah thought that she was smart and therefore not an **imbecile.**

   a. stupid person   b. shy person   c. loud person   d. young person

2. Darren used his **wits** to win the trivia game.

   a. muscles   b. friends   c. quick thinking   d. jokes

3. The celebrity was surprised by an **ambush** of demanding reporters.

   a. meal   b. attack   c. gift   d. hug

4. I felt **idiotic** when I arrived at school and realized that I had forgotten my backpack!

   a. confused   b. stupid   c. sad   d. happy

5. With great **cunning,** the detective tricked the suspect into telling the truth.

   a. skill in fooling   b. skill in fighting   c. skill in shouting   d. skill in running

B. Use the **Words to Know** to fill in the blanks. After you have finished, use the boxed letters to fill in the answer to the bonus question.

If you want to fool somebody, you want to be this.   ☐ __ __ __ __ __ __

This is something that would take you by surprise.   __ __ __ __ __ ☐ __

You can use these to get yourself out of a sticky situation.   __ ☐ __ __

The town fool could also be called this.   __ __ __ __ __ __ ☐ __

I felt this way after I dropped the meal on the ground.   __ __ ☐ __ __ __

What is the Chinese word for "good omen" that the old astrologer talked about? _____

Writing Activity
Write a three- or four-line rap, using at least two of the **Words to Know.**

HIGH AS HAN HSIN

A. Complete each statement by filling in the circle beside the correct answer.

1. On the night that Han Hsin is born, one star rises in the sky
○ a. while many others fall.   ○ b. along with many others.   ○ c. and then crashes to earth.

2. This is a sign that Han Hsin
○ a. will be born palsied.   ○ b. will be a great shen.   ○ c. will be a great man.

3. The first sign that Han Hsin will be great comes when he
○ a. builds a bridge for some ants.
○ b. drops Prince Chin's spear.
○ c. splits the millstone around the bamboo.

4. Han Hsin becomes a general in King Kao Lin's army after he
○ a. injures Prince Chin with his spear.
○ b. writes a new detailed muster roll.
○ c. wins one great battle after another.

5. Han Hsin defeats Prince Chin's first army by
○ a. clothing scarecrows and putting them in the battle line.
○ b. crossing the river on bamboo rafts and surprising Chin's men.
○ c. making a sandbag stairway and capturing the army from behind.

6. Han Hsin defeats Prince Chin's second army by
○ a. writing "The Battle Is Lost" with honey and ants.
○ b. crossing the river on bamboo rafts and surprising Chin's men.
○ c. scaring Chin's troops with a kite and some fireflies.

7. Han Hsin defeats Prince Chin's third army by
○ a. making a sandbag stairway and capturing the army from behind.
○ b. crossing the river on bamboo rafts and surprising Chin's men.
○ c. scaring Chin's troops with a kite, fireflies, honey, and ants.

8. In time Han Hsin becomes
○ a. a much taller man.   ○ b. the king of his land.   ○ c. the Shen of the Sky.

9. According to this tale, Han Hsin is best remembered today as the man who
○ a. first made kites.   ○ b. ruled his country well.   ○ c. defeated Chin's armies.

B. In your own words, explain why Han Hsin is able to defeat others.

_____

_____

Focus Skills

SkillBuilder Copymasters

Assessment

Readability Scores

DRP	LEXILE	DALE-CHALL
50	550	5.2

FOR WANT OF A HORSESHOE NAIL

adapted from James Baldwin

They are only two horseshoe nails. Yet they cost a king everything. Discover what happens behind the scenes of a battle.

Connect to Your Life

In the title of the selection, the word *want* means "being without something necessary." When has *not* having something hurt you?

Key to the Story

This story takes place when horses were very important in wartime. Blacksmiths made metal tools for riders and to be used for horses.

Vocabulary Preview

Words to Know
determine   rein
advancing
retreat

 Reading Coach CD-ROM selecti

190 Unit 6 The Battle Is On!

Connect to Your Life

You may want to have students discuss this topic in pairs. As they describe their wants and needs, have them consider how things might be different today if they could have gotten what they needed.

Key to the Story

Remind students that even though this story is based on things that really happened in the past, the author used his imagination to fill in the plot with dialogue and events that make the story more interesting.

Vocabulary Preview

Words to Know
determine *v.* decide
advancing *v.* moving forward
retreat *v.* withdraw from attack
reins *n.* straps used to control a horse

 For direct instruction on Words to Know, see page T248.

A battle is about to begin. Find out about the quick decision that someone makes.

King Richard the Third was preparing for the fight of his life. An army led by Henry, Earl of Richmond, was marching against him. The contest would determine who would rule England. A

The morning of the battle, Richard sent a groom to make sure his favorite horse was ready.

"Shoe him quickly," the groom told the blacksmith. "The king wishes to ride at the head of his troops."

10 "You'll have to wait," the blacksmith answered. "I've shoed the king's whole army the last few days, and now I've got to go get more iron."

"I can't wait," the groom shouted impatiently. "The king's enemies are advancing right now, and we must meet them on the field. Make do with what you have."

So the blacksmith bent to his task. From 20 a bar of iron he made four horseshoes. He hammered and shaped and fitted them to the horse's feet. Then he began to nail them on. But after he had fastened three shoes, he found he did not have enough nails for the fourth.

"I need one or two more nails," he said, "and it will take some time to hammer them out."

"I told you I can't wait," the groom said impatiently. "I hear the trumpets now. 30 Can't you just use what you've got?"

determine
(dĭ tûr′ mĭn)
v. decide

shoed
(shōōd)
fitted with a horseshoe

advancing
(ăd văns′ ing)
v. moving forward

Vocabulary Strategy

Multiple-Meaning Words Remind students that a single word can have more than one meaning, and that to figure out which meaning an author is using, students must use context. Read these sentences aloud, then ask what *nail* means in each.

1. We have to find a <u>nail</u> strong enough to hold up this mirror.
2. While watching a scary movie, Alex chewed on his <u>nails</u>.

For more on Multiple-Meaning Words, see page T248.

Building Background

Richard III became king of England in 1483, when he had the 12-year-old King Edward V and his little brother Richard put in prison (some say he had the boys killed). He lost the Battle of Bosworth Field in 1485 and was killed. This is the battle described in the story.

COMPREHENSION

FOCUS SKILL: Summarizing

Remind students that to **summarize** a story is to restate, in one's own words, only the most important elements of the plot, leaving out details.

For direct instruction on Summarizing, see page T247.

A **Teacher Modeling: Summarizing** Say: Here's how I would summarize what has happened up to this point of the story. I'll try to use as few words as possible.

King Richard the Third is in a battle to continue ruling England. He sends his groom to a blacksmith to have new shoes put on his horse. The blacksmith runs out of nails just as the groom is running out of time. He urges the blacksmith to finish, despite the fact that there aren't enough nails for the fourth horseshoe.

LITERATURE

FOCUS SKILL: Historical Fiction

Explain that even though this **historical fiction** story is based on events that really happened in the past, it contains fictional elements, such as description and dialogue.

For direct instruction on Historical Fiction, see page T247.

Use questions like this one to encourage literary analysis.

A What are some clues that tell you that this story is going to be historical fiction? *(King Richard and Henry—who really existed—are preparing to go to battle to see who will rule England. The battle will take place on horseback, which suggests that it took place long ago.)* **historical fiction**

VOCABULARY

FOCUS SKILL: Multiple-Meaning Words

As students come across the **multiple-meaning words** in this story, such as *iron* and *bar*, have them use context clues and a dictionary to figure out which meaning applies.

A **groom** means "one who takes care of a horse"

B **head** means "front"

FOR ENGLISH LEARNERS

Help students understand the following expressions and idioms:

Line 1: the fight of his life
Line 11: shoed the king's whole army
Line 17: Make do with what you have
Line 19: bent to his task

"I can put the shoe on, but it won't be as secure as the others."

"Will it hold?" asked the groom.

"It should," answered the blacksmith, "but I can't be certain."

"Well, then, just nail it on," the groom cried. "And hurry, or King Richard will be angry with us both."

THINK IT THROUGH
What does the groom tell the blacksmith to do?

FOCUS
Read on to discover how the groom's decision affects the battle.

The armies clashed, and Richard was in the thick of
40 the battle. He rode up and down the field, cheering his men and fighting his foes. "Press forward! Press forward!" he yelled, urging his troops toward Henry's lines.

Far away, at the other side of the field, he saw some of his men falling back. If others saw them, they too might **retreat**. So Richard spurred his horse and galloped toward the broken line, calling on his soldiers to turn and fight.

He was barely halfway across the field
50 when one of the horse's shoes flew off. The horse stumbled and fell, and Richard was thrown to the ground.

Before the king could grab at the **reins**, the frightened animal rose and galloped away. Richard looked around him. He saw

retreat
(rĭ trēt')
v. withdraw from attack

reins
(rānz)
n. straps used to control a horse

192 Unit 6 The Battle Is On!

that his soldiers were turning and running, and Henry's troops were closing around him.

He waved his sword in the air. "A horse!" he shouted. "A horse! My kingdom for a horse!"
60 But there was no horse for him. His army had fallen to pieces, and his troops were busy trying to save themselves. A moment later Henry's soldiers were upon Richard, and the battle was over.

And since that time, people have said,

For want of a nail, a shoe was lost,
For want of a shoe, a horse was lost,
For want of a horse, a battle was lost,
For want of a battle, a kingdom was lost,
And all for the want of a horseshoe nail.

THINK IT THROUGH
1. Why does King Richard lose the battle?
2. What do you think the king is feeling at the point that he offers to trade his kingdom for a horse?
3. Reread from line 65 to the end. What lesson do you think the writer of the story wants readers to understand?

For Want of a Horseshoe Nail 193

COMPREHENSION

B **THINK IT THROUGH** What does the groom tell the blacksmith to do? *(He tells the blacksmith to hurry up and shoe the king's horse with fewer nails than he needs.)* **summarizing**

C **THINK IT THROUGH**

1. Why does King Richard lose the battle? *(His horse's shoe falls off, which causes the horse to fall and then run away. When Richard's army sees him in trouble, they begin retreating. Henry's troops are soon upon Richard, and the battle comes to an end.)* **summarizing**

2. What do you think the king is feeling at the point that he offers to trade his kingdom for a horse? *(Possible answers: desperate, afraid, defeated, angry)* **making inferences**

3. Reread from line 65 to the end. What lesson do you think the writer of the story wants readers

to understand? *(Possible answers: Small details matter as much as big ones do; preparedness is everything; one small error or oversight can cause everything to crumble—and can even cost you your life.)* **theme**
LITERATURE

Option for Writing Students can write a paragraph that tells what lesson they think the writer of this story wants readers to understand. Does the lesson have personal meaning for students? If so, have them explain.

LITERATURE

B Ask students what they could do to find out how much of this story is fact and how much was made up. *(Students could read about this incident in different reference sources to see what really happened.)* **historical fiction**

VOCABULARY

C **thick** Have students look in the dictionary to find the correct meaning of *thick:* "most active part."

FOR ENGLISH LEARNERS

Help students understand the following expressions and idioms:

Line 47: the broken line
Line 57: closing around him
Line 59: My kingdom for a horse
Line 61: fallen to pieces

1. COMPREHENSION

Comprehension SkillBuilder   Name _____

FOR WANT OF A HORSESHOE NAIL

Summarizing

Summarizing means retelling the important ideas from a text in a shortened form and in your own words.

Write in the blanks in each box to state the most important ideas and details from "For Want of a Horseshoe Nail." Then complete the summary in the last box. Use as few words as possible to write the summary while still including the important ideas.

Richard the Third's army was about to _____	Richard's horse needed _____	The blacksmith didn't have enough _____ so one of the horse's shoes was not _____

As Richard rode his horse in battle _____, and Richard was thrown from the horse.	Without Richard to encourage them, his troops _____ and lost the _____

Summary:
When Richard's horse's shoe lost a nail during an important battle, _____

Copyright © McDougal Littell Inc.

For Want of a Horseshoe Nail **T249**

Summarizing

Direct Instruction Tell students that **summarizing** means retelling in their own words the important ideas in a text. Explain that a good summary includes only the most important information. It is short and to the point, sometimes as short as one or two sentences long.

Read this paragraph from "For Want of a Horseshoe Nail" and have the students summarize it.

> Far away, at the other side of the field, he saw some of his men falling back. If others saw them, they too might retreat. So Richard spurred his horse and galloped toward the broken line, calling on his soldiers to turn and fight.

Compare their summaries with the summary that follows. Together, decide whether their summaries include the most important information in the fewest possible words.

> When some men started retreating, Richard rode toward them, shouting at them to turn back and fight.

Comprehension SkillBuilder Answer Key:

Richard III's army was about to meet Henry's army in an important battle.
Richard's horse needed new shoes.
The blacksmith didn't have enough nails, so one of the horse's shoes was not fastened securely.
As Richard rode his horse in battle, the horse's shoe fell off, and Richard was thrown from the horse.
Without Richard to encourage them, his troops fell apart and lost the battle.
Possible summary: *When Richard III's horse's shoe lost a nail during an important battle, the shoe came off and Richard was thrown to the ground, losing both the battle and the kingdom.*

2. LITERATURE

Literary SkillBuilder   Name _____

FOR WANT OF A HORSESHOE NAIL

Historical Fiction

Historical fiction is a blend of fact and fiction. It is set in a real time and place in the past. But the writer imagines many of the thoughts, feelings, and words of the characters. Some parts of historical fiction are factual. Other parts are made up by the writer.

Read each passage below from "For Want of a Horseshoe Nail." Decide if it tells something that can probably be found in records or something that the writer has made up. Put a check in the correct column.

Passage from "For Want of a Horseshoe Nail"	Facts from records	Made up by writer
1. King Richard the Third was preparing for the fight of his life. An army led by Henry, Earl of Richmond, was marching against him. The contest would determine who would rule England.		
2. "You'll have to wait," the blacksmith answered. "I've shoed the king's whole army the last few days, and now I've got to get more iron."		
3. "I can't wait," the groom shouted impatiently. "The king's enemies are advancing right now, and we must meet them on the field. Make do with what you have."		
4. The armies clashed, and Richard was in the thick of the battle. He rode up and down the field, cheering his men and fighting his foes.		
5. He was barely halfway across the field when one of the horse's shoes flew off. The horse stumbled and fell, and Richard was thrown to the ground.		
6. His army had fallen to pieces, and his troops were busy trying to save themselves. A moment later Henry's soldiers were upon Richard, and the battle was over.		

Copyright © McDougal Littell Inc.

T250 Unit 6 The Battle Is On!

Historical Fiction

Direct Instruction Tell students that **historical fiction** is a combination of historical fact and the writer's imagination. Explain that writers often get their inspiration from interesting people and events of the past. Then they imagine how the people who were part of important events must have felt and what they might have said. Point out that writers of historical fiction usually create characters who never really lived. These characters often meet actual historical figures or take part in events that are part of historical record.

Read aloud these passages from a story about a pioneer in a wagon train headed west. Help students see that the writer probably made up the first one, and the second one could most likely be proven by searching through records.

- Josh was nervous and excited as he climbed into the covered wagon. He took one last look at the busy city of St. Louis and then shouted, "Oregon or bust!"
- The rough-and-ready mountain man Jim Bridger was a trusted guide for Oregon-bound wagon trains like this one.

Literary SkillBuilder Answer Key:

1. *fact* **2.** *made up* **3.** *made up* **4.** *fact* **5.** *fact* **6.** *fact*

3. VOCABULARY

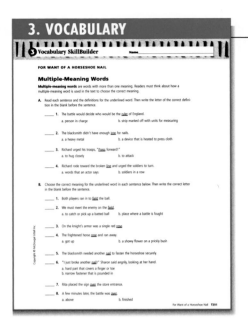

Multiple-Meaning Words

Direct Instruction Tell students that if a word has more than one meaning, it is a **multiple-meaning word.** To understand the meaning the writer intended, readers should pay attention to clues in the context—the phrases and sentences before and after the word. Explain that readers need to try out the possible meanings within the context to see which meaning makes the most sense.

Discuss this example from "For Want of a Horseshoe Nail."

The morning of the battle, Richard sent a **groom** to make sure his favorite horse was ready.

The dictionary lists at least two meanings for the word *groom: person whose job it is to take care of horses* or *man about to be married or just married.* Have students try each of these meanings in the sentence. It should be clear that the first meaning is the one that fits best.

Vocabulary SkillBuilder Answer Key:	
A.	**B.**
1. *a* **2.** *a* **3.** *b* **4.** *b*	**1.** *a* **2.** *b* **3.** *b* **4.** *a*
	5. *b* **6.** *a* **7.** *a* **8.** *b*

4. WORDS TO KNOW

Words to Know

Direct Instruction As you present the **Words to Know,** here are some points you might want to cover. For Section A, begin by reading aloud the poem with the words scripted underneath the blanks. Then have students place the synonyms in the blanks, and

have them read the poem aloud.

Homophones are briefly reviewed in Section C. You may choose to cover other examples as well (*soar* and *sore, knight* and *night, bear* and *bare,* etc.).

Words to Know SkillBuilder Answer Key:		
A.	**B.**	**C.**
1. determine	**1.** *b*	**1.** *rein*
2. Advancing	**2.** *c*	**2.** *reigns*
3. reins	**3.** *a*	
4. retreat	**4.** *a*	

5. SELECTION TEST

Selection Test Answer Key:
A. 1. *b* **2.** *c* **3.** *a* **4.** *a*
B. *Enemy soldiers got him, and he lost everything.*

FOR WANT OF A HORSESHOE NAIL

Summarizing

Summarizing means retelling the important ideas from a text in a shortened form and in your own words.

Write in the blanks in each box to state the most important ideas and details from "For Want of a Horseshoe Nail." Then complete the summary in the last box. Use as few words as possible to write the summary while still including the important ideas.

Richard the Third's army was about to _____ _____ _____ _____ .	Richard's horse needed _____ .	The blacksmith didn't have enough _____ so one of the horse's shoes was not _____ _____ .

As Richard rode his horse in battle, _____ _____ , and Richard was thrown from the horse.	Without Richard to encourage them, his troops _____ _____ and lost the _____ .

Summary:

When Richard's horse's shoe lost a nail during an important battle,

_____

_____

_____

_____ .

FOR WANT OF A HORSESHOE NAIL

Historical Fiction

Historical fiction is a blend of fact and fiction. It is set in a real time and place in the past. But the writer imagines many of the thoughts, feelings, and words of the characters. Some parts of historical fiction are factual. Other parts are made up by the writer.

Read each passage below from "For Want of a Horseshoe Nail." Decide if it tells something that can probably be found in records or something that the writer has made up. Put a check in the correct column.

Passage from "For Want of a Horseshoe Nail"	Facts from records	Made up by writer
1. King Richard the Third was preparing for the fight of his life. An army led by Henry, Earl of Richmond, was marching against him. The contest would determine who would rule England.	_____	_____
2. "You'll have to wait," the blacksmith answered. "I've shoed the king's whole army the last few days, and now I've got to get more iron."	_____	_____
3. "I can't wait," the groom shouted impatiently. "The king's enemies are advancing right now, and we must meet them on the field. Make do with what you have."	_____	_____
4. The armies clashed, and Richard was in the thick of the battle. He rode up and down the field, cheering his men and fighting his foes.	_____	_____
5. He was barely halfway across the field when one of the horse's shoes flew off. The horse stumbled and fell, and Richard was thrown to the ground.	_____	_____
6. His army had fallen to pieces, and his troops were busy trying to save themselves. A moment later Henry's soldiers were upon Richard, and the battle was over.	_____	_____

FOR WANT OF A HORSESHOE NAIL

Multiple-Meaning Words

Multiple-meaning words are words with more than one meaning. Readers must think about how a multiple-meaning word is used in the text to choose the correct meaning.

A. Read each sentence and the definitions for the underlined word. Then write the letter of the correct definition in the blank before the sentence.

_____ **1.** The battle would decide who would be the <u>ruler</u> of England.

    a. person in charge   b. strip marked off with units for measuring

_____ **2.** The blacksmith didn't have enough <u>iron</u> for nails.

    a. a heavy metal   b. a device that is heated to press cloth

_____ **3.** Richard urged his troops, "<u>Press</u> forward!"

    a. to hug closely   b. to attack

_____ **4.** Richard rode toward the broken <u>line</u> and urged the soldiers to turn.

    a. words that an actor says   b. soldiers in a row

B. Choose the correct meaning for the underlined word in each sentence below. Then write the correct letter in the blank before the sentence.

_____ **1.** Both players ran in to <u>field</u> the ball.

_____ **2.** We must meet the enemy on the <u>field</u>.

    a. to catch or pick up a batted ball   b. place where a battle is fought

_____ **3.** On the knight's armor was a single red <u>rose</u>.

_____ **4.** The frightened horse <u>rose</u> and ran away.

    a. got up   b. a showy flower on a prickly bush

_____ **5.** The blacksmith needed another <u>nail</u> to fasten the horseshoe securely.

_____ **6.** "I just broke another <u>nail</u>!" Sharon said angrily, looking at her hand.

    a. hard part that covers a finger or toe
    b. narrow fastener that is pounded in

_____ **7.** Rita placed the sign <u>over</u> the store entrance.

_____ **8.** A few minutes later, the battle was <u>over</u>.

    a. above   b. finished

FOR WANT OF A HORSESHOE NAIL

Words to Know

retreat   advancing   determine   reins

A. Write the word that is most like the **boldfaced** word below each blank in the following poem.

We are human.
We are brave.

We _____ which adventures
                    decide
will be ours.

_____ toward the wide world of the sun
                    Traveling
like wild horses,

and one day we will pull on the _____
                                        straps

and _____ into wet caves,
                    withdraw
holding onto the warmth.

B. Circle the letter next to the word or words that answer each question correctly.

1. What is the opposite of **advancing?**
   a. moving forward   b. turning back   c. following

2. If you put **reins** on an animal, what do you hope to do?
   a. clean it   b. feed it   c. steer it

3. Which of the following might make you **retreat?**
   a. barking dog   b. birthday present   c. kitchen table

4. If you **determine** which book you will read, which do you do?
   a. decide   b. wonder   c. ignore

C. Sometimes you come across words that sound alike but have different spellings and definitions. These are called **homophones.** For example:

   rein *n.* leather strap used to control a horse
   reign *v.* to hold power over something (like a king over a country)
   rain *n.* falling water

Place the correct homophone in the following sentences.

1. Hold on to the horse's _____ so you won't fall off.

2. In my family, my mother _____ over the dinner table.

FOR WANT OF A HORSESHOE NAIL

A. Answer each question by filling in the circle beside the correct answer.

1. When and where does this story take place?
- ○ a. in modern-day England
- ○ b. many years ago in England
- ○ c. In England during the future

2. Why were Richard the Third and Henry, Earl of Richmond, going to battle?
- ○ a. to settle a fight that they had earlier
- ○ b. to determine who would rule the world
- ○ c. to determine who would rule England

3. Why did Richard's horse lose its shoe during the battle?
- ○ a. The blacksmith didn't have time to put it on with enough nails.
- ○ b. The horse's hoof hit a tree root, and its shoe came off.
- ○ c. The groom and the blacksmith arranged for it to fall off.

4. What happened when Richard's troops saw him without a horse?
- ○ a. They turned around and ran away.
- ○ b. They started laughing at him.
- ○ c. They rushed to give him a new horse.

B. In your own words, tell what happened to Richard in the end.

_____

_____

Focus Skills

COMPREHENSION
Visualizing

LITERATURE
Descriptive Details

VOCABULARY
Prefixes and Suffixes

SkillBuilder Copymasters

 Reading Comprehension:
1 Visualizing p. T262

 Literary Analysis:
2 Descriptive Details p. T263

 Vocabulary:
3 Prefixes and Suffixes p. T264
4 Words to Know p. T265

Assessment

 5 Selection Test p. T266

Readability Scores

DRP	LEXILE	DALE-CHALL
51	490	4.2

Reading Fluency

 ★ Reading Fluency p. T267

For English Learners

This selection about the Vietnam War contains specialized vocabulary related to military flight equipment. You may want to introduce some or all of these terms before students read: *two-man F-4 Phantom jet, weapons-systems operator, air-to-air missiles, cockpit, eject, ejection lever, surface-to-air missiles, automatic rifle fire, mini-guns.*

by Don L. Wulffso[n]

More About the Vietnam War

In an attempt to help prevent the spread of Communism in Southeast Asia, President Lyndon Johnson sent the first U.S. ground troops to Vietnam in 1965 to fight on the side of South Vietnam. Many people opposed America's involvement in the war—so much so that they criticized and shunned returning veterans. In 1975, the United States withdrew from the war, and South Vietnam surrendered to North Vietnam. In 1976, the two areas were united into the single country of Vietnam.

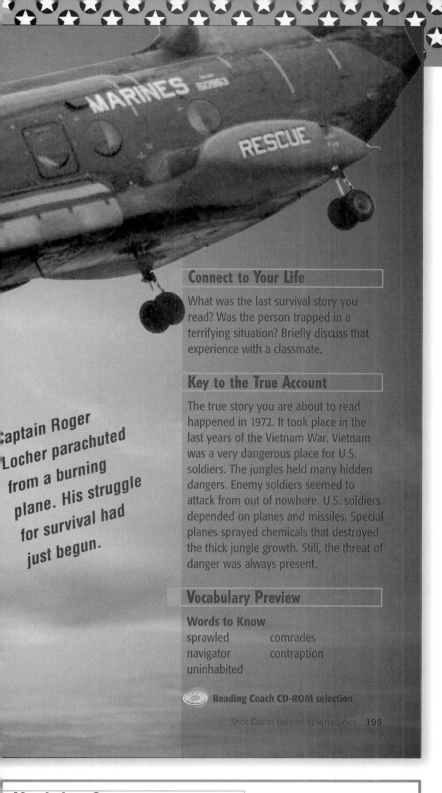

Captain Roger Locher parachuted from a burning plane. His struggle for survival had just begun.

Connect to Your Life

What was the last survival story you read? Was the person trapped in a terrifying situation? Briefly discuss that experience with a classmate.

Key to the True Account

The true story you are about to read happened in 1972. It took place in the last years of the Vietnam War. Vietnam was a very dangerous place for U.S. soldiers. The jungles held many hidden dangers. Enemy soldiers seemed to attack from out of nowhere. U.S. soldiers depended on planes and missiles. Special planes sprayed chemicals that destroyed the thick jungle growth. Still, the threat of danger was always present.

Vocabulary Preview

Words to Know

sprawled   comrades
navigator   contraption
uninhabited

 Reading Coach CD-ROM selection

Shot Down Behind Enemy Lines   195

Connect to Your Life

As partners discuss survival stories, have them tell each other what they thought was the scariest or most suspenseful part of the story, and what made it so. Was the story fiction, or did it really happen?

Key to the True Account

If students know people who served in Vietnam, they may know some stories about those people's experiences. Invite them to share what they learned about the Vietnam War from those who actually served in it.

Vocabulary Preview

Words to Know
sprawled *v.* spread out
navigator *n.* one who tells a pilot where to go
uninhabited *adj.* without people
comrades *n.* persons sharing the same activity
contraption *n.* mechanical device

For direct instruction on Words to Know, see page T261.

Building Background

On May 10, 1972, Captain Roger Locher's Phantom II jet was hit by a heat-seeking missile that had been launched from a MiG-21 fighter plane. Locher ejected from his burning jet and landed deep within enemy territory, 40 miles northwest of Hanoi, North Vietnam's capital city. Completely surrounded by the enemy, unable to use his radio, and without provisions, Locher knew that the only thing he could do was lie down and hide. "If they're going to capture me," he said, "they'll have to step on me." Although this selection mentions only two choppers in Locher's rescue, it actually involved the coordinated effort of 38 aircraft.

Vocabulary Strategy: Preteaching

Prefixes and Suffixes Remind students that a **prefix** is a word part that can be added to the beginning of a base word, and a **suffix** is a word part that can be added to the end. Copy the following chart, and have students add at least one more word to each row in the last column.

Prefix	Meaning	Examples
dis-	not; the absence of	dislike, disagreement, _____
Suffix	**Meaning**	**Examples**
-ly	in a certain way	slowly, warmly, _____

 For more on Prefixes and Suffixes, see page T261.

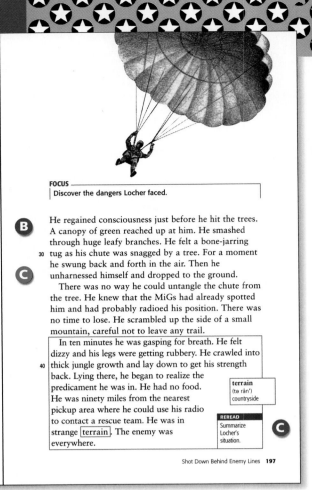

FOCUS
Find out what happened to Captain Locher's jet.

Below sprawled the jungles of North Vietnam. As he drifted down in his parachute, Captain Roger Locher's only thought was, *This can't be!* Getting shot down was something that happened to others. Like all fliers, he had never believed it could happen to him. But it had. Unreal as it seemed, it had happened to him!

A

Locher had taken off that morning from the airbase on his 407th mission. In the rear of the two-man F-4 Phantom jet, he was the navigator and weapons-systems operator. With air-to-air missiles, he had already knocked out three MiG-21s.

Suddenly he felt a numbing explosion. "We're hit!" yelled the pilot. The ship flipped over in a ball of flame. It tumbled out of control through space as smoke filled the cockpit.

A

"I'm going to have to eject," Locher shouted. He pulled hard on the ejection lever. He heard a blast as he was shot earthward. Then there was another blast, a great explosion as the plane disintegrated, taking with it the life of the pilot. An instant later Locher's parachute opened. He blacked out.

B

sprawled
(sprôld)
v. spread out; past tense of *sprawl*

navigator
(năv′ ĭ gā′ tər)
n. one who tells a pilot where to go

MiG-21s
(mĭg′ twĕn′tē wŭnz′)
enemy fighter planes

disintegrated
(dĭs′ ĭn′ tĭ grā′ tĭd)
broke apart

THINK IT THROUGH
What serious trouble was Locher in?

FOCUS
Discover the dangers Locher faced.

B

He regained consciousness just before he hit the trees. A canopy of green reached up at him. He smashed through huge leafy branches. He felt a bone-jarring tug as his chute was snagged by a tree. For a moment he swung back and forth in the air. Then he unharnessed himself and dropped to the ground.

C

There was no way he could untangle the chute from the tree. He knew that the MiGs had already spotted him and had probably radioed his position. There was no time to lose. He scrambled up the side of a small mountain, careful not to leave any trail.

In ten minutes he was gasping for breath. He felt dizzy and his legs were getting rubbery. He crawled into thick jungle growth and lay down to get his strength back. Lying there, he began to realize the predicament he was in. He had no food. He was ninety miles from the nearest pickup area where he could use his radio to contact a rescue team. He was in strange terrain. The enemy was everywhere.

terrain
(tə rān′)
countryside

REREAD
Summarize Locher's situation.

C

COMPREHENSION

FOCUS SKILL: Visualizing

Remind students that when they **visualize,** they use details that the author provides to help them form mental pictures of things, people, or events.

For direct instruction on Visualizing, see page T260.

A Ask students, What details help you to visualize or "see" what has happened? *(Possible answers: the words* flipped *and* tumbled*)* **details**

B **THINK IT THROUGH** What serious trouble was Locher in? *(His jet had been hit, and he was on his way down to landing behind enemy lines.)* **summarizing**

C **REREAD** Summarize Locher's situation. *(He had been shot down 90 miles from the nearest pickup area, he had no provisions, and he was surrounded by the enemy.)* **summarizing**

LITERATURE

FOCUS SKILL: Descriptive Details

Explain that **descriptive details** are details that appeal to senses and help readers visualize how things look, sound, smell, taste, and feel.

For direct instruction on Descriptive Details, see page T260.

Use the following questions to encourage literary analysis.

A What descriptive details help you know what Locher felt, saw, heard, and smelled when his jet was hit? *(felt—explosion, jet tumbling out of control, heat from the flame; saw—ball of flame, smoke; heard—explosion, pilot yelling; smelled—smoke)* **descriptive details**

B What did the trees look like just before Locher hit them? *(a canopy of green reaching up at him)* **descriptive details**

VOCABULARY

FOCUS SKILL: Prefixes and Suffixes

Remind students that knowing the meanings of different **prefixes** and **suffixes** can help them understand unfamiliar words. Have them separate the words into base words and affixes, to explain their meaning.

A **unreal** = un- + real = not real

B **earthward** = earth + -ward = toward earth

C **unharnessed** = un- + harnessed = not in a harness

FOR ENGLISH LEARNERS

Help students understand the following expressions and idioms:

Line 26: blacked out
Line 28: canopy of green

Crash Diet

When U.S. Air Force Captain Scott O'Grady's plane went down in 1995 during the war in Bosnia, he had to eat ants to survive. He smashed them against his backpack and ate them raw. After he had survived for six days on sour ants, grass, and leaves, rescuers found him. Guess what he did as soon as he got on the rescue chopper? Eat, of course!

With a compass and a map to guide him, Locher carefully set out southwest. Each step had to be checked for boot prints, broken twigs, or other signs that could give him away.

C

At noon he suddenly froze. He heard excited yelling coming straight at him. It was a search party of Vietnamese soldiers! He crawled into some thick brush. He lay still as the enemy came into view. He could see their faces. He could see their guns and sharp bayonets. Locher held his breath as the soldiers walked by within a few feet of his hiding place.

bayonets
(bā′ ə nǐts)
blades on the ends of rifles

The next day it happened again. He heard screams, shouts, rifle fire. *They're trying to scare me, flush me out like a game bird,* he thought. *Stay put. They've practically got to step on you to* 70 *find you.*

Hunger was beginning to take its toll on Locher. All he could find to eat were a few pieces of unripe jungle fruit. Water was no problem. It rained almost every night. But in the mornings he had to dry out, being careful not to let his boots and socks rot.

D

Mosquitoes and other insects tormented him endlessly. His skin was covered with red welts and stinging bites. Too, leeches crawled up inside his clothing. Time and 80 again he would pull up his pants to find his legs covered with the ugly things. Their

leeches
(lē′ chǐz)
worms that suck people's blood

198   Unit 6 The Battle Is On!

slimy black bodies were bloated with his blood. With disgust, he tore them from his flesh and crushed them.

D

E **THINK IT THROUGH**
What were some of the dangers Locher had to deal with during two days in the jungle?

FOCUS
Locher's struggle continued. Read about new problems he faced.

E

One nightmarish day passed into the next. Locher grew steadily weaker. He stumbled on through the jungle, not always sure of where he was going. Razor-sharp elephant grass slashed him. Dense brush often blocked his way. Sometimes he pushed through miles of jungle in order to make only a few yards of 90 headway. On the twelfth day he found a wide, well-worn path leading south. With newfound spirit he headed down it. It was a real relief from pushing through jungle brush.

The path led down into a narrow valley. It seemed uninhabited. But suddenly Locher saw two children coming right at him. They were herding water buffalo to pasture. He dove into some bushes. For the rest of the day he lay there in hiding, not daring to 100 move. In the evening, the children began herding the buffalo home. One of the beasts passed within a few feet of Locher. It stepped on a sapling, whacking it down on his ankles. He opened his mouth in pain but stifled any sound.

uninhabited
(ŭn′ ĭn hăb′ ĭ tĭd)
adj. without people

sapling
(săp′ lĭng)
young tree

Shot Down Behind Enemy Lines   **199**

COMPREHENSION

D Ask: What details help you visualize what the insects were doing to Locher? *(His skin was covered with red welts and bites, and slimy black leeches covered his legs and were bloated with his blood.)* **visualizing**

E **THINK IT THROUGH** What were some of the dangers Locher had to deal with during two days in the jungle? *(Vietnamese soldiers were everywhere, trying to scare and capture him; he was hungry; he had to dry out his clothes every morning; insects tormented him.)* **details**

LITERATURE

C Have students reread lines 54–65. Ask, to which senses do the descriptive details in these lines mostly appeal? *(hearing—excited yelling, soldiers walking; sight—soldiers' faces, guns, and bayonets)* **descriptive details**

VOCABULARY

Have students break the words into bases and affixes.

D **endlessly** = end + -less + -ly = in a manner without end

E **nightmarish** = nightmare + -ish = like a nightmare

FOR ENGLISH LEARNERS

Help students understand the following expressions and idioms:

Line 53: give him away
Line 68: flush me out like a game bird
Line 69: Stay put
Line 71: take its toll
Line 79: Time and again

After dark he wormed his way up the side of a mountain which overlooked a village. Hiding there, he spent a miserable night.

When morning finally came, he pulled a damp, crumbling map from his pocket. With difficulty, he
110 studied it. He found that in twelve days he had gone only seven miles! Ahead of him lay the Red River plain. It was nearly twenty miles wide and filled with small villages. He knew he could never cross it without being captured.

> **REREAD**
> How long might it have taken Locher to cross the valley?

F

Very weak, and not knowing what else to do, Locher remained in his hiding place. One day fused with another. On the twentieth day he knew he was wasting away. He squeezed skinny arms and legs.
D 120 He rubbed his buttocks and found only skin and bone. Slowly, the jungle was doing what the enemy could not. It was killing him.

G

THINK IT THROUGH
Why did Locher get discouraged? In what ways was the jungle killing Locher?

FOCUS

Read to find out what finally happened to Locher.

He drifted in and out of sleep. One afternoon he suddenly awoke to the flashes of surface-to-air missiles. They were being fired from the village below at U.S. aircraft. Even if it meant giving his position away to the enemy, he had to let his comrades know he was still alive. He pressed the transmitter button on his radio.
130 Both frightened and excited, he spoke into

> **comrades**
> (kom' rādz)
> *n.* persons sharing an activity

the radio: "Any U.S. aircraft that reads Oyster One Bravo, please come in."

He switched to receive and heard, "Go ahead, Oyster One Bravo."
The voice startled him. For a long moment Locher did not know what to say. He laughed. "Hey, I'm still down here after twenty-two days!" said Locher. "Relay that I'm okay."

> **REREAD**
> What do you think happened next?

H

He switched back to receive. The radio
140 remained silent. He repeated his message. Again there was no reply. His heart sank. No one had heard him. For a long while he hung his head. Then suddenly he was startled to hear another voice on the radio. It was saying, "We've got your position, buddy. Rescue forces on the way. Hold on. We're coming in."

Magically, helicopters appeared on the horizon. They came in high, then swooped down toward where Locher stood. He signalled the choppers by flashing a mirror. He was sure he was only moments away from
150 being rescued. But in the next instant MiGs appeared, their cannons blazing at the helicopters. Then, from the village, antiaircraft weapons joined the battle. In disbelief, Locher watched as the helicopters swooped down low to escape the deadly fire. They slipped over a ridge, then were gone.

> **REREAD**
> Is this what you thought would happen? Why?

F

I

It's all over, Locher told himself. He thought sadly of the loved ones he would never see. He thought of the pilots who had risked their lives for him. Sick and near
160 death, he sat down. He rolled onto his side in the jungle muck, waiting to die. He drowsed fitfully the rest of the afternoon and through the night.

J

THINK IT THROUGH
Why did Locher lose hope here?

200 Unit 6 The Battle Is On!

Shot Down Behind Enemy Lines 201

In his sleep Locher heard the steady beat of helicopter rotors. He opened his eyes. It was morning. Another pair of choppers was headed toward him! He thought he was dreaming. He blinked. The choppers were real. One slid in toward him. The other held back, ready to act in an emergency.

170   The lead helicopter hovered fifty feet above him. It began lowering a penetrator, a torpedo-shaped device with enough weight to break through the thick jungle growth.

> **rotors**
> (rō' tərz)
> spinning parts
> of machines

Automatic rifle fire broke out from the village. The second chopper went into action. It swept down and sideways. Rockets hissed, snaked toward the enemy. Explosions of red and orange billowed skyward, swept back over the village. Mini-guns blazed at the hidden foe.

E

180   The penetrator smashed through the overhanging trees. Broken leaves floated down with it like huge green birds. Locher grabbed the contraption. Trying to hold it steady, he pulled down the seat. He struggled to get into the seat. He slipped and fell. He grabbed the seat again, swivelled sideways into it. Then he felt himself floating, being lifted skyward. The jungle faded below. He looked up. He watched himself being reeled into the chopper.

> **contraption**
> (kən trăp' shən)
> n. mechanical
> device

G

190   "Brother, do you look awful!" laughed one man as another pulled him on board. Locher did not know what to say. He was too weak—and too happy—to say anything.

The ride home was the most beautiful journey of his life. The whole way he kept smiling. He looked at the crew and wanted somehow to say thank you. *But how* 200 *do you thank people for saving your life?* he wondered. There was nothing he could do but look at them with a big loving grin and let the tears roll down through his beard.

Captain Roger Locher smiles a short time after his rescue.

K

THINK IT THROUGH

1. How did the pilots rescue Locher?
2. What part of Locher's time in the jungle seemed the most dangerous? Give a reason for your opinion.

COMPREHENSION

K **THINK IT THROUGH**

1. How did the pilots rescue Locher? *(While one helicopter sent a penetrator down to pick him up, another helicopter protected it by firing rockets and guns at the enemy.)* **problem and solution**

2. What part of Locher's time in the jungle seemed the most dangerous? Give a reason for your opinion. *(Students can read portions of the text aloud as they explain their opinions.)* **drawing conclusions**

Option for Speaking and Listening: Have students ever been so overwhelmed that they couldn't speak? Invite them to discuss what Locher might have been thinking and feeling as he rode home in silence in the helicopter.

LITERATURE

E Have students list details that describe what the rockets looked and sounded like during the second chopper's attack. *(They snaked toward the enemy, and their explosions were red and orange; they made hissing noises.)* **descriptive details**

VOCABULARY

G **skyward** Remind students that they read *earthward* earlier and it meant "toward earth." Have students use the meaning of the suffix *-ward* to help them figure out what this words means.

FOR ENGLISH LEARNERS

Help students understand the following expressions and idioms:

Line 176: snaked toward the enemy
Line 188: The jungle faded below
Line 191: pulled him on board

RETEACHING

If students have trouble understanding **Prefixes and Suffixes,** use pages T613–T614.

1. COMPREHENSION

Comprehension SkillBuilder   Name _____

SHOT DOWN BEHIND ENEMY LINES

Visualizing

To **visualize** a scene means to see it in your mind. Drawing a sketch helps you place details correctly in a scene.

Review the final part of "Shot Down Behind Enemy Lines," after the pilot saw the children outside a village. Find answers to the following questions about the scene. Correct the sketch below as needed.

1. Did the pilot find a hiding place at the bottom of a mountain, partway up, or at the top? Draw an **X** in the sketch to show where Locher was.

2. Where was the village—at the top or near the bottom of the mountain? Draw a square in the sketch to stand for the village.

3. The first time helicopters tried to rescue Locher, they were driven off by enemy planes and ground fire. How many helicopters came the second time? If there are too many helicopters in the sketch, cross off the extra ones.

4. How did Locher get to the helicopter? Complete these steps.
   a. First, the helicopter dropped _____
   b. Second, Locher _____
   c. Last, the helicopter _____

T262   Unit 6 The Battle Is On!

Visualizing

Direct Instruction Remind students that **visualizing** means picturing a scene in one's imagination. A reader uses visualization to make sure he or she has examined the details carefully enough to bring them all together correctly.

Read aloud, or have a volunteer read aloud, the first three paragraphs of "Shot Down Behind Enemy Lines." Encourage students to imagine themselves in the position of Captain Locher. Ask: Before your plane is shot down, what do you see around you? After you eject, what do you see above and below you? What do you hear and feel after you eject? Remind students to call on their own experiences as well as the text in visualizing. In this case, for example, both plane rides and amusement park rides could help students picture and understand what Locher was going through.

Comprehension SkillBuilder Answer Key:

1. *The X should be drawn at or near the top of the mountain.*
2. *The square should be on the plain, some distance from the bottom of the mountain.*
3. *Three of the five helicopters should be crossed off.*
4. *(Wording may vary.)*
   a. *First, the helicopter dropped a penetrator that broke through the tree branches.*
   b. *Second, Locher pulled a seat down from the penetrator and got into it.*
   c. *Last, the helicopter pulled up the seat with Locher in it.*

---

2. LITERATURE

Literary SkillBuilder   Name _____

SHOT DOWN BEHIND ENEMY LINES

Descriptive Details

Writers often want to make a person, place, thing, or event seem real to readers. To do that, they include **descriptive details** about how a thing looks, sounds, feels, smells, or tastes.

Fill in the following cluster graph with descriptive details from "Shot Down Behind Enemy Lines." If you want to write more details from the story, add boxes.

(Cluster graph with center "Captain Locher in Vietnam" and branches: What he saw, What he heard, What he felt)

Shot Down Behind Enemy Lines T263

Descriptive Details

Direct Instruction Explain that when writers describe a person, place, thing, or event, they often use **descriptive details**. These bits of information about how a thing looks, sounds, smells, feels, or tastes help readers form a mental picture or experience a sensation.

Read this paragraph from "Shot Down Behind Enemy Lines." Ask students to identify which senses its descriptive details appeal to.

Mosquitoes and other insects tormented him endlessly. His skin was covered with red welts and stinging bites. Too, leeches crawled up inside his clothing. Time and again he would pull up his pants to find his legs covered with the ugly things. Their slimy black bodies were bloated with his blood.

Descriptive details that appeal to the sense of touch: *mosquitoes, stinging bites, slimy leeches crawling inside his clothing.* Descriptive details that appeal to the sense of sight: *red welts, stinging bites, slimy black bodies bloated with blood.*

Literary SkillBuilder Answer Key:

Details will vary. Possible answers:

What he saw: *green branches, thick brush, slimy black leeches, wide path, narrow valley, children herding water buffalo, damp map, missiles flashing, helicopters on the horizon, explosions*

What he heard: *pilot shouting, blast, yelling of soldiers, screams, shouts, rifle fire, voice on radio, beat of helicopter rotors, rockets' hiss*

What he felt: *explosion, tug as chute snags tree, dizzy, rubbery legs, mosquitoes, welts and bites, leeches crawling inside his clothes, sharp grass, sapling slapping his ankles, floating feeling*

3. VOCABULARY

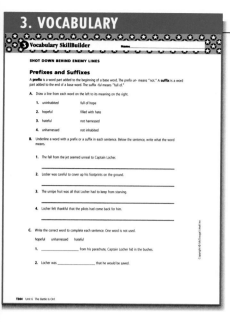

Prefixes and Suffixes

Direct Instruction Remind students that a **prefix** is a word part that is added to the beginning of a base word. A **suffix** is a word part added to the end of a base word. Point out that each prefix or suffix has a meaning of its own. Explain that when you add a prefix or a suffix to a base word, you make a new word with a meaning different from that of the base word alone.

Write the following words on the board and have students find the base word and the prefix or suffix: *graceful, unhappy, replay, slowly, careless*.

Present this chart of common prefixes and suffixes and their meanings.

Prefix or Suffix	Meaning	Example	Meaning
re-	again	rewrite	write again
un-	not	unjust	not just
-ly	in a certain way	quickly	in a quick way
-ful	full of	wonderful	full of wonder
-less	without	hairless	without hair

Vocabulary SkillBuilder Answer Key:

A.
1. *not inhabited*
2. *full of hope*
3. *filled with hate*
4. *not harnessed*

B.
1. *unreal, not real*
2. *careful, full of care*
3. *unripe, not ripe*
4. *thankful, full of thanks*

C.
1. *Unharnessed*
2. *hopeful*

4. WORDS TO KNOW

Words to Know

Direct Instruction As you present the **Words to Know,** here are some points you might want to cover. Help students to identify the parts of the vocabulary words. Stress the importance of finding the base of each word. Help students remove prefixes and suffixes first.
un- + **inhabit** + -ed = *uninhabited*
navigate + -or = *navigator*

-or: suffix meaning "one who performs a specified action"
sprawl + -ed = *sprawled* (past-tense form of *sprawl*)

Writing Activity Pair students or allow them to work in groups to complete the exercise. Have volunteers read their creations aloud.

Words to Know SkillBuilder Answer Key:

A.
1. *sprawled*
2. *contraption*
3. *navigator*
4. *comrades*
5. *uninhabited*

B.
1. *c*
2. *b*
3. *c*
4. *a*

5. SELECTION TEST

Selection Test Answer Key:
A. 1. *false* 2. *false* 3. *true* 4. *true* 5. *false* 6. *true* 7. *true* 8. *false* 9. *true*
B. *One fought off the enemy while the other picked Locher up.*

SHOT DOWN BEHIND ENEMY LINES

Visualizing

To **visualize** a scene means to see it in your mind. Drawing a sketch helps you place details correctly in a scene.

Review the final part of "Shot Down Behind Enemy Lines," after the pilot saw the children outside a village. Find answers to the following questions about the scene. Correct the sketch below as needed.

1. Did the pilot find a hiding place at the bottom of a mountain, partway up, or at the top? Draw an **X** in the sketch to show where Locher was.

2. Where was the village—at the top or near the bottom of the mountain? Draw a square in the sketch to stand for the village.

3. The first time helicopters tried to rescue Locher, they were driven off by enemy planes and ground fire. How many helicopters came the second time? If there are too many helicopters in the sketch, cross off the extra ones.

4. How did Locher get to the helicopter? Complete these steps.

a. First, the helicopter dropped _____

_____

b. Second, Locher _____

_____

c. Last, the helicopter _____

_____

SHOT DOWN BEHIND ENEMY LINES

Descriptive Details

Writers often want to make a person, place, thing, or event seem real to readers. To do that, they include **descriptive details** about how a thing looks, sounds, feels, smells, or tastes.

Fill in the following cluster graph with descriptive details from "Shot Down Behind Enemy Lines." If you want to write more details from the story, add boxes.

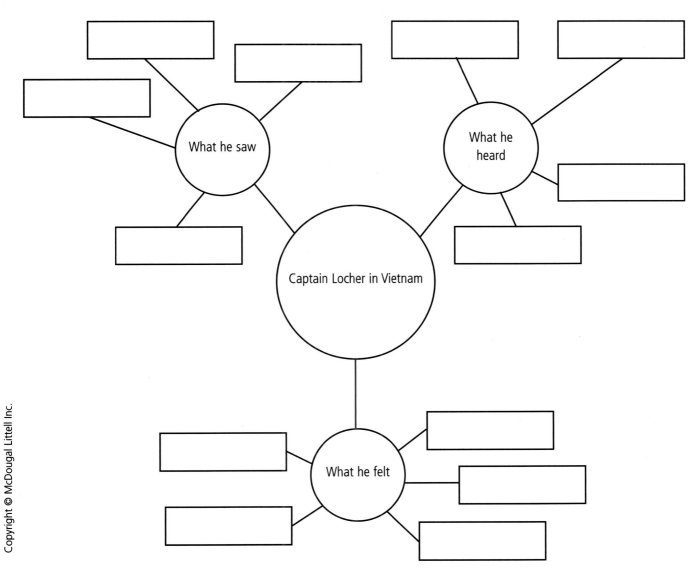

SHOT DOWN BEHIND ENEMY LINES

Prefixes and Suffixes

A **prefix** is a word part added to the beginning of a base word. The prefix *un-* means "not." A **suffix** is a word part added to the end of a base word. The suffix *-ful* means "full of."

A. Draw a line from each word on the left to its meaning on the right.

1. uninhabited   full of hope

2. hopeful   filled with hate

3. hateful   not harnessed

4. unharnessed   not inhabited

B. Underline a word with a prefix or a suffix in each sentence. Below the sentence, write what the word means.

1. The fall from the jet seemed unreal to Captain Locher.

    _____

2. Locker was careful to cover up his footprints on the ground.

    _____

3. The unripe fruit was all that Locher had to keep from starving.

    _____

4. Locher felt thankful that the pilots had come back for him.

    _____

C. Write the correct word to complete each sentence. One word is not used.

hopeful   unharnessed   hateful

1. _____ from his parachute, Captain Locher hid in the bushes.

2. Locher was _____ that he would be saved.

SHOT DOWN BEHIND ENEMY LINES

Words to Know

sprawled   navigator   contraption   uninhabited   comrades

A. Write in the blank the word from the list that best completes the sentence.

1. I came home from school to find my cat _____ on the couch.

2. Natasha tried her hardest to open the strange boxlike _____.

3. I drove the car, but my cousin was the _____, reading the map.

4. The army generals were close friends, a group of

   _____.

5. The little house in the woods was empty and looked _____.

B. Circle the letter next to the word that doesn't belong. Use the dictionary, if you need to.

1. a. uninhabited   b. empty   c. crowded

2. a. machine   b. bread   c. contraption

3. a. enemies   b. rivals   c. comrades

4. a. folded   b. spread out   c. sprawled

Writing Activity
Skywriters are pilots. Their job is to write messages in the sky with a trail of smoke from their planes. If you were to send a message to your city by a skywriter, what would it say? Use at least one word from the **Words to Know.**

SHOT DOWN BEHIND ENEMY LINES

A. Write **true** or **false** on the line next to each statement.

_____ **1.** Although this selection is fiction, it is based on things that really happened in the past.

_____ **2.** The setting of this selection is an African jungle.

_____ **3.** Captain Roger Locher's jet got shot down behind enemy lines.

_____ **4.** When he parachuted out of the jet, he landed ninety miles from the nearest pickup area.

_____ **5.** With a compass and a map, Locher had an easy time making his way back to safety.

_____ **6.** In twelve days, he had covered only seven miles.

_____ **7.** One afternoon Locher heard U.S. aircraft overhead.

_____ **8.** He was unable to radio them, though, so he wasn't rescued that day.

_____ **9.** The next morning a pair of U.S. choppers located Locher.

B. In your own words, explain how the pilots rescued Locher.

_____

_____

Reading Fluency SkillBuilder

Name_____

Reader directions:

Cut this paper in half. Practice reading the passage aloud until you don't make any mistakes.
Then have someone listen to you read. Use your voice to show the unusual actions.

from "Crash Diet"

When U.S. Air Force Captain Scott O'Grady's plane went down in 1995 during the war in Bosnia, he had to eat ants to survive. He smashed them against his backpack and ate them raw. After he had survived for six days on sour ants, grass, and leaves, rescuers found him. Guess what he did as soon as he got on the rescue chopper? Eat, of course!

✂ cut along dotted line

Checker directions:

Follow along as the passage is read. Make a dot under each word the reader misses.
Show the reader the missed words. Erase the dots and repeat for each reading.

from "Crash Diet"

When U.S. Air Force Captain Scott O'Grady's plane went down in 1995 during the war in Bosnia, he had to eat ants to survive. He smashed them against his backpack and ate them raw. After he had survived for six days on sour ants, grass, and leaves, rescuers found him. Guess what he did as soon as he got on the rescue chopper? Eat, of course!

Use this chart for Timed Readings and Repeated Readings.

Reading	1	2	3	4	5
Time (minutes/seconds)					
Words Missed					

Focus Skills

COMPREHENSION
Problem and Solution

LITERATURE
Climax

VOCABULARY
Context Clues: Synonyms

SkillBuilder Copymasters

 Reading Comprehension:
1 Problem and Solution p. T276

 Literary Analysis:
2 Climax p. T277

 Vocabulary:
3 Context Clues p. T278
4 Words to Know p. T279

Assessment

 5 Selection Test p. T280

Readability Scores

DRP	LEXILE	DALE-CHALL
55	570	5.2

Reading Fluency

 ★ Reading Fluency p. T281

For English Learners

Students may wonder what the title "Fa Mulan" means. Explain that in the Chinese culture, a person's last name, or family name, comes before his or her first name. Put another way, if Mulan had been born in the United States, her name would have been Mulan Fa.

Fa Mulan
by Robert D. San Souci

204   Unit 6 The Battle Is On!

Vocabulary Strategy: Preteaching

Context Clues: Synonyms Tell students that one kind of context clue that can help unlock the meaning of an unfamiliar word is a synonym. Remind them that a **synonym** is a word that has the same, or nearly the same, meaning as another word.

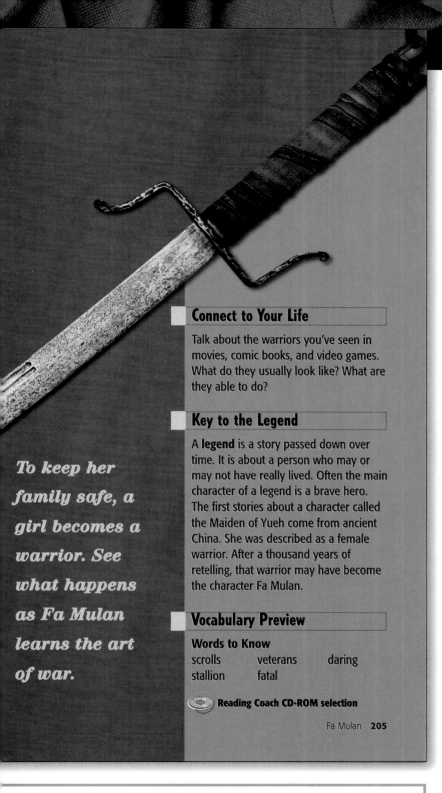

To keep her family safe, a girl becomes a warrior. See what happens as Fa Mulan learns the art of war.

Connect to Your Life

Talk about the warriors you've seen in movies, comic books, and video games. What do they usually look like? What are they able to do?

Key to the Legend

A **legend** is a story passed down over time. It is about a person who may or may not have really lived. Often the main character of a legend is a brave hero. The first stories about a character called the Maiden of Yueh come from ancient China. She was described as a female warrior. After a thousand years of retelling, that warrior may have become the character Fa Mulan.

Vocabulary Preview

Words to Know

scrolls   veterans   daring
stallion   fatal

 Reading Coach CD-ROM selection

Fa Mulan **205**

Connect to Your Life

As you guide students in a discussion about warriors they've seen, tally up the number of males versus females. What does this say about people's perceptions of warriors? Also ask if there are any physical or mental qualities that all of the warriors share.

Key to the Legend

Remind students that most legends are based on real people whose behavior and accomplishments get more and more exaggerated as their stories are retold. As students read this selection, tell them to think about how and why Fa Mulan became a legendary character.

Vocabulary Preview

Words to Know
scrolls *n.* rolls of paper, usually with writing on them
stallion *n.* adult male horse
veterans *n.* soldiers with long experience
fatal *adj.* deadly
daring *n.* boldness

For direct instruction on Words to Know, see page T275.

Building Background

In order to write his book *Fa Mulan*, author Robert D. San Souci did extensive research into the life of the real Fa Mulan. For the plot of the story, San Souci followed the events in a ballad called *The Song of Fa Mulan*, which is thought to have been written between A.D. 420 and A.D. 589. San Souci based Mulan's victorious plan of attack on information that he found in *The Art of War*, a book of military strategy that was written more than 2300 years ago, and that he believes Fa Mulan actually studied. This book is still used in China today.

Write these sentences. Have students identify the synonym in context for each underlined word.

1. Fa Mulan was so <u>anxious</u> for her father's safety that she worried about what she could do to help him.

2. Fa Mulan's <u>deeds</u> as a soldier have been remembered long after the actions of the men she fought beside.

 For more on Context Clues: Synonyms, see page T275.

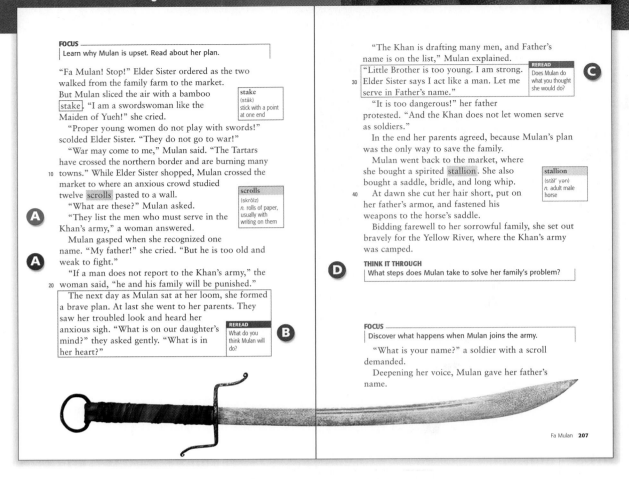

FOCUS

Learn why Mulan is upset. Read about her plan.

"Fa Mulan! Stop!" Elder Sister ordered as the two walked from the family farm to the market. But Mulan sliced the air with a bamboo stake. "I am a swordswoman like the Maiden of Yueh!" she cried.

stake
(stāk)
stick with a point at one end

"Proper young women do not play with swords!" scolded Elder Sister. "They do not go to war!"

"War may come to me," Mulan said. "The Tartars have crossed the northern border and are burning many

10 towns." While Elder Sister shopped, Mulan crossed the market to where an anxious crowd studied twelve scrolls pasted to a wall.

"What are these?" Mulan asked.

scrolls
(skrōlz)
n. rolls of paper, usually with writing on them

 "They list the men who must serve in the Khan's army," a woman answered.

Mulan gasped when she recognized one name. "My father!" she cried. "But he is too old and weak to fight."

 "If a man does not report to the Khan's army," the

20 woman said, "he and his family will be punished."

The next day as Mulan sat at her loom, she formed a brave plan. At last she went to her parents. They saw her troubled look and heard her anxious sigh. "What is on our daughter's mind?" they asked gently. "What is in her heart?"

REREAD
What do you think Mulan will do?

B

"The Khan is drafting many men, and Father's name is on the list," Mulan explained.

30 "Little Brother is too young. I am strong. Elder Sister says I act like a man. Let me serve in Father's name."

REREAD
Does Mulan do what you thought she would do?

C

"It is too dangerous!" her father protested. "And the Khan does not let women serve as soldiers."

In the end her parents agreed, because Mulan's plan was the only way to save the family.

Mulan went back to the market, where she bought a spirited stallion. She also bought a saddle, bridle, and long whip.

stallion
(stăl′ yən)
n. adult male horse

40 At dawn she cut her hair short, put on her father's armor, and fastened his weapons to the horse's saddle.

Bidding farewell to her sorrowful family, she set out bravely for the Yellow River, where the Khan's army was camped.

THINK IT THROUGH

What steps does Mulan take to solve her family's problem?

D

FOCUS

Discover what happens when Mulan joins the army.

"What is your name?" a soldier with a scroll demanded.

Deepening her voice, Mulan gave her father's name.

Fa Mulan **207**

COMPREHENSION

FOCUS SKILL: Problem and Solution

Tell students that in this legend, Mulan and her family have a **problem.** To solve their problem, Mulan comes up with a risky and clever **solution.**

For direct instruction on Problem and Solution, see page T274.

A Ask, What is Mulan's problem? *(Her father has been drafted to serve in the Khan's army, but he's too old and weak to fight. Further, if he doesn't show up to fight, he and his family will be punished.)* **problem and solution**

B REREAD What do you think Mulan will do? *(Most students will predict that Mulan will try to help her father in some way.)* **predicting**

C REREAD Does Mulan do what you thought she would do? *(Have students confirm their predictions.)* **predicting**

D **THINK IT THROUGH** What steps does Mulan take to solve her family's problem? *(She outfits herself and goes to join the army.)* **problem and solution**

LITERATURE

FOCUS SKILL: Climax

Tell students that a story's **climax** is its turning point—the point in the plot during which the main conflict, or problem, is resolved and the outcome becomes clear.

For direct instruction on Climax, see page T274.

VOCABULARY

FOCUS SKILL: Synonyms

Remind students that a **synonym** is a word that has the same or nearly the same meaning as another word.

A **serve** Help students skim the page to see that in this context, the word *fight* (line 18) is a synonym of *serve.*

FOR ENGLISH LEARNERS

Help students understand the following expressions and idioms:

Line 3: sliced the air
Line 31: in Father's name
Line 35: In the end

50 The man nodded, marked his list, and waved her away.

Leading her stallion to the water, Mulan whispered, "I am afraid, but also excited." She pointed her sword at the setting sun.

(A) "I will be like the Maiden of Yueh, the greatest swordswoman."

Before sunrise, the army marched to Black Mountain. In that lonely place, the only sound was the cry of birds and the whicker of wild horses. But as **(B)** 60 the troops marched north across the grasslands beyond, to join with other armies that the Khan had raised, Mulan heard a new sound: the jangle of Tartar bridles and armor.

Soon the Tartars swept over the plain. Spotting the Khan's forces, the enemy halted. The two armies faced each other.

208 Unit 6 The Battle Is On!

Shouting orders, the Chinese generals positioned their troops. Mulan and other new soldiers were placed beside veterans. Then the **(E)** 70 sudden pounding of drums filled the air— the signal to attack! With a shout, Mulan **(C)** urged her steed at the enemy. An armored Tartar rider raced to meet her. The shock of their clashing spears nearly unseated Mulan. But she imagined how the Maiden of Yueh would react. She struck the Tartar's shield and helmet. Her mount suddenly lurched sideways, forcing the enemy's horse to buck and rear, unsettling his rider. Taking this advantage, Mulan delivered a fatal 80 thrust, and the man tumbled into the dust.

(B) Soon after this, the Khan's forces broke the Tartar line. As the Chinese surged forward, Mulan helped drive the enemy back.

veterans
(vĕt' ər ənz)
n. soldiers with long experience

fatal
(fāt' l)
adj. deadly

(F) THINK IT THROUGH
What helps Mulan to survive her first battle?

FOCUS
Mulan gains more experience in war. Find out how she wins the respect of her fellow warriors.

In the months that followed, Mulan increased her strength and improved her swordplay. "You excel because you balance female and male energies," one veteran told her. "A good swordsman should appear as calm as a fine lady, but he must be capable of quick action like a surprised tiger."
90 Mulan studied the art of war to learn how great generals planned and carried out battles. Her courage

Fa Mulan 209

COMPREHENSION

(E) Ask students to predict what will happen next. *(Accept any predictions that students can support with clues from the text.)* **predicting**

(F) THINK IT THROUGH What helps Mulan to survive her first battle? *(She imagines how the Maiden of Yueh would react and tries to imitate her.)* **problem and solution**

LITERATURE

Use these questions to encourage literary analysis.

(A) How do Mulan's behavior and actions make her the perfect family member to fight in her father's place? *(She pretends to be a swordswoman like the Maiden of Yueh, and Elder Sister says that she acts like a man.)* **character**

(B) How do you know that Mulan will be a great warrior? *(Before her first battle she is afraid but also excited; during the battle she tries to be like the Maiden of Yueh, and she fights bravely and skillfully.)* **character**

VOCABULARY

(B) troops Students can skim to find out that the word *armies* (line 65) is a synonym of *troops.*

(C) steed Have students find synonyms of *steed.* (*mount,* line 76, and *horse,* line 77)

FOR ENGLISH LEARNERS

Help students understand the following expressions and idioms:

Line 59: the whicker of wild horses
Line 64: swept over the plain
Line 79: delivered a fatal thrust
Line 81: broke the Tartar line
Line 83: drive the enemy back
Line 90: the art of war

and skill with a sword were praised by soldiers, officers, and even officials sent by the Khan.

D Mulan missed her family. She kept apart from the soldiers of her squad, her "fire companions," because of her secret. But sometimes one or another of the brave, handsome young men would touch her heart. She would dream of leaving the battlefield for the fields of home, of becoming a bride, a wife, a
100 mother. However, duty to family and country, and her sense of honor, pushed all these dreams aside.

> **REREAD**
> What other kind of life has Mulan put aside? **G**

Each time the Khan's armies met the Tartars, Mulan was in the thick of battle, encouraging her fellow warriors, setting a brave example, and driving back the enemy.

Valor and ability won her the command of a company, then of a small troop that made surprise raids on the Tartars. Mulan
110 rose in rank until she became a general, commanding one of three armies preparing for what promised to be the deciding battle of the twelve-year war.

> **valor**
> (văl′ ər)
> courage

H **THINK IT THROUGH**
How does Mulan become a general?

FOCUS
The general prepares her warriors for battle. Find out the news she learns afterwards.

Meeting with the other generals, Mulan outlined a plan that the others quickly approved. "We will follow the classic wisdom that says, 'Act like a shy maiden to make the enemy think you are no threat.

210   Unit 6   The Battle Is On!

Then surprise them like a hare just let loose, and catch them off guard.'"

> **hare**
> (hâr)
> animal similar to a rabbit

The Khan's army separated, one group
120 heading east, the other west. Mulan's troops marched north toward the Tartar force. She ordered her soldiers to march ragtag so they looked like a mob, not a real army.

When the two armies faced off, the Tartars laughed to see Mulan's troops looking so disorganized. They thundered across the plain like hounds after a hare. But the hare had a surprise waiting. At Mulan's command, her foot soldiers formed crisp battle lines. Then her cavalry galloped to meet the enemy, who
130 were caught off guard. The Tartars, reeling from Mulan's attack, were crushed in the jaws of her deadly trap, as the Khan's other troops charged in from the east and west. At the height of the victory celebration, messengers arrived and informed Mulan that

> **REREAD**
> How did Mulan fool the enemy in this battle? **I**

C she must appear before the Khan in the royal
140 city of Loyang.

Fa Mulan   211

She feared that the Khan might have discovered that one of his generals was a woman. If so, he might punish her and her family for her daring.

| daring |
| (dâr′ ĭng) |
| n. boldness |

(J) THINK IT THROUGH
Why does Mulan feel both pride and fear?

FOCUS
Read to see how the Khan reacts to Mulan.

When she reached the royal city, Mulan was immediately brought to the palace. She bowed before the Khan's throne. "General," the Khan began, "you have served me well and have brought honor to your
150 family. Your deeds are enough to fill twelve books. I give you a thousand strings of copper coins as a reward. What else do you wish?"

"Now that the kingdom is safe," Mulan answered, "I ask only to return home and take up my old life. And I request the loan of your swiftest mount to carry me there."

A small honor guard of her fire companions accompanied Mulan home. What excitement there was at her arrival! Father, Mother, Elder Sister, and
160 Little Brother—how grown he was!—showered her with tears and smiles.

In her room, Mulan changed her armor and boots for a silk robe and brocade slippers. She powdered her face and arranged her hair like a soft cloud.

(D) At last Mulan stepped into the room where her fire companions and family waited. Her comrades were amazed and confused.

212 Unit 6 The Battle Is On!

"Our general is a woman!" cried one.

Smiling, Mulan said, "When the male rabbit
170 bounds across the meadow, and the female runs beside him, no one can tell which is which. So it is when soldiers fight side by side."

The companion who had spoken—the one Mulan felt closest to—returned her smile, saying, "In the field, what is the need of telling he-rabbit from she-rabbit? But when they return to their burrow, the rabbits know which partner is husband and which is wife. So they build a life together."

REREAD
What does Mulan's closest companion really mean?

(K)

180 To Mulan, his words hinted at a bright, shared tomorrow. Then each of her fire companions bowed to her, acknowledging all she had achieved and their loyalty to their former general. Mulan bowed to them in turn.

Finally Father said, "We have all heard of famous warrior women, like the Maiden of Yueh. But my daughter's fame will outshine and outlive them all."

(L) THINK IT THROUGH
1. What is Mulan's reward?
2. How do Mulan's fire companions react to her as a female?
3. Mulan is a woman warrior. If she had been a man in this war, would she have been as successful in this war? Explain your opinion.

Fa Mulan 213

---

1. COMPREHENSION

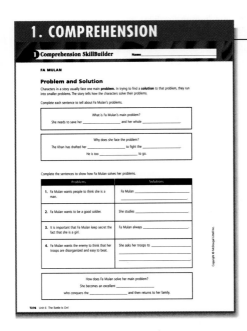

Problem and Solution

Direct Instruction Tell students that the characters in a story usually face one major problem and several related minor problems. Point out that in "Fa Mulan," as in other stories, the main problem is introduced early in the story. The rest of the story tells how she finds a solution to her problem. When discussing problems and solutions in a story, readers should try to answer questions such as the following:

- Which characters have the problem? Which characters solve it?
- What exactly is the problem? What smaller problems must be solved before the major problem can be solved? How is the problem solved? Discuss the problems and solutions in familiar stories such as folk tales that the students know well or in the plots of popular movies. Encourage students to be brief and specific when they state problems and solutions.

Comprehension SkillBuilder Answer Key:

She needs to save her <u>father</u> *and her whole* <u>family</u>.

The Khan has drafted her <u>father</u> *to fight the* <u>Tartars</u>. *He is too* <u>old and weak</u> *to go.*

1. *Fa Mulan* <u>cuts her hair and talks in a deep voice</u>.
2. *She studies* <u>the art of war</u>.
3. *Fa Mulan always* <u>keeps apart from the soldiers of her squad</u>.
4. *She asks her troops to* <u>walk out of step, like a mob of people instead of an army</u>. *She becomes an excellent* <u>soldier</u> *who conquers the* <u>Tartars</u> *and then returns to her family.*

2. LITERATURE

Climax

Direct Instruction Tell students that the **climax** is the turning point in a story. Point out that the climax usually involves a crucial decision, a discovery, or an event that changes the lives of the characters. Remind students of the plot diagram that was introduced in Unit 1. Draw the plot diagram on the board.

Direct students' attention to the climax on the diagram. Lead them to see how the story builds in complexity and tension until the climax, the highest point on the diagram. Point out that the rising action leg of the triangle is longer than the falling action leg, to correspond to the many story events that happen before the climax and the few events that wrap up the story after the climax.

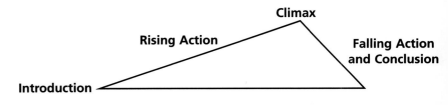

Literary SkillBuilder Answer Key:

A. **Introduction:** *a;* **Rising Action:** *b, c, d, e, f, g;* **Climax:** *h;* **Falling Action and Conclusion:** *i, j*

B. *Possible answer: The men learned that they had been led by a woman*

3. VOCABULARY

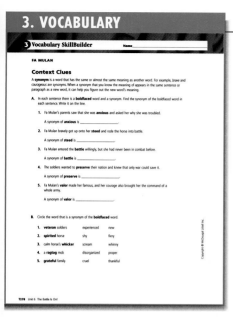

Context Clues: Synonyms

Direct Instruction Explain that a **synonym** is a word that means the same, or nearly the same, as another word. Tell students that when they don't understand a word, they should look for a synonym in the sentences or paragraphs that surround the unfamiliar word. If they know the meaning of the synonym, they will understand the new word.

Read these sentences aloud and ask students to find the synonym of the underlined word in each:

- Ken enjoyed being out in the <u>gale</u>, even though trying to walk against the strong wind was difficult. (The synonym of *gale* is *wind*.)
- Fa Mulan's parents felt <u>grief</u> when she left, but their sorrow turned to joy when she came back. (The synonym of *grief* is *sorrow*.)
- Some people thought the cocoa was <u>scalding</u>, but it wasn't too hot for me to drink. (The synonym of *scalding* is *hot*.)

Vocabulary SkillBuilder Answer Key:

A.
1. *troubled*
2. *horse*
3. *combat*
4. *save*
5. *courage*

B.
1. *experienced*
2. *fiery*
3. *whinny*
4. *disorganized*
5. *thankful*

---

4. WORDS TO KNOW

Words to Know

Direct Instruction Instruct students to complete the first exercise using the context clues.

Lead them through Section B orally, and if they find a statement to be false, encourage them to explain why.

Writing Activity Pair students or allow them to work in groups to complete the exercise. Have volunteers read their creations aloud.

Words to Know SkillBuilder Answer Key:

A.
1. *stallion*
2. *daring*
3. *scrolls*
4. *veterans*
5. *fatal*

B.
1. *false*
2. *false*
3. *true*
4. *true*
5. *false*

---

5. SELECTION TEST

Selection Test Answer Key:

A. 1. *scrolls* **2.** *Khan's* **3.** *fight* **4.** *general* **5.** *plan*
   6. *off guard* **7.** *copper coins* **8.** *fire companions* **9.** *future*
B. *She would become more famous than all other warrior women.*

FA MULAN

Problem and Solution

Characters in a story usually face one main **problem.** In trying to find a **solution** to that problem, they run into smaller problems. The story tells how the characters solve their problems.

Complete each sentence to tell about Fa Mulan's problems.

What is Fa Mulan's main problem?
She needs to save her _____ and her whole _____ .

Why does she face the problem?
The Khan has drafted her _____ to fight the _____ .
He is too _____ to go.

Complete the sentences to show how Fa Mulan solves her problems.

Problems	Solutions
1. Fa Mulan wants people to think she is a man.	Fa Mulan _____ _____ .
2. Fa Mulan wants to be a good soldier.	She studies _____ .
3. It is important that Fa Mulan keep secret the fact that she is a girl.	Fa Mulan always _____ .
4. Fa Mulan wants the enemy to think that her troops are disorganized and easy to beat.	She asks her troops to _____ _____ _____ .

How does Fa Mulan solve her main problem?
She becomes an excellent _____
who conquers the _____ and then returns to her family.

Name_____

FA MULAN

Climax

In a story, tension builds until the climax. The **climax** is the turning point. Tension falls after the climax until the story draws to a close.

A. Read this list of events from "Fa Mulan" carefully. Then look at the plot diagram at the bottom of this page. Write the letter of each event in the correct place on the diagram. There is one blank line for each story event.

   a. Fa Mulan discovers that her father has been drafted.

   b. Fa Mulan goes to war in his place, keeping secret the fact that she is a girl.

   c. Fa Mulan fights bravely in her first battles.

   d. Fa Mulan studies how great generals win wars.

   e. Fa Mulan fights so bravely and so well that she is made a general.

   f. Fa Mulan leads her troops in a clever plan and defeats the enemy.

   g. The Khan sends for Mulan. She is afraid that he knows her secret and wants to punish her, but the Khan just wants to thank her. He rewards her by sending her home.

   h. At home, Fa Mulan reveals to her fellow soldiers that she is a woman.

   i. Fa Mulan's fellow soldiers bow to her.

   j. Her father says that she is the greatest woman warrior of all.

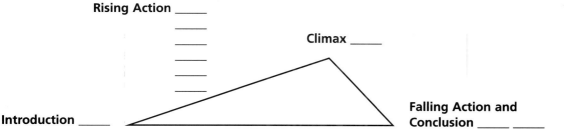

B. Reread the event that you chose as the climax. What was exciting to you about this turning point?

_____

_____

FA MULAN

Context Clues

A **synonym** is a word that has the same or almost the same meaning as another word. For example, *brave* and *courageous* are synonyms. When a synonym that you know the meaning of appears in the same sentence or paragraph as a new word, it can help you figure out the new word's meaning.

A. In each sentence there is a **boldfaced** word and a synonym. Find the synonym of the boldfaced word in each sentence. Write it on the line.

1. Fa Mulan's parents saw that she was **anxious** and asked her why she was troubled.

   A synonym of **anxious** is _____.

2. Fa Mulan bravely got up onto her **steed** and rode the horse into battle.

   A synonym of **steed** is _____.

3. Fa Mulan entered the **battle** willingly, but she had never been in combat before.

   A synonym of **battle** is _____.

4. The soldiers wanted to **preserve** their nation and knew that only war could save it.

   A synonym of **preserve** is _____.

5. Fa Mulan's **valor** made her famous, and her courage also brought her the command of a whole army.

   A synonym of **valor** is _____.

B. Circle the word that is a synonym of the **boldfaced** word.

1. **veteran** soldiers   experienced   new

2. **spirited** horse   shy   fiery

3. calm horse's **whicker**   scream   whinny

4. a **ragtag** mob   disorganized   proper

5. **grateful** family   cruel   thankful

FA MULAN

Words to Know

scrolls   stallion   veterans   fatal   daring

A. In each blank, write the word that best fits the sentence.

1. The sun shone off the strong back of the _____ as he galloped across the beach.

2. Laura was a brave skateboarder; her tricks were very _____.

3. The museum guide would not unroll the _____ because the paper was too old.

4. Todd's grandfathers are _____ because they are no longer in the army.

5. Typhoid fever is a dangerous disease that can be _____.

B. Write **true** or **false** in the blanks.

_____ **1.** People who have just entered the army are called **veterans**.

_____ **2.** **Stallions** can give birth to baby horses.

_____ **3.** If you are trying something new or dangerous, you are **daring.**

_____ **4.** Losing a lot of blood can be **fatal.**

_____ **5.** If you'd like to see **scrolls,** you can go to the video store and rent some.

Writing Activity
Imagine you are a reporter for a newspaper during a war. Using one or two of the **Words to Know,** write a headline for something you might see during a battle.

FA MULAN

A. Complete the paragraph by filling in each blank with the appropriate word or phrase from the list.

future	fire companions	plan
off guard	copper coins	Khan's
general	fight	scrolls

Fa Mulan lived with her family in China. One day when she and Elder Sister were at the market, Mulan

saw twelve **(1)** _____ pasted to a wall. As she read the list of those who

must serve in the **(2)** _____ army, she saw her father's name. Since he

was too old and weak, Mulan went to **(3)** _____ in his place. Mulan

became a skillful warrior, and in time she became a **(4)** _____. For the

most important battle of the twelve-year war, Mulan had a brilliant **(5)** _____.

She and her troops took the Tartars **(6)** _____ and defeated

them with a surprise attack. After the war, the Khan gave Mulan a thousand strings of

(7) _____ and sent her home with a group of her

(8) _____. At home, Mulan changed clothes and surprised

her comrades. The companion to whom Mulan felt closest hinted at a bright, shared

(9) _____.

B. In your own words, tell what Mulan's father said about her at the end of the story.

_____

_____

Reader directions:
Cut this paper in half. Practice reading the passage aloud until you don't make any mistakes.
Then have someone listen to you read. Try to sound like you're reading a magazine.

from **"Roberto Clemente: Hero and Friend"**

The Clementes could not buy any luxuries—not even a baseball for Roberto. Instead, Roberto and his friends used sticks to practice batting cans. They had no gloves, pads, or even a real bat. They simply loved the game. To Roberto, baseball players were heroes. He dreamed of becoming a great player someday. Roberto was determined to work hard to make his dream come true.

In high school, Roberto joined the baseball team. Roberto was a top runner, but he knew that speed was not enough. Baseball players needed strong arms to throw the ball fast and hit it hard.

✂ **cut along dotted line**
- -

Checker directions:
Follow along as the passage is read. Make a dot under each word the reader misses.
Show the reader the missed words. Erase the dots and repeat for each reading.

from **"Roberto Clemente: Hero and Friend"**

The Clementes could not buy any luxuries—not even a baseball for Roberto. Instead, Roberto and his friends used sticks to practice batting cans. They had no gloves, pads, or even a real bat. They simply loved the game. To Roberto, baseball players were heroes. He dreamed of becoming a great player someday. Roberto was determined to work hard to make his dream come true.

In high school, Roberto joined the baseball team. Roberto was a top runner, but he knew that speed was not enough. Baseball players needed strong arms to throw the ball fast and hit it hard.

Use this chart for Timed Readings and Repeated Readings.

Reading	1	2	3	4	5
Time (minutes/seconds)					
Words Missed					

Focus Skills and SkillBuilder Copymasters

Decisions Don't Come Easily

Unit 7

Fiction

Ketchup or mustard? Paper or plastic? These are small decisions. Some decisions in life are tough. They may mean the difference between winning and losing—or between life and death.

In this unit, you'll read three selections. One of them is an allegory. An **allegory** is a story in which the characters and setting stand for something else. Often they stand for real people at a certain time in history.

Meet a few characters who are forced to make tough decisions.

214

Reading Fluency

  ★ Reading Fluency pp. T295, T323

Pacing Guide

SELECTION	TOTAL DAYS	PREREADING	READING	POST READING	
				SELECTIVE OPTIONS	ALL OPTIONS
Two Were Left	2–2.5	1	.5	.5	1
Terrible Things: An Allegory of the Holocaust	2.5–3	1	1	.5	1
The Lady or the Tiger?	2.5–3	1	1	.5	1

215

More About Fiction

These stories provide students with rich opportunities to reinforce their knowledge of story grammar. In addition, students will appreciate that when woven together well, the elements of plot, character, setting, and theme have the power to excite readers and leave them wanting to know a story's outcome. In each of these stories, a character must make a crucial decision. After reading, students might engage in discussions about the apparent outcomes.

Technology Resources

Audio CD
The following selections in this unit are featured in the Audio Library: "Two Were Left," "Terrible Things," and "The Lady or the Tiger?"

Reading Coach CD-ROM
The following selections are part of the Reading Coach: "Two Were Left" and "The Lady or the Tiger?" You may use Reading Coach selections as a group activity, as an individual activity, or as a tutorial for students who might benefit from this format or who have missed class.

Building Bridges: Closing the Reading Gap
This video is intended for teacher use only. It gives instructions and tips on how to help middle school readers become strategic readers.

Assessment

Selection Tests
pp. T294, T308, T322

**Assessment Booklet
Progress Check Units 5–8**
Administer this test after the units 5 through 8 of the book have been read. It covers skills taught in all four units.

Focus Skills

COMPREHENSION
Predicting

LITERATURE
Suspense

VOCABULARY
Structural Analysis

SkillBuilder Copymasters

 Reading Comprehension:
1 Predicting p. T290

Literary Analysis:
2 Suspense p. T291

Vocabulary:
3 Structural Analysis p. T292
4 Words to Know p. T293

Assessment

 5 Selection Test p. T294

Readability Scores

DRP	LEXILE	DALE-CHALL
52	600	4.2

Reading Fluency

★ Reading Fluency p. T295

For English Learners

Write the following words on the chalkboard: *ominously, suspiciously, incredulously.* Discuss the meanings of these words, which are defined in the selection, to add to students' appreciation of the suspense of the story.

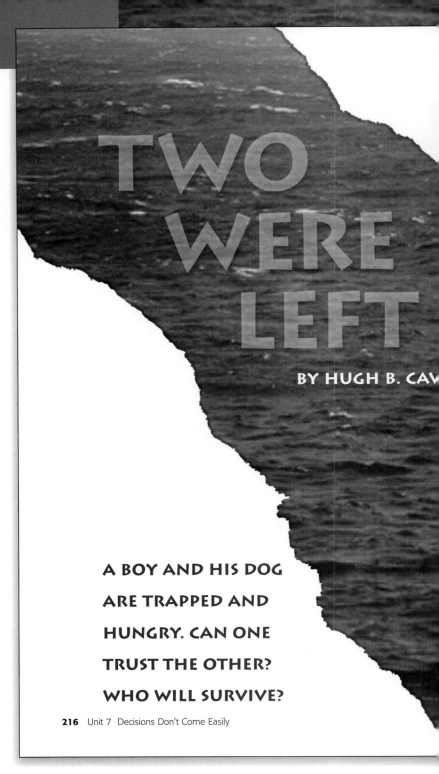

TWO WERE LEFT

BY HUGH B. CAV

A BOY AND HIS DOG ARE TRAPPED AND HUNGRY. CAN ONE TRUST THE OTHER? WHO WILL SURVIVE?

216 Unit 7 Decisions Don't Come Easily

Vocabulary Strategy: Preteaching

Structural Analysis Remind students that they can begin to understand an unfamiliar word by separating it into smaller parts. To illustrate the following points, you might wish to write each example word shown on the next page on the chalkboard. Then conclude by informing students that if necessary, they should use dictionaries to check the meaning of an unfamiliar word or word part.

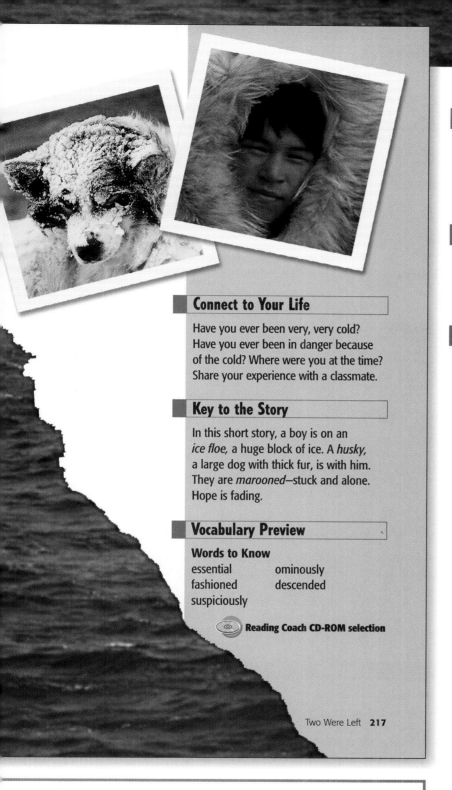

Connect to Your Life

Have you ever been very, very cold? Have you ever been in danger because of the cold? Where were you at the time? Share your experience with a classmate.

Key to the Story

In this short story, a boy is on an *ice floe,* a huge block of ice. A *husky,* a large dog with thick fur, is with him. They are *marooned*—stuck and alone. Hope is fading.

Vocabulary Preview

Words to Know

essential   ominously
fashioned   descended
suspiciously

💿 **Reading Coach CD-ROM selection**

To analyze a word:

- Look at the base word to try to figure out its meaning. mis•state•ment
- Look at any prefixes and suffixes for hints to the word's meaning. mis•state•ment
- If a word includes more than one base word, as in a compound word, those base words can be separated, and the meaning of each of them may be known. earth•quake

 For more on Structural Analysis, see page T289.

Connect to Your Life

If students have no direct experience with the extreme conditions of cold weather, encourage them to share experiences they've heard or read about.

Key to the Story

As a way of setting a purpose for reading, have students predict what the boy and his dog might do to survive.

Vocabulary Preview

Words to Know
essential *adj.* necessary
fashioned *v.* shaped or formed
suspiciously *adv.* without trust
ominously *adv.* in a threatening way
descended *v.* moved from a higher to a lower place

For direct instruction on Words to Know, see page T289.

Building Background

Nimuk, the dog in this story, is a Siberian husky. Siberian huskies are purebred dogs that are members of a group of Arctic sled dogs that includes the Alaskan malamute, the Eskimo dog, and the Samoyed. Huskies have amazing strength and stamina. They also have double coats of fur, which help them endure extreme Arctic temperatures. Beneath their longer outer coat is a shorter undercoat that allows the dogs to sleep outside in temperatures as low as −70°F.

In some cultures, dog meat is a delicacy. In others, eating dogs is taboo. In the Arctic culture described in this story, eating dogs—even those considered devoted companions—is sometimes necessary for survival. How do students feel about this issue? Invite them to share their thoughts.

FOCUS

Noni and Nimuk are in great danger. Find out the awful decision that Noni faces.

On the third night of hunger Noni thought of the dog. Nothing of flesh and blood lived upon the floating ice island except those two.

In the breakup of the iceberg, Noni had lost his sled, his food, his fur, even his knife. He had saved only Nimuk, his devoted husky. And now the two marooned on the ice eyed each other warily—each keeping his distance.

 Noni's love for Nimuk was real, very real—as real
10 as the hunger and cold nights and the gnawing pain of his injured leg in its homemade brace. But the men of his village killed their dogs when food was scarce, didn't they? And without thinking twice about it.

And Nimuk, he told himself, when hungry enough, would seek food. One of us will soon be eating the other, Noni thought. So . . .

REREAD
What problem is upsetting Noni?

 He could not kill the dog with his bare hands. Nimuk was powerful and much fresher
20 than he. A weapon, then, was essential.

essential
(Ĭ sĕn′ shəl)
adj. necessary

Removing his mittens, he unstrapped the brace from his leg. When he had hurt his leg a few weeks before, he had fashioned the brace from bits of harness and two thin strips of iron.

fashioned
(făsh′ ənd)
v. shaped or formed; past tense of *fashion*

Kneeling now, he wedged one of the iron strips into a crack in the ice and began to rub the other against it with firm, slow strokes.

Nimuk watched him intently, and it seemed to Noni
30 that the dog's eyes glowed more brightly as night waned.

218 Unit 7 Decisions Don't Come Easily

He worked on, trying not to remember why. The slab of iron had an edge now. It had begun to take shape. Daylight found his task completed.

THINK IT THROUGH
What has Noni decided to do? Why?

FOCUS

Read to find out who survives.

Noni pulled the finished knife from the ice and thumbed its edge. The sun's glare, reflected from it, stabbed at his eyes and momentarily blinded him.

Noni steeled himself.
40 "Here, Nimuk!" he called softly.
The dog watched him suspiciously.
"Come here," Noni called.
Nimuk came closer. Noni read fear in the animal's gaze. He read hunger and suffering in the dog's labored breathing and awkward, dragging crouch. His heart wept. He hated himself and fought against it.

steeled
(stēld)
prepared to do something hard

suspiciously
(sə spĭsh′ əs lē)
adv. without trust

Closer Nimuk came, wary of his intentions. Now Noni felt a thickening in his throat. He
50 saw the dog's eyes and they were wells of suffering.
Now! Now was the time to strike!

REREAD
What do you think Noni will do next?

A great sob shook Noni's kneeling body. He cursed the knife. He swayed blindly; flung the weapon far from him. With empty hands outstretched he stumbled toward the dog, and fell.

Two Were Left 219

COMPREHENSION

FOCUS SKILL: Predicting

Tell students that **predicting** is guessing what will happen next in a story based on clues and information that the author provides.

For direct instruction on Predicting, see page T288.

A **REREAD** What problem is upsetting Noni? *(Noni loves his dog very much, so it's upsetting him to think about eating Nimuk in order to keep from starving. Nor does he want Nimuk to eat him.)* **making inferences**

B Ask: What do you think Noni is going to do with his leg brace? Why? *(He will make a weapon; the text says he can't kill Nimuk with his bare hands and that a weapon is essential.)* **predicting**

C **THINK IT THROUGH** What has Noni decided to do? Why? *(He's decided to kill his dog with the knife he has made because he is starving.)* **drawing conclusions**

D **REREAD** What do you think Noni will do next? *(Some students will predict that he will kill and eat Nimuk. Others will predict that he won't be able to go through with it.)* **predicting**

LITERATURE

FOCUS SKILL: Suspense

Explain that **suspense** is the growing tension and excitement that a reader feels while reading a story. Writers create suspense by raising questions in the reader's mind about what might happen next.

For direct instruction on Suspense, see page T288.

Use questions such as this one to encourage literary analysis.

A What is the setting of this story? How does the setting add to the story's suspense? *(The setting is a floating ice floe. Noni and his dog are alone and starving to death on the floe. They are eyeing each other to see which one will be eating the other first.)* **suspense**

VOCABULARY

FOCUS SKILL: Structural Analysis

Structural analysis involves looking at the meanings of an unfamiliar word's prefix, suffix, and base word to figure out the meaning of the word.

A **powerful** Students can understand this word by taking it apart and thinking about the meanings of its base word and suffix. *(power + -ful)*

FOR ENGLISH LEARNERS

Help students understand the following expressions and idioms:

Line 2: of flesh and blood
Line 7: eyed each other
Line 10: gnawing pain
Line 18: with his bare hands
Line 30: as night waned
Line 36: thumbed its edge
Line 37: stabbed at his eyes

The dog growled **ominously** as he warily circle the boy's body. And Noni was sick with fear.

B 60   In flinging away his knife he had left himself defenseless. He was too weak to crawl after it now. He was at Nimuk's mercy, and Nimuk was hungry.

ominously
(ŏm' ə nəs lē)
adv. in a threatening way

REREAD
What trouble is Noni in?

E

   The dog circled him and was creeping up from behind. Noni shut his eyes, praying that the attack might be swift. He felt the dog's feet against his leg, the hot rush of Nimuk's breath against his neck. A scream gathered in the boy's throat.

   Then he felt the dog's hot tongue caressing his face.

B 70   Noni's eyes opened, staring **incredulously**. Crying softly, he thrust out an arm and drew the dog's head down against his own. . . .

incredulously
(ĭn krĕj' ə ləs lē)
in disbelief

   The plane came out of the south an hour later. Its pilot looked down and saw the large, floating floe. And he saw something flashing.

   It was the sun gleaming on something shiny which moved. His curiosity aroused, the pilot banked his ship and **descended**, circling 80 the floe. Now he saw a dark, still shape that appeared to be human. Or were there two shapes?

descended
(dĭ sĕn' dĭd)
v. moved from a higher to a lower place; past tense of *descend*

   He set his ship down in a water lane and investigated. There were two shapes, boy and dog. The boy was unconscious but alive. The dog whined feebly but was too weak to move. **C**

   The gleaming object which had trapped the pilot's attention was a crudely fashioned knife stuck into the ice a little distance away and quivering in the wind. **F**

G **THINK IT THROUGH**

1. Do you think the decisions both the boy and dog make are believable? Why or why not?
2. How do you think *you* would act if you were Noni?

COMPREHENSION

E **REREAD** What trouble is Noni in? *(Noni now has no way to protect himself should Nimuk attack him.)* **summarizing**

F Ask: Do the predictions you made earlier match what actually happens? Why or why not? *(Explain that in order to build suspense, the author deliberately kept readers guessing. Review the story, however, for clues that might have helped students predict more accurately.)* **predicting**

G **THINK IT THROUGH**

1. Do you think the decisions both the boy and dog make are believable? Why or why not? *(Some students will say yes, because they love each other that much. Others will say no, because under those conditions, the need to survive takes over.)* **making judgments**

2. How do you think *you* would act if you were Noni? *(Possible*

answers: Like Noni, I would not have hurt my dog; Nimuk seemed dangerous. I would have done what I needed to do to survive, especially if he had attacked me first.) **making judgments**

RETEACHING

If students need more help understanding **Predicting,** use pages T653–T655.

LITERATURE

B How does the author build suspense in lines 60–68? *(He describes the scene almost as if it were happening in slow motion, and he tells us what Noni is thinking.)* **suspense**

C At what point do you feel that the suspense starts to fade? *(Answers will vary. Many students might say it's when the pilot finds Noni and Nimuk still alive.)* **suspense**

VOCABULARY

B **incredulously** Students can understand this word by taking it apart. Point out that *in-* means "not," *credul* is a Latin root meaning "belief," *-ous* means "having," and *-ly* means "in a certain way." *Incredulously* means "in an unbelieving way."

FOR ENGLISH LEARNERS

Help students understand the following expressions and idioms:

Line 83: water lane
Line 87: trapped the pilot's attention
Line 88: crudely fashioned

RETEACHING

If students need more help understanding **Structural Analysis,** use page T623.

1. COMPREHENSION

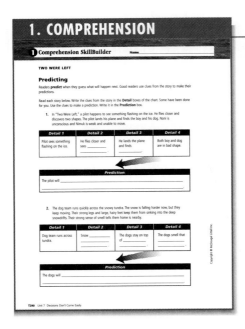

Predicting

Direct Instruction Remind the students that readers can use clues from a story to guess what will happen next. Such a guess is called a **prediction**. When readers know something about the story already, they can better predict what is likely to follow. Review some of the story clues that can help students to predict:

Characters: How have the characters acted so far? What qualities do the characters possess that help you determine what they will do next?

Setting: When and where does the story take place? What is a logical outcome in that setting?

Plot: What events have happened so far? What event would make sense next?

Mood: If the author has written a story full of suspense, such as "Two Were Left," the next event probably will add to that feeling.

Comprehension SkillBuilder Answer Key:

Wording will vary.

1. *Detail 2: two shapes; Detail 3: a boy and a dog; Prediction: The pilot will take the boy and dog to a hospital or other place where they will be cared for.*
2. *Detail 2: is falling but doesn't stop dogs; Detail 3: the snow; Detail 4: home is near; Prediction: The dogs won't stop until they get to their home.*

---

2. LITERATURE

Suspense

Direct Instruction Direct the students to think of a popular movie that is filled with suspense. Ask: What makes the movie so suspenseful? *(setting, plot, dialogue, background music)* Tell the class that writers of suspense stories also use many of these elements to create a mood or tone that leaves the reader anxious to discover what will happen next.

Draw the students' attention to the following elements:

Setting: Does the setting present a conflict or problem that adds to the suspense?

Plot: Do the events seem to build to new levels of excitement?

Mood: How does the author use certain words to create a feeling of uneasiness or suspense, much like the scary background music in the movies?

Literary SkillBuilder Answer Key:

A.

1. *"One of us will soon be <u>eating</u> the other, Noni thought. <u>So</u>..."*
5. *"The dog <u>growled</u> . . . as he . . . circled the boy's body. And Noni was <u>sick with fear</u>."*
3. *When Noni finished the knife, he called to Nimuk. "<u>Now</u>!" he thought. "Now was the time to <u>strike</u>!"*
2. *As Noni sharpened the slab of iron, "it seemed …that the <u>dog's eyes glowed more brightly</u> as night waned."*
6. *"He felt the dog's feet against his leg, the <u>hot rush</u> of Nimuk's breath <u>against his neck</u>."*
4. *Noni threw the knife away and with "<u>empty hands</u> outstretched he <u>stumbled</u> toward the dog , and <u>fell</u>."*

B. *Answers will vary, but should include several of these details: that the boy and dog were alone, on ice, in the middle of freezing water for three days, with no food.*

---

3. VOCABULARY

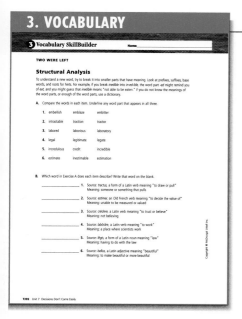

Structural Analysis

Direct Instruction Recall that unfamiliar words can often be broken into smaller parts to discover their meanings. Point out that, usually, prefixes and suffixes can easily be separated from base words, and their meanings are often known. In some words, taking away the affixes may make it easy to recognize the base words to determine their meaning alone, and then to determine the meaning of the word with the affixes added. If a word includes more than one base word, as in a compound, those base words can be separated, and the meaning of each of them may be known. If the word is based on a root from another language and that root appears in many other familiar words, the meaning of that word part, too, may be figured out.

Point out that there are two other techniques students can use to determine the meaning of the new word: compare a possible meaning with context clues, and look up the word in a dictionary. Note that when a word is based on an unfamiliar root, using the dictionary may be necessary.

Vocabulary SkillBuilder Answer Key:

A.
1. *em*
2. *tract*
3. *labor*
4. *leg*
5. *cred*
6. *estim*

B.
1. *tractor*
2. *inestimable*
3. *incredulous*
4. *laboratory*
5. *legal*
6. *embellish*

4. WORDS TO KNOW

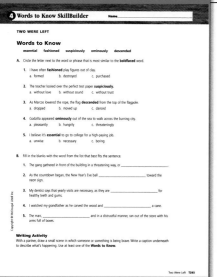

Words to Know

Direct Instruction As you present the **Words to Know,** here are some points you might want to cover. Help students to identify the parts of the vocabulary words. Stress the importance of finding the base of each word. Help students remove prefixes and suffixes first.

ominous + -ly = *ominously*
fashion + -ed = *fashioned*
suspicious + -ly = *suspiciously*
descend + -ed = *descended*
Essential is related to the word *essence,* meaning "the indispensable properties that serve to identify something."

Writing Activity
Pair students to work on a sketch of a situation involving bravery. Inform students that they may interpret this in any way they choose. Then, instruct them to add a caption to the drawing, using at least one of the **Words to Know.**

Words to Know SkillBuilder Answer Key:
A. 1. *a* **2.** *c* **3.** *a* **4.** *c* **5.** *b*
B. 1. *ominously* **2.** *descended* **3.** *essential* **4.** *fashioned* **5.** *suspiciously*

5. SELECTION TEST

Selection Test Answer Key:
A. 1. *Nimuk* **2.** *supplies* **3.** *starving* **4.** *scarce* **5.** *weapon*
　　6. *kill* **7.** *flung* **8.** *swift* **9.** *licked*
B. *The pilot saw a knife.*

TWO WERE LEFT

Predicting

Readers **predict** when they guess what will happen next. Good readers use clues from the story to make their predictions.

Read each story below. Write the clues from the story in the **Detail** boxes of the chart. Some have been done for you. Use the clues to make a prediction. Write it in the **Prediction** box.

1. In "Two Were Left," a pilot happens to see something flashing on the ice. He flies closer and discovers two shapes. The pilot lands his plane and finds the boy and his dog. Noni is unconscious and Nimuk is weak and unable to move.

Detail 1	Detail 2	Detail 3	Detail 4
Pilot sees something flashing on the ice.	He flies closer and sees _____ _____ .	He lands the plane and finds _____ .	Both boy and dog are in bad shape.

Prediction
The pilot will _____ _____ .

2. The dog team runs quickly across the snowy tundra. The snow is falling harder now, but they keep moving. Their strong legs and large, hairy feet keep them from sinking into the deep snowdrifts. Their strong sense of smell tells them home is nearby.

Detail 1	Detail 2	Detail 3	Detail 4
Dog team runs across tundra.	Snow _____ _____ _____ .	The dogs stay on top of _____ _____ .	The dogs smell that _____ _____ .

Prediction
The dogs will _____ _____ .

TWO WERE LEFT

Suspense

Suspense is the growing feeling of tension and excitement felt by a reader. In "Two Were Left," the writer uses the plot and setting to create suspense. One event builds upon another, leaving the reader guessing at what will happen next. The writer carefully chooses words and details to add more suspense.

A. Number the events from "Two Were Left" in the correct order. Then underline at least one word in each sentence that adds to the suspense. The first item in the list has been marked for you.

1   "One of us will soon be <u>eating</u> the other, Noni thought. <u>So</u> . . ."

_____ "The dog growled . . . as he . . . circled the boy's body. And Noni was sick with fear."

_____ When Noni finished the knife, he called to Nimuk. Now! Now was the time to strike!

_____ As Noni sharpened the slab of iron, "it seemed . . . that the dog's eyes glowed more brightly as night waned."

_____ "He felt the dog's feet against his leg, the hot rush of Nimuk's breath against his neck."

_____ Noni threw the knife away and with "empty hands outstretched he stumbled toward the dog, and fell."

B. In your own words, tell how the setting of "Two Were Left" adds to the suspense.

_____

_____

_____

_____

_____

TWO WERE LEFT

Structural Analysis

To understand a new word, try to break it into smaller parts that have meaning. Look at prefixes, suffixes, base words, and roots for hints. For example, if you break *inedible* into *in-ed-ible,* the word part *-ed* might remind you of *eat,* and you might guess that *inedible* means "not able to be eaten." If you do not know the meanings of the word parts, or enough of the word parts, use a dictionary.

A.   Compare the words in each item. Underline any word part that appears in all three.

1. embellish   emblaze   embitter

2. intractable   traction   tractor

3. labored   laborious   laboratory

4. legal   legitimate   legate

5. incredulous   credit   incredible

6. estimate   inestimable   estimation

B.   Which word in Exercise A does each item describe? Write that word on the blank.

_____ **1.** Source: *tractus,* a form of a Latin verb meaning "to draw or pull"
Meaning: someone or something that pulls

_____ **2.** Source: *estimer,* an Old French verb meaning "to decide the value of"
Meaning: unable to be measured or valued

_____ **3.** Source: *crēdere,* a Latin verb meaning "to trust or believe"
Meaning: not believing

_____ **4.** Source: *labōrāre,* a Latin verb meaning "to work"
Meaning: a place where scientists work

_____ **5.** Source: *lēgis,* a form of a Latin noun meaning "law"
Meaning: having to do with the law

_____ **6.** Source: *bellus,* a Latin adjective meaning "beautiful"
Meaning: to make beautiful or more beautiful

TWO WERE LEFT

Words to Know

essential   fashioned   suspiciously   ominously   descended

A. Circle the letter next to the word or phrase that is most similar to the **boldfaced** word.

1. I have often **fashioned** play figures out of clay.
   a. formed   b. destroyed   c. purchased

2. The teacher looked over the perfect test paper **suspiciously.**
   a. without love   b. without sound   c. without trust

3. As Marcos lowered the rope, the flag **descended** from the top of the flagpole.
   a. dropped   b. moved up   c. danced

4. Godzilla appeared **ominously** out of the sea to walk across the burning city.
   a. pleasantly   b. hungrily   c. threateningly

5. I believe it's **essential** to go to college for a high-paying job.
   a. unwise   b. necessary   c. boring

B. Fill in the blanks with the word from the list that best fits the sentence.

1. The gang gathered in front of the building in a threatening way, or _____.

2. As the countdown began, the New Year's Eve ball _____ toward the neon sign.

3. My dentist says that yearly visits are necessary, as they are _____ for healthy teeth and gums.

4. I watched my grandfather as he carved the wood and _____ a cane.

5. The man, _____ and in a distrustful manner, ran out of the store with his arms full of boxes.

Writing Activity

With a partner, draw a small scene in which someone or something is being brave. Write a caption underneath to describe what's happening. Use at least one of the **Words to Know.**

TWO WERE LEFT

A. Complete each sentence with the correct word from the list.

kill	swift	licked
supplies	Nimuk	weapon
flung	starving	scarce

1. Noni and his dog, _____, were marooned on an ice floe.

2. When the iceberg broke up, Noni lost all his _____.

3. Now he and his dog were _____ to death.

4. Noni had heard that when food was _____, the men of his village ate their dogs.

5. Thinking he might have to do the same, Noni used a piece of his leg brace to make a

   _____.

6. When the time came, however, he couldn't _____ his dog with it.

7. Instead, he _____ it far away and waited for Nimuk to attack him.

8. Noni hoped that Nimuk's attack would be _____.

9. But instead of attacking, Nimuk _____ Noni's face.

B. In your own words, what was the object that captured the pilot's attention?

_____

_____

Reader directions:
Cut this paper in half. Practice reading the passage aloud until you don't make any mistakes.
Then have someone listen to you read. Try to sound like a story narrator.

from "Two Were Left"

Noni pulled the finished knife from the ice and thumbed its edge. The sun's glare, reflected
from it, stabbed at his eyes and momentarily blinded him.

Noni steeled himself.

"Here, Nimuk!" he called softly.

The dog watched him suspiciously.

"Come here," Noni called.

Nimuk came closer. Noni read fear in the animal's gaze. He read hunger and suffering in
the dog's labored breathing and awkward, dragging crouch. His heart wept. He hated
himself and fought against it.

Closer Nimuk came, wary of his intentions. Now Noni felt a thickening in his throat. He
saw the dog's eyes and they were wells of suffering.

✂ **cut along dotted line**
- -

Checker directions:
Follow along as the passage is read. Make a dot under each word the reader misses.
Show the reader the missed words. Erase the dots and repeat for each reading.

from "Two Were Left"

Noni pulled the finished knife from the ice and thumbed its edge. The sun's glare, reflected
from it, stabbed at his eyes and momentarily blinded him.

Noni steeled himself.

"Here, Nimuk!" he called softly.

The dog watched him suspiciously.

"Come here," Noni called.

Nimuk came closer. Noni read fear in the animal's gaze. He read hunger and suffering in
the dog's labored breathing and awkward, dragging crouch. His heart wept. He hated
himself and fought against it.

Closer Nimuk came, wary of his intentions. Now Noni felt a thickening in his throat. He
saw the dog's eyes and they were wells of suffering.

Use this chart for Timed Readings and Repeated Readings.

Reading	1	2	3	4	5
Time (minutes/seconds)					
Words Missed					

Focus Skills

Cause and Effect

Theme

Syllabication

SkillBuilder Copymasters

 Reading Comprehension:
1 Cause and Effect p. T304

 Literary Analysis:
2 Theme p. T305

 Vocabulary:
3 Syllabication p. T306
4 Words to Know p. T307

Assessment

 5 Selection Test p. T308

Readability Scores

DRP	LEXILE	DALE-CHALL
52	550	5.0

For English Learners

In a general sense, the term *holocaust* means "widespread destruction" or "complete destruction by fire." In the context of World War II, the Holocaust refers to the Nazis' systematic annihilation of about six million Jews from 1933 to 1945.

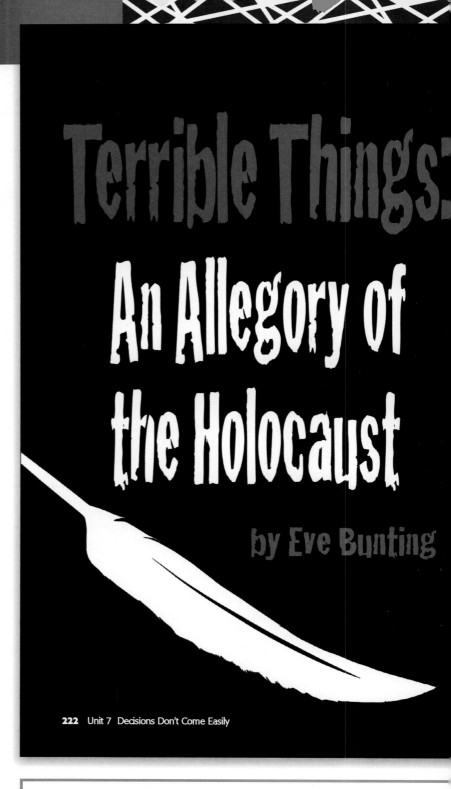

Terrible Things: An Allegory of the Holocaust

by Eve Bunting

222 Unit 7 Decisions Don't Come Easily

Vocabulary Strategy: Preteaching

Syllabication Remind students that breaking a word into parts, or **syllables**, can help them figure it out. Review the rules shown on this and the next page. Then have students syllabicate these words from the selection: rab•bits, rum•ble, clear•ing, ter•ri•ble, por•cu•pines.

1. If a word has a **prefix,** such as *pre-, mis-,* or *un-,* divide the word after the prefix; if a word has a **suffix,** such as *-ment, -tion, -less,* or *-ly,* divide the word before the suffix.

Each time the Terrible Things come, an awful change happens. Learn a lesson about the damage done by doing nothing.

Connect to Your Life

What do you know about Nazi Germany of the 1930s and 1940s? What group of people did not fit the Nazi view of a "master race"? What terrible things did the Nazis do to those who didn't fit in? In small groups, discuss what you know about this period of history.

Key to the Story

"Terrible Things" is an allegory. In an **allegory,** the characters and events stand for something else. Often they stand for *real* people at a certain time in history.

"Terrible Things" features animal characters in a forest. As you read the story, think about the Nazis and the terror they once caused. Think about the Holocaust, the deliberate killing of millions of people. The main targets were the Jewish people, yet there were other groups of victims, too. Think about what fear causes people to do—or not do.

Vocabulary Preview

Words to Know

clearing   quills
content   bristled
shimmering

Terrible Things   223

Connect to Your Life

You might choose to have students use a K-W-L chart to record what they know. See page T666. Tell students that in addition to exterminating about six million Jews, the Nazis killed almost five million other people, including Gypsies, Slavs, Poles, Jehovah's Witnesses, criminals, German opponents of Nazism, and resistance fighters from every nation.

Key to the Story

As students read this allegory, have them think about why the author chose to tell this story through animals. Also, ask them to consider why the Terrible Things don't have a specific breed or name as the other characters do.

Vocabulary Preview

Words to Know
clearing *n.* land from which trees have been removed
content *adj.* satisfied
shimmering *adj.* shining with a flickering light
quills *n.* sharp, hollow spines, like pointed needles
bristled *v.* stiffened

 For direct instruction on Words to Know, see page T303.

Building Background

In the introduction to her book *Terrible Things,* Eve Bunting states: "In Europe, during World War II, many people looked the other way while terrible things happened. They pretended not to know that their neighbors were being taken away and locked in concentration camps. They pretended not to hear their cries for help. The Nazis killed millions of Jews and others in the Holocaust. If everyone had stood together at the first sign of evil would this have happened? Standing up for what you know is right is not always easy. Especially if the one you face is bigger and stronger than you. It is easier to look the other way. But if you do, terrible things can happen."

---

2. If a word has **two consonants in the middle,** divide the word *between* them.
3. If a word ends with a **consonant + *le,*** divide the word *before* the consonant.
4. If a word has a **consonant between two vowels,** first try dividing the word *before* the consonant and giving the first vowel a long sound. If that doesn't work, divide the word *after* the consonant and give the first vowel a short sound.

 For more on Syllabication, see page T303.

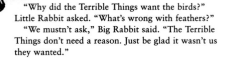

FOCUS

Read to find out what happens when the Terrible Things first appear in a quiet forest clearing.

The clearing in the woods was home to the small forest creatures. The birds and squirrels shared the trees. The rabbits and porcupines shared the shade beneath the trees and the frogs and fish shared the cool brown waters of the forest pond. They were content.

clearing
(klîr' ĭng)
n. land from which trees have been removed

content
(kən tĕnt')
adj. satisfied

Until the day the Terrible Things came.

Little Rabbit saw their terrible shadows

10 before he saw them. They stopped at the edge of the clearing and their shadows blotted out the sun.

"We have come for every creature with feathers on its back," the Terrible Things thundered.

"We don't have feathers," the frogs said.

"Nor we," said the squirrels.

"Nor we," said the porcupines.

"Nor we," said the rabbits.

The little fish leaped from the water to show the shine of their scales, but the birds twittered nervously

20 in the tops of the trees. Feathers! They rose in the air, then screamed away into the blue of the sky.

But the Terrible Things had brought their terrible nets and they flung them high and caught the birds and carried them away.

The other forest creatures talked nervously among themselves.

"Those birds were always too noisy," Old Porcupine said. "Good riddance, I say."

30 "There's more room in the trees now," the squirrels said.

REREAD
Is this the reaction you expected? Explain.

224 Unit 7 Decisions Don't Come Easily

"Why did the Terrible Things want the birds?" Little Rabbit asked. "What's wrong with feathers?"

"We mustn't ask," Big Rabbit said. "The Terrible Things don't need a reason. Just be glad it wasn't us they wanted."

THINK IT THROUGH

What do the Terrible Things want? Why are they able to get what they want?

FOCUS

The Terrible Things return. Find out how Big Rabbit reacts.

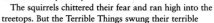

Now there were no birds to sing in the clearing. But life went on almost as before. Until the day the Terrible Things came back.

40 Little Rabbit heard the thump of their terrible feet before they came into sight.

"We have come for every bushy-tailed creature who lives in the clearing," the Terrible Things thundered.

"We have no tails," the frogs said.

"Nor do we. Not real tails," the porcupines said.

The little fish leaped from the water to show the smooth shine of their finned tails and the rabbits turned their rumps so the Terrible Things could see for themselves.

50 "Our tails are round and furry," they said. "By no means are they bushy."

The squirrels chittered their fear and ran high into the treetops. But the Terrible Things swung their terrible

Terrible Things 225

COMPREHENSION

FOCUS SKILL: Cause and Effect

Tell students that they can identify the **causes** and **effects** in this story by asking, What happened? and What caused it to happen?

For direct instruction on Cause and Effect, see page T302.

Ⓐ REREAD Is this the reaction you expected? Explain. *(Most students probably will say no because until then, the animals were content to live together and share. Instead of trying to help the birds, the other animals turn their backs on them.)* **evaluating**

Ⓑ THINK IT THROUGH What do the Terrible Things want? Why are they able to get what they want? *(the birds; because the animals fear the Terrible Things and don't fight back)* **cause and effect**

LITERATURE

FOCUS SKILL: Theme

Remind students that the **theme** of a story is an author's message about life or human nature. Sometimes a theme is stated outright. At other times, however, students must infer the theme based on what the characters think, feel, say, and do.

For direct instruction on Theme, see page T302.

Use questions such as this one to encourage literary analysis.

Ⓐ Why do the animals almost seem to be showing off here? In what situation might human beings behave like this? *(Possible answers: The animals feel safe because they aren't what the Terrible Things are after. They want to set themselves apart from the hunted animals. In a situation in which human beings feel threatened, they may try to set themselves apart from a targeted person or group. Students familiar with the Holocaust may discuss the indifferent attitudes of those not victimized by the Nazis.)* **theme**

VOCABULARY

FOCUS SKILL: Syllabication

As students read this selection, remind them to break unfamiliar words into smaller parts, or **syllables,** in order to figure them out.

Ⓐ squirrels, shadows (line 9), **nervously** (line 19), **riddance** (line 28): If necessary, review the syllabication rules that you introduced earlier. Then help students syllabicate these words. *(squir•rels, shad•ows, ner•vous•ly, rid•dance)*

FOR ENGLISH LEARNERS

Help students understand the following expressions and idioms:

Line 11: blotted out the sun
Line 13: the Terrible Things thundered
Line 28: good riddance
Line 50: by no means

nets higher than the squirrels could run and wider than the squirrels could leap and they caught them all and carried them away.

B "Those squirrels were greedy," Big Rabbit said. "Always storing away things for themselves. Never sharing."

REREAD
What attitude does Big Rabbit show here?

C

60 "But why did the Terrible Things take them away?" Little Rabbit asked. "Do the Terrible Things want the clearing for themselves?"

"No. They have their own place," Big Rabbit said. "But the Terrible Things don't need a reason. Just mind your own business, Little Rabbit. We don't want them to get mad at us."

D **THINK IT THROUGH**
What advice does Big Rabbit give Little Rabbit? Why?

FOCUS
Discover why Big Rabbit feels safe from the visits of the Terrible Things.

Now there were no birds to sing or squirrels to chitter in the trees. But life in the clearing went on almost as before. Until the day the Terrible Things
70 came again.

Little Rabbit heard the rumble of their terrible voices.

"We have come for every creature that swims," the Terrible Things thundered.

"Oh, we can't swim," the rabbits said quickly.

"And we can't swim," the porcupines said.

B The frogs dived deep in the forest pool and ripples spiraled like corkscrews on the dark, brown water. The little fish darted this way
80 and that in streaks of silver. But the Terrible Things threw their terrible nets down into the depths and they dragged up the dripping frogs and the shimmering fish and carried them away.

spiraled
(spī' rəld)
moved in circles or coils

"Why did the Terrible Things take them?" Little Rabbit asked. "What did the frogs and the fish do to them?"

"Probably nothing," Big Rabbit said. "But the Terrible Things don't need a reason. Many creatures
90 dislike frogs. Lumpy, slimy things. And fish are so cold and unfriendly. They never talk to any of us."

shimmering
(shĭm' ər ĭng)
adj. shining with a flickering light

Now there were no birds to sing, no squirrels to chitter, no frogs to croak, no fish to play in the forest pool. A nervous silence filled the clearing. But life went on almost as usual. Until the day the Terrible Things came back.

REREAD
Try to picture this scene in your mind. How does it compare to the opening scene of the story?

E

COMPREHENSION

C **REREAD** What attitude does Big Rabbit show here? *(To disguise his fear, sadness, and relief, Big Rabbit turns on the squirrels and acts happy that they're gone.)* **making inferences**

D **THINK IT THROUGH** What advice does Big Rabbit give Little Rabbit? Why? *(Mind your own business and don't make them mad. Big Rabbit doesn't want to draw any attention to the rabbits.)* **theme** LITERATURE

E **REREAD** Try to picture this scene in your mind. How does it compare to the opening scene of the story? *(The clearing is still and silent. Most of the animals are gone, and the ones left aren't content but nervous.)* **compare and contrast**

LITERATURE

B **Teacher Modeling: Figurative Language** Use lines 78–81 to model how to recognize descriptive language. Remind students that writers use description to create clear pictures in readers' minds.
You might say: *This paragraph contains some very vivid words and phrases. "Spiraled like corkscrews" helps me to imagine how the water rippled when the frogs dove into it. I can almost see the twists and swirls in the water. The frogs left in a way that seemed as if they were trying to escape. The word darted and the phrase "streaks of silver" paint a picture for me of how quickly the fish went away. They seemed fearful, too. The writer might have simply written, "The frogs and fish left quickly." The way she did describe the actions helps me to sense the fear and confusion caused by the Terrible Things.*

VOCABULARY

B **greedy, chitter** (lines 57 and 68), **silver** (line 80), **shimmering** (line 83): Have students syllabicate and pronounce these words. *(greed•y, chit•ter, sil•ver, shim•mer•ing)*

FOR ENGLISH LEARNERS

Help students understand the following expressions and idioms:

Line 65: mind your own business
Line 78: corkscrews
Line 80: in streaks of silver

Little Rabbit smelled their terrible smell before they came into sight. The rabbits and the porcupines
100 looked everywhere, except at each other.

"We have come for every creature that sprouts quills," the Terrible Things thundered.

The rabbits stopped quivering. "We don't have quills," they said, fluffing their soft, white fur.

C The porcupines bristled with all their strength. But the Terrible Things covered them with the curl of their terrible nets
110 and the porcupines hung in them like flies
F in a spider's web as the Terrible Things carried them away.

"Those porcupines always were bad tempered," Big Rabbit said shakily. "Prickly, stickly things!"

> **quills**
> (kwĭlz)
> *n.* sharp, hollow spines, like pointed needles

> **bristled**
> (brĭs′ əld)
> *v.* stiffened; past tense of *bristle*

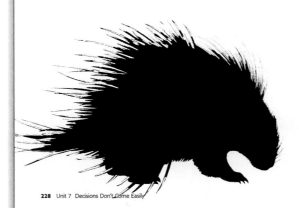

228 Unit 7 Decisions Don't Come Easily

This time Little Rabbit didn't ask why. By now he knew that the Terrible Things didn't need a reason. The smell still filled the clearing, though the Terrible Things had gone.

"I liked it better when there were all kinds of
120 creatures in our clearing," he said. "And I think we should move. What if the Terrible Things come back?"

"Nonsense," Big Rabbit said. "Why should we move? This has always been our home. And the Terrible Things won't come back. We are the White Rabbits. It couldn't happen to us."

C

THINK IT THROUGH
G Big Rabbit thinks he knows the Terrible Things. Do you think he knows as much as he thinks he does? Use evidence from this part of the story to support your view.

FOCUS
The Terrible Things return. Read to discover what Little Rabbit learns.

As day followed peaceful day Little Rabbit thought Big Rabbit must be right. Until the day the Terrible Things came back.

Little Rabbit saw the terrible gleam of their terrible
130 eyes through the forest darkness. And he smelled again the terrible smell.

"We have come for any creature that is white," the Terrible Things thundered.

"There are no white creatures here but us," Big Rabbit said.

"We have come for you," the Terrible Things said.

The rabbits scampered in every direction. "Help!" they screamed. "Somebody help!" But there was no

Terrible Things 229

COMPREHENSION

F Name all the creatures that are now missing. *(birds, squirrels, frogs, fish, and porcupines—all but the rabbits)* **details; summarizing**

G **THINK IT THROUGH** Big Rabbit thinks he knows the Terrible Things. Do you think he knows as much as he thinks he does? Use evidence from this part of the story to support your view. *(Most students will agree that Big Rabbit's arrogance and ignorance when he says "We are the White Rabbits. It couldn't happen to us" are giving him a false sense of security. Based on what has happened to the others, Big Rabbit should be following Little Rabbit's suggestion.)* **making judgments**

LITERATURE

C From the Terrible Things' first appearance, Little Rabbit has been watching and learning about them. What has Little Rabbit noticed about the forest and the Terrible Things that no one else has spoken about? *(He sees how the forest has changed. He sees that the Terrible Things don't have a reason for choosing the groups they capture.)* **theme**

VOCABULARY

C **bristled, better** (lines 107 and 119), **nonsense** (line 122), **happen** (line 125), **darkness** (line 130): Have students syllabicate these words. *(bris•tled, bet•ter, non•sense, hap•pen, dark•ness)*

one left to help. And the big, circling nets dropped
140 over them and the Terrible Things carried them away.

All but Little Rabbit, who was little enough to hide
in a pile of rocks by the pond and smart enough to
stay so still that the Terrible Things thought he was a
rock himself.

When they had all gone Little Rabbit crept into the
middle of the empty clearing. I should have tried to
help the other rabbits, he thought. If only we
creatures had stuck together, it could have been
different.

150 Sadly, Little Rabbit left the clearing. He'd go tell
other forest creatures about the Terrible Things. He
hoped someone would listen.

H **THINK IT THROUGH**

1. Little Rabbit thinks it could have been different.
   Why didn't the animals stick together? Review the
   story for evidence to support your answer.
2. The writer of this tale bases it on the time when
   the Nazis caused terror. The Nazis sent groups of
   people to death camps. What do you think is this
   tale's theme or message?
3. Why do you think the writer tells a fictional story
   with animal characters instead of describing the
   real events?

Speech by Parson Martin Niemöller

The Nazis came first for the Communists.
But I wasn't a Communist,
so I didn't speak up.
Then they came for the Jews,
5 but I wasn't a Jew,
so I didn't speak up.
Then they came for the trade unionists,
but I wasn't a trade unionist
so I didn't speak up.
10 Then they came for the Catholics,
but I was a Protestant
so I didn't speak up.
Then they came for me.
By that time there was no one left.

COMPREHENSION

H **THINK IT THROUGH**

1. Little Rabbit thinks it could have
   been different. Why didn't the
   animals stick together? Review the
   story for evidence to support your
   answer. *(Fear was the biggest reason. Other reasons include superior
   attitudes, lack of concern for others,
   and prejudice.)* **cause and effect**

2. The writer of this tale bases it on
   the time when the Nazis caused
   terror. The Nazis sent groups of
   people to death camps. What do
   you think is this tale's theme, or
   message? *(Possible answer: Evil
   happens when no one stands to
   fight it.)* **theme** LITERATURE

3. Why do you think the writer tells
   a fictional story with animal characters instead of describing the
   real events? *(Possible answer: She
   wanted to teach a big lesson in a
   simple, powerful way.)* **author's
   purpose**

Option for Writing Have students
write a paragraph that explains their
interpretation of the theme, or message, of this allegory. Also have them
tell how this theme applies to the
world today.

RETEACHING

If students need more help understanding **Cause and Effect,** use
pages T642–T646.

RELATED READING

Background Information Martin
Niemöller (1892–1984) was a
Lutheran pastor who opposed Hitler.
After the Nazi era, Niemöller traveled
the world, promoting intellectual freedom. He ended many of his speeches
with the words in this selection.

1. What message do you think
   Niemöller is trying to give with
   these words? *(Possible answer: If
   you don't speak up in defense of
   others, their problems will someday
   be yours.)* **theme**

2. How are Niemöller's thoughts and
   actions similar to Big Rabbit's? *(As
   long as the Terrible Things and the
   Nazis weren't coming for the rabbits
   and a certain person, Big Rabbit and
   that person didn't speak up. But in
   the end when they came for Big
   Rabbit and that person, there was
   no one left to help them.)* **compare
   and contrast**

VOCABULARY

RETEACHING

If students need more help understanding **Syllabication,** use pages
T625–T633.

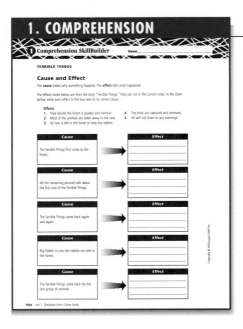

1. COMPREHENSION

Cause and Effect

Direct Instruction Remind students that events in a story often are related by cause and effect. A **cause** gives the reason *why* the event happened and an **effect** tells *what* happened.

Read the first three paragraphs of "Terrible Things," ending with "their shadows blotted out the sun." Ask: *If blotting out the sun is the effect, what is the cause?* Remind the students to ask themselves, Why did this event happen? (to find the cause) and What happened as a result of this event? (to find the effect).

> **Comprehension SkillBuilder Answer Key:**
> **Effects:**
>
> *The birds are captured and removed.*
>
> *They decide the forest is quieter and roomier.*
>
> *Most of the animals are taken away in the nets.*
>
> *He will not listen to any warnings.*
>
> *No one is left in the forest to help the rabbits.*

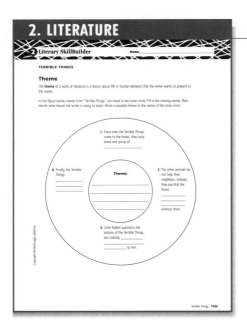

2. LITERATURE

Theme

Direct Instruction Recall that the **theme** of a work of literature is a lesson, or message, about human life. Explain to the students that a writer usually does not tell the theme directly. An author uses the actions and words of the characters and the events of the story to state the theme in an indirect way. Remind the students that one way to discover the theme of a story is to ask themselves, What lesson about life did the characters in the story learn? Can I apply this message to my life? Stress that the theme is valid only if it can be supported by details in the story.

> **Literary SkillBuilder Answer Key:**
> *Sentence completions:*
> **1.** *animals*
> **2.** *is better*
> **3.** *listens/pays attention*
> **4.** *take away the rabbits*
>
> *Themes may vary. Possible answer: By not speaking out against evil toward a few, all will eventually suffer.*

Direct Instruction
for SkillBuilder Copymasters

---

3. VOCABULARY

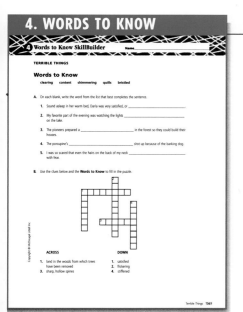

Syllabication

Direct Instruction Recall that **syllables** are word parts that contain a vowel sound. Write *storing, peaceful, matter, unfriendly* on the board. Ask the students how many vowel sounds they hear in each word and where each should be divided into syllables. *(Answers: stor/ing, peace/ful, mat/ter, un/friend/ly)* Elicit from the students some of the guidelines for syllabication:

- A one-syllable prefix, such as *un-*, forms a separate syllable.
- A one-syllable suffix, such as *-ing*, *-ful*, or *-ly*, forms a separate syllable.
- A word with double consonants between vowels is divided between the double consonants.
  Encourage students to use the dictionary for help in dividing words into syllables.

Vocabulary SkillBuilder Answer Key:

A.
1. *clear – ing*
2. *squir – rels*
3. *rid – dance*
4. *dis – like*
5. *prick – ly*

B. *(Order may vary.)* *porcupine, nervously, shimmering, terrible*

C.
1. *shimmering*
2. *nervously*
3. *terrible*
4. *porcupine*

---

4. WORDS TO KNOW

Words to Know

Direct Instruction As you present the **Words to Know,** here are some points you might want to cover. Help students to identify the parts of the vocabulary words. Stress the importance of finding the base of each word. Help students remove prefixes and suffixes first.

　clear + -ing = *clearing*
　shimmer + -ing = *shimmering*
　bristle + -ed = *bristled*

Point out to students that a good rule to remember is to drop the silent e from the base word when you add a suffix beginning with a y or a vowel.

For Exercise B, review the concept of the crossword puzzle. Students may find the use of a dictionary helpful.

Words to Know SkillBuilder Answer Key:

A.
1. *content*
2. *shimmering*
3. *clearing*
4. *quills*
5. *bristled*

B.
1 **across:** *clearing*
3 **across:** *quills*
1 **down:** *content*
2 **down:** *shimmering*
4 **down:** *bristled*

---

5. SELECTION TEST

Selection Test Answer Key:
A. 1. *a* 2. *a* 3. *c* 4. *b* 5. *b* 6. *b* 7. *a* 8. *c* 9. *c*
B. *Little Rabbit decides to tell other creatures about the Terrible Things.*

TERRIBLE THINGS

Cause and Effect

The **cause** states why something happens. The **effect** tells what happened.

The effects listed below are from the story "Terrible Things." They are not in the correct order. In the chart below, write each effect in the box next to its correct cause.

Effects

1. They decide the forest is quieter and roomier.
2. Most of the animals are taken away in the nets.
3. No one is left in the forest to help the rabbits.
4. The birds are captured and removed.
5. He will not listen to any warnings.

Cause	Effect
The Terrible Things first come to the forest.	
All the remaining animals talk about the first visit of the Terrible Things.	
The Terrible Things come back again and again.	
Big Rabbit is sure the rabbits are safe in the forest.	
The Terrible Things come back for the last group of animals.	

TERRIBLE THINGS

Theme

The **theme** of a work of literature is a lesson about life or human behavior that the writer wants to present to the reader.

In the figure below, events from "Terrible Things" are listed in the outer circle. Fill in the missing words. Then decide what lesson the writer is trying to teach. Write a possible theme in the center of the inner circle.

1. Every time the Terrible Things come to the forest, they carry away one group of _____.

Theme:

_____

_____

_____

_____

4. Finally, the Terrible Things _____ _____ _____.

2. The other animals do not help their neighbors. Instead, they say that the forest _____ _____ _____ without them.

3. Little Rabbit questions the actions of the Terrible Things, but nobody _____ _____ _____ to him.

TERRIBLE THINGS

Syllabication

A **syllable** is a word part with one vowel sound. A word is broken into syllables between doubled consonants, as in *mat-ter*. A syllable break usually falls between a base word and a prefix or suffix, as in *re-wind-ing*. Use a dictionary to find syllable breaks in other words.

A. Break these words into syllables. Write the syllables on the lines.

1. clearing   _____   _____

2. squirrels   _____   _____

3. riddance   _____   _____

4. dislike   _____   _____

5. prickly   _____   _____

B. Choose one syllable from each column to form a word found in the story.

Column 1	Column 2	Column 3	Three-Syllable Word
por	ri	ing	
ner	mer	pine	
shim	cu	ly	
ter	vous	ble	

C. Use the three-syllable words from Exercise B to complete the following sentences.

1. The shiny scales on the fish were _____ in the sunlight.

2. He was shaking with fear as he _____ paced back and forth.

3. People in the village suffered during the _____ storm.

4. The quills of the _____ have barbs, or hooks, at the tip.

TERRIBLE THINGS

Words to Know

clearing   content   shimmering   quills   bristled

A. On each blank, write the word from the list that best completes the sentence.

1. Sound asleep in her warm bed, Darla was very satisfied, or _____.

2. My favorite part of the evening was watching the lights _____ on the lake.

3. The pioneers prepared a _____ in the forest so they could build their houses.

4. The porcupine's _____ shot up because of the barking dog.

5. I was so scared that even the hairs on the back of my neck _____ with fear.

B. Use the clues below and the **Words to Know** to fill in the puzzle.

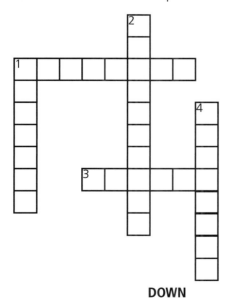

ACROSS

1. land from which trees have been removed
3. sharp, hollow spines

DOWN

1. satisfied
2. flickering
4. stiffened

TERRIBLE THINGS

A. Complete each statement by filling in the circle beside the letter of the correct answer.

1. **In the beginning of this story, all of the animals**
   - ○ a. share the woods and are content.
   - ○ c. are waiting for the Terrible Things to arrive.
   - ○ b. dislike each other and fight all the time.

2. **One day, the Terrible Things arrive and**
   - ○ a. take away the birds.
   - ○ c. take over the animals' land.
   - ○ b. steal the animals' food.

3. **The Terrible Things keep returning to the woods and**
   - ○ a. taking over more land.
   - ○ c. taking away more animals.
   - ○ b. taking away more food.

4. **Every time the Terrible Things leave, Little Rabbit asks,**
   - ○ a. "Why do the Terrible things take our food?"
   - ○ c. "Why do the Terrible Things want our land?"
   - ○ b. "Why did the Terrible Things take them away?"

5. **And every time, Big Rabbit answers,**
   - ○ a. "The Terrible Things get very hungry."
   - ○ c. "The Terrible Things need more room to live."
   - ○ b. "The Terrible Things don't need a reason."

6. **Finally, when only the rabbits are left, Little Rabbit says,**
   - ○ a. "There's nothing left to eat. We should find more food."
   - ○ b. "We should move. What if the Terrible Things come back?"
   - ○ c. "The Terrible Things eat rabbits. We should make some stew."

7. **But Big Rabbit answers,**
   - ○ a. "They won't come back. It couldn't happen to us."
   - ○ b. "They don't like stew. Let's make something else."
   - ○ c. "Don't worry. The Terrible Things are bringing food."

8. **One day, the Terrible Things come back and**
   - ○ a. move onto the animals' land.
   - ○ b. have a huge party.
   - ○ c. take away the rabbits.

9. **Little Rabbit is sorry because**
   - ○ a. the forest creatures have nowhere to live.
   - ○ c. the forest creatures didn't help each other
   - ○ b. the animals' land is completely destroyed.

B. In your own words, tell what Little Rabbit decides to do at the end of the story.

_____

THE LADY
OR
THE TIGER?

by Frank L. Stockton, retold by Sue Baugh

Focus Skills

COMPREHENSION
Evaluating

LITERATURE
Motive

VOCABULARY
Context Clues: Definition

SkillBuilder Copymasters

 Reading Comprehension:
1 Evaluating p. T318

 Literary Analysis:
2 Motive p. T319

 Vocabulary:
3 Context Clues p. T320
4 Words to Know p. T321

Assessment

 5 Selection Test p. T322

Readability Scores

DRP	LEXILE	DALE-CHALL
50	550	3.6

Reading Fluency

 ★ Reading Fluency p. T323

For English Learners

In some languages, different words represent different kinds of love. So the fact that *love* refers to both parental and spousal love in this story might be confusing to students learning English. If necessary, discuss the differences between the kind of love that the king and his daughter have for each other and the kind of love that the princess and the servant have for each other.

Vocabulary Strategy: Preteaching

Context Clues Explain that several of the words in this selection are surrounded by context clues that provide definitions of the words. Write the examples shown on this and the next page on the board. Then have students use the context clues to give a definition for each word.

Connect to Your Life

Have you ever had to choose something you could not see? What did you choose? Where you happy or unhappy with your choice?

Key to the Story

Long ago, rulers held big contests in arenas. An *arena* is an open area surrounded by seats. A sports stadium is an arena. As you read this short story, imagine you have a front-row seat to all that happens. The narrator will speak to you directly. Pay attention to the details. You will be asked to make a decision.

Vocabulary Preview

Words to Know

barbarians	savage	jealousy
gladiators	willful	

 Reading Coach CD-ROM selection

A beautiful woman

    waits behind one door.

A deadly tiger

    waits behind another.

Will the servant

    choose love or doom?

The Lady or the Tiger? **233**

Connect to Your Life

Encourage students to use the title, pictures, and teaser in the lower right corner to predict what the story will be about.

Key to the Story

Explain to students that as readers of this story, they will be like fans at a ball game. Suggest that they look for similarities between the entertainment in the story and modern sporting or entertainment events. Encourage them to study the characters as they read.

Vocabulary Preview

Words to Know

  barbarians *n.* brutal people
  gladiators *n.* men who fought each other as a public show
  savage *adj.* fiercely wild
  willful *adj.* always wanting to get one's own way
  jealousy *n.* fear of losing one's love to another person

 For direct instruction on Words to Know, see page T317.

Building Background

When the American writer Frank R. Stockton (1834–1902) published "The Lady or the Tiger?" in 1882, it became instantly popular for its unusual open-ended conclusion. Despite the fact that Stockton would never reveal the ending, people have been arguing about it for decades. "The Lady or the Tiger?" has been included in many short-story anthologies and was dramatized in 1966 as part of the Broadway musical *The Apple Tree*, whose cast included Alan Alda and Karen Black.

---

1. The <u>barbarians</u>, a cruel and brutal people, defeated the villagers. *(definition: cruel and brutal people)*
2. The king said he cared about <u>justice</u>—that is, fair and equal treatment. *(definition: fair and equal treatment)*

 For more on Context Clues, see page T317.

FOCUS
A king has complete control of his kingdom. Find out how he deals with those who break his rules.

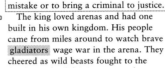 In the days of old there lived a king and his beautiful daughter. The king admired his neighbors, who lived in the Roman Empire, and even copied some of their ways. But his ancestors had been barbarians. They rode where they wanted. They took what they wanted and answered to no one but themselves. The king had settled down, but he still had the blood of his ancestors in his veins.

> **barbarians**
> (bär bär′ ē ənz)
> *n.* brutal people

10 He would think of the wildest schemes and ideas for his kingdom. Then, with his power and wealth, he would make them happen. The king was known for getting whatever he wanted.

He also watched over his kingdom with a sharp eye. When his household and government worked smoothly, the king smiled. And when something went wrong, he smiled even more. Nothing made him happier than to crush a mistake or to bring a criminal to justice.

> **REREAD**
> What kind of man is the king?

20 The king loved arenas and had one built in his own kingdom. His people came from miles around to watch brave gladiators wage war in the arena. They cheered as wild beasts fought to the death. But he didn't just copy other people's arenas. He added something of his own to improve the minds of his people.

> **gladiators**
> (glăd′ ē ā′ tərz)
> *n.* men who fought each other as a public show

On the inside of the arena, he had two 30 doors built. They looked alike and stood side by side. Behind one was a savage,

> **savage**
> (săv′ ĭj)
> *adj.* fiercely wild

hungry tiger. Behind the other waited a beautiful lady. The inside of each door was covered in thick curtains. That way, no sound of the lady or tiger could reach the outside.

You might ask why the king did this.

He believed that people accused of a crime should choose their own punishment or reward. Luck would decide if the person was guilty or innocent. The 40 people watching would see justice done. What could be more fair?

> **THINK IT THROUGH**
> How has the king made his arena different?

FOCUS
Find out how the king decides legal cases.

Not every crime caught the king's interest. But when one did, the king would set a trial day. The royal jailers would bring the accused person to the arena. Hundreds of people would fill the seats to see this trial. High above the arena, the king sat on his throne, with the princess and all his royal followers around him. At the king's signal, a door far below the throne opened. The accused person stepped out into 50 the harsh light of the arena.

He would see the two doors waiting for him. It was his duty and honor to walk right up to these doors and open one of them. If he chose the door with the tiger, that proved he was guilty. The tiger would spring out and tear him apart. At his death, iron bells would ring, and the people would wail and cry. Why

---

COMPREHENSION

FOCUS SKILL: Evaluating

Tell students that when they **evaluate** a piece of literature, they judge part or all of it in areas such as its believability, its originality, and its ability to entertain, inform, persuade, or describe.

For direct instruction on Evaluating, see page T316.

A REREAD What kind of man is the king? *(He is a schemer who has firm control over his kingdom.)* **evaluating**

B THINK IT THROUGH How has the king made his arena different? *(He has had two doors built side by side. Behind one door is a hungry tiger; behind the other is a beautiful lady.)* **details**

LITERATURE

FOCUS SKILL: Motive

Explain that a character's **motive** is his or her reason for thinking, feeling, or acting a certain way. Some characters' motives are stated directly, but others are implied.

For direct instruction on Motive, see page T316.

Use these questions to encourage literary analysis.

A Why did the king copy the ways of his neighbors in the Roman Empire? *(He admired the Romans and wanted to be like them.)* **motive**

B Consider what you know about the king so far. Why do you think he made his arena different? *(Not only did he want people to choose their own punishment or reward, he probably also wanted to have a better, more exciting arena than anyone else's.)* **motive**

VOCABULARY

FOCUS SKILL: Context Clues

Remind students to use **context clues**—particularly those that provide definitions—to figure out any words they don't know.

A savage Students can use the clues (found later in the text on p. 238) *bigger and stronger, claws could tear through armor,* and *teeth could stab like knives* to figure out what *savage* means.

FOR ENGLISH LEARNERS

Help students understand the following expressions and idioms:

Line 1: the days of old
Line 7: answered to no one but themselves
Line 14: with a sharp eye
Line 19: bring a criminal to justice
Line 42: caught the king's interest

did one so young and fair, or one so old and respected, have to die like that?

If he chose the door with the lady, that proved he 60 was innocent. The man and woman would be married right then and there. The king always chose a lady of the right age and social rank for the man. What joy! Brass bells rang out the news. The people shouted and laughed! As the man led his new wife home, children threw rose petals along their path. It didn't matter if the man loved someone else or if he was already married. The king's word was law.

REREAD
Why might the choice of the lady be an unhappy one?

C

70 Think of it! No judge, no jury, no trial, no lawyers. Just one person choosing life or death. And it all depended on luck or chance! The accused person could not know which door hid the tiger or the lady. In this arena, the king believed, everyone got what he deserved.

The whole kingdom looked forward to the king's trial days. When people came to the arena, they never knew what would happen. Would they see a bloody 80 death or a joyful wedding?

REREAD
What does this tell you about the people in the kingdom?

D

The king felt no one could find anything wrong with this system. After all, the accused person had his life in his own hands, didn't he? The king was very pleased with himself for thinking up this idea.

E

Now, remember the king had a daughter. The princess was so beautiful that people turned and stared at her wherever she went. She was also as strong and willful as her father. The king loved her more than anyone or 90 anything in his kingdom.

willful
(wĭl′ fəl)
adj. always wanting to get one's own way

236 Unit 7 Decisions Don't Come Easily

Among the king's royal servants was a young man so handsome and brave that he had no equal. The daughter fell in love with him—how could she help herself? They kept their love secret for many months. The royal daughter wasn't supposed to be seeing a lowly servant. Then one day the king found out about them.

C

Oh, the cries of rage and doom! The king threw the young man into prison and set a day for his trial in the arena. Of course, this was a special event. Never 100 before had a lowly subject of the king dared to love his daughter. Everyone talked about the case for days, wondering how it would all turn out.

subject
(sŭb′ jĭkt)
one who is under the rule of another

D

The king ordered his servants to search for the most savage tiger in the kingdom. He also ordered them to search for the most beautiful woman they could find. His servants obeyed and brought both to the king's arena. At last, everything was ready.

THINK IT THROUGH
For this trial, why do you think the king wants the *most* beautiful woman and the *most* savage tiger?

F

The Lady or the Tiger? 237

COMPREHENSION

C **REREAD** Why might the choice of the lady be an unhappy one? *(A man who chose the lady was forced to live with the choice, no matter what.)* **clarifying**

D **REREAD** What does this tell you about the people of the kingdom? *(They care more about entertainment than they care about the cruel nature of the event.)* **evaluating**

E Ask: The author has given several clues and examples to describe the king. What is your opinion of the king so far? *(Most students probably will say that he is unkind and unfair, and he seems to enjoy making people suffer.)* **evaluating**

F **THINK IT THROUGH** For this trial, why do you think the king wants the *most* beautiful woman and the *most* savage tiger? *(Since this "crime" involves the person the king loves most, he wants to punish both his daughter and his ser-*

vant in the cruelest way possible.) **drawing conclusions**

LITERATURE

C **Teacher Modeling: Motive**
Use lines 97–103 to demonstrate how to analyze motive.
You might say: *The character I know the best so far is the king. From what I've read, it's clear he has total control of the kingdom and over life and death. Control means more to him than justice. It is fun for him to manipulate lives and watch people squirm as he does so. I know he loves his daughter and was furious that a lowly servant could get close to her. I know the king's a cruel character. So you have to expect that his reasons for punishing the servant will somehow be influenced by his cruel ways.*

D Is this what you think the king wanted for the princess? Explain. *(Most students will say yes, that he wanted the princess to suffer and be sorry for falling in love with a lowly servant.)* **motive**

VOCABULARY

FOR ENGLISH LEARNERS

Help students understand the following expressions and idioms:

Line 62: social rank
Line 63: rang out the news
Line 92: he had no equal
Line 93: how could she help herself?
Line 102: how it would all turn out

The day of the trial arrives. Read to discover how the young man prepares himself.

The day of the trial, people came from every part of
110 the kingdom to watch. They pushed their way into
the arena and filled the seats. When there were no
seats left, people stood outside the walls and listened
eagerly for the trial to begin. The king and his court
took their places. Across the arena stood the two
doors with their awful secret.

Then the people fell silent. Every eye was fixed on **B**
the king. He raised his hand and gave the signal.
Beneath the royal throne, a door opened, and the
young man stepped into the dusty circle. People saw
120 how handsome he was. No wonder the princess loved
him. What a terrible thing for him to be there!

The young man walked to the center of the arena.
He turned and bowed to the king. But his eyes were
on the princess. He thought, "She must know which
door hides the tiger and which one hides the lady."

He was right. As soon as the king had set the trial
day, the princess had worked day and night to find
out. She knew the men who were in charge of the
doors. But which one would tell her what she wanted
130 to know? She promised them gold and other fine
things. Day after day the princess came. Finally, one
of the men told her the secret.

At last she knew behind which door lay the tiger
and which one stood the lady, waiting to be chosen.
She learned that the tiger was bigger and stronger
than any tiger in the arena before. His claws could
tear through armor, and his teeth could stab like
knives.

238 Unit 7 Decisions Don't Come Easily

The princess also knew who the beautiful lady was
140 and hated her. The lady was from the royal court.
Often the princess had seen this lady—or thought she
had seen her—looking at the young man. Sometimes
she thought her young man even returned the look.

E Now and then the princess had seen them talking
together. It was only for a minute or two, but much
can be said in a minute or two. Maybe they were
talking about the weather. Maybe they were agreeing
to meet later. How could the princess know?

Now she sat in the arena beside the king. Her lover
150 turned and looked up at her. He knew her strong
nature. She would never rest until the
secret, hidden even from the king, was
hers.

His eyes asked, "Which door should I
choose?"

> **REREAD**
> What do you think the princess is feeling? **G**

The question was as plain as if he had shouted it
from where he stood. There was no time to lose. She
must answer quickly.

Her right arm lay on a soft cushion in front of her.
160 She raised her hand and made a slight, quick motion
to the right. No one but the young man saw it.
Everyone else was looking at him.

He turned and walked quickly across the empty
arena. Every heart stopped beating, every breath was
held, every eye was fixed on his handsome face.
Without a thought, he went to the door on the right
and opened it.

Now, the point of the story is this: Did the tiger
come out of that door, or did the lady?

THINK IT THROUGH
H The young man follows the motion the princess makes without a thought. What does this show about him?

The Lady or the Tiger? **239**

COMPREHENSION

G **REREAD** What do you think the princess is feeling? *(She's confused and jealous and is beginning to doubt the servant's feelings for her.)* **making inferences**

H **THINK IT THROUGH** The young man follows the motion the princess makes without a thought. What does this show about him? *(He trusts her totally and believes she wants to save his life.)* **drawing conclusions**

LITERATURE

E What possible motive would the princess have for pointing to the door with the tiger behind it? *(her suspicion of a relationship between the servant and beautiful lady, which causes her to feel jealous)* What motive would she have for pointing to the door with the beautiful woman behind it? *(her love for the servant, which would cause her to save his life and lose him to the beautiful woman)* **motive**

VOCABULARY

B **every eye was fixed on** Explain to students that this idiom means that everyone was watching with close attention.

FOR ENGLISH LEARNERS

Help students understand the following expressions and idioms:

Line 114: took their places
Line 116: fell silent
Line 123: his eyes were on the princess
Line 143: returned the look
Line 168: the point of the story

Read to find out about a choice you'll have to make.

C 170 The more we think about this question, the harder it is to answer. We have to search deep into the human heart, which is not easy. Put yourself in the place of the princess. She is torn between love and jealousy. She has lost him, but who should have him? She has an awful choice to make.

jealousy
(jĕl' ə sē)
n. fear of losing one's love to another person

Oh, many times she had dreamed of that tiger! In her nightmares she saw her lover opening the door. She heard the tiger's roar and saw
180 its powerful body leap on the man. She cried out in terror as the tiger sank its teeth into her lover's neck.

But she had dreamed of the other door more often. She saw the look of delight on his face when he opened it, and the beautiful lady was waiting for him. The princess felt jealousy burn like fire in her body. She saw him rush to meet the woman, and she felt hatred twist inside as the woman smiled in victory. How could the princess stand to see them married right before her eyes? How could she stand to hear
190 the joyful shouts from the crowd? The brass bells would ring out. The crowd would cheer madly. She would watch the happy couple walking on the rose petals as they went to their home. The noise would drown out her own scream of rage and loss.

D

Wouldn't it be better for him to die at once? Then he and the princess would be together after death.

And yet, that awful tiger, those screams, that blood! She had spent days and nights trying to decide which door he should open. She had known he would
I 200 ask. Finally, the princess knew how she would answer. That was why she moved her hand to the right.

F

Her choice is not one to be taken lightly. As the author, I'm really not the one to answer such a hard question. So I leave it with all of you:

Which came out of the opened door—the lady, or the tiger?

J THINK IT THROUGH

1. What do you think came out of the opened door? Use evidence from the story to support your answer.
2. What is your reaction to the ending? Explain.
3. Review the actions of the princess. What do you think she should have done? Give a reason for your answer.

COMPREHENSION

I Ask: Based on the author's description of the princess, what is your opinion of her? *(Responses will vary. Some students may think she is selfish and jealous and doesn't really love the servant. Others may say that she is feeling what any person who loves someone fiercely would feel.)* **evaluating**

J THINK IT THROUGH

1. What do you think came out of the opened door? Use evidence from the story to support your answer. *(Some students might point to lines 139–143 and 182–196 as clues that the princess led the servant to the tiger. Others might point to lines 177–181 and line 197 as clues that she led him to the lady.)* **drawing conclusions**

2. What is your reaction to the ending? Explain. *(Answers will vary, but most students are likely to respond that they wish the writer had revealed the servant's fate.)* **evaluating**

3. Review the actions of the princess. What do you think she should have done? Give a reason for your answer. *(Most students will agree that the princess should have shown the servant the door with the beautiful woman. They might cite a possible reason that her love should have been stronger than her feelings of jealousy. In addition, the princess would not have wanted to see the servant killed by a savage tiger right before her eyes.)* **drawing conclusions**

Option for Writing Have students review the details of this story and then write their own ending. If any students share the same idea about how the story might turn out, you might have them work together to write an ending.

LITERATURE

F Why do you think there is so much description of the princess's motives for choosing either door? *(Possible answers: The author wants to drag out the suspense about the princess's final decision. The author wants to show how the princess struggled in the days before the event.)* **motive**

VOCABULARY

C **search deep into the human heart** Make sure students understand that this idiom means to closely examine the source of certain emotions.

D **crowd would cheer madly** Explain that in this context, *madly* means "wildly."

RETEACHING

If students need more help understanding **Context Clues,** use pages T608–T611.

1. COMPREHENSION

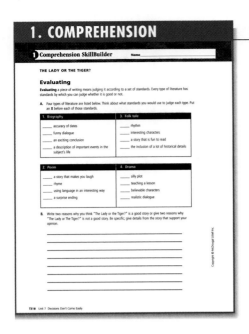

Evaluating

Direct Instruction Tell students that when they study a piece of literature carefully and judge its value, they are **evaluating** the piece. To make an evaluation, they must compare a selection to a set of standards. Those standards change, depending on the type of literature. For example, the students should evaluate a short story on the basis of whether or not it has believable characters, has a plot that holds their attention, and is entertaining. If a story has these elements, it is a good story. They would not use these standards to evaluate a nonfiction selection. For that type of writing, students would judge whether the piece was accurate and the facts were presented in a clear, easy-to-understand way.

Discuss what standards should be used to evaluate "The Lady or the Tiger?" Make sure the students include interesting characters and plot devices and any other aspect they feel is appropriate to judge the story. Then have the students evaluate the story on the basis of these standards.

Comprehension SkillBuilder Answer Key:

A. **1.** *accuracy of dates, a description of important events in the subject's life*

  2. *rhyme, using language in an interesting way*

  3. *interesting characters, a story that is fun to read*

  4. *believable characters, realistic dialogue*

B. *Answers will vary but must cite evidence from the story.*

2. LITERATURE

Motive

Direct Instruction Tell the students that characters in stories often behave like people in real life. As in real life, the characters have reasons for behaving the way they do. These reasons are called **motives.** Usually, a character's actions are clear, but readers may have to look for hints that will tell them the reasons for those actions. "The Lady or the Tiger?" is unique because the motives for the princess's choice are clear, but readers have to look for hints as to what her choice was.

Point out to the students that although the situation in the story is not realistic, the idea that someone might have reasons to act in totally opposite ways is true to life. Ask the students if they have ever been in a situation where they have had conflicting motivations that have made it difficult to make choices. For example, they may have been tempted to cheat because they were motivated to get a good grade. On the other hand, they may have not wanted to cheat because they would like to be thought of as honest.

Literary SkillBuilder Answer Key:

2a. *The whole kingdom* looked forward to / enjoyed / attended *the trial days.*

2b. *The people wanted to find out if they would see* a death *or a* wedding.

3a. *The* princess *fell in love with a young man.*

3b. *He was very* handsome.

4a. *he looked at the* princess.

4b. *He hoped she would let him know* which door hid the tiger and which door hid the beautiful lady.

5a. *that hid the* tiger.

5b. *She did not want the young man to* marry the lady.

6a. *that hid the* lady.

6b. *She did not want the young man to* be killed.

3. VOCABULARY

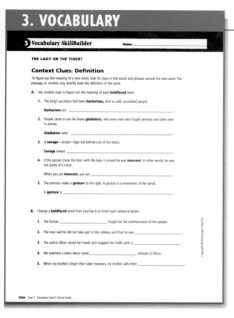

Context Clues: Definition

Direct Instruction Remind students that **context** is the sentence or paragraph in which you find a word. Some writers realize that their readers may not understand a certain word, so they give clues to its meaning. These clues are called **context clues.** One type of context clue is the **definition clue,** in which the writer tells the meaning of the new word. Tell students to look for these common signal words for definition clues: *is, which is, who is, that is,* and *in other words.* Sometimes, punctuation marks such as commas and dashes are used as signals. Write these sentences on the board and discuss how the punctuation marks set off the definitions:

> The young man was led into the arena, the place where the trial would take place.
> A dilemma—a difficult choice—faced the princess.

Vocabulary SkillBuilder Answer Key:

A. 1. *wild, uncivilized people*
2. *men who fought animals and other men in arenas*
3. *brutal*
4. *not guilty of a crime*
5. *a movement of the hands*

B. 1. *gladiators*
2. *innocent*
3. *gesture*
4. *savage*
5. *barbarians*

---

4. WORDS TO KNOW

Words to Know

Direct Instruction As you present the **Words to Know,** here are some points you might want to cover. Help students to identify the parts of the vocabulary words. Stress the importance of finding the root of each word for easier decoding.

barbarian is in the same family of words as *barbarous* and *barbaric*
gladiator is derivative of the Celtic word, *gladius,* meaning "sword"
will + -ful = willful, or "full of will"
Will is defined as "determination."
jealous + -y = jealousy

Writing Activity
Pair students or allow them to work in small groups to write a short ad for anything they choose. Have the students present the ad to the class upon finishing. Poll the class as to whether they would buy the product based on the students' advertisement.

Words to Know SkillBuilder Answer Key:
A. 1. *jealousy* 2. *willful* 3. *savage* 4. *gladiators* 5. *barbarians*
B. 1. *false* 2. *false* 3. *true* 4. *true* 5. *false*

---

5. SELECTION TEST

Selection Test Answer Key:
A. 1. *true* 2. *false* 3. *false* 4. *true* 5. *true* 6. *true* 7. *false* 8. *true* 9. *false*
B. *No one knows what the servant discovers. What is behind the door is not revealed.*

THE LADY OR THE TIGER?

Evaluating

Evaluating a piece of writing means judging it according to a set of standards. Every type of literature has standards by which you can judge whether it is good or not.

A. Four types of literature are listed below. Think about what standards you would use to judge each type. Put an **X** before each of those standards.

1. Biography	3. Folk tale
_____ accuracy of dates	_____ rhythm
_____ funny dialogue	_____ interesting characters
_____ an exciting conclusion	_____ a story that is fun to read
_____ a description of important events in the subject's life	_____ the inclusion of a lot of historical details

2. Poem	4. Drama
_____ a story that makes you laugh	_____ silly plot
_____ rhyme	_____ teaching a lesson
_____ using language in an interesting way	_____ believable characters
_____ a surprise ending	_____ realistic dialogue

B. Write two reasons why you think "The Lady or the Tiger?" is a good story or give two reasons why "The Lady or The Tiger?" is not a good story. Be specific; give details from the story that support your opinion.

_____

_____

_____

_____

_____

_____

_____

_____

THE LADY OR THE TIGER?

Motive

Characters in stories act for specific reasons. These reasons are called **motives.**

Fill in the motives for these characters from "The Lady or the Tiger?" The first one is done for you.

The character's action (or possible)	The character's motive, or reason for the action
1a. The king forced the accused person to choose between two doors; behind one was a _____tiger_____, behind the other, a _____a beautiful lady_____ .	**1b.** The king believed that _____luck_____ would decide if the person was _____innocent_____ or _____guilty_____ .
2a. The whole kingdom _____ _____ the trial days. _____ .	**2b.** The people wanted to find out if they would see a _____ or a _____ .
3a. The _____ fell in love with a young man.	**3b.** The young man was very _____ .
4a. When the young man was brought into the arena, he looked at the _____ .	**4b.** He hoped she would let him know _____ _____ _____ .
5a. The princess might point to the door that hid the _____ .	**5b.** She was jealous and did not want the young man to _____ _____ .
6a. The princess might point to the door that hid the _____ .	**6b.** She did not want the young man to _____ .

THE LADY OR THE TIGER?

Context Clues: Definition

To figure out the meaning of a new word, look for clues in the words and phrases around the new word. The passage, or context, may directly state the definition of the word.

A. Use context clues to figure out the meaning of each **boldfaced** word.

1. The king's ancestors had been **barbarians,** that is, wild, uncivilized people.

   Barbarians are _____ .

2. People came to see the brave **gladiators,** who were men who fought animals and other men in arenas.

   Gladiators were _____ .

3. A **savage**—brutal—tiger hid behind one of the doors.

   Savage means _____ .

4. If the person chose the door with the lady, it proved he was **innocent.** In other words, he was not guilty of a crime.

   When you are **innocent,** you are _____ .

5. The princess made a **gesture** to the right. A gesture is a movement of the hands.

   A **gesture** is _____ .

B. Choose a **boldfaced** word from Exercise A to finish each sentence below.

1. The Roman _____ fought for the entertainment of the people.

2. The man said he did not take part in the robbery and that he was _____ .

3. The police officer raised her hands and stopped the traffic with a _____ .

4. We watched a video about some _____ animals in Africa.

5. When my brothers forget their table manners, my mother calls them _____ .

THE LADY OR THE TIGER?

Words to Know

barbarians   **gladiators**   **savage**   **willful**   **jealousy**

A. Fill in the blanks with the word from the list that best completes the sentence.

1. I was surprised by my feelings of _____ when my girlfriend went to the movies with somebody else.

2. My father says that I am a demanding, _____ person who can't take no for an answer.

3. It's amazing that my gentle pet cat is related to the fierce and _____ tiger.

4. Roman _____ fought each other in many games and challenges.

5. In the movie, the brutal _____ killed the beasts in the nastiest battle I've ever seen.

B. Write **true** or **false** in the blanks.

_____ **1.** Gladiators work with plants and flowers.

_____ **2.** If you always follow another person's rules, you are willful.

_____ **3.** Barbarians are wild and sometimes cruel people.

_____ **4.** You may feel some jealousy if your parents give your brother more attention than you.

_____ **5.** Some of the most savage animals are the mouse, turtle, and duck.

Writing Activity
Work with a group and write a two- or three-sentence advertisement. You are trying to convince someone to buy something. It can be anything you choose. Use at least one of the **Words to Know.**

Name_____

THE LADY OR THE TIGER?

A. Write **true** or **false** on the line next to each statement.

_____ **1.** This story takes place in a kingdom in the past.

_____ **2.** The king is a refined nobleman in the Roman Empire.

_____ **3.** The king rules his land with fairness and kindness.

_____ **4.** His idea of fairness is to let accused people choose their own punishment or reward.

_____ **5.** They do this by choosing what is behind one of the doors in the arena that the king built.

_____ **6.** No one speaks out against the king's system of punishment.

_____ **7.** One day the king discovers that his daughter is in love with the royal court adviser.

_____ **8.** The king uses his usual system to punish the couple.

_____ **9.** When the young man goes to choose his door, the princess tells him to choose the one on the left.

B. In your own words, tell what the young man discovers behind the door.

_____

_____

_____

_____

_____

Reader directions:

Cut this paper in half. Practice reading this passage aloud until you don't make any mistakes.
Then have someone listen to you read. Try to sound the way you think an old-fashioned storyteller would sound.

from **The Lady or the Tiger?**

Among the king's royal servants was a young man so handsome and brave that he had no equal. The daughter fell in love with him—how could she help herself? They kept their love secret for many months. The royal daughter wasn't supposed to be seeing a lowly servant. Then one day the king found out about them.

Oh, the cries of rage and doom! The king threw the young man into prison and set a day for his trial in the arena. Of course, this was a special event. Never before had a lowly subject of the king dared to love his daughter.

✂ **cut along dotted line**

— —

Checker directions:

Follow along as the passage is read. Make a dot under each word the reader misses.
Show the reader the missed words. Erase the dots and repeat for each reading.

from **The Lady or the Tiger?**

Among the king's royal servants was a young man so handsome and brave that he had no equal. The daughter fell in love with him—how could she help herself? They kept their love secret for many months. The royal daughter wasn't supposed to be seeing a lowly servant. Then one day the king found out about them.

Oh, the cries of rage and doom! The king threw the young man into prison and set a day for his trial in the arena. Of course, this was a special event. Never before had a lowly subject of the king dared to love his daughter.

Use this chart for Timed Readings and Repeated Readings.

Reading	1	2	3	4	5
Time (minutes/seconds)					
Words Missed					

Focus Skills and SkillBuilder Copymasters

Hard to Believe

Unit 8

Nonfiction

Are there alligators in our subways? Are there squirrels that can fly? Clear thinking or science can explain some things. The truth behind other strange things is still unknown.

In this unit, you'll read about some hard-to-believe events. Look for what's fact and what might be opinion.

As you read, feel free to form your own opinions. Ask questions. Seeing isn't always believing.

242

Pacing Guide

SELECTION	TOTAL DAYS	PREREADING	READING	POST READING	
				SELECTIVE OPTIONS	ALL OPTIONS
Ships That Could Think	2.5–3	1	1	.5	1
Earthquakes	3–3.5	1	1.5	.5	1
Sparky	2–2.5	1	.5	.5	1
The Roswell Incident	2.5–3	1	1	.5	1

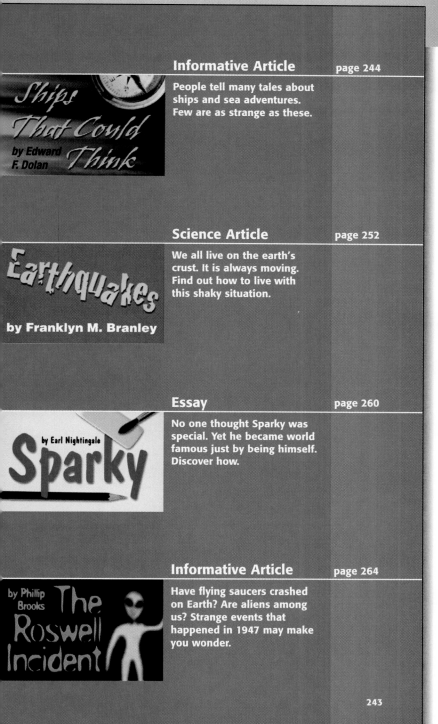

More About Nonfiction

The selections in this unit challenge students to think critically. As students sift through details—in particular, facts about unusual occurrences—they will be encouraged to question what they read and to make judgments. Reading a non-narrative science article will provide a chance for students to explore the kind of text features they regularly encounter in content areas apart from language arts materials.

Technology Resources

Audio CD
All selections in this unit are featured in the Audio Library.

Reading Coach CD-ROM
The following selections are part of the Reading Coach: "Ships That Could Think," "Sparky," and "The Roswell Incident." You may use Reading Coach selections as a group activity, as an individual activity, or as a tutorial for students who might benefit from this format or who have missed class.

Building Bridges: Closing the Reading Gap
This video is intended for teacher use only. It gives instructions and tips on how to help middle school readers become strategic readers.

Assessment

Selection Tests
pp. T337, T349, T359, T369

Assessment Booklet
Progress Check Units 5–8
Administer this test after the units 5 through 8 of the book have been read. It covers skills taught in all four units.

Focus Skills

COMPREHENSION
Drawing Conclusions
Author's Argument and Evidence

LITERATURE
Informative Nonfiction

VOCABULARY
Specialized Vocabulary

SkillBuilder Copymasters

 Reading Comprehension:
1 Drawing Conclusions p. T333
2 Author's Argument and
Evidence p. T334

 Vocabulary:
3 Specialized Vocabulary p. T335
4 Words to Know p. T336

Assessment

 5 Selection Test p. T337

Readability Scores

DRP	LEXILE	DALE-CHALL
51	570	5.6

For English Learners

It's likely that students will not be familiar with the different types of ships mentioned in "Ships That Could Think." If an encyclopedia or visual dictionary is available, have students look at drawings of different ships to get an idea of ships' varying shapes, sizes, and purposes.

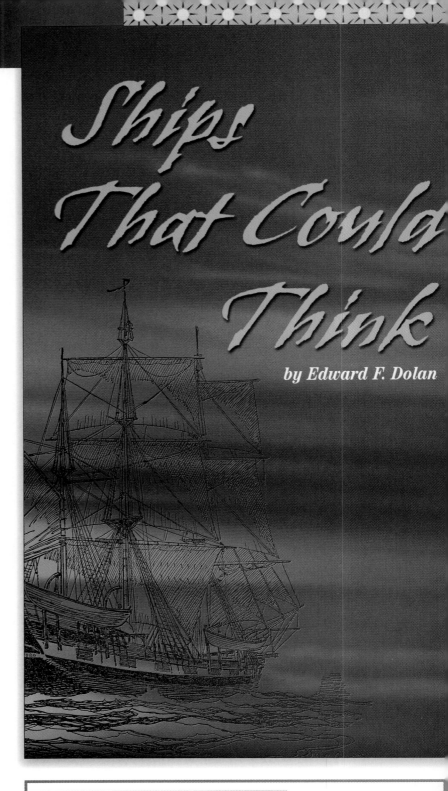

Ships That Could Think

by Edward F. Dolan

More About Informative Nonfiction

Point out to students that this type of writing is found in textbooks, newspapers, magazines, pamphlets, books, encyclopedias, and so on. Informative articles are usually written from an objective viewpoint. It's usually easy to separate facts from opinions. However, when a topic is unusual or presents unproved facts, readers should take an additional step and question even the facts themselves.

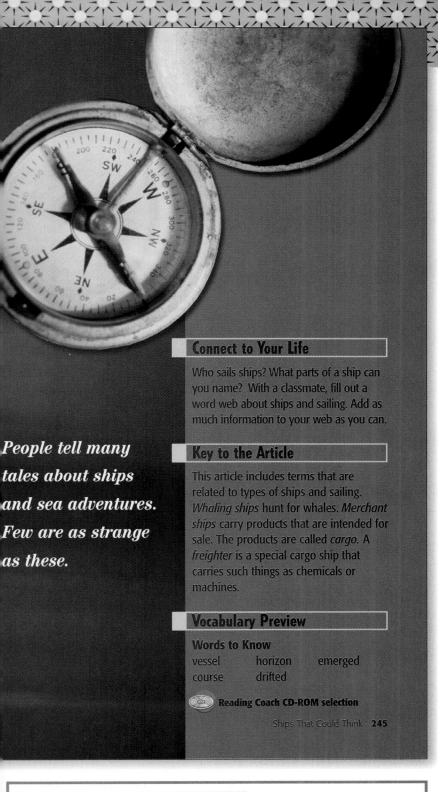

People tell many tales about ships and sea adventures. Few are as strange as these.

Connect to Your Life

Who sails ships? What parts of a ship can you name? With a classmate, fill out a word web about ships and sailing. Add as much information to your web as you can.

Key to the Article

This article includes terms that are related to types of ships and sailing. *Whaling ships* hunt for whales. *Merchant ships* carry products that are intended for sale. The products are called *cargo.* A *freighter* is a special cargo ship that carries such things as chemicals or machines.

Vocabulary Preview

Words to Know

vessel   horizon   emerged

course   drifted

 Reading Coach CD-ROM selection

Ships That Could Think   **245**

Connect to Your Life

If students need help with their word webs, you might suggest the following categories: Kinds of Ships, Uses for Ships, Parts of a Ship, Crew Members and Their Duties, Famous Ships, and Nautical Terms and Their Meanings.

Key to the Article

Help students understand that *whaling ship, merchant ship, cargo, freighter,* and *cargo ship* are called specialized vocabulary words because they all relate to the topic of this selection, ships. Have students notice the writer's choice of words and the types of statements he makes as they read "Ships That Could Think."

Vocabulary Preview

Words to Know

vessel *n.* boat

course *n.* route

horizon *n.* line where the earth seems to meet the sky

drifted *v.* wandered

emerged *v.* came into view

For direct instruction on Words to Know, see page T332.

Building Background

Not to be confused with its smaller cousin the *boat,* a *ship* is any large oceangoing vessel. The first "ships" probably were logs used for crossing small bodies of water. With the Egyptians' discovery of sails in about 3000 B.C., however, and their use of wood planks to build boats, they gained the ability to cross oceans, and true sailing ships were born. In this selection, the *Canton* was a three-masted sailing ship used for hunting whales. It rescued sailors evacuated from a merchant ship, which had been carrying items to be traded to other countries. The *Frigorifique* was a steamer, powered by a steam engine; and the *Rumney* was a freighter, a cargo ship, carrying coal.

Vocabulary Strategy: Preteaching

Specialized Vocabulary Tell students that special words are often related to the topic of a nonfiction selection. Write the following, having students circle the word that helps them figure out meaning.

1. Whenever seamen talk about a (ship), they use the words *she* and *her.* You'll hear these words even when the <u>vessel</u> has a man's name.
2. The *Canton* gave her <u>skipper</u> no more trouble. She obediently followed the course that the (captain) had set for St. Helena.

 For more on Specialized Vocabulary, see page T332.

FOCUS

Read to discover the mysterious actions of an American ship.

Sailors have always looked on ships as being alive. This is because ships seem to act like human beings. For instance, they often move through the sea with such womanly grace that sailors have come to think of them as women. Whenever seamen talk about a ship, they use the words "she" and "her." You'll hear these words even when the **A** vessel bears a man's name.

Further, like some humans, many ships
10 seem to get along well with the people around them. They cooperate with their crews and are a joy to sail. Others prove hard to handle at all times. Some seem to live happy lives. Others seem forever dogged by bad luck.

Some ships even seem to have minds of their own. They have been the cause of some very odd happenings. A perfect example here is the three-masted whaling ship, *Canton*.

vessel
(vĕs' əl)
n. boat

three-masted
having three poles that support the sails

A Strange Three Days

Built in 1835, the *Canton* was an
20 American ship. She was known as a vessel that handled easily. She always answered quickly to any turn of the wheel. But, for three days in 1867, while sailing the South Atlantic, she refused to obey her captain. The whaler set her own **B** course and went where she wanted to go.

It happened as the ship was traveling to the island of St. Helena after capturing several whales. Once there, she was to take on food and water. But, suddenly, the *Canton* seemed
30 dead against going to the island. She veered off to the

course
(kôrs)
n. route

side and headed in another direction. The captain brought her back on course. Then a puzzled look crossed his face. Though he was gripping the wheel tightly, the *Canton* swung to the side once more.

Again, the captain brought her back on course. Again, the ship defied him. Off she went in her own direction. She continued to do so, no matter how often he turned the wheel back to the original heading.

The captain was a deeply religious man. A thought
40 struck him. Perhaps God, for some reason, wanted the ship to travel in the new direction. If so, the captain was not about to argue. He decided to let the *Canton* go where she wished.

C **REREAD**
How do the captain's actions change? Why?

For the next three days, he allowed the *Canton* to pursue her own course. Then his men sighted a cluster of black dots on the horizon. The *Canton* sped to them. They turned out to be lifeboats. They were
50 crowded with half-starved seamen.

On being taken aboard, the men explained that they were from a merchant ship. They had been sailing near Africa when their vessel had caught fire days ago. No sooner had they taken to the lifeboats than the blazing ship went to the bottom. The captain estimated that they had drifted more than 150 miles before he came to their rescue.

No. *He* hadn't rescued them. His *ship*
60 had. The *Canton* had sought out the exact spot where they were floating in the vast Atlantic. Perhaps God had guided her to that spot. Or perhaps she herself had somehow known where it was. The captain was never able to tell.

horizon
(hə rī' zən)
n. line where the earth seems to meet the sky

drifted
(drĭf' tĭd)
v. wandered; past tense of *drift*

246 Unit 8 Hard to Believe

Ships That Could Think **247**

FOCUS SKILL 1: Drawing Conclusions

Remind students that they can **draw conclusions** about what they read by combining facts and details from the text with their own knowledge to make logical judgments or decisions.

 For direct instruction on Drawing Conclusions, see page T331.

FOCUS SKILL 2: Author's Argument and Evidence

Explain that an **author's argument** is the side, or perspective, he or she takes regarding a particular topic or issue. The facts and information that the author presents to support the argument are called **evidence.**

 For direct instruction on Author's Argument and Evidence, see page T331.

A Ask: In what ways do ships seem to act like humans? *(They move through the sea with womanly grace; they seem to get along well with their crews or are hard to handle; they seem lucky or unlucky;*

they seem to have minds of their own.) **comparing and contrasting**

B Ask: Why do you think the author describes the *Canton* in this section? *(to provide evidence for his argument that ships seem to have minds of their own)* **author's argument and evidence**

C **REREAD** How do the captain's actions change? Why? *(He lets the ship do what it wants to do. Because he is religious, he thinks there may be some spiritual force guiding the ship.)* **cause and effect**

LITERATURE

FOCUS SKILL: Informative Nonfiction

Tell students that **informative nonfiction** is writing that gives facts and details about real people, places, events, and things—in the case of this selection, ships that seem to think.

VOCABULARY

FOCUS SKILL: Specialized Vocabulary

Remind students to use context clues, their prior knowledge of nautical terms, and any reference sources necessary to figure out the specialized vocabulary in this selection.

FOR ENGLISH LEARNERS
Help students understand the following expressions and idioms:

Line 1: looked on
Line 4: have come to think of them
Line 8: bears a man's name
Line 14: dogged by bad luck
Line 29: seemed dead against going
Line 32: a puzzled look crossed his face
Line 39: A thought struck him
Line 54: No sooner had they taken to the lifeboats than . . . bottom.

Once the men were saved, the *Canton* gave her skipper no more trouble. She obediently followed the course that he set for St. Helena.

THINK IT THROUGH
Where does the *Canton* finally lead the captain? What can't anyone explain about what happened?

(D)

FOCUS
Notice how a French freighter acts differently from the *Canton*.

Looking for Revenge

(A) The *Canton* helped a group of sailors. The French steamer, *Frigorifique,* did exactly the opposite. She
70 terrified the men on a British freighter one March day in 1884. Their ship had accidentally wounded her and she seemed to be looking for revenge.

The *Frigorifique* was heading home along the French coast with a cargo from Spain that March day. She was moving slowly through a heavy fog. Suddenly, the men on deck heard a ship's whistle echoing across the water. Then there was the throbbing sound of approaching engines. And then they saw a ship stumble blindly
80 out of the mist. It was the British coal freighter, *Rumney*. It was coming straight at them.

REREAD
What do you think will happen next?

(E)

(B) Up on the bridge, the French captain yelled for the steersman to change course. The sailor spun the wheel hard. The *Frigorifique* began swinging away to safety. But it was too late. With a grinding crash, the *Rumney* steamed into the *Frigorifique's* side.

248 Unit 8 Hard to Believe

The French ship reeled to a halt. The *Rumney* was undamaged and backed off. The
90 *Frigorifique* was left with a jagged rip in her hull. Seawater rushed into the holds. The *Frigorifique* began to list and sink. The captain knew immediately that his ship would go to the bottom in minutes. He and his men put lifeboats over the side. They rowed to the *Rumney*.

(C)
(F)

hull
lower body of a ship

list
tilt to one side

Once safely on board, the French sailors looked back at their stricken ship. Standing with the English crew, they watched the *Frigorifique* struggle back into
100 the fog. Her engines were still running because there hadn't been time to shut them down. They would carry her on for a mile or so before she finally sank. All the men knew that they would never see the ship again.

How wrong they were! The *Rumney* began inching her way through the mist. She had gone but two miles when there were gasps all along the deck. For out of the mist burst a ship. It was the *Frigorifique*. Smoke poured from her stack. She came directly at the
110 *Rumney*. She looked like a charging warrior.

The *Rumney* escaped to the side. The French vessel steamed past, missing a collision by just a few yards. Back into the fog she disappeared.

REREAD
Retell what happens in your own words.

(G)

The frightened British and French crewmen stared at each other. The *Frigorifique* should have gone to the bottom. by now.

Ships That Could Think 249

COMPREHENSION

(D) THINK IT THROUGH Where does the *Canton* finally lead the captain? What can't anyone explain about what happened? *(to a cluster of lifeboats that had escaped a burning merchant ship; whether God had guided the ship to that spot or whether the ship had somehow known where it was)* **author's argument and evidence**

(E) REREAD What do you think will happen next? *(Based on clues in the text, students should predict that the* Frigorifique *will try to harm a group of sailors rather than help them as the* Canton *did.)* **predicting**

(F) Ask: Does the *Rumney* do what you predicted? Explain. *(Most students will have predicted that the* Rumney *would encounter the* Frigorifique *but not in so forceful a way.)* **predicting**

(G) REREAD Retell what happened in your own words. *(When the* Rumney *had gone two miles, her crew was shocked to see that the* Frigorifique *had not sunk but was heading right for them. The* Rumney *moved to the side, and the* Frigorifique *missed her by only a few yards.)* **summarizing**

VOCABULARY

(A) steamer Help students use the context to realize that *steamer* is a specialized vocabulary word, and refers to a kind of ship driven by steam.

(B) bridge Have students notice the context clues "Up on the bridge" and "the . . . captain" to reason that the *bridge* must be a place high on the ship where the captain stands.

(C) holds Point out context clues— "Seawater rushed into the holds"—and help students use a dictionary to understand that this specialized word means "the lower part of a ship where cargo is stored."

FOR ENGLISH LEARNERS

Help students understand the following expressions and idioms:

Line 72: looking for revenge
Line 73: heading home
Line 79: stumble blindly
Line 88: reeled to a halt
Line 97: on board
Line 102: a mile or so
Line 105: inching her way
Line 106: gone but two miles

120 But she was still afloat and steaming hard. She had looked as if she were trying to attack the ship that had harmed her. She had *actually* looked that way! Was it possible that she had been seeking revenge?

It was a question that made the men nervous for the next two miles. Then there were fresh cries of alarm. Once again, the *Frigorifique* broke out of the fog. Again, she came charging at the *Rumney*. Again, the Britisher tried to swing away—but failed this time. The *Frigorifique* smashed into her and tore a gaping 130 hole in her side.

THINK IT THROUGH
> What was frightening about the actions of the *Frigorifique*?

FOCUS
> Discover a possible explanation for the *Frigorifique's* actions.

The *Rumney* was now as badly wounded as her attacker. The French and English crews took to the lifeboats as she quickly sank beneath the waves. As for the *Frigorifique*, she continued on her way. She faded back into the fog, leaving a doomed ship behind. Did she have a look of satisfaction about her as she disappeared? The sailors wondered.

The lifeboats set out for the nearby French coast. 140 Fifteen minutes later, they emerged into sunlight—only to see the *Frigorifique* come sailing out of the fog after them. She did not, however, aim for the boats. Rather, she passed close-by along a circling route.

> **emerged**
> (ĭ mûrjd')
> *v.* came into view; past tense of *emerge*

Both the British and French captains decided to board the ship. They wanted to know why she was

still afloat. And, if possible, they wanted to learn why she had twice sought out the *Rumney* as if on a mission of revenge.

> **mission of revenge**
> special journey to deliver punishment

They found the answers soon after they 150 brought the lifeboats alongside and climbed aboard. There was a simple reason why the *Frigorifique* had not yet sunk. The seawater was pouring in more slowly than was first thought. But, with each passing minute, it was coming faster. The ship did not have long to live.

And why had she twice attacked the *Rumney*? The captains discovered the answer on the bridge. After the *Frigorifique* had been hit, the steersman had found her too hard to handle. He had 160 pulled the wheel over and had lashed it down. This had caused the vessel to sail in a wide circle—a circle that had twice brought her to the *Rumney*.

> **lashed**
> tied with ropes

The captains returned to the lifeboats. They rowed to a safe distance and watched the *Frigorifique* plunge beneath the sea. Then they told their crews about the lashed wheel. The doomed ship hadn't attacked the *Rumney* after all. She hadn't been angrily looking for revenge.

170 But was this the truth of the matter? Many of the nervous sailors were never sure.

THINK IT THROUGH
> 1. What answers did the two captains find on the *Frigorifique*?
> 2. Both stories tell of ships that seemed to think. In your opinion, is this possible? Use details from the selection to support your opinion.

COMPREHENSION

H **THINK IT THROUGH** What was frightening about the actions of the *Frigorifique*? *(The ship seemed to be deliberately attacking the* Rumney. *It was as if the ship were angry about the first crash. It kept charging.)* **clarifying**

I Ask: Why do you think the author describes the *Frigorifique* in this section? *(to provide evidence for the other side of his argument that ships seem to have minds of their own)* **author's argument and evidence**

J **THINK IT THROUGH**

1. What answers did the two captains find on the *Frigorifique*? *(The ship hadn't sunk because not enough water had poured in. The ship's steering wheel had been tied down. This caused it to travel in a circle, which made the attacks look as if they were on purpose.)* **author's argument and evidence**

2. Both stories tell of ships that seemed to think. In your opinion, is this possible? Use details from the selection to support your opinion. *(Whichever side students take, be sure the evidence they present strongly supports their argument.)* **drawing conclusions**

Option for Speaking and Listening Have students argue for or against the idea that ships can think for themselves. Tell students to be sure they support their arguments with plenty of evidence from prior knowledge or experience, this selection, or other sources.

VOCABULARY

FOR ENGLISH LEARNERS

Help students understand the following expressions and idioms:

Line 132: took to the lifeboats
Line 136: a look of satisfaction about her
Line 147: twice sought
Line 165: plunge beneath the sea
Line 170: the truth of the matter

1. COMPREHENSION

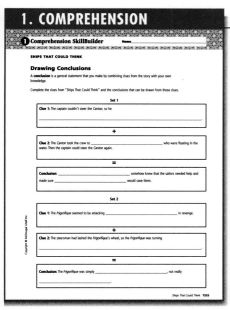

Drawing Conclusions

Direct Instruction Tell students that **conclusions** are general statements that readers make after thinking about clues or details in the text combined with their own knowledge. Explain that writers carefully choose which details and clues to include to lead readers to certain conclusions.

Read aloud the following clues from "Ships That Could Think" and have students suggest the conclusion that the writer wants readers to draw.

Clue 1: The *Rumney* rammed the *Frigorifique,* and the *Frigorifique* started to sink.
Clue 2: After the sailors left the ship and boarded the *Rumney,* the injured ship came at the *Rumney* once, until the *Rumney* started to sink too. *(Possible conclusion: The* Frigorifique *was angry at the* Rumney *and wanted revenge.)*

Comprehension SkillBuilder Answer Key:
Set 1: *Possible answers:*
The captain couldn't steer the Canton, *so he* <u>let her go where she wanted to go</u>.
The Canton *took the crew to* <u>some half-starved sailors</u> *who were floating in the water. Then the captain could steer the* Canton *again.*
Conclusion: <u>It seemed that the</u> Canton *somehow knew that the sailors needed help and made sure* <u>the captain and the crew</u> *would save them.*

Set 2: *Possible answers:*
The Frigorifique *seemed to be attacking* <u>the</u> Rumney *in revenge.*
The steersman had lashed the Frigorifique's *wheel, so the* Frigorifique *was turning* <u>in circles</u>.
Conclusion: The Frigorifique *was simply* <u>turning in circles</u>, *not really* <u>attacking the</u> <u>Rumney</u>.

2. COMPREHENSION

Author's Argument and Evidence

Direct Instruction Tell students that writers sometimes want to persuade readers to agree with their point of view. To lead readers to a particular conclusion, they present an argument. Explain that an **argument** is a series of statements intended to lead readers to a particular conclusion. An argument may begin with a general statement, followed by **evidence,** facts that support the statement.

Read aloud this example of an argument:

General statement: Our candidate is the best person for the job, and you should vote for our candidate.

Supporting evidence: Our candidate has served as a senator for 12 years, and so she has plenty of experience in governing.
Supporting evidence: In her writings, our candidate has proved that she is intelligent and understands foreign affairs.
Supporting evidence: Our candidate's speeches show that she has many good ideas about how to change the government to make it work even better.

The argument may end with a conclusion that restates the general statement.

Comprehension SkillBuilder Answer Key:
1. *d*   **2.** *c*   **3.** *b*

3. VOCABULARY

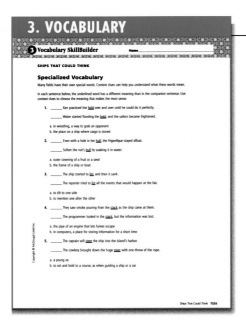

Specialized Vocabulary

Direct Instruction Tell students that people in different fields often use special words to identify things and ideas peculiar to their profession. Discuss with students the special terms that are used only in specific sports or games, such as *touchdown* in football and *home run* in baseball. Point out that people sometimes coin, or invent, words and terms to describe new concepts in their fields. Such coinages include the terms *byte* and *serial port,* used in the computer field.

Vocabulary SkillBuilder Answer Key:

1. *a; b*

2. *b; a*

3. *a; b*

4. *a; b*

5. *b; a*

---

4. WORDS TO KNOW

Words to Know

Direct Instruction As you present the **Words to Know,** you might want to help students identify the word parts. Stress the importance of finding the base of each word. Help students remove prefixes and suffixes to identify the base.

- **vessel,** from the Latin *vās,* is also defined as "a hollow utensil used as a container for liquids"; it can also refer to a blood vessel.
- **course,** from the Latin *currere,* "to run," has many other definitions, as students will learn in the Writing Activity.

- **horizon** is from the Greek *horos,* "boundary."
- **drifted** = *drift* + *-ed; drift* can also be a noun, as in "a drift of snow."
- **emerged** (*emerge* + *-ed)* is from the Latin *ex-* + *mergere,* "to immerse."

Writing Activity Help students to use the words correctly with different meanings. You may pair students so that they may assist each other. Have volunteers read their sentences aloud.

Words to Know SkillBuilder Answer Key:

A.

   1. *vessel*   **2.** *drifted*   **3.** *horizon*   **4.** *course*   **5.** *emerged*

B.

Instruct students to provide evidence for their conclusions, particularly if they believe the statement to be false.

   1. *true*   **2.** *false*   **3.** *true*   **4.** *false*   **5.** *false*

---

5. SELECTION TEST

Selection Test Answer Key:

A. 1. *true* **2.** *false* **3.** *false* **4.** *true*

B. Possible answer: *whether the* Frigorifique *attacked the* Rumney *on purpose.*

SHIPS THAT COULD THINK

Drawing Conclusions

A **conclusion** is a general statement that you make by combining clues from the story with your own knowledge.

Complete the clues from "Ships That Could Think" and the conclusions that can be drawn from those clues.

Set 1

Clue 1: The captain couldn't steer the *Canton,* so he

_____.

+

Clue 2: The *Canton* took the crew to _____ who were floating in the water. Then the captain could steer the *Canton* again.

=

Conclusion: _____ somehow knew that the sailors needed help and

made sure _____ would save them.

Set 2

Clue 1: The *Frigorifique* seemed to be attacking _____ in revenge.

+

Clue 2: The steersman had lashed the *Frigorifique*'s wheel, so the *Frigorifique* was turning

_____.

=

Conclusion: The *Frigorifique* was simply _____, not really

_____.

SHIPS THAT COULD THINK

Author's Argument and Evidence

When writers want to persuade readers to agree with them, they present arguments. An **argument** is a series of statements meant to lead readers to a certain conclusion. In their statements, writers give **evidence** that proves their conclusion.

Circle the letter of the statement in each group that does <u>not</u> support the writer's argument.

1. The writer wants readers to come to this conclusion: **This year's weather was bad for farmers.**

    a. Late spring rains flooded the fields and washed out the farmers' seeds.

    b. A lack of rain during June made many crops wither and die.

    c. A hailstorm in August knocked down plants.

    d. Farmers in this area are used to bad weather.

2. The writer wants readers to come to this conclusion: **The buffalo was important in the lives of Native Americans who lived on the Great Plains.**

    a. Plains tribes used buffalo hides to make their homes.

    b. Plains tribes hunted buffalo for their meat.

    c. Plains tribes hunted buffalo on horseback.

    d. Plains tribes used the sharpened bones of buffalo as sewing needles.

3. The writer wants readers to come to this conclusion: **Ships seem to act like humans.**

    a. The *Canton* took her captain and crew to half-starved sailors who needed to be rescued.

    b. The *Canton* was a three-masted whaling ship that was traveling near the island of St. Helena.

    c. The *Canton* would not go in the direction the captain steered her.

    d. Even though the *Frigorifique* was sinking and no one was aboard her, twice she came at the ship that had run into her.

SHIPS THAT COULD THINK

Specialized Vocabulary

Many fields have their own special words. Context clues can help you understand what these words mean.

In each sentence below, the underlined word has a different meaning than in the companion sentence. Use context clues to choose the meaning that makes the most sense.

1. _____ Ken practiced the hold over and over until he could do it perfectly.

_____ Water started flooding the hold, and the sailors became frightened.

a. in wrestling, a way to grab an opponent
b. the place on a ship where cargo is stored

2. _____ Even with a hole in her hull, the *Frigorifique* stayed afloat.

_____ Soften the nut's hull by soaking it in water.

a. outer covering of a fruit or a seed
b. the frame of a ship or boat

3. _____ The ship started to list, and then it sank.

_____ The reporter tried to list all the events that would happen at the fair.

a. to tilt to one side
b. to mention one after the other

4. _____ They saw smoke pouring from the stack as the ship came at them.

_____ The programmer looked in the stack, but the information was lost.

a. the pipe of an engine that lets fumes escape
b. in computers, a place for storing information for a short time

5. _____ The captain will steer the ship into the island's harbor.

_____ The cowboy brought down the huge steer with one throw of the rope.

a. a young ox
b. to set and hold to a course, as when guiding a ship or a car

Name_____

SHIPS THAT COULD THINK

Words to Know

vessel   course   horizon   drifted   emerged

A. Fill in each blank with the correct word from the **Words to Know.**

1. The beautiful _____ sailed off into shimmering waters.

2. The fallen tree branch _____ to the river's shore.

3. Sam and I sat on the hill, watching the sun melt into the _____.

4. The car sped down the _____.

5. My sister _____ from her room, dressed in her prom dress.

B. Write **true** or **false** in the blanks before each statement.

_____ 1. A **course** is a route.

_____ 2. The **horizon** is the part of the eye next to the retina.

_____ 3. If you've come into view, you've **emerged.**

_____ 4. If your raft has **drifted** upstream, it has stayed where you left it.

_____ 5. A **vessel** is something you use to keep your clothing in.

Writing Activity
Use your dictionary to find three meanings for *vessel* and three meanings for *course*. Write three sentences, each using *vessel* with a different meaning. Then write three sentences, each using *course* with a different meaning.

SHIPS THAT COULD THINK

A. Write **true** or **false** next to each statement.

_____ **1.** Even when a ship has a man's name, sailors will refer to the ship as *she.*

_____ **2.** The *Canton* was known as a very stubborn ship that always gave her captain a difficult time.

_____ **3.** In 1835, the *Canton* was seeking her revenge.

_____ **4.** Some people believed that the *Frigorifique* deliberately smashed into the *Rumney* and tore a hole in her side.

B. Complete this sentence with words that make it a true statement.

Even though the sailors heard evidence that the steering wheel of the *Frigorifique* was tied, they would never be sure

_____

_____.

Focus Skills

COMPREHENSION
Main Idea and Supporting Details
Text Structure

LITERATURE
Informative Nonfiction (Science)

VOCABULARY
Context Clues

SkillBuilder Copymasters

 Reading Comprehension:
1 Main Idea and Supporting
Details p. T345
2 Text Structure p. T346

 Vocabulary:
3 Context Clues p. T347
4 Words to Know p. T348

Assessment

 5 Selection Test p. T349

Readability Scores

DRP	LEXILE	DALE-CHALL
54	670	4.0

For English Learners

Students may find it confusing that
four earthquakes from the last century are discussed out of sequence
in the article. Help students to pin-
point each earthquake by construct-
ing a time line of these events. Also
in the article, mentions of earthquakes in Japan and Italy are not
accompanied by dates. These examples need not be examined.

Earthquakes

by Franklyn M. Branley

We all live on the
earth's crust. It is
always moving.
Find out how to
live with this
shaky situation.

252 Unit 8 Hard to Believe

Vocabulary Strategy: Preteaching

Context Clues Remind students that the words and phrases that provide hints about a word's meaning are called **context clues.** Then write
the following sentences on the board, and have students tell or circle
which words or phrases help them figure out the meaning of each
underlined word.

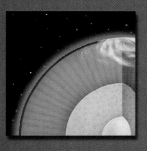

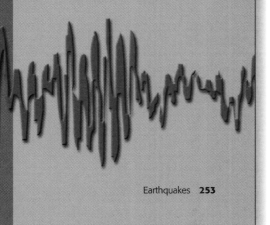

Connect to Your Life

Recall the last earthquake report you heard. Where did it happen and how strong was it? What damage did it cause?

Key to the Article

This science article is similar to what you'd find in an earth science textbook. As you read facts about earthquakes, look for special terms in bold type. Pay close attention to the diagrams. The terms and diagrams explain how earthquakes form and how their strength is measured.

Vocabulary Preview

Words to Know

continent   erupt
buckles   satellites
topple

Earthquakes **253**

Connect to Your Life

Guide students in a discussion of the last earthquake report they heard. If any of your students personally witnessed an earthquake, invite them to describe what happened, as well as what they were thinking and feeling during and after the quake.

Key to the Article

Tell students that previewing a piece of nonfiction will help them understand it better when they actually read it. Have them begin by looking at the title and teaser on page 252. Tell students that science writing usually has specific features designed to help readers understand scientific ideas. Have students point out examples of these features in "Earthquakes": boldface type, illustrations, diagrams, and photos.

Vocabulary Preview

Words to Know
  continent *n.* one of the seven large land areas on earth
  buckles *v.* crumples
  topple *v.* push over
  erupt *v.* explode
  satellites *n.* man-made objects that orbit the Earth

 For direct instruction on Words to Know, see page T344.

1. Parts of the earth are always moving. Whole mountains move. Even whole <u>continents</u> move. Right now (North America and Europe) are moving apart.
2. Earthquakes often occur where there are volcanoes. Melted rock deep under the earth pushes upward, making the area shake and rumble. These are warnings that a volcano may <u>erupt</u>, or (explode violently).

 For more on Context Clues, see page T344.

FOCUS

Discover what causes an earthquake.

Parts of the Earth are always moving. That's hard to believe, but they are. The movements are so small and so slow, we usually cannot feel them.

Whole mountains move. Big sections of a continent like North America can move. Even whole continents move. Right now North America and Europe are moving apart. They move slowly, only as fast as your fingernails grow. So we don't feel the motion.

10 When parts of the Earth move quickly, there may be an earthquake. Every day there are at least a thousand earthquakes on our planet. Most are small, but each year there are a few earthquakes large enough to knock down buildings.

The strength of an earthquake can be measured. We use something called the Richter scale, named after C. F. Richter, an American scientist. Anything that measures less than 2 is a small quake, and 8 or higher is a 20 very big one.

REREAD
What is the main idea of this paragraph?

A

Every earthquake has a center. That's where it all begins. Parts of the Earth move up and down or go sideways, and make waves that spread out and go through the whole Earth.

They are called **seismic waves.** The word comes from *seismos*, a Greek word meaning to shake. Scientists all over the 30 world measure the waves on **seismometers.**

A

> **continent**
> (kŏn' tə nənt)
> *n.* one of the seven large land areas on earth

Scientists read information from seismometers like this one.

254 Unit 8 Hard to Believe

We live on the outer part of Earth. It is called Earth's **crust.** In some places the crust is 30 or 40 miles thick. If Earth were an apple, the crust would be only as thick as the skin of the apple. Most earthquakes occur in 40 the crust.

Large sections of the Earth's crust are always moving. Sometimes two sections push against each other. The place where they meet is called a **fault.** When the sections cannot pass, the Earth bends and buckles. Suddenly the bend releases, and a whole section may move four or five feet at once. That's what happened twelve miles below the surface in 50 Mexico in 1985. The seismic waves from the earthquake's center were strong enough to topple buildings in Mexico City, 220 miles away, and kill several thousand people. The quake measured 8.1 on the Richter scale.

THINK IT THROUGH
Why do earthquakes happen? What do seismic waves show?

B

> **Cutaway Image of the Earth**
> outer core   mantle   crust
> inner core
>
> **LOOK CLOSELY** Notice how thin the earth's crust is compared to the other sections.

B

> **buckles**
> (bŭk' əlz)
> *v.* crumples

> **topple**
> (tŏp' əl)
> *v.* push over

B

FOCUS

What results of earthquakes also cause deaths?

Sometimes two sections of the crust scrape alongside each other. That makes a fault too. The San Andreas Fault is a crack in the Earth that runs north

Earthquakes 255

COMPREHENSION

FOCUS SKILL 1: Main Idea and Supporting Details

Tell students that a **main idea** is the most important idea in a section of text. Other sentences in the section give details that tell more about or support the main idea. Depending on the selection, students might encounter a different main idea in each paragraph or other section, or they might find only a single main idea.

For direct instruction on Main Idea and Supporting Details, see page T343.

FOCUS SKILL 2: Text Structure

Explain that **text structure** is the way a piece of nonfiction is organized. Since this selection describes the causes and effects of several important earthquakes, its main text structure is cause and effect. Other text structures include description, sequential order, compare and contrast, and problem and solution.

For direct instruction on Text Structure, see page T343.

A REREAD What is the main idea of this paragraph? *(An earthquake's strength can be measured.)* **main idea and supporting details**

B THINK IT THROUGH Why do earthquakes happen? What do seismic waves show? *(When large sections of the earth's crust push against each other, the earth bends and buckles and then releases. During this release, the earth moves and causes an earthquake. Seismic waves show where and how strong the quake is.)* **summarizing**

LITERATURE

FOCUS SKILL: Informative Nonfiction (Science)

Review with students that **informative nonfiction** gives facts and details about real people, places, and events and that "Earthquakes" contains scientific facts and details about different earthquakes, what caused them, and the damage they caused.

VOCABULARY

FOCUS SKILL: Context Clues

A seismometers Students can use the context clues *to shake* and *measure the waves* to figure out that seismometers measure shaking seismic waves during an earthquake.

B fault Students can use context clues to figure out that a *fault* is the place where two large sections of the earth's crust meet and push against each other.

FOR ENGLISH LEARNERS

Help students understand the following expressions and idioms:

Line 11: at least a thousand
Line 57: runs north and south

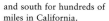

and south for hundreds of miles in California.

60 In 1906 there was an earthquake along a section of the San Andreas Fault. In seconds, the crust on the west side of the fault moved twenty feet. San Francisco and the area around the city shook and trembled. Fires started, and most of the city 70 burned down.

Most earthquakes occur along the shores of the Pacific Ocean, where the crust moves a lot. Japan has about 7,000 quakes a year. Luckily, most are small.

There are volcanoes in this part of the world too. Earthquakes often occur in places where there are 80 volcanoes. Melted rock deep under the Earth pushes upward, making the area shake and rumble. These are warnings that a volcano may erupt or that there may be a big earthquake.

In southern Europe there are several volcanoes. There are also many earthquakes. In Pozzuoli, Italy, a small town not far from Mount Vesuvius, there were 4,000 quakes in one year. Mount Vesuvius is a volcano that has erupted 90 from time to time for several thousand years.

| erupt |
| (ĭ rŭpt′) |
| v. explode |

The San Andreas Fault extends from north of San Francisco to southern California.

In 1939 a big fault opened up in the bottom of the sea, causing an earthquake just off the coast of Chile in South America. Water rushed into the opening. After it was filled, water kept rushing toward the fault. The water piled high, making a huge wave that traveled toward the shore. The wave was a wall of water called a *tsunami*, a Japanese word. People ran to the hills to escape, but a landslide caused by the quake swept them back into the sea. This was a big 100 undersea earthquake.

THINK IT THROUGH
What two other natural forces can be connected to a quake?

FOCUS
What steps can people take to protect lives and property? Read to find out.

In a small quake, dishes rattle. Ceiling lights swing. The ground jiggles a bit as if a big truck were going by. It's all over in a few seconds.

During a big earthquake, many buildings fall down. There are also fires. Pipes that carry gas to homes are broken. A spark may set the gas afire. Sometimes firefighters can't fight the flames because water pipes have broken.

During an earthquake, dams may break too. Rivers 110 may be blocked by landslides. So there is often flooding in the area of an earthquake.

In many parts of the world where there are big earthquakes, new buildings are made of steel instead of wood. They are built where the ground is solid so seismic waves will not knock them down. Old bridges

---

COMPREHENSION

C Ask: What is the main idea of this paragraph? Give one detail that supports the main idea. *(Main idea: There are many volcanoes and earthquakes in southern Europe. Supporting detail: In Pozzuoli there were 4,000 quakes in a year, or Mount Vesuvius has erupted for several thousand years.)* **main idea and supporting details**

D **Reciprocal Teaching Suggestion: Visualizing Teacher Modeling** To demonstrate the Active Reading Strategy of visualizing, focus on the paragraph at the top of page 257. You could say: *When I picture the scene described in the beginning sentences of this paragraph, I see a huge hole with water rushing into it. Then I see a tall wave sweeping over that hole and heading toward the shore.*

Student Modeling Have a volunteer read the last two sentences of the paragraph and tell what picture comes to his or her mind. The student should describe people trying to run up hills and being swept back down, toward the sea, by the landslide.

E **THINK IT THROUGH** What two other natural forces can be connected to a quake? *(volcanoes and tsunamis)* **cause and effect**

VOCABULARY

C **trembled** Students can use context to figure out that *trembled* is a synonym of *shook.*

D **jiggles** Students can use the example *as if a big truck were going by* to figure out the meaning of this word.

FOR ENGLISH LEARNERS

Help students understand the following expressions and idioms:

Line 90: from time to time
Line 106: afire
Line 107: fight the flames

and dams are made stronger with extra steel and concrete.

120 In 1989, there was a serious earthquake near San Francisco. It was the worst in the area since 1906. Sixty-seven people were killed. Bridges and roadways were damaged, and many buildings were destroyed. Because of the way it was built, the famous Golden Gate Bridge swayed in the quake, but it did not collapse.

REREAD How does this 1989 San Francisco quake compare to the one in 1906? **F**

The Golden Gate Bridge wasn't damaged in the 1989 earthquake. However, the Bay Bridge was. This bridge connects the city of Oakland to San Francisco.

Earthquakes happen without any warning. However, scientists are working to find ways to predict quakes. They use satellites to measure even the smallest motion along 130 faults. These small motions can often become larger.

satellites
(săt′ l ĭts′)
n. man-made objects that orbit the Earth

The crust of our planet is always moving, so we will continue to have earthquakes. Most of them, fortunately, will be small ones.

G **THINK IT THROUGH**

1. Name at least three things you can do to try to survive an earthquake.
2. Make a cause-and-effect chart to show what happened in the 1939 earthquake described at the top of page 257.
3. This article shows many dangers that happen because of earthquakes. Name several effects that are damaging or deadly.

Earthquakes **259**

COMPREHENSION

F **REREAD** How does this 1989 San Francisco quake compare to the one in 1906? *(Most of San Francisco burned down in the 1906 quake. In the 1989 quake, 67 people were killed, bridges and roadways were damaged, and many buildings were destroyed.)* **compare and contrast**

G **THINK IT THROUGH**

1. Name at least three things you can do to try to survive an earthquake. *(Possible answers: When outside, stay away from objects that could fall on you, and go to an open space if possible. When inside, stay there; stay away from windows; follow a teacher's instructions; keep water, food, and equipment handy.)* **main idea and supporting details**

2. Make a cause-and-effect chart to show what happened in the 1939 earthquake described at the top of page 257. *(A big fault opened in the bottom of the sea and caused an undersea earthquake. • Water rushed into the open fault. • Water kept rushing toward the fault even after it was full. • The rushing water made a huge tsunami, which traveled toward the shore. A landslide swept people into the sea.)* **cause and effect**

3. This article shows many dangers that happen because of earthquakes. Name several effects that are damaging or deadly. *(Earthquakes may cause volcanoes or tsunamis. Earthquakes can damage or destroy buildings, endangering people nearby. Earthquakes can damage power lines, which, when exposed, are dangerous.)* **cause and effect**

RETEACHING

If students need more help understanding **Main Idea and Supporting Details,** use pages T635–T638.

VOCABULARY

RETEACHING

If students need more help understanding **Context Clues,** use pages T608–T611.

1. COMPREHENSION

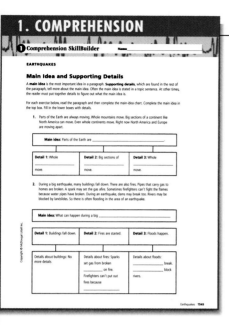

Main Idea and Supporting Details

Direct Instruction Tell students that the **main idea** is the most important idea in a paragraph. Point out that the main idea is often, but not always, stated in a topic sentence. Other sentences give **details** that tell more about, or support, the main idea.

Read the following paragraph aloud and have students find the sentence that states the main idea. Ask them to find details that tell more about the main idea.

In 1989, there was a serious earthquake near San Francisco. It was the worst in the area since 1906. Sixty-seven people were killed. Bridges and roadways were damaged, and many buildings were destroyed.

Now read the following paragraph aloud. Tell students that it has no topic sentence and that they must figure out the main idea from details in the paragraph.

In a small quake, dishes rattle. Ceiling lights swing. The ground jiggles a bit as if a big truck were going by. It's all over in a few seconds. (Main idea: what happens during a small earthquake)

> **Comprehension SkillBuilder Answer Key:**
> 1. Main idea: *Parts of the Earth are <u>always moving</u>.* Detail 1: *Whole <u>mountains</u> move.* Detail 2: *Big sections of <u>continents</u> move.* Detail 3: *Whole <u>continents</u> move.*
> 2. Main idea: *What can happen during a big <u>earthquake</u>*
>   Details about fires: *Sparks set gas from broken <u>gas pipes</u> on fire. Firefighters can't put out fires because <u>water pipes are broken.</u>*
>   Details about floods: *<u>Dams</u> break. <u>Landslides</u> block rivers.*

2. COMPREHENSION

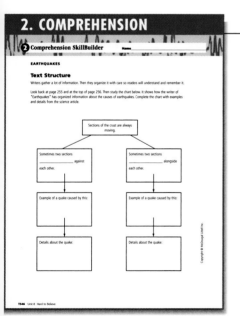

Text Structure

Direct Instruction Tell students that writers do a great deal of research. Explain that if writers simply listed all the facts they know about their topics, the lists might be boring, and readers might not understand or remember what they had read. To make the information interesting, easy to understand, and easy to remember, writers carefully choose which information to include, and they order the information in logical ways.

Point out that the writer of "Earthquakes" organizes information by presenting a fact and then supplying a specific example.

- Fact: Earthquakes often occur in places where there are volcanoes.
- Example: In Pozzuoli, Italy, a small town not far from Mount Vesuvius, there were 4,000 quakes in one year. Mount Vesuvius is a volcano that has erupted from time to time for several thousand years.

> **Comprehension SkillBuilder Answer Key:**
> Sometimes two sections <u>push</u> against each other. Example: *earthquake in Mexico in 1985.* Details about the quake: *It killed several thousand people. It measured 8.1 on the Richter scale.*
>
> Sometimes two sections <u>scrape</u> alongside each other. Example: *earthquake in San Francisco in 1906.* Details about the quake: *Fires started and most of the city burned down.*

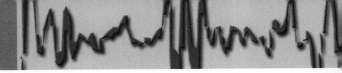

3. VOCABULARY

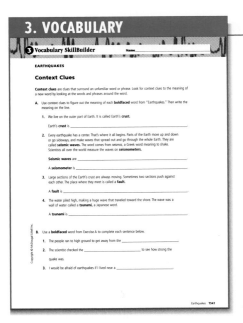

Context Clues

Direct Instruction Tell students that they can use clues in the text called **context clues** to figure out the meaning of unfamiliar words. Context clues are usually found in the same sentence or paragraph as the new word. Writers of nonfiction know that many words they use may be new to readers. For that reason, they often clearly define new words. Urge students to look for definitions in the text when they come upon unfamiliar words.

Point out that sometimes context clues only hint at a word's meaning, as in this example: The weather forecaster checked the <u>anemometer</u> to find out how strong the wind was. Context clues suggest to readers that an anemometer must be an instrument for measuring wind speed and force.

Vocabulary SkillBuilder Answer Key:

A.
1. *the outer part of Earth*
2. *waves that spread out from the center of an earthquake and go through the whole Earth, an instrument to measure seismic waves*
3. *a place where two sections of Earth's crust meet*
4. *a huge wave that travels toward the shore*

B.
1. *tsunami*
2. *seismometer*
3. *fault*

---

4. WORDS TO KNOW

Words to Know

Direct Instruction As you present the **Words to Know,** you might want to cover these points .

- **continent,** from the Latin *continēre,* "to hold together," is also an adjective meaning "exercising self-restraint."
- **buckles** *(buckle + -s)* is from the Latin *buccula,* "chin strap of a helmet," itself from *bucca,* "cheek"; *buckle* is also defined as "a clasp for fastening two ends, as in a belt."
- **erupt** is from the Latin *ex-* + *rumpere,* "to break."
- **satellites** *(satellite + -s)* is from the Latin *satelles; satellite* is also defined as "a subservient follower" and "an urban or suburban community located near a big city."

Writing Activity Pair students or allow them to work in groups to complete the exercise. Have volunteers read their sentences aloud.

Words to Know SkillBuilder Answer Key:

A.
1. *continent*
2. *topple*
3. *satellites*
4. *buckles*
5. *erupt*

B.
1. *topple*
2. *buckles*
3. *continent*
4. *erupt*
5. *satellites*

---

5. SELECTION TEST

Selection Test Answer Key:
A. 1. *c* **2.** *a* **3.** *b* **4.** *a* **5.** *a* **6.** *b* **7.** *c* **8.** *b* **9.** *a*
B. Possible answer: *because the earth's crust is always moving*

EARTHQUAKES

Main Idea and Supporting Details

A **main idea** is the most important idea in a paragraph. **Supporting details,** which are found in the rest of the paragraph, tell more about the main idea. Often the main idea is stated in a topic sentence. At other times, the reader must put together details to figure out what the main idea is.

For each exercise below, read the paragraph and then complete the main-idea chart. Complete the main idea in the top box. Fill in the lower boxes with details.

1. Parts of the Earth are always moving. Whole mountains move. Big sections of a continent like North America can move. Even whole continents move. Right now North America and Europe are moving apart.

Main idea: Parts of the Earth are _____.

| **Detail 1:** Whole _____ move. | **Detail 2:** Big sections of _____ move. | **Detail 3:** Whole _____ move. |

---

2. During a big earthquake, many buildings fall down. There are also fires. Pipes that carry gas to homes are broken. A spark may set the gas afire. Sometimes firefighters can't fight the flames because water pipes have broken. During an earthquake, dams may break too. Rivers may be blocked by landslides. So there is often flooding in the area of an earthquake.

Main idea: What can happen during a big _____

| **Detail 1:** Buildings fall down. | **Detail 2:** Fires are started. | **Detail 3:** Floods happen. |

| Details about buildings: No more details | Details about fires: Sparks set gas from broken _____ on fire. Firefighters can't put out fires because _____ | Details about floods: _____ break. _____ block rivers. |

EARTHQUAKES

Text Structure

Writers gather a lot of information. Then they organize it with care so readers will understand and remember it.

Look back at page 255 and at the top of page 256. Then study the chart below. It shows how the writer of "Earthquakes" has organized information about the causes of earthquakes. Complete the chart with examples and details from the science article.

```
                    ┌─────────────────────────────┐
                    │  Sections of the crust are   │
                    │        always moving.        │
                    └─────────────────────────────┘
                       /                        \
  ┌──────────────────────────┐      ┌──────────────────────────┐
  │ Sometimes two sections   │      │ Sometimes two sections   │
  │ _____ against     │      │ _____ alongside   │
  │ each other.              │      │ each other.              │
  └──────────────────────────┘      └──────────────────────────┘
              │                                  │
  ┌──────────────────────────┐      ┌──────────────────────────┐
  │ Example of a quake       │      │ Example of a quake       │
  │ caused by this:          │      │ caused by this:          │
  │                          │      │                          │
  └──────────────────────────┘      └──────────────────────────┘
              │                                  │
  ┌──────────────────────────┐      ┌──────────────────────────┐
  │ Details about the quake: │      │ Details about the quake: │
  │                          │      │                          │
  │                          │      │                          │
  └──────────────────────────┘      └──────────────────────────┘
```

EARTHQUAKES

Context Clues

Context clues are clues that surround an unfamiliar word or phrase. Look for context clues to the meaning of a new word by looking at the words and phrases around the word.

A. Use context clues to figure out the meaning of each **boldfaced** word from "Earthquakes." Then write the meaning on the line.

1. We live on the outer part of Earth. It is called Earth's **crust.**

   Earth's **crust** is _____.

2. Every earthquake has a center. That's where it all begins. Parts of the Earth move up and down or go sideways, and make waves that spread out and go through the whole Earth. They are called **seismic waves.** The word comes from *seismos,* a Greek word meaning to shake. Scientists all over the world measure the waves on **seismometers.**

   Seismic waves are _____.

   A **seismometer** is _____.

3. Large sections of the Earth's crust are always moving. Sometimes two sections push against each other. The place where they meet is called a **fault.**

   A **fault** is _____.

4. The water piled high, making a huge wave that traveled toward the shore. The wave was a wall of water called a **tsunami,** a Japanese word.

   A **tsunami** is _____.

B. Use a **boldfaced** word from Exercise A to complete each sentence below.

1. The people ran to high ground to get away from the _____.

2. The scientist checked the _____ to see how strong the

   quake was.

3. I would be afraid of earthquakes if I lived near a _____.

EARTHQUAKES

Words to Know

continent   buckles   topple   erupt   satellites

A. In each blank, write the word from the list that best completes the sentence.

1. My parents were born somewhere within the African _____.

2. My little cousin loves to _____ the blocks after her mother sets them up.

3. Many countries send _____ to orbit the earth to watch the weather.

4. The shelf _____ because there is too much weight on it.

5. I have only seen volcanoes _____ in photographs.

B. Fill in each blank with a word from the list at the top of the page.

1. If you knock something over, you _____.

2. A person faints from the heat and falls, or _____.

3. Asia's land mass makes it the largest _____.

4. If you shake a bottle of soda and then open it, it might

   _____.

5. We get cable television and keep an eye on our weather through _____.

Writing Activity

Have you ever experienced an earthquake or another force of nature such as a tornado or a hurricane? If so, what was it like? If not, what do you imagine it would be like? Write three sentences using at least three of the **Words to Know.**

EARTHQUAKES

A. Complete each statement by filling in the circle beside the letter of the correct answer.

1. According to this selection, parts of the earth are
- ○ a. always disappearing.
- ○ b. always growing.
- ○ c. always moving.

2. Earthquakes can occur when
- ○ a. parts of the earth move quickly.
- ○ b. parts of the earth move slowly.
- ○ c. parts of the earth stand still.

3. To describe the strength of an earthquake, scientists use
- ○ a. seismometers.   ○ b. the Richter scale.   ○ c. a fault meter.

4. Very large quakes measure 8 or higher. A small quake measures
- ○ a. less than 2.   ○ b. less than 4.   ○ c. less than 7.

5. We live on the outer part of the earth, which is called its
- ○ a. crust.   ○ b. core.   ○ c. fault.

6. The place where two large sections of earth meet and push against each other is called a
- ○ a. landslide.   ○ b. fault.   ○ c. tsunami.

7. Most earthquakes occur along the shores of the
- ○ a. Atlantic Ocean.   ○ b. Indian Ocean.   ○ c. Pacific Ocean.

8. Earthquakes often occur in places where there are
- ○ a. tornadoes.   ○ b. volcanoes.   ○ c. mudslides.

9. To try to predict when earthquakes will occur, scientists use
- ○ a. satellites.   ○ b. the Richter scale.   ○ c. seismometers.

B. In your own words, explain why we will continue to have earthquakes.

_____

Focus Skills

COMPREHENSION
Evaluating

LITERATURE
Essay

VOCABULARY
Using the Dictionary

SkillBuilder Copymasters

 Reading Comprehension:
1 Evaluating p. T355

 Literary Analysis:
2 Essay p. T356

 Vocabulary:
3 Using the Dictionary p. T357
4 Words to Know p. T358

Assessment

 5 Selection Test p. T359

Readability Scores

DRP	LEXILE	DALE-CHALL
57	600	5.0

by Earl Nightingale

Sparky

No one thought Sparky was special. Yet he became world famous just by being himself. Discover how.

Connect to Your Life

When was the last time you heard someone called a loser? Did you think that description was fair or unfair? Explain your answer to a classmate.

Key to the Essay

"Sparky" was the creator of a comic strip called "Peanuts." The main character is named Charlie Brown. See what Sparky and Charlie Brown have in common.

Vocabulary Preview

Words to Know
submitted
rejection

 Reading Coach CD-ROM selec

260 Unit 8 Hard to Believe

Connect to Your Life

Before students break into pairs to discuss the last time they heard someone called a loser, you may want to have the class discuss their feelings about using such a label. Are there any students who feel that it's never fair to call someone a loser? If so, encourage them to explain their feelings.

Key to the Essay

You may wish to limit or skip prior discussion of the "Peanuts" comic strip. The writer does not reveal the identity of the essay's subject—Charles Schulz—until the conclusion.

Vocabulary Preview

Words to Know
submitted *v.* presented for approval
rejection *n.* the act of being refused

 For direct instruction on Words to Know, see page T354.

FOCUS

Read to find out about Sparky's childhood.

For Sparky, school was all but impossible. He failed
every subject in the eighth grade. He flunked physics
in high school, getting a grade of zero. Sparky also
flunked Latin, algebra and English. He didn't do
much better in sports. Although he did manage to
make the school's golf team, he promptly lost the only
important match of the season. There was a
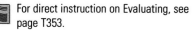 consolation match; he lost that, too.

> **consolation match**
> contest for those
> who lose the first
> prize

Throughout his youth Sparky was
10 awkward socially. He was not actually
disliked by the other students; no one cared
that much. He was astonished if a classmate
ever said hello to him outside of school hours. There's
no way to tell how he might have done at dating.
Sparky never once asked a girl to go out in high
school. He was too afraid of being turned down.

Sparky was a loser. He, his classmates . . . everyone
knew it. So he rolled with it. Sparky had made up his
mind early in life that if things were meant to
20 work out, they would. Otherwise he would
content himself with what appeared to be his
inevitable mediocrity.

> **inevitable mediocrity**
> average ability
> that can't be
> avoided

THINK IT THROUGH

Why did everyone consider Sparky a loser?

Sparky **261**

COMPREHENSION

FOCUS SKILL: Evaluating

Tell students that **evaluating** a piece
of writing involves judging its worth
by asking questions and forming
opinions about it.

For direct instruction on Evaluating, see
page T353.

 Ask: In your opinion, do the
examples that the author gives
clearly support the main idea that
Sparky was a loser? Why or why
not? *(Students probably will say
that the examples do support the
main idea because they show several ways in which Sparky consis-
tently failed.)* **evaluating**

THINK IT THROUGH Why did
everyone consider Sparky a loser?
*(He failed every subject in eighth
grade and several classes in high
school, he wasn't good at sports,
he was socially awkward, and he
never dated in high school.)* **cause
and effect**

LITERATURE

FOCUS SKILL: Essay

Explain that an **essay** is a short work
of nonfiction that deals with a single
subject. Also explain that the essay
that students are about to read is
called a **biographical essay** because
it describes several incidents in the
life of a person nicknamed Sparky.

For direct instruction on Essay, see page
T353.

VOCABULARY

FOCUS SKILL: Using a Dictionary

match Have students use a dictionary to find out that in this
context, *match* means "game or
competition."

astonished Have students use a
dictionary to discover that *astonished* means "shocked."

FOR ENGLISH LEARNERS

Help students understand the following expressions and idioms:

Line 1: all but impossible
Line 5: manage to make
Line 6: promptly
Line 15: asked a girl to go out
Line 16: turned down
Line 18: rolled with it
Line 21: content himself

However, one thing was important to Sparky—drawing. He was proud of his artwork. Of course, no one else appreciated it. In his senior year of high school, he submitted some cartoons to the editors of the yearbook. The cartoons were turned down. Despite this particular rejection, Sparky was so
30 convinced of his ability that he decided to become a professional artist.

After completing high school, he wrote a letter to Walt Disney Studios. He was told to send some samples of his artwork, and the subject for a cartoon was suggested. Sparky drew

submitted
(səb mĭt′ ĭd)
v. presented for approval; past tense of *submit*

rejection
(rĭ jĕk′ shən)
n. act of being refused

"Sparky" at his drawing board

262 Unit 8 Hard to Believe

the proposed cartoon. He spent a great deal of time on it and on all the other drawings he submitted.

Finally, the reply came from Disney Studios. He had been rejected once again. Another loss for the loser.
40 So Sparky decided to write his own autobiography in cartoons. He described his childhood self—a little boy loser and chronic underachiever. The cartoon character would soon become famous worldwide. For Sparky, the boy who had such lack of success in school and whose work was rejected again and again, was Charles Schulz. He created the "Peanuts" comic strip and the little cartoon character whose kite would never fly and who never succeeded in kicking a
50 football, Charlie Brown.

chronic underachiever
one who has performed poorly for a long time

THINK IT THROUGH

1. By what name did the world come to know Sparky?
2. What do you think was the key to Sparky's success? Find details in the essay to support your answer.
3. This essay once appeared in the book *Chicken Soup for the Teenaged Soul.* What message do you think the writer wants to send in telling Sparky's story?

Sparky 263

COMPREHENSION

C Ask: What did Sparky do that finally helped him turn his failures into worldwide success? *(He created the comic strip "Peanuts," which featured Charlie Brown, a character he based on himself.)* **cause and effect**

D THINK IT THROUGH

1. By what name did the world come to know Sparky? *(Charles Schulz)* **details**

2. What do you think was the key to Sparky's success? Find details in the essay to support your answer. *(Possible answers: Sparky did not let rejection stop him; he worked hard and had faith in himself; he saw that a comic strip about a loser could capture people's hearts; he took lemons and made lemonade.)* **evaluating**

3. This essay once appeared in the book *Chicken Soup for the Teenaged Soul.* What message do you think the writer wants to send in telling Sparky's story? *(Possible answers: Have faith in yourself, no matter what others think of you; don't give up on your dreams; if at first you don't succeed, try, try again; turn your failures into success; even people who are considered losers can triumph in the end.)* **theme** LITERATURE

Option for Writing Have students write a paragraph in which they describe either the key to Charles Schulz's success or the writer's message in this essay. When students have finished, invite volunteers to share their writing with the class.

VOCABULARY

C **subject . . . proposed** Have students use a dictionary to find out that in the context of this paragraph, *subject* means "topic or idea" and *proposed* means "planned or suggested."

D **chronic** Have students use a dictionary to find out that *chronic* means "constant or habitual."

FOR ENGLISH LEARNERS

Help students understand the following expressions and idioms:

Line 28: Despite
Line 33: Walt Disney Studios
Line 41: childhood self
Line 45: lack of success

1. COMPREHENSION

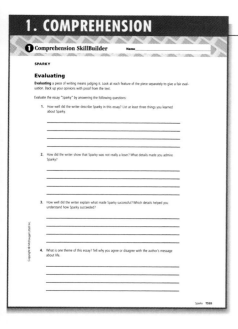

Evaluating

Direct Instruction Ask students to name a comic strip they like. Have them describe one thing they like about the strip. Explain that when they gave their opinions about comic strips and pinpointed what they enjoyed, they were evaluating. Tell students that **evaluating** means judging a work and explaining the ways in which it meets or fails to meet your standards.

Point out that evaluating requires more than simply saying whether you like or dislike a thing. Fair evaluations consider each important aspect of the subject.

Have students ask these questions in evaluating an essay:
- Is the writer's point of view expressed clearly?
- Are the writer's reasons for his or her opinions logical?
- Does the writer support his or her opinions with facts?

Comprehension SkillBuilder Answer Key:

Answers will vary. Possible answers:

1. *Sparky didn't do many things well. He always had confidence in his ability to draw. He tried to get a job with Disney but failed. Then he achieved success with "Peanuts," a cartoon about himself as loser.*
2. *The writer told how Sparky kept trying. I admire Sparky because he was strong and didn't let other people get him down.*
3. *The writer didn't tell how Sparky got his cartoon noticed. That would have made it easier to understand how he succeeded. Details that explained his success were his persistence and his faith in himself.*
4. *One theme is that people can't see what is inside a person by looking at his or her outside. Another theme is that other people's opinions of you don't count; what matters is how you see yourself.*

2. LITERATURE

Essay

Direct Instruction Tell students that an **essay** is a short piece of nonfiction writing in which the writer shares his or her opinions about a particular topic. Point out that essays may also have a theme, or message, about life and human behavior.

Explain that because an essay is short, writers usually concentrate on only one limited topic. They tell the reasons why they feel as they do as briefly as possible.

Lead students to see that in "Sparky" the writer presents several details that support the view of Sparky as a loser in many ways. Help students recognize the writer's admiration for the way Sparky finally achieved success.

Literary SkillBuilder Answer Key:

Answers may vary. Possible answers:

Sparky was a loser at school because he <u>failed many courses.</u>

Sparky was a loser at sports because he <u>lost the important golf match and the consolation match.</u>

Sparky was a loser in relationships because he <u>didn't have any friends and never asked a girl out on a date in high school.</u>

Sparky never lost faith in his ability to <u>draw</u>.

Sparky became a success when he <u>started drawing "Peanuts."</u>

Possible Message: *Don't be discouraged if you aren't always a winner. You will be a winner if you keep trying.*

3. VOCABULARY

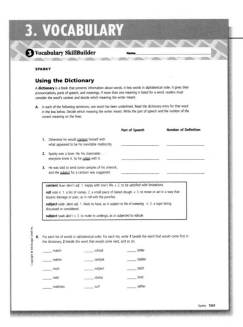

Using the Dictionary

Direct Instruction Tell students that a **dictionary** is a book that offers a wealth of information about words. Point out that a dictionary entry not only gives a word's meaning; it also gives the word's pronunciation, its part of speech, its history and origins, and often even a sentence or phrase showing how the word is used.

Remind students that words in a dictionary are listed in alphabetical order. Remind them also that guide words at the top of each page indicate the first and last words found on that page. If possible, make a dictionary available to each student and point out the respellings of several words and the pronunciation key at the bottom of the page.

Point out the abbreviations for the parts of speech and the numbers for the various meanings. Explain to students that many words have more than one meaning (and may even act as more than one part of speech). The most common meaning is usually listed first. Tell students to consider a word's context in deciding which meaning the writer intended.

Vocabulary SkillBuilder Answer Key:

A.
1. *v., 2*
2. *v., 3*
3. *n., 2*

B. col. 1: *1, 2, 5, 4, 3;*
col. 2: *2, 1, 4, 3, 5;*
col. 3: *4, 1, 2, 5, 3*

4. WORDS TO KNOW

Words to Know

Direct Instruction As you present the **Words to Know,** you might want to help students identify the word parts. Stress the importance of finding the base of each word. Help students remove prefixes and suffixes to identify the base.

• **submitted** *(submit + t + -ed)* is from the Latin *sub + mittere,* "to cause to go."

• **rejection** *(reject + -ion)* is from the Latin *re + iacere,* "to throw."

Writing Activity Pair students or allow them to work in groups to complete the exercise. Have volunteers share their cartoons.

Words to Know SkillBuilder Answer Key:

A. 1. *submitted* **2.** *rejection*
B. *Students may work together on this exercise.* **1.** *subside* **2.** *repulsed*
    3. *submarine* **4.** *reproduce*

5. SELECTION TEST

Selection Test Answer Key:
A. 1. *loser* **2.** *success* **3.** *autobiography* **4.** *Charlie Brown*
B. *Sparky was Charles Schulz.*

SPARKY

Evaluating

Evaluating a piece of writing means judging it. Look at each feature of the piece separately to give a fair evaluation. Back up your opinions with proof from the text.

Evaluate the essay "Sparky" by answering the following questions:

1. How well did the writer describe Sparky in this essay? List at least three things you learned about Sparky.

    _____

    _____

    _____

    _____

2. How did the writer show that Sparky was not really a loser? What details made you admire Sparky?

    _____

    _____

    _____

    _____

3. How well did the writer explain what made Sparky successful? Which details helped you understand how Sparky succeeded?

    _____

    _____

    _____

    _____

4. What is one theme of this essay? Tell why you agree or disagree with the author's message about life.

    _____

    _____

    _____

    _____

SPARKY

Essay

An **essay** is a short work in which the writer explains his or her opinion. The writer may also share a message about life. In "Sparky," the writer shares his thoughts about a loser who became a winner.

Fill in the missing details from the essay "Sparky." Then write the message that you think the author is sharing.

Sparky was a loser at school because he _____

_____

_____

Sparky was a loser at sports because he _____

_____

_____

Writer's message _____

_____

_____

_____

_____

Sparky became a success when he _____

_____

_____

Sparky was a loser in relationships because he _____

_____

_____

Sparky never lost faith in his ability to _____

_____

_____

SPARKY

Using the Dictionary

A **dictionary** is a book that presents information about words. It lists words in alphabetical order. It gives their pronunciations, parts of speech, and meanings. If more than one meaning is listed for a word, readers must consider the word's context and decide which meaning the writer meant.

A. In each of the following sentences, one word has been underlined. Read the dictionary entry for that word in the box below. Decide which meaning the writer meant. Write the part of speech and the number of the correct meaning on the lines.

	Part of Speech	Number of Definition
1. Otherwise he would <u>content</u> himself with what appeared to be his inevitable mediocrity.	_____	_____
2. Sparky was a loser. He, his classmates . . . everyone knew it. So he <u>rolled</u> with it.	_____	_____
3. He was told to send some samples of his artwork, and the <u>subject</u> for a cartoon was suggested.	_____	_____

---

content (kən tĕnt') *adj*. 1. happy with one's life. *v.* 2. to be satisfied with limitations.

roll (rōl) *n*. 1. a list of names. 2. a small piece of baked dough. *v.* 3. to move or act in a way that lessens damage or pain, as in *roll with the punches.*

subject (sŭb' jĕkt) *adj*. 1. likely to have, as in *subject to fits of sneezing.* *n.* 2. a topic being discussed or considered.

subject (səb jĕkt') *v.* 3. to make to undergo, as in *subjected to ridicule.*

B. Put each list of words in alphabetical order. For each list, write **1** beside the word that would come first in the dictionary, **2** beside the word that would come next, and so on.

_____ match	_____ school	_____ letter
_____ matter	_____ sample	_____ ladder
_____ mutt	_____ subject	_____ latch
_____ melt	_____ stamp	_____ limit
_____ mattress	_____ surf	_____ lather

SPARKY

Words to Know

submitted   rejection

A. In each blank, write the word from the list that best completes the sentence.

1. I _____ my homework to my teacher at the end of class.

2. My family says that I have to learn how to handle _____.

B. **Prefixes** The prefix **sub-** means "below" or "almost." The prefix **re-** means "again" or "backward." The following words have a **sub-** or **re-** prefix. Read the definitions, then complete each sentence by writing the correct word on the line.

submarine   *n.* a boat that goes underwater

subside   *v.* to sink to a lower or normal level

repulsed   *adj.* driven back or pushed away

reproduce   *v.* to make a copy of

1. Her screams and tears began to _____, and

   she felt much more like herself.

2. I was _____ by all of the smoke in the

   hallway and didn't enter the room.

3. The spies used a _____ to move into enemy

   waters.

4. Luz wanted to _____ the magazine article, so

   she used a photocopy machine.

Writing Activity
Draw your own cartoon. Write a caption using one of the **Words to Know.**

SPARKY

A. In each blank, write the correct word or name from the list below.

Charlie Brown   autobiography   loser   success

1. Throughout grade school and high school, Sparky was considered a _____.

2. Sparky finally gained _____ when he created the "Peanuts" comic strip.

3. The comic strip was Sparky's _____ in cartoons.

4. The cartoon character _____ was based on Sparky's childhood self.

B. In your own words, reveal who Sparky actually was.

_____

Focus Skills

COMPREHENSION
Fact and Opinion
Author's Perspective

LITERATURE
Informative Nonfiction

VOCABULARY
Word Origins: Greek Roots

SkillBuilder Copymasters

 Reading Comprehension:
1 Fact and Opinion p. T365
2 Author's Perspective p. T366

 Vocabulary:
3 Word Origins: Greek Roots
   p. T367
4 Words to Know p. T368

Assessment

 5 Selection Test p. T369

Assessment Booklet
Progress Check Units 5–8

Readability Scores

DRP	LEXILE	DALE-CHALL
54	670	5.2

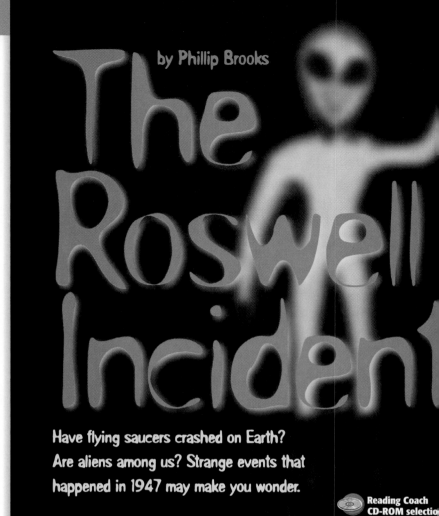

by Phillip Brooks

The Roswell Incident

Have flying saucers crashed on Earth?
Are aliens among us? Strange events that
happened in 1947 may make you wonder.

 **Reading Coach
CD-ROM selectio**

Connect to Your Life

When you hear the words
flying saucer, what images
come to your mind?
Briefly discuss why people
are so interested in the
idea of visitors from other
planets.

Key to the Article

When the topic is flying
saucers, it's often hard to
find solid facts. Read this
selection carefully. Notice
how the writer presents
the information. Judge the
facts and evidence.

**Vocabulary
Preview**

Words to Know
authorities
spindly
bizarre
procedure
rumor

264 Unit 8 Hard to Believe

Connect to Your Life

Students can break into small groups to
share their ideas about flying saucers.
Encourage them to discuss whether they
believe flying saucers and aliens exist,
and why or why not.

Key to the Article

Before students begin reading, make
sure they understand the difference
between a fact and an opinion.
Encourage them to keep track of the
facts and opinions in this selection. Why
do they think the author includes both?

Vocabulary Preview

Words to Know
authorities *n.* persons who have
power
spindly *adj.* slender and long
bizarre *adj.* strange
procedure *n.* way of doing something
rumor *n.* unproved information spread
by word of mouth

For direct instruction on Words to Know,
see page T364.

In 1947, Mac Brazel made an amazing discovery. Read on for the details.

Date: July 3, 1947
Place: Roswell, New Mexico

William "Mac" Brazel rode his horse across the dry desert land of his ranch. He thought about the explosion he had heard last night during a storm. Now he wanted to find out what had caused it.

Something silver glinted in the sunlight, catching Mac's eye. The ground around him was littered with shiny metal pieces. He stopped to pick one up.

10 The fragment was extremely lightweight but unbendable. And it was covered with hieroglyphs.

 A

A hieroglyphs
(hī′ ər ə glĭfs′)
picture symbols used for writing

Mac felt uneasy. The metal looked like nothing on earth. He telephoned the air force base at nearby Roswell.

Staff from the Roswell base arrived at Mac's ranch. They posted guards around the area where the metal was found.

20 On July 8, the air force base issued an amazing news statement—they said that the wreckage was from a flying saucer!

Later that day, the base released a second statement. It said that the first story was a mistake. The crashed object was in fact a weather balloon. But was it? Were the authorities covering something up?

authorities
(ə thôr′ Ĭ tēz)
n. persons who have power

THINK IT THROUGH
B From the information you've read so far, which statement do you think is true? Explain.

The Roswell Incident **265**

Vocabulary Strategy:
Preteaching

Word Origins: Greek Roots
Explain to students that many English words are made up of parts from ancient Greek or Latin words. Write the following items on the board. Have volunteers add one or two words to the list of examples:

Skopein means "to see" in Greek.

English words that come from *skopein: telescope, periscope*

(Students might supply microscope *or* stethoscope.)

Tell students that learning about a word's **origins** will not only give them deeper knowledge of the word but also help them understand the meanings of related words.

For more on Word Origins, see page T364.

COMPREHENSION

FOCUS SKILL 1: Fact and Opinion

Help students review that a **fact** is a statement that can be proved and thus is not debatable. An **opinion,** however, is a statement that cannot be proved. Therefore, it can be debated.

For direct instruction on Fact and Opinion, see page T363.

FOCUS SKILL 2: Author's Perspective

Tell students that an **author's perspective** includes his or her viewpoint, beliefs, and attitudes about a particular topic.

For direct instruction on Author's Perspective, see page T363.

A Ask: Is the statement "The fragment was extremely lightweight but unbendable" a fact or an opinion? How do you know? *(It is a fact because it can be proved.)*
fact and opinion

B **THINK IT THROUGH** From the information you've read so far, which statement do you think is true? Explain. *(Most students may respond that the first statement about the flying saucer seems truthful, because the second statement sounds like a cover-up story. Other students may think that the second statement, which may have been made after further investigation, is more believable.)* **drawing conclusions**

LITERATURE

FOCUS SKILL: Informative Nonfiction

Explain that **informative nonfiction** is writing that gives facts and details about real people, places, and events.

VOCABULARY

FOCUS SKILL: Word Origins: Greek Roots

A **hieroglyphs, telephoned** (lines 12 and 14) Have students use a dictionary to find out that *hieroglyphs* comes from the Greek words *hieros,* meaning "sacred," and *gluphē,* meaning "carving." The first part of the word *telephone* comes from the Greek word *tēle,* meaning "far."

FOR ENGLISH LEARNERS

Help students understand the following expressions and idioms:

Line 7: catching Mac's eye
Line 13: looked like nothing on earth
Line 17: posted guards
Line 24: weather balloon
Line 26: covering something up

FOCUS

Grady Barnett found something very strange 100 miles from Roswell. Read to discover how the Roswell legend grew.

Soon there were stories of a second crash site about 100 miles west of Roswell.

30 An engineer named Grady Barnett said he was working in the desert when he saw a large metal disk on the ground. Scattered around the crumpled disk were five small, gray bodies. They appeared to be dead.

As Grady stood staring, a military vehicle drove up. An officer jumped out. He told Grady to leave at once and, more importantly, never speak about what he had seen.

As he was hustled away, Grady glanced over his shoulder. One of the creatures
40 seemed to open an eye and look back at him.

> **REREAD**
> What questions do you have about this event?

 C

Grady Barnett said later that the bodies were "like humans, but they were not humans." They were small, with spindly arms and legs. Their heads were large, with sunken eyes and no teeth.

> **spindly**
> (spĭnd' lē)
> *adj.* slender and long

In the fifty years since the actual event, various witnesses have come forward with bizarre stories about the aliens. Some
50 claim the alien bodies were taken to the Roswell Air Force Base.

> **bizarre**
> (bĭ zär')
> *adj.* strange

One story told how doctors at the Roswell Army Hospital had been ordered on duty at short notice. The shocked doctors were told to cut open and examine the bodies of the dead aliens in a procedure called an

> **procedure**
> (prə sē' jər)
> *n.* way of doing something

B autopsy.

266 Unit 8 Hard to Believe

This is the front page of a Roswell newspaper that appeared in 1947. The major headline describes the actions of the Roswell Army Air Force (RAAF).

When the bodies were cut open, a terrible smell filled the room. Several doctors became too sick to
60 carry on.

The story took another twist in the 1990s, when a video tape was released. The film was supposed to date from 1947 and show the alien autopsy. But many people believe that the film is a fake and the autopsy never happened.

The Roswell legend has continued to grow. New details have been added, including a rumor that the alien bodies were frozen in ice and kept at a top-secret air force base
70 called Area 51.

> **rumor**
> (rōō' mər)
> *n.* unproved information spread by word of mouth

It seems certain that something did crash at Roswell in 1947. Does the air force know more than it is telling? Were the stories fake? We may never know.

D

E **THINK IT THROUGH**

1. Do you think aliens came to earth in 1947? Use evidence from the selection to support your opinion.
2. The writer supports his story with many facts and details. Why do you think he does this?
3. Why do you think the Roswell incident has been talked about for so many years?

The Roswell Incident 267

COMPREHENSION

C **REREAD** What questions do you have about this event? *(Possible questions: How large was the disk? Was it flat or hollow? Was the disk a flying saucer? Were the five bodies human or alien? Why did the officer tell Grady to leave and to never speak about what he had seen? Why didn't Grady refuse to leave? Did the creature that seemed to open its eye survive? If so, what happened to it?)* **questioning**

D Ask: Is the statement "We may never know" a fact or an opinion? How do you know? *(It is an opinion because it is the author's belief. It can't be proved, and it can be debated.)* **fact and opinion**

E **THINK IT THROUGH**

1. Do you think aliens came to earth in 1947? Use evidence from the selection to support your opinion. *(Accept any answers that students can justify. Encourage them to use examples from the text to support their conclusions.)* **evaluating**

2. The writer supports his story with many facts and details. Why do you think he does this? *(He wants to appear to be objective or to have a balanced view about an unsolved mystery.)* **author's perspective**

3. Why do you think the Roswell incident has been talked about for so many years? *(It's a mystery that remains unsolved, and people are fascinated with the idea of UFOs and aliens.)* **drawing conclusions**

RETEACHING

If students need more help understanding **Fact and Opinion,** use pages T656–T658.

VOCABULARY

B **autopsy** Help students use a dictionary to find out that *autopsy* comes from the Greek word *autopsiā*, which means "a seeing for oneself"; *auto-* means "self," and *opsis* means "a seeing." Have students look at the entries surrounding *autopsy* in the dictionary to find other words containing *auto-*.

FOR ENGLISH LEARNERS

Help students understand the following expressions and idioms:

Line 38: hustled away
Line 48: come forward
Line 53: ordered on duty at short notice
Line 60: carry on
Line 61: took another twist
Line 64: a fake
Line 66: legend has continued to grow

1. COMPREHENSION

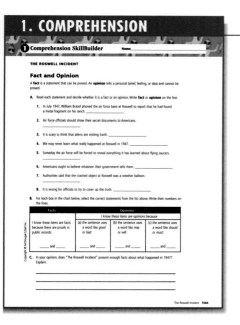

Comprehension SkillBuilder   Name_____

THE ROSWELL INCIDENT

Fact and Opinion
A **fact** is a statement that can be proved. An **opinion** tells a personal belief, feeling, or idea and cannot be proved.

A. Read each statement and decide whether it is a fact or an opinion. Write **fact** or **opinion** on the line.

1. In July 1947, William Brazel phoned the air force base at Roswell to report that he had found a metal fragment on his ranch. _____
2. Air force officials should show their secret documents to Americans. _____
3. It is scary to think that aliens are visiting Earth. _____
4. We may never learn what really happened at Roswell in 1947. _____
5. Someday the air force will be forced to reveal everything it has learned about flying saucers. _____
6. Americans ought to believe whatever their government tells them. _____
7. Authorities said that the crashed object at Roswell was a weather balloon. _____
8. It is wrong for officials to try to cover up the truth. _____

B. For each box in the chart below, select the correct statements from the list above. Write their numbers on the lines.

Fact and Opinion

Direct Instruction Tell students that a **fact** is a statement that can be proved. An **opinion** tells a personal belief, feeling, or idea and cannot be proved.

Read the following statements aloud to students and have them decide whether the statements are facts or opinions. When students say that a statement is a fact, have them suggest ways in which the fact can be verified.

- William Brazel lived near the Roswell Air Force Base in 1947. *(F)*
- The air force should investigate every report of a UFO. *(O)*
- It is silly to think that aliens are visiting Earth. *(O)*
- Humans will someday speak to creatures from other galaxies. *(O)*

Explain to students that these clue words often signal opinions:

- *should, ought to, must.* These words mean that what is said is not always so.
- *may, will.* If an event has not yet happened, the statement is a prediction. A prediction is a type of opinion.
- judgment words such as *better, best, bad, worst, wonderful,* and *ridiculous.* Judgments cannot be proved and so cannot be classified as facts.

> **Comprehension SkillBuilder Answer Key:**
> **A. 1.** *fact* **2.** *opinion* **3.** *opinion* **4.** *opinion* **5.** *opinion* **6.** *opinion*
>   **7.** *fact* **8.** *opinion*
> **B. Facts:** *1 and 7* **Opinions:** *(a) 3 and 8 (b) 5 and 4 (c) 2 and 6*
> **C.** *Accept whatever reasonable opinions students express about the article.*

2. COMPREHENSION

Comprehension SkillBuilder   Name_____

THE ROSWELL INCIDENT

Author's Perspective
The **author's perspective** is the way he or she feels about a question or topic. Writing that gives only one side of a question is described as **biased**. Writing that presents both sides is described as **balanced**.

A. Read each paragraph. Decide whether it is biased or balanced. Circle your choice.

1. The silly people who believe in flying saucers just will not give up, it seems. Even though patient air force officials have told them over and over again that there are no UFOs, they keep making trouble. When will these pitiful losers get a life?

   biased   balanced

2. Many believers in UFOs say that the air force is covering up the truth about what happened at Roswell. Air force officials insist that they have shared all they know about reports of flying saucers. The debate will likely go on for years.

   biased   balanced

3. Starting in 1947 with the famous Roswell discovery of an alien spaceship, the air force has shown a terrible lack of respect for the people of the United States. Of course, any thinking person knows that officials are covering up important secrets about visits from other planets. What are they trying to hide?

   biased   balanced

B. Read this paragraph and answer the question below.

Foolish scientists are sending out radio messages into space, hoping that someday a creature in outer space will hear them and answer back. This waste of time and money has been going on for far too long. I say forget about imaginary space creatures and concentrate on problems in the real world.

What is the author's perspective about sending radio messages into space?

Author's Perspective

Direct Instruction Tell students that the **author's perspective** is the way he or she looks at a subject or feels about an issue. Explain that when authors present only one side of a question or issue, their writing is said to be **biased.** In biased writing authors make no attempt to hide their point of view. Biased writing often includes opinions, not just facts.

Tell students that when writers present both sides of a question and allow readers to draw their own conclusions, the writing is said to be **balanced,** or **unbiased.** Point out that "The Roswell Incident" is balanced because it presents both sides of the issue in a factual, objective way.

> **Comprehension SkillBuilder Answer Key:**
> **A.**
>   **1.** *biased*
>   **2.** *balanced*
>   **3.** *biased*
>
> **B.** *The author is against sending radio messages into space. He or she thinks it is a foolish waste of time and money.*

3. VOCABULARY

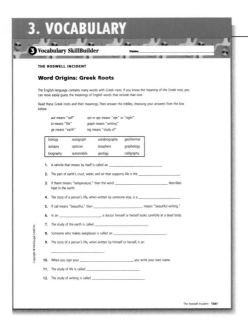

Word Origins: Greek Roots

Direct Instruction Tell students that many English words have Greek roots. Explain that some English words are combinations of two Greek words. For example, *microscope* combines *micro*, from a Greek word meaning "small," and *scope*, from a Greek word meaning "to see." When you understand the word's two Greek roots, you can guess that a microscope helps people examine small objects.

Tell students that they may have to study a word carefully to spot a familiar Greek root. It could appear at the beginning, in the middle, or at the end of the word. Remind students that although knowing the meaning of the Greek root will help them understand the meaning of the English word, they must try out the meaning in context to see if they have guessed correctly. Remind students to refer to the dictionary if they have trouble figuring out the word's meaning.

Vocabulary SkillBuilder Answer Key:

1. *automobile*
2. *biosphere*
3. *geothermal*
4. *biography*
5. *calligraphy*
6. *autopsy*
7. *geology*
8. *optician*
9. *autobiography*
10. *autograph*
11. *biology*
12. *graphology*

4. WORDS TO KNOW

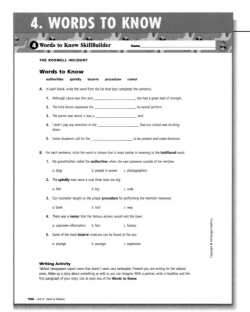

Words to Know

Direct Instruction As you present the **Words to Know,** you might want to help students identify the word parts. Stress the importance of finding the base of each word. Help students remove prefixes and suffixes to identify the base.

- **authorities** (authority – y + -ie + -s) is derived from the Latin *auctor*, "creator," and belongs to a family of related words (such as *author* and *authentic).*
- **spindly** is derivative of *spindle.*
- **procedure** belongs to a family of words related to *process*, from the Latin *prōcēdere,* "to advance"; other words in this family include *proceed, procession,* and *processor.*
- **rumor** is from the Latin *rūmor.*

Writing Activity Showing students an example of a tabloid newspaper may help them understand the model. Pair or group students together to work on the project. Have volunteers share their creations.

Words to Know SkillBuilder Answer Key:

A.
1. *spindly* 2. *procedure* 3. *bizarre* 4. *rumor* 5. *authorities*

B.
1. *b* 2. *a* 3. *c* 4. *a* 5. *a*

5. SELECTION TEST

Selection Test Answer Key:

A. 1. *false* 2. *false* 3. *true* 4. *true*

B. Possible answer: *The legend has continued to grow.*

THE ROSWELL INCIDENT

Fact and Opinion

A **fact** is a statement that can be proved. An **opinion** tells a personal belief, feeling, or idea and cannot be proved.

A. Read each statement and decide whether it is a fact or an opinion. Write **fact** or **opinion** on the line.

1. In July 1947, William Brazel phoned the air force base at Roswell to report that he had found a metal fragment on his ranch. _____

2. Air force officials should show their secret documents to Americans. _____

3. It is scary to think that aliens are visiting Earth. _____

4. We may never learn what really happened at Roswell in 1947. _____

5. Someday the air force will be forced to reveal everything it has learned about flying saucers. _____

6. Americans ought to believe whatever their government tells them. _____

7. Authorities said that the crashed object at Roswell was a weather balloon. _____

8. It is wrong for officials to try to cover up the truth. _____

B. For each box in the chart below, select the correct statements from the list above. Write their numbers on the lines.

Facts	Opinions		
	I know these items are opinions because		
I know these items are facts because there are proofs in public records:	(a) the sentence uses a word like *good* or *bad*:	(b) the sentence uses a word like *may* or *will*:	(c) the sentence uses a word like *should* or *must*:
_____ and _____	_____ and _____	_____ and _____	_____ and _____

C. In your opinion, does "The Roswell Incident" present enough facts about what happened in 1947? Explain.

_____

_____

_____

THE ROSWELL INCIDENT

Author's Perspective

The **author's perspective** is the way he or she feels about a question or topic. Writing that gives only one side of a question is described as **biased.** Writing that presents both sides is described as **balanced.**

A. Read each paragraph. Decide whether it is biased or balanced. Circle your choice.

1. The silly people who believe in flying saucers just will not give up, it seems. Even though patient air force officials have told them over and over again that there are no UFOs, they keep making trouble. When will these pitiful losers get a life?

         biased   balanced

2. Many believers in UFOs say that the air force is covering up the truth about what happened at Roswell. Air force officials insist that they have shared all they know about reports of flying saucers. The debate will likely go on for years.

         biased   balanced

3. Starting in 1947 with the famous Roswell discovery of an alien spaceship, the air force has shown a terrible lack of respect for the people of the United States. Of course, any thinking person knows that officials are covering up important secrets about visits from other planets. What are they trying to hide?

         biased   balanced

B. Read this paragraph and answer the question below.

Foolish scientists are sending out radio messages into space, hoping that someday a creature in outer space will hear them and answer back. This waste of time and money has been going on for far too long. I say forget about imaginary space creatures and concentrate on problems in the real world.

What is the author's perspective about sending radio messages into space?

_____

_____

_____

THE ROSWELL INCIDENT

Word Origins: Greek Roots

The English language contains many words with Greek roots. If you know the meaning of the Greek root, you can more easily guess the meanings of English words that include that root.

Read these Greek roots and their meanings. Then answer the riddles, choosing your answers from the box below.

aut means "self"   *opt* or *ops* means "eye" or "sight"

bi means "life"   *graph* means "writing"

ge means "earth"   *log* means "study of"

biology	autograph	autobiography	geothermal
autopsy	optician	biosphere	graphology
biography	automobile	geology	calligraphy

1. A vehicle that moves by itself is called an _____.

2. The part of earth's crust, water, and air that supports life is the _____.

3. If *therm* means "temperature," then the word _____ describes heat in the earth.

4. The story of a person's life, when written by someone else, is a _____.

5. If *call* means "beautiful," then _____ means "beautiful writing."

6. In an _____, a doctor himself or herself looks carefully at a dead body.

7. The study of the earth is called _____.

8. Someone who makes eyeglasses is called an _____.

9. The story of a person's life, when written by himself or herself, is an

   _____.

10. When you sign your _____, you write your own name.

11. The study of life is called _____.

12. The study of writing is called _____.

THE ROSWELL INCIDENT

Words to Know

authorities   spindly   bizarre   procedure   rumor

A. In each blank, write the word from the list that best completes the sentence.

1. Although Laura was thin and _____, she had a great deal of strength.

2. The kind doctor explained the _____ he would perform.

3. The parrot was weird; it was a _____ bird.

4. I didn't pay any attention to the _____ that our school was shutting down.

5. Some situations call for the _____ to be present and make decisions.

B. For each sentence, circle the word or phrase that is most similar in meaning to the **boldfaced** word.

1. My grandmother called the **authorities** when she saw someone outside of her window.

   a. dogs   b. people in power   c. photographers

2. The **spindly** man wore a coat three sizes too big.

   a. thin   b. big   c. rude

3. Our counselor taught us the proper **procedure** for performing the Heimlich maneuver.

   a. book   b. tool   c. way

4. There was a **rumor** that the famous actress would visit the town.

   a. unproven information   b. fact   c. history

5. Some of the most **bizarre** creatures can be found at the zoo.

   a. strange   b. average   c. expensive

Writing Activity

Tabloid newspapers report news that doesn't seem very believable. Pretend you are writing for the tabloid press. Make up a story about something as wild as you can imagine. With a partner, write a headline and the first paragraph of your story. Use at least two of the **Words to Know.**

THE ROSWELL INCIDENT

A. Write **true** or **false** next to each statement.

_____ **1.** This selection contains only facts that can be researched and proved.

_____ **2.** William "Mac" Brazel found shiny metal pieces on his farm in Roswell, Nevada.

_____ **3.** In a first statement, the air force base said that the wreckage was from a flying saucer.

_____ **4.** The base issued a second statement, however, that said it was a crashed weather balloon.

B. In your own words, tell what has happened to the legend of Roswell.

_____

Focus Skills and SkillBuilder Copymasters

The Jade Stone p. T372
COMPREHENSION
Predicting p. T381
LITERATURE
Conflict p. T382
VOCABULARY
Latin Roots p. T383
Words to Know p. T384

The Stolen Party p. T386
COMPREHENSION
Making Judgments p. T395
LITERATURE
Theme p. T396
VOCABULARY
Multiple-Meaning Words p. T397
Words to Know p. T398

Acceptance p. T400
COMPREHENSION
Cause and Effect p. T408
Author's Purpose p. T409
VOCABULARY
Context Clues p. T410
Words to Know p. T411

Growing Up in a World of Darkness p. T414
COMPREHENSION
Main Idea p. T424
Problem and Solution p. T425
VOCABULARY
Syllabication p. T426
Words to Know p. T427

Making Adjustments

Unit 9
Mixed Genres

Adjustments are changes designed to make something work or fit. Think of adjustments as improvements. That's why there is a volume control on a TV and movable straps on a backpack. You can also adjust your own attitude. This kind of adjustment can help you look at problems differently.

In this unit, you'll be reading a **play,** a **short story,** an **informative article,** and a **biography.** The people who make adjustments come from very different places and time periods. Each one makes an adjustment and discovers a new way of "seeing."

268

Reading Fluency

 ★ Reading Fluency pp. T413, T429

Pacing Guide

SELECTION	TOTAL DAYS	PREREADING	READING	POST READING	
				SELECTIVE OPTIONS	ALL OPTIONS
The Jade Stone	3–3.5	1	1.5	.5	1
The Stolen Party	2.5–3	1	1	.5	1
Acceptance	2–2.5	1	.5	.5	1
Growing Up in a World of Darkness	2.5–3	1	1	.5	1

More About Mixed Genres

One unusual piece students will encounter in this unit is an example of Readers Theater, a play that can be performed without the complicated trappings of dramatic presentations. The main characters and the two real-life figures in the selections face particular difficulties. Through their individual responses to their problems, readers come to understand the importance of adaptability.

Technology Resources

Audio CD
All selections in this unit are featured in the Audio Library.

Reading Coach CD-ROM
All five selections in this unit are part of the Reading Coach. You may use Reading Coach selections as a group activity, as an individual activity, or as a tutorial for students who might benefit from this format or who have missed class.

Building Bridges: Closing the Reading Gap
This video is intended for teacher use only. It gives instructions and tips on how to help middle school readers become strategic readers.

Assessment

Selection Tests
pp. T385, T399, T412, T428

Assessment Booklet
End-of-Year Skills Test Units 1–12
Administer this test when students have completed the book. It covers skills taught in all the units.

Focus Skills

COMPREHENSION
Predicting

LITERATURE
Conflict

VOCABULARY
Latin Roots

SkillBuilder Copymasters

 Reading Comprehension:
1 Predicting p. T381

 Literary Analysis:
2 Conflict p. T382

 Vocabulary:
3 Latin Roots p. T383
4 Words to Know p. T384

Assessment

 5 Selection Test p. T385

Readability Scores

DRP	LEXILE	DALE-CHALL
52	N/A	4.6

THE JADE STONE

by Caryn Yacowitz, adapted by Aaron Shepard

An emperor demands a carving of "a dragon of wind and fire." Find out what the stone carver creates instead.

Connect to Your Life

Think about a time you saw a painting or statue that you thought was a work of art. What do you think caused the artist to create that work?

Key to the Play

Of course, you can read this play silently. However, it was meant to be read aloud. This special kind of drama is called **Readers Theater.** To perform the play, actors simply read it while sitting on chairs or standing. Ordinary plays usually have no narrator and lots of stage directions. Here, four narrators describe most of the settings and actions.

Vocabulary Preview

Words to Know
apprentice
entangled
defy

 Reading Coach CD-ROM selection

The Jade Stone **271**

Connect to Your Life

As you guide students in a discussion of several works of art, have them give a few different reasons why they think each artist might have created his or her painting or statue. Also encourage students to discuss how each work makes them feel.

Key to the Play

Before students begin reading, you may want to point out that if this play were written as a story containing dialogue, the narrators' lines often would be the parts of the story that are found *outside* the quotation marks. For example, in a story, lines 10 through 12 would be written like this: "I always listen to the stone," replied Chan Lo. "The stone tells me what it wants to be."

Vocabulary Preview

Words to Know
apprentice *n.* one who is learning a job
entangled *adj.* twisted together
defy *v.* resist with boldness

 For direct instruction on Words to Know, see page T380.

Building Background

It is no surprise that one of the "stars" of this play is a beautiful jade stone. Jade is very strong, which makes it well-suited for carving into delicate patterns and shapes. In ancient China, where the play takes place, jade was considered more precious than gold—so precious that the Chinese buried it with their dead. Two minerals, jadeite and nephrite, are both classified as jade. However, it is nephrite, which comes in green, white, yellow, gray, red, and black, that the early Chinese used for carving.

Vocabulary Strategy: Preteaching

Latin Roots Tell students that many of the English words we use today come from **Latin root words.** These words have changed slightly from the ancient Latin, but their original roots are still present. To illustrate, have students look up the word *celestial* in a dictionary. Help them find the word's Latin roots, as well as what they mean. (Celestial *comes from the Latin words* caelestis *and* caelum, *both of which mean "sky."*)

 For more on Latin Roots, see page T380.

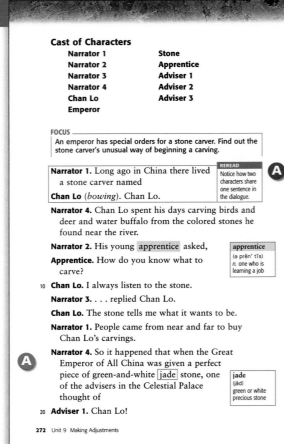

Cast of Characters

Narrator 1	Stone
Narrator 2	Apprentice
Narrator 3	Adviser 1
Narrator 4	Adviser 2
Chan Lo	Adviser 3
Emperor	

FOCUS

An emperor has special orders for a stone carver. Find out the stone carver's unusual way of beginning a carving.

Narrator 1. Long ago in China there lived a stone carver named

REREAD Notice how two characters share one sentence in the dialogue. A

Chan Lo (*bowing*). Chan Lo.

Narrator 4. Chan Lo spent his days carving birds and deer and water buffalo from the colored stones he found near the river.

Narrator 2. His young apprentice asked,

> apprentice
> (ə prĕn' tĭs)
> *n.* one who is learning a job

Apprentice. How do you know what to carve?

10 **Chan Lo.** I always listen to the stone.

Narrator 3. . . . replied Chan Lo.

Chan Lo. The stone tells me what it wants to be.

Narrator 1. People came from near and far to buy Chan Lo's carvings.

A **Narrator 4.** So it happened that when the Great Emperor of All China was given a perfect piece of green-and-white jade stone, one of the advisers in the Celestial Palace thought of

> jade
> (jād)
> green or white precious stone

20 **Adviser 1.** Chan Lo!

272 Unit 9 Making Adjustments

Narrator 2. The humble stone carver was brought before the Great Emperor of All China. Chan Lo bowed deeply.

Emperor. I want you to carve a dragon.

Narrator 3. . . . the emperor commanded.

Emperor. A dragon of wind and fire.

Chan Lo. I will do my best to please you.

Narrator 1. The emperor's men carried the precious stone to Chan Lo's garden. B

30 **Narrator 4.** Chan Lo had never seen such a perfect piece of jade. The green-and-white of the stone was like moss-entangled-in-snow.

> entangled
> (ĕn tăng' gəld)
> *adj.* twisted together

A **Narrator 2.** The great emperor had commanded, "a dragon of wind and fire." Chan Lo wondered if that was what the stone wanted to be. He spoke to it.

Chan Lo.
Here I stand, O Noble Stone,
to carve a creature of your own.
40 Whisper signs and sounds from rock
that I, your servant, may unlock.

REREAD What does Chan Lo want to know? B

Narrator 3. Chan Lo bent down and put his ear to the stone. From deep inside came a gentle sound.

Stone (*softly*). Pah-tah. Pah-tah. Pah-*tah*.

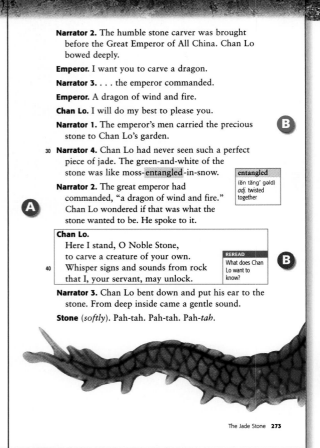

The Jade Stone 273

COMPREHENSION

FOCUS SKILL: Predicting

Tell students that **predicting** is guessing what will happen in a story—or in this case, a play—based on clues and information that the author provides.

For direct instruction on Predicting, see page T379.

A **REREAD** Notice how two characters share one sentence in the dialogue. *(Make sure students understand the setup of the lines.)*

B **REREAD** What does Chan Lo want to know? *(He is asking the stone what it wants to be carved into.)* **making inferences**

LITERATURE

FOCUS SKILL: Conflict

Tell students that a **conflict** is a struggle between two opposing forces. In an **internal conflict,** the struggle goes on in a character's own mind as the character struggles with himself or herself. In an **external conflict,** the struggle is between two characters or between a character and some outside force, such as nature.

For direct instruction on Conflict, see page T379.

Use the questions that follow to encourage literary analysis.

A What conflict is beginning to develop for Chan Lo? Is it internal or external? Explain. *(Chan Lo wants to do the emperor's bidding, but he also wants to carve the stone into what it wants to be. The conflict is internal because it is in Chan Lo's mind.)* **conflict**

VOCABULARY

FOCUS SKILL: Latin Roots

Remind students that many of the English words that we use today come from Latin words.

A **Emperor** Help students use a dictionary to find out that *emperor* originally comes from the Latin roots *in-* (meaning "in") and *parāre* (meaning "to prepare"). An emperor is a person who is prepared to rule or command.

B **precious** Help students find out that *precious* originally comes from the Latin word *pretium* (meaning "price"), and that something precious has a high price.

FOR ENGLISH LEARNERS

Help students understand the following expressions and idioms:

Line 4: spent his days
Line 23: bowed deeply
Line 27: do my best to please you

Chan Lo. Do dragons make that sound?

Narrator 1. . . . Chan Lo wondered.

Chan Lo. Perhaps the dragon's tail splashing in the ocean says "Pah-tah, pah-*tah*."

Narrator 4. But he was not sure.

THINK IT THROUGH
How does Chan Lo usually decide what to carve? What is different this time?

FOCUS
The stone carver examines the jade stone again. Read to find out what he hears.

50 **Narrator 2.** That evening, Chan Lo thought about dragons.

Narrator 3. But late at night, in his dreams, he heard,

Stone. Pah-tah. Pah-tah.

Stone and Chan Lo. Pah-*tah*.

Narrator 1. The next morning, Chan Lo went to the garden.

Narrator 4. The stone was spring-water-green in the morning light.

Chan Lo.
60   Here I stand, O Noble Stone,
to carve a creature of your own.
Whisper signs and sounds from rock that I, your servant, may unlock.

Narrator 2. Chan Lo put his ear to the green-and-white jade and listened.

Narrator 3. Softly the sounds came.

Stone (*softly*). Bub-bub-bubble. Bub-bub-bubble.

70 **Chan Lo.** Do dragons make that sound?

Narrator 1. . . . Chan Lo asked himself.

Chan Lo. Perhaps a dragon rising from the wild waves blows bubbles through his nostrils.

Narrator 4. But these were not mighty dragon bubbles that were coming from the rock. They were gentle, lazy, playful sounds.

REREAD
What other creatures might make such sounds?

D

Narrator 2. That evening, Chan Lo tried again to think about dragons.

80 **Narrator 3.** But when he went to bed, he heard in his dreams the sound of

Stone. Bub-bub-bubble. Bub-bub-bubble.

Stone and Chan Lo. Bub-bub-bubble.

B

Narrator 1. In the middle of the night, Chan Lo awoke. He walked into the moonlit garden.

Narrator 4. The stone shone silvery-green in the moonlight.

Chan Lo.
Here I stand, O Noble Stone,
90   to carve a creature of your own.
Whisper signs and sounds from rock that I, your servant, may unlock.

Narrator 2. He put his ear to the stone. Silence.

Narrator 3. Chan Lo ran his hands over the jade. His fingers felt tiny ridges, and the ridges made a sound.

COMPREHENSION

C **THINK IT THROUGH** How does Chan Lo usually decide what to carve? What is different this time? (*He listens to the object he will carve. The difference this time is that he has been told what to carve by the emperor.*) **compare and contrast**

D **REREAD** What other creatures might make such sounds? (*Possible answers: fish, frogs, or crocodiles moving underwater*) **making inferences**

LITERATURE

B If you were doing a Readers Theater performance of this play, how would you read the lines belonging to the Stone? Why? (*Based on the text and the stage directions, the lines should be read softly and in a gentle, lazy, playful voice.*) **Readers Theater**

VOCABULARY

FOR ENGLISH LEARNERS

Help students understand the following expression:

Line 57: spring-water-green

Stone (*softly*). S-s-s-ah, S-s-s-s-s-ah, S-s-s-s-s-s-s-ah.

Chan Lo. Do dragons have ridges?

C **Narrator 1.** . . . . Chan Lo pondered.

Chan Lo. Yes. They have scales. Scales on
100   their tails and bodies. And their scales
might say, "S-s-s-ah, S-s-s-s-s-ah, S-s-s-s-
s-s-s-ah," if one dared to touch them.

> **pondered**
> (pŏn' dərd)
> thought over
> carefully

Narrator 4. But Chan Lo knew these small, delicate
ridges were *not* dragon scales. **D**

Narrator 2. Chan Lo could not carve what he did not
hear, but he was afraid to disobey the emperor.

Narrator 3. His fear weighed in him like a great stone
as he picked up his tools and began to carve.

E **THINK IT THROUGH**
What do you think Chan Lo will carve? Use lines from the
play to support your opinion.

FOCUS
What does the stone carver make from the jade stone?

Narrator 1. Chan Lo worked slowly and carefully for a
110   year and a day.

Narrator 4. Finally, the carving was complete.

Narrator 2. Early in the morning, before the birds were
awake, Chan Lo and his apprentice wrapped the jade
carving in a cloth and set out for the Celestial Palace.

Narrator 3. Chan Lo entered the Great Hall, where the
three advisers sat waiting for the Great Emperor of
All China. He placed the jade stone on the table in
the center of the room.

276   Unit 9 Making Adjustments

Narrator 1. Soon the emperor's advisers grew curious.
120   They scurried to the jade stone and
peeked under the cloth.

> **scurried**
> (skûr' ēd)
> went with
> running steps;
> past tense of
> *scurry*

Adviser 1 (*surprised*). No dragon!

Adviser 2 (*louder*). *No dragon!*

Adviser 3 (*loudest*). NO DRAGON!

Narrator 4. At that moment, the emperor himself
entered the Great Hall.

Emperor. Show me my dragon of wind and fire!

Narrator 2. The advisers whisked the cloth away.

Emperor (*thundering*). *This* is not my dragon!

130   **Adviser 1** (*pointing at Chan Lo*). Punish him!   **E**

Adviser 2. *Punish him!*

Adviser 3. PUNISH HIM!

Narrator 3. Chan Lo's knees shook like
ginkgo leaves in the wind.

> **ginkgo leaves**
> (gĭng' kō lēvz')
> fan-shaped
> leaves of a tree
> native to China

Chan Lo. O mighty emperor, there *is* no
dragon of wind and fire. I did not *hear* it!
I heard these three carp fish swimming
playfully in the reeds in the pool of the Celestial
Palace.   **C**

140   **Emperor.** *Hear* them? You did not *hear* them!

Adviser 1. Chop off his head!

Adviser 2. *Boil him in oil!*

Adviser 3. CUT HIM IN A THOUSAND PIECES!

D **Narrator 1.** But the emperor was so angry, he could
not decide which punishment to choose.

F **THINK IT THROUGH**
Why is the emperor angry? What does he plan to do about it?

The Jade Stone   277

COMPREHENSION

E **THINK IT THROUGH** What do you
think Chan Lo will carve? Use
lines from the play to support
your opinion. *(Predictions will vary;
some might guess fish, but most
will say that he will not carve a
dragon. Clues include "scales,"
"delicate ridges were not dragon
scales," "could not carve what he
did not hear," "fear weighed on
him.")* **predicting**

F **THINK IT THROUGH** Why is the
emperor angry? What does he
plan to do about it? *(He can't
believe Chan Lo disobeyed him. He
wants to choose a good punishment.)* **cause and effect**

LITERATURE

C How does Chan Lo resolve his
internal conflict? *(He carves the
fish, not the dragon.)* **conflict**

D What kind of conflict is the
emperor having? Explain. *(He's
having an internal conflict because
he's struggling with himself about
how to punish Chan Lo.)* **conflict**

VOCABULARY

C **ponder** Help students find out
that *ponder* comes from the Latin
word *ponderāre* (meaning
"weigh") and that to *ponder*
means "to weigh an issue or
think about it very carefully."

D **delicate** Help students find out
that *delicate* comes from the Latin
word *dēlicātus* (meaning "pleasing") and that something that is
delicate is pleasing and must be
treated with special care.

E **punish** Help students use a
dictionary to find out that *punish*
and *punishment* (line 145) come
from the Latin word, *pūnīre*,
which means "to punish."

FOR ENGLISH LEARNERS

Help students understand the following idioms and expressions:

Line 107: his fear weighed in him
Line 128: whisked the cloth away

Emperor. I will let my *dreams* decide his punishment. Now, take him away! And remove that stone from the Celestial Palace!

150 **Narrator 4.** Chan Lo was dragged down many flights of stairs and thrown into a black prison cell. The carving was placed outside, near the reeds of the reflecting pool.

F

Narrator 2. That evening, the emperor thought about dragons.

Narrator 3. But late that night, in his sleep, the emperor dreamed of fish playfully slapping their tails in green water.

Stone. Pah-tah. Pah-tah.

Stone and Emperor. Pah-*tah*.

160 **Narrator 1.** In the morning, the emperor's advisers asked,

Adviser 1. What punishment have you chosen?

Narrator 4. But the emperor said,

Emperor. My dreams have not yet decided.

Narrator 2. That evening, the emperor again tried to think about dragons.

Narrator 3. But when he went to bed, the emperor dreamed of fish gliding smoothly through deep, clear water.

Stone. Bub-bub-bubble. Bub-bub-bubble.

170 **Stone and Emperor.** Bub-bub-bubble.

Narrator 1. In the morning, the emperor's advisers again asked him,

E

Adviser 2. What punishment have your dreams chosen?

278 Unit 9 Making Adjustments

Narrator 4. But the emperor told them,

Emperor. My dreams have still not decided.

G

THINK IT THROUGH
How is the emperor now like Chan Lo?

FOCUS
The emperor has again delayed Chan Lo's punishment. Read to find out what he finally decides.

Narrator 2. On the third night, the emperor groaned and tossed in his sleep, but he did not dream.

Narrator 3. He awoke in the darkest hour of the night. A strange sound filled the room.

180 **Stone.** S-s-s-ah, S-s-s-s-s-ah, S-s-s-s-s-s-s-ah.

Narrator 1. The emperor got out of bed and went toward the sound. He hurried down the corridors, through the Great Hall, and out into the moonlit garden.

Narrator 4. There by the reflecting pool was the jade stone. Next to it stood the apprentice, running his fingers down the scales of the three carp fish.

Stone. S-s-s-ah, S-s-s-s-s-ah, S-s-s-s-s-s-s-ah.

Narrator 2. When the apprentice had gone,
190 the emperor sat near the pool and gazed at the jade stone. The shining scales of the jade carp glowed in the moonlight. The fishes' slippery bodies were reflected in the pool. They seemed ready to flick their tails and swim among the reeds.

REREAD
What do you think the emperor is thinking?

H

The Jade Stone 279

G **THINK IT THROUGH** How is the emperor now like Chan Lo? *(Instead of acting right away, he is waiting for an answer to come to him in his dreams.)* **compare and contrast**

H **REREAD** What do you think the emperor is thinking? *(He realizes that Chan Lo was right—the stone wanted to be fish and not a dragon.)* **making inferences**

E Why do you think the advisers keep asking if the emperor has decided on a punishment? *(They're jealous, or shallow, or anxious to see a punishment.)* **motive**

F **reflecting** Help students find out that *reflect*—the base word in *reflecting* and *reflected* (line 193)—comes from the Latin word *reflectere* (meaning "bend back"), and that *reflect* means "show back."

FOR ENGLISH LEARNERS

Help students understand the following expressions and idioms:

Line 149: many flights of stairs
Line 186: running his fingers down the scales
Line 194: flick their tails

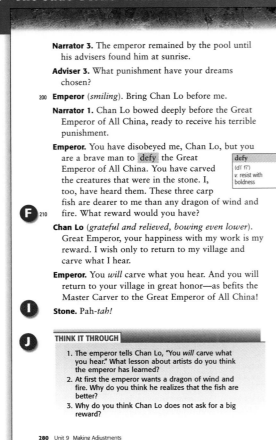

Narrator 3. The emperor remained by the pool until his advisers found him at sunrise.

Adviser 3. What punishment have your dreams chosen?

200 **Emperor** (*smiling*). Bring Chan Lo before me.

Narrator 1. Chan Lo bowed deeply before the Great Emperor of All China, ready to receive his terrible punishment.

Emperor. You have disobeyed me, Chan Lo, but you are a brave man to defy the Great Emperor of All China. You have carved the creatures that were in the stone. I, too, have heard them. These three carp fish are dearer to me than any dragon of wind and fire. What reward would you have?

defy
(dĭ fī')
v. resist with boldness

210 **Chan Lo** (*grateful and relieved, bowing even lower*). Great Emperor, your happiness with my work is my reward. I wish only to return to my village and carve what I hear.

Emperor. You *will* carve what you hear. And you will return to your village in great honor—as befits the Master Carver to the Great Emperor of All China!

Stone. Pah-*tah!*

THINK IT THROUGH

1. The emperor tells Chan Lo, "You *will* carve what you hear." What lesson about artists do you think the emperor has learned?
2. At first the emperor wants a dragon of wind and fire. Why do you think he realizes that the fish are better?
3. Why do you think Chan Lo does not ask for a big reward?

280 Unit 9 Making Adjustments

RELATED READING for THE JADE STONE

by Lucille Clifton

the carver
for fred

sees the man
in the wood and
calls his name and
the man in the wood
5 breaks through the bark and
the nations of wood call
the carver
Brother

The Jade Stone 281

COMPREHENSION

I Tell students to think back to the predictions they made while reading and tell which matched what actually happened. **predicting**

J THINK IT THROUGH

1. The emperor tells Chan Lo, "You *will* carve what you hear." What lesson about artists do you think the emperor has learned? *(By following their heart and their inspiration, artists create their best work.)* **theme** LITERATURE

2. At first the emperor wants a dragon of wind and fire. Why do you think he realizes that the fish are better? *(He dreams of the fish himself. He also sees them in his garden and probably realizes they are better for that setting than a dragon.)* **making inferences**

3. Why do you think Chan Lo does not ask for a big reward? *(Possible answer: He is more interested in having the freedom to create his art*

than he is in having lots of money.) **drawing conclusions**

Option for Speaking and Listening Have students practice reading sections of the play aloud, encouraging them to work on making the narrators' words follow the other characters' words fluently.

RETEACHING

If students need more help understanding **Predicting,** use pages T653–T655.

LITERATURE

F How does the emperor resolve his internal conflict? *(He listens to his dreams and resolves that Chan Lo was right; he rewards Chan Lo instead of punishing him.)* **conflict**

RELATED READING

Explain that the title of the poem is also its first line, so the poem actually begins, "the carver / sees the man / in the wood. . . . "

1. Who is the "man in the wood"? *(Possible answer: the spirit of the material to be carved)* **making inferences**

2. Why do you think the nations of wood call the carver Brother? *(They know that he loves and respects them as if they were part of his family.)* **making inferences**

3. How are Chan Lo and the carver alike? *(Both Chan Lo and the carver respect the material they carve and ask permission to carve it.)* **compare and contrast**

1. COMPREHENSION

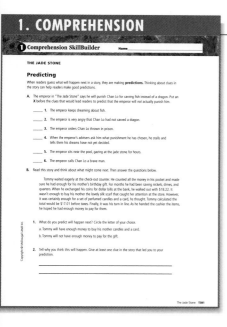

Predicting

Direct Instruction Tell students that **predicting** means guessing what might happen next by examining the clues in the story. Making predictions helps readers think about the story and remember it better, even if their predictions turn out to be wrong. Encourage the students to look for the following clues:

Characters: What do you know about the characters? How have these characters behaved so far in the story?

Setting: What do you know about the time and place of the story? What outcome would make sense in that setting?

Plot: What has happened in the story so far? What would be the next logical event?

Mood: What mood has the writer created in the story? Is it serious or humorous? What event would keep the same mood? For example, in "The Jade Stone," which has a serious mood, it would not make sense to predict that the emperor would start telling jokes.

> **Comprehension SkillBuilder Answer Key:**
>
> **A.** *1, 4, 5, 6*
>
> **B. 1.** *b*
> **2.** *(Wording will vary.) Possible responses: Tommy is worried that he may not have enough money. The total cost with taxes may be more than $18.22.*

2. LITERATURE

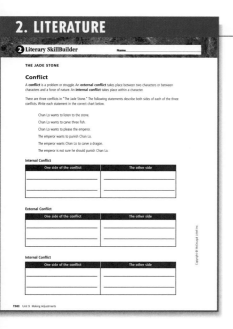

Conflict

Direct Instruction Remind students that characters in every story face some kind of struggle or problem. This struggle is called **conflict.** There are two types of conflicts—external and internal. An **external conflict** takes place between two characters or between a character and a force of nature. An **internal conflict** takes place within a character and often involves a difficult decision the character must make. Point out that many stories have several conflicts, both external and internal.

Discuss the last few stories that the class has read, asking the students to name the characters, the conflicts they face, and whether the conflicts are external or internal.

> **Literary SkillBuilder Answer Key:**
>
> *(Order of Internal Conflicts may vary; order of statements within each chart may vary.)*
>
> **Internal Conflict:** *Chan Lo wants to listen to the stone.* **AND** *Chan Lo wants to please the emperor.*
>
> **External Conflict:** *The emperor wants Chan Lo to carve a dragon.* **AND** *Chan Lo wants to carve three fish.*
>
> **Internal Conflict:** *The emperor wants to punish Chan Lo.* **AND** *The emperor is not sure he should punish Chan Lo.*

3. VOCABULARY

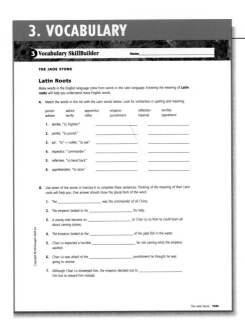

Latin Roots

Direct Instruction Tell students that many words in English have **Latin roots;** in other words, many words in the English language are based on words in the Latin language. The meanings of the English words are related to the meanings of the Latin words. Write the following English words from "The Jade Stone" and Latin words on the board.

English word	Latin word	Meaning of Latin word
celestial	caelum	sky
curious	cūriōsus	inquisitive, careful

Discuss how the meanings of the English words are related to the meanings of the Latin words. Also point out that the spelling of the English and Latin words are similar.

Point out to the students that once they know the meaning of a root, they can look for that root in words whose meanings they do not know. Knowing Latin roots often helps unlock the meaning of English words.

Vocabulary SkillBuilder Answer Key:

A.
1. *terrify, terrible*
2. *punish, punishment*
3. *advice, adviser*
4. *emperor, imperial*
5. *reflection, reflex*
6. *apprehend, apprentice*

B.
1. *emperor*
2. *advisers*
3. *apprentice*
4. *reflection*
5. *punishment*
6. *terrible*
7. *punish*

4. WORDS TO KNOW

Words to Know

Direct Instruction As you introduce the **Words to Know,** here are some points you might want to cover.
- **apprentice** Especially in the past, young people learned a trade by becoming an apprentice to a craftsman. This is still done in some fields, such as plumbing.

- **entangle** can also mean "to complicate; confuse"
- **defy**, from the Latin *dis-* ("not") + *fīdus* ("faithful") = "not faithful"

Writing Activity Encourage students to be creative. Have volunteers read their creations aloud.

Words to Know SkillBuilder Answer Key:

A.	**B.**	**C.**
1. *entangled*	1. *b*	1. *c*
2. *apprentice*	2. *c*	2. *a*
3. *defy*	3. *a*	3. *b*

5. SELECTION TEST

Selection Test Answer Key:
A. **1.** *China* **2.** *carvings* **3.** *listened* **4.** *jade* **5.** *dragon*
   6. *year* **7.** *fish* **8.** *punishment* **9.** *right*
B. *He accepted that Chan Lo carved what he heard and let him return to his village with honor.*

THE JADE STONE

Predicting

When readers guess what will happen next in a story, they are making **predictions.** Thinking about clues in the story can help readers make good predictions.

A. The emperor in "The Jade Stone" says he will punish Chan Lo for carving fish instead of a dragon. Put an **X** before the clues that would lead readers to predict that the emperor will *not* actually punish him.

_____ **1.** The emperor keeps dreaming about fish.

_____ **2.** The emperor is very angry that Chan Lo had not carved a dragon.

_____ **3.** The emperor orders Chan Lo thrown in prison.

_____ **4.** When the emperor's advisers ask him what punishment he has chosen, he stalls and tells them his dreams have not yet decided.

_____ **5.** The emperor sits near the pool, gazing at the jade stone for hours.

_____ **6.** The emperor calls Chan Lo a brave man.

B. Read this story and think about what might come next. Then answer the questions below.

Tommy waited eagerly at the check-out counter. He counted all the money in his pocket and made sure he had enough for his mother's birthday gift. For months he had been saving nickels, dimes, and quarters. When he exchanged his coins for dollar bills at the bank, he walked out with $18.22. It wasn't enough to buy his mother the lovely silk scarf that caught her attention at the store. However, it was certainly enough for a set of perfumed candles and a card, he thought. Tommy calculated the total would be $17.01 before taxes. Finally, it was his turn in line. As he handed the cashier the items, he hoped he had enough money to pay for them.

1. What do you predict will happen next? Circle the letter of your choice.

a. Tommy will have enough money to buy his mother candles and a card.

b. Tommy will not have enough money to pay for the gift.

2. Tell why you think this will happen. Give at least one clue in the story that led you to your prediction.

_____

_____

THE JADE STONE

Conflict

A **conflict** is a problem or struggle. An **external conflict** takes place between two characters or between characters and a force of nature. An **internal conflict** takes place within a character.

There are three conflicts in "The Jade Stone." The following statements describe both sides of each of the three conflicts. Write each statement in the correct chart below.

Chan Lo wants to listen to the stone.

Chan Lo wants to carve three fish.

Chan Lo wants to please the emperor.

The emperor wants to punish Chan Lo.

The emperor wants Chan Lo to carve a dragon.

The emperor is not sure he should punish Chan Lo.

Internal Conflict

One side of the conflict	The other side

External Conflict

One side of the conflict	The other side

Internal Conflict

One side of the conflict	The other side

THE JADE STONE

Latin Roots

Many words in the English language come from words in the Latin language. Knowing the meaning of **Latin roots** will help you understand many English words.

A. Match the words in this list with the Latin words below. Look for similarities in spelling and meaning.

punish	advice	apprentice	emperor	reflection	terrible
adviser	terrify	reflex	punishment	imperial	apprehend

1. *terrēre,* "to frighten"   _____   _____

2. *pūnīre,* "to punish"   _____   _____

3. *ad-,* "to" + *vidēre,* "to see"   _____   _____

4. *imperātor,* "commander"   _____   _____

5. *reflectere,* "to bend back"   _____   _____

6. *apprehendere,* "to seize"   _____   _____

B. Use seven of the words in Exercise A to complete these sentences. Thinking of the meaning of their Latin roots will help you. One answer should show the plural form of the word.

1. The _____ was the commander of all China.

2. The emperor looked to his _____ for help.

3. A young man became an _____ to Chan Lo so that he could learn all about carving stones.

4. The emperor looked at the _____ of the jade fish in the water.

5. Chan Lo expected a horrible _____ for not carving what the emperor wanted.

6. Chan Lo was afraid of the _____ punishment he thought he was going to receive.

7. Although Chan Lo disobeyed him, the emperor decided not to _____ him but to reward him instead.

THE JADE STONE

Words to Know

apprentice   entangled   defy

A. Fill in the blanks with a word from the list above that best completes the sentence.

1. I couldn't say a word—it was as if my tongue had become _____.

2. I wanted to learn the work, so I became an _____ in the shop.

3. It's not a good idea to _____ my father's orders.

B. Match the word with its correct definition.

_____ **1.** apprentice   a. resist with boldness

_____ **2.** entangled   b. one who is learning a job

_____ **3.** defy   c. twisted together

C. Circle the word or phrase that is most similar to the **boldfaced** word.

1. The cranky old man yelled at the **apprentice** after he dropped the instrument.

    a. veteran   b. boss   c. beginner

2. Soon I found myself **entangled** in the wires, unable to move.

    a. twisted   b. loose   c. asleep

3. I **defy** the advice of my friends and do just what I want to.

    a. obey   b. resist   c. respect

Writing Activity

Write a couple of sentences about something you've done that you're especially proud of. Use at least one of the **Words to Know.**

THE JADE STONE

A. Complete each statement with a word from the list below. One of the choices is not an answer.

jade	listened	fish	right	dragon
China	carvings	honored	punishment	year

1. Long ago in _____ there lived an artist named Chan Lo.

2. People came from near and far to buy Chan Lo's stone _____.

3. When asked how he knew what to create, Chan Lo said he always _____ to the stone.

4. The emperor gave Chan Lo a beautiful piece of green and white _____.

5. He told Chan Lo to carve him a _____ of wind and fire.

6. Chan Lo worked on the stone for a _____ and a day.

7. But when he showed his carving to the emperor, it was three _____ instead.

8. The emperor was so angry that he said he'd let his dreams decide Chan Lo's

    _____.

9. But his dreams told him that Chan Lo had been _____.

B. In your own words, tell what the emperor did instead of punishing Chan Lo.

_____

_____

Focus Skills

COMPREHENSION
Making Judgments

LITERATURE
Theme

VOCABULARY
Multiple-Meaning Words

SkillBuilder Copymasters

 Reading Comprehension:
1 Making Judgments p. T395

 Literary Analysis:
2 Theme p. T396

 Vocabulary:
3 Multiple-Meaning Words
p. T397
4 Words to Know p. T398

Assessment

 5 Selection Test p. T399

Readability Scores

DRP	LEXILE	DALE-CHALL
50	510	4.2

For English Learners

Students may wonder or question how a party can be stolen. Explain to them that the meaning behind the title has a great significance to the main character in this short story. As students read, tell them to think about the way the title can be interpreted. Point out that the title can mean something different to each reader. At the end of the story, ask them if the title fits the selection.

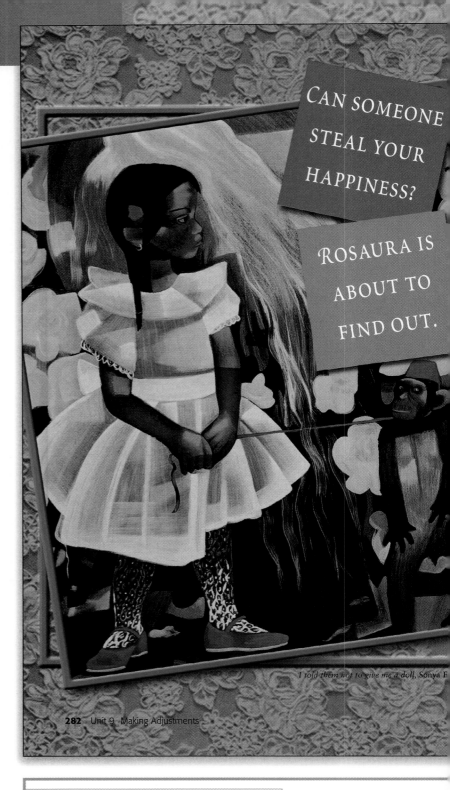

CAN SOMEONE STEAL YOUR HAPPINESS?

ROSAURA IS ABOUT TO FIND OUT.

I told them not to give me a doll, Sonya F

282 Unit 9 Making Adjustments

Vocabulary Strategy: Preteaching

Multiple-Meaning Words Tell students that a single word can have more than one meaning. For example, the word *bridge* can mean "structure built over water" or "game played with cards" or "upper part of the nose." To figure out which meaning an author is using, students must use context. To illustrate, you can use *cross,* a multiple-meaning word found in "The Stolen Party."

The STOLEN PARTY

by *Liliana Heker*
translated by *Alberto Manguel*

Connect to Your Life

Has someone ever believed something about you because of how you dressed or where you were born? What did he or she think? How did you feel about it?

Key to the Story

This story takes place in Argentina. In the past there were only two classes of people in that country—the rich and the poor. Poor people often worked as servants for the rich. The rich did not mix with the poor. The two groups lived very separate lives. In "The Stolen Party," a poor girl, Rosaura, believes that she and a girl from a rich family are friends.

Vocabulary Preview

Words to Know

approve   employee
offended   compliment
boisterous

💿 **Reading Coach CD-ROM selection**

The Stolen Party **283**

Connect to Your Life

Before students discuss what someone believed about them and how it made them feel, remind them to recall positive as well as negative situations. Did students do anything to try to change or encourage the other person's way of thinking? Why or why not?

Key to the Story

As students read this story, tell them to look for ways in which Rosaura is treated differently because she is poor.

Vocabulary Preview

Words to Know
  approve *v.* think to be right or good
  offended *v.* hurt
  boisterous *adj.* active and noisy
  employee *n.* person who works for pay
  compliment *n.* words of praise

 For direct instruction on Words to Know, see page T394.

Building Background

Because "The Stolen Party" was translated from Spanish into English, it may contain some unfamiliar words and phrases. Tell students that the title *Señora* refers to a married woman and is equal to *Mrs.* If necessary, help students pronounce the names *Luciana* (lōō syä' nä), *Rosaura* (rō sou' rä), and *Herminia* (ĕr mē' nyä), and explain that the phrase *get away with you* means "don't be ridiculous."

Read these sentences aloud. Then ask what *cross* means in each one.

1. On our trip to San Francisco, we got to <u>cross</u> the Golden Gate Bridge in our car.
2. Anita has been in a very <u>cross</u> mood since her fight with Carla.
3. For Aldo's birthday, his mother gave him a gold <u>cross</u> and a chain to wear it on.

 For more on Multiple-Meaning Words, see page T394.

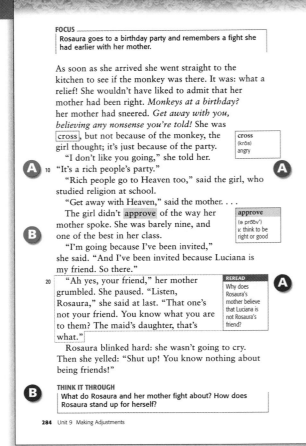

FOCUS

Rosaura goes to a birthday party and remembers a fight she had earlier with her mother.

As soon as she arrived she went straight to the kitchen to see if the monkey was there. It was: what a relief! She wouldn't have liked to admit that her mother had been right. *Monkeys at a birthday?* her mother had sneered. *Get away with you, believing any nonsense you're told!* She was cross, but not because of the monkey, the girl thought; it's just because of the party.

> **cross**
> (krôs)
> angry

"I don't like you going," she told her.

10 "It's a rich people's party."

"Rich people go to Heaven too," said the girl, who studied religion at school.

"Get away with Heaven," said the mother. . . .

The girl didn't approve of the way her mother spoke. She was barely nine, and one of the best in her class.

> **approve**
> (ə prōōv′)
> v. think to be right or good

"I'm going because I've been invited," she said. "And I've been invited because Luciana is my friend. So there."

20 "Ah yes, your friend," her mother grumbled. She paused. "Listen, Rosaura," she said at last. "That one's not your friend. You know what you are to them? The maid's daughter, that's what."

> **REREAD**
> Why does Rosaura's mother believe that Luciana is not Rosaura's friend?

Rosaura blinked hard: she wasn't going to cry. Then she yelled: "Shut up! You know nothing about being friends!"

THINK IT THROUGH

What do Rosaura and her mother fight about? How does Rosaura stand up for herself?

284 Unit 9 Making Adjustments

FOCUS

Read to learn why Rosaura believes she and Luciana are friends.

30 Every afternoon she used to go to Luciana's house and they would both finish their homework while Rosaura's mother did the cleaning. They had their tea in the kitchen and they told each other secrets. Rosaura loved everything in the big house, and she also loved the people who lived there.

"I'm going because it will be the most lovely party in the whole world, Luciana told me it would. There will be a magician, and he will bring a monkey and everything."

The mother swung around to take a 40 good look at her child, and pompously put her hands on her hips.

> **pompously**
> (pŏm′ pəs lē)
> with too much pride

"Monkeys at a birthday?" she said. "Get away with you, believing any nonsense you're told!"

Rosaura was deeply offended. She thought it unfair of her mother to accuse other people of being liars simply because they were rich. Rosaura too wanted to be rich, of course. If one day 50 she managed to live in a beautiful palace, would her mother stop loving her? She felt very sad. She wanted to go to that party more than anything else in the world.

> **offended**
> (ə fĕn′ dĭd)
> v. hurt; past tense of *offend*

> **REREAD**
> What conflict is going on inside Rosaura?

"I'll die if I don't go," she whispered, almost without moving her lips.

And she wasn't sure whether she had been heard, but on the morning of the party she discovered that her mother had starched her Christmas dress. And in the afternoon, after washing her hair, her mother

The Stolen Party 285

COMPREHENSION

FOCUS SKILL: Making Judgments

Tell students that when they read, they must use clues from the story as well as their own knowledge and opinions in order to **make judgments,** or decisions, about whether something is accurate or inaccurate, true or false, or right or wrong.

 For direct instruction on Making Judgments, see page T393.

A REREAD Why does Rosaura's mother believe that Luciana is not Rosaura's friend? *(because Luciana is rich and Rosaura is poor, and the two classes don't mix)* **making inferences**

B THINK IT THROUGH What do Rosaura and her mother fight about? How does Rosaura stand up for herself? *(whether or not Luciana is Rosaura's friend; Rosaura yells at her mother and tells her she knows nothing about being friends)* **making judgments**

C REREAD What conflict is going on inside Rosaura? *(Rosaura feels that her mother is against rich people and may someday dislike her if she becomes rich.)* **making inferences**

LITERATURE

FOCUS SKILL: Theme

Remind students that the **theme** of a story is an author's message about life or human nature. Sometimes a theme is stated outright. At other times, however, students must infer the theme, based on what the characters think, feel, say, and do.

 For direct instruction on Theme, see page T393.

Use questions such as the following to encourage literary analysis.

A Why do you think Rosaura's mother is trying to discourage her daughter from going to the party? *(Rosaura's mother is well aware of the class system; she might be trying to save Rosaura from being hurt when she's treated differently at the party.)* **motive**

VOCABULARY

FOCUS SKILL: Multiple-Meaning Words

As students come across the multiple-meaning words in this story, remind them to use context clues to figure out which meaning the author is using.

A rich Have students come up with at least one other meaning than the one used in this story (e.g., "having a strong aroma," "warm and strong in color").

B class Have students come up with at least one other meaning than the one used in this story (e.g., "a kind or category," "social rank").

FOR ENGLISH LEARNERS

Help students understand the following expressions and idioms:

Line 5: sneered
Line 58: starched

I told them not to give me a doll, Sonya Fe.

60 rinsed it in apple vinegar so that it would be all nice and shiny. Before going out, Rosaura admired herself in the mirror, with her white dress and glossy hair, and thought she looked terribly pretty.

THINK IT THROUGH

D How does Rosaura feel about Luciana and her family? about other rich people?

FOCUS

Read to learn how Luciana's family treats Rosaura at the party.

Señora Ines also seemed to notice. As soon as she saw her, she said:

> **Señora Ines**
> (sĕ nyō' rä ē nĕs')
> Mrs. Ines,
> Luciana's mother

"How lovely you look today, Rosaura."

Rosaura gave her starched skirt a slight toss with her hands and walked into the party with a firm step. She said hello to Luciana and asked about
70 the monkey. Luciana put on a secretive look and whispered into Rosaura's ear:

> **secretive**
> (sĕ' krĭ tĭv)
> not open; as if
> keeping a secret

"He's in the kitchen. But don't tell anyone, because it's a surprise."

Rosaura wanted to make sure. Carefully she entered the kitchen and there she saw it: deep in thought, inside its cage. It looked so funny that the girl stood there for a while, watching it, and later, every so

286 Unit 9 Making Adjustments

C often, she would slip out of the party unseen and go and admire it. Rosaura was the only one allowed into
80 the kitchen. Señora Ines had said: "You yes, but not the others, they're much too boisterous, they might break something." Rosaura had never broken anything. She even managed the jug of orange juice, carrying it from the kitchen into the dining-room. She held it carefully and didn't spill a single drop. And Señora Ines had said:

> **boisterous**
> (boi' stər əs)
> *adj.* active and
> noisy

D "Are you sure you can manage a jug as big as that?" Of course she could manage. She wasn't a butterfingers, like the others. Like that
90 blonde girl with the bow in her hair. As soon as she saw Rosaura, the girl with the bow had said:

> **butterfingers**
> (bŭt' ər fĭng' gərz)
> person who drops
> things

"And you? Who are you?"

"I'm a friend of Luciana," said Rosaura.

"No," said the girl with the bow, "you are not a friend of Luciana because I'm her cousin and I know all her friends. And I don't know you."

THINK IT THROUGH

E How does Señora Ines treat Rosaura?

FOCUS

Read to find out how Rosaura responds to Luciana's cousin.

"So what," said Rosaura. "I come here every afternoon with my mother and we do our homework together."
100 "You and your mother do your homework together?" asked the girl, laughing.

The Stolen Party 287

COMPREHENSION

D THINK IT THROUGH How does Rosaura feel about Luciana and her family? about other rich people? *(She loves Luciana and her family; she says, "Rich people go to Heaven too" and wants to be rich herself someday.)* **details**

E THINK IT THROUGH How does Señora Ines treat Rosaura? *(Señora Ines shows that she trusts Rosaura in the kitchen with the monkey and with the jug of orange juice. She also feels that Rosaura is not noisy like the others.)* **drawing conclusions**

VOCABULARY

C slip Have students use context clues to figure out the appropriate meaning of this word. Then have them come up with at least one other meaning (e.g., to lose one's balance; a slight error).

D drop Have students come up with at least one other meaning than the one used in this story (e.g., the act of falling; to descend from one level to another).

FOR ENGLISH LEARNERS

Help students understand the following expressions and idioms:

Line 63: terribly pretty
Line 75: deep in thought
Line 98: So what

"I and Luciana do our homework together," said Rosaura, very seriously.

The girl with the bow shrugged her shoulders.

"That's not being friends," she said. "Do you go to school together?"

"No."

"So where do you know her from?" said the girl, getting impatient.

110   Rosaura remembered her mother's words perfectly. She took a deep breath.

"I'm the daughter of the employee," she said.

Her mother had said very clearly: "If someone asks, you say you're the daughter of the employee; that's all." She also told her to add: "And proud of it." But Rosaura thought that never in her life would she dare say something of the sort.

120   "What employee?" said the girl with the bow. "Employee in a shop?"

"No," said Rosaura angrily. "My mother doesn't sell anything in any shop, so there."

"So how come she's an employee?" said the girl with the bow.

Just then Señora Ines arrived saying *shh shh*, and asked Rosaura if she wouldn't mind helping serve out the hot-dogs, as she knew the house so much better than the others.

130   "See?" said Rosaura to the girl with the bow, and when no one was looking she kicked her in the shin.

> **employee**
> (ĕm ploi' ē)
> *n.* person who works for pay

> **REREAD**
> Why does her mother tell Rosaura to say this?

THINK IT THROUGH
What reasons does Rosaura give to show that she and Luciana are friends? Why doesn't the cousin believe her?

FOCUS
Read to find out why Rosaura enjoys the party.

Apart from the girl with the bow, all the others were delightful. The one she liked best was Luciana, with her golden birthday crown; and then the boys. Rosaura won the sack race, and nobody managed to catch her when they played tag. When they split into two teams to play charades, all the boys wanted her for their side. Rosaura felt she had never been so happy in all her life.

140   But the best was still to come. The best came after Luciana blew out the candles. First the cake. Señora Ines had asked her to help pass the cake around, and Rosaura had enjoyed the task immensely, because everyone called out to her, shouting "Me, me!" Rosaura remembered a story in which there was a queen who had the power of life or death over her subjects. She had always loved that, having the power of life or death. To Luciana and the boys she gave the largest pieces, and to the

150 girl with the bow she gave a slice so thin one could see through it.

After the cake came the magician, tall and bony, with a fine red cape. A true magician: he could untie handkerchiefs by blowing on them and make a chain with links that had no openings. He could guess what cards were pulled out from a pack, and the monkey was his assistant. He called the monkey "partner." "Let's see here, partner," he would say, "Turn over a card." And, "Don't run away,

160 partner: time to work now."

The final trick was wonderful. One of the children had to hold the monkey in his arms and the magician said he would make him disappear.

> **charades**
> (shə rädz')
> a game in which people act out words or phrases and others try to guess them

> **REREAD**
> What do you think Rosaura likes about serving the cake?

COMPREHENSION

F **REREAD** Why does her mother tell Rosaura to say this? *(because she wants her daughter to be proud of her mother's job and not embarrassed by it)* **making inferences**

G **THINK IT THROUGH** What reasons does Rosaura give to show that she and Luciana are friends? Why doesn't the cousin believe her? *(Rosaura says they do their homework every afternoon and she knows the house better than the others. The cousin knows all of Luciana's friends but doesn't know Rosaura; she says that doing homework together isn't being friends.)* **details**

H **REREAD** What do you think Rosaura likes about serving the cake? *(She likes that it gives her power over the others.)* **making inferences**

LITERATURE

B How do you think Rosaura feels about being "the daughter of the employee"? *(She does not seem embarrassed by it; she probably doesn't think it matters; otherwise she would not have mentioned it to the girl.)* **theme**

VOCABULARY

E **subjects** Have students use context clues to figure out the appropriate meaning of this word. Then have them come up with at least one other meaning (e.g., a course of study; the persons or things being described).

F **pack** Have students come up with at least one other meaning than the one used in this story (e.g., a bundle arranged for carrying, especially on the back of a person).

FOR ENGLISH LEARNERS

Help students understand the following expressions and idioms:

Line 132: apart from the girl with the bow

Line 135: sack race

"What, the boy?" they all shouted.

"No, the monkey!" shouted back the magician.

170 Rosaura thought that this was truly the most amusing party in the whole world.

The magician asked a small fat boy to come and help, but the small fat boy got frightened almost at once and dropped the monkey on the floor. The magician picked him up carefully, whispered 180 something in his ear, and the monkey nodded almost as if he understood.

"You mustn't be so unmanly, my friend," the magician said to the fat boy.

"What's unmanly?" said the fat boy.

The magician turned around as if to look for spies.

"A sissy," said the magician. "Go sit down."

Then he stared at all the faces, one by one. Rosaura felt her heart tremble.

"You, with the Spanish eyes," said the magician.

190 And everyone saw that he was pointing at her.

I told them not to give me a doll, Sonya Fe.

 THINK IT THROUGH
What happens to make Rosaura feel she is special?

290 Unit 9 Making Adjustments

Read to learn what Rosaura tells her mother about the party.

She wasn't afraid. Neither holding the monkey, nor when the magician made him vanish; not even when, at the end, the magician flung his red cape over Rosaura's head and uttered a few magic words . . . and the monkey reappeared, chattering happily, in her arms. The children clapped furiously. And before Rosaura returned to her seat, the magician said:

"Thank you very much, my little countess."

She was so pleased with the compliment 200 that a while later, when her mother came to fetch her, that was the first thing she told her.

"I helped the magician and he said to me, 'Thank you very much, my little countess.'"

It was strange because up to then Rosaura had thought that she was angry with her mother. All along Rosaura had imagined that she would say to her: "See that the monkey wasn't a lie?" But instead she was so thrilled that she told her mother all about the wonderful magician.

210 Her mother tapped her on the head and said: "So now we're a countess!"

But one could see that she was beaming.

And now they both stood in the entrance, because a moment ago Señora Ines, smiling, had said: "Please wait here a second."

Her mother suddenly seemed worried.

"What is it?" she asked Rosaura.

"What is what?" said Rosaura. "It's nothing; she just wants to get the presents for those who are leaving, see?"

countess
(koun' tĭs)
woman of noble rank

compliment
(kŏm' plə mənt)
n. words of praise

 THINK IT THROUGH
How does Rosaura feel toward her mother now? How does her mother react?

The Stolen Party 291

COMPREHENSION

I THINK IT THROUGH What happens to make Rosaura feel she is special? *(The magician picks her to help him with his trick.)* **cause and effect**

J THINK IT THROUGH How does Rosaura feel toward her mother now? How does her mother react? *(Rosaura isn't angry with her mother anymore. Her mother taps her on the head and beams at her; she seems happy and proud.)* **making inferences**

LITERATURE

C Why does Rosaura consider it such a compliment when the magician calls her "countess"? How is this compliment unusual for Rosaura? *(Countess is the title of a rich person from the upper class. It's unusual because it's the opposite of what Rosaura really is—but the magician doesn't know that.)* **theme**

VOCABULARY

G furiously Have students use context clues—and if necessary, a dictionary—to figure out the appropriate meaning of this word. Have students come up with at least one other meaning than the one used in this story (e.g., angrily; violently).

FOR ENGLISH LEARNERS

Help students understand the following expressions and idioms:

Line 188: felt her heart tremble
Line 210: tapped her on the head
Line 212: she was beaming

FOCUS

Learn what Rosaura hopes she will get from Señora Ines.

220 She pointed at the fat boy and at a girl with pigtails who were also waiting there, next to their mothers. And she explained about the presents. She knew, because she had been watching those who left before her. When one of the girls was about to leave, Señora Ines would give her a bracelet. When a boy left, Señora Ines gave him a yo-yo. Rosaura preferred the yo-yo because it sparkled, but she didn't mention that to her mother. Her mother might have said: "So why don't you ask for one, you blockhead?" That's

230 what her mother was like. Rosaura didn't feel like explaining that she'd be horribly ashamed to be the **odd one out**. Instead she said:

> **odd one out** person who is different from others in a group

"I was the best-behaved at the party."

And she said no more because Señora Ines came out into the hall with two bags, one pink and one blue.

First she went up to the fat boy, gave him a yo-yo out of the blue bag, and the fat boy left with his mother. Then she went up to the girl and gave her a

240 bracelet out of the pink bag, and the girl with the pigtails left as well.

Finally she came up to Rosaura and her mother. She had a big smile on her face and Rosaura liked that. Señora Ines looked down at her, then looked up at her mother, and then said something that made Rosaura proud:

"What a **marvelous** daughter you have, Herminia."

> **marvelous** (mär′ və ləs) wonderful

For an instant, Rosaura thought that

250 she'd give her two presents: the bracelet and the yo-yo. Señora Ines bent down as if about to look for

292 Unit 9 Making Adjustments

something. Rosaura also leaned forward, stretching out her arm. But she never completed the movement.

(L) Señora Ines didn't look in the pink bag. Nor did she look in the blue bag. Instead she rummaged in her purse. In her hand appeared two bills.

> **REREAD**
> What is Señora Ines paying Rosaura for?

(K)

"You really and truly earned this," she said handing them over. "Thank you for all your help, my pet."

260 Rosaura felt her arms stiffen, stick close to her body, and then she noticed her mother's hand on her shoulder. Instinctively she pressed herself against her mother's body. That was all. Except her eyes. Rosaura's eyes had a cold, clear look that fixed itself on Señora Ines's face.

(D) Señora Ines, motionless, stood there with her hand outstretched. As if she didn't dare draw it back. As if the slightest change might shatter an **infinitely delicate balance**.

> **infinitely delicate balance** something that can easily be disturbed

(M) **THINK IT THROUGH**

1. What does Rosaura expect to get? How does she feel about being offered money?
2. How do you think Rosaura happened to come to the party in the first place?
3. In what ways do you think this party changes Rosaura?

The Stolen Party 293

COMPREHENSION

(K) **REREAD** What is Señora Ines paying Rosaura for? *(helping her with the party)* **drawing conclusions**

(L) Ask: Do you think Señora Ines was wrong to give Rosaura money instead of a bracelet? *(Many students will say yes, that she was treating Rosaura as a servant and made her feel terrible. Others will say no, that she was just trying to be kind and didn't know she was going to hurt Rosaura.)* **making judgments**

(M) **THINK IT THROUGH**

1. What does Rosaura expect to get? How does she feel about being offered money? *(a bracelet; Possible feelings: shocked, embarrassed, offended, let down, betrayed)* **cause and effect**

2. How do you think Rosaura happened to come to the party in the first place? *(Possible answer: Luciana may have asked Rosaura as*

a friend without her mother's knowing it, and the mother then assumed she was there to help. Señora Ines may have asked Luciana to ask Rosaura to help at the party, but Luciana's invitation may not have mentioned helping. At any rate, Rosaura's appearance there seems to be the result of a misunderstanding.) **conflict** LITERATURE

3. In what ways do you think this party changes Rosaura? *(Possible answers: She might feel that her mother was right to think that Señora Ines and Luciana saw her only as the "maid's daughter." She might be disappointed in rich people and no longer want to be one of them.)* **making inferences**

LITERATURE

(D) In your opinion, what is the theme, or message, that the author is trying to communicate in this story? *(Possible answers:*

Sometimes the way we see ourselves is very different from the way others see us; regardless of what we're like inside, people often judge us by our circumstances.) **theme**

VOCABULARY

RETEACHING

If students need more help understanding **Multiple-meaning Words,** use pages T620–T621.

FOR ENGLISH LEARNERS

Help students understand the following expressions and idioms:

Line 220: pigtails
Line 229: blockhead
Line 255: rummaged

1. COMPREHENSION

Making Judgments

Direct Instruction Tell students that when they read, they bring their own values to the reading. Using their own ideas of right and wrong, they can decide if characters are good or bad, if events are right or wrong, if statements are true or not. This is called **making judgments.** If their judgments are based on details in the story, their opinions are valid.

Have a student read aloud the passage on page 290 that begins with "The magician asked a small fat boy to come and help" and ends with "'A sissy,' said the magician. 'Go sit down.'"

Ask the class: Do you think the magician was right or wrong to call the boy a sissy? Why? Accept judgments backed by reasons.

Comprehension SkillBuilder Answer Key:

(Opinions and answers may vary.)

Possible answers:

1. *disagree; I feel this way because she does not believe that the rich girl could be friends with Rosaura; does not believe Rosaura about the monkey.*

2. *agree; I feel this way because she thinks she is like a queen giving out the cake; kicks the girl for questioning her about Luciana.*

3. *agree; I feel this way because Rosaura comes to the party as a friend of Luciana's and should be treated the same as the other girls.*
   disagree; I feel this way because Rosaura helps serve at the party and should be rewarded for the extra work.

4. *disagree; I feel this way because when Señora Ines offers Rosaura money, she makes her feel that she has been invited to the party as a maid, not a guest, so the fun of the party is stolen from her.*

2. LITERATURE

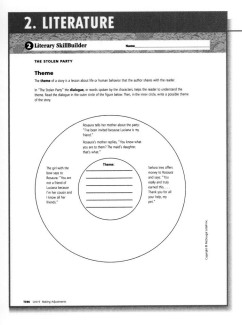

Theme

Direct Instruction Recall that the **theme** of a work of literature is a lesson or message about human life or behavior. Explain that the writer usually states the theme in an indirect way through the actions of the characters and events of the story. Note that sometimes the words spoken by the characters, or **dialogue,** are especially important in defining the theme. Students can ask themselves, "What lesson about life did the characters in the story learn?" Remind the students that the theme must be supported by facts and details in the story.

Literary SkillBuilder Answer Key:

Answers may vary. Some possible themes:

Sometimes appearances deceive people.

It's easy to misinterpret events if you look at them with a particular idea in mind.

People do not always have good intentions; you have to learn whom you can and can't trust.

3. VOCABULARY

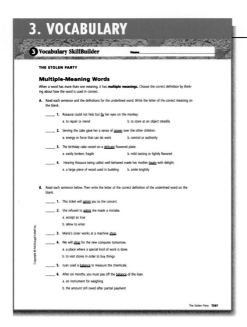

Multiple-Meaning Words

Direct Instruction Ask the students for the definition of *bank.* Elicit as many responses as possible. *(institution that deals in money; ground along riverside; to tilt, as an airplane; a heap; to cover [a fire] with ashes; place where reserves are kept; a set or row of things)* Note that the word has more than one meaning; that is, it has **multiple meanings.** Remind the class that good readers look at the context of the sentence to determine the meaning intended by the author. Write the following sentences on the board:

The pilot needed to <u>bank</u> the plane to avoid the treetops.

Take the money you earned and put it in the <u>bank.</u>

Discuss which definition fits *bank* best in each sentence.

Vocabulary SkillBuilder Answer Key:

A.
1. *b*
2. *b*
3. *a*
4. *b*

B.
1. *b*
2. *a*
3. *a*
4. *b*
5. *a*
6. *b*

4. WORDS TO KNOW

Words to Know

Direct Instruction Many students probably have not had exposure to analogies. Explain to students that analogies show relationships between pairs of words. Work together with students to complete the analogies in Exercise B. Try to elicit the relationship between the words in the first part of the analogy from students. If necessary help them:

1. A chef works in a restaurant just as an _____ works in a company.
2. *Quiet* and *silent* mean the same thing. What word means the same as *noisy?*
3. *Understand* and *misunderstand* are opposites. What is the opposite of *disapprove?*

Words to Know SkillBuilder Answer Key:

A.
1. *compliment*
2. *employee*
3. *offended*
4. *approve*
5. *boisterous*

B.
1. *employee*
2. *boisterous*
3. *approve*

C.
1. *complement* 2. *compliment*

5. SELECTION TEST

Selection Test Answer Key:
A. **1.** *birthday* **2.** *monkey* **3.** *friend* **4.** *maid's* **5.** *dress* **6.** *important* **7.** *magician* **8.** *presents* **9.** *money*
B. *Possible answer: Rosaura feels offended by the money.*

THE STOLEN PARTY

Making Judgments

When you **judge** an element of a story, such as a character or the character's actions, you decide whether you approve or disapprove. To make a fair judgment, you must not only think of how you feel. You must also find details in the story that support your judgment.

Read each statement below from "The Stolen Party" and circle **agree** or **disagree**. Then tell why you feel this way. Use a detail from the story to support your judgment.

1. Rosaura's mother is an open-minded person.   **agree**   **disagree**

   I feel this way because

   _____

   _____

   _____

2. Rosaura is too pleased with herself during the party.   **agree**   **disagree**

   I feel this way because

   _____

   _____

   _____

3. It is wrong for Señora Ines to offer money to Rosaura at the end of the party.   **agree**   **disagree**

   I feel this way because

   _____

   _____

   _____

4. The title of this story doesn't fit the story.   **agree**   **disagree**

   I feel this way because

   _____

   _____

   _____

THE STOLEN PARTY

Theme

The **theme** of a story is a lesson about life or human behavior that the author shares with the reader.

In "The Stolen Party" the **dialogue,** or words spoken by the characters, helps the reader to understand the theme. Read the dialogue in the outer circle of the figure below. Then, in the inner circle, write a possible theme of the story.

Rosaura tells her mother about the party: "I've been invited because Luciana is my friend."

Rosaura's mother replies, "You know what you are to them? The maid's daughter, that's what."

Theme:

_____

_____

_____

_____

_____

The girl with the bow says to Rosaura: "You are not a friend of Luciana because I'm her cousin and I know all her friends."

Señora Ines offers money to Rosaura and says: "You really and truly earned this. . . . Thank you for all your help, my pet."

THE STOLEN PARTY

Multiple-Meaning Words

When a word has more than one meaning, it has **multiple meanings.** Choose the correct definition by thinking about how the word is used in context.

A. Read each sentence and the definitions for the underlined word. Write the letter of the correct meaning on the blank.

_____ **1.** Rosaura could not help but <u>fix</u> her eyes on the monkey.

  a. to repair or mend   b. to stare at an object steadily

_____ **2.** Serving the cake gave her a sense of <u>power</u> over the other children.

  a. energy or force that can do work   b. control or authority

_____ **3.** The birthday cake rested on a <u>delicate</u> flowered plate.

  a. easily broken; fragile   b. mild tasting or lightly flavored

_____ **4.** Hearing Rosaura being called well-behaved made her mother <u>beam</u> with delight.

  a. a large piece of wood used in building   b. smile brightly

B. Read each sentence below. Then write the letter of the correct definition of the underlined word on the blank.

_____ **1.** This ticket will <u>admit</u> you to the concert.

_____ **2.** She refused to <u>admit</u> she made a mistake.

  a. accept as true

  b. allow to enter

_____ **3.** Maria's sister works at a machine <u>shop</u>.

_____ **4.** We will <u>shop</u> for the new computer tomorrow.

  a. a place where a special kind of work is done

  b. to visit stores in order to buy things

_____ **5.** Juan used a <u>balance</u> to measure the chemicals.

_____ **6.** After six months, you must pay off the <u>balance</u> of the loan.

  a. an instrument for weighing

  b. the amount still owed after partial payment

THE STOLEN PARTY

Words to Know

approve   employee   compliment   offended   boisterous

A. Fill in the blanks with the word from the list that best completes the sentence.

1. Natalie received a _____ from the teacher on her research paper.

2. I was hired as an _____ of the local grocery store.

3. Jackson was _____ by the hurtful remarks made by his friends.

4. My grandmother did not _____ of my new hair color.

5. Nikki tried to calm the _____ kids she babysat by giving them ice cream.

B. **Analogies** An analogy shows a relationship between words:

poodle : dog :: goldfish : fish

A poodle **is to** a dog **as a** goldfish **is to** a fish.

A poodle is a type of dog; a goldfish is a type of fish.

To complete an analogy, look at the first pair of words and decide how they are related. Then find a word that relates to the word in the second part in the same way.

Use a word from the **Words to Know** list above to fill in the analogies below.

1. chef : restaurant :: _____ : company

2. quiet: silent :: noisy: _____

3. understand: misunderstand :: _____ : disapprove

C. **Homophones** are words that sound alike but have different spellings and definitions. For example:

compliment (noun) words of praise, admiration, or congratulations

complement (noun) something that completes or fills; makes a whole

Fill in the blanks with the correct homophone.

1. A soda or drink will _____ a large, thin-crust pizza.

2. The doctor gave me a _____ on my recovery.

THE STOLEN PARTY

A. Complete the paragraph below by filling in each blank with the appropriate word from the list.

dress	important	stared	birthday	presents
monkey	friend	maid's	money	magician

Rosaura is invited to a **(1)** _____ party at Luciana's house. She is very excited

about going. She tells her mother that there will be a **(2)** _____

at the party, but her mother doesn't believe her. She tells Rosaura that she shouldn't go to the party

because she is not Luciana's **(3)** _____. She says that Rosaura is nothing more

to Luciana's family than the **(4)** _____ daughter. In spite of her feelings,

Rosaura's mother starches Rosaura's **(5)** _____ and helps her get ready for the

party. Rosaura feels very **(6)** _____ at the party as she carries the juice and

passes out the cake. She even gets to help the **(7)** _____, who calls her

his little countess. At the end of the party, Rosaura waits while Señora Ines gets the

(8) _____. But instead of giving her what she gives the other girls, she gives

Rosaura some **(9)** _____. Rosaura doesn't accept what Señora Ines offers.

B. In your own words, tell how Rosaura reacts to what Señora Ines tries to give her.

_____

_____

Focus Skills

COMPREHENSION
Cause and Effect
Author's Purpose

LITERATURE
Informative Article

VOCABULARY
Context Clues

SkillBuilder Copymasters

 Reading Comprehension:
1 Cause and Effect p. T408
2 Author's Purpose p. T409

 Vocabulary:
3 Context Clues p. T410
4 Words to Know p. T411

Assessment

 5 Selection Test p. T412

Readability Scores

DRP	LEXILE	DALE-CHALL
56	850	5.8

Reading Fluency

 ★ Reading Fluency p. T413

For English Learners

Many of the sentences in this selection begin with phrases or dependent clauses. If necessary, read a section of the selection aloud and show students how they can invert the sentences in order to understand them. For example, the first sentence can be changed to *Jane observed chimps from the mountain peak for nearly two months.*

ACCEPTANCE

BY J. A. SENN

"I think I expected to be torn to pieces," Jane Goodall once said. This animal watcher has faced dangers. Discover why she took such risks.

294 Unit 9 Making Adjustments

Vocabulary Strategy: Preteaching

Context Clues Remind students that when they come to a word they don't know, they can often figure it out by looking at the context clues surrounding it. Write the sentences shown on the next page on the board, and have students tell you the meaning of each underlined word. Then have them tell you which context clues helped them figure out the meaning.

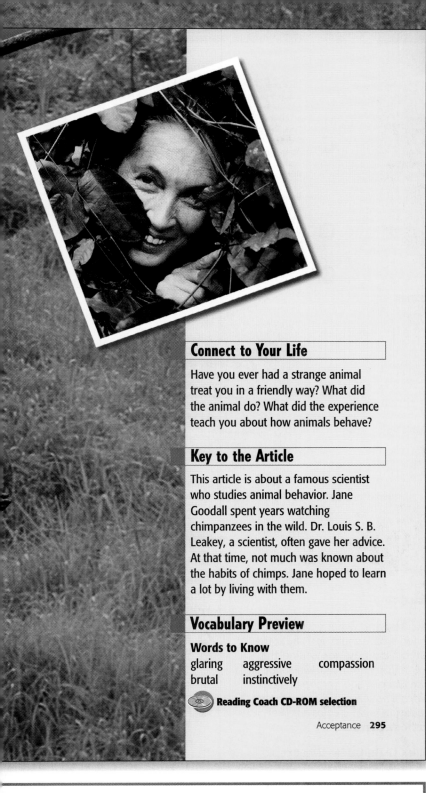

Connect to Your Life

Have you ever had a strange animal treat you in a friendly way? What did the animal do? What did the experience teach you about how animals behave?

Key to the Article

This article is about a famous scientist who studies animal behavior. Jane Goodall spent years watching chimpanzees in the wild. Dr. Louis S. B. Leakey, a scientist, often gave her advice. At that time, not much was known about the habits of chimps. Jane hoped to learn a lot by living with them.

Vocabulary Preview

Words to Know

glaring	aggressive	compassion
brutal	instinctively	

 Reading Coach CD-ROM selection

Acceptance **295**

Connect to Your Life

Guide students in a discussion of animals that treated them in a friendly way. How did they feel about what was happening? Did their encounter change their feelings about the animals?

Key to the Article

To set a purpose for reading, have students tell whether the statements in this **anticipatory guide** are true or false. Then have them revisit the questions when they've read the article.
1. The chimpanzee population is increasing.
2. Chimpanzees eat fruit and nuts.
3. Chimpanzees never attack unless they are attacked first.

See page T405 for after-reading follow-up.

Vocabulary Preview

Words to Know
glaring *adj.* staring in anger
brutal *adj.* extremely rough
aggressive *adj.* forceful
instinctively *adv.* by natural action; without thinking
compassion *n.* concern for the suffering of others

For direct instruction on Words to Know, see page T407.

Building Background

Jane Goodall was born in London in 1934. She left school at the age of 18 and worked various jobs until she could pay her way to Africa. (She later earned a Ph.D. from Cambridge University.) In 1960 she set up a camp in the Gombe Stream Game Reserve in Tanzania and began a 40-year study of the local chimpanzees. This now-famous study became the longest continuous study of any animal in the world. Through her observations, Goodall learned that rather than being vegetarians as scientists had previously thought, chimps ate animals as well. She also learned that chimps make and use tools, and that they have social behaviors that are quite similar to humans', including love, compassion, and even a sense of humor.

---

1. Jane needed to <u>broaden</u> her work with the chimpanzees. Instead of just focusing on the chimps in Gombe, she began working with chimps all around the world.
2. Jane is trying to help save the world's <u>dwindling</u> chimpanzee population, which has dropped to only 175,000.

For more on Context Clues, see page T407.

FOCUS
Jane Goodall gets ready to watch chimps in the wild. Find out what happens.

For nearly two months, Jane observed chimps from the mountain peak. Then she slowly and cautiously moved down the mountain to be closer to them. Soon she noticed that the chimps were more curious about her than they were afraid. But that curiosity quickly turned to unmistakable boldness. Instead of running away like before, they would climb into the trees, rock the branches, and stare at her in silence. This went on for several months.

The Excitement of Danger

10 At one time during those months, Jane decided to follow a group of chimpanzees through a thick part of the forest. As she stopped to get her bearings, she heard a branch snap right beside her. As she swung around, she saw a young chimp sitting in a tree almost directly over her head. Then she saw two females nearby. Suddenly she realized that chimps were all around her—she was surrounded!

 A

REREAD
How do you think Jane feels during this first meeting? **A**

Jane sat down and tried to remain still.
20 Then she heard a low "huh" sound in the thick vegetation to her right. Soon another "huh" came from behind her, and another from in front of her. These nervous chimpanzee calls continued for approximately 10 minutes. But Jane would only occasionally catch a glimpse of a large hand or a pair of glaring eyes.

vegetation
(vĕj′ ĭ tā′ shən)
plant growth

Suddenly the calls grew louder, until the chimps were almost screaming. Then six

glaring
(glâr′ ĭng)
adj. staring in anger

296 Unit 9 Making Adjustments

30 large males rushed out of their hiding places. As each chimp became excited, he shook nearby tree branches and snapped off twigs. One chimp, named Goliath for his great size and strength, even climbed on a bush near Jane. She could see his hair standing on end as he wildly swayed back and forth. At one point, she thought he was going to land on top of her. Jane later confessed, "I think I expected to be torn to pieces."

B **B**

REREAD
Try to picture what is happening to Jane.

40 Then, just as quickly as this display of anger had begun, it ended. Quietly, the males joined the females and their young and left. Years later, Jane wrote, "My knees were shaking when I got up. But there was the sense of excitement that comes when danger has come and left one unharmed. And the chimpanzees were surely less afraid of me now."

C

THINK IT THROUGH
What could have happened to Jane?

D

"I THINK I EXPECTED TO BE TORN TO PIECES."
-JANE GOODALL

Acceptance 297

COMPREHENSION

FOCUS SKILL 1: Cause and Effect

Remind students that they can identify the **causes** and **effects** in this article by asking, What happened? and What caused it to happen?

 For direct instruction on Cause and Effect, see page T406.

FOCUS SKILL 2: Author's Purpose

Tell students that an **author's purpose** is his or her reason or reasons for writing something. Those reasons are usually to entertain, persuade, inform, and/or express an opinion.

For direct instruction on Author's Purpose, see page T406.

A **REREAD** How do you think Jane feels during this first meeting? *(Possible answer: probably afraid and uncertain but also excited at being so close to the animals she's been watching for so long)* **making inferences**

B **REREAD** Try to picture what is happening to Jane. *(Tell students*

to look for clues that help them understand what Jane is seeing, hearing, feeling, and thinking.)* **visualizing**

C Say: Based on what you've read so far, what would you say is the author's purpose for writing this article? *(to inform readers about Jane Goodall and her experiences with chimpanzees; also to inform readers of what chimps are like)* **author's purpose**

D **THINK IT THROUGH** What could have happened to Jane? *(She could have been killed and torn to pieces.)* **cause and effect**

LITERATURE

FOCUS SKILL: Informative Article

Review with students that an **informative article** gives facts and details about real people, places, and events, and that this selection is about the famous scientist Jane Goodall and her studies on chimpanzees.

VOCABULARY

FOCUS SKILL: Context Clues

Remind students to try to use context clues to figure out any words they don't know.

A **surrounded** Students can use the clue *chimps were all around her* to figure out what *surrounded* means.

B **swayed** Students can use *back and forth* to figure out what *swayed* means.

FOR ENGLISH LEARNERS

Help students understand the following expressions and idioms:

Line 12: get her bearings
Line 34: hair standing on end

Jane Goodall continues her work. Read about another experience that holds danger for her.

Another Frightening Experience

Another time, however, Jane was not so lucky. She was waiting for some chimps to pass by a ripe fruit tree when she heard footsteps in the leaves behind her. Trying not to scare the chimps, she lay down on the
50 ground. When the footsteps got closer, they stopped. Then Jane heard a worried "Hoo! Hoo!" from one of the chimps.

Like a flash of lightning, a large male jumped into the tree directly over her. Soon the chimp started to show his rage by hitting the tree's trunk and shaking its branches wildly. His hoots became louder, until he was uttering high-pitched screams of anger. Overcome by fear, Jane remained motionless.

All at once the angry chimp seemed to disappear into
60 the thick vegetation. After a moment of silence, however, he rushed toward Jane and let out a horrifying and brutal scream. She suddenly felt his hand slam down on the back of her head. Though dazed and fearful, she slowly sat up and looked around. When the chimp saw her move, he quickly ran off.

> **brutal**
> (brōōt′ l)
> *adj.* extremely rough

Later she guessed that he must not have recognized her, because she was lying down. The plastic sheet she was wearing to protect herself against the rain
70 also could have confused him. When she discussed this incident with Dr. Leakey, he said, "If you had waved your arms, shouted, or shown anger in any way, you might have been killed. He was merely testing to find out if you were an enemy or not."

> **REREAD**
> How does Jane's reaction to danger help her?

This is one of the many chimps Jane Goodall studied.

Dr. Leakey must have been right, because gradually over the next several months, the apes became less aggressive. In fact, Jane was eventually greeted almost as if she were a
80 chimpanzee herself. Sometimes the chimps would show excitement by hooting and shaking the branches. At other times, they showed no interest in her at all.

> **aggressive**
> (ə grĕs′ ĭv)
> *adj.* forceful

THINK IT THROUGH
How does the chimps' attitude toward Jane change over time?

COMPREHENSION

E **Teacher Modeling: Predicting**
Use lines 46–58 to model how to use clues to predict what will happen to Jane when she encounters another chimp.
You could say: *In line 46, I learn that Jane had another encounter with a chimp, but this time she wasn't so lucky. Immediately, I know something bad is going to happen. If I read on, I learn that Jane was careful not to scare the chimps, but something upsets one of them. The chimp goes wild and starts to hit the tree's trunk. Then he shakes the tree's branches wildly. His screams grow louder and louder the angrier he becomes. Jane must be full of fear as she tries to remain still. From these clues, I can predict that the chimp will attack her this time.*

F Ask: For what reason does Jane think the chimp attacked her? *(He didn't recognize her because she was lying down and wearing a plastic sheet.)* **cause and effect**

G **REREAD** How does Jane's reaction to danger help her? *(By staying very still, she shows the chimps that she is not an enemy and doesn't mean them any harm. This keeps them from attacking and killing her.)* **cause and effect**

H **THINK IT THROUGH** How does the chimps' attitude toward Jane change over time? *(They begin to greet her almost as if she's a chimp herself.)* **details**

VOCABULARY

C **gradually** Students can use the clue *over the next several months* to figure out what *gradually* means.

FOR ENGLISH LEARNERS

Help students understand the following expressions and idioms:

Line 53: Like a flash of lightning
Line 74: merely testing

FOCUS
Read to discover how a chimp called David Graybeard deals with Jane.

Physical Contact

Although the chimps no longer seemed to be afraid of Jane, she was still not able to establish any personal relationships with them. That changed, however, one day about a year after her arrival in Gombe. On that day, Jane was sitting near David Graybeard by a tiny stream in the forest. On the
90 ground she saw a ripe red palm nut. Slowly she picked it up and held it out to him on her open palm. At first he turned his head away. But Jane moved a little closer to him. Once again she held out her hand. This time he looked at the fruit, at Jane, and then back at the fruit. He reached out his hand and held her hand firmly but gently. After a moment, he released her hand and watched the nut drop to the ground.

REREAD
Try to picture this scene in your mind. What might the chimp be trying to "say" to Jane?

Jane Goodall and a friend

300   Unit 9 Making Adjustments

100   "At that moment I didn't need a scientist to explain what had happened," Jane later wrote in her notes. "David Graybeard had communicated with me. It was as if he had said, 'Everything is going to be okay.' And for those few seconds, the wall between human and chimpanzee was broken down. It was a reward far beyond my greatest hopes." David had become the first chimpanzee to fully accept Jane. . . .

THINK IT THROUGH
Why is this moment with David Graybeard important to Jane?

FOCUS
Read to find out how Jane's purpose changes.

Championing the Rights of Chimps

After her husband's death, Jane realized that she needed to broaden her work with
110 the chimpanzees. "For years I was selfishly concerned only with the Gombe chimps," she once said. "Now, I'm worried about the treatment and survival of chimps everywhere."

As a result, she founded the Jane Goodall Institute in Tucson, Arizona, in 1977. The purpose of the institute is to help save the world's dwindling chimpanzee population. Poaching, hunting, and the destruction of chimpanzee habitats have caused the
120 world population of chimps to drop to 175,000. Since 1977, Jane has been lecturing one month a year at the institute. She also spends much of her time raising money throughout the world for her cause. . . .

championing
(chăm' pē ə nĭng)
strongly defending

poaching
(pō' chĭng)
hunting animals where it is forbidden to do so

Acceptance   301

I **REREAD** Try to picture this scene in your mind. What might the chimp be trying to "say" to Jane? *(Possible answer: "I accept your offer of friendship.")* **making inferences**

J **THINK IT THROUGH** Why is this moment with David Graybeard important to Jane? *(It is the first time that any of the chimps has accepted her and communicated with her personally.)* **cause and effect**

K Have students tell why Jane founds the Jane Goodall Institute in Tucson. *(She wants to improve the treatment and survival of chimps everywhere.)* **cause and effect**

D **communicated** Students can use the clue *It was as if he had said* to figure out what *communicated* means.

FOR ENGLISH LEARNERS

Help students understand the following expressions and idioms:

Line 104: the wall between human and chimpanzee
Line 119: chimpanzee habitats
Line 123: raising money
Line 124: for her cause

At the end of many of her lectures and talks, Jane usually tells the story about an eight-year-old chimp named Old Man. At the zoo, he was placed on a human-made island with three females. After he had been there for several years, a young man named
130 Marc Cusano was hired to feed the chimps. He was warned at the time not to go near them. "Those brutes are vicious," he was told. "They'll kill you."

E

Although he was cautious at first, Marc soon started going closer and closer to the chimps. One day, while he was sitting in his boat, Old Man reached out and gently took a banana from Marc's hand. At that moment Marc and Old Man began a very special friendship that just kept growing. Eventually, Marc even groomed and played with
140 Old Man.

One day when Marc slipped and fell, he startled an infant chimp. Screaming, the infant ran to its mother. To protect her baby, the mother instinctively leaped on Marc and bit his neck. As he lay there, the other two females rushed up and joined in the attack. Then, just when Marc thought he was going to die, Old Man charged toward the three females. He pushed them away and stayed close to
150 Marc. With Old Man's help, Marc was finally able to get into his boat and row away to safety. There is no question in Marc's mind that Old Man saved his life.

> **instinctively**
> (ĭn stĭngk′ tĭv lē)
> *adv.* by natural action; without thinking

> **REREAD**
> How do you think Old Man feels about Marc?

L

Jane Goodall concludes the story with the following challenge. "If a chimpanzee—one, moreover, who has been abused by humans—can reach out across the species barrier to help a human friend in need,

> **species**
> (spē′ shēz)
> particular kind of animal

then surely we, with our deeper capacity for
160 compassion and understanding, can reach out to help the chimpanzees who need us, so desperately, today. Can't we?"

> **compassion**
> (kəm păsh′ ən)
> *n.* concern for the suffering of others

M

THINK IT THROUGH

1. What has become Jane's new purpose? How is her telling of Marc's story related to that purpose?
2. Reread the last paragraph. What does Jane think we can learn from chimps?
3. Review the article. What are the dangers of working with wild animals? What are the rewards?
4. Tell three facts you learned about chimps.

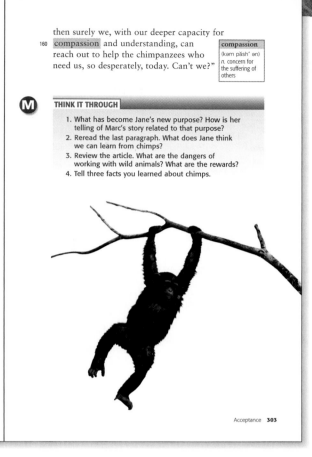

COMPREHENSION

L **REREAD** How do you think Old Man feels about Marc? *(He loves and trusts Marc and wants to protect him.)* **making inferences**

M **THINK IT THROUGH**

1. What has become Jane's new purpose? How is her telling of Marc's story related to that purpose? *(saving the world's shrinking chimp population; It might have proved that chimps are caring creatures that can help humans—and that need humans' help in return.)* **cause and effect**

2. Reread the last paragraph. What does Jane think we can learn from chimps? *(how to reach out across the species barrier to help each other)* **main idea**

3. Review the article. What are the dangers of working with wild animals? What are the rewards? *(Dangers: It's hard to predict their behavior, especially when instinct* takes over; they can become dangerous or deadly at any time. Rewards: They can teach us many things—about themselves as well as ourselves.) **author's purpose**

4. Tell three facts you learned about chimps. *(Possible facts: Chimps will attack when they feel afraid or threatened; they protect those who are close to them; they can form relationships with humans.)* **fact and opinion**

Have students revisit the statements in the anticipatory guide on page T401. The answers are *false, true, false.*

RETEACHING

If students need more help understanding **Cause and Effect,** use pages T642–T646.

VOCABULARY

E **vicious** Students can use the context clues *brutes* and *"They'll kill you"* to figure out the meaning of this word.

FOR ENGLISH LEARNERS

Help students understand the following expressions and idioms:

Line 152: no question in Marc's mind

RETEACHING

If students need more help understanding **Context Clues,** use pages T608–T611.

1. COMPREHENSION

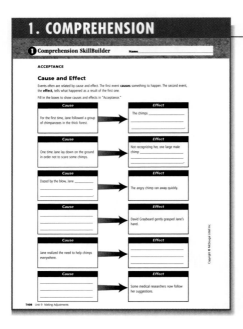

Cause and Effect

Direct Instruction Tell students that events are often joined by cause and effect. The **cause** is the first event, "why" something happens. The **effect** is the second event and tells the result.

Refer students to the second to last paragraph of "Acceptance." Say: Jane tells the story of the friendship between Marc and Old Man. If the cause is that Marc fell and startled the infant chimp, what is the effect? *(Answer: The females attacked Marc.)* If the effect is that Marc was able to get to safety, what is the cause? *(Answer: Old Man came to Marc's rescue.)* Direct students to find the cause by asking themselves, Why did this happen? Tell them to find the effect by questioning, What is the result?

Comprehension SkillBuilder Answer Key:

(Wording may vary.)

Effect: *The chimps surrounded her.*

Effect: *Not recognizing her, one large male chimp hit her in the back of the head.*

Cause: *Dazed by the blow, Jane slowly sat up and looked around.*

Cause: *Jane offered a palm nut to David Graybeard.*

Effect: *She founded the Jane Goodall Institute.*

Cause: *Jane told researchers how chimps could have a better life.*

2. COMPREHENSION

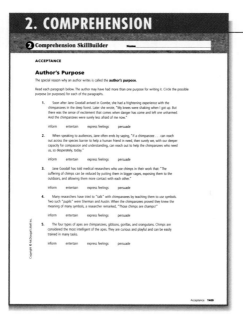

Author's Purpose

Direct Instruction Remind students that writers have a reason for writing what they write. The reason is called the **author's purpose.** List the four main purposes: to inform or teach, to express feelings, to entertain or bring enjoyment, and to persuade the reader to think or feel in a certain way. Say: What is the most likely purpose of each of the following articles about chimpanzees? "101 Chimpanzee Jokes" *(to entertain)*; "Foods of the Mountain Chimpanzees" *(to inform)*; "Jane Goodall's Personal Diary of Favorite Chimps" *(to share feelings)*; "Chimps Facing Extinction: What You Must Do to Help" *(to persuade)*

Comprehension SkillBuilder Answer Key:

1. *express feelings*
2. *persuade*
3. *inform/persuade*
4. *entertain/inform*
5. *inform*

3. VOCABULARY

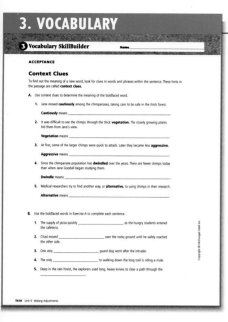

Context Clues

Direct Instruction Tell students to use context clues when they come across a new or unfamiliar word in their reading. **Context clues** are words or phrases in the sentence near the new word. List the following helpful hints:

- Look for words and phrases such as *is, which is, that is, who is.* These words signal that a definition follows. For example: Isaac was a *herpetologist,* that is, one who studies reptiles.

- Look for a synonym of the new word. For example: The flood *precluded,* or prevented, us from crossing the river.
- Look for an antonym of the new word. For example: Lake Maude was *placid* before the storm, but afterward it was not calm at all.
- Look for general clues about the word. For example: The *trek* on the mountain trail took longer than we thought, since we had to walk so slowly and carefully.

Vocabulary SkillBuilder Answer Key:	
A.	**B.**
1. *taking care to be safe*	**1.** *dwindled*
2. *growing plants*	**2.** *cautiously*
3. *quick to attack*	**3.** *aggressive*
4. *become smaller, lessen*	**4.** *alternative*
5. *another way*	**5.** *vegetation*

4. WORDS TO KNOW

Words to Know

Direct Instruction As you present the **Words to Know,** here are some points you might want to cover. Help students to identify the parts of the vocabulary words. Stress the importance of finding the base of each word. Help students remove prefixes and suffixes first.

glare + *-ing* = *glaring*
aggress + *-ive* = *aggressive*
brute + *-al* = *brutal*
instinct + *-ive* + *-ly* = *instinctively*

Writing Activity Students may want to use an encyclopedia to get information about an animal.

Words to Know SkillBuilder Answer Key:	
A.	**B.**
1. *instinctively*	**1.** *e*
2. *compassion*	**2.** *c*
3. *brutal*	**3.** *b*
4. *glaring*	**4.** *d*
5. *aggressive*	**5.** *a*

5. SELECTION TEST

Selection Test Answer Key:
A. 1. *Africa* **2.** *surrounded* **3.** *head* **4.** *communicated*
B. *save the world's chimpanzee population.*

ACCEPTANCE

Cause and Effect

Events often are related by cause and effect. The first event **causes** something to happen. The second event, the **effect,** tells what happened as a result of the first one.

Fill in the boxes to show causes and effects in "Acceptance."

Cause	Effect
For the first time, Jane followed a group of chimpanzees in the thick forest.	The chimps _____ _____ _____.

Cause	Effect
One time Jane lay down on the ground in order not to scare some chimps.	Not recognizing her, one large male chimp _____ _____ _____.

Cause	Effect
Dazed by the blow, Jane _____ _____ _____.	The angry chimp ran away quickly.

Cause	Effect
_____ _____ _____	David Graybeard gently grasped Jane's hand.

Cause	Effect
Jane realized the need to help chimps everywhere.	_____ _____ _____

Cause	Effect
_____ _____ _____	Some medical researchers now follow her suggestions.

ACCEPTANCE

Author's Purpose

The special reason why an author writes is called the **author's purpose.**

Read each paragraph below. The author may have had more than one purpose for writing it. Circle the possible purpose (or purposes) for each of the paragraphs.

1.   Soon after Jane Goodall arrived in Gombe, she had a frightening experience with the chimpanzees in the deep forest. Later she wrote, "My knees were shaking when I got up. But there was the sense of excitement that comes when danger has come and left one unharmed. And the chimpanzees were surely less afraid of me now."

   inform   entertain   express feelings   persuade

2.   When speaking to audiences, Jane often ends by saying, "If a chimpanzee . . . can reach out across the species barrier to help a human friend in need, then surely we, with our deeper capacity for compassion and understanding, can reach out to help the chimpanzees who need us, so desperately, today."

   inform   entertain   express feelings   persuade

3.   Jane Goodall has told medical researchers who use chimps in their work, "The suffering of chimps can be reduced by putting them in bigger cages, exposing them to the outdoors, and allowing them more contact with each other."

   inform   entertain   express feelings   persuade

4.   Many researchers have tried to "talk" with chimpanzees by teaching them to use symbols. Two such "pupils" were Sherman and Austin. When the chimpanzees proved they knew the meaning of many symbols, a researcher remarked, "Those chimps are champs!"

   inform   entertain   express feelings   persuade

5.   The four types of apes are chimpanzees, gibbons, gorillas, and orangutans. Chimps are considered the most intelligent of the apes. They are curious and playful and can be easily trained in many tasks.

   inform   entertain   express feelings   persuade

ACCEPTANCE

Context Clues

To find out the meaning of a new word, look for clues in words and phrases within the sentence. These hints in the passage are called **context clues.**

A. Use context clues to determine the meaning of the boldfaced word.

1. Jane moved **cautiously** among the chimpanzees, taking care to be safe in the thick forest.

   Cautiously means _____.

2. It was difficult to see the chimps through the thick **vegetation.** The closely growing plants hid them from Jane's view.

   Vegetation means _____.

3. At first, some of the larger chimps were quick to attack. Later they became less **aggressive.**

   Aggressive means _____.

4. The chimpanzee population has **dwindled** over the years. There are fewer chimps today than when Jane Goodall began studying them.

   Dwindle means _____.

5. Medical researchers try to find another way, or **alternative,** to using chimps in their research.

   Alternative means _____.

B. Use the boldfaced words in Exercise A to complete each sentence.

1. The supply of pizza quickly _____ as the hungry students entered the cafeteria.

2. Chad moved _____ over the rocky ground until he safely reached the other side.

3. One very _____ guard dog went after the intruder.

4. The only _____ to walking down the long trail is riding a mule.

5. Deep in the rain forest, the explorers used long, heavy knives to clear a path through the _____.

ACCEPTANCE

Words to Know

glaring   aggressive   compassion   brutal   instinctively

A. On each blank, write the word from the list that best fits the sentence.

1. Flying south is what birds do naturally, or _____.

2. My grandmother worked at an animal shelter because she had such _____ for animals.

3. Mr. Chen thought boxing was far too violent, cruel, and _____.

4. My sister's _____ eyes showed that she was angry.

5. The kids who forced their way to the front of the line were very _____.

B. On the blank, write the letter of the correct definition. Use the dictionary if you need to.

_____ **1.** compassion   a. extremely rough

_____ **2.** glaring   b. forceful

_____ **3.** aggressive   c. staring in anger

_____ **4.** instinctively   d. by natural action; without thinking

_____ **5.** brutal   e. concern for the suffering of others

Writing Activity

Suppose you are an animal expert. Write three sentences about one animal. Use at least one of the **Words to Know.**

ACCEPTANCE

A. Complete the paragraph by filling in each blank with the correct word from the list.

population   communicated   surrounded
Africa   head

While observing chimpanzees in the forests of **(1)** _____,

Jane Goodall had some interesting experiences. One time when several chimps

(2) _____ her, she thought she was going to be torn

to pieces. Another time, an angry chimp rushed toward her and hit her on the back of the

(3) _____. Eventually the chimps got used to seeing Jane,

and they began relaxing around her. After a year, she and a chimp named David Graybeard finally

(4) _____ when she tried to hand him a palm nut.

B. Complete the second sentence.

In 1977, Jane started the Jane Goodall Institute in Arizona. The purpose of the institute is to help

_____

_____

Reader directions:

Cut this paper in half. Practice reading the passage aloud until you don't make any mistakes.
Then have someone listen to you read. Try to sound the way you think an old-fashioned storyteller would sound.

from "The Lady, or the Tiger?"

Among the king's royal servants was a young man so handsome and brave that he had no equal. The daughter fell in love with him—how could she help herself? They kept their love secret for many months. The royal daughter wasn't supposed to be seeing a lowly servant. Then one day the king found out about them.

Oh, the cries of rage and doom! The king threw the young man into prison and set a day for his trial in the arena. Of course, this was a special event. Never before had a lowly subject of the king dared to love his daughter.

✂ **cut along dotted line**

- -

Checker directions:

Follow along as the passage is read. Make a dot under each word the reader misses.
Show the reader the missed words. Erase the dots and repeat for each reading.

from "The Lady, or the Tiger?"

Among the king's royal servants was a young man so handsome and brave that he had no equal. The daughter fell in love with him—how could she help herself? They kept their love secret for many months. The royal daughter wasn't supposed to be seeing a lowly servant. Then one day the king found out about them.

Oh, the cries of rage and doom! The king threw the young man into prison and set a day for his trial in the arena. Of course, this was a special event. Never before had a lowly subject of the king dared to love his daughter.

Use this chart for Timed Readings and Repeated Readings.

Reading	1	2	3	4	5
Time (minutes/seconds)					
Words Missed					

Focus Skills

COMPREHENSION
Main Idea
Problem and Solution

VOCABULARY
Syllabication

SkillBuilder Copymasters

 Reading Comprehension:
1 Main Idea p. T424
2 Problem and Solution p. T425

 Vocabulary:
3 Syllabication p. T426
4 Words to Know p. T427

Assessment

 5 Selection Test p. T428

Readability Scores

DRP	LEXILE	DALE-CHALL
56	920	4.4

Reading Fluency

 ★ Reading Fluency p. T429

For English Learners

In this selection Stevie Wonder describes the self-consciousness that he felt at growing up not only blind but black. Invite students to discuss times when they felt uncomfortable because of a physical impairment or their ethnic, religious, social, or educational background.

Growing Up
in a World
of Darkness
by James Haskins

304 Unit 9 Making Adjustments

Vocabulary Strategy

Syllabication Tell students that when they come to a word they don't know, one way they can figure out how to pronounce it is to break it into parts, or **syllables.** Review the syllabication rules shown on this and the next page with students. Then have them syllabicate these words from the selection: hap•pens, peo•ple, per•son, giv•en, mu•sic.

1. If a word has **two consonants in the middle,** divide the word *between* the two consonants: bet•ter, gos•pel.

A child who is blind learns all about sounds. Then sounds lead him to explore making music. Discover how Stevie Wonder became a wonder of the world.

Growing Up in a World of Darkness **305**

Connect to Your Life

Guide students in a discussion of blind people whom they have observed. In what situations did students observe them? What did the blind people do to compensate for the fact that they couldn't see?

Key to the Biography

Be sure students understand that although a **biography** tells about a person's life, it is not written by that person. For example, this biography of Stevie Wonder's early years is written by an author named James Haskins. Haskins includes quotations from Stevie Wonder to add interest and authenticity.

Vocabulary Preview

Words to Know
  handicaps *n.* physical disabilities
  encouraged *adj.* given a sense of hope
  mimicking *n.* imitating
  self-conscious *adj.* very aware of one's own actions and appearance
  audition *n.* performance to show a skill

For direct instruction on Words to Know, see page T423.

Building Background

This selection ends with ten-year-old Stevie Morris signing his first record contract with Hitsville USA, which later became known as Motown Records. Because Stevie could play so many instruments, Berry Gordy dubbed him Little Stevie Wonder, and his career soon took off. Within eight months Stevie's third single, "Fingertips, Part 2," became his first #1 hit, topping both the pop and R&B music charts.

2. If a word ends with a **consonant + le,** divide the word *before* the consonant: ta•ble, tur•tle.
3. If a word has a **consonant between two vowels,** if the first vowel has a long sound, divide the word *before* the consonant: to•tal, hu•man. If the first vowel has a short sound, divide the word *after* the consonant: hon•est, nev•er.

 For more on Syllabication, see page T423.

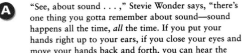

FOCUS

Read about Stevie Wonder's first memories of his blindness.

A "See, about sound . . . ," Stevie Wonder says, "there's one thing you gotta remember about sound—sound happens all the time, *all* the time. If you put your hands right up to your ears, if you close your eyes and move your hands back and forth, you can hear the sound getting closer and farther away. . . . Sound bounces off everything, there's always something happening."

A 10 Stevie Wonder was born Steveland Morris on May 13, 1950, in Saginaw, Michigan. He was the third boy in a family that would eventually include five boys and one girl. All except Stevie were born without handicaps. He was

B born prematurely, and his early birth led to his total blindness.

> **handicaps**
> (hăn′ dē kăps′)
> *n.* physical disabilities

"I guess that I first became aware that I was blind," Stevie recalls, "—and I just vaguely remember this—when I'd be wallowing around in the grass back of the house, and I'd get myself and my 20 clothes soiled. My mother would get on me about that. She explained that I couldn't move about so much, that I'd have to try and stay in one place.

B "When I was young," he says, "my mother taught me never to feel sorry for myself, because handicaps are really things to be used, another way to benefit yourself and others in the long run." This was the best possible advice Stevie's mother could have given. He learned to 30 regard his blindness in more than one way. It could be a hindrance, but it could also

> **REREAD**
> What attitude is Stevie's mother giving him?

> **hindrance**
> (hĭn′ drəns)
> something that prevents progress

be a special gift. He was able to accept this idea, sometimes better than his mother could.

"I know it used to worry my mother," Stevie recalls, "and I know she prayed for me to have sight someday, and so finally I just told her that I was *happy* being blind, and I thought it was a gift from God, and I think she felt better after that."

C **THINK IT THROUGH**

What does the author think about Stevie and his mother?

FOCUS

Stevie continues to learn ways of dealing with blindness. Read to find out more about his discoveries.

C Stevie was a lucky child in many 40 ways. He was lucky to have two brothers close enough to him in age not to understand at first about his blindness and to expect him to do many of the things they did. He was also lucky to have a mother and a father, and occasionally an uncle, who understood how important sound was to him, and how important it was for him to learn to identify things he 50 could not see by their sound. He recalls:

"I remember people dropping money on the table and saying, 'What's that, Steve?' That's a dime— buh-duh-duh-da; that's a quarter—buh-duh-duh-duh-da; that's a nickel. I could almost always get it right except a penny and a nickel confused me.

"I don't really feel my hearing is any better than yours," Stevie says now; "we all have the same

306 Unit 9 Making Adjustments

Growing Up in a World of Darkness **307**

COMPREHENSION

FOCUS SKILL 1: Main Idea

Remind students that the **main idea** is the most important idea in a section of text. Depending on the selection, students might find a different main idea in each paragraph or section of text, or the whole selection might have a single main idea.

 For direct instruction on Main Idea, see page T422.

FOCUS SKILL 2: Problem and Solution

Tell students that in life, as in fiction, people have **problems.** To solve their problems, they often try different **solutions.** By the end, they usually come up with a result—the **outcome.**

 For direct instruction on Problem and Solution, see page T422.

A Have a volunteer state the main idea of the first paragraph. *(Sound happens all the time.)* **main idea**

B **REREAD** What attitude is Stevie's mother giving him? *(Stevie's mother is being positive about his handicap. She wants him to make the best of his situation and not feel sorry for himself.)* **main idea**

C **THINK IT THROUGH** What does the author think about Stevie and his mother? *(The author admires both mother and son.)* **making inferences**

VOCABULARY

FOCUS SKILL: Syllabication

As students read this selection, remind them to break unfamiliar words into smaller parts, or **syllables,** in order to figure them out. If necessary, review the syllabication rules that you introduced earlier.

A **eventually** Help students syllabicate this word. Explain that it can be broken into five parts. *(e•ven•tu•al•ly)*

B **prematurely** Point out that this word begins with the prefix *pre-* and ends in the suffix *-ly.* Tell students to look for prefixes and suffixes in words and then break the word into its parts. *(pre•ma•ture•ly)*

C **occasionally** Tell students that this word is the word *occasion* + the suffixes *-al* and *-ly.* It can be broken into five parts. *(oc•ca•sion•al•ly)*

FOR ENGLISH LEARNERS

Help students understand the following expressions and idioms:

Line 20: get on me
Line 27: in the long run
Line 41: close enough to him in age

abilities, you know. The only difference is how much you use it." Encouraged by his
60 family, Stevie used his hearing more and more as he grew older. He learned how to tell birds apart by their calls, and to tell trees apart by the sound their leaves made as they rustled in the wind. He learned to tell when people were tired or annoyed or pleased by listening to the tone of their voices.

D His world of sound grew larger and larger, and the most frightening experience for him was silence. He depended so on sound that
70 silence, for him, was like total darkness for deaf children. It is hard for sighted and hearing people to understand this. Perhaps the best way to understand is to imagine being shut up in a dark, soundproof box. People need to feel that they are part of the world around them. It is hard enough to do so when one cannot see, or when one cannot hear; but it is doubly hard for a blind person in a silent room or a deaf person in total darkness.
80 He also spent a lot of time beating on things, to make sounds and to make music. Although his mother was a gospel singer, the family was not especially musical. But Stevie had shown musical interest and ability very young. By the time he was two years old his favorite toys were two spoons, with which he would beat
90 rhythmically on pans and tabletops and anything else his

> **encouraged**
> (ĕn kûr' ījd)
> *adj.* given a
> sense of hope

> **REREAD**
> Can you imagine what it would be like in a dark, soundproof box?

D

mother would let him beat on. When she began to worry about her furniture, she bought him cardboard drums from the dime store. None of them lasted very long. "I'd beat 'em to death," Stevie says with a chuckle. But there would always be a new drum, and there were other toy instruments as
100 well.

E "One day someone gave me a harmonica to put on my key chain, a little four-hole harmonica," Stevie recalls. He managed to get a remarkable range of sounds from that toy instrument.

"Then one day my mother took me to a picnic and someone sat me behind my first set of drums. They put my foot on the pedal and I played. They gave me a quarter. I liked the sound of quarters."

At a very early age, too, Stevie began to sing. All
110 voices were very important to him, for they brought him closer to the world around him, a world he could not see. As he grew older, his own voice became particularly important to him, especially at night when the rest of the house was silent.

F He learned the endless possibilities of the human voice by experimenting with his own, and by mimicking others'.

Music itself, not necessarily made by
120 him, became very important to him. He loved to listen to the radio; his earliest memory is of hearing Johnny Ace singing "Pledging My Love" on the radio. Shortly before he entered school he was given a small transistor radio for his very own. From then on, that radio was his constant

> **REREAD**
> Why do you think Stevie uses his voice when his house is still?

E

> **mimicking**
> (mĭm' ĭ kĭng)
> *n.* imitating

308 Unit 9 Making Adjustments

Growing Up in a World of Darkness **309**

COMPREHENSION

D **REREAD** Can you imagine what it would be like in a dark, sound-proof box? *(Responses may vary. Being inside a dark, soundproof box might make someone feel helpless and afraid.)* **making inferences**

E **REREAD** Why do you think Stevie uses his voice when his house is still? *(It helps him feel connected to his surroundings and not shut off from them.)* **problem and solution**

VOCABULARY

D **frightening** Help students syllabicate and pronounce this word. Point out the suffix *-ing*. *(fright•en•ing)*

E **harmonica** Tell students that this word can be broken down into four parts. *(har•mon•i•ca)*

F **possibilities . . . experimenting** Help students syllabicate and pronounce these words. *(pos•si•bil•i•ties, ex•per•i•ment•ing)*

FOR ENGLISH LEARNERS

Help students understand the following expressions and idioms:

Line 62: tell birds apart; tell trees apart

Line 65: the tone of their voices

Line 75: hard enough to do so

Line 97: I'd beat 'em to death

Growing Up in a World of Darkness   PE 308–309 • **T417**

companion. He even slept with it under his pillow at night. It played softly, providing sounds for him in an otherwise silent apartment. When he started school, he insisted on taking it to school with him.

F

THINK IT THROUGH
Why does music become important to Stevie? Use examples from this section to explain.

FOCUS
The radio plays an important part in Stevie's life. Read to find out how it helps him.

G

130 Stevie was enrolled in special classes for the blind in the Detroit public school system. A special bus picked him up every morning and brought him back every afternoon. Stevie wished he could walk to school as his brothers did, and go to their neighborhood school. But he was learning to adjust to the fact that he must lead a different life, and in his special classes he was taught many things that would help him lead as normal a life as possible.

140 Sighted children attended the same school, and they often whispered about "the blind kids" as they passed by. Adults did the same thing. Somehow, normal people have the idea that blind people cannot hear them. It was hard to deal in an honest way with sighted people or even with his partially sighted classmates.

H

Being blind is to be exposed to constant frustrations. Dropping something, especially something small, means having to grope about with little chance of finding 150 it. Some blind children won't even bother looking for an object they have dropped

frustrations
(frŭ strā' shənz)
feelings of hopelessness at not being able to do what one wants

G

because they are embarrassed to be seen groping about for it.

I

Stevie had an additional problem in getting along with other children. Not only was he blind; he was also black. At first it might seem that the idea of skin color should not be very important to a child who has never seen color. But blackness is not just skin color; it is a culture, a way of looking at things. People 160 divide themselves into "Us" and "Them" because of skin color, but that is not the only division. We also divide ourselves because of religion, education, economic class. If everyone in the entire world were blind, people would still divide themselves into "Us" and "Them"; it just would not be on the basis of appearance.

REREAD
This is the author's opinion. Do you agree?

H

A

At home, Stevie heard his brothers and their friends talk about the white kids they knew. Before long, even 170 though Stevie could not himself see color, he was very aware of skin color, and in addition to being self-conscious because of his blindness he was a little bit ashamed of being black.

self-conscious
(sĕlf' kŏn' shəs)
adj. very aware of one's own actions and appearance

"I remember when I was little," says Stevie, "I used to listen to this black radio station in Detroit on my way to school. Like I was the only black kid on the bus, and I would always turn the 180 radio down, because I felt ashamed to let them hear me listening to B.B. King. But I *loved* B.B. King. Yet I felt ashamed because—because I was

310 Unit 9 Making Adjustments

Growing Up in a World of Darkness 311

COMPREHENSION

F **THINK IT THROUGH** Why does music become important to Stevie? Use examples from this section to explain. *(Possible responses: The sound of music, especially singing, brought Stevie closer to the world he could not see. His own voice helped him fill the silence at night, so he experimented with the endless possibilities it offered him. His transistor radio also helped Stevie fill the silence. It became his constant companion, and he would even take it with him to school.)* **drawing conclusions**

G Have students tell how school was different for Stevie than it was for his brothers. *(Stevie was enrolled in special classes for the blind and had to take a bus every morning and afternoon. His brothers walked to school and went to the neighborhood school.)* **compare and contrast**

H **REREAD** This is the author's opinion. Do you agree? *(Students should use their own experiences as well as the text to support their opinions.)* **making judgments**

LITERATURE

Use this question to encourage literary analysis.

A How did Stevie become aware of his skin color? How did this self-awareness make him feel? *(Stevie heard his brothers and their friends talk about the white kids they knew. He felt a little bit ashamed of being black.)* **internal conflict**

VOCABULARY

G **neighborhood** Tell students that the word *neighborhood* is a compound word made up of the words *neighbor + hood*. It can be broken into three parts. *(neigh•bor•hood)*

H **partially** Point out that the word *partially* ends in the suffix *-ly*. Have students syllabicate and pronounce this word. *(par•tial•ly)*

I **additional** Have students syllabicate this word. Tell them to look for any suffixes or prefixes to help them break it into its parts. *(ad•di•tion•al)*

FOR ENGLISH LEARNERS

Help students understand the following expressions and idioms:

Line 144: partially sighted
Line 149: to grope about
Line 167: basis of appearance

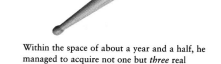

different enough to want to hear him and because I had never heard him anywhere else."

J Stevie was not about to stop listening to B.B. King; he simply played his radio softly in situations where he felt uncomfortable. That radio meant more to him than just about anything else in the world.

190 "I spent a lot of time listening to the radio," Stevie recalls, "and I was able to relate to the different instruments and know what they were. I began to know them by name. I used to listen to this program on station WCHB . . . called 'Sundown.' The disc jockey was named Larry Dixon and he always played a lot of old songs. There was one thing he played, it was his theme song . . . da da duh duh *dommm* da duh . . . da da da da *dommm dommm* da da duh. . . . Oh, it's really a bad tune, really a beautiful song—

200 can't think of the name right now, but I could never forget that tune."

I He would sing the words of the songs quietly to himself. He would hum the tunes. He would tap out the beats on his toy drums and try to play the melodies on his four-note

K harmonica. It frustrated him not to have real,

210 grown-up instruments to play on, and it was hard for him to accept the fact that his mother just did not have enough money to buy real instruments for him. But luck soon proved to be with Stevie.

Young Stevie Wonder with his harmonica

Within the space of about a year and a half, he managed to acquire not one but *three* real
220 instruments.

J **THINK IT THROUGH**
How does the radio help Stevie to develop an interest in music?

FOCUS
Discover the changes in Stevie's life when he receives three special gifts.

Every year the Detroit Lions Club gave a Christmas party for blind children, and at Christmastime during his first-grade year at school Stevie went to one. Each child received a gift, and someone must have told the Detroit Lions Club about Stevie's interest in music, for his gift—he could hardly believe it—was a set of real drums! Stevie sat down and began to pound on them right then and there.

Later a neighborhood barber gave Stevie a
230 harmonica—a real one. He practiced and practiced until he had mastered that.

Then, when he was seven, Stevie became the proud owner of a real piano. A neighbor was moving out of the housing project, and she really did not want to take her piano. Knowing how much Stevie loved music, she decided to give it to him. Stevie

312 Unit 9 Making Adjustments

Growing Up in a World of Darkness **313**

COMPREHENSION

I **Teacher Modeling: Connecting**
To model how to use the Active Reading Strategy of connecting, focus on lines 202–216.
You could say: *After reading this paragraph, I think I can understand Stevie's frustration about not being able to play real instruments. Even though he practiced on his toy drums and his harmonica, he wasn't completely satisfied. I remember when I was younger, I wanted to play sports, but I couldn't because I was ill. I could play catch, but I wasn't allowed to run and play basketball. I felt frustrated and angry that I couldn't do more. This memory helps me relate to what Stevie felt about not being able to play a real instrument.*

J **THINK IT THROUGH** How does the radio help Stevie to develop an interest in music? *(It helps him pay attention to lyrics, learn melodies and rhythms, and identify different instruments.)* **making inferences**

VOCABULARY

J **situations . . . uncomfortable**
Have students syllabicate these words. *(sit•u•a•tions, un•com•fort•a•ble)*

K **frustrated** Have students syllabicate this word. *(frus•tra•ted)*

FOR ENGLISH LEARNERS

Help students understand the following expressions and idioms:

Line 199: a bad tune
Line 204: tap out the beats
Line 218: within the space of about a year and a half
Line 219: managed to acquire
Line 231: until he had mastered that
Line 234: housing project

remembers, "I kept asking, 'When they gonna bring the piano over, Mamma?' I never realized how important that was going to be to me." When the piano finally arrived, it was like all the birthdays Stevie could remember all rolled into one. He ran his hands along the smooth wooden top, down the sides and around the back, down the slim legs, around to the cold metal of the pedals, and back up to the keys, some flat, some raised. He asked his mother to open the top of the piano, so he could feel the strings inside. He asked her what color they were.

REREAD What do you think Stevie is trying to do here?

 K

They were kind of gold, and the small wooden blocks between them were light brown. What color was the piano? A dark brown. From that moment on, dark brown, although he had not ever seen it and would never see it, meant something nice to Stevie. And since, he had been told, his skin was a sort of dark brown, too, he began to feel much better about his skin color.

L

THINK IT THROUGH
Why are the three musical gifts important to Stevie's life?

FOCUS
Read to find out where Stevie's love of music leads him.

By the time he was nine or ten Stevie was a very popular member of the neighborhood. He was certainly the most gifted musically, and he spent many Saturdays and after-school hours on the front porches of neighbors' houses on Horton Street. By this time Stevie had a set of bongo drums, which he had

mastered as he had every other instrument to which he had been exposed. Often he would play his bongos; sometimes it would be the harmonica. Everyone would join in the singing, but Stevie's clear, strong voice always took the lead. Without exception the music was rhythm and blues, the kind the people listened to on WCHB.

One of his favorite singing partners was a boy about his age named John Glover. John Glover had a grown-up cousin named Ronnie White, who lived in another part of the city. Ronnie White was a member of the singing group the Miracles, which had enjoyed great success recording with a company named Hitsville USA. Of course, John Glover was very proud to have a cousin like Ronnie White, and he often boasted about him. John Glover was also proud to have a friend like Stevie. "You oughta hear my friend Stevie," he kept telling his cousin. But naturally White was busy, and he didn't really believe this kid Stevie was anything special. Then, one day in 1960, he happened to drop by to visit his relatives on Horton Street, and Stevie just happened to be having one of his front-porch sessions at the time. White did not

---

COMPREHENSION

K **REREAD** What do you think Stevie is trying to do here? *(He's trying to "see" the piano. He's using his other senses to understand what it looks like and how it works.)* **drawing conclusions**

L **THINK IT THROUGH** Why are the three musical gifts important to Stevie's life? *(They help him learn more about music and how to make it; knowing his piano was dark brown helps him feel proud of his own skin color.)* **main idea**

VOCABULARY

FOR ENGLISH LEARNERS

Help students understand the following expressions and idioms:

Line 241: all rolled into one
Line 283: happened to drop by

The adult Stevie Wonder performs at a Grammy Awards show.

have to listen very long to realize that his little cousin was right. This kid was something!

White arranged with the president of Hitsville USA, Berry Gordy, to take Stevie to the company's
290 recording studio and to give him an
audition , and one exciting afternoon Stevie was taken to the place that would be like a second home to him for the next ten years.

> **audition**
> (ô dǐsh′ ən)
> *n.* performance to show a skill

Stevie will never forget that afternoon. White took him around the studio, helping him to the different instruments and sound equipment, letting him touch them. It seemed to Stevie that every wonderful instrument in the world was right there in that sound

300 studio, and he never wanted to leave it. Then he was introduced to Berry Gordy. Gordy listened to him sing, and play the harmonica and drums, and hired him on the spot, which says a lot for Gordy. Few, if any, other record-company owners would have taken such a chance back in 1960. But then, few, if any, other record companies had or would have the history of Gordy's. No other black-owned label would prevail as his would, and perhaps this was because once they were established,
310 those other labels were too busy holding on to their position to take any risk or to try anything new.

> **prevail**
> (prǐ vāl′)
> succeed

Anyway, signing an artist brought in by a performer already with the company has become a common, and famous, practice of Gordy's. The Supremes were discovered by the Temptations. Diana Ross discovered the Jackson Five.

Of course, Stevie's mother actually signed Stevie's contract with Hitsville, for he was underage. There
320 was little talk of money or other conditions. Stevie's family was so excited, so grateful for this opportunity for him, that they would have agreed to anything!

 THINK IT THROUGH

1. Why was Berry Gordy taking a chance when he signed Stevie Wonder?
2. How did Stevie's family and community help make him a star? Think of several ways.
3. Do you think Stevie Wonder would have become a musician if he had been able to see? Use evidence from the biography to support your opinion.

COMPREHENSION

Ⓜ THINK IT THROUGH

1. Why was Berry Gordy taking a chance when he signed Stevie Wonder? *(Gordy was doing something that no one had ever done before: Stevie was only ten years old, and he was blind.)* **making inferences**

2. How did Stevie's family and community help make him a star? Think of several ways. *(His family taught him about sounds and bought him a radio and toy instruments; the community gave him real instruments; his friend's cousin got Stevie an audition with a record company.)* **problem and solution**

3. Do you think Stevie Wonder would have become a musician if he had been able to see? Use evidence from the biography to support your opinion. *(Accept any answers that students can support with evidence from the text.)* **making judgments**

Option for Speaking and Listening Suggest that students form small groups to discuss the ways in which Stevie's family and community helped to make him a star. Be sure they give reasons for why each action was significant.

RETEACHING

If students need more help understanding **Main Idea,** use pages T635–T638.

VOCABULARY

FOR ENGLISH LEARNERS

Help students understand the following expressions and idioms:

Line 287: this kid was something
Line 302: hired him on the spot
Line 310: holding on to their position
Line 319: for he was underage

RETEACHING

If students need more help understanding **Syllabication,** use pages T625–T633.

1. COMPREHENSION

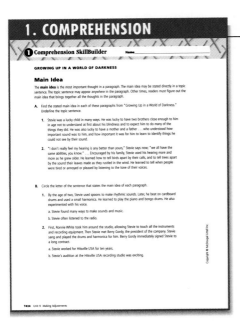

Main Idea

Direct Instruction Remind students that the **main idea** is the most important thought in a paragraph. Often the main idea is stated in the topic sentence. Note that the main idea can be found anywhere in the paragraph. Read the following paragraph from "Growing Up in a World of Darkness":

> Being blind is to be exposed to constant frustrations. Dropping something, especially something small, means having to grope about with little chance of finding it. Some blind children won't even bother looking for an object they have dropped because they are embarrassed to be seen groping about for it.

Direct the students to find the main idea in this paragraph. *(First sentence)* Note how the other sentences support this main idea.

Remind students that not every paragraph has a stated main idea. In paragraphs without a topic sentence, the reader must think about all the information in the paragraph and decide how these ideas belong together. The relationship between the ideas is the main idea of the paragraph. Reread the above paragraph without the first sentence, and have students express the main idea in their own words.

Comprehension SkillBuilder Answer Key:

A.
  1. *Stevie was a lucky child in many ways.*
  2. *Encouraged by his family, Stevie used his hearing more and more as he grew older.*
B. 1. *a* **2.** *b*

---

2. COMPREHENSION

Problem and Solution

Direct Instruction Tell students that characters in stories often face problems, just as we do. The writer introduces the problem and shows how the character works to solve it. This organization of events is called **problem and solution.** Note that this kind of organization is used in both fiction and nonfiction. Discuss some common problems (examples: missing the last school bus, lack of money to buy a ticket to a basketball game) and possible solutions. Tell students that when identifying the problems or solutions in a story, they should be as precise as possible without retelling the whole story.

Comprehension SkillBuilder Answer Key:

1. Problem: *Stevie became blind as a baby.*
2. Solution: *He made his own sounds by singing/playing his radio softly.*
3. Problem: *Stevie's mother worried about him.*
4. Solution: *He went to a special school for the blind.*
5. Problem: *Stevie's mother could not afford to buy him real musical instruments.*
6. Solution: *He turned the radio down so only he could hear it.*

Direct Instruction
for SkillBuilder Copymasters

---

3. VOCABULARY

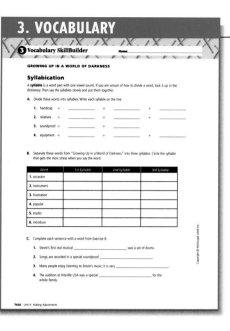

Syllabication

Direct Instruction Tell students that dividing unfamiliar words into syllables can help them unlock the meanings of those words. They may recognize the word when they say each syllable. By separating prefixes and suffixes and by separating compound words, they may understand the word or realize that they know the word.

State this rule for dividing multisyllable words: when one vowel comes between two consonants and the vowel sound is long, divide the word before the second consonant. Have students discuss where this rule can be applied to the sample words, and review other syllabication rules that apply. Challenge students to divide the sample words into syllables. *(ma•ple, so•da, ra•di•o, mel•o•dy)* Remind the students to use the dictionary if in doubt.

> **Vocabulary SkillBuilder Answer Key:**
> **A. 1.** *hand•i•cap*   **2.** *rel•a•tives*   **3.** *sound•proof*   **4.** *e•quip•ment*
>
> **B.** *(Boldfaced syllable should be circled.)*
>   **1.** *oc•**ca**•sion*   **2.** ***in**•stru•ment*   **3.** *frus•**tra**•tion*   **4.** ***pop**•u•lar*
>   **5.** ***stu**•di•o*   **6.** *in•tro•**duce***
>
> **C. 1.** *instrument*   **2.** *studio*   **3.** *popular*   **4.** *occasion*

---

4. WORDS TO KNOW

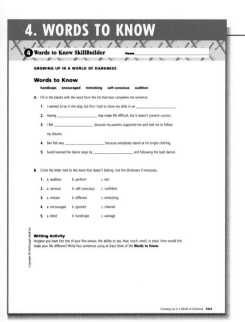

Words to Know

Direct Instruction As you present the **Words to Know,** here are some points you might want to cover. Help students to identify the parts of the vocabulary words. Stress the importance of finding the base of each word. Help students remove prefixes and suffixes first.
- **handicap** + -s = *handicaps*
- **encourage** + -ed = *encouraged*
- **mimic** + k + -ing = *mimicking,* from Latin *mīmicus,* "mimic"
- self- + **conscious** = *self-conscious*; *conscious* is from the Latin *cōnscius,*

from *com-* + *scīre,* "to know"
- **audition** is in a family of words stemming from the Latin *audīre,* "to hear" (e.g., *auditorium,* audible, audio, auditor, audience)

Writing Activity Have students select one of the five senses and write a paragraph on the circumstances that go along with not having that sense. Have volunteers read their sentences aloud.

> **Words to Know SkillBuilder Answer Key:**
> **A.**
>   **1.** *audition*   **4.** *self-conscious*
>   **2.** *handicaps*   **5.** *mimicking*
>   **3.** *encouraged*
>
> **B.**
>   **1.** *c*   **2.** *c*   **3.** *b*   **4.** *b*   **5.** *c*

---

5. SELECTION TEST

> **Selection Test Answer Key:**
> **A. 1.** *b*   **2.** *c*   **3.** *b*   **4.** *a*   **5.** *a*   **6.** *b*   **7.** *c*   **8.** *a*   **9.** *c*
> **B.** *Stevie performed in an audition for the president of Hitsville USA.*

GROWING UP IN A WORLD OF DARKNESS

Main Idea

The **main idea** is the most important thought in a paragraph. The main idea may be stated directly in a topic sentence. The topic sentence may appear anywhere in the paragraph. Other times, readers must figure out the main idea that brings together all the thoughts in the paragraph.

A. Find the stated main idea in each of these paragraphs from "Growing Up in a World of Darkness." Underline the topic sentence.

   1. Stevie was a lucky child in many ways. He was lucky to have two brothers close enough to him in age not to understand at first about his blindness and to expect him to do many of the things they did. He was also lucky to have a mother and a father . . . who understood how important sound was to him, and how important it was for him to learn to identify things he could not see by their sound.

   2. "I don't really feel my hearing is any better than yours," Stevie says now; "we all have the same abilities, you know." . . . Encouraged by his family, Stevie used his hearing more and more as he grew older. He learned how to tell birds apart by their calls, and to tell trees apart by the sound their leaves made as they rustled in the wind. He learned to tell when people were tired or annoyed or pleased by listening to the tone of their voices.

B. Circle the letter of the sentence that states the main idea of each paragraph.

   1. By the age of two, Stevie used spoons to make rhythmic sounds. Later, he beat on cardboard drums and used a small harmonica. He learned to play the piano and bongo drums. He also experimented with his voice.

     a. Stevie found many ways to make sounds and music.

     b. Stevie often listened to the radio.

   2. First, Ronnie White took him around the studio, allowing Stevie to touch all the instruments and recording equipment. Then Stevie met Berry Gordy, the president of the company. Stevie sang and played the drums and harmonica for him. Berry Gordy immediately signed Stevie to a long contract.

     a. Stevie worked for Hitsville USA for ten years.

     b. Stevie's audition at the Hitsville USA recording studio was exciting.

GROWING UP IN A WORLD OF DARKNESS

Problem and Solution

In most stories, characters meet problems in their lives. They must find ways to solve the problems they face. The events in a story or article may be organized to describe a **problem** and then show its **solution.**

The biography "Growing Up in a World of Darkness" describes several problems that Stevie Wonder had to solve. In the chart below, either the problem or a solution is listed. Fill in the missing problems and solutions.

Problem	Solution
1. _____ _____ _____	1. As a child, Stevie developed his sense of hearing so he could identify things by the way they sounded.
2. Sometimes at night, Stevie did not feel part of the world when everything around him was silent.	2. _____ _____ _____
3. _____ _____ _____	3. Stevie told his mother that he was happy being blind. He said it was a gift from God.
4. In order to live as normal a life as possible, Stevie needed to learn many things not taught to children with sight.	4. _____ _____ _____
5. _____ _____ _____	5. Stevie received a drum set from the Lions Club. Friendly neighbors gave him a real harmonica and piano.
6. On the school bus, Stevie felt a little ashamed because he listened to a black radio station.	6. _____ _____ _____

GROWING UP IN A WORLD OF DARKNESS

Syllabication

A **syllable** is a word part with one vowel sound. If you are unsure of how to divide a word, look it up in the dictionary. Then say the syllables slowly and put them together.

A. Divide these words into syllables. Write each syllable on the line.

1. handicap   =   _____ + _____ + _____

2. relatives   =   _____ + _____ + _____

3. soundproof =   _____ + _____

4. equipment   =   _____ + _____ + _____

B. Separate these words from "Growing Up in a World of Darkness" into three syllables. Circle the syllable that gets the most stress when you say the word.

Word	1st Syllable	2nd Syllable	3rd Syllable
1. occasion			
2. instrument			
3. frustration			
4. popular			
5. studio			
6. introduce			

C. Complete each sentence with a word from Exercise B.

1. Stevie's first real musical _____ was a set of drums.

2. Songs are recorded in a special soundproof _____.

3. Many people enjoy listening to Stevie's music; it is very _____.

4. The audition at Hitsville USA was a special _____ for the whole family.

GROWING UP IN A WORLD OF DARKNESS

Words to Know

handicaps   encouraged   mimicking   self-conscious   audition

A. Fill in the blanks with the word from the list that best completes the sentence.

1. I wanted to be in the play, but first I had to show my skills in an _____.

2. Having _____ may make life difficult, but it doesn't prevent success.

3. I felt _____ because my parents supported me and told me to follow

   my dreams.

4. Ben felt very _____ because everybody stared at his bright clothing.

5. Sarah learned the dance steps by _____ and following the lead dancer.

B. Circle the letter next to the word that doesn't belong. Use the dictionary if necessary.

1. a. audition   b. perform   c. eat

2. a. nervous   b. self-conscious   c. confident

3. a. imitate   b. different   c. mimicking

4. a. encouraged   b. ignored   c. cheered

5. a. blind   b. handicaps   c. average

Writing Activity

Imagine you have lost one of your five senses: the ability to see, hear, touch, smell, or taste. How would this make your life different? Write four sentences using at least three of the **Words to Know.**

GROWING UP IN A WORLD OF DARKNESS

A. Complete each statement by filling in the circle next to the letter of the correct answer.

1. Stevie Wonder's real name is
   ○ a. Morris May.   ○ b. Steveland Morris.   ○ c. Steve Wonderland.

2. Stevie is totally blind because he was
   ○ a. born that way.   ○ b. injured as a child.   ○ c. born prematurely.

3. When Stevie was young, he told his mother that his blindness was
   ○ a. a terrible problem.   ○ b. a gift from God.   ○ c. not important.

4. Stevie's relatives dropped coins on the table to teach him how to
   ○ a. tell the difference in the sounds the coins made.
   ○ b. count how many coins they had dropped.
   ○ c. add up how much the coins were worth.

5. The most frightening thing to Stevie was
   ○ a. being in total silence.   ○ b. being in total darkness.   ○ c. hearing constant noise.

6. The first toy instruments Stevie ever got were
   ○ a. a piano and some bongo drums.
   ○ b. cardboard drums and a harmonica.
   ○ c. a drum set and a piano.

7. Stevie learned a lot about music by listening to his
   ○ a. mother.   ○ b. drums.   ○ c. radio.

8. According to the author, if everyone were blind, people would
   ○ a. still divide themselves into "Us" and "Them."
   ○ b. not divide themselves into different groups.
   ○ c. not care what anyone else looked like.

9. When Stevie was told that his new piano was dark brown, he
   ○ a. asked to have it painted.   ○ b. said he didn't want it.   ○ c. felt better about his skin color.

B. Answer the following question in a complete sentence.

How did Stevie get his first recording contract?

_____

_____

Reader directions:

Cut this paper in half. Practice reading the passage aloud until you don't make any mistakes.
Then have someone listen to you read. Try to sound the way you think a narrator would sound.

from "Growing Up in a World of Darkness"

He would sing the words of the songs quietly to himself. He would hum the tunes. He
would tap out the beats on his toy drums and try to play the melodies on his four-note
harmonica. It frustrated him not to have real, grown-up instruments to play on, and it was
hard for him to accept the fact that his mother just did not have enough money to buy
real instruments for him. But luck soon proved to be with Stevie. Within the space of
about a year and a half, he managed to acquire not one but *three* real instruments.

✂ **cut along dotted line**

- -

Checker directions:

Follow along as the passage is read. Make a dot under each word the reader misses.
Show the reader the missed words. Erase the dots and repeat for each reading.

from "Growing Up in a World of Darkness"

He would sing the words of the songs quietly to himself. He would hum the tunes. He
would tap out the beats on his toy drums and try to play the melodies on his four-note
harmonica. It frustrated him not to have real, grown-up instruments to play on, and it was
hard for him to accept the fact that his mother just did not have enough money to buy
real instruments for him. But luck soon proved to be with Stevie. Within the space of
about a year and a half, he managed to acquire not one but *three* real instruments.

Use this chart for Timed Readings and Repeated Readings.

Reading	1	2	3	4	5
Time (minutes/seconds)					
Words Missed					

Focus Skills and SkillBuilder Copymasters

Appearances Can Fool You

Unit 10
Poetry

Many things and people are not what they seem. You cannot judge them by how they look. The poems in this unit invite you to look at familiar things in different ways.

Some of the poets use rhyme and rhythm to give a musical sound to their poems. One uses **free verse,** poetry without rhyme and rhythm. All the poems have a **speaker,** the voice that talks to the reader. Sometimes the voice uses **humor** to make you laugh. Sometimes the voice gives an important message about life, called a **theme.** Take a new look at some familiar things.

318

Pacing Guide

The suggested Post Reading time varies, depending on how you use it. For example, you might have the class complete each SkillBuilder after reading the corresponding poem, or you might have them complete all the SkillBuilders in one session at the end of this unit.

SELECTION	TOTAL DAYS	PREREADING	READING	POST READING
Appearances Can Fool You (all poems)	3.5–4	1	2	.5–1

More About Poetry

The poems in this unit will make students think about whether things really are what they seem to be. Most students thier age enjoy the mental gymnastics involved in analyzing appearances. Students will analyze poems' themes and points of view along with the elements of rhythm and rhyme, free verse, speaker, figurative language, and humor. You might teach all the elements first and then read the poems, or teach each element with its corresponding poem. Either way, use suggestions in Presenting the Poem to help students enjoy and appreciate the sounds of poetry. Refer students to pages 462–463 in the Student Resources section for a review of poetry terms.

Technology Resources

Audio CD
The following poetry selections in this unit are featured in the Audio Library: "Some People," "Almost Human," and "Nikki-Rosa."

Reading Coach CD-ROM
The following poetry selections are part of the Reading Coach: "Some People" and "Nikki-Rosa." You may use Reading Coach selections as a group activity, as an individual activity, or as a tutorial for students who might benefit from this format or who have missed class.

Building Bridges: Closing the Reading Gap
This video is intended for teacher use only. It gives instructions and tips on how to help middle school readers become strategic readers.

Assessment

Unit Test
Unit 10 poetry is assessed on pages T452–T453.

Assessment Booklet
End-of-Year Skills Test Units 1–12
Administer this test when students have completed the book. It covers skills taught in all the units.

Focus Skill

LITERATURE

Theme

SkillBuilder Copymaster

 Literary Analysis:
1 Theme p. T435

Assessment

2 All Unit 10 poetry is assessed on pages T452–T453.

Some People

By Rachel Field

Some people make you feel good and some people don't. Do you know someone who belongs in this poem?

 **Reading Coach CD-ROM selection**

Connect to Your Life

Do you know someone who always has something nice to say? Think of something that person said recently. How did it make you feel?

Key to the Poem

Some poems use contrasts to help give the main message. **Contrasts** are differences, almost opposites. For example, a soft voice is a contrast to a very loud voice. This poem gives its message through contrast.

320 Unit 10 Appearances Can Fool You

Connect to Your Life

As students discuss how someone's kind words made them feel, be sure they give reasons for why the person's words made them feel that way. Use chart paper to list kind words and phrases that come up during the discussion. Keep the chart on display as a reference when students are writing.

Key to the Poem

Be sure students understand that when they contrast two things or people, they are looking at how those things or people are different, rather than alike. If necessary, explain that contrasting differences is the opposite of comparing similarities.

Some People
By Rachel Field

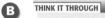

> Isn't it strange some people make
>   You feel so tired inside,
> Your thoughts begin to shrivel up
>   Like leaves all brown and dried!
>
> 5 But when you're with some other ones,
>   It's stranger still to find
> Your thoughts as thick as fireflies
>   All shiny in your mind!

B

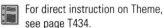
THINK IT THROUGH

1. How are the people in the first half of the poem different from the people in the second half?
2. In lines 3 and 4, what are thoughts compared to? What are they compared to in lines 7 and 8?
3. What is the poem's message, or theme, about how people can affect you?

Some People **321**

Presenting the Poem

Read the poem aloud in an expressive, conversational tone—as if talking to your best friend. Have students listen for what they like about the poem and how it makes them feel. Then allow volunteers to choose a stanza to read. Have them pretend that they are talking to their friends. Encourage a conversational rhythm. After a few readings, have students find the rhyming words in the first stanza (inside-dried); the second stanza (find-mind). Then proceed to the focus skill instruction.

LITERATURE

FOCUS SKILL: Theme

Tell students that the **theme** of a poem is the message about life or human nature that the poet is trying to convey. Sometimes the theme is stated outright. At other times, however, readers must infer it.

For direct instruction on Theme, see page T434.

Use the following questions to encourage literary analysis.

A **Teacher Modeling: Simile** To help students understand similes, say: *Wow, I like the similes that the poet uses to contrast thoughts about being with different people. The first simile helps me understand what happens to thoughts around people who "drain the life out of you." Picturing the life draining out of a fallen leaf helps me imagine a thought slowly fading as it dies. But the second simile helps me understand what happens to thoughts around people who "set you on fire."*

Now read the second stanza and find the second simile. *(thoughts as thick as fireflies)*

B **THINK IT THROUGH**

1. How are the people in the first half of the poem different from the people in the second half? *(The people in the first half make you feel bad, while the people in the second half make you feel good.)* **compare and contrast**
   COMPREHENSION

2. In lines 3 and 4, what are thoughts compared to? What are they compared to in lines 7 and 8? *(In lines 3 and 4 thoughts are compared to shriveled, brown leaves; in lines 7 and 8 they are compared to shiny fireflies.)* **simile**

3. What is the poem's message, or theme, about how people can affect you? *(Some people can make you feel tired and unhappy, while others can make you feel alive and joyous.)* **theme**

1. LITERATURE

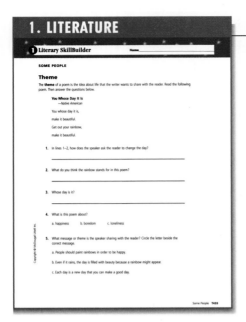

Theme

Direct Instruction Review the definition of theme. Tell students that the **theme** is the message or idea about life that the poet shares with the reader. The message can be stated directly in the poem or it can be hidden from the reader. When it is hidden, the reader must look at the poem as a whole and put together the clues that the poet leaves behind. Tell students that the poet may concentrate on an image or a specific word that is full of meaning. Some words and images can represent something deeper and more meaningful. For example, a red rose may stand for beauty or love.

In fiction, the theme is sometimes revealed by the actions or the development of the main character. Point out that the speaker in a poem is like the character in a short story; the speaker may also reveal something about the theme. Sometimes, if the speaker is the poet, he or she may be sharing a piece of advice with the reader.

Literary SkillBuilder Answer Key:

1. *Possible response: The speaker asks the reader to make the day beautiful.*
2. *Possible response: The rainbow can stand for a smile or any act of goodness.*
3. *The reader's (or listener's)*
4. *a*
5. *c*

SOME PEOPLE

Theme

The **theme** of a poem is the idea about life that the writer wants to share with the reader. Read the following poem. Then answer the questions below.

> **You Whose Day It Is**
> *—Native American*
>
> You whose day it is,
>
> make it beautiful.
>
> Get out your rainbow,
>
> make it beautiful.

1. In lines 1–2, how does the speaker ask the reader to change the day?

   _____

2. What do you think the rainbow stands for in this poem?

   _____

3. Whose day is it?

   _____

4. What is this poem about?

   a. happiness   b. boredom   c. loneliness

5. What message or theme is the speaker sharing with the reader? Circle the letter beside the correct message.

   a. People should paint rainbows in order to be happy.

   b. Even if it rains, the day is filled with beauty because a rainbow might appear.

   c. Each day is a new day that you can make a good day.

Focus Skill

LITERATURE
Speaker

SkillBuilder Copymaster

 Literary Analysis:
1 Speaker p. T440

Assessment

 2 All Unit 10 poetry is assessed
on pages T452–T453.

For English Learners

If any of your students have never
attended a water show at a zoo, an
aquarium, or a theme park, you
may want to have those who have
attended one share what happens.
In particular, have them explain
what is being described in lines
15–22 of the poem.

Almost Human

by Pat Moon

Can dolphins talk?

To find out, why not

just ask them?

322 Unit 10 Appearances Can Fool You

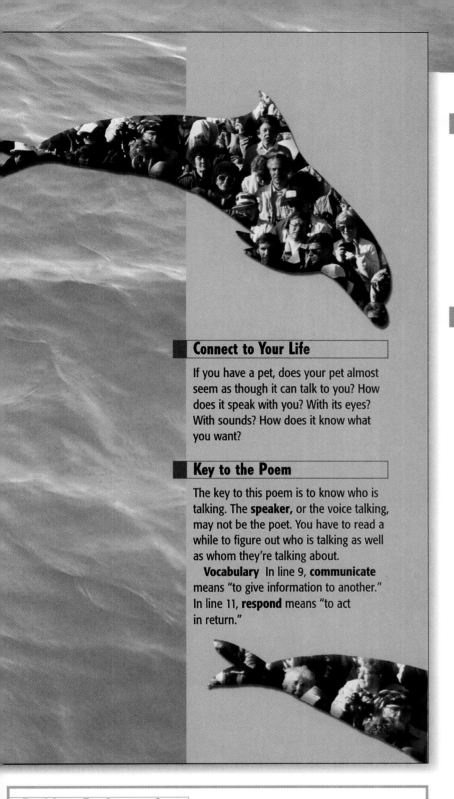

Connect to Your Life

If you have a pet, does your pet almost seem as though it can talk to you? How does it speak with you? With its eyes? With sounds? How does it know what you want?

Key to the Poem

The key to this poem is to know who is talking. The **speaker,** or the voice talking, may not be the poet. You have to read a while to figure out who is talking as well as whom they're talking about.

Vocabulary In line 9, **communicate** means "to give information to another." In line 11, **respond** means "to act in return."

Connect to Your Life

Have students form small groups to discuss the different ways in which they and their pets communicate with them. Encourage students to explain how they can tell whether their pets understand them and what their pets do to be understood. Have students read the title of the poem and speculate on what it means.

Key to the Poem

Students learned in Unit 3 that even though a poem may contain the words *I, me,* and *my,* the speaker of the poem is not necessarily the person who wrote it. Help students understand that poets sometimes choose to write poems spoken by someone—or something—else in order to present a different or unique point of view.

Presenting the Poem

Do not tell students that this poem is told from an animal's point of view and is about people. It will be more rewarding for students if they discover this on their own. Ask students what animal they think this poem will be about. (Most will say a dolphin.) Elicit students' experiences watching dolphins at the zoo, in the movies, or on TV. Have students listen for what they like about the poem as you read the poem aloud with expression. Don't be surprised if you are asked to read it again. Allow time for students to discuss what they like about the poem and then proceed to the focus-skill instruction.

Building Background

Many scientists regard the dolphin as one of the most intelligent animals. Some scientists even believe that dolphins make different sounds in different situations. For example, scientists believe that dolphins send out different kinds of distress calls for different kinds of trouble. Because of dolphins' intelligence, hundreds of them have been trained to perform in water shows. Their tricks include jumping through hoops, throwing balls through nets, "walking" backwards on their flukes, and jumping out of the water to ring bells or take food from a trainer's mouth.

Almost Human

by Pat Moon

Come and see the people dear.
Oh, look how they sit!
Aren't they sweet
The way they laugh?
5 I really must admit
That they seem quite intelligent.
Just hear the sound they make;
You could almost believe
They're trying to communicate.

A

10 They're very easily trained
And respond to simple rules.
Just watch how they point and wave
As we swim around the pool.
See how they stand and clap
15 When we dive through the hoop?
And the noise they make
When we walk on our tails
Or leap the bar in one swoop!

Just watch how they jump and shout
20 In my favorite part of the shows
When we dive and splash the water
All over the front few rows.

B

It's time to leave them now, dear,
They've had enough for one day.
25 It's quite amazing what people can do
If you treat them in the right way.

C

THINK IT THROUGH

1. Who is speaking in the poem? Whom is the speaker talking about?
2. What does the speaker think of people? Give examples to explain your opinion.
3. What would the speaker probably say about the intelligence of animals and people?

LITERATURE

FOCUS SKILL: Speaker

Remind students that the speaker of a poem is not necessarily the person who wrote it, even when the speaker uses *I* and *me*.

 For direct instruction on Speaker, see page T439.

Use the following questions to encourage literary analysis.

A What is ironic, or unexpected, about the ideas presented in lines 12–22? *(The speaker seems to be implying that the responses of the audience—pointing, waving, standing and clapping, and so on—are a result of their being trained to act that way. In actuality, however, it is the dolphins who have been trained to dive, "walk," and splash. The audience is just reacting to the dolphins' tricks.)* **irony**

B Share the following with students. Sometimes a poet will make the speaker of a poem someone—or something—else in order to make a particular point.

That is what Pat Moon does in "Almost Human." By looking at a water show through the eyes of a dolphin, Moon seems to be sending the message that maybe some animals are more intelligent than we think, and that maybe they have their own opinions about human behavior and intelligence. **speaker**

C **THINK IT THROUGH**

1. Who is speaking in the poem? Whom is the speaker talking about? *(The speaker is a dolphin or whale and it is talking about humans.)* **speaker**

2. What does the speaker think of people? Give examples to explain your opinion. *(They are not as smart as animals. Examples may include: "They (people) seem quite intelligent; They (the people) have had enough for one day; It's quite amazing what people can do.")* **speaker**

3. What would the speaker probably say about the intelligence of animals and people? *(The speaker probably would say that animals are more intelligent than humans.)* **theme**

VOCABULARY

FOR ENGLISH LEARNERS

Help students understand the following expressions and idioms:

Line 15: through the hoop
Line 17: walk on our tails
Line 18: leap the bar in one swoop
Line 24: had enough for one day

1. LITERATURE

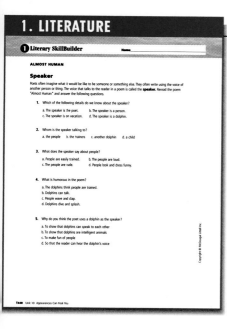

Speaker

Direct Instruction Review with students the definition of *speaker*. Tell them that the **speaker** is the voice that talks to the reader. The speaker may or may not be the poet, but often the speaker will express the poet's own feelings. Point out that the identity of the speaker is not always obvious. Explain that readers must pay attention to clues to understand who is speaking. Readers can learn how the speaker feels about a certain subject. They can learn other details about the speaker like his or her age, gender, and occupation.

Tell students that the speaker is not always a human. Sometimes poets choose animals or objects as speakers to send a strong message. Ask students what they know about dolphins. Then ask: *Do you think the poet is trying to make a statement about the way people treat dolphins? What clues tell you so?* (Students may point to the title and suggest that the poet has strong feelings about dolphins.)

Literary SkillBuilder Answer Key:

1. *d* **4.** *a*

2. *c* **5.** *b*

3. *a*

ALMOST HUMAN

Speaker

Poets often imagine what it would be like to be someone or something else. They often write using the voice of another person or thing. The voice that talks to the reader in a poem is called the **speaker.** Reread the poem "Almost Human" and answer the following questions.

1. Which of the following details do we know about the speaker?

   a. The speaker is the poet.   b. The speaker is a person.
   c. The speaker is on vacation.   d. The speaker is a dolphin.

2. Whom is the speaker talking to?

   a. the people   b. the trainers   c. another dolphin   d. a child

3. What does the speaker say about people?

   a. People are easily trained.   b. The people are loud.
   c. The people are rude.   d. People look and dress funny.

4. What is humorous in the poem?

   a. The dolphins think people are trained.
   b. Dolphins can talk.
   c. People wave and clap.
   d. Dolphins dive and splash.

5. Why do you think the poet uses a dolphin as the speaker?

   a. To show that dolphins can speak to each other
   b. To show that dolphins are intelligent animals
   c. To make fun of people
   d. So that the reader can hear the dolphin's voice

Focus Skill

LITERATURE
Point of View

SkillBuilder Copymaster

 Literary Analysis:
1 Point of View p. T445

Assessment

 2 All Unit 10 poetry is assessed on pages T452–T453.

POINT OF VIEW

BY SHEL SILVERSTEIN

Everyone loves a holiday meal! Well, maybe not everyone. . . .

Connect to Your Life

Sometimes you see things one way and a friend sees them another way. When is it okay for friends to have different opinions about the same thing?

Key to the Poem

Notice that the title of this poem is "Point of View." **Point of view** means the way someone sees something. Two people can have two different ways of thinking about the same thing. Imagine how different the points of view of an animal and a person would be. This poem contrasts two very different points of view, indeed.

326 Unit 10 Appearances Can Fool You

Connect to Your Life

If necessary, provide students with scenarios for which there might be strong views pro and con *(wearing a coat made from animal fur, hanging out past curfew, playing pranks on a friend, and so on)*. Discuss what the different points of view might be. Encourage students to consider both sides of each issue.

Key to the Poem

As students learned when they read "Some People," when contrasting two things or people, look at how they are different. In this poem, students will read about contrasting viewpoints—the viewpoints of people and the animals they eat.

POINT OF VIEW

BY SHEL SILVERSTEIN

A
B
Thanksgiving dinner's sad and thankless
Christmas dinner's dark and blue
When you stop and try to see it
From the turkey's point of view.

5 Sunday dinner isn't sunny
Easter feasts are just bad luck
When you see it from the viewpoint
Of a chicken or a duck.

C
D
Oh how I once loved tuna salad
10 Pork and lobsters, lamb chops too
Till I stopped and looked at dinner
From the dinner's point of view.

E

THINK IT THROUGH

1. How does line 4 make the reader laugh?
2. How is the speaker's point of view different from the animals' points of view?
3. Why does the speaker stop enjoying dinners?

Point of View **327**

FOCUS SKILL: Point of View

Explain to students that **point of view** is the way in which a poem, story, or article is told. In the first-person point of view, a character is talking. The speaker uses the words *I, me,* or *my.* We learn about the subject through what the speaker says. We learn about the speaker too— what he or she thinks and feels.

 For direct instruction on Point of View, see page T444.

Use the following questions to encourage literary analysis.

A Which lines rhyme in each stanza? *(lines 2 and 4)* What is similar about the rhyming lines in the first and third stanzas? *(Lines 2 and 4 in the first stanza rhyme with lines 2 and 4 in the third stanza.)* **rhyme**

B **Teacher Modeling: Ironic Humor**
To help students understand the humor in this poem you might say: *When I read the first two lines of the first stanza, I think, No way, holiday dinners aren't sad and blue; they're fun. Then I read the next two lines and realize the speaker's describing the poor turkey's point of view. This unexpected twist makes me laugh as I think about ways turkeys might show that they do not enjoy holiday dinners. Even though I feel sorry for the turkey, pictures in my mind of a turkey revolt—turkeys jumping off the tables, drumsticks kicking forks away—make me laugh.*

Encourage volunteers to share their versions of the humor in the remaining two stanzas. **humor**

C How do we know that this poem is told in the first-person point of view? *(speaker says I)* **point of view**

D What other point of view is the speaker asking us to consider? *(animals'/dinner's)* **point of view**

E **THINK IT THROUGH**

1. How does line 4 make the reader laugh? *(Line 4 makes the reader suddenly think about the turkey victim's point of view.)* **humor**

2. How is the speaker's point of view different from the animals' points of view? *(The speaker gets to eat the animals, so he or she is happy; the animals are miserable because they're the ones being eaten.)* **point of view**

3. Why does the speaker stop enjoying dinners? *(He or she starts looking at things from the animals' points of view.)* **cause and effect** COMPREHENSION

1. LITERATURE

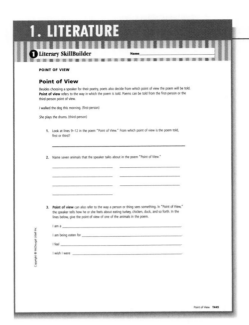

Point of View

Direct Instruction Tell students that **point of view** refers to the way in which a poem is told. In the first-person point of view, the speaker uses the pronouns *I, me,* and *my.* In the third-person point of view, the speaker uses the pronouns *he* or *she.* Explain that in the first-person point of view, the reader learns more about the speaker: how he or she feels and thinks. In the third-person point of view, the reader learns how the speaker feels about another person or thing.

To help students understand point of view, have them use the first-person and third-person points of view to write a sentence about each of the following topics: school, television, sports, the Internet.

Literary SkillBuilder Answer Key:
1. *first-person*
2. *turkey, chicken, duck, tuna, pig, lobster, lamb*
3. *Accept all reasonable responses. Possible answer: turkey; Thanksgiving dinner; terrified; somewhere else*

POINT OF VIEW

Point of View

Besides choosing a speaker for their poetry, poets also decide from which point of view the poem will be told. **Point of view** refers to the way in which the poem is told. Poems can be told from the first-person or the third-person point of view.

I walked the dog this morning. (first-person)

She plays the drums. (third-person)

1. Look at lines 9–12 in the poem "Point of View." From which point of view is the poem told, first or third?

   _____

2. Name seven animals that the speaker talks about in the poem "Point of View."

   _____   _____

   _____   _____

   _____   _____

   _____

3. **Point of view** can also refer to the way a person or thing sees something. In "Point of View," the speaker tells how he or she feels about eating turkey, chicken, duck, and so forth. In the lines below, give the point of view of one of the animals in the poem.

   I am a _____.

   I am being eaten for _____.

   I feel _____.

   I wish I were _____.

Focus Skill

LITERATURE
Free Verse

SkillBuilder Copymasters

Literary Analysis:
1 Free Verse p. T450

Vocabulary:
2 All Unit 10 vocabulary is covered on p. T451.

Assessment

3 All Unit 10 poetry is assessed on pages T452–T453.

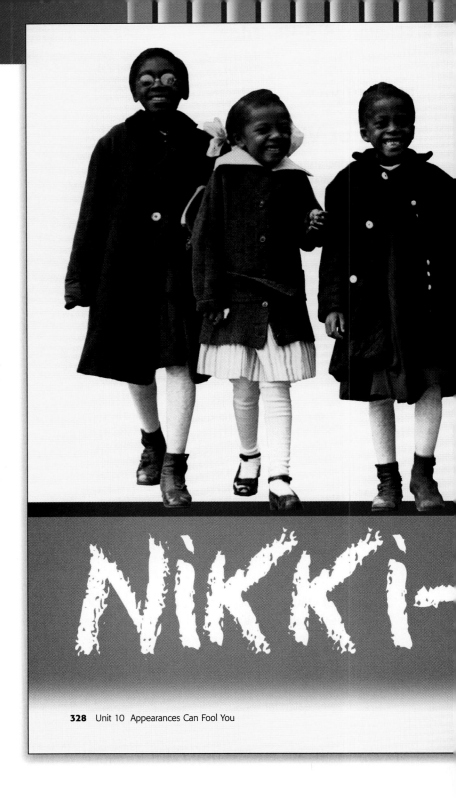

328 Unit 10 Appearances Can Fool You

Connect to Your Life

Do other people see you the way you see yourself? How is their view different from yours?

Key to the Poem

In **free verse,** the poet does not have to use rhyming words or a strong rhythm. This poet expresses thoughts freely, without rhyme or a beat. Notice that the lines are different lengths, depending on what is said. They take the shape of the writer's feelings as they flow onto the paper.

In "Nikki-Rosa" free verse is used to express feelings. Look for the speaker's feelings about childhood.

Vocabulary In line 17, **biographers** means "people who write the life stories of famous people." In line 20, **poverty** means "the state of being poor."

 Reading Coach CD-ROM selection

BY NIKKI GIOVANNI

We all have

childhood memories.

What feelings go

along with those

memories?

Nikki-Rosa **329**

Building Background

Nikki Giovanni (born 1943) is an African-American poet, essayist, lecturer, and teacher. She has received numerous awards for her writing as well as for her recordings. At 28 she produced an album of her readings called *Truth Is on Its Way.* In her early work, Giovanni often wrote about her political views and her feelings about civil rights. Later, however, she began to focus more on family and relationships. In 1987 she was the subject of a PBS documentary called *Spirit to Spirit: The Poetry of Nikki Giovanni.*

NiKKi-ROSA
BY NiKKi GiOVANNi

(A) childhood remembrances are always a drag
if you're Black
you always remember things like living in Woodlawn
with no inside toilet
5 and if you become famous or something
(B) they never talk about how happy you were to have
your mother
all to yourself and
how good the water felt when you got your bath
10 from one of those
big tubs that folk in chicago barbecue in
and somehow when you talk about home
it never gets across how much you
understood their feelings
15 as the whole family attended meetings about
   Hollydale
and even though you remember
your biographers never understand
your father's pain as he sells his stock
and another dream goes

20 And though you're poor it isn't poverty that
concerns you
and though they fought a lot
it isn't your father's drinking that makes any difference
but only that everybody is together and you
(C) 25 and your sister have happy birthdays and very good
Christmases
and I really hope no white person ever has cause
to write about me
because they never understand
30 Black love is Black wealth and they'll
probably talk about my hard childhood
and never understand that
all the while I was quite happy

(D) **THINK IT THROUGH**

1. In what ways might the speaker's childhood seem hard?
2. How does the speaker really feel about her childhood?
3. What message, or theme, does the speaker give about her childhood?

330 Unit 10 Appearances Can Fool You

Nikki-Rosa **331**

LITERATURE

FOCUS SKILL: Free Verse

Remind students that because a poem written in **free verse** has no regular pattern of rhyme, rhythm, or line length, it often sounds like conversation. Also explain that the speaker in this poem is actually the poet, and she is conversing with her audience about her own life.

 For direct instruction on Free Verse, see page T449.

Use the following questions to encourage literary analysis.

(A) Point out that lines 1–3 sound like conversation because the speaker is using "you" and talking directly to the reader. **free verse**

(B) How does the poet feel about her mother? *(She loves her mother and enjoys having her attention.)* **details COMPREHENSION**

(C) What are the poet's feelings about birthdays and Christmas in her childhood? *(They were very happy times because everyone was together and the celebrations were filled with love.)* **making inferences COMPREHENSION**

(D) **THINK IT THROUGH**

1. In what ways might the speaker's childhood seem hard? *(Possible answers: no inside toilet, baths in a tub designed for barbecuing meat, father's lost dreams, being poor, parents fighting, and father drinking)* **cause and effect COMPREHENSION**

2. How does the speaker really feel about her childhood? *(She feels that it was quite happy.)* **details COMPREHENSION**

3. What message, or theme, does the speaker give about her childhood? *(Possible answers: You don't have to have a lot to have a happy life. It's love, not money, that makes people happy.)* **theme**

VOCABULARY

FOR ENGLISH LEARNERS

Help students understand the following expressions and idioms:

Line 1: a drag
Line 4: inside toilet
Line 11: big tubs that folk in chicago barbecue in (large galvanized tubs)
Line 13: never gets across
Line 30: Black love is Black wealth

1. LITERATURE

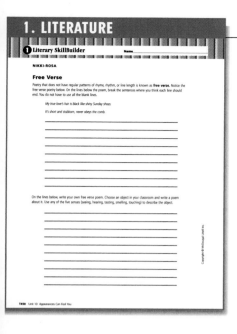

Free Verse

Direct Instruction Tell students that much modern poetry is written in **free verse.** Free verse is poetry that contains no regular pattern of rhyme, rhythm, or line length. The lines in free verse often flow more naturally than those that have rhythm and rhyme; free verse sounds more like a conversation. Explain that in free verse, poets determine where lines break based on where pauses are required or on how the poem will look on the page. A line can be as short as one word, or it can be a complete sentence. Modern poets also often experiment with line breaks, form, and word choice to create a mood or feeling.

Write the following sentences on the board and ask volunteers to break them into lines of free verse: *On my first day of school, I stand before the class and face the silent stares of the jury. I breathe deeply and hold onto life with both hands.* Make sure students understand that there is more than one way to break the lines.

Literary SkillBuilder Answer Key:
Accept all forms of free verse. Have volunteers share their work with the class.

2. VOCABULARY

Vocabulary

Direct Instruction The vocabulary words in this SkillBuilder come from the following poems:
shrivel: "Some People"
communicate and *respond:* "Almost Human"
biographers and *poverty:* "Nikki-Rosa"

When presenting the words to students, you might discuss these word origins.

- **communicate** comes from the Latin *commūnicāre,* meaning "to share."
- **respond** comes from the Latin *re-,* meaning "back" and *spondēre,* meaning "to pledge."
- **poverty** comes from the Latin *paupertās,* meaning "poverty."
- **biographers** comes from the Greek *bio-,* meaning "life" and *-graphiā,* meaning "writing."

Vocabulary Skillbuilder Answer Key:

1. *poverty*
2. *shrivel*
3. *biographers*
4. *communicate*
5. *respond*

6. *communicate*
7. *poverty*
8. *biographers*
9. *shrivel*
10. *respond*

3. UNIT TEST

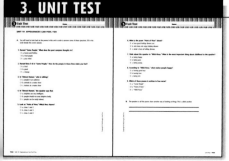

Unit Test

Tell the students that they will need to look back at the poems in this unit while answering these questions.

Unit Test Answer Key:
A. 1. *a* **2.** *b* **3.** *b* **4.** *c* **5.** *c* **6.** *b* **7.** *a* **8.** *b* **9.** *c*
B. *point of view.*

NIKKI-ROSA

Free Verse

Poetry that does not have regular patterns of rhyme, rhythm, or line length is known as **free verse.** Notice the free verse poetry below. On the lines below the poem, break the sentences where you think each line should end. You do not have to use all the blank lines.

My true love's hair is black like shiny Sunday shoes.

It's short and stubborn, never obeys the comb.

_____

_____

_____

_____

_____

_____

_____

_____

On the lines below, write your own free verse poem. Choose an object in your classroom and write a poem about it. Use any of the five senses (seeing, hearing, tasting, smelling, touching) to describe the object.

_____

_____

_____

_____

_____

_____

_____

_____

UNIT 10 POETRY

You read the following words in the poems in this unit. They are words you can learn.

shrivel *v.* dry up

communicate *v.* give information to another

respond *v.* act in return

biographers *n.* people who write the life stories of famous people

poverty *n.* the state of being poor

Write the correct word from the list above.

1. What is the opposite of wealth? _____

2. What is the opposite of grow? _____

3. When you become rich and famous, who will write about you? _____

4. What do people do when they speak and write? _____

5. If someone asks you a question, what should you do? _____

6. What do people do when they use a telephone? _____

7. People work hard for money to avoid living in what? _____

8. Who might write about a president? _____

9. Grapes do what to become raisins? _____

10. If you are invited to a party, what should you do? _____

UNIT 10 APPEARANCES CAN FOOL YOU

A. You will need to look back at the poems in this unit in order to answer some of these questions. Fill in the circle beside the correct answer.

1. Reread "Some People." What does the poet compare thoughts to?
   ○ a. leaves and fireflies
   ○ b. tired people
   ○ c. your mind

2. Reread lines 5–8 in "Some People." How do the people in those lines make you feel?
   ○ a. tired
   ○ b. good
   ○ c. strange

3. In "Almost Human," who is talking?
   ○ a. a person in an audience
   ○ b. an animal in a water show
   ○ c. a trainer at a water show

4. In "Almost Human," the speaker says that
   ○ a. dolphins are very intelligent.
   ○ b. people should not treat dolphins badly.
   ○ c. people can be easily trained.

5. Look at "Point of View." Which lines rhyme?
   ○ a. Lines 1 and 2
   ○ b. Lines 2 and 3
   ○ c. Lines 2 and 4

6. **What is the poem "Point of View" about?**
   - ○ a. how good holiday dinners are
   - ○ b. who does not enjoy holiday dinners
   - ○ c. what is best at holiday dinners

7. **Think about the speaker in "Nikki-Rosa." What is the most important thing about childhood to the speaker?**
   - ○ a. being happy
   - ○ b. being poor
   - ○ c. being young

8. **According to "Nikki-Rosa," what makes people happy?**
   - ○ a. having good toys
   - ○ b. having love
   - ○ c. being rich

9. **Which of these poems is written in free verse?**
   - ○ a. "Some People"
   - ○ b. "Point of View"
   - ○ c. "Nikki-Rosa"

B. The speakers in all the poems show another way of looking at things. This is called another

_____

_____

Focus Skills and SkillBuilder Copymasters

Reading Fluency

Bridges to History

Unit 11

Mixed Genres

Think of the history of the United States as a patchwork quilt. There are patches for all the people and events. The brightest patches are for the dreams that came true.

History is made up of stories, and stories are told in many different ways. In this unit you'll read **historical fiction** as well as **informative articles.** You'll also read a **ballad**—a story in the form of a poem that was sung aloud. Finally you'll read a **folk tale** that someone recorded. As you read all of these pieces, you need to separate fact from fiction.

332

Pacing Guide

SELECTION	TOTAL DAYS	PREREADING	READING	POST READING	
				SELECTIVE OPTIONS	ALL OPTIONS
The Invaders	2.5–3	1	1	.5	1
Weapons of War	2.5–3	1	1	.5	1
The New Mother	3–3.5	1	1.5	.5	1
The Ballad of John Henry	2	1	.5	.5	1
from California Gold Days	3.5–4	1	2	.5	1
Rabbit Foot: A Story of the Peacemaker	2–2.5	1	.5	.5	1

More About Mixed Genres

Selections in this unit shed light on the beginnings of European exploration in the Americas, the emergence of the United States as a nation, and U.S. expansion into the West. Stirring times are illuminated through facts, sometimes mixed with imaginative details. A wide array of genres suitably reflects the diverse American experience. The offerings include a Native American oral history, a fictionalized episode in the life of a highly respected president, and a well-known ballad about a folk hero. Students will be exposed to stirring events of American history and will gain a sense of the hardships involved in building an enduring nation.

Technology Resources

Audio CD
All selections in this unit are featured in the Audio Library.

Reading Coach CD-ROM
All six selections in this unit are part of the Reading Coach. You may use Reading Coach selections as a group activity, as an individual activity, or as a tutorial for students who might benefit from this format or who have missed class.

Building Bridges: Closing the Reading Gap
This video is intended for teacher use only. It gives instructions and tips on how to help middle school readers become strategic readers.

Assessment

Selection Tests
pp. T466, T479, T495, T503, T516, T528

Assessment Booklet
End-of-Year Skills Test Units 1–12
Administer this test when students have completed the book. It covers skills taught in all the units.

Focus Skills

COMPREHENSION
Author's Purpose

LITERATURE
Point of View

VOCABULARY
Suffix *-ly*

SkillBuilder Copymasters

 Reading Comprehension:
1 Author's Purpose p. T462

 Literary Analysis:
2 Point of View p. T463

Vocabulary:
3 Suffix *-ly* p. T464
4 Words to Know p. T465

Assessment

5 Selection Test p. T466

Readability Scores

DRP	LEXILE	DALE-CHALL
53	670	4.4

For English Learners

Since the identity of the invaders is not revealed until the last paragraph of this story, discuss what students know about these terms after they have finished reading: *Pilgrims, Miles Standish, Plymouth Colony.*

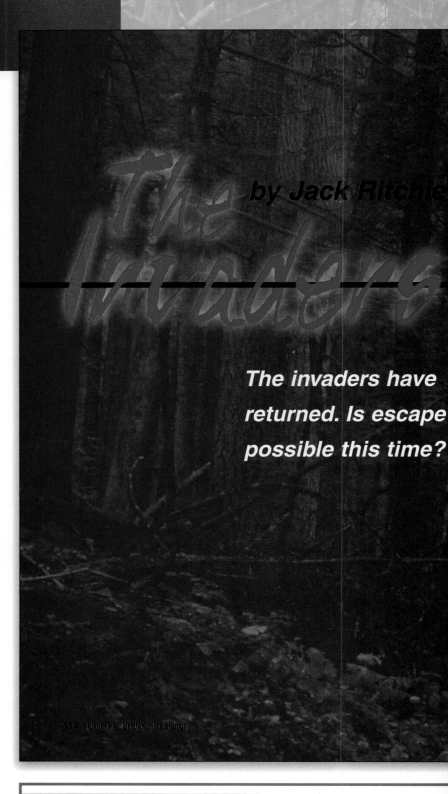

The **Invaders**

by Jack Ritchie

The invaders have returned. Is escape possible this time?

334 Unit 11 Bridges to History

Vocabulary Strategy: Preteaching

Suffix *-ly* Tell students that when they come across a word ending in the suffix *-ly*, they should understand that the suffix often indicates an adverb meaning "in a certain way." For example, *bravely* is an adverb meaning "acting in a brave manner." Review that adverbs usually tell more about the verb, explaining how the action happens. Not all words that end in *-ly* are adverbs, however; *friendly* is an adjective describing a noun.

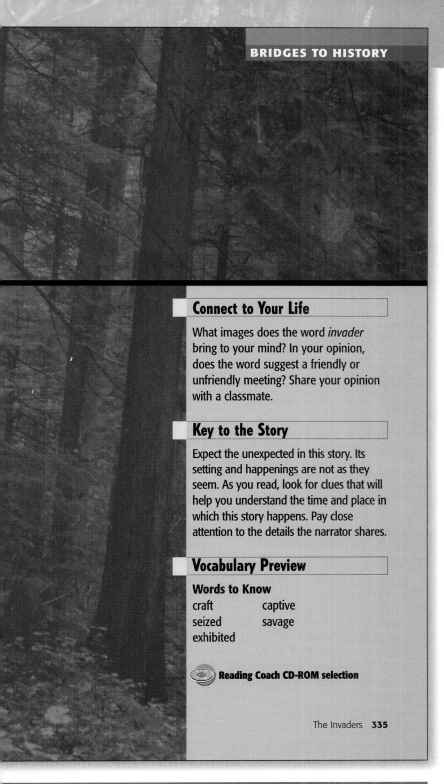

Connect to Your Life

What images does the word *invader* bring to your mind? In your opinion, does the word suggest a friendly or unfriendly meeting? Share your opinion with a classmate.

Key to the Story

Expect the unexpected in this story. Its setting and happenings are not as they seem. As you read, look for clues that will help you understand the time and place in which this story happens. Pay close attention to the details the narrator shares.

Vocabulary Preview

Words to Know

craft   captive
seized   savage
exhibited

 Reading Coach CD-ROM selection

The Invaders **335**

Connect to Your Life

To help partners discuss the word *invader,* you may want to have them create a word map that includes the categories *Meaning, Examples,* and *Synonyms.*

Key to the Story

To set a purpose for reading, ask a volunteer to read aloud the first four paragraphs of the story. Then have students predict who or what the invaders might be, and what they might do. When students finish the story, have them check their predictions.

Vocabulary Preview

Words to Know
 craft *n.* ship
 seized *v.* captured by force
 exhibited *v.* presented for others to see
 captive *n.* prisoner
 savage *n.* fierce, brutal person

For direct instruction on Words to Know, see page T461.

Building Background

Share this information *after* students have finished reading:

When the colonists arrived in America, they were first referred to by Native Americans as the Old Comers and then later as the Forefathers. It wasn't until 200 years after their arrival that they were first called the Pilgrim Fathers. At that time a manuscript written by Plymouth Colony's second governor, William Bradford, was discovered, in which he called the colonists "saints" who had come to America as "pilgrimes." The famous orator Daniel Webster liked Bradford's words so much that in a speech he gave at a bicentennial celebration in 1820, he called the colonists the Pilgrim Fathers. The name was so well-received that it has been used ever since.

As students come across unfamiliar words ending in *-ly,* they should remove the suffix and figure out what the base word means. Then they can add "in such a manner" to the meaning of the base word to understand the whole word.

 For more on Suffix *-ly,* see page T461.

FOCUS

As you read this section, look for clues that hint at who is speaking and what is happening.

None of them left the ship on the first day of its arrival, but I knew that they would be watching carefully for signs of human life.

The skies were dark with scudding clouds, and the cold wind moved high in the trees. Thin snow drifted slowly to the ground.

 From the cover of the forest, I now watched as a small, heavily armed group of them left the large craft. When they reached the edge of
10 the woods, they hesitated for a few moments and then moved cautiously forward.

craft
(krăft)
n. ship

I had seen them before and I knew that in appearance, at least, they were not monsters. They looked very much like us. There were some differences, of course, but all in all, we were really quite similar to them.

REREAD
Make predictions: Who are *they*? Who are *we*?

I met them first when I was almost a boy and I had been without caution. I
20 approached them and they seemed friendly, but then suddenly they seized me and carried me off in their strange ship.

It was a long journey to their land and when our ship made a landing, I was shown about and exhibited as though I were some kind of animal.

I saw their cities, and I was shown plants and animals completely strange to me. I learned to wear their clothing and even to
30 eat their food.

seized
(sēzd)
v. captured by force; past tense of *seize*

exhibited
(ĭg zĭb' ĭt ĭd)
v. presented for others to see; past tense of *exhibit*

They taught me to communicate in their strange and difficult tongue until I could, at times, even think in their language.

I had almost given up the hope of ever seeing my home again, but they one day put me back on one of their ships and told me that they were returning me because they wished to establish friendly relations with my people. But by now, I knew enough of them to know that this was not true. However, I nodded
40 and smiled and watched for my opportunity to escape.

When the ship landed, I went out with the first search party. It was near evening and as the darkness gathered, I edged away from them and finally I fled into the blackness and safety of the forest.

They came after me, of course, but I was hidden deep in the woods where they could not find me.

Finally they gave up and I watched their ship become smaller and finally disappear, and I
50 hoped fervently that they would never return.

But now they were back again.

fervently
(fûr' vənt lē)
with great emotion

THINK IT THROUGH
Why does the narrator flee from the invaders?

FOCUS
Look for clues about who the invaders are.

I felt a coldness inside of me as I watched them moving slowly through the trees. They seemed somehow different from the others who had been here before. It was not so much in their appearance as in

---

COMPREHENSION

FOCUS SKILL: Author's Purpose

Remind students that an **author's purpose** is his or her reason for writing something. That purpose is usually to entertain, persuade, inform, or express an opinion. An author may have more than one purpose for writing, but usually has one main purpose.

For direct instruction on Author's Purpose, see page T460.

Ⓐ REREAD Make predictions: Who are *they*? Who are *we*? (*Based on the clues that the invaders have arrived in a ship, are watching for human life, and are not monsters, students may predict that the invaders are space aliens being watched by a human being.*) **predicting**

Ⓑ THINK IT THROUGH Why does the narrator flee from the invaders? (*He doesn't like or trust them, and he doesn't want to help them. He just wants to be back in his own land with his own people.*) **cause and effect**

LITERATURE

FOCUS SKILL: Point of View

Remind students that when a story is told from a **first-person point of view,** the narrator is a character in the story and uses *I, me,* and *my* to tell the story. When a story is told from a **third-person point of view,** the narrator is not a character in the story and uses words such as *he, she, it,* and *they.*

For direct instruction on Point of View, see page T460.

Use the following questions to encourage literary analysis.

Ⓐ From what point of view is this story being told? How do you know? (*first person; the narrator is a character in the story and uses* I, me, *and* my *as he describes what happens to him*) **point of view**

VOCABULARY

FOCUS SKILL: Suffix -*ly*

Remind students that a **suffix** is a word part that is added to the end of a word. Words ending in *-ly* are often adverbs meaning "in a ____ way."

Ⓐ cautiously Have students break this word into its base and suffix (*cautious* + *ly*) to understand that it means "in a cautious or careful manner."

FOR ENGLISH LEARNERS

Help students understand the following expressions and idioms:

Line 3: signs of human life
Line 7: From the cover of the forest
Line 8: heavily armed
Line 15: all in all

the air about them—the way they walked, the way they looked about with speculating eyes.

B
60 Slowly and instinctively, I realized that this time they were not here on just another raid for a captive or two.

This time they had come to stay.

What could we do now? Could we lure them deeper into the forest and kill them? Could we take their weapons and learn how to use them?

C
No, I thought despairingly. There were so many more of the invaders on the ship. And more weapons. They would come out and hunt us down
70 like animals. They would hunt us down and kill us all.

I sighed. We must find out what it was that they wanted this time and whatever it might be, we must learn to adjust and to hope for the best.

REREAD
Why is the narrator losing hope?

C

But I still retreated silently before them, afraid to approach. I watched them search the ground ahead of them and knew they were looking for footprints, for some signs of life. But there was
80 not yet enough snow on the ground to track us down.

Their strangely colored eyes glanced about warily. They were cautious, yes.

They could be a cruel race, I knew. I had seen with my own eyes how they treated their animals and even their own kind.

I sighed again. Yes, we could be cruel, too. In this respect we could not claim to be superior to the invaders.

They paused now in a clearing, their eyes gleaming
90 beneath their helmets.

captive
(kăp' tĭv)
n. prisoner

lure
(lo͝or)
attract in order to trick

338 Unit 11 Bridges to History

It was time for me to approach them.

I took a deep breath and stepped into the open. Their weapons quickly pointed at me.

"Welcome," I said.

They stared at me, and then one of them turned to their bearded leader. "It appears that this savage can speak some English, Captain Standish."

B
"Welcome," I said again. But I
100 wondered what they would do to my land and my people now.

REREAD
Miles Standish is an English ship captain. How might this be a clue to what is happening?

D

savage
(săv' ĭj)
n. fierce, brutal person

E **THINK IT THROUGH**

1. Who is the narrator? Who are the invaders? Review the story to find details to support your answer.
2. The narrator says, "We must learn to adjust and to hope for the best." Why do you think the narrator decides to talk to the invaders?
3. As you read, who did you think the invaders were? Were you surprised? Explain.

The True Invaders

This story is based on a real event in history. It is also based on two real people. The narrator is a combination of two Native Americans. One was Samoset. In 1620, Samoset watched newcomers land on the Massachusetts coast. These people were called the Pilgrims. Samoset welcomed the Pilgrims and introduced them to the second Native American, Squanto. Squanto was captured by English fishermen and taken to England. There he learned to speak the language. After several years, Squanto was able to escape to America.

The Invaders 339

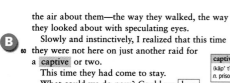

COMPREHENSION

C **REREAD** Why is the narrator losing hope? *(He knows that the invaders have come to stay, have them outnumbered, and can kill them with their weapons.)* **cause and effect**

D **REREAD** Miles Standish is an English ship captain. How might this be a clue to what is happening? *(The captain's name may suggest to students that he is probably a figure from England.)* **making inferences**

E **THINK IT THROUGH**

1. Who is the narrator? Who are the invaders? Review the story to find details to support your answer. *(The narrator is a Native American. The invaders are the Pilgrims. Captain Standish is Miles Standish, who came to America on the Mayflower.)* **making inferences**

2. The narrator says, "We must learn to adjust and to hope for the best." Why do you think the narrator talks to the invaders? *(Possible answers: He realizes that the invaders have come to stay and that fighting them would be futile. He welcomes them to show that he and his people are friendly and mean no harm.)* **making inferences**

3. As you read, who did you think the invaders were? Were you surprised? Explain. *(Have students recall their predictions. Have them discuss exactly when they figured out who the invaders were—if they figured it out. Point out that the writer is intentionally vague to leave room for a variety of speculations.)* **predicting**

LITERATURE

B Why do you think the author wrote this story from the narrator's point of view? *(He wanted to keep readers guessing about the invaders right up until the end and to show the Native Americans' point of view about the Pilgrims' arriving in their land.)* **point of view**

VOCABULARY

B **instinctively** Have students break this word into its base word and suffixes *(instinct + -ive + -ly)* to see that it means "in a manner based on instinct."

C **despairingly** Have students break this word into its base word and suffixes *(despair + -ing + -ly)* to see that it means "in a manner full of despair."

1. COMPREHENSION

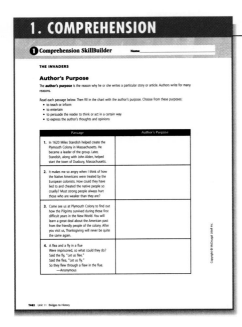

Author's Purpose

Direct Instruction Tell students that the reason an author writes something is called the **author's purpose.** Authors' purposes include the following:

- to entertain readers
- to inform readers
- to express the author's opinions or feelings on a topic
- to persuade readers to think, feel, or act in a certain way

Explain that a piece of writing may fulfill more than one purpose. As an example, point out how some children's programs on TV both teach and entertain. Explain that "The Invaders" could be said to accomplish all four purposes. It entertains with a suspenseful story, it teaches how the Native Americans might have viewed the coming of the Europeans, it persuades the reader to see the event from the Native Americans' point of view, and it expresses the feelings of the author about how unfairly the Native Americans were treated. Discuss which of these purposes students feel was the central one for the author of "The Invaders."

> **Comprehension SkillBuilder Answer Key:**
> 1. *to teach or inform*
> 2. *to express the author's thoughts and opinions*
> 3. *to persuade the reader to think or act in a certain way*
> 4. *to entertain*

2. LITERATURE

Point of View

Direct Instruction Tell students that the narrator is the one who tells the story. Tell them that if the narrator is a character in the story, the story is told from the **first-person point of view.** The narrator uses first-person pronouns such as *I* and *we.* If the narrator is someone outside the story, the story is told from the **third-person point of view.** The narrator uses third-person pronouns such as *he, she,* and *they.*

Have students find the pronouns used by the narrator in each of these paragraphs, and determine the point of view from which each paragraph is written.

(1) The ship had been in the harbor for more than a day when the invaders finally came out. The Native American watched them row their small boat to the shore and step onto his homeland. There were at least eight men in the party, all armed and dangerous-looking. Some say this was the beginning of a tragic chapter in history.

(2) I can feel someone's eyes upon us. However, when I look into the dark forest, I see only trees. It is so silent. I don't hear any birds. It is so cold, much colder than my native England. I wonder if I will ever feel comfortable here.

> **Literary SkillBuilder Answer Key:**
> **A.1.** *the Native American; first-person point of view*
> **2.** *someone outside the story; third-person point of view*
> **3.** *one of the invaders; first-person point of view*
>
> **B.** *Answers may vary. Possible answers: I felt frightened when the invaders pointed their weapons at me. The Native American looked frightened when we pointed our guns at him.*

3. VOCABULARY

[SkillBuilder worksheet]

③ Vocabulary SkillBuilder Name_____

THE INVADERS

Suffix -ly

A **suffix** is a word part added to the end of a word. The suffix *-ly* means "in a certain way." For example, *brightly* means "in a bright way." When adding *-ly* to a word ending in *y*, first change the *y* to *i* (example: *angry + -ly = angrily*).

A. Add the suffix *-ly* to each of the words below. Write the new word on the first line. Then write the meaning of the word on the second line.

1. cautious _____ _____
2. crazy _____ _____
3. pretty _____ _____
4. fervent _____ _____
5. silent _____ _____
6. cozy _____ _____
7. wary _____ _____
8. cruel _____ _____

B. Add a word that ends with the suffix *-ly* to complete each sentence. The meaning of the word is in parentheses.

1. The invaders walked _____ (in a slow way) through the forest.
2. The man hiding behind the tree watched them _____ (in a wary way).
3. The snow was falling _____ (in a light way).
4. If snow had been falling more _____ (in a heavy way), no one would have seen him run away.
5. The invaders had treated him _____ (in a cruel way) before.
6. The man was _____ (in a final way) sure that the invaders had come to stay.
7. He stepped forward _____ (in a bold way) and said _____ (in a loud way), "Welcome."

T464 Unit 11 Bridges to History

Suffix *-ly*

Direct Instruction Tell students that separating a long word into its parts is a good way to understand the meaning of the word. Often a word that ends in the suffix *-ly* is an adverb explaining how, or in what manner, something is done. Demonstrate how they can separate *carefully* into its parts: *care + -ful + -ly*. They can then think through the meaning: "in a way full of care."

Point out that when *ly* is added to a word that ends in *y*, the *y* becomes *i* (*pretty + -ly = prettily*).

> **Vocabulary SkillBuilder Answer Key:**
>
> **A.1.** *cautiously; in a cautious way*
> **2.** *crazily; in a crazy way*
> **3.** *prettily; in a pretty way*
> **4.** *fervently; in a fervent way*
> **5.** *silently; in a silent way*
> **6.** *cozily; in a cozy way*
> **7.** *warily; in a wary way*
> **8.** *cruelly; in a cruel way*
>
> **B. 1.** *slowly* **2.** *warily* **3.** *lightly*
> **4.** *heavily* **5.** *cruelly* **6.** *finally*
> **7.** *boldly, loudly*

4. WORDS TO KNOW

[SkillBuilder worksheet]

④ Words to Know SkillBuilder Name_____

THE INVADERS

Words to Know

craft seized exhibited captive savage

A. Circle the word or phrase that is most similar to the **boldfaced** word. Use a dictionary, if you need to.

1. I **exhibited** my art project in front of the rest of the class.
   a. made b. presented c. hid
2. I think it was cruel to hold the firefly **captive** in a glass jar.
   a. prisoner b. king c. comedian
3. The sailors boarded the **craft** and began their work.
   a. animal b. ship c. car
4. The lawyer called the criminal a **savage**.
   a. shy person b. smart person c. brutal person
5. The pirate **seized** the ship from the explorers.
   a. borrowed b. captured c. bought

B. Write **true** or **false** in the blanks.

_____ 1. You can see a **craft** speeding down the highway.
_____ 2. If you are **seized**, you have been taken by force.
_____ 3. A painting in a museum is usually **exhibited** on the wall.
_____ 4. A **captive** is a businessman.
_____ 5. A **savage** would work well with others.

Writing Activity
Imagine you are stuck on a desert island. Write a note to send off in a bottle to rescuers. Use all of the **Words to Know**.

The Invaders **T465**

Words to Know

Direct Instruction As you present the **Words to Know,** here are some points you might want to cover. Help students identify the parts of the vocabulary words. Stress the importance of finding the base of each word. Help students remove prefixes and suffixes.

- **seize** + -ed = *seized,* past tense of *seize,* from Old French *seisir,* "to take possession"
- **exhibit** + -ed = *exhibited,* past tense of *exhibit,* from Latin *ex- + habēre,* "to hold"
- **captive** is from the Latin *capere,* "to seize."
- **savage** can be used either as an adjective or as a noun (as it is used in "The Lady or the Tiger?") and is from the Latin *silva,* "forest."
- **craft,** from Old English *cræft,* has multiple meanings:
  a. *n.* skill in doing or making something, as in the arts; proficiency
  b. *n.* skill in evasion or deception; guile (as in *crafty*)
  c. *n.* an occupation or trade requiring manual dexterity or skilled artistry
  d. *n.* a boat, ship, or aircraft
  e. *v.* to make or construct something

Writing Activity Pair students or have them work in small groups to complete the exercise. Have volunteers read their creations aloud.

> **Words to Know SkillBuilder Answer Key:**
> **A.**
> **1.** *b* **2.** *a* **3.** *b* **4.** *c* **5.** *b*
> **B.**
> **1.** *false* **2.** *true* **3.** *true* **4.** *false* **5.** *false*

5. SELECTION TEST

[Selection Test worksheet]

> **Selection Test Answer Key:**
> **A. 1.** *kidnapped* **2.** *animal* **3.** *friendly* **4.** *escaped*
> **B.** *The invaders turn out to be Captain Standish, an English captain, and some of the crew from his ship.*

THE INVADERS

Author's Purpose

The **author's purpose** is the reason why he or she writes a particular story or article. Authors write for many reasons.

Read each passage below. Then fill in the chart with the author's purpose. Choose from these purposes:
- to teach or inform
- to entertain
- to persuade the reader to think or act in a certain way
- to express the author's thoughts and opinions

Passage	Author's Purpose
1. In 1620 Miles Standish helped create the Plymouth Colony in Massachusetts. He became a leader of the group. Later, Standish, along with John Alden, helped start the town of Duxbury, Massachusetts.	
2. It makes me so angry when I think of how the Native Americans were treated by the European colonists. How could they have lied to and cheated the native people so cruelly? Must strong people always hurt those who are weaker than they are?	
3. Come see us at Plymouth Colony to find out how the Pilgrims survived during those first difficult years in the New World. You will learn a great deal about the American past from the friendly people of the colony. After you visit us, Thanksgiving will never be quite the same again.	
4. A flea and a fly in a flue Were imprisoned, so what could they do? Said the fly, "Let us flee." Said the flea, "Let us fly." So they flew through a flaw in the flue. 　　—Anonymous	

THE INVADERS

Point of View

The **narrator** of a story is the person who is telling it. If the narrator is a character in the story, the story is told in the **first-person point of view.** The narrator uses pronouns such as *I* and *we.* If the narrator is outside the story, the story is told in the **third-person point of view.** The narrator uses pronouns such as *he, she,* and *they.*

A. Read each of these passages based on "The Invaders." Decide who is the speaker in each one; circle your answer. Then write whether the paragraph is written in the first-person or third-person point of view.

1. I met them first when I was almost a boy and I had been without caution. I approached them and they seemed friendly, but then suddenly they seized me and carried me off in their strange ship.

   Speaker: one of the invaders   the Native American   someone outside the story

   Point of view: _____

2. The invaders walked slowly through the forest. It had been a long journey to the New World. Some of the men were glad to be walking on solid ground after so many weeks at sea. But they were also cautious. No one knew if the natives in this land would be friendly or hostile.

   Speaker: one of the invaders   the Native American   someone outside the story

   Point of view: _____

3. I was greatly surprised when the native stepped out from the woods and said, "Welcome." Was it possible? Here, thousands of miles from England, a strangely dressed man was speaking to me in my own language. What a wonderful new land!

   Speaker: one of the invaders   the Native American   someone outside the story

   Point of view: _____

B. Rewrite this third-person sentence in the first-person point of view.

The Native American felt frightened when the invaders pointed their weapons at him.

_____

_____

THE INVADERS

Suffix -*ly*

A **suffix** is a word part added to the end of a word. The suffix -*ly* means "in a certain way." For example, *brightly* means "in a bright way." When adding -*ly* to a word ending in *y,* first change the *y* to *i* (example: *angry* + -*ly* = *angrily).*

A. Add the suffix -*ly* to each of the words below. Write the new word on the first line. Then write the meaning of the word on the second line.

1. cautious _____   _____

2. crazy   _____   _____

3. pretty   _____   _____

4. fervent _____   _____

5. silent   _____   _____

6. cozy   _____   _____

7. wary   _____   _____

8. cruel   _____   _____

B. Add a word that ends with the suffix -*ly* to complete each sentence. The meaning of the word is in parentheses.

1. The invaders walked _____ (in a slow way) through the forest.

2. The man hiding behind the tree watched them _____ (in a wary way).

3. The snow was falling _____ (in a light way).

4. If snow had been falling more _____ (in a heavy way), no one would have seen him run away.

5. The invaders had treated him _____ (in a cruel way) before.

6. The man was _____ (in a final way) sure that the invaders had come to stay.

7. He stepped forward _____ (in a bold way) and said

   _____ (in a loud way), "Welcome."

THE INVADERS

Words to Know

craft   seized   exhibited   captive   savage

A. Circle the word or phrase that is most similar to the **boldfaced** word. Use a dictionary, if you need to.

1. I **exhibited** my art project in front of the rest of the class.

    a. made   b. presented   c. hid

2. I think it was cruel to hold the firefly **captive** in a glass jar.

    a. prisoner   b. king   c. comedian

3. The sailors boarded the **craft** and began their work.

    a. animal   b. ship   c. car

4. The lawyer called the criminal a **savage.**

    a. shy person   b. smart person   c. brutal person

5. The pirate **seized** the ship from the explorers.

    a. borrowed   b. captured   c. bought

B. Write **true** or **false** in the blanks.

_____ **1.** You can see a **craft** speeding down the highway.

_____ **2.** If you are **seized,** you have been taken by force.

_____ **3.** A painting in a museum is usually **exhibited** on the wall.

_____ **4.** A **captive** is a businessman.

_____ **5.** A **savage** would work well with others.

Writing Activity
Imagine you are stuck on a desert island. Write a note to send off in a bottle to rescuers. Use all of the **Words to Know.**

THE INVADERS

A. Complete the paragraph by filling in each blank with the correct word from the list.

escaped   friendly   kidnapped   animal

The narrator first met the invaders when they **(1)** _____

him. They took him to their land and showed him about as if he were some sort of

(2) _____. They finally returned him to his home because

they wanted to form **(3)** _____ relations with his people.

Upon returning, the narrator **(4)** _____, and the invaders

finally sailed away. When the invaders returned with Captain Standish, the narrator realized they

had come to stay.

B. In your own words, tell who the invaders turn out to be.

_____

_____

_____

Focus Skills

COMPREHENSION
Compare and Contrast
Patterns of Organization

LITERATURE
Informative Nonfiction

VOCABULARY
Context Clues: Definition Clues

SkillBuilder Copymasters

 Reading Comprehension:
1 Compare and Contrast
   p. T475
2 Patterns of Organization
   p. T476
 Vocabulary:
3 Context Clues p. T477
4 Words to Know p. T478

Assessment

 5 Selection Test p. T479

Readability Scores

DRP	LEXILE	DALE-CHALL
49	480	4.4

For English Learners

To set a purpose before students begin reading, you may want to have them discuss what they already know about some or all of these terms: *American Revolution, colonists, British Redcoats, King George III, General George Washington.*

WEAPONS OF WAR

by Shirley Jordan

In any war, the choice of weapons is important. Find out how a secret weapon helped in the American Revolution.

340 Unit 11 Bridges to History

Vocabulary Strategy: Preteaching

Context Clues Remind students that the **context clues** surrounding an unknown word can help them understand the word's meaning. Explain that in this selection the context clues often give an unknown word's definition. Write on the board the sentences shown on the facing page. Then have students point out the context clues that define each underlined word.

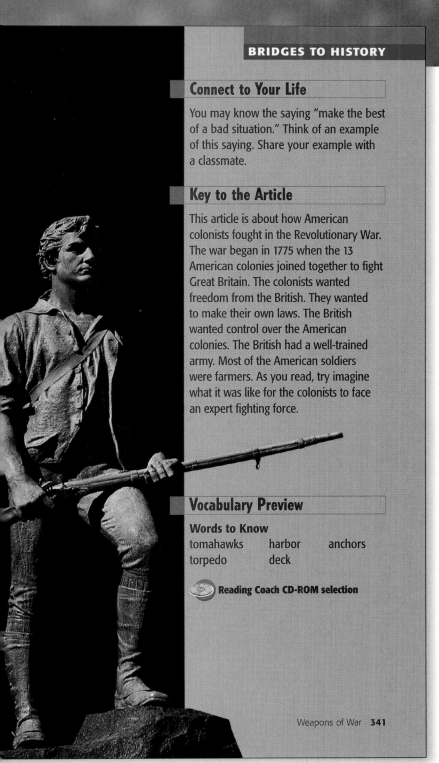

Connect to Your Life

You may know the saying "make the best of a bad situation." Think of an example of this saying. Share your example with a classmate.

Key to the Article

This article is about how American colonists fought in the Revolutionary War. The war began in 1775 when the 13 American colonies joined together to fight Great Britain. The colonists wanted freedom from the British. They wanted to make their own laws. The British wanted control over the American colonies. The British had a well-trained army. Most of the American soldiers were farmers. As you read, try imagine what it was like for the colonists to face an expert fighting force.

Vocabulary Preview

Words to Know

tomahawks   harbor   anchors

torpedo   deck

 Reading Coach CD-ROM selection

Weapons of War **341**

Connect to Your Life

If partners have trouble thinking of examples in which they personally made the best of a bad situation, tell them to describe the experience of someone they have heard about, read about, or seen on TV or in a movie. Did that person or character succeed? Why or why not?

Key to the Article

As students read this article, they will be comparing and contrasting the British and American armies during the Revolutionary War. Before they begin, you may want to have them create a **comparison chart** that they can fill in as they read. See page T647 for instructions and page T648 for a copymaster.

Vocabulary Preview

Words to Know

tomahawks *n.* lightweight axes used as tools or weapons

torpedo *n.* cigar-shaped weapon that can explode

harbor *n.* area of shelter where ships may anchor

deck *n.* main level of the outside of a ship

anchors *n.* heavy weights attached to a connecting rope that are used to keep ships in place

For direct instruction on Words to Know, see page T474.

Building Background

The Revolutionary War between Great Britain and its thirteen American colonies began in 1775. The British army and navy were highly skilled and well-equipped. The colonists, on the other hand, had no army or navy when the war began. Two advantages that they did have, however, were the help of the French—who provided them with much-needed money and equipment—and the fact that the British had to wait for their supplies and troops to arrive from across the Atlantic. This caused the British to keep losing momentum, while the colonists kept re-forming and fighting. They finally fought their way to independence from Great Britain in 1783.

1. In the Revolution, most fighting was done by the <u>infantry</u>, the men on the front lines of battle.
2. The <u>flintlock</u> was a metal wheel that turned and set off sparks.

 For more on Context Clues, see page T474.

FOCUS

Colonists in America have to prepare for war. Find out some of the problems these soldiers face.

America's success in the American Revolution was a surprise to many. Mostly to King George III.

You see, the colonists were not soldiers. Few of them had done any fighting at all.

 England's Redcoats, however, knew about war. They were part of a trained army.

In the early years, the colonists had no uniforms. Each man carried whatever kind of gun he might own. There were few bullets. So the colonists melted
10 pots and eating tools to make bullets.

There were few cannons or other large weapons in America. Earlier fighting in the colonies had been against the Indians. Cannons did not roll well over the rough ground. They would not fit between the trees in the forests, where the Indians hid.

In the Revolution, most fighting was done by the *infantry*, the men on the front lines of battle. The British Redcoats were well trained in this kind of battle. The Americans had no choice but to fight this way too.

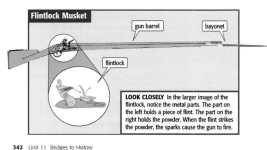

Flintlock Musket

gun barrel

bayonet

flintlock

LOOK CLOSELY In the larger image of the flintlock, notice the metal parts. The part on the left holds a piece of flint. The part on the right holds the powder. When the flint strikes the powder, the sparks cause the gun to fire.

342 Unit 11 Bridges to History

20   In battle, both sides formed a battle line. Until everything was ready, the line stood still. They waited where the enemy cannons could not reach them. Then, when the order came, the men marched toward the enemy. They looked just like a parade.

REREAD
Picture the battle scene in your mind.

A

When there was nothing else to use, the Americans carried hunting rifles. These were not a good weapon. They took too long to reload. And a knife, or *bayonet*, could not be fastened to the front
30   of them.

After 1776, the colonists had uniforms and better weapons. But there weren't always enough to go around.

THINK IT THROUGH The colonists had problems. In what ways were the colonists not as ready for war as the British?

FOCUS

Read about the weapons used.

A fighting gun—the flintlock musket with a bayonet—was the main weapon of the war. These early muskets were six or seven feet long! And they weighed 40 pounds!

They were loaded from the muzzle with the soldier standing up. After each shot, the man had to reload.
40   The *flintlock* was a metal wheel that turned and set off sparks. The sparks lit the powder in the barrel of the gun. A soldier carried extra gunpowder and lead balls in a leather shoulder bag.

Weapons of War 343

COMPREHENSION

FOCUS SKILL 1: Compare and Contrast

Tell students that **comparing** means looking at how two or more things, people, or events are alike. To **contrast** means to look at how two or more things, people, or events are different.

For direct instruction on Compare and Contrast, see page T473.

FOCUS SKILL 2: Patterns of Organization

Tell students that this selection follows two **patterns of organization.** One pattern is **main idea and supporting details.** The other is **chronological order,** which is the time order of a series of events. Explain that other organizational patterns of nonfiction include cause and effect, problem and solution, and compare and contrast.

For direct instruction on Patterns of Organization, see page T473.

Ⓐ **REREAD** Picture the battle scene in your mind. *(Ask: What words help you visualize what is happening?)* **visualize**

Ⓑ **THINK IT THROUGH** The colonists had problems. In what ways were the colonists not as ready for war as the British? *(The British troops were part of a trained army and had experience in fighting. The colonists weren't soldiers, so they didn't know how to fight as a military unit, they had no uniforms, and their weapons were inadequate and in short supply.)* **compare and contrast**

LITERATURE

FOCUS SKILL: Informative Nonfiction: Historical Writing

Tell students that **historical writing** is nonfiction that gives facts, dates, and other information about people who lived and things that happened in the past.

VOCABULARY

FOCUS SKILL: Context Clues

As students read this selection, remind them to use **context clues**—especially ones that provide definitions—to figure out any unknown words.

Ⓐ **Redcoats** Students should use context clues to determine that Redcoats were soldiers who were part of the English army.

Ⓑ **bayonet** Students should notice that the word *bayonet* is defined as "knife" in the sentence.

FOR ENGLISH LEARNERS

Help students understand the following expressions and idioms:

Line 23: when the order came
Line 32: enough to go around
Line 38: loaded from the muzzle

Some officers had *breech-loading* rifles. These could be loaded from the side. Men with these fast rifles did not have to stand up to reload.

Hunting swords and small knives were worn by officers. A long, heavy weapon—the *saber*—was used by men on horses. These *cavalrymen* could
50 reach farther from their horses with the saber.

American patriots who had no bayonets often used tomahawks. The Indians had taught them how.

> **tomahawks**
> (tŏm′ ə hŏks′)
> *n.* lightweight axes used as tools or weapons

THINK IT THROUGH
The colonists had a few decent weapons. What made each weapon hard to use?

FOCUS
You've seen how the colonists fought on land. Read to find out about a special weapon used at sea.

Attack from Under the Sea
This might seem strange. But America's first submarine was part of the American Revolution.

David Bushnell was a young college student with a big idea. He knew the American patriots had few ships. And that the British navy was mighty. Perhaps,
60 he thought, he could find a way to stop some of the British ships.

Bushnell built a special underwater boat of oak. It was shaped like a walnut. And it was big enough for a man to climb in and sit down.

The wood was wrapped with iron bands. Bushnell called his invention the *Turtle.*

> **REREAD**
> What are two main differences between this submarine and modern ones?

344 Unit 11 Bridges to History

To push it through the water, the man inside turned
70 a set of blades, or *propellers.*

The plan was to get close to a British warship and drill a small hole in the side. Then the man in the submarine would stick a torpedo in the hole.

> **torpedo**
> (tôr′ pē′ dō)
> *n.* cigar-shaped weapon that can explode

The torpedo was filled with gunpowder. After the *Turtle* left, the powder would blow up.

General George Washington liked the plan. The British had control of the waters around New York. If
80 the Americans could blow up a few ships, maybe the frightened British would take their other ships away.

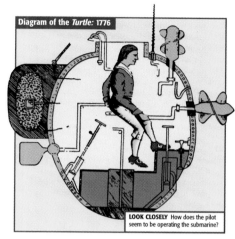

Diagram of the *Turtle*: 1776

LOOK CLOSELY How does the pilot seem to be operating the submarine?

Weapons of War 345

Bushnell chose the *Eagle*. It was the largest ship in the harbor.

On the day of the attack, David Bushnell was sick. So General Ezra Lee was chosen to take his place.

Lee knew the plan. He would use a carpenter's drill attached to the front of the *Turtle*. He would stick the torpedo into the ship. And he would
90 quickly set a timer. The blast would come after the submarine had moved away.

General Lee climbed into the *Turtle*. Quietly, he moved close to the warship. Now it was time to drill a hole just deep enough to hide a torpedo. He tried. But it wasn't working.

"Why won't this work?" he wondered. "I just know this ship is made of wood!"

Unfortunately, he had chosen a spot that was covered with copper. The drill would never go in. But
100 Lee didn't know that.

The darkness of night was almost gone. There was no time to try another spot.

General Lee started back toward land. By now, sailors on the warship's deck had seen him.

The sailors said, "What is that strange thing just under the water?"

The *Eagle* sent out a small boat to see. Alarmed, Lee shot off a torpedo through the water.
110 He did his best to aim it toward the ship.

He missed the *Eagle*. But as the torpedo exploded, water flew high into the air. Men on all the nearby ships begin to shout and run about.

harbor
(här′ bər)
n. area of shelter where ships may anchor

deck
(dĕk)
n. main level of the outside of a ship

346 Unit 11 Bridges to History

The British were terrified. They raised their anchors. Soon, all their ships were sailing out of New York's harbor.

The Redcoats had no idea what had attacked them. And they didn't know how
120 many of the enemy there were.

The *Turtle* never sank any ships. But it showed that man could attack from underwater.

A new military weapon was born!

anchors
(ăng′ kərs)
n. heavy weights attached to a connecting rope that are used to keep ships in place

THINK IT THROUGH

1. The *Turtle's* torpedo missed the ship. Why was the *Turtle* still a success?
2. Why was the *Turtle's* victory a good sign for the American fighters?
3. Look again at the diagram of the musket on page 342 and its description on page 343. Why was the gun so hard to use?

Weapons of War 347

H Why didn't Lee know about the copper? *(Possible answer: He was unfamiliar with the way British ships were built.)* **making inferences**

I How did the *Turtle's* intended plan differ from what actually happened? *(Bushnell was sick, so Lee went in his place. Lee couldn't drill a hole, so he started back toward land. When the* Eagle *sent a boat out, Lee shot a torpedo. It scared the British, and they all left the harbor.)* **compare and contrast**

J THINK IT THROUGH

1. The *Turtle's* torpedo missed the ship. Why was the *Turtle* still a success? *(Instead of attacking one ship, the* Turtle *inadvertently scared all the British ships out of the harbor.)* **problem and solution**

2. Why was the *Turtle's* victory a good sign for the American fighters? *(It showed that troops could attack from underwater, and it gave them a new weapon for fighting the British.)* **problem and solution**

3. Look again at the diagram of the musket on page 342 and its description on page 343. Why was the gun so hard to use? *(The musket was too long and heavy. Soldiers had to reload it after every shot.)* **understanding visuals**

Discuss the **comparison chart** that students filled in as they read this selection.

RETEACHING

If students need more help understanding **Compare and Contrast,** use pages T647–T649.

FOR ENGLISH LEARNERS

Help students understand the following:

Line 86: take his place
Line 90: set a timer

RETEACHING

If students need more help understanding **Context Clues,** use pages T608–T611.

1. COMPREHENSION

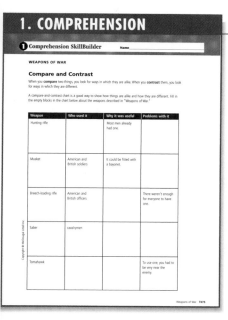

Compare and Contrast

Direct Instruction Tell students that to **compare** means to look for ways in which things are alike. To **contrast** means to look for ways in which things are different. Point out that in a nonfiction article such as "Weapons of War," the writer presents a great deal of information. One good way to organize and remember that information is by comparing and contrasting.

To familiarize students with a compare-and-contrast chart, draw a simple three-column chart on the board. Give the columns these headings: *Type of Vehicle, Advantages, Disadvantages.* Under *Type of Vehicle,* write *Car* in the first row and *Truck* and *SUV* in the next two rows. Then lead students in a discussion of the advantages and disadvantages of these vehicles. After filling in the chart, point out the ways in which the vehicles are alike and different.

> **Comprehension SkillBuilder Answer Key:**
>
> *Answers may vary. Possible answers:*
>
> *Hunting rifle—Who used it: American soldiers; Problems: It took too long to reload. A bayonet could not be fastened to the front of it.*
>
> *Musket—Problems: It was long and heavy. It took a long time to reload.*
>
> *Breech-loading rifle—Why it was useful: It could be reloaded quickly. Men with these fast rifles did not have to stand up to reload.*
>
> *Saber—Why it was useful: It was long, so people on horseback could reach their enemy more easily than with a short sword or knife; Problems: It was too long and heavy for anyone but a cavalryman to carry.*
>
> *Tomahawk—Who used it: American soldiers; Why it was useful: It was light. Many Americans could easily make one to use.*

2. COMPREHENSION

Patterns of Organization

Direct Instruction Tell students that writers can choose different ways in which to organize their writing. The way the ideas or facts are arranged is called the **pattern of organization.** Point out that in a long piece of writing, a writer may use more than one pattern of organization. The writer chooses the type of organization that best fits his or her specific topic.

Tell students that these two common patterns of organization are found in "Weapons of War."

- **Chronological order** The writer describes events in the order in which they happened. This pattern may extend over several paragraphs.
- **Main idea** The writer makes sure that all of the sentences in a paragraph or a group of paragraphs relate to the main idea. Every detail tells more about the main idea.

> **Comprehension SkillBuilder Answer Key:**
>
> **1.** *main idea*
> **2.** *chronological order*
> **3.** *main idea*
> **4.** *chronological order*

3. VOCABULARY

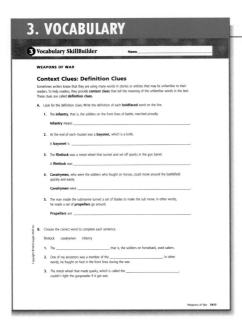

Context Clues: Definition Clues

Direct Instruction Tell students that they can often find clues to the meaning of new or unfamiliar words in the sentences or paragraphs surrounding the words. Such clues are called **context clues.** Explain that one type of context clue is called a definition clue. A **definition clue** tells the meaning of the new word. The following words and phrases are often used to introduce definition clues:

- **is**—A saber is a long, heavy sword.

- **who is**—The captain, who is the leader of an army unit, ordered his men into battle.
- **which is**—David Bushnell made an early submarine, which is a boat that can move underwater.
- **in other words**—Bushnell planned to destroy the man-of-war. In other words, he wanted to destroy the warship.
- **that is**—Some American soldiers used tomahawks, that is, light axes.

Vocabulary SkillBuilder Answer Key:

A.1. *the soldiers on the front lines of battle*
2. *a knife*
3. *a metal wheel that turned and set off sparks in the gun barrel*
4. *the soldiers who fought on horses*
5. *a set of blades*

B.1. *cavalrymen*
2. *infantry*
3. *flintlock*

4. WORDS TO KNOW

Words to Know

Direct Instruction As you present the **Words to Know,** here are some points you might want to cover.
- **torpedo**, from the Latin *torpēre*, "to be stiff"
- **harbor** is also defined as a verb: "to provide a place, home, or habitat for" or "to entertain or nourish (a specified thought or feeling)."

- **deck** is also defined as a verb: "to clothe with finery; adorn"; often used with *out: We were all decked out for the party.*
- **anchor** is also defined as a verb: "to narrate or coordinate (a newscast)."

Writing Activity Encourage students to be creative. Have volunteers read their paragraphs aloud.

Words to Know SkillBuilder Answer Key:

A.
1. *anchors*
2. *Tomahawks*
3. *deck*
4. *harbor*
5. *torpedo*

B.
1. *anchors*
2. *tomahawks*
3. *harbor*
4. *deck*
5. *torpedo*

Bonus Question: *saber*

5. SELECTION TEST

Selection Test Answer Key:
A. 1. *true* **2.** *true* **3.** *false* **4.** *false* **5.** *true* **6.** *false* **7.** *true* **8.** *true* **9.** *false*
B. *He accidentally scared all the British ships out of the harbor.*

WEAPONS OF WAR

Compare and Contrast

When you **compare** two things, you look for ways in which they are alike. When you **contrast** them, you look for ways in which they are different.

A compare-and-contrast chart is a good way to show how things are alike and how they are different. Fill in the empty blocks in the chart below about the weapons described in "Weapons of War."

Weapon	Who used it	Why it was useful	Problems with it
Hunting rifle		Most men already had one.	
Musket	American and British soldiers	It could be fitted with a bayonet.	
Breech-loading rifle	American and British officers		There weren't enough for everyone to have one.
Saber	cavalrymen		
Tomahawk			To use one, you had to be very near the enemy.

WEAPONS OF WAR

Patterns of Organization

Writers organize information to make it easier to understand and remember. One way to organize is by arranging facts and events in **chronological order,** or time order. Another pattern of organization is having all sentences in a paragraph or group of paragraphs relate to a **main idea.**

Read these parts of "Weapons of War." On the line, tell which pattern of organization the writer used—chronological order or main idea.

1. There were few cannons or other large weapons in America. Earlier fighting in the colonies had been against the Indians. Cannons did not roll well over the rough ground. They would not fit between the trees in the forests, where the Indians hid.

    This part of the article is organized using _____.

2. General Lee climbed into the *Turtle*. Quietly, he moved close to the warship. Now it was time to drill a hole just deep enough to hide a torpedo. He tried. But it wasn't working. "Why won't this work?" he wondered. "I just know this ship is made of wood!"

    This part of the article is organized using _____.

3. Muskets were loaded from the muzzle with the soldier standing up. After each shot, the man had to reload. The *flintlock* was a metal wheel that turned and set off sparks. The sparks lit the powder in the barrel of the gun. A soldier carried extra gunpowder and lead balls in a leather shoulder bag.

    This part of the article is organized using _____.

4. General Lee started back toward land. By now, sailors on the warship's deck had seen him. The sailors said, "What is that strange thing just under the water?" The *Eagle* sent out a small boat to see. Alarmed, Lee shot off a torpedo through the water. He did his best to aim it toward the ship. He missed the *Eagle*. But as the torpedo exploded, water flew high into the air. Men on all the nearby ships begin to shout and run about.

    This part of the article is organized using _____.

WEAPONS OF WAR

Context Clues: Definition Clues

Sometimes writers know that they are using many words in stories or articles that may be unfamiliar to their readers. To help readers, they provide **context clues** that tell the meaning of the unfamiliar words in the text. These clues are called **definition clues.**

A. Look for the definition clues. Write the definition of each **boldfaced** word on the line.

1. The **infantry**, that is, the soldiers on the front lines of battle, marched proudly.

   Infantry means _____.

2. At the end of each musket was a **bayonet,** which is a knife.

   A **bayonet** is _____.

3. The **flintlock** was a metal wheel that turned and set off sparks in the gun barrel.

   A **flintlock** was _____.

4. **Cavalrymen,** who were the soldiers who fought on horses, could move around the battlefield quickly and easily.

   Cavalrymen were _____.

5. The man inside the submarine turned a set of blades to make the sub move. In other words, he made a set of **propellers** go around.

   Propellers are _____.

B. Choose the correct word to complete each sentence.

flintlock   cavalrymen   infantry

1. The _____, that is, the soldiers on horseback, used sabers.

2. One of my ancestors was a member of the _____. In other words, he fought on foot in the front lines during the war.

3. The metal wheel that made sparks, which is called the _____, couldn't light the gunpowder if it got wet.

WEAPONS OF WAR

Words to Know

tomahawks   torpedo   harbor   deck   anchors

A. Fill in each blank with the correct word from the list above.

1. Once the ship reached shore, the settlers dropped the _____ to keep the ship in one place.

2. _____ are tools very much like axes.

3. The sailors gathered together on the large _____ of the ship.

4. My father has a boat that he keeps at our town's _____.

5. My little brother ran around the house at full speed, pretending he was a

_____ that could explode.

B. Use the **Words to Know** to fill in the blanks. Then use the boxed letters to complete the sentence below the puzzle.

1. What would you use to weigh down a ship?   __ __ __ __ __ [__]

2. Native American peoples invented these.   __ __ [__] __ __ __ __ __

3. This is home base for boats.   __ __ __ [__] __ __

4. This is the main level on a ship.   __ [__] __ __

5. This is an underwater weapon.   __ __ [__] __ __ __ __

Answer the question with the word that the boxed letters spell out.

What is the name for the long, heavy weapon cavalrymen used? _____

Writing Activity
Write two sentences describing a boat of some kind. Use at least two of the **Words to Know.**

Name_____

WEAPONS OF WAR

A. Write **true** or **false** on the line next to each statement.

_____ **1.** America's success in the Revolutionary War was surprising because the colonists didn't know how to fight.

_____ **2.** The British Redcoats, on the other hand, were part of a trained army and knew all about war.

_____ **3.** The colonists did have many weapons, however, which they quickly learned to use well.

_____ **4.** One of the colonists' most useful weapons was the cannon.

_____ **5.** Another weapon was their first submarine, the *Turtle*.

_____ **6.** The *Turtle* was developed by General Ezra Lee, a college professor.

_____ **7.** The *Turtle* was made of oak and was shaped like a walnut.

_____ **8.** David Bushnell came up with a plan to blow up a few British ships with his submarine.

_____ **9.** When Bushnell tried to drill a hole into the side of the *Eagle,* however, he got scared and couldn't do it.

B. In your own words, answer the following question.

What happened when General Lee shot a torpedo from the submarine?

_____

_____

_____

Focus Skills

COMPREHENSION
Main Idea

LITERATURE
Historical Fiction

VOCABULARY
Multiple-Meaning Words

SkillBuilder Copymasters

 Reading Comprehension:
1 Main Idea p. T491

 Literary Analysis:
2 Historical Fiction p. T492

 Vocabulary:
3 Multiple-Meaning Words
p. T493
4 Words to Know p. T494

Assessment

 5 Selection Test p. T495

Readability Scores

DRP	LEXILE	DALE-CHALL
54	450	4.6

For English Learners

Because Abe Lincoln and his family lived in Kentucky in the early 1800s, their speech reflects the patterns and pronunciations used in that setting. If you think students will have trouble understanding the dialect in the selection, you may want to preview the story with them and explain some of the more difficult words and expressions.

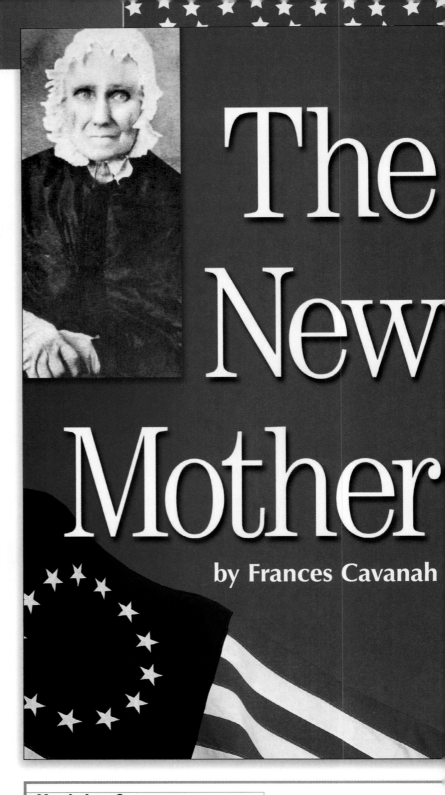

The New Mother
by Frances Cavanah

Vocabulary Strategy: Preteaching

Multiple-Meaning Words Remind students that a single word can have more than one meaning, and that to figure out which meaning an author is using, students can use context clues. To illustrate, you can use *brush,* a **multiple-meaning word** from this story. Read the sentences on the next page aloud, then ask what *brush* means in each one.

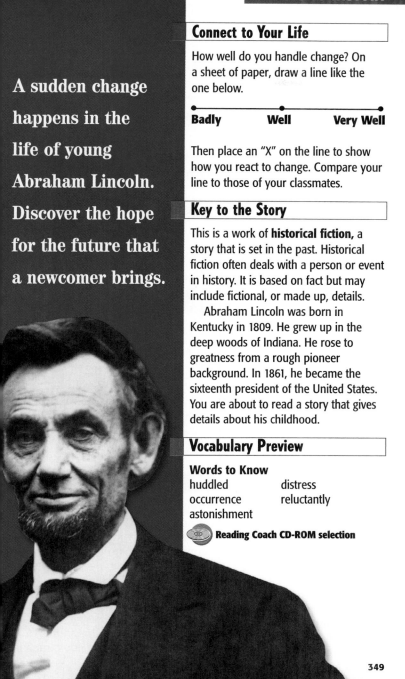

A sudden change happens in the life of young Abraham Lincoln. Discover the hope for the future that a newcomer brings.

Connect to Your Life

How well do you handle change? On a sheet of paper, draw a line like the one below.

Badly   **Well**   **Very Well**

Then place an "X" on the line to show how you react to change. Compare your line to those of your classmates.

Key to the Story

This is a work of **historical fiction,** a story that is set in the past. Historical fiction often deals with a person or event in history. It is based on fact but may include fictional, or made up, details.

Abraham Lincoln was born in Kentucky in 1809. He grew up in the deep woods of Indiana. He rose to greatness from a rough pioneer background. In 1861, he became the sixteenth president of the United States. You are about to read a story that gives details about his childhood.

Vocabulary Preview

Words to Know
huddled   distress
occurrence   reluctantly
astonishment

 Reading Coach CD-ROM selection

349

Connect to Your Life

As partners share their diagrams, ask them to explain why they placed their "X" where they did. Have them share examples that illustrate the way they handle change.

Key to the Story

Tell students that the dialogue, or conversations, in this story are different from the narration because they contain **dialect,** a regional variety of English. The author used dialect to show how Abe Lincoln and his family probably spoke when Abe was a boy.

Vocabulary Preview

Words to Know
huddled v. crowded together
occurrence n. event
astonishment n. amazement
distress n. suffering
reluctantly adv. unwillingly

For direct instruction on Words to Know, see page T490.

Building Background

Abraham Lincoln's mother, Nancy Hanks Lincoln, died in October 1818 of "milk sickness," which probably was caused by bacteria in cows' milk she had drunk. On December 2, 1819, Thomas Lincoln married Sarah Bush Johnston, a widow he had known since before her first marriage. Sarah's own children were 12, 8, and 5 at the time of the marriage. Despite the shaky start between Abe and Sarah described in "The New Mother," the two grew to love and respect each other greatly—so much so that Abe referred to Sarah as his "angel mother." Sarah really did encourage young Abe's love for reading and learning, even though she and Abe's father were basically illiterate.

1. It was so windy at the beach that John kept having to <u>brush</u> the sand off his blanket.
2. I <u>brush</u> my hair every night before I go to bed.
3. With no rain for a month, the trees got so dry that the smallest spark would start a <u>brush</u> fire.

 For more on Multiple-Meaning Words, see page T490.

FOCUS

Unexpected company arrives one night at the Lincoln cabin. Read to find out who comes to the cabin and why.

Inside the cabin the only light came from a feeble fire in the mammoth fireplace. The dirt floor felt cold under her moccasined feet as Sarah Lincoln paused in the doorway. Tom, her husband, cleared his throat in some embarrassment. He had only recently married the Widow Johnston, and he knew this home was not what she and her three children had expected.

mammoth
(măm′ əth)
huge

10 "Sally, Abe, this is your new mammy," he called. "I've been back to Kaintuck to git myself a wife."

 A

It was then that Sarah, peering through the gloom, saw the Lincoln children. They huddled on low stools near the fire, looking up at her out of frightened gray eyes. Sarah gasped at the sight of their thin soiled clothing, their dark matted hair, their pinched gray faces smudged with soot.

Kaintuck
the state of Kentucky

huddled
(hŭd′ ld)
v. crowded together; past tense of *huddle*

20 "Howdy!" She tried to smile, but they only huddled closer together. "Don't you want to meet my young'uns?"

B

"Mamma, I don't like it here," said Johnny Johnston.

"Sh!" Sarah warned. She nudged Betsy and Mathilda, who stopped staring long enough for each to make an awkward curtsy. Sally, after one glance at their pretty linsey-woolsey dresses and neat leather moccasins, tried to hide her bare toes under the stool.

30 Abe said, "Howdy," somewhere down inside his stomach.

350 Unit 11 Bridges to History

A THINK IT THROUGH

Who is Sarah, and why is she there?

FOCUS

Read to see how Sarah tries to unite her new family.

From the moment Sarah laid aside her hood and shawl, things began to happen in the Lincoln cabin. First, she announced cheerfully, she and Sally would have some victuals on the table, quicker than anyone could say "Jack Robinson." Tom went out to the wagon to unhitch the horses, and when he came

40 back he was carrying a slab of bacon and a comb of honey.

victuals
(vĭt′ ls)
food

A

Dennis Hanks, an older cousin who made his home with the Lincolns, brought in some firewood. Abe and Mathilda started for the spring, swinging the water pail between

B

50 them. A few minutes later Sally had forgotten her soiled dress and her bare feet, as she and Betsy mixed batter and set corn bread to bake on the hearth.

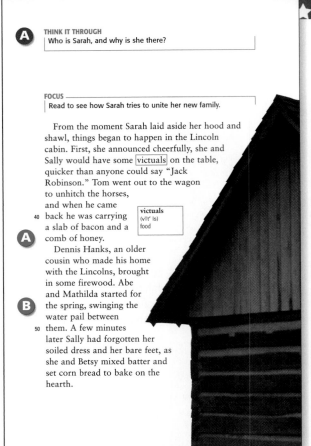

COMPREHENSION

FOCUS SKILL: Main Idea

Remind students that a **main idea** is the most important idea in a section of text.

For direct instruction on Main Idea, see page T489.

A **THINK IT THROUGH** Who is Sarah, and why is she there? *(She's Tom's new wife and Abe's new stepmother. She is there because Tom has brought her from Kentucky to live with him and his children.)* **main idea**

LITERATURE

FOCUS SKILL: Historical Fiction

Explain that even though this **historical fiction** story is based on real events in Abe Lincoln's life, it contains fictional elements, such as description and dialogue, that the author made up in her imagination.

For direct instruction on Historical Fiction, see page T489.

Use the following questions to encourage literary analysis.

A Identify some clues that tell you that this story is historical fiction. *(Possible answers: The story is based on Abe Lincoln and other people who really lived; they live in a cabin with a dirt floor, wear moccasins instead of shoes, and speak in a dialect that reflects that time and that part of the country. It gives their words and thoughts, so it must be fiction.)* **historical fiction**

B Based on what you've read so far, what kind of person do you think Sarah Lincoln is? *(Possible answers: She's polite and cheerful, and she's trying to make the best of the situation.)* **character**

VOCABULARY

FOCUS SKILL: Multiple-Meaning Words

As students come across the **multiple-meaning words** in this story, remind them that they can use context clues to figure out which meaning the author is using.

A **comb** Have students discuss several meanings of *comb*. They should conclude that in this selection, the word *comb* means "honeycomb."

B **spring** Students can use context clues or a dictionary to figure out which meaning is used in this selection.

FOR ENGLISH LEARNERS

Help students understand the following expressions and idioms:

Line 3: moccasined feet
Line 13: peering through the gloom
Line 19: pinched gray faces
Line 30: somewhere down inside his stomach
Line 44: made his home

B Keep 'em busy. Get 'em working together, said Sarah to herself. They'll soon forgit they're shy.

Soon the magic smell of frying bacon filled the air. The table was rather crowded with eight people 60 gathered around it, but no one seemed to mind. Under the influence of a hearty meal, Sally and her stepsisters chattered like old friends. Only Abe ate in silence, his eyes on the slab of bark which served him as a plate.

"I declare," said Dennis, as he sopped up some of the golden honey on his corn bread. "I ain't et like this since Cousin Nancy died."

C Abe jumped up and started for the cabin door. A little choking sound escaped him.

70 Tom tried to hide his embarrassment in a show of anger. "Abe Lincoln, you set right down and finish your corn bread."

Abe shook his head. "I . . . I can't, Pa."

Tom was on his feet now. "This is a purty way to treat your new ma—after she goes and gits all these good victuals ready. You clean up your plate, or I'll give you a hiding."

The young Johnstons gasped. Sally, twisting the hem of her dress, cast an 80 appealing glance at her new stepmother.

appealing
(ə pē′ lĭng)
begging

Sarah's heart seemed to turn over. Abe looked so miserable and scared. He was frightened not only of his father but of the strange woman who had come, without warning, to take his mother's place. She never would get next to him if Tom was not careful.

REREAD
What do Sarah's thoughts tell about her?

D

"Please, let the boy be," she said.

"I won't stand for him treatin' you that way."

Sarah smiled, more brightly than she felt. "Abe and 90 I'll have plenty of chance to git acquainted. I reckon all of us are through."

C She arose, her hands on her hips, surveying the dirty room. "Thar's a sight o' things to be done here before we unpack my plunder from the wagon. Fust, I'll need lots of hot water. Who wants to go to the spring?"

plunder
(plŭn′ dər)
Sarah Lincoln's name for her household items. Usually, *plunder* means "stolen items."

Her glance rested on Abe.

"I'll go, ma'am." He grabbed the wooden bucket and made his escape.

E THINK IT THROUGH

Why is Abe so willing to get water from the spring?

FOCUS

Read to discover the other changes Sarah Lincoln brings.

100 Abe made several trips to the spring that afternoon. Each pailful of water was poured into one of the huge iron kettles over the fireplace. Higher and higher **D** roared the flames, and when Sarah wasn't asking for more water, she was asking for more wood. She would hear the steady chop-chop of Abe's ax in the **E** clearing. Every few minutes, it seemed, he was bringing in a fresh armful of wood. His woebegone expression was giving way to one of curiosity—curiosity at all the strange 110 goings-on in the Lincoln cabin.

woebegone
(wō′ bĭ gôn′)
deeply sad

For even Dennis was working. Under Sarah's direction he washed the cabin walls, while the girls scrubbed the table and the few three-legged

---

COMPREHENSION

B Ask: Besides the fact that Sarah needs help, what is her reason for giving all the children something to do? *(She wants to keep them busy and working together so they'll have to get to know one another.)* **main idea**

C Ask: Why do you think Abe leaves the table? *(Possible answers: He still misses his mother and the mention of her name upsets him; he is having trouble accepting his new stepmother.)* **making inferences**

D REREAD What do Sarah's thoughts tell about her? *(that she's sensitive to Abe's feelings; that she's trying to understand him and doesn't want to hurt or upset him)* **characterization**

E THINK IT THROUGH Why is Abe so willing to get water from the spring? *(Possible answers: It gives him a chance to get away from Sarah and the discomfort and embarrassment he feels around her. It also gives him a chance to make up to her for his earlier behavior.)* **making inferences**

VOCABULARY

C **surveying** Students can use context clues, prior knowledge, and/or a dictionary to figure out which meaning of the word the author is using.

D **roared** Students should use context clues to figure out the meaning of the word *roared* (to make a loud, prolonged noise).

E **clearing** Students can use the context clues of chopping wood and the setting to figure out which meaning the author is using.

FOR ENGLISH LEARNERS

Help students understand the following expressions and idioms:

Line 76: I'll give you a hiding
Line 85: get next to him
Line 93: Thar's a sight o' things to be done
Line 110: goings-on

stools. Not since Nancy died had the cabin had such a thorough going-over.

At length Sarah climbed the peg ladder to peer into the loft. "Tssch! Tssch!" she said when she saw the cornhusks and dirty bearskins on which the boys had been sleeping. "Take 'em out and burn 'em, 120 Tom."

"Burn 'em?" he protested.

C "Burn those kivers on the bed downstairs, too. We're startin' fresh in this house."

Tom sighed, but did as he was asked.

Within a few hours the cabin fairly shone. Then came the most remarkable occurrence of that remarkable afternoon— the unloading of Sarah Lincoln's plunder.

"Tom, you oughter git the walnut 130 bureau in fust," she suggested. "I'm most particular about that."

With much heaving and grunting Tom and Dennis carried in the bureau, setting it in the place of honor against the wall opposite the bed. "This-here bureau cost forty-five dollars," Tom announced in an undertone.

Forty-five dollars! Abe gasped. Sarah saw him run a finger over the shining dark wood. She 140 noticed his startled expression when he **D** saw his reflection in the little mirror which she hung above the bureau. Most likely he had never seen a looking glass before.

F The wagon yielded other pieces of furniture—a larger table, chairs with real backs, a spinning wheel,

> **occurrence**
> (ə kûr′ əns)
> *n.* event

> **bureau**
> (byŏŏr′ ō)
> a dresser for holding clothes

> **REREAD**
> Read Tom's words aloud. Use your voice to show his feelings.

> **startled**
> (stär′ tld)
> surprised; past tense of *startle*

a big chest filled with clothes. Mrs. Lincoln's pots and pans shone. Her pewter dishes 150 were spotless.

G Most remarkable of all were the feather beds. One was laid on the pole bed in the corner. Another was placed on a clean bearskin in another corner to provide a sleeping place for the girls. The third was carried to the loft. Sarah handed Abe one end of a 160 homespun blanket. "If you'll help me spread these blankets, you and Dennis can turn in. I reckon you won't mind if Johnny bunks with you."

"Yes'm—I mean, no'm," said Abe.

She saw his look of astonishment when he felt the warmth of soft wool between his fingers. It had been a long time since he had slept under a blanket. He almost smiled as he punched his fist into the feather bed.

Within a few minutes gentle snores could be heard 170 coming from the loft. The three girls on the makeshift bed in the corner were already asleep. Sarah sank down into one of her own chairs before the fire, a pile of sewing in her lap.

H Thar's nothin' wrong with Sally that soap and water and a little lovin' won't fix, she thought. Did my heart good to hear her call me Mamma, jes' like my own young'uns. But Abe—

> **astonishment**
> (ə stŏn′ ĭsh mənt)
> *n.* amazement

> **makeshift**
> (māk′ shĭft′)
> temporary substitute

F **REREAD** Read Tom's words aloud. Use your voice to show his feelings. *(Encourage a volunteer to read Tom's lines with a feeling of pride.)* **oral interpretation**

G Ask: What do the items in Sarah's "plunder" tell you about her old life? *(that she lived a comfortable life and had many nice things)* **making inferences**

H Ask: What kind of new family do you think Sarah wants to have? *(one in which everyone feels loved and is happy with the new situation)* **making inferences**

C **Teacher Modeling: Theme** Say: *When Sarah says, "We're startin' fresh in this house," I think she means it in more than one way. In the obvious ways, she means that they're cleaning the place and making it fresh in that way. But I also think she means that both families are getting a fresh start as a blended family, and that things are going to be different for them all.*

D What about Sarah's plunder, or belongings, helps you know that this story takes place in the past? *(Possible answers: First, people don't usually use the words* plunder, bureau, *and* looking glass *anymore. Also, Sarah's most prized possession, her dresser, cost only forty-five dollars; Abe has never seen a mirror; and Sarah uses a spinning wheel to spin her own blankets and cloth.)* **historical fiction**

F **yielded, chest** For each of these words, students can use context clues to figure out that *yielded* means "gave up" and *chest* is a large wooden box for storing clothes.

FOR ENGLISH LEARNERS

Help students understand the following expressions and idioms:

Line 122: kivers
Line 125: the cabin fairly shone
Line 145: chairs with real backs
Line 161: turn in

Sarah paused to thread her bone needle.

180　Abe's harder to figure out, she went on talking to herself. Thar's a lonesome place in his heart. Still a little skittish of havin' a new mammy, I reckon. Jes' have to be patient.

REREAD
Read Sarah's thoughts. What do they show about her?

The bearskin at the door was pushed aside and Tom entered, his arms filled with wood. He started to dump the whole armful on the floor near the fireplace. Then, seeming to think better of it, he arranged the logs in a neat pile.

190　"By cracky"—he gave a look around the room— "you sure did a heap of fixin' here today."

Sarah laughed softly. "Why, Tom, we ain't started yit. You won't know the place when we git through. I reckon you and Dennis will want to split and smooth some logs and lay a puncheon floor. Folks shouldn't live on a dirt floor, not this day and age."

There was a look of distress, almost of anguish, on Tom's face as his wife continued to outline the changes she

200　expected in the cabin. "But, Sairy!" he protested.

"Yes, Tom?" Sarah looked up from her sewing.

Under her level gaze, he began to squirm. "Nothin' much. I jes' figured maybe Dennis and I'll go huntin' tomorrow. That slab of bacon is all the meat we have."

distress
(dĭ strĕs')
n. suffering

THINK IT THROUGH
What things are now better because of Sarah? Use details from this section to support your answer.

356　Unit 11 Bridges to History

FOCUS
Read to find out what Sarah learns as she turns her attention to Abe himself.

The next morning Sarah was pleased to have the men out of the house. "Abe," she said, "today I aim to make you two young'uns look more human."

210　Abe looked startled, but at his stepmother's request he carried several pails of water from the spring. He poured it into the kettles to boil. He dragged a big wooden tub inside. Then mumbling something about having to chop more wood, he disappeared through the door. Sarah smiled as the sharp, steady sound of his chopping was borne to her on the crisp air.

Two hours later she stood in the doorway watching the girls trip gaily down the path.

220　Sally, her hair in two neat pigtails, was wearing her stepmother's shawl over one of Betsy's dresses. She was taking her new sisters to call on one of the neighbors.

Sarah shaded her eyes with her hand and peered off into the woods. "Abe! Oh, Abe," she shouted.

The only answer was the sound of an ax biting into wood—faster and faster.

"You heerd me, Abe," she called.

He came then, reluctantly. Leaving

230　his ax by the door, he edged into the room.

borne
(bôrn)
carried

reluctantly
(rĭ lŭk' tənt lē)
adv. unwillingly

The New Mother　357

COMPREHENSION

I **REREAD** Read Sarah's thoughts. What do they show about her? *(She wants to win Abe over, but she realizes he is still recovering from the loss of his mother. She understands that she will have to be patient with him.)* **making inferences**

J **THINK IT THROUGH** What things are now better because of Sarah? Use details from this section to support your answer. *(Sarah has made the house cleaner and more comfortable with her cooking and cleaning, her furnishings, and her new beds.)* **cause and effect**

K Ask: In the two hours that Sarah worked on Sally, how did she make her look "more human"? *(Sarah bathed her, put her hair in pigtails, and gave her Betsy's dress and her own shawl to wear.)* **details**

LITERATURE

E Tom begins to protest Sarah's changes but then changes his mind. What does this tell you about him? *(Possible answers: He likes the changes that Sarah is making and suggesting, even though it means more work for him; he too would like to make things better for his new family, but he is escaping the work by going hunting.)* **character**

VOCABULARY

G **outline** Have students come up with at least one other meaning than the one used in this selection (e.g., a short summary of a subject; a line that traces the outer limits of an object or figure).

H **trip** Have students use context clues to figure out which meaning the author is using.

FOR ENGLISH LEARNERS

Help students understand the following expressions and idioms:

Line 182: skittish
Line 190: By cracky
Line 195: lay a puncheon floor
Line 203: Under her level gaze
Line 216: borne to her on the crisp air
Line 230: he edged into the room

"Sally's had her bath," said Sarah firmly. "Now I've got a tub of good hot water and a gourdful of soap waiting' for you. Skedaddle out of those old clothes and throw 'em in the fire—"

"I . . . I ain't got any others." Abe looked terrified.

Sarah laughed. "I don't aim to pluck your feathers without giving you some new ones. I set up late last night, cutting
240 down a pair of Mr. Johnston's old pants. I got one of his shirts, too."

> **REREAD**
> Is Sarah a tough person or a gentle one? Explain.

L

Abe slowly started taking off his shirt. He walked toward the fire, edging along the wall, keeping as far away as possible from the tub of hot water.

"That tub won't bite," Sarah reminded him. "Now I'm a-goin' down to the spring. When I git back, I want you to have yourself scrubbed all over."

Abe stuck one toe into the water, said "Ouch!" and
250 drew it out again. Finally, screwing up his courage, he put in his whole foot. He put in his other foot. Then he sat down in the tub. By the time Sarah returned he was standing before the fire dressed in the cut-down trousers and homespun shirt of the late Mr. Johnston.

Sarah surveyed him critically. "You look different already. Those trousers look a mite too big, but you'll soon grow into 'em."

> **surveyed**
> (sər vād′)
> inspected

Abe was somewhat surprised to find how good it
260 felt to be clean. "Thank you, ma'am. Now I reckon I'd better finish my chopping."

"No," said Sarah. "You set yourself down on that stool and let me git at your hair."

M Sarah not only washed his hair but some of the places Abe himself had overlooked. His neck had not

358 Unit 11 Bridges to History

had such a scrubbing for more than a year.
I He submitted silently, only screwing up his
270 eyes a little tighter when Sarah dug in behind his ears. But when she opened the top drawer of the bureau and took out a haw comb and a pair of scissors, he jumped up in alarm.

> **submitted**
> (səb mĭt′ ĭd)
> surrendered to

"Thar's no call to be skeered," she told him, with another look at his mop of unruly black hair. "I'm jes' goin' to cut away some of that brush heap on top of your head."

"Then how folks know I'm me?" he asked plaintively.

> **plaintively**
> (plān′ tĭv lē)
> in a sorrowful way

"What do you mean, Abe?"

"When we came to Indiany, Pappy marked
280 off our claim by pilin' brush along the boundary lines. He said he wanted everyone to know this here was our farm. I figured that brush heap atop of me is my boundary line. How folks know I'm Abe Lincoln, if you clear it away?"

It was the first time Sarah had heard him say more than "Yes'm" or "No'm," and such a long speech took her by surprise. Was he joking? It was hard to tell, he was such a solemn-looking boy. Or was he still frightened? He sat

> **solemn**
> (sŏl′ əm)
> deeply serious

J quietly as she snipped off lock after lock of the unruly black hair. She tried not to pull, but once he said, "Ouch!" She patted his shoulder and waited a moment before she attacked the next tangle.

COMPREHENSION

L **REREAD** Is Sarah a tough person or a gentle one? Explain.
(Students may say she's both. She gives orders, but she's not mean or unreasonable. Rather, she is trying to make things better for her new family, especially Abe.) **making judgments**

M Ask: Why do you think Abe's neck hasn't had a good scrubbing for more than a year?
(Possible answers: That's about how long Abe's mother has been gone, and his father doesn't look after the children the way she did; people's health and hygiene habits were much different in Abe's time.) **making inferences**

VOCABULARY

I **submitted** Have students come up with at least one other meaning than the one used in this selection (e.g., to leave to the judgment or approval of someone else).

J **lock** Have students use context clues to figure out which meaning the author is using.

FOR ENGLISH LEARNERS

Help students understand the following expressions and idioms:

Line 234: Skedaddle
Line 250: screwing up his courage
Line 256: look a mite too big
Line 267: screwing up his eyes
Line 274: brush heap

"Thar!" she said at last. "It's all over. S'pose you mosey over to the lookin' glass and tell me if that's Abe Lincoln you see."

He gazed at his reflection, a pleased expression in his eyes. "It's Abe, I reckon. I still ain't the purtiest boy in Pigeon Creek. On
300 t'other hand, thar ain't quite so much of me to be ugly, now you cleared away the brush heap."

RERED What does Abe show about himself here? **N**

Suddenly he grinned, and Sarah laughed in relief. "You're a caution, Abe. Smart, too. Had much schoolin'?"

caution
(kô' shən)
someone who is surprising

Abe shook his head, serious again. "I've just been to school by littles."

"Have you a mind to go again?"

"There ain't any school since Master
310 Crawford left. Anyhow, Pappy don't set much store by eddication."

set much store by
see as valuable

Sarah looked at him sharply. "Can you read?"

"Yes'm. But I haven't any books."

"Now, that's peculiarsome," said Sarah. "You can **O** read and you haven't any books. I have books and can't read."

Abe stared at her, amazed. "You have books?"

She walked over to the bureau and came back **K** 320 carrying four worn-looking volumes. "Books are a right good thing to have, so I brung 'em along. You set yourself down thar at the table and I'll show you."

THINK IT THROUGH
P What does Sarah discover about Abe? What does he discover about her?

360 Unit 11 Bridges to History

FOCUS
Sarah and Abe continue talking. Find out what happens as she learns more about him.

Abe, his brown cheeks flushed with pleasure, spelled out the titles: "Rob-in-son Cru-soe, Pil-grim's Prog-ress, Sin-bad the Sail-or, Ae-sop's Fa-bles. Oh, ma'am, this here book is one Master Crawford told us about."

Master
teacher or schoolmaster

Sarah sat down beside him and turned the pages. "The stories look like little bitty ones.
330 Could you read one of 'em to me, Abe?"

The book was open to the story of "The Crow and the Pitcher." Abe, his shorn head bent above the page, **L** began to read. "A crow was almost dead of—of th-thirst, when he found a p-pitcher with a little water in the bottom."

It had been so long since Abe had seen a book that he stumbled over a few of the words, but he gained more confidence as he went along. "'The crow reached in his bill to take a drink. He
340 tried and tried, but he could not reach the water. He was al-most ready to give up, when he had an i-dea. He picked up a peb-ble in his bill and dropped it into the pit-cher. He picked up an-other pebble and an-other . . .

bill
beak

"'With every pebble that he dropped, the water in **M** the pitcher rose a little high-er. At last the water rose so high that the crow could reach it with his bill. He took a long drink, and so was a-ble to q-q-quench his thirst and save his life.'"

350 "You read right well," said Sarah.

Abe laughed delightedly. "It says something else here. 'Mo-ral,'" he read. **F** "'Little by little does the trick.'"

moral
(môr' al)
the lesson taught by a fable or story

The New Mother 361

COMPREHENSION

N **REREAD** What does Abe show about himself here? *(Possible responses: He has a sense of humor, he doesn't take himself too seriously, he is becoming less uncomfortable around Sarah, he is grateful for what she has done.)* **making judgments**

O Say: Think about when Sarah grew up. Why do you think she can't read? *(When Sarah was young, education wasn't valued—especially for girls.)* **making inferences**

P **THINK IT THROUGH** What does Sarah discover about Abe? What does he discover about her? *(Sarah discovers that Abe is a bright boy with a good sense of humor who loves to read. Abe discovers that Sarah has books but can't read.)* **details**

LITERATURE

F In what way does "little by little" apply to Abe and Sarah's relationship? *(Little by little they are getting to know, understand, trust, and like each other.)* **theme**

VOCABULARY

K **volumes** Students should use context clues to figure out that the word *volumes* in this selection means "books."

L **pitcher** Have students use context clues to figure out which meaning the author is using. Then have them come up with a second meaning of the word.

M **rose** Have students use context clues to figure out which meaning the author is using.

FOR ENGLISH LEARNERS

Help students understand the following expressions and idioms:

Line 307: by littles
Line 308: Have you a mind
Line 323: flushed with pleasure
Line 332: shorn head bent above the page
Line 337: stumbled over a few of the words

Abe took the book closer to the fireplace where it was easier to see the words. He read story after story, pausing only now and then to throw
360 another log on the fire. As Sarah went about her household tasks, she watched him closely, a puzzled frown in her honest gray eyes.

This photograph of Sarah Lincoln was taken in the 1860s. At this point, her stepson had already been president.

Abe was different from what her John would ever be. He was different from any boy she had ever seen. She pulled a chair closer to the fire and picked up her knitting. "Which
370 story do you like best?" she asked.

Q

REREAD
In what ways do you think Abe is different?

Abe looked up with a start. "The one about the smart crow that filled up the pitcher with pebbles so he could git himself a drink."

"That story sorta reminds me of you," she told him.

"How come, ma'am?"

"Didn't that Mr. Aesop say, 'Little by little does the trick'? Wall, you go to school by littles. Each time you l'arn something. I figure those little bits of l'arnin' are
380 like pebbles. Keep on pilin' 'em up higher, and you'll make something of yourself."

Abe shook his head. "I reckon I won't ever git to go to school agin."

"I wouldn't say that. Lots of new folks are a-comin' to Pigeon Creek, and the more folks, the more likely another schoolmaster is to come."

362 Unit 11 Bridges to History

"But Pappy says I already know how to read and write and cipher. He says I have more eddication than he ever had. I—I can't
390 help it, ma'am. I want to know more'n Pappy knows."

cipher
(si' fər)
to solve number problems

"Your pappy's a good man," said Sarah, "and the next time a school keeps in these parts, I'm a-goin' to ask him to let you and the other young'uns go. That's a promise, Abe."

Again Abe could only stare.

"Meanwhile, you can l'arn right smart jes' by reading these-here books."

R "I can read 'em—any time I like?"

"I'm a-giving 'em to you to keep."

"Oh, Mamma," said Abe. The name slipped out as though he had always been used to saying it.

G Only the fire crackling softly on the hearth broke the long silence. "You're my boy now, Abe," said Sarah softly, "and I'm a-goin' to help you all I can."

Abe did not answer. He did not need to. His shining eyes told Sarah all she wished to know. And he had called her Mamma of his own free will. **N**

S

THINK IT THROUGH

1. Abe and Sarah talk about stories. They discuss the moral that "Little by little does the trick." How does Sarah use the story to help Abe?
2. What kind of person is Sarah Lincoln? Support your answer with details from the story.
3. Think about the qualities young Abe Lincoln shows in this story. In your opinion, which of these qualities could be helpful to him later when he is president of the United States?

The New Mother 363

Q **REREAD** In what ways do you think Abe is different? *(Possible answers: He is very sensitive and serious for his age, and he has a desire for learning that Sarah has never seen. She thinks he will do more with himself than even her own son will do.)* **character**

R Ask: Why do you think Sarah gives Abe her books? *(Possible answers: She sees how important books and reading are to Abe, and she can't read anyway. Also, by giving Abe the books, she is encouraging him to read.)* **making inferences**

S **THINK IT THROUGH**

1. Abe and Sarah talk about stories. They discuss the moral that "Little by little does the trick." How does Sarah use this story to help Abe? *(She tells him that if he keeps getting his education "by littles," he'll make something of himself.)* **cause and effect**

2. What kind of person is Sarah Lincoln? Support your answer with details from the story. *(She is kind, caring, and fair; freely shares her love and possessions with her new family; and treats her stepchildren as if they were her own. She also sees there's something special about Abe, and she tries to bring it out.)* **character** LITERATURE

3. Think about the qualities young Abe Lincoln shows in this story. In your opinion, which of these qualities could be helpful to him later when he is president of the United States? *(He is observant and curious, has a strong desire to learn, is thoughtful, and seems to show a kind of wisdom. He is also hardworking and has a strong sense of himself.)* **character** LITERATURE

RETEACHING

If students need more help understanding **Main Idea,** use pages T635–T638.

G Reread lines 394–406 and identify the lines that you think tell the climax of the story. *(lines 401–402: Abe accepts Sarah as his new mother.)* **climax**

N **will** Students should be able to figure out that in this context, the meaning of *will* that the author is using is "choice."

FOR ENGLISH LEARNERS

Help students understand the following expressions and idioms:

Line 393: keeps in these parts
Line 403: broke the long silence

RETEACHING

If students need more help understanding **Multiple-Meaning Words,** use pages T620–T621.

1. COMPREHENSION

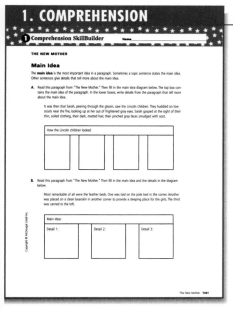

Main Idea

Direct Instruction Tell students that the **main idea** of a paragraph or passage is its most important idea. Explain that **supporting details** tell more about the main idea.

Before reading this passage from "The New Mother" aloud to the students, point out that the main idea is stated in the first sentence of the passage. Ask students to identify the details that support the main idea.

From the moment Sarah laid aside her hood and shawl, things began to happen in the Lincoln cabin. . . . Dennis Hanks, an older cousin who made his home with the Lincolns, brought in some firewood. Abe and Mathilda started for the spring, swinging the water pail between them. A few minutes later Sally had forgotten her soiled dress and her bare feet, as she and Betsy mixed batter and set corn bread to bake on the hearth.

Comprehension SkillBuilder Answer Key:

A. *First detail box: huddled on stools, looking at Sarah with frightened eyes*
Second detail box: wearing soiled clothing
Third detail box: dark, matted hair
Fourth detail box: pinched gray faces smudged with soot

B. *Main Idea: The remarkable featherbeds or Where the featherbeds were put*
Detail 1: One was laid on the bed in the corner.
Detail 2: One was placed on a bearskin in another corner.
Detail 3: The third one was carried to the loft.

2. LITERATURE

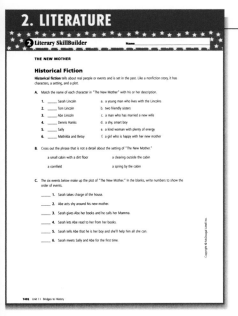

Historical Fiction

Direct Instruction Tell students that **historical fiction** takes place in the past. Historical fiction often tells about a real person or event in history. Explain that writers of historical fiction base their stories on known facts, but they imagine the words, actions, and feelings of the people involved. In "The New Mother" the writer uses dialect to show the way people spoke during Lincoln's time. Explain that historical fiction has the same elements as fiction: characters, setting, and plot.

Literary SkillBuilder Answer Key:

A. 1. *e* **2.** *c* **3.** *d* **4.** *a* **5.** *f* **6.** *b*

B. *Cross out: a cornfield*

C. 1. *3* **2.** *2* **3.** *5* **4.** *4* **5.** *6* **6.** *1*

3. VOCABULARY

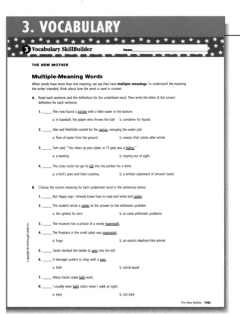

Multiple-Meaning Words

Direct Instruction Tell students that some words have more than one meaning, or **multiple meanings.** Explain that context clues help readers understand the intended meaning. Tell students that if they consult a dictionary to find out the meaning of a word as it is used in a story or article, they will need to try out the various meanings in context and choose the correct one.

Discuss this example from "The New Mother."

With much heaving and grunting Tom and Dennis carried in the <u>bureau</u>, setting it in the place of honor against the wall opposite the bed.

The dictionary lists at least two meanings for the word *bureau*: "a chest of drawers" and "a department of an organization." Have students try each of these meanings in the sentence. Help them see that the first meaning is the one that fits.

Vocabulary SkillBuilder Answer Key:

A.1. *b* **2.** *a* **3.** *a* **4.** *a*

B. 1. *b* **2.** *a* **3.** *b* **4.** *a* **5.** *a* **6.** *b*
7. *a* **8.** *b*

4. WORDS TO KNOW

Words to Know

Direct Instruction As you introduce the **Words to Know,** here are some points you might want to cover. Help students identify the parts of the vocabulary words. Stress the importance of finding the base of each word. Help students remove the suffixes first.

- **huddle** + -ed = *huddled,* past tense of *huddle*
- **occur** + -ence = *occurrence,* derivative of *occur,* from Latin *occurrere,* from *ob-,* "toward" and *currere,* "to run"

- **astonish** + -ment = *astonishment,* derivative of *astonish,* from Latin *ex- + tonāre,* "to thunder"
- **distress,** from the Latin *distringere,* "to hinder"
- **reluctant** + -ly = *reluctantly,* adverb form of *reluctant,* from Latin *re- + luctārī,* "to struggle"

Writing Activity Encourage students to be creative. Have volunteers read their paragraphs aloud.

Words to Know SkillBuilder Answer Key:

A.
1. *reluctantly*
2. *astonishment*
3. *huddled*
4. *occurrence*
5. *distress*

B.
1. *occurrence—synonyms*
2. *distress—antonyms*
3. *astonishment—synonyms*
4. *reluctantly—antonyms*
5. *huddled—antonyms*

5. SELECTION TEST

Selection Test Answer Key:
A. 1. *b* **2.** *a* **3.** *c* **4.** *b* **5.** *c* **6.** *a* **7.** *b* **8.** *c* **9.** *a*
B. *"Little by little" applies to the way Sarah and Abe got to know each other.*

THE NEW MOTHER

Main Idea

The **main idea** is the most important idea in a paragraph. Sometimes a topic sentence states the main idea. Other sentences give details that tell more about the main idea.

A. Read this paragraph from "The New Mother." Then fill in the main idea diagram below. The top box contains the main idea of the paragraph. In the lower boxes, write details from the paragraph that tell more about the main idea.

> It was then that Sarah, peering through the gloom, saw the Lincoln children. They huddled on low stools near the fire, looking up at her out of frightened gray eyes. Sarah gasped at the sight of their thin, soiled clothing, their dark, matted hair, their pinched gray faces smudged with soot.

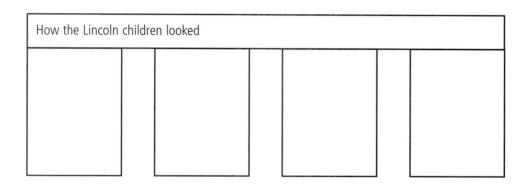

How the Lincoln children looked

B. Read this paragraph from "The New Mother." Then fill in the main idea and the details in the diagram below.

> Most remarkable of all were the feather beds. One was laid on the pole bed in the corner. Another was placed on a clean bearskin in another corner to provide a sleeping place for the girls. The third was carried to the loft.

Main Idea:		
Detail 1:	Detail 2:	Detail 3:

THE NEW MOTHER

Historical Fiction

Historical fiction tells about real people or events and is set in the past. Like a nonfiction story, it has characters, a setting, and a plot.

A. Match the name of each character in "The New Mother" with his or her description.

1. _____ Sarah Lincoln
2. _____ Tom Lincoln
3. _____ Abe Lincoln
4. _____ Dennis Hanks
5. _____ Sally
6. _____ Mathilda and Betsy

a. a young man who lives with the Lincolns
b. two friendly sisters
c. a man who has married a new wife
d. a shy, smart boy
e. a kind woman with plenty of energy
f. a girl who is happy with her new mother

B. Cross out the phrase that is not a detail about the setting of "The New Mother."

a small cabin with a dirt floor   a clearing outside the cabin

a cornfield   a spring by the cabin

C. The six events below make up the plot of "The New Mother." In the blanks, write numbers to show the order of events.

_____ **1.** Sarah takes charge of the house.

_____ **2.** Abe acts shy around his new mother.

_____ **3.** Sarah gives Abe her books and he calls her Mamma.

_____ **4.** Sarah lets Abe read to her from her books.

_____ **5.** Sarah tells Abe that he is her boy and she'll help him all she can.

_____ **6.** Sarah meets Sally and Abe for the first time.

THE NEW MOTHER

Multiple-Meaning Words

When words have more than one meaning, we say they have **multiple meanings.** To understand the meaning the writer intended, think about how the word is used in context.

A. Read each sentence and the definitions for the underlined word. Then write the letter of the correct definition for each sentence.

1. _____ The crow found a <u>pitcher</u> with a little water in the bottom.

  a. in baseball, the player who throws the ball   b. container for liquids

2. _____ Abe and Mathilda started for the <u>spring</u>, swinging the water pail.

  a. flow of water from the ground   b. season that comes after winter

3. _____ Tom said, "You clean up your plate, or I'll give you a <u>hiding</u>."

  a. a beating   b. staying out of sight

4. _____ The crow could not get its <u>bill</u> into the pitcher for a drink.

  a. a bird's jaws and their covering   b. a written statement of amount owed

B. Choose the correct meaning for each underlined word in the sentences below.

1. _____ But Pappy says I already know how to read and write and <u>cipher</u>.

2. _____ The student wrote a <u>cipher</u> as the answer to the arithmetic problem.

  a. the symbol for zero   b. to solve arithmetic problems

3. _____ The museum has a picture of a wooly <u>mammoth</u>.

4. _____ The fireplace in the small cabin was <u>mammoth</u>.

  a. huge   b. an extinct elephant-like animal

5. _____ Sarah climbed the ladder to <u>peer</u> into the loft.

6. _____ A teenager prefers to shop with a <u>peer</u>.

  a. look   b. social equal

7. _____ Many hands make <u>light</u> work.

8. _____ I usually wear <u>light</u> colors when I walk at night.

  a. easy   b. not dark

THE NEW MOTHER

Words to Know

huddled　　**occurrence**　　**astonishment**　　**distress**　　**reluctantly**

A. In each blank, write the word from the list that best completes the sentence.

1. Although she didn't like it, the cat _____ allowed me to put her in the box.

2. There was a look of _____ on his face when everyone jumped up and yelled, "Surprise!"

3. We _____ together closely for warmth in the back seat of the car.

4. We have not had one _____ of cheating since the tests were put on a computer.

5. Laurence felt much _____ over the loss of his goldfish.

B. **Synonyms** are words that have nearly the same meaning. **Antonyms** are opposites. Beside each word, write a word from the list above that is **either** a synonym **or** an antonym for the word. Then circle "synonyms" or "antonyms" to describe the word pair.

1. event　　_____ synonyms / antonyms

2. comfort　_____ synonyms / antonyms

3. surprise　_____ synonyms / antonyms

4. eagerly　_____ synonyms / antonyms

5. separated　_____ synonyms / antonyms

Writing Activity
Write a paragraph about a major change in your life. Use at least two of the **Words to Know.**

THE NEW MOTHER

A. Complete each sentence by filling in the circle beside the letter of the correct answer.

1. This historical fiction story is
○ a. based on made-up people and events.   ○ c. completely true and factual.
○ b. based on real people and events.

2. Sarah Lincoln
○ a. really did become Abraham Lincoln's stepmother.
○ b. is a made-up character who didn't really exist.
○ c. doesn't appear in any true stories about Abe Lincoln.

3. When Sarah first arrived at her new home, she
○ a. started to cry when she saw what it looked like.
○ b. acted very mean to her new stepchildren.
○ c. began to cook and clean and make a fresh start.

4. When Abe first met Sarah, he
○ a. loved her immediately and called her Mamma.
○ b. was very upset and had trouble accepting her.
○ c. did all that he could to make her feel welcome.

5. In order to make Abe and Sally "look more human," Sarah
○ a. cut their nails and hair, which had grown very long.
○ b. taught them how to hold a fork and a spoon.
○ c. bathed them, washed their hair, and gave them new clothes.

6. When Sarah showed Abe her books,
○ a. Abe told her that he loved to read.   ○ c. she read Abe her favorite story.
○ b. she told Abe to never touch them.

7. The story of the crow reminded Sarah of Abe because
○ a. Abe had black hair, and the crow had black feathers.
○ b. they both got what they wanted "by littles."
○ c. the crow was greedy, and so was Abe.

8. When Abe said he wanted to know more than his father knew, Sarah
○ a. scolded Abe for being disrespectful.   ○ c. promised Abe she'd try to send him to school.
○ b. told Abe that he already did.

9. When Sarah gave Abe her books, he said,
○ a. "Oh, Mamma."   ○ b. "Thank you, Sarah."   ○ c. "Are you serious?"

B. In your own words, tell what "little by little" means in terms of Abe and Sarah's relationship.

_____

_____

Focus Skills

COMPREHENSION
Sequence

LITERATURE
Narrative Poetry

SkillBuilder Copymasters

 Reading Comprehension:
1 Sequence p. T501

 Literary Analysis:
2 Narrative Poetry p. T502

Assessment

 3 Selection Test p. T503

For English Learners

Help students understand that poets use rhyme and rhythm in ballads to create the lyrical quality of a song. Read "John Henry" aloud with students a few times and help them hear the rhyme and rhythm. Discuss how the repeated lines in the poem are like the refrain, or chorus, of a song. If available, obtain a recording of the ballad to play for students.

364

More About Narrative Poetry

A **narrative poem** tells a story. Like a short story or a novel, a narrative poem has the following elements: setting, characters, and a sequence of related events, or plot. A **ballad** is a type of narrative poem. Ballads tell a story about ordinary people who have unusual adventures or have performed daring deeds. Traditional ballads are characterized by regular stanzas, refrains, and other repetitions. For instance, "The Ballad of John Henry" uses repetition to create a strong, steady rhythm that mimics the sound of a pounding hammer.

The Ballad of John Henry
by Anonymous

"A man ain't nothing but a man," says John Henry. Can a hero be bigger than life?

Connect to Your Life

Think of someone you admire, someone you'd call a hero. What makes this person special? If you could write a song about this person, what actions would you describe?

Key to the Ballad

This is a **ballad**, a poem that tells a story. Each block of five lines is called a **stanza.** Many ballads were first shared as songs.

After the Civil War, railroads began to stretch from the Midwest into the West. Tough railroad workers laid countless miles of track. They carved or blasted tunnels through rock. They often risked their lives. Then machines began to take over some of this work. This ballad is about John Henry, a worker who may or may not have really lived. He shows the qualities of many bold and strong railroad workers.

 Reading Coach CD-ROM selection

The Ballad of John Henry **365**

Connect to Your Life

As you guide students in a discussion of the actions and qualities of different heroes, you may want to remind them that heroes come in all shapes, sizes, and ages—and that some heroes are animals.

Key to the Ballad

Help students understand that a **ballad** can be a song as well as a poem, and that ballads tell stories in a very concise way, using much action and few words. Before people began writing ballads down, they passed them on by word of mouth or by singing. Perhaps as a way of helping people remember their ballads, poets included rhyme and repetition in them.

Building Background

This ballad is based on an actual event that took place in the 1870s. An African American named John Henry worked on the Big Bend Tunnel of the Chesapeake and Ohio Railroad. One day a man brought a steam drill to the site and said it could dig faster than twenty workers with hammers. John Henry decided to race the drill to prove that a man could dig faster than a machine. In the ballad, John Henry dies from exhaustion right after winning the race. However, the real John Henry is said to have been crushed after winning by a rock that fell from the tunnel's ceiling. John Henry's heroic act has come to stand for all workers' fight against industrialization.

FOCUS
Find out how railroad worker John Henry reacts to the coming of the steam drill.

When John Henry was about three days old,
A-sittin' on his pappy's knee,
He gave one loud and lonesome cry:
"The hammer'll be the death of me,
5   The hammer'll be the death of me."

Well, the captain said to John Henry one day:
"Gonna bring that steam drill 'round,
Gonna take that steam drill out on the job,
Gonna whop that steel on down,
10   Gonna whop that steel on down."

John Henry said to the captain:
"Well, the next time you go to town
Just bring me back a twelve-pound hammer
And I'll beat your steam drill down,
15   And I'll beat your steam drill down."

John Henry said to the captain:
"Well, a man ain't nothin' but a man,
And before I let a steam drill beat me down
Gonna die with the hammer in my hand,
20   Gonna die with the hammer in my hand."

THINK IT THROUGH
Why do you think John Henry wants to compete against the steam drill?

FOCUS
Read to discover the unforgettable actions of John Henry.

John Henry went to the tunnel,
And they put him in the lead to drive,
The rock so tall and John Henry so small,
He laid down his hammer and he cried
25   He laid down his hammer and he cried.

John Henry said to his shaker:
"Shaker, why don't you sing?
For I'm swingin' twelve pounds from the hips on down,
Just listen to that cold steel ring,
30   Just listen to that cold steel ring."

COMPREHENSION

FOCUS SKILL: Sequence

Remind students that **sequence** is the order in which events happen. The signal words that the poet uses help readers understand the sequence of events in this ballad.

For direct instruction on Sequence, see page T500.

Ⓐ Ask: What signal words help you understand how old John Henry is at the beginning of this ballad? *(When John Henry was about three days old)* **sequence**

Ⓑ Ask: What signal words help you know that John Henry is a grown man when he is talking to the captain? *(one day)* **sequence**

Ⓒ Ask: Who or what do you predict will win the contest? Why? *(Accept any prediction that students can support with clues from the poem. However, given what John Henry says in the first stanza, and the fact that he cries, most*

students probably will predict that the steam drill will win.) **predicting**

Ⓓ **THINK IT THROUGH** Why do you think John Henry wants to compete against the steam drill? *(He wants to prove that a man and his hammer are better and faster than a steam drill.)* **drawing conclusions**

LITERATURE

FOCUS SKILL: Narrative Poetry

Tell students that **narrative poetry** is poetry that tells a story. It contains elements of fiction—such as character, setting, plot, and theme—as well as elements of poetry, such as rhyme, rhythm, and figurative language. Ballads are a form of narrative poetry.

For direct instruction on Narrative Poetry, see page T500.

Use the following questions to encourage literary analysis.

Ⓐ **Teacher Modeling: Character** Say: *John Henry is only three days old when he says his first words. And not only does he speak, he foretells his own death. That tells me right away that John Henry is capable of doing some pretty amazing things. I wonder what else he'll do.*

Ⓑ Who is the captain in this ballad? *(Students should be able to use context clues to figure out that the captain is the head of John Henry's railroad crew.)* **character**

John Henry told his captain:
"Look-a yonder what I see—
Your drill's done broke and your hole's done choke',
And you can't drive steel like me,
35   And you can't drive steel like me."

> Well, the man that invented the steam drill,
> He thought he was mighty fine,
> But John Henry drove his fifteen feet,
> And the steam drill only made nine,
> 40   And the steam drill only made nine.

REREAD
Who won the contest?

E

John Henry looked up at the mountain,
And his hammer was striking fire,
Well, he hammered so hard that he broke his poor old heart,
He laid down his hammer and he died,
45   He laid down his hammer and he died.

They took John Henry to the graveyard,
And they laid him in the sand,
Three men from the east and a woman from the west
Came to see that old steel-drivin' man,
50   Came to see that old steel-drivin' man.

They took John Henry to the graveyard,
And they laid him in the sand,
C And every | locomotive | comes a-roarin' by
Says: "There lies a steel-drivin' man,"
55   Says: "There lies a steel-drivin' man."

locomotive
(lō' kə mō' tĭv)
train

F **THINK IT THROUGH**

1. This poem describes a contest between a man and a machine. Who do *you* think won? Explain your answer.
2. Find details in the ballad that show the kind of person John Henry was.
3. In the ballad, John Henry died from his efforts. Machines did take over the work. In your opinion, were John Henry's actions worth doing?

Unit 11 Bridges to History

The Ballad of John Henry **369**

E **REREAD** Who won the contest? *(John Henry, by six feet)* **details**

F **THINK IT THROUGH**

1. This poem describes a contest between a man and a machine. Who do *you* think won? Explain your answer. *(Some students may feel that John Henry won because he drove his hammer fifteen feet while the steam drill went only nine feet. Other students may feel that the machine won because it ultimately replaced humans.)* **drawing conclusions**

2. Find details in the ballad that show the kind of person John Henry was. *(Possible responses: Lines 11–15 show that John Henry was strong and hard-working. Lines 16–20 show that John Henry was proud and brave. Lines 37–47 show that John Henry was heroic.)* **character** LITERATURE

3. In the ballad, John Henry died from his efforts. Machines did eventually take over the work of many railroad workers. In your opinion, were John Henry's actions worth doing? *(Some students will say yes, because he did what he set out to do. Others will say no, because even though John Henry won, machines still took over in the end.)* **drawing conclusions**

RETEACHING

If students need more help understanding **Sequence,** use pages T639–T641.

LITERATURE

C Narrative poetry tells a story. In your own words, recall the main events of this poem's story. *(John Henry's captain tells him he has a steam drill that can break through a mountain faster than John Henry can. John Henry accepts the challenge and outperforms the drill fifteen feet to nine. Because of the strain he puts on his heart, however, John Henry dies after the contest.)* **narrative poetry**

The Ballad of John Henry   PE 368–369 • **T499**

Direct Instruction
for SkillBuilder Copymasters

1. COMPREHENSION

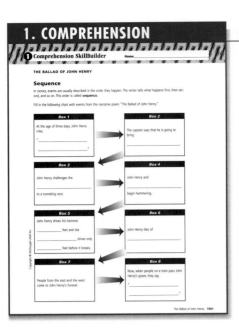

Sequence

Direct Instruction Tell students that since narrative poems tell stories, the events in the poems are usually related in the order they happen. We say the events are described in **sequence.**

Point out that in "The Ballad of John Henry," the writer has not used the usual signal words to make the sequence clear. Explain that events are simply described one after the other, leaving the reader to figure out that the events happen in that same order. Each stanza tells about an event that happens after the one in the preceding stanza. Point out that the time elapsed between stanzas can vary greatly. For example, in the first stanza, John Henry is only three days old. In the next stanza, he is an adult who is working on a railroad.

> **Comprehension SkillBuilder Answer Key:**
> *At the age of three days, John Henry cries, "The hammer'll be the death of me."* *The captain says that he is going to bring a steam drill around. John Henry challenges the steam drill to a tunneling race. John Henry and the steam drill begin hammering. John Henry drives his hammer 15 feet, and the steam drill drives only nine feet before it breaks. John Henry dies of a broken heart. Now, when people on a train pass John Henry's grave, they say, "There lies a steel-drivin' man."*

2. LITERATURE

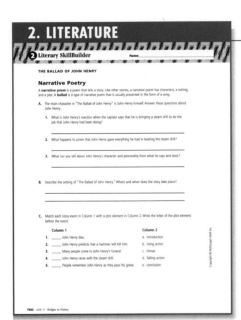

Narrative Poetry

Direct Instruction Tell students that a **narrative poem** is a poem that tells a story. Like other stories, a narrative poem has characters, a setting, and a plot, a series of events connected to one another.

Point out the stanzas of the poem. Explain that each stanza moves the story along by describing another event.

Point out that because "The Ballad of John Henry" is a poem, not just a story, it relies heavily on rhythm, rhyme, and repetition. Explain further that a ballad is a kind of narrative poem that was originally presented as a song. Explain that the words the poet has used were selected with care. The poet paid attention both to meanings of the words and to their sounds.

> **Literary SkillBuilder Answer Key:**
> **A.1.** *John Henry says he'll beat the steam drill at doing the job.*
> **2.** *John Henry dies on the job after beating the steam drill.*
> **3.** *Answers will vary. Possible answer: John Henry is strong, brave, proud, and hard-working. He never backs down when he says he will do something.*
>
> **B.** *The story takes place in a mountainous area near a town, probably sometime soon after the Civil War.*
>
> **C. 1.** *c* **2.** *a* **3.** *d* **4.** *b* **5.** *e*

3. SELECTION TEST

> **Selection Test Answer Key:**
> **A. 1.** *true* **2.** *true* **3.** *false* **4.** *true*
> **B.** *Possible responses: broke his heart; died of a heart attack; died with a hammer in his hand.*

THE BALLAD OF JOHN HENRY

Sequence

In stories, events are usually described in the order they happen. The writer tells what happens first, then second, and so on. This order is called **sequence.**

Fill in the following chart with events from the narrative poem "The Ballad of John Henry."

Box 1

At the age of three days, John Henry cries,

" _____

_____."

Box 2

The captain says that he is going to bring

_____.

Box 3

John Henry challenges the

_____

to a tunneling race.

Box 4

John Henry and

_____

begin hammering.

Box 5

John Henry drives his hammer

_____ feet and the

_____ drives only

_____ feet before it breaks.

Box 6

John Henry dies of

_____.

Box 7

People from the east and the west come to John Henry's funeral.

Box 8

Now, when people on a train pass John Henry's grave, they say,

" _____

_____."

THE BALLAD OF JOHN HENRY

Narrative Poetry

A **narrative poem** is a poem that tells a story. Like other stories, a narrative poem has characters, a setting, and a plot. A **ballad** is a type of narrative poem that is usually presented in the form of a song.

A. The main character in "The Ballad of John Henry" is John Henry himself. Answer these questions about John Henry.

   1. What is John Henry's reaction when the captain says that he is bringing a steam drill to do the job that John Henry had been doing?

     _____

   2. What happens to prove that John Henry gave everything he had in beating the steam drill?

     _____

   3. What can you tell about John Henry's character and personality from what he says and does?

     _____

B. Describe the setting of "The Ballad of John Henry." Where and when does the story take place?

   _____

   _____

C. Match each story event in Column 1 with a plot element in Column 2. Write the letter of the plot element before the event.

Column 1	Column 2
1. _____ John Henry dies.	a. introduction
2. _____ John Henry predicts that a hammer will kill him.	b. rising action
3. _____ Many people come to John Henry's funeral.	c. climax
4. _____ John Henry races with the steam drill.	d. falling action
5. _____ People remember John Henry as they pass his grave.	e. conclusion

THE BALLAD OF JOHN HENRY

A. Write **true** or **false** next to each statement.

_____ **1.** John Henry knew all his life that he would die with a hammer in his hand.

_____ **2.** John Henry is known as the "steel-drivin' man."

_____ **3.** The steam drill was more powerful than John Henry.

_____ **4.** People came to see John Henry's grave from the east and the west.

B. Complete this sentence with words that make it a true statement.

John Henry hammered so hard that he _____

_____

_____

Focus Skills

COMPREHENSION
Main Idea
Understanding Visuals

LITERATURE
Informative Nonfiction

VOCABULARY
Specialized Vocabulary

SkillBuilder Copymasters

 Reading Comprehension:
1 Main Idea p. T512
2 Understanding Visuals p. T513

 Vocabulary:
3 Specialized Vocabulary p. T514
4 Words to Know p. T515

Assessment

 5 Selection Test p. T516

Readability Scores

DRP	LEXILE	DALE-CHALL
48	460	3.0

For English Learners

You might spend time discussing the basic background of the California Gold Rush. Explain how the discovery of gold led to the growth of the West. In this selection, students will become acquainted with the terms *Forty-Niners, prairie schooners,* and *Conestoga wagon.* They will also encounter many words related to life on the frontier.

Reading Fluency

 ★ Reading Fluency p. T517

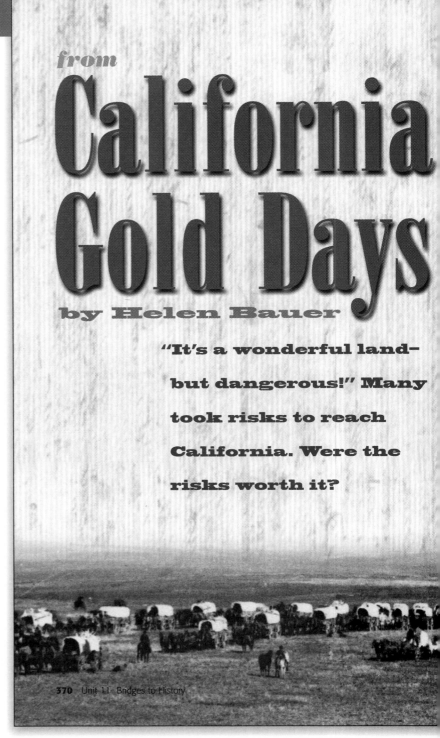

from
California Gold Days

by Helen Bauer

"It's a wonderful land— but dangerous!" Many took risks to reach California. Were the risks worth it?

370 Unit 11 Bridges to History

Vocabulary Strategy: Preteaching

Specialized Vocabulary Tell students that when they read nonfiction, they might come across words that look familiar but have unexpected meanings. For example, in this selection about traveling west during the Gold Rush, *party* is a **specialized vocabulary word.** Rather than meaning "a celebration" in this selection, *party* means "a group of people organized to do something." Explain that students can figure out a specialized word's meaning by looking at the context and using their prior knowledge.

Connect to Your Life

Imagine you are moving to a new place. It is far from your present home. Each family member can take only a few things. What would you take with you? Make a list to show to a classmate.

Key to the Article

In 1848 in California, an ordinary worker discovered gold. This started the California Gold Rush. By 1849, the exciting news had attracted thousands to the West. Some wanted to find gold. Most simply wanted to find a new chance in life.

These fortune seekers were called "Forty-Niners." They traveled to the West in covered wagons that looked almost like sailboats. They traveled in large groups called *wagon trains*. This article gives details about the kinds of journeys the Forty-Niners had.

Vocabulary Preview

Words to Know
plains   barrels   passes

 Reading Coach CD-ROM selection

371

Connect to Your Life

You may want to set a limit on the number of items that students can add to their lists. As they jot down each item, remind them to think about what would make that item something that they just couldn't do without.

Key to the Article

Point out the photograph extending across the bottom of these two pages. Tell students that it shows four lines of wagons that were traveling through territory that later became the bordering states of North Dakota and South Dakota.

To help set a purpose for reading, you may want to have students begin a **K-W-L chart** on the California Gold Rush. See page T664 for instructions and page T666 for a copymaster.

Vocabulary Preview

Words to Know
plains *n.* large, treeless land
barrels *n.* large, round containers, usually made of wood
passes *n.* ways around, over, and through mountains

 For direct instruction on Words to Know, see page T511.

Building Background

The California Gold Rush was the greatest gold rush in United States history, and it played an important part in the development of California. It began when a carpenter named James W. Marshall discovered gold while working at John Sutter's mill on January 24, 1848. News of Marshall's discovery spread like wildfire, and people from all over the world soon began flocking to California. Thanks to those "Forty-Niners" (most arrived during 1849), California's population grew from 15,000 to more than 100,000 in less than two years. This growth spurt gave California enough people to be admitted into the Union. It became the 31st state on September 9, 1850.

Write the following sentences on the board and have students choose the meanings that would fit this selection.
1. We came to a <u>fork</u> in the road and decided to go south.
   a. instrument used for eating   b. place where something divides
2. They formed several <u>companies</u> before they left for California.
   a. groups of people joined for a purpose   b. businesses

 For more on Specialized Vocabulary, see page T511.

FOCUS
Thousands rush toward one place—California. Discover what makes this place such a powerful attraction.

About forty thousand people came to California by sea in 'forty-nine and 'fifty. An even larger number came overland. This was a harder way to go than by ship. It did not take much money to go this way, but it took lots of courage. The trip across the plains, mountains, and desert took six months. Because of the snow, the gold seekers could not go in winter.

> plains
> (plānz)
> *n.* large, treeless area of land

Most of the overland gold seekers left
10 from St. Joseph or Independence, Missouri. By April 1849, the first twenty thousand people from all over the United States were waiting to start. Tents could be seen everywhere along the riverbanks. "How many miles to California from St. Joe?" could be heard on all sides. "Two thousand miles," was the answer. "They are long, hard miles too!"

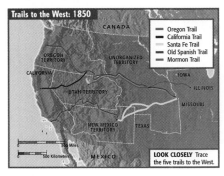

Trails to the West: 1850

— Oregon Trail
— California Trail
— Santa Fe Trail
— Old Spanish Trail
— Mormon Trail

CANADA
OREGON TERRITORY
CALIFORNIA
UNORGANIZED TERRITORY
UTAH TERRITORY
IOWA
ILLINOIS
MISSOURI
NEW MEXICO TERRITORY
TEXAS
MEXICO

500 Miles
500 Kilometers

LOOK CLOSELY Trace the five trails to the West.

All of the people were eager to start. Some of them were old; most of them were young. There were wives, mothers, children. All were going for gold.
20 More important than that, they were looking for a better life than they had known. California was to be their new home.

The trails were fairly well known by this time. For the most part, they followed the trails of early trappers and fur traders. One trail went southwest to Santa Fe (New Mexico). Here the trail made a fork. One fork led through the desert. The other went by way of South Pass in the
30 Rocky Mountains. Almost all took this trail.

> fork
> point at which one road divides into two

REREAD
Which colored trail from the map on page 372 did most people take?
A

THINK IT THROUGH
Besides money, what excites the Forty-Niners about California?
B

FOCUS
Find out how the Forty-Niners prepare for the journey.

C
A
The Forty-Niners made careful plans before starting. While waiting in the camps, parties and companies were formed. They agreed that it was safer to have ten to thirty wagons in a train. It would take about six yoke or pairs of oxen to each wagon. A captain would be the head of each party. His orders were to be obeyed by all. He was to guide them over the plains
40 and into California. In all ways he was to treat everyone fairly. It was his duty to keep all as well and happy as possible. Each man in the party was given certain duties. Young men would go ahead as scouts

> yoke
> bars connecting two working animals

B

COMPREHENSION

FOCUS SKILL 1: Main Idea

Tell students that a **main idea** is the most important idea in a section of text. Often the main idea is stated in a **topic sentence** that comes at the beginning or the end of a section of text.

 For direct instruction on Main Idea, see page T510.

FOCUS SKILL 2: Understanding Visuals

Tell students that **visuals** are the pictures, tables, graphs, and diagrams that are often found in nonfiction. Visuals help readers understand what they're reading by using both words and pictures to explain information, rather than by using just words.

 For direct instruction on Understanding Visuals, see page T510.

A **REREAD** Which colored trail from the map on page 372 did most people take? *(Based on both the text and the map, students will probably conclude that the Santa Fe Trail—yellow on the map—is the one*

most people took. As the map shows, this trail leads to New Mexico and has a fork that reconnects at the point where the Old Spanish Trail begins.)* **understanding visuals**

B **THINK IT THROUGH** Besides money, what excites the Forty-Niners about California? *(the promise of adventure and a better life than they had known)* **main idea**

C Ask: Which sentence states the main idea of lines 32–46? *(The Forty-Niners made careful plans before starting.)* **main idea**

LITERATURE

FOCUS: Informative Nonfiction

Review with students that **informative nonfiction** gives facts and details about real people, places, and events, and that this selection describes the hardships the Forty-Niners faced as they traveled west during the California Gold Rush.

VOCABULARY

FOCUS SKILL: Specialized Vocabulary

Remind students to use context clues, visuals, their prior knowledge, and any reference sources necessary to figure out the **specialized vocabulary** in this selection.

A **train** Tell students that to travel together, covered wagons lined up like the cars of a railroad train.

B **scouts** Students should use context to figure out that the job of scouts was to keep a wagon train progressing safely by riding ahead and watching for danger.

FOR ENGLISH LEARNERS

Help students understand the following expressions and idioms:

Line 2: in 'forty-nine and 'fifty
Line 24: For the most part
Line 29: went by way of
Line 33: parties and companies were formed
Line 37: the head of each party

The Inside of a Conestoga Wagon

- canvas roof with patch
- butter churn
- kerosene lamp
- spinning wheel
- chest of silverware

LOOK CLOSELY Notice how much is packed into the wagon. What items do you think didn't survive the trip?

to find the best trails. It would be their duty to look for good camping places each night. Each man was to take turns guarding day and night.

The camps were noisy with men trying to sell supplies and food. "Buy now—or have nothing!" they called. The Forty-Niners did not know what to 50 believe. So they bought—and bought. They took as much food as they could carry: barrels of flour, sacks of beans, rice, coffee, dried fruit. They had frying pans, buckets, axes, hammers, tools, guns. Some of the wagons were loaded with trunks and even furniture. They thought the West was wild. They must be prepared. So they took more than they should have taken.

> **barrels**
> (băr′ əls)
> *n.* large, round containers, usually made of wood

374 Unit 11 Bridges to History

Now it was May—and the grass showed green. It 60 was the time they had been waiting for so the cattle would have food. All made ready to start at once. Everyone was busy now—men, women, and children. There was cooking, baking, packing, hitching up of oxen and mules. Excitement was in the air! They were headed for the "land of gold." Different signs could be seen on the white canvas "prairie schooners":

> **hitching up**
> (hĭch′ ĭng ŭp)
> connecting animals to a wagon

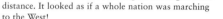

BOUND FOR CALIFORNIA
TO THE LAND OF GOLD
70 **CALIFORNIA OR BUST**
MEET ME AT SUTTER'S FORT

They were glad to go—but it was hard to leave, too. "Remember, there's an Indian behind every tree!" some warned. "Be careful out there! It's a wonderful land—but dangerous!" But no one wanted to turn back.

At last there was the creaking of the heavy white-topped wagons. Yoke chains clanked. Oxen bawled and moved slowly forward. Mules brayed. Men yelled and whips cracked. "All's set! Let's get going! Keep 80 the wagons moving!" was the captain's command. Drivers walked by their wagons. Men with guns rode beside the wagons to keep watch for Indians. Soon there was only a white line of wagons moving into the distance. It looked as if a whole nation was marching to the West!

THINK IT THROUGH
Excitement was in the air! Do the Forty-Niners seem to be thinking clearly? Explain.

from California Gold Days 375

COMPREHENSION

D Ask: What does the photo help you understand? *(what a covered wagon looked like and how much could fit inside it)* Which items do you think did not survive the trip? *(probably the chest of silverware, the armchair, anything "extra")* **understanding visuals**

E **Teacher Modeling: Questioning** Say: *Since this article focuses on the experiences of those who are looking to find new homes out West, I'd wondered when any mention of the people who already lived there would come up. It's fine to see the journey from the point of view of the Forty-Niners, but you have to remember that others may have felt the impact of the sudden changes. I asked myself if the Forty-Niners' fears about Native Americans would prove to be based on fact or on fear of the unknown. As I continue reading, I plan to look for other refer-ences to the Native Americans. How did they respond to all these newcomers?*

F **THINK IT THROUGH** Excitement was in the air! Do the Forty-Niners seem to be thinking clearly? Explain. *(Students should give examples from the text to explain how the Forty-Niners did and didn't act sensibly. Have them discuss modern situations in which people are as excited and caught up in the adventure as the Forty-Niners were.)* **making inferences**

VOCABULARY

C **prairie schooner** Explain that a *prairie* is a wide area of treeless, rolling land, and that a *schooner* is a small-sized sailboat. Tell students that the sight of wagon trains traveling across the prairie, with their canvas coverings flapping in the breeze, looked like schooners sailing on rolling waves.

FOR ENGLISH LEARNERS

Help students understand the following expressions and idioms:

Line 61: made ready to start at once
Line 75: turn back
Line 79: whips cracked

FOCUS
Read to find out what challenges the Forty-Niners face during their journeys.

The people seemed to enjoy the excitement of the journey at first. Meadows were covered with spring wild flowers. Grass was green and thick for the cattle. Rushing streams were beautiful but hard to cross with
90 heavy wagons. So they went slowly each day—about fifteen miles. Day after day, wagons rolled on to the West.

About sundown each day the captain blew a horn. The wagons were placed in a circle, tongues out. The animals were put outside to graze, with guards to watch them. The camp inside the circle was just like a fort. All felt safer that way. Then with fear forgotten, evenings were spent around the campfire
100 inside the circle. Sometimes they sang and made up their own words for songs they knew:

> tongues
> poles attached to the fronts of wagons

 A

"Oh Susanna!
O don't you cry for me!
I'm on my way to Californy
With my wash-bowl on my knee!"

OR

"California!
You're the land for me!
There's plenty of gold, so I've been told
110 In Cali—for—ny—ee!"

G

The Indians did not bother the first parties. Those who came in 1850 had more trouble with them. But the Forty-Niners had other things to worry them.

376 Unit 11 Bridges to History

Many of the travelers became ill; some died. The wagons were much too heavy for hard travel. Many things were thrown away along the overland trail to make the wagons lighter. Others who came later could pick up what was needed along the way—if there was room to carry it. Most of the wagons were too loaded
120 to carry anything more.

On and on across the plains went the wagons. Then they came to the buffalo country. The buffaloes had nibbled the grass short. Cattle of the overland train could not get enough to eat. They bellowed with hunger. Later trains found even less grass. Most of the grass had been eaten by the ox trains before them. Sometimes the buffalo herds came racing toward the wagons. Some of the buffaloes were killed for meat. The rest of the herd was scared away by
130 guns. If this did not work, a fire was built to drive them away. In this way, the wagon train was saved from harm.

> REREAD
> How does this scene contrast to the start of the trip?

H

Notice the weary expressions on the faces of these travelers. Days on the trail were rough.

from California Gold Days 377

COMPREHENSION

G **Teacher Modeling: Clarifying**
Say: *Okay, I've found the spot where Native Americans are mentioned again. This answers one of the questions I had earlier about how the Native Americans would react to the Forty-Niners' pouring into their territory. Not much is said about the Native Americans here. Apparently, meeting them along the way wasn't the dramatic experience that the earlier statements about the Native Americans implied. At least, not for the time period the article covers.*

H **REREAD** How does this scene contrast to the start of the trip? *(At the start people were excited and happy, wagons were filled to overflowing, the cattle were healthy; now people are ill and tired and have thrown out items to make the wagons lighter, cattle are starving, and buffalo charge the wagons.)* **compare and contrast**

LITERATURE

A Inform students that Stephen Foster's folk song "Oh! Susannah" was a very popular tune of its time (1848). If students are unfamiliar with this song, you may want to obtain the song lyrics or play a recording. **historical detail**

VOCABULARY

FOR ENGLISH LEARNERS

Help students understand the following:

Line 122: buffalo country
Line 124: bellowed with hunger
Line 129: scared away
Line 132: saved from harm

The longer the journey, the harder it became. There was always the fear that they would be caught in the mountains by snow. Everyone was tired, but they had to keep going. Food ran low. One had to share with another. Sometimes they could find no water. All suffered as they crossed the desert. In the mountains, the passes were almost too
140 narrow to get through. It was very hard to climb these steep mountains with wagons.

Sometimes it was even worse to go down the other side. Often heavy ropes were tied around the trees and the wagons let down by the ropes. The trip seemed never to end. But when the mountains were crossed, the worst was over.

passes
(păs′ əs)
n. ways around, over, or through mountains

REREAD
Picture this challenge in your mind. What does this show about the Forty-Niners?

I

One party made a trip that made California history.
This company was led by young William Manly.
150 When he first heard of gold, he decided to seek his fortune. On the way to California his party met a man who had a new map. It showed a shorter way to go. This they followed. In time they came to a lonely valley. The low desert valley had high mountain walls around it. There was not a blade of grass there. Not a drop of water was seen. All were hungry and thirsty—people and beast. The party went slower and slower. Food was almost gone, so they ate the oxen. What could they do next? Manly and another young man
160 agreed to go for help. Sixteen were left behind by a little spring they had found. At last Manly came to Mission San Fernando in southern California. From there the two young men started back with food. They were surprised to find any of the party still alive. Sometime after their return they started on. As they looked back at the camping place, they said,

J

D

K "Goodbye, Death Valley!" And the place has had that name to this day. By the time they came to Mission San Fernando, they had been a whole year on the
170 way. The gold fields were still six hundred miles away!

When the overland gold seekers finally came to the diggings, they were tired, ragged, and hungry. Hundreds had died on the way. But those who came by land were better able to stand the life at the mines. They were used to rough, outdoor life. Nothing could have been harder than the long overland trip they had taken.

L **THINK IT THROUGH**

1. Why do you think the Forty-Niners were able to survive in Death Valley?
2. Think of the mood of the Forty-Niners before they made their trip. Think of their mood at the end. What caused the change? Use details from the article to support your answer.
3. How might the Forty-Niners have prepared themselves better for the trip? Give reasons for your answer.

COMPREHENSION

I **REREAD** Picture this challenge in your mind. What does this show about the Forty-Niners? *(They were tough problem solvers who were willing to face hardships they probably hadn't imagined at the start of their journey.)* **making judgments**

J Ask: Which sentence states the main idea of lines 148–171? *(One party made a trip that made California history.)* **main idea**

K Ask: How did William Manly's party make history? *(They named Death Valley in California.)* **main idea and supporting details**

L **THINK IT THROUGH**

1. Why do you think the Forty-Niners were able to survive in Death Valley? *(They had already learned some survival skills along the way. They knew to use their oxen for food and to send out scouts. Staying near the spring probably*

kept the party supplied with water.) **making inferences**

2. Think of the mood of the Forty-Niners before they made their trip. Think of their mood at the end. What caused the change? Use details from the article to support your answer. *(Students should use details that illustrate the fact that before the trip the Forty-Niners were excited, encouraged, and happy. But by the end they were tired, ragged, and hungry. The change was caused by all of the hardships that the travelers had to endure.)* **compare and contrast**

3. How might the Forty-Niners have prepared themselves better for the trip? Give reasons for your answer. *(Knowing what to expect would have helped the Forty-Niners plan better. They should have talked to others who had made the trip to find out which supplies to take and which routes to travel.)* **drawing conclusions**

Help students complete the **K-W-L chart** that they began before reading.

RETEACHING

If students need more help understanding **Main Idea,** use pages T635–T638.

VOCABULARY

D **spring** Students can use context clues and prior knowledge to figure out the specialized meaning of this word.

FOR ENGLISH LEARNERS

Help students understand the following:

Line 136: Food ran low
Line 147: the worst was over
Line 148: a trip that made California history
Line 168: to this day

1. COMPREHENSION

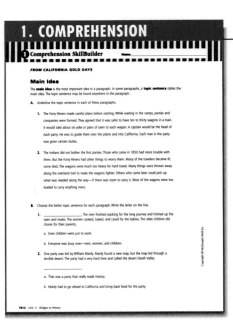

Main Idea

Direct Instruction Tell students that the **main idea** is the most important idea in a paragraph and that a sentence that states the main idea is called the **topic sentence.** Other sentences in the paragraph tell more about the main idea. Point out that not every paragraph has a topic sentence. Explain that although the topic sentence is often the first sentence, it may appear anywhere in the paragraph.

Read the following paragraph aloud. Have students find the topic sentence and identify details that support the main idea.

<u>The longer the journey, the harder it became</u>. There was always the fear that they would be caught in the mountains by snow. Everyone was tired, but they had to keep going. Food ran low. Sometimes they could find no water. All suffered as they crossed the desert. In the mountains, the passes were almost too narrow to get through. It was very hard to climb these steep mountains with wagons. Sometimes it was even worse to go down the other side.

> **Comprehension SkillBuilder Answer Key:**
> **A. 1.** *The Forty-Niners made careful plans before starting.*
>   **2.** *But the Forty-Niners had other things to worry them.*
>
> **B. 1.** *b*   **2.** *a*

2. COMPREHENSION

Understanding Visuals

Direct Instruction Tell students many nonfiction articles, and even some stories, are accompanied by illustrations, drawings, maps, and other graphics that present information in a visual way. Explain that these pictures are sometimes called **visuals.** Visuals help readers understand information in the text.

Point out the visuals that accompany this excerpt from "California Gold Days." Ask students to describe what they learn from each visual. Have them find the paragraphs or sentences in which information that is shown in the visual is mentioned.

Comprehension SkillBuilder Answer Key:

	Oregon Trail	California Trail	Santa Fe Trail	Mormon Trail	Old Spanish Trail
Goes to Salt Lake City				✔	
Goes to Vancouver					
Ends in Sacramento		✔			
Ends in Los Angeles					✔
Goes farthest north	✔				
Goes farthest south					✔

Direct Instruction
for SkillBuilder Copymasters

3. VOCABULARY

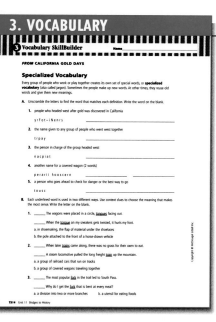

Specialized Vocabulary

Direct Instruction Tell students that to communicate, groups of people who are doing the same job or participating in the same game or hobby often make up new words to talk about what they are interested in. They may also reuse a familiar word, changing its meaning slightly. These words with meanings that relate to a particular field are called **specialized vocabulary.**

Examples of words created for a particular field are terms such as *gainer, pike,* and *swan dive,* all terms used in the sport of diving. Examples of words that were reused and given new, specialized meanings are these words used by the Forty-Niners in their journey west: *tongue, captain,* and *scout.*

Vocabulary SkillBuilder Answer Key:

A. 1. *Forty-Niners*
   2. *party*
   3. *captain*
   4. *prairie schooner*
   5. *scout*

B. 1. *b, a*
   2. *b, a*
   3. *a, b*

---

4. WORDS TO KNOW

Words to Know

Direct Instruction As you present the **Words to Know,** here are some points you might want to cover.
- **plain,** from Latin *plānus*
  Plain has multiple meanings, as students will practice in Exercise C. It also has a homophone, **plane.**
- **barrel,** from Old French *baril*
  Barrel has multiple meanings, as students will practice in Exercise C.

- **pass,** from Latin *passus,* "step"
  Pass has multiple meanings, as students will practice in Exercise C. Review analogies with students, and help them think their way through the reasoning.

Writing Activity Encourage students to be creative. Have volunteers read their creations aloud.

Words to Know SkillBuilder Answer Key:

A.
  1. *passes*
  2. *barrels*
  3. *plains*

B.
  1. *plains*
  2. *passes*
  3. *barrels*

C.
*Plain can be defined as an adjective and a noun. **Barrel** can be defined as a noun and a verb. **Pass** can be defined as a noun and a verb. Pair or group students together to find these definitions in a dictionary.*

---

5. SELECTION TEST

Selection Test Answer Key:
A. 1. *c* **2.** *a* **3.** *c* **4.** *b*
B. *The Forty-Niners began the trip to the West feeling hopeful and strong. They ended up almost worn out, but they were tougher.*

FROM **CALIFORNIA GOLD DAYS**

Main Idea

The **main idea** is the most important idea in a paragraph. In some paragraphs, a **topic sentence** states the main idea. The topic sentence may be found anywhere in the paragraph.

A. Underline the topic sentence in each of these paragraphs.

1. The Forty-Niners made careful plans before starting. While waiting in the camps, parties and companies were formed. They agreed that it was safer to have ten to thirty wagons in a train. It would take about six yoke or pairs of oxen to each wagon. A captain would be the head of each party. He was to guide them over the plains and into California. Each man in the party was given certain duties.

2. The Indians did not bother the first parties. Those who came in 1850 had more trouble with them. But the Forty-Niners had other things to worry them. Many of the travelers became ill; some died. The wagons were much too heavy for hard travel. Many things were thrown away along the overland trail to make the wagons lighter. Others who came later could pick up what was needed along the way—if there was room to carry it. Most of the wagons were too loaded to carry anything more.

B. Choose the better topic sentence for each paragraph. Write the letter on the line.

1. _____. The men finished packing for the long journey and hitched up the oxen and mules. The women cooked, baked, and cared for the babies. The older children did chores for their parents.

   a. Even children were put to work.

   b. Everyone was busy now—men, women, and children.

2. One party was led by William Manly. Manly found a new map, but the map led through a terrible desert. The party had a very hard time and called the desert Death Valley.

   _____.

   a. That was a party that really made history.

   b. Manly had to go ahead to California and bring back food for the party.

FROM **CALIFORNIA GOLD DAYS**

Understanding Visuals

Visuals are drawings, pictures, charts, and maps that help readers understand the text.

Use the map from "California Gold Days" to fill in the chart below.

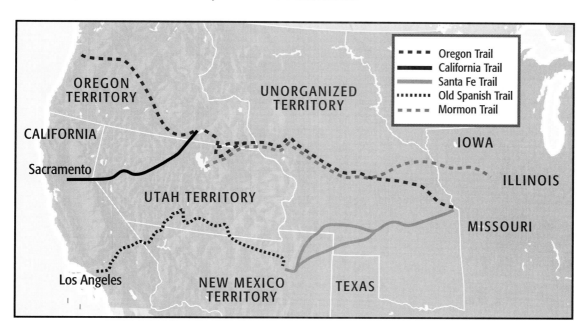

Read each description of the trails on the left. If the description matches the trail, put a check under the trail's name.

	Oregon Trail	California Trail	Santa Fe Trail	Mormon Trail	Old Spanish Trail
Goes to Salt Lake City					
Goes to Vancouver					
Ends in Sacramento					
Ends in Los Angeles					
Goes farthest north					
Goes farthest south					

FROM CALIFORNIA GOLD DAYS

Specialized Vocabulary

Every group of people who work or play together creates its own set of special words, or **specialized vocabulary** (also called jargon). Sometimes the people make up new words. At other times, they reuse old words and give them new meanings.

A. Unscramble the letters to find the word that matches each definition. Write the word on the blank.

1. people who headed west after gold was discovered in California

   y r F o t – i N e n r s   _____

2. the name given to any group of people who went west together

   t r p a y   _____

3. the person in charge of the group headed west

   n a c p i a t   _____

4. another name for a covered wagon (2 words)

   p e r a r i i   h o o s c e r n   _____   _____

5. a person who goes ahead to check for danger or the best way to go

   t o u s c   _____

B. Each underlined word is used in two different ways. Use context clues to choose the meaning that makes the most sense. Write the letter on the blank.

1. _____ The wagons were placed in a circle, <u>tongues</u> facing out.

   _____ When the <u>tongue</u> on my sneakers gets twisted, it hurts my foot.

   a. in shoemaking, the flap of material under the shoelaces

   b. the pole attached to the front of a horse-drawn vehicle

2. _____ When later <u>trains</u> came along, there was no grass for their oxen to eat.

   _____ A steam locomotive pulled the long freight <u>train</u> up the mountain.

   a. a group of railroad cars that run on tracks

   b. a group of covered wagons traveling together

3. _____ The most popular <u>fork</u> in the trail led to South Pass.

   _____ Why do I get the <u>fork</u> that is bent at every meal?

   a. a division into two or more branches   b. a utensil for eating foods

FROM CALIFORNIA GOLD DAYS

Words to Know

plains   barrels   passes

A. Fill in each blank with the word from the list that best completes the sentence.

1. Our family drove through the _____ of the Great Smoky Mountains.

2. The circus uses _____ to hold food for the elephants.

3. You can find _____ in states that have much farmland.

B. Complete the following analogies with the words from the list. Remember to say "Water is to lakes as grass is to *blank*."

1. WATER : LAKES :: grass : _____

2. _____: mountains :: PATHS : PARKS

3. boxes: _____ :: FORKS : SPOONS

C. Using the Dictionary: Multiple Meanings

All three of the **Words to Know** are plural nouns. But if we drop the final **s,** they all have other meanings. Using your dictionary, fill in two definitions for each word.

plain:

barrel:

pass:

Writing Activity
Write a short paragraph telling whether you would have enjoyed traveling by wagon train to California. Use at least one of the **Words to Know.**

FROM CALIFORNIA GOLD DAYS

A. For each item, fill in the circle next to the letter of the correct answer.

1. Why were the Forty-Niners so eager to get to California?
- ○ a. They were hoping to find gold and become rich.
- ○ b. They were looking for a better life than they had known.
- ○ c. Both of the above answers are correct.

2. In what month did the Forty-Niners leave Missouri, and why?
- ○ a. May—so the cattle would have lots of green grass to eat
- ○ b. July—so they could celebrate New Year's Eve out West
- ○ c. January—so they could enjoy their summer in California

3. What were conditions like when the Forty-Niners reached the buffalo country?
- ○ a. It was scorching hot, and there were no buffalo in sight.
- ○ b. There were beautiful flowers and green grass everywhere.
- ○ c. There was hardly any grass, and the buffalo were fierce.

4. How did William Manly's party make California history?
- ○ a. They named California's football team.
- ○ b. They named California's Death Valley.
- ○ c. They named the California Gold Rush.

B. Answer the question below.

Many Forty-Niners were tired, ragged, and hungry when they finally reached California. How did the Forty-Niners change from the beginning to the end of their journey?

_____

_____

_____

Reader directions:

Cut this paper in half. Practice reading this passage aloud until you don't make any mistakes.
Then have someone listen to you read. Try to sound very positive and hopeful.

from "California Gold Days"

All of the people were eager to start. Some of them were old; most of them were young.
There were wives, mothers, children. All were going for gold. More important than that,
they were looking for a better life than they had known. California was to be their new
home.

The trails were fairly well known by this time. For the most part, they followed the trails
of early trappers and fur traders. One trail went southwest to Santa Fe (New Mexico). Here
the trail made a fork. One fork led through the desert. The other went by way of South
Pass in the Rocky Mountains. Almost all took this trail.

✂ **cut along dotted line**

- -

Checker directions:

Follow along as the passage is read. Make a dot under each word the reader misses.
Show the reader the missed words. Erase the dots and repeat for each reading.

from "California Gold Days"

All of the people were eager to start. Some of them were old; most of them were young.
There were wives, mothers, children. All were going for gold. More important than that,
they were looking for a better life than they had known. California was to be their new
home.

The trails were fairly well known by this time. For the most part, they followed the trails
of early trappers and fur traders. One trail went southwest to Santa Fe (New Mexico). Here
the trail made a fork. One fork led through the desert. The other went by way of South
Pass in the Rocky Mountains. Almost all took this trail.

Use this chart for Timed Readings and Repeated Readings.

Reading	1	2	3	4	5
Time (minutes/seconds)					
Words Missed					

Focus Skills

COMPREHENSION
Making Inferences

LITERATURE
Theme

VOCABULARY
Syllabication

SkillBuilder Copymasters

 Reading Comprehension:
1 Making Inferences p. T524

 Literary Analysis:
2 Theme p. T525

 Vocabulary:
3 Syllabication p. T526
4 Words to Know p. T527

Assessment

 5 Selection Test p. T528

Readability Scores

DRP	LEXILE	DALE-CHALL
54	830	4.2

For English Learners

The author of this story uses a style and a format that are slightly different from the way people talk and write today. If you think this will pose problems for students, you may want to have them follow along silently while you read the story aloud. Pause when necessary to check students' understanding or to explain the author's meaning.

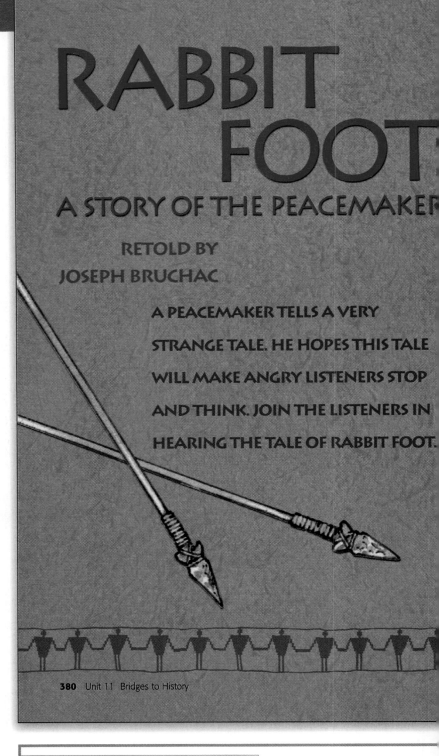

RABBIT FOOT

A STORY OF THE PEACEMAKER

RETOLD BY
JOSEPH BRUCHAC

A PEACEMAKER TELLS A VERY
STRANGE TALE. HE HOPES THIS TALE
WILL MAKE ANGRY LISTENERS STOP
AND THINK. JOIN THE LISTENERS IN
HEARING THE TALE OF RABBIT FOOT.

380   Unit 11 Bridges to History

Vocabulary Strategy: Preteaching

Syllabication Remind students that **syllables** are word parts with one vowel sound each. One way to understand an unfamiliar word is to separate it into syllables. Sound out each syllable, and then put the syllables together to read the entire word.

The following rules are helpful when separating words into syllables.

1. Prefixes such as *un-* and *re-* are separate syllables.
2. Suffixes such as *-ly* and *-ful* are separate syllables.
3. In words with double consonants, separate the syllables between the consonants, as in *saddle* (sad•dle) and *fallen* (fal•len).

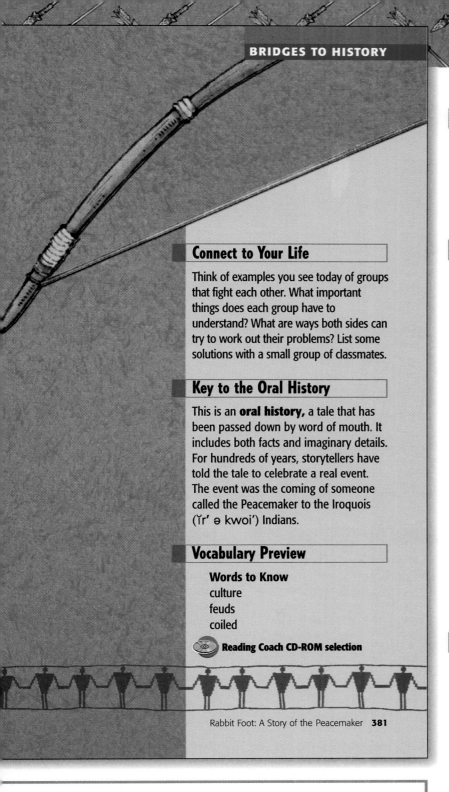

Connect to Your Life

Think of examples you see today of groups that fight each other. What important things does each group have to understand? What are ways both sides can try to work out their problems? List some solutions with a small group of classmates.

Key to the Oral History

This is an **oral history,** a tale that has been passed down by word of mouth. It includes both facts and imaginary details. For hundreds of years, storytellers have told the tale to celebrate a real event. The event was the coming of someone called the Peacemaker to the Iroquois (ĭr′ ə kwoi′) Indians.

Vocabulary Preview

Words to Know
culture
feuds
coiled

 Reading Coach CD-ROM selection

Rabbit Foot: A Story of the Peacemaker **381**

Connect to Your Life

When all of the groups have finished their lists of solutions, have them share their ideas to see how they are alike and different. Are there any groups or solutions that showed up on every list?

Key to the Oral History

Point out to students that there is no written account of what was actually said during the coming of the Peacemaker. Most Native Americans passed down their history orally. This oral history may have begun with someone who witnessed the event and then told others. The shared details of the event spread throughout the group and have since spanned many generations. To help students understand the background for this oral history, you may wish to read aloud the opening paragraph on page 382. It is actually a headnote that provides background information about the Iroquois tribes. It explains the nature of their conflict and the steps taken to make peace. In describing the formation of the Five Nations of the Iroquois, the headnote actually reveals what happened as the result of the Peacemaker's efforts.

Vocabulary Preview

Words to Know
  culture *n.* the ideas, customs, and skills shared by a certain people
  feuds *n.* bitter fights
  coiled *adj.* wound into a series of rings

For direct instruction on Words to Know, see page T523.

4. One sure way to separate words into syllables correctly is to look them up in the dictionary.

Write the following words on the board. Have volunteers draw a slash between each syllable. If necessary, review an appropriate rule and have students consult dictionary entries to correct errors.

re/run   **loud/ly**   **tear/ful/ly**   **strug/gled**

 For more on Syllabication, see page T523.

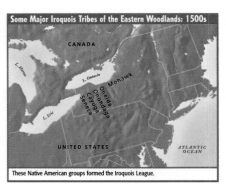

Several Iroquois tribes once lived in the northern section of New York. They made the worst kind of war—against each other. They attacked neighbors' villages. They stole food **(A)** and took prisoners. In the 1500s, a man named Deganawida (the Peacemaker) met with the tribes. He wanted to convince them to make peace. With the help of a young **(A)** chief named Hiawatha, the tribes listened. They joined together, forming the Iroquois League. They created a body of laws called the Great Law of Peace. A long period of peace followed.

FOCUS

Find out why the Peacemaker has come to the Iroquois people.

Many hundreds of years ago
before the Europeans came
the Five Nations of the Iroquois,
Mohawk and Oneida, Onondaga, Cayuga and Seneca,
were always at war with one another.

Although they had a common [culture]
and languages that were much the same
no longer did they remember
they had been taught to live
(B) 10 as sisters and brothers.

> **culture**
> (kŭl' chər)
> *n.* the ideas, customs, and skills shared by a certain people

Once they had shared the beautiful land
from Niagara to the eastern mountains,
(A) but now only revenge was in their hearts
and blood [feuds] had made every trail
a path leading to war.

> **feuds**
> (fyo͞odz)
> *n.* bitter fights

Some Major Iroquois Tribes of the Eastern Woodlands: 1500s

CANADA

L. Huron
L. Ontario
Mohawk
Oneida
Onondaga
Cayuga
Seneca
L. Erie
UNITED STATES
ATLANTIC OCEAN

These Native American groups formed the Iroquois League.

So it was that the Great Creator
(B) sent once again a messenger,
a man who became known
to all of the Five Nations
20 by the name of the Peacemaker.

THINK IT THROUGH
(B) How had life among the tribes changed?

COMPREHENSION

FOCUS SKILL: Making Inferences

Remind students that **inferences** are logical conclusions that they can draw based on information in the text and their own experiences.

> For direct instruction on Making Inferences, see page T522.

(A) Ask: Why do you think the tribes are fighting? *(Possible answers: Each tribe wants power and control over the others; rather than wanting to share the land they lived on, each tribe may have wanted to own all the land and its resources.)* **making inferences**

(B) **THINK IT THROUGH** How had life among the tribes changed? *(Instead of living in peace as they had in the past, the tribes are all at war with one another.)* **compare and contrast**

LITERATURE

FOCUS SKILL: Theme

Remind students that a **theme** is a message about life or human nature that an author is trying to convey. Sometimes a theme is stated outright. At other times, however, readers must infer the theme based on what the characters do and say.

> For direct instruction on Theme, see page T522.

Use the following questions to encourage literary analysis.

(A) What is the setting of this story? *(the northern section of what is now New York; the 1500s, before Europeans arrived in America)* **setting**

(B) From what point of view is this story being told? How do you know? *(Third person; the narrator is a character outside the story and uses the pronouns* they *and* their.*)* **point of view**

VOCABULARY

FOCUS SKILL: Syllabication

Remind students that breaking a word into parts, or **syllables,** can often help them figure out its pronunciation and meaning.

(A) **revenge** Have students break this word into syllables for understanding. *(re•venge)*

(B) **messenger** Have students syllabicate *messenger. (mes•sen•ger)*

FOR ENGLISH LEARNERS

Help students understand the following expressions and idioms:

Line 2: before the Europeans came
Line 7: much the same
Line 10: as sisters and brothers

The Peacemaker tells a tale. Read to find out what a boy called Rabbit Foot sees.

To help the people once again
make their minds straight
he told them stories
about peace and war.
This is one of his tales.

Once there was a boy named Rabbit Foot.
He was always looking and listening.
He knew how to talk to the animals
so the animals would talk to him.

30 One day as he walked out in the woods
he heard the sound of a great struggle
coming from a clearing just over the hill.
So he climbed that hilltop to look down.

What he saw surprised him.
There was a great snake
coiled in a circle.
It had caught a huge frog
and although the frog struggled
C the snake was slowly swallowing its legs.

coiled
(koild)
adj. wound into a
series of rings

40 Rabbit Foot came closer
and spoke to the frog.
"He has really got you, my friend."
The frog looked up at Rabbit Foot.
"Wa'he! That is so," the frog said.

Rabbit Foot nodded, then said to the frog,
"Do you see the snake's tail there,
just in front of your mouth?
Why not do to him what he's doing to you?"

Then the huge frog reached out
50 and grabbed the snake's tail.
He began to stuff it into his mouth
C as Rabbit Foot watched both of them.

The snake swallowed more of the frog
the frog swallowed more of the snake
and the circle got smaller and smaller
until both of them swallowed one last
time
and just like that, they both were gone.

REREAD
Why do you
think the snake
and frog go so
far?

D

They had eaten each other,
the Peacemaker said.
60 And in much the same way,
unless you give up war
and learn to live together in peace,
C that also will happen to you.

E **THINK IT THROUGH**

1. The Peacemaker delivers his message in the form of a tale. Why might this choice have had a stronger effect on the listeners?
2. How could the Iroquois tribes' shared culture and language help them learn to live together?
3. This tale was first told many years ago. Do you think it could be used to help other fighting groups today? Explain.

COMPREHENSION

C Ask: How are Rabbit Foot and the Peacemaker alike and different? *(They are alike in that they both give advice to someone or something that is fighting. They are different in that only the Peacemaker tries to bring about peace.)* **compare and contrast**

D **REREAD** Why do you think the snake and frog go so far? *(They are so caught up in destroying each other that they don't realize they are ultimately destroying themselves.)* **making inferences**

E **THINK IT THROUGH**

1. The Peacemaker delivers his message in the form of a tale. Why might this choice have had a stronger effect on the listeners? *(By shifting the focus from the tribes and using animals to tell the story, the Peacemaker addressed the problem without causing anyone to get defensive or stop listening. Instead he gave them a chance to see themselves in the tale and make their*

own inferences about what would happen if they didn't stop destroying each other.) **making inferences**

2. How could the Iroquois tribes' shared culture and language help them learn to live together? *(They already understood each other's customs, and their similar language would allow them to discuss problems and make laws.)* **making inferences**

3. This tale was first told many years ago. Do you think it could be used to help other fighting groups today? Explain. *(Most students will say yes, because there are still wars going on today, and the same message still applies.)* **making inferences**

RETEACHING

If students need more help understanding **Making Inferences,** use pages T650–T652.

LITERATURE

C What message was the Peacemaker trying to send? *(Possible answers: Whatever you do to someone else will also be done to you; you can't hurt another without also hurting yourself; if you don't learn to live in peace, you will destroy one another.)* **theme**

VOCABULARY

C **swallowing** Have students break this word into syllables. *(swal•low•ing)*

FOR ENGLISH LEARNERS

Help students understand the following expressions and idioms:

Line 22: make their minds straight
Line 32: coming from a clearing
Line 51: stuff it into his mouth
Line 57: just like that
Line 61: give up war

1. COMPREHENSION

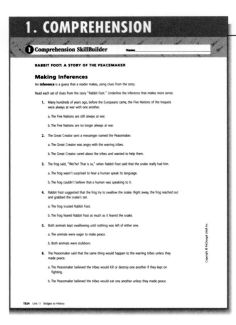

Making Inferences

Direct Instruction Explain to students that an **inference** is a logical guess a reader makes using clues in the text. Tell students that as readers, they can use small details about characters—such as their expressions, words, and tone of voice—to make inferences about how they think and feel.

Have students figure out what inference can be made using the clues in the following examples.

- Clue #1: All of the tribe's weapons are old and rusty.
  Inference #1: The weapons have not been used recently because the tribe has not gone to war.
- Clue #2: People have been telling this story over and over again for years.
  Inference #2: Many people like this story and feel it has value for future generations.

> **Comprehension SkillBuilder Answer Key:**
> **1.** *b* **2.** *b* **3.** *a* **4.** *a* **5.** *b* **6.** *a*

2. LITERATURE

Theme

Direct Instruction Tell students that the **theme** of a story is the lesson it teaches about life and human nature. Explain that usually the theme is not stated; readers must figure out the theme by paying attention to clues such as characters' words and thoughts, along with story events and outcomes. To give students an example of a theme, discuss the lesson that the familiar fairy tale "Snow White" teaches: "Goodness and kindness win over evil," or "Don't let your own physical beauty become too important in your life. There is always someone who is better looking than you."

Point out that in "Rabbit Foot," the theme is stated clearly and is found at the end of the story, after the frog and the snake eat each other up:

> And in much the same way,
> unless you give up war
> and learn to live together in peace,
> that also will happen to you.

> **Literary SkillBuilder Answer Key:**
> *Answers will vary. Possible answers: People who keep fighting will someday be destroyed or When people fight, no one wins. Everyone loses.*

Direct Instruction
for SkillBuilder Copymasters

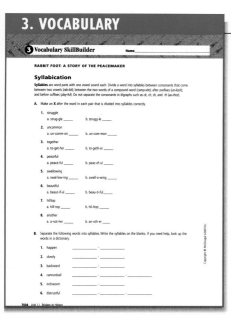

3. VOCABULARY

Syllabication

Direct Instruction Remind students that when they come to a long word while reading, breaking the word into syllables is one strategy for pronouncing and understanding the word. Tell them that a **syllable** is a word part with only one vowel sound. *Hill* has one syllable. *Hilltop* has two syllables. Give students the following rules for dividing words into syllables. Explain that while these rules usually work, they do not hold true 100% of the time. Tell students that to be sure a word has been divided correctly, they should look it up in a dictionary.

- Divide words between two consonants that come between two vowels. Example: *pic-nic.*
- Divide each compound word between the two words that make it up. Example: *birth-day.*
- Prefixes such as *dis-, re-,* and *un-* are separate syllables. Example: *dis-like.*
- Suffixes such as *-ly* and *-ful* are separate syllables. Example: *kind-ly.*
- Do not separate the two consonants in digraphs. Review the meaning of the term *digraph.* Say: *A digraph is made up of two letters that represent one sound.* Examples of digraphs are *ch, ck, ph, sh,* and *th.* Example: *ei-ther.*

Vocabulary SkillBuilder Answer Key:

A. **1.** *a* **2.** *b* **3.** *b* **4.** *a* **5.** *a* **6.** *b*
 7. *a* **8.** *b*

B. **1.** *hap-pen* **2.** *slow-ly*
 3. *back-ward* **4.** *can-non-ball*
 5. *inch-worm* **6.** *dis-trust-ful*

---

4. WORDS TO KNOW

Words to Know

Direct Instruction As you present the **Words to Know,** here are some points you might want to cover. Help students to identify the parts of the vocabulary words. Stress the importance of finding the base of each word. Help students remove prefixes and suffixes first.

- **coil** + -ed = *coiled,* from the Latin *colligere*
 Coil is a verb as well as a noun.
- **culture** is from the Latin *colere.* *Culture* can also be defined as "the growing of microorganisms, tissue cells, or other living matter in a specially prepared nutrient medium."
- **feud** + -s = *feuds*
- Instruct students to provide evidence for their conclusions in the *True* and *False* section (B), particularly if they believe a statement to be false.

Writing Activity Pair students or have them work in small groups to complete the exercise. Have volunteers read their creations aloud.

Words to Know SkillBuilder Answer Key:

A.
 1. *feuds* **2.** *coiled* **3.** *culture* **4.** *coiled* **5.** *feuds* **6.** *culture*

B.
 1. *false* **2.** *true* **3.** *false*

---

5. SELECTION TEST

Selection Test Answer Key:

A. **1.** *Nations* **2.** *Great* **3.** *Peacemaker* **4.** *understood*
B. *He compared their disappearance to what could happen to the fighting tribes.*

RABBIT FOOT: A STORY OF THE PEACEMAKER

Making Inferences

An **inference** is a guess that a reader makes, using clues from the story.

Read each set of clues from the story "Rabbit Foot." Underline the inference that makes more sense.

1. Many hundreds of years ago, before the Europeans came, the Five Nations of the Iroquois were always at war with one another.

   a. The Five Nations are still always at war.

   b. The Five Nations are no longer always at war.

2. The Great Creator sent a messenger named the Peacemaker.

   a. The Great Creator was angry with the warring tribes.

   b. The Great Creator cared about the tribes and wanted to help them.

3. The frog said, "Wa'he! That is so," when Rabbit Foot said that the snake really had him.

   a. The frog wasn't surprised to hear a human speak its language.

   b. The frog couldn't believe that a human was speaking to it.

4. Rabbit Foot suggested that the frog try to swallow the snake. Right away, the frog reached out and grabbed the snake's tail.

   a. The frog trusted Rabbit Foot.

   b. The frog feared Rabbit Foot as much as it feared the snake.

5. Both animals kept swallowing until nothing was left of either one.

   a. The animals were eager to make peace.

   b. Both animals were stubborn.

6. The Peacemaker said that the same thing would happen to the warring tribes unless they made peace.

   a. The Peacemaker believed the tribes would kill or destroy one another if they kept on fighting.

   b. The Peacemaker believed the tribes would eat one another unless they made peace.

Name_____

RABBIT FOOT: A STORY OF THE PEACEMAKER

Theme

The **theme** of a story is the lesson it teaches about life, human nature, and how we should treat one another.

Read the events from "Rabbit Foot" in the outer circle below. Think about them and then write a possible theme for the story in the inner circle.

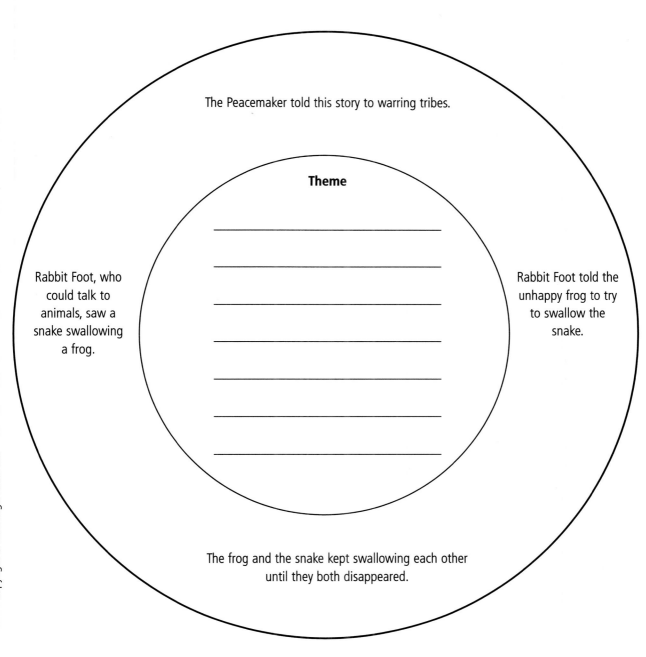

The Peacemaker told this story to warring tribes.

Theme

_____

_____

_____

_____

_____

_____

Rabbit Foot, who could talk to animals, saw a snake swallowing a frog.

Rabbit Foot told the unhappy frog to try to swallow the snake.

The frog and the snake kept swallowing each other until they both disappeared.

RABBIT FOOT: A STORY OF THE PEACEMAKER

Syllabication

Syllables are word parts with one vowel sound each. Divide a word into syllables between consonants that come between two vowels (*rab-bit*); between the two words of a compound word (*camp-site*); after prefixes (*un-lock*); and before suffixes (*play-ful*). Do not separate the consonants in digraphs such as *ck, ch, sh,* and *th* (*au-thor*).

A. Make an **X** after the word in each pair that is divided into syllables correctly.

1. struggle

   a. strug-gle _____   b. strugg-le _____

2. uncommon

   a. un-comm-on _____   b. un-com-mon _____

3. together

   a. to-get-her _____   b. to-geth-er _____

4. peaceful

   a. peace-ful _____   b. peac-ef-ul _____

5. swallowing

   a. swal-low-ing _____   b. swall-o-wing _____

6. beautiful

   a. beaut-if-ul _____   b. beau-ti-ful_____

7. hilltop

   a. hill-top _____   b. hil-ltop _____

8. another

   a. a-not-her _____   b. an-oth-er ____

B. Separate the following words into syllables. Write the syllables on the blanks. If you need help, look up the words in a dictionary.

1. happen   _____ - _____

2. slowly   _____ - _____

3. backward   _____ - _____

4. cannonball   _____ - _____ - _____

5. inchworm   _____ - _____

6. distrustful   _____ - _____ - _____

RABBIT FOOT: A STORY OF THE PEACEMAKER

Words to Know

culture   feuds   coiled

A. Fill in each blank with the word from the list that best completes the sentence.

1. There are _____ that have existed between countries for hundreds of years.

2. I found the hose _____ up on the edge of the driveway.

3. Take pride in your _____; it's part of your identity.

4. I use my curling iron if I want my hair to be _____.

5. My mother was upset about the longtime _____ that went on in our family.

6. My parents and I travel a lot, so I get to experience much _____ from around the world.

B. Write **true** or **false** in each blank.

_____ **1.** A person's **culture** is his or her education.

_____ **2. Feuds** are bitter fights.

_____ **3.** Examples of things that are **coiled** are steps, walls, and roofs.

Writing Activity
Imagine you are a peacemaker. Write down a list of five ways in which you could keep peace between groups of people. Use at least one of the **Words to Know.**

RABBIT FOOT: A STORY OF THE PEACEMAKER

A. Complete the paragraph by filling in each blank with the correct word from the list.

peace   understood   Nations
Great   Peacemaker

Many hundreds of years ago, the Five **(1)** _____ of the Iroquois

were always at war with one another. So the **(2)** _____ Creator sent

a messenger to help the people. The **(3)** _____ told the people a

story about a snake and a frog that swallowed each other up. When he finished the story, the people

(4) _____.

B. To what did the Peacemaker compare what happened to the snake and frog?

_____

_____

_____

Teacher's Notes

Focus Skills and SkillBuilder Copymasters

Reader's Choice

Longer Selections for Independent Reading

Unit 12

Mixed Genres

When does reading become an adventure? It can happen when you suddenly get "lost" in a strange setting. It can happen when you meet an unusual character. And it certainly happens when you find yourself at the center of an amazing event.

When you read a longer selection, your adventure can last longer, too. You get to spend more time with that interesting person. You are able to enjoy the details of the exciting event. So get ready to explore the longer pieces in this unit, and let the adventure begin!

386

Reading Fluency

 ★ Reading Fluency p. T549

Pacing Guide

SELECTION	TOTAL DAYS	PREREADING	READING	POST READING	
				SELECTIVE OPTIONS	ALL OPTIONS
from Hiroshima	5–5.5	1	3	1	1.5
from Anne Frank: Child of the Holocaust	4.5–5	1	2.5	1	1.5
Black Whiteness	5–5.5	1	3	1	1.5

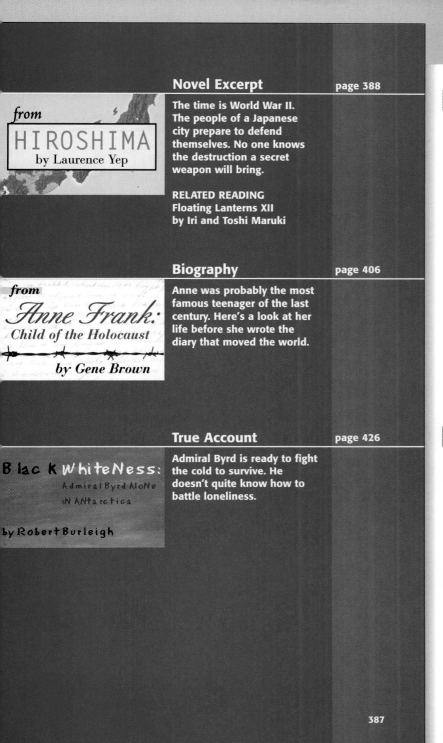

387

In this unit, the longer fiction pieces give students an opportunity to use the skills they have learned and to build their confidence as independent readers. You can assign these selections at any time to students who are ready to handle more independent reading. Or you can allow them to choose one to read independently. However, you can also choose to teach a selection to the class. Each story comes with full teaching apparatus.

Before students begin a selection, you might want to help them understand the context, setting, and characters involved. Point out that with a longer story, readers can get to know the characters better and discover how they handle some very tough problems.

Technology Resources

Audio CD
The following selections in this unit are featured in the Audio Library: "from *Hiroshima*," "from *Anne Frank: Child of the Holocaust*," and "Black Whiteness."

Reading Coach CD-ROM
The excerpt from *Anne Frank: Child of the Holocaust* is part of the Reading Coach. You may use the Reading Coach selection as a group activity, as an individual activity, or as a tutorial for students who might benefit from this format or who have missed class.

Building Bridges: Closing the Reading Gap
This video is intended for teacher use only. It gives instructions and tips on how to help middle school readers become strategic readers.

Assessment

Selection Tests
pp. T548, T567, T587

Assessment Booklet
End-of-Year Reading Test
Administer the End-of-Year Reading Test (pp. 21–28 in the Assessment Booklet) to determine student gains in reading progress since the Placement Test.

End-of-Year Skills Test Units 1–12
Administer this test when students have completed the book. It covers skills taught in all the units.

Focus Skills

 COMPREHENSION
Compare and Contrast

 LITERATURE
Plot

 VOCABULARY
Latin Roots

SkillBuilder Copymasters

 Reading Comprehension:
1 Compare and Contrast
p. T544

Literary Analysis:
2 Plot p. T545

Vocabulary:
3 Latin Roots p. T546
4 Words to Know p. T547

Assessment

5 Selection Test p. T548

Readability Scores

DRP	LEXILE	DALE-CHALL
55	630	4.8

Reading Fluency

 ★ Reading Fluency p. T549

from

HIROSHIMA

by Laurence Yep

The time is World War II. The people of a Japanese city prepare to defend themselves. No one knows the destruction a secret weapon will bring.

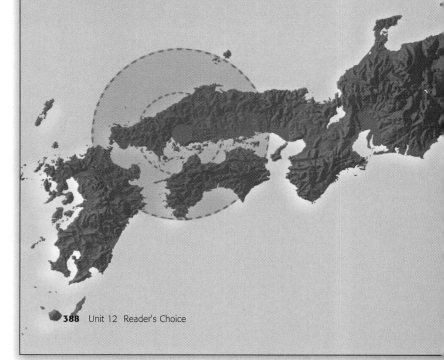

388 Unit 12 Reader's Choice

Vocabulary Strategy: Preteaching

Latin Roots Tell students that words that have the same origin, or root, usually have related meanings. For example, all of the words on the chart on the facing page belong to the same **word family.** They are related because they all come from the Latin word *corpus,* which means "body." Have students use a dictionary to fill in the meanings of the words on the chart.

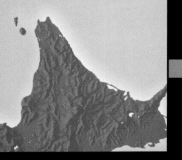

Connect to Your Life

Think about bombings you have heard about in your lifetime. How powerful were the bombs? What kinds of damage did they cause? Discuss your answers in a small group.

Key to the Novel Excerpt

This selection is a work of historical fiction. This means it tells a story using real events. The story takes place in 1945, toward the end of World War II. The United States and its partners, or allies, have defeated Germany. The war against Japan is not over. The United States plans to end the war quickly. The military drops an atomic (or atom) bomb on the Japanese city of Hiroshima. The bomb causes horrible damage that still affects people's lives today.

As you read, keep track of the events. The plot of this story shows the same event from two viewpoints. One shows what the pilots see as they drop the bomb. The other shows what two young girls, Riko and Sachi, experience on the ground.

Vocabulary Preview

Words to Know

routine	devastated
colonel	radioactive
anxiously	

from Hiroshima **389**

Words That Come from Latin *Corpus*

Word	Meaning
corpse	a dead human body
corporation	_____
corporal	_____
corps	_____
corpuscle	_____

 For more on Latin Roots, see page T543.

Connect to Your Life

To help students understand the selection, have them fill out a **K-W-L chart** (see page T666 for copymaster). In the *K* column, have students write what they already know about bombs. In the *W* column, have them write what they want to find out. Then while they read the selection, have them record what they learn in the *L* column.

Key to the Novel Excerpt

Students can keep the events in this selection straight by making a two-column chart and creating a sequence chain for each plot line. When they finish, they will have one sequence chain for the events in the air and one for the events on the ground.

Vocabulary Preview

Words to Know
routine *adj.* regular
colonel *n.* a military officer
anxiously *adv.* nervously
devastated *v.* destroyed
radioactive *adj.* containing particles of radiation

 For direct instruction on Words to Know, see page T543.

Building Background

The decision to drop the atom bomb on Hiroshima came from Harry Truman, who had been president of the United States for less than four months. While Truman was in Germany meeting with Winston Churchill and Joseph Stalin, he received word that scientists on the Manhattan Project had successfully tested the first atom bomb in New Mexico. Seeing a way to end World War II, Truman ordered American fliers to drop an atom bomb on Japan. The first bomb, "Little Boy," fell on Hiroshima on August 6, 1945. A second bomb, "Fat Man," was dropped on Nagasaki on August 9. Six days later Japan agreed to end the war, and Japan officially surrendered on September 2.

FOCUS

Early one morning, a pilot makes special preparations. Read to find out what he is getting ready to do.

The Bomb

 Early in the morning of August 6, 1945, a big American bomber roars down the runway on a tiny island called Tinian. The pilot is Colonel Tibbets. He has named the plane after his mother, Enola Gay. On a routine mission, a B-29 would carry 4000 to 16,000 pounds of bombs. The *Enola Gay* is on a special mission. It carries a single bomb. It is an atom bomb that weighs 8900 pounds. Everyone hopes the atom
10 bomb will finally end a long and horrible war.

routine
(rōō tēn')
adj. regular

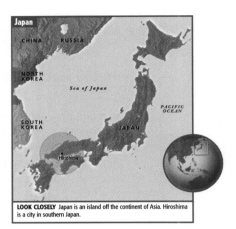

Japan

CHINA   RUSSIA

NORTH
KOREA

Sea of Japan

PACIFIC
OCEAN

SOUTH
KOREA   JAPAN

Hiroshima

LOOK CLOSELY Japan is an island off the continent of Asia. Hiroshima is a city in southern Japan.

Four years before, on December 7, 1941, Japanese planes attacked American ships in Hawaii without warning. Caught by surprise, many ships and planes were wrecked at the naval base, Pearl Harbor. The United States declared war on Japan and Japan's ally, Germany. With other countries, they fight a war called World War II.

By 1945, Germany has given up. Only Japan fights on. But the United States has a secret weapon—the
20 atom bomb. Nothing is as powerful and as awful. The atom bomb is so terrible that the United States hopes it will make Japan stop fighting.

Two other bombers follow the *Enola Gay*. These planes only carry cameras and special instruments to measure the explosion. Together the three bombers turn over the Pacific Ocean and speed through the darkness toward Japan.

THINK IT THROUGH

Why does the United States plan to drop the atom bomb?

FOCUS

Read to find out what is happening on that morning in Hiroshima.

The City

It is only seven o'clock in the morning, but the air is already hot and muggy in
30 Hiroshima. People go to work. Children hurry to school. Some soldiers and women go out with baskets to shop. A peddler wheels his cart carefully through the crowd. A colonel exercises his white horse.

muggy
(mŭg' ē)
damp

colonel
(kûr' nəl)
n. a military officer

COMPREHENSION

FOCUS SKILL: Compare and Contrast

Tell students that **comparing** means looking at how two or more things, people, or events are alike. **Contrasting** means looking at how two or more things, people, or events are different.

For direct instruction on Compare and Contrast, see page T542.

Ⓐ Ask: How does the *Enola Gay*'s mission compare to other, routine missions? (*Routine missions carry 4,000 to 16,000 pounds of bombs, but the* Enola Gay *carries a single 8,900-pound bomb—the first atom bomb—which everyone hopes will end a war.*) **compare and contrast**

Ⓑ **THINK IT THROUGH** Why does the United States plan to drop the atom bomb? (*The government hopes it will make Japan stop fighting, which will put an end to World War II.*) **problem and solution**

LITERATURE

FOCUS SKILL: Plot

Remind students that a **plot** is the sequence of related events that make up a story. Most plots revolve around a **conflict,** or problem, and what the characters do to solve it. Tell students to pay close attention while they read this story, because it has two plots that are woven together.

For direct instruction on Plot, see page T542.

Use questions such as this one to encourage literary analysis.

Ⓐ What is the main conflict, or problem, in this story so far? (*The Germans have given up fighting World War II, but their ally, Japan, won't stop fighting.*) **plot**

VOCABULARY

FOCUS SKILL: Latin Roots

As students read this selection, remind them to think about how some of the words are related. Knowing which **word family** certain words belong to will help students understand their meanings.

Ⓐ **bomber . . . bombs** You may want to have students add these words to the chart that they began in the Vocabulary Strategy. Then have them use a dictionary to find out that the words *bomber* and *bombs* belong to a word family related to the Latin word *bombus,* meaning "a booming sound."

FOR ENGLISH LEARNERS

Help students understand the following expressions and idioms:

Line 2: roars down the runway
Line 13: Caught by surprise
Line 15: Japan's ally
Line 18: given up; fights on
Line 32: A peddler wheels his cart

There are about 320,000 people in Hiroshima that morning.

Two sisters walk sleepily in the crowd. Riko is sixteen and her little sister, Sachi, is twelve. They have stayed up all night hiding from American bombers.
40 Up until now, though, the airplanes have always bombed other cities. Some people believe that Hiroshima is so beautiful that the Americans have decided to spare it.

Riko and Sachi stop by a shrine. They say a prayer for their father, who is in the army. Looking at the calm, forgiving face of Buddha, they begin to feel at peace.

Buddha
(bōō′ də)
a statue of the founder of a religion practiced in Japan

• • •

An American bomber flies ahead of the *Enola Gay* and its companions. This bomber
50 is called the *Straight Flush*. It will check the weather over Hiroshima. If there are clouds over Hiroshima, the *Straight Flush* will tell the *Enola Gay* to attack another city.

The crew of the *Straight Flush* scans the sky anxiously for Japanese fighter planes. However, the Japanese are saving their airplanes for the invasion that everyone expects. So there are no Japanese planes today.

At first, the *Straight Flush* only sees clouds. Then,
60 the crew spots a big hole in the clouds directly over Hiroshima. The sunlight pours right through the hole on to the city.

Green hills surround the city and the seven rivers shine like ribbons.

Hiroshima is a perfect target.

anxiously
(ăngk′ shəs lē)
adv. nervously

B

The *Straight Flush* tells the *Enola Gay* to continue to Hiroshima.

In the meantime, down below in Hiroshima, someone spots the *Straight Flush* and sounds the
70 alarm.

The siren shrieks in short blasts. Everywhere, people stop whatever they are doing. A streetcar rumbles to a halt. Its passengers run for the air-raid shelter.

Sachi and Riko leave the shrine and join the others. "Put on your hood, Sachi," Riko tells her. From their emergency bags, the two sisters pull out air-raid hoods. Putting them over their heads, they tie them tight. If the bombs start fires, the hoods are supposed to
80 protect them from burning sparks.

With the other people, they go down the steps to hide in the darkness.

However, the *Straight Flush* passes harmlessly over the city.

REREAD
What do the people of Hiroshima think the *Straight Flush* is going to do?

C

C

C REREAD What do the people of Hiroshima think the *Straight Flush* is going to do? *(They think the Straight Flush is going to bomb the city. They don't know it's only checking the weather.)* **making inferences**

B This story has two different plot lines. One plot line will follow what happens to two sisters named Riko and Sachi. What will the other one follow? *(what the crew of two American bombers named* Enola Gay *and* Straight Flush *experience)* **plot**

C Why do you think the author chose to tell two stories in one? *(He wants to tell the story from two different points of view—one from the Americans in the air and one from the Japanese on the ground.)* **point of view**

FOR ENGLISH LEARNERS

Help students understand the following expressions and idioms:

Line 43: decided to spare it
Line 50: *Straight Flush*
Line 54: scans the sky
Line 60: spots a big hole
Line 71: shrieks in short blasts
Line 73: rumbles to a halt

Work

When the *Straight Flush* finally leaves, the siren announces that it is safe. Breathing sighs of relief, the people leave the bomb shelters. They hurry to finish their interrupted chores. They go back to their homes to cook breakfast. The shopkeepers reopen their
90　stores. The streetcars rumble along the tracks again.

Everyone believes that they are safe now. They do not think more bombers will come so soon after the *Straight Flush*.

THINK IT THROUGH

D The people in Hiroshima think they're safe. What don't they know?

A view from the air of Hiroshima before the bombing

394　Unit 12　Reader's Choice

FOCUS
Discover more about people's daily lives in wartime Hiroshima.

Sachi takes off her hood as soon as she is on the street. "I hate to wear it," she says and stuffs it into her emergency bag.

"We're going to be late," Riko tells Sachi. Lunches and emergency bags bouncing, the two girls start to run.

At the corner, Riko makes Sachi stop. "Don't forget
100　to wear your hood," she reminds her sister.

Sachi hurries to school and gathers in the yard with her classmates. They will not study in the classroom today. As members of the labor service corps, they have been assigned tasks outdoors to help defend Japan against the American invasion.

D The older children work in the factories. Others, like Riko, record phone messages at the army headquarters, located in an old castle. They have taken the place of the
110　soldiers who are needed to fight the Americans.

REREAD
How do students help defend the city?
E

F Sachi and her classmates work outside in the streets tearing down houses. It is a sad sight for the owners, but they know it is necessary to lose their houses to support the war effort.

Many of the Japanese buildings are wood and paper. In other cities, American planes have dropped bombs and started fires that have devastated large areas. As yet, this has not
120　happened to Hiroshima, but since no one wants to take chances, the army and city officials have decided to make fire lanes. The empty spaces will help stop the fires from spreading. The lanes will also provide avenues

devastated
(dĕv′ ə stāt′ ĕd) *v.* destroyed; past tense of *devastate*

from Hiroshima　395

COMPREHENSION

D **THINK IT THROUGH** The people in Hiroshima think they're safe. What don't they know? *(that the Straight Flush was just checking; the Enola Gay is on the way.)* **details**

E **REREAD** How do students help defend the city? *(They sit in for the soldiers and record phone messages at army headquarters.)* **problem and solution**

F **Teacher Modeling** To show students the Active Reading Strategy of visualization, focus on lines 112–124.
You could say: *When I read the author's description of Sachi and her classmates "tearing down houses" and making fire lanes to "help stop the fires from spreading," I imagine a lot of people working together as fast as possible. The city must look broken down, as if a natural disaster had just hit it.*

LITERATURE

D Remind students that although the events in historical fiction are usually factual, the writer makes up dialogue and sometimes characters, who act in a way that the writer thinks people would have done. Ask whether this paragraph is factual. *(yes)* Have students reread the dialogue at the top of the page, and ask them whether it is factual or made up. *(made up)* **historical fiction**

VOCABULARY

FOR ENGLISH LEARNERS

Help students understand the following expressions and idioms:

Line 85: the siren announces
Line 101: gathers in the yard
Line 103: labor service corps
Line 115: support the war effort
Line 121: take chances
Line 122: fire lanes

for fire-fighting equipment as well as escape routes for people fleeing the flames.

Sachi and her classmates help the adults wreck houses. They sort through the remains, looking for
130 useful parts they can save and reuse, such as roof tiles. It is hot, dusty work and the muggy air makes the dust stick to their sweaty faces. To make the work go faster, the children chant in time as they wield their shovels.

REREAD
What are Sachi and her classmates doing?

Sachi's best friend pulls on white gloves to protect her hands. Several children tie headbands around their foreheads to keep the sweat from their eyes.

Everyone is busy as the *Enola Gay* approaches.

THINK IT THROUGH
What steps does the city take to defend itself?

FOCUS
How bad do you think the atom bomb will be? Read to see if you are right.

The Attack

All over Japan, there are observers who look out
140 for the American bombers. Nineteen miles east of Hiroshima, an observer spots the *Enola Gay* and its two companions. Hurriedly, he calls the army headquarters in Hiroshima.

Riko answers the phone and takes down the report. She is shocked to learn that there are more bombers coming. Angrily, she thinks it is a sneaky trick to catch people outside the shelters.

She dials the radio station immediately and asks the announcers to warn everyone.

396 Unit 12 Reader's Choice

The *Enola Gay* is a B-29 bomber.

150 Riko thinks she is safe deep inside the ancient castle. But she prays for her mother at home and Sachi out in the street tearing down houses.

ancient
(ān' shənt) of times long past

In the meantime, people go on calmly with their lives. They eat their breakfasts. They begin their work. Outside their homes, the very small children begin to play. A colonel rides his horse across a bridge.

On the *Enola Gay*, Colonel Tibbets orders,
160 "On glasses." His crew pull on goggles to protect their eyes. However, Colonel Tibbets must see clearly to steer the bomber. He does not put on goggles. Neither does the bombardier.

bombardier
(bŏm' bər dîr') member of a bomber crew who releases the bombs

REREAD
Picture and compare these two scenes.

Everyone is tense and excited. No one is sure if the bomb will go off. Yesterday on Tinian, Colonel Tibbets tested the gunlike device that sets off the bomb. It did not work then.

Now the bombardier looks through his bombsight
170 and guides the *Enola Gay* the last few miles to its target.

from Hiroshima **397**

COMPREHENSION

G **REREAD** What are Sachi and her classmates doing? *(They help wreck houses and sort through the remains looking for parts that can be reused.)* **details**

H **THINK IT THROUGH** What steps does the city take to defend itself? *(All citizens, including children, have jobs. The city is tearing down houses and building fire lanes, which will provide avenues for fire-fighting equipment and will serve as escape routes for people.)* **problem and solution**

I **REREAD** Picture and compare these two scenes. *(In the first, people are calmly going about their lives, unaware of what will soon happen. In the second, the crew prepare to bomb the city and are probably very nervous and excited.)* **compare and contrast**

LITERATURE

E How does the author build suspense in the moments before the bomb is dropped? *(Possible answer: He describes what Riko does and thinks after she receives the observer's message. Then he tells what Colonel Tibbets and the crew do and think just before they drop the bomb.)* **suspense**

VOCABULARY

B **bombardier . . . bombsight** Students can add these words under *bombus* on their charts. Have them use a dictionary, if necessary, to fill in the meaning of each word.

FOR ENGLISH LEARNERS

Help students understand the following expressions and idioms:

Line 128: sort through the remains
Line 133: chant in time; wield their shovels
Line 144: takes down the report

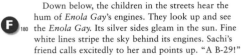

Doors snap open on the belly of the plane.

The bombardier sees his landmark. It is a bridge shaped like a T. On the bridge, a Japanese colonel rides his horse.

The bombardier presses a button to release the bomb.

Down below, the children in the streets hear the hum of *Enola Gay*'s engines. They look up and see

F 180 the *Enola Gay*. Its silver sides gleam in the sun. Fine white lines stripe the sky behind its engines. Sachi's friend calls excitedly to her and points up. "A B-29!"

"B-29! B-29!" a teacher shouts.

Sachi remembers her sister's warning. From her emergency bag, she pulls out her special hood and puts it on.

Another teacher blows a whistle. It is a signal for the children to go to the air-raid shelter.

In the *Enola Gay*, the bombardier shouts, "Bomb

G 190 away!"

The huge, heavy bomb drops from the airplane. Suddenly the *Enola Gay* is much lighter, and it jerks up into the air. Colonel Tibbets is skillful. He keeps control of the airplane and swings it to the right.

The bomb whistles as it plunges down, down through the air.

On the *Enola Gay*, a crewman flips a switch on a special radio. It sends a signal to a special gun inside the bomb.

200 This time the gun works. It shoots a cone-shaped bullet of uranium into a larger ball of uranium.

Everything is made up of tiny particles called atoms. They are so small they are invisible to the eye. The atoms are also made up of even smaller parts.

Energy holds these parts together like glue. When the atom breaks up into its parts, the energy goes free and there is a big explosion.

Inside the bomb, one uranium atom collides with another. Those atoms both break up. Their parts

210 smash into more atoms and split them in turn.

This is called a chain reaction. There are millions and millions of atoms inside the bomb. When they all break up, it is believed that the atom bomb will be equal to 20,000 tons of dynamite. In 1945, it is the most powerful weapon ever made.

REREAD Summarize how the atom bomb works. **J**

As the chain reaction builds, the bomb falls faster and faster. But it does not go off over the bridge. It explodes over a hospital instead.

220 There is a blinding light like a sun.

There is a boom like a giant drum.

There is a terrible wind. Houses collapse like boxes. Windows break everywhere. Broken glass swirls like angry insects.

The wind strikes Sachi's back like a hammer and picks her up. She feels as if she has fallen into boiling oil. It tears away her special hood and even her clothes. The wind sweeps her into the whirlwind of glass.

230 There is no time to scream. There is no one to hear. There is only the darkness. . . .

And Sachi mercifully passes out.

THINK IT THROUGH
At this point in the story, why do you think the author gives details about what happens to only one person? **K**

COMPREHENSION

J **REREAD** Summarize how the atom bomb works. *(When one uranium atom collides with another, it causes the millions of other atoms inside the bomb to collide and break up in a chain reaction. This causes the bomb's explosion to be as powerful as 20,000 tons of dynamite.)* **summarizing**

K **THINK IT THROUGH** At this point in the story, why do you think the author gives details about what happens to only one person? *(Possible answers: He wants to give a personal account of the effects of the bomb, rather than just a factual explanation. Through Sachi, he is able to let readers know what many other people were thinking, feeling, and experiencing at the time of the explosion.)* **author's purpose**

LITERATURE

F What is happening on the ground? *(Sachi's friend sees the* Enola Gay *and shouts "A B-29!" Sachi puts on her special hood, and everyone heads for the air-raid shelter.)* **plot**

G What is happening in the air? *(The bombardier has pressed a button to release the bomb and shouts "Bomb away!," and the bomb drops from the plane. A crewman sends a signal to the bomb.)* **plot**

VOCABULARY

FOR ENGLISH LEARNERS

Help students understand the following:

Line 172: belly of the plane
Line 232: passes out

This is a photograph of the mushroom cloud produced by the Hiroshima bombing.

FOCUS

Find out the other effects of this deadly explosion.

The Mushroom Cloud

The *Enola Gay* circles. The same wind that carries Sachi through the air almost knocks the bomber from the sky. Colonel Tibbets manages to right his airplane. The two companion bombers begin to take pictures and record the explosion.

right
put in upright or correct position

C

240 Up until then, no single bomb has ever caused so much damage or so many deaths.

Out of 76,327 buildings, over 50,000 are destroyed.

Up to 125,000 people will die on that first day or will die soon.

REREAD
Review these facts. Why was all the work done by the citizens of Hiroshima wasted?

L

The wind mixes their dust with the dirt and debris. Then it sends everything boiling upward in a tall purple-gray column. When the top of the dust cloud spreads out, it looks like a strange, giant mushroom.

400 Unit 12 Reader's Choice

250 The bottom of the mushroom cloud is a fiery red. All over the city fires spring up. They rise like flames from a bed of coals.

The bomb goes off 580 meters above the ground. The temperature reaches several million degrees Celsius immediately. It is so hot that the hospital below and everyone inside it disappears.

Two hundred yards away, people vanish. However, in that instant, their outlines are burnt into the cement like shadows.

260 The army headquarters and all the soldiers and Riko and her classmates are destroyed.

One mile away, the fierce heat starts fires.

Even two miles away, people are burned by the heat.

On the *Enola Gay*, the tail gunner tries to count the fires. But he gives up because there are too many.

Everyone in the crew has flown on bombers. They have helped drop tons of regular bombs. On each flight, they have seen death and destruction.

But no one has ever seen anything as 270 powerful as this one bomb.

The copilot writes a note to himself: "What have we done?"

D

REREAD
What might the crew be feeling at this time?

M

When the bomb's uranium breaks up, bits of atoms zip away. They go right through people's skin and hurt their bodies inside. This is called radiation. It will make thousands of people sick. Many will die later that day. More will fall ill and die in a year. Some will die in five years, or ten, or twenty. People are still dying today.

THINK IT THROUGH

Review the section "The Mushroom Cloud." List all of the effects of the bombing.

N

from Hiroshima 401

COMPREHENSION

L **REREAD** Review these facts. Why was all the work done by the citizens of Hiroshima wasted? *(No amount of preparation could have spared them from such devastation. With that single bomb, almost three-fourths of the city's buildings were destroyed, and more than one-third of the population died, either on that day or in the near future.)* **making inferences**

M **REREAD** What might the crew be feeling at this time? *(Possible answers: shock, regret, sorrow, guilt, sadness)* **making inferences**

N **THINK IT THROUGH** Review the section "The Mushroom Cloud." List all of the effects of the bombing. *(The wind from the bomb almost knocks the* Enola Gay *out of the sky; more than 50,000 buildings are destroyed; up to 125,000 people die; fires start all over the city and up to one mile away; the hospital disappears; people and buildings vanish; and many people get sick or die from radiation. They were still dying decades later.)* **cause and effect**

VOCABULARY

C **destroyed** Have students use a dictionary to find the Latin ancestor of this word. *(dēstruere, "to destroy")*

D **destruction** Point out that this word has the same Latin root as *destroy*. Then have the students add the words *destroyed* and *destruction* to their chart, along with a few others in the same word family.

FOR ENGLISH LEARNERS

Help students understand the following:

Line 251: fires spring up
Line 264: tail gunner

FOCUS

Discover more of what is happening to the people of Hiroshima.

Destruction

280 Sachi wakes a few minutes later when she hears someone screaming. At first, there is so much smoke and dust she feels as if she is staring at a black wall. Then the smoke and dust rise like a curtain. She is stunned when she sees all the damage. One moment there was a city here. Now all the buildings are destroyed. The streets are filled with rubble and ruins.
H She does not know what could cause such wide destruction.

290 Shocked, Sachi stumbles through the wasteland until she stops upon a lawn. From the wrecked buildings, people call for help. Before she can help anyone, the buildings go up in flames.

It is so hot around her that the grass catches fire. She crouches down and waits and hopes. The sheet of fire

The ruined city of Hiroshima a few months after the atom bomb was dropped

402   Unit 12 Reader's Choice

retreats. Flames shoot out of the nearby houses. People continue to scream. Everywhere, there is a sea of fire.

Sachi follows some people as they run into a cemetery. She jumps over tombstones. The pine trees around them catch fire with a great crackling noise.

300 Ahead she sees a river. People jump into it to get away from the fire. In the panic, some people are crushed. Others drown. Sachi cannot swim. She jumps in anyway. Then she sees a wooden bucket drifting by. She grabs it and holds on desperately.

Soon the water is full of bodies.

The hot ash from all the fires soars high, high into the sky. When the fiery ash mixes with the cold air, it causes rain. It is a horrible kind of rain.

The rain falls in drops as big as marbles.
310 The drops are black and greasy with dust. The drops sting like falling pebbles.

The rain leaves black, oily spots wherever it falls.

The rain is radioactive. It will make people sick, too. They will also die.

> **radioactive**
> (rā′ dē ō ăk′ tĭv)
> *adj.* containing particles of radiation

> **REREAD**
> How is this rain different from regular rainfall?
> **P**

After about an hour, the rain puts out the fires. Somebody finds Sachi and brings her to the hospital.

The people living just outside Hiroshima think they
320 are safe. They search through the deadly wasteland for family and friends. They do not know about
E radiation. Some of these searchers will also fall ill. Many of them will die.

One mother hunts all over the city for her children. Finally, she stops at a hospital.

The bodies of schoolchildren are piled up on a hallway bench. The mother looks through the bodies

from Hiroshima **403**

COMPREHENSION

O Imagine yourself a reporter on this scene. What words would you use to describe the image you see? (*Possible answers: horrible, terrible, unreal, unbelievable, frightening, shocking, nightmarish, devastation, destruction*) **understanding visuals**

P **REREAD** How is this rain different from regular rainfall? (*Regular rainfall is colorless and harmless. This rainfall is mixed with deadly radioactive particles and ash, and it falls in black, oily, stinging drops that are as big as marbles.*) **compare and contrast**

LITERATURE

H **Teacher Modeling: Visualizing** Model for students how to use visualizing to understand the changed setting of the selection.

You could say: *When I read lines 280–286, I can picture an image in my mind of what has just happened to Hiroshima. Before the bomb was dropped, there was an entire city with houses and buildings. But after the bomb, there is so much smoke and dust. Line 286 says, "The streets are filled with rubble and ruins." The city of Hiroshima must have been completely destroyed immediately after the bombing.*

Remind students to visualize scenes when they are reading.

VOCABULARY

E **radiation** Point out that both *radiation* and *radioactive* contain the root of the Latin word *radius,* "spoke of a wheel." Ask for other words in the same family. (*radium, radius*) Suggest that students add these words to their word-family chart.

FOR ENGLISH LEARNERS

Help students understand the following:

Line 294: sheet of fire retreats
Line 296: sea of fire

for her daughter. She hears a groan. Someone is alive. It is
330 Sachi.

However, Sachi has terrible burns on her face. She cannot even smile. It is as if she has no face. One arm is bent permanently. Of all her classmates, only she has survived.

I

Despite America's terrible new weapon, Japanese
340 military leaders still refuse to give up.

Three days later, on August 9, 1945, the Americans drop another bomb, this time on the city of Nagasaki. Much of that city is also destroyed. Seventy thousand people die.

At last, on August 15, Japan surrenders. World War II is finally over.

The A-Bomb Dome is located in Hiroshima. It is dedicated to the victims of the bombings of Hiroshima and Nagasaki.

Q

THINK IT THROUGH

1. Why do you think the author wanted you to know Sachi's story?
2. Do you think the crew of the *Enola Gay* knew what the bomb would do? Support your answer with details from the story.
3. This piece shows the tragedy caused by the dropping of the atom bomb. Do you think ending the war made up for this tragedy?

FLOATING LANTERNS XII

Written by Iri and Toshi Maruki
Translated from the Japanese by
Nancy Hunter with Yasuo Ishikawa

On August sixth every year
        the seven rivers of Hiroshima
        are filled with lanterns
Painted with the names of
5   fathers, mothers, and sisters
        they float on their way to the sea

Almost there, pushed back
        flame snuffed out
Darkly coming back in pieces
10 Tossed by ocean waves

That time, years past
        these same rivers were filled
With the corpses of those
        fathers, mothers, and sisters

COMPREHENSION

Q THINK IT THROUGH

1. Why do you think the author wanted you to know Sachi's story? *(Possible answers: because it's not only Sachi's story but the story of hundreds of thousands of Japanese who were injured or killed that day; because the author wanted to show how humans were affected by the bombing)* **author's purpose**

2. Do you think the crew of the *Enola Gay* knew what the bomb would do? Support your answer with details from the story. *(No. There had never been a bomb as powerful as the atom bomb, so no one knew what it would do. Also, after they dropped the bomb, the copilot wrote, "What have we done?")* **drawing conclusions**

3. This piece shows the tragedy caused by the dropping of the atom bomb. Do you think ending the war made up for this tragedy? *(Students' opinions will vary. Accept all answers that students can reasonably support.)* **making judgments**

Have students complete the last column of the **K-W-L chart** that they began before reading.

RETEACHING

If students need more help understanding **Compare and Contrast**, use pages T647–T649.

LITERATURE

I If Sachi could send the world a message about war, what do you think it might be? *(Possible answers: There are other ways to solve our problems than with guns and bombs. The decisions that are made can change the world forever.)* **theme**

RELATED READING

1. In what ways are the lanterns like the people they represent? *(Possible answers: The lanterns had their flames snuffed out as they were hit by the ocean's waves; the people had their lives snuffed out as they were hit by the bomb's wind. Also, the lanterns that now fill the rivers stand for the people who filled them on the day of the bombing.)* **compare and contrast**

2. If a crew member of the *Enola Gay* were to read this poem today, how do you think he would feel? *(Responses will vary. Encourage students to use their own feelings as well as information from the novel excerpt to explain their answers.)* **making inferences**

1. COMPREHENSION

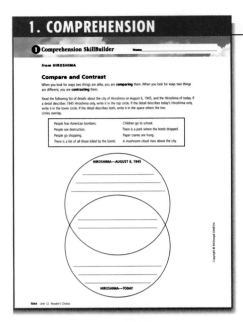

Compare and Contrast

Direct Instruction Remind students that when they look for what two people or things have in common, they are **comparing** the people or things. When they are looking for ways two people or things are different, they are **contrasting** them. Tell students that one way to understand a selection better is to compare and contrast the people and things in the selection.

Have the students compare and contrast their own lives to the lives the two sisters, Riko and Sachi, were leading before the bomb fell. Ask: *What activities do both you and the sisters engage in? Which of your activities are different?*

> **Comprehension SkillBuilder Answer Key:**
>
> **Hiroshima—August 6, 1945:** *people fear American bombers, people see destruction, a mushroom cloud rises above the city*
>
> **Both:** *people go shopping, children go to school*
>
> **Hiroshima—Today:** *there is a park where the bomb dropped, paper cranes are hung, there is a list of all those killed by the bomb*

2. LITERATURE

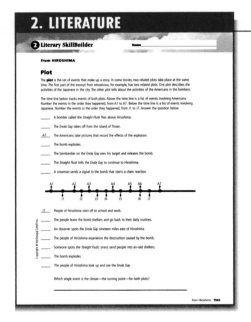

Plot

Direct Instruction Remind students that the **plot** is the sequence of events that make up a story. Usually these events are told in time order. In some stories, two related sets of events, or plots, take place at the same time. Different characters take part in each plot, but these two sets of characters often move toward one or more shared events. The characters take a different path to the event that is shared, and the event has different effects on them. The action of a story may jump between the two plots as the writer describes what the two sets of characters are doing.

Point out to the students that situation comedies often have two plots involving characters who are working against each other unknowingly. For example, a family is trying to find their lost dog while their neighbors are taking care of the dog, which followed them home; the two groups repeatedly miss chances to discuss their activities. Finally, at the end of the program, they get together and straighten things out. Ask students to recall and describe stories they have seen—comic or serious—that involve two plots developing at the same time.

> **Literary SkillBuilder Answer Key:**
> **American events:** *A2, A1, A7, A6, A4, A3, A5*
> **Japanese events:** *J1, J3, J4, J7, J2, J6, J5*
> **Turning point**: *The bomb explodes.*

3. VOCABULARY

Latin Roots

Direct Instruction Tell students that many words in the English language come from words in the Latin language. The meanings of the English words are related to the meanings of the Latin words. Write the following English and Latin words from *Hiroshima* on the board.

English	Latin	Latin Meaning
observer	observāre	to guard
chant	cantāre	to sing
ceremony	caerimōnia	a rite or solemn act

Discuss how the meanings of the English words are related to the meanings of the Latin words. Also point out that the spellings of the words are similar.

Point out to the students that once they know the meaning of a root, they can look for that root in words that are unfamiliar to them. Knowing Latin roots often helps unlock the meaning of English words.

Vocabulary SkillBuilder Answer Key:

A. *(Order of words in each family may vary.)*

1. *bomb, bomber, bombardier*   2. *corps, corpse, corporation*   3. *radiation, radioactive, radiant*   4. *office, officer, officious*   5. *mile, million, millennium*

B.

1. *radiation*   2. *bomber*   3. *corpse*   4. *officer*   5. *bombardier*   6. *radioactive*   7. *million*   8. *mile*

4. WORDS TO KNOW

Words to Know

Direct Instruction As you present the **Words to Know,** here are some points you might want to cover. Help students identify the parts of the vocabulary words. Stress the importance of finding the base of each word. Help students remove prefixes and suffixes first.

- **colonel,** from the Latin *columna,* "column"
- **anxious** + -ly = *anxiously,* from the Latin *angere,* "to torment"
- **devastate** + -ed = *devastated,* from the Latin *dē* + *vāstāre,* "to lay waste"

- **radioactive** contains the prefix *radio-,* which is related to the words *radiate, radiant, radial, radar, radius,* etc. *Radioactive* can be used informally to mean "extremely sensitive or controversial."

Writing Activity Pair students or have them work in small groups to complete the exercise. Have volunteers read their creations aloud.

Words to Know SkillBuilder Answer Key:

A. 1. *anxiously*   **2.** *devastated*   **3.** *routine*   **4.** *radioactive*   **5.** *colonel*

B. *Instruct students to provide evidence for their conclusions on the true and false section (B), particularly if they believe the statement to be false.*

1. *false*   2. *true*   3. *false*   4. *true*   5. *true*

5. SELECTION TEST

Selection Test Answer Key:

A. 1. *c* **2.** *a* **3.** *c* **4.** *b* **5.** *a* **6.** *b* **7.** *c* **8.** *b* **9.** *a*

B. *Possible answers: The rain is black and gray. It is radioactive and will make people sick.*

from **HIROSHIMA**

Compare and Contrast

When you look for ways two things are alike, you are **comparing** them. When you look for ways two things are different, you are **contrasting** them.

Read the following list of details about the city of Hiroshima on August 6, 1945, and the Hiroshima of today. If a detail describes 1945 Hiroshima only, write it in the top circle. If the detail describes today's Hiroshima only, write it in the lower circle. If the detail describes both, write it in the space where the two circles overlap.

People fear American bombers.	Children go to school.
People see destruction.	There is a park where the bomb dropped.
People go shopping.	Paper cranes are hung.
There is a list of all those killed by the bomb.	A mushroom cloud rises above the city.

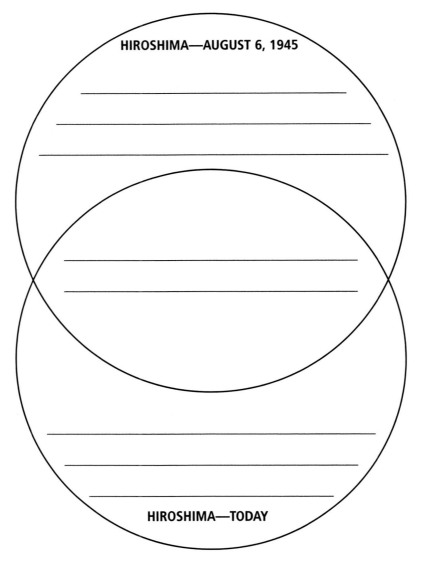

HIROSHIMA—AUGUST 6, 1945

HIROSHIMA—TODAY

from **HIROSHIMA**

Plot

The **plot** is the set of events that make up a story. In some stories, two related plots take place at the same time. The first part of the excerpt from *Hiroshima*, for example, has two related plots. One plot describes the activities of the Japanese in the city. The other plot tells about the activities of the Americans in the bombers.

The time line below tracks events of both plots. Above the time line is a list of events involving Americans. Number the events in the order they happened, from A1 to A7. Below the time line is a list of events involving Japanese. Number the events in the order they happened, from J1 to J7. Answer the question below.

_____ A bomber called the *Straight Flush* flies above Hiroshima.

_____ The *Enola Gay* takes off from the island of Tinian.

__A7___ The Americans take pictures that record the effects of the explosion.

_____ The bomb explodes.

_____ The bombardier on the *Enola Gay* sees his target and releases the bomb.

_____ The *Straight Flush* tells the *Enola Gay* to continue to Hiroshima.

_____ A crewman sends a signal to the bomb that starts a chain reaction.

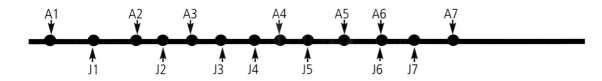

__J1___ People of Hiroshima start off to school and work.

_____ The people leave the bomb shelters and go back to their daily routines.

_____ An observer spots the *Enola Gay* nineteen miles east of Hiroshima.

_____ The people of Hiroshima experience the destruction caused by the bomb.

_____ Someone spots the *Straight Flush;* sirens send people into air-raid shelters.

_____ The bomb explodes.

_____ The people of Hiroshima look up and see the *Enola Gay.*

Which single event is the climax—the turning point—for both plots?

_____

from HIROSHIMA

Latin Roots

Many words in the English language come from words in the Latin language. Knowing the meaning of Latin roots will help you understand many English words.

A. Each Latin word listed below is related to three English words in the box. Write each English word on the line after the related Latin word. Look for similarities in spelling and meaning.

radiant	corpse	office	bomb	million
bomber	radioactive	bombardier	millennium	corporation
officious	radiation	mile	corps	officer

1. *bombus,* "a deep, hollow sound"

_____

2. *corpus,* "body"

_____

3. *radius,* "spoke of a wheel"

_____

4. *officium,* "service or duty"

_____

5. *mīlle,* "thousand"

_____

B. Choose from the words in Exercise A to complete these sentences.

1. The atom bomb put out rays, called _____, that caused death.

2. A plane that carries bombs is a _____.

3. After the bomb dropped, survivors tried to bury each dead body, or _____.

4. The duty of Colonel Tibbets was to be the _____ who piloted the *Enola Gay.*

5. The crew member called the _____ decides when to drop a bomb.

6. Anything that is _____ gives off energy in the form of rays.

7. The number shown by a one followed by six zeroes, which means a thousand thousand, is one

_____.

8. Our _____ was originally based on a distance of a thousand steps.

from **HIROSHIMA**

Words to Know

routine   colonel   anxiously   devastated   radioactive

A. Fill in the blanks with the word from the list that best completes the sentence.

1. I _____ approached the principal's office.

2. The remains of the _____ village showed that a fire had destroyed the town.

3. The ride back and forth from school was a _____ trip.

4. We pretended our couch was a battlefield and the pillows were _____ missiles.

5. The _____ yelled at the officer because he had disobeyed orders.

B. Write **true** or **false** in the blanks.

_____ **1.** A **colonel** is the head librarian.

_____ **2.** If you **anxiously** wait for something, you are nervous.

_____ **3.** Something that is **radioactive** is against the law.

_____ **4.** Something that normally happens is **routine.**

_____ **5.** A city with crumbled buildings is **devastated.**

Writing Activity

The events in the excerpt from *Hiroshima* really happened. Using the true events, write about someone you make up who was in Hiroshima the day the atom bomb was dropped. Write at least one paragraph, and use at least three of the **Words to Know.**

from HIROSHIMA

A. Answer each question by filling in the circle beside the correct answer.

1. Where does this selection take place?

   ○ a. in the air over Hiroshima, Japan   ○ c. in the air and on the ground in Hiroshima, Japan

   ○ b. on the ground in Hiroshima, Japan

2. When does this selection take place?

   ○ a. on August 6, 1945   ○ b. on December 9, 1960   ○ c. on August 15, 1994

3. Who is Colonel Tibbets?

   ○ a. the man exercising his horse on a bridge   ○ c. the pilot of a B-29 called the *Enola Gay*

   ○ b. the horse that the man is exercising

4. What special mission is the United States planning?

   ○ a. to burn down all of Hiroshima   ○ c. to surprise Hiroshima with a ground attack

   ○ b. to drop an atom bomb on Hiroshima

5. What is the job of the *Straight Flush*?

   ○ a. to check weather conditions over Hiroshima   ○ c. to drop an atom bomb over Hiroshima

   ○ b. to flush people out of their homes with bombs

6. Why do Sachi and Riko put on their hoods?

   ○ a. to keep their hair from getting wet in the pouring rain

   ○ b. to protect them from burning sparks during a bombing

   ○ c. to keep dust out of their faces

7. Why aren't Sachi and Riko in school?

   ○ a. It is summer, and there is no school.   ○ c. They are both helping to defend Hiroshima.

   ○ b. They are practicing their air-raid procedures.

8. Why are people wrecking homes in Hiroshima?

   ○ a. so they can build a landing strip for their planes

   ○ b. to keep fires from spreading during a bombing

   ○ c. to replace them with sturdier homes of brick

9. What happens when the *Enola Gay* drops the atom bomb on Hiroshima?

   ○ a. More than 50,000 buildings are destroyed.

   ○ b. Japan surrenders, and World War II ends.

   ○ c. The blast knocks the *Enola Gay* out of the sky.

B. Describe the rain that falls after the bomb hits Hiroshima.

_____

_____

Reader directions:

Cut this paper in half. Practice reading this passage aloud until you don't make any mistakes. Then have someone listen to you read. Imagine that you are a storyteller or a narrator telling about the events that happened in Hiroshima.

from Hiroshima

It is only seven o'clock in the morning, but the air is already hot and muggy in Hiroshima. People go to work. Children hurry to school. Some soldiers and women go out with baskets to shop. A peddler wheels his cart carefully through the crowd. A colonel exercises his white horse. There are about 320,000 people in Hiroshima that morning.

Two sisters walk sleepily in the crowd. Riko is sixteen and her little sister, Sachi, is twelve. They have stayed up all night hiding from American bombers. Up until now, though, the airplanes have always bombed other cities. Some people believe that Hiroshima is so beautiful that the Americans have decided to spare it.

✂ **cut along dotted line**

- -

Checker directions:

Follow along as the passage is read. Make a dot under each word the reader misses. Show the reader the missed words. Erase the dots and repeat for each reading.

from Hiroshima

It is only seven o'clock in the morning, but the air is already hot and muggy in Hiroshima. People go to work. Children hurry to school. Some soldiers and women go out with baskets to shop. A peddler wheels his cart carefully through the crowd. A colonel exercises his white horse. There are about 320,000 people in Hiroshima that morning.

Two sisters walk sleepily in the crowd. Riko is sixteen and her little sister, Sachi, is twelve. They have stayed up all night hiding from American bombers. Up until now, though, the airplanes have always bombed other cities. Some people believe that Hiroshima is so beautiful that the Americans have decided to spare it.

Use this chart for Timed Readings and Repeated Readings.

Reading	1	2	3	4	5
Time (minutes/seconds)					
Words Missed					

Focus Skills

COMPREHENSION
Patterns of Organization

LITERATURE
Biography

VOCABULARY
Context Clues

SkillBuilder Copymasters

 Reading Comprehension:
1 Patterns of Organization, Part I
p. T563
2 Patterns of Organization, Part II
p. T564

 Vocabulary:
3 Context Clues p. T565
4 Words to Know p. T566

Assessment

 5 Selection Test p. T567

Readability Scores

DRP	LEXILE	DALE-CHALL
55	750	5.2

For English Learners

Since Anne Frank's diary has been translated into many languages, you may want to have students read it in their first language to learn more about Anne and her life. You also may want to discuss the following terms with students before they read this biography: *Anne Frank, Adolf Hitler, Nazis, Jews, Holocaust.*

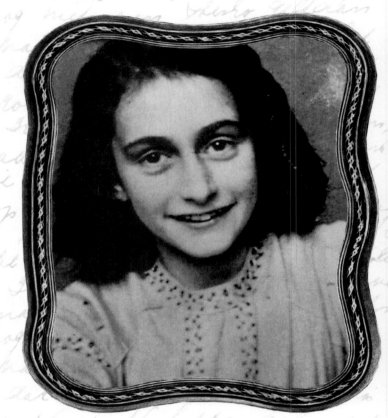

from

Anne Frank:
Child of the Holocaust

by Gene Brown

Vocabulary Strategy: Preteaching

Context Clues Remind students that the **context clues** surrounding an unknown word can help them understand what the word means. Explain that in this selection the context clues often give a word's meaning, or they give the opposite meaning.

Anne was probably the most famous teenager of the last century. Here's a look at her life before she wrote the diary that moved the world.

Connect to Your Life

Think of news stories about people who become heroes. What kinds of situations make heroes out of everyday people? What qualities did the people show?

Key to the Biography

Anne Frank grew up during the 1930s and 1940s. The Nazi Party rose to power in Germany at the same time. Jewish people became the main targets of Nazi threats. Anne's family tried to escape by hiding in a secret place. While she was there, she kept a diary. The family hid successfully for two years. Then the Franks were arrested, and all were sent to prison camps. Only Anne's father survived. He published Anne's diary in 1947.

As you read the biography, notice the words in dark type. They are important words to remember about this time in history. They are defined in the text.

Vocabulary Preview

Words to Know

tolerant   torture
secure   synagogues

 **Reading Coach
CD-ROM selection**

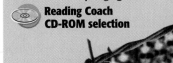

Connect to Your Life

This biography includes several examples that illustrate the kind of person Anne Frank was. To help students fully appreciate her personality, you may want to have them begin a **Character Profile** for Anne that they can fill in as they read. See page T665 for instructions and page T673 for copymaster.

Key to the Biography

This biography gives excellent historical background about what led up to World War II. It also easily defines many historic terms that students should learn. Suggest that they keep a list of the vocabulary words in bold that are defined in the selection, starting with *Holocaust,* which is mentioned on page 408. They will have several chances during reading to make time lines of events.

Vocabulary Preview

Words to Know
   tolerant *adj.* respectful of the beliefs or customs of others
   secure *adj.* free from danger
   torture *n.* the causing of physical pain as punishment
   synagogues *n.* places of worship for Jews

   For direct instruction on Words to Know, see page T562.

Building Background

Thanks to Anne Frank's writings, the world knows much about the time that she and seven others spent hiding from the Nazis. What became of Anne after she left the secret Annex is not as well documented, however. On August 4, 1944, the *Grüne Polizei* (Security Police) raided the Annex after receiving an anonymous tip. After Anne and the others were arrested, they were sent to the concentration camp at Auschwitz in Poland. After a month there, Anne and Margot were transferred to Bergen-Belsen in Germany. Both girls contracted typhus and died in March 1945—just weeks before the camp was liberated by the British on April 15. Otto Frank was the only Annex resident to survive the camps. He died in 1980.

Write the following sentences on the board, and have students tell whether the context around each underlined word gives the word's meaning or its opposite meaning—or both.

  1. The Nazis also built <u>concentration camps</u>—large prisons—for those who opposed them.
  2. One out of every four persons in Frankfurt was <u>unemployed.</u> Those still working worried that they might be the next to become jobless.

   For more on Context Clues, see page T562.

FOCUS
Read to discover the different sides of Anne Frank.

Why would anyone want to read about the most private thoughts of a 13-year-old girl? That's what Anne Frank asked herself as she wrote in her dairy in the early 1940s. She was, after all, an ordinary 13-year-old. Her parents didn't seem to understand her. She often couldn't figure out the boys she knew. And she did not care for some of her teachers.

A 10 Anne wasn't even known as a good writer. One of her teachers said that "the compositions that Anne wrote in school were just ordinary, no better than average."

Yet millions of people have read Anne's diary and seen the play and movie based on it. Most were deeply moved. The diary has been translated into many languages, and Anne Frank's name is known all over the world. The place in the Netherlands where she wrote her famous diary is now a museum.

the Netherlands
(nĕ*th*′ ər lăndz)
country near
Germany in Western
Europe, also called
Holland

Anne is famous because she was able to
20 write about a subject for which the world's best writers have been unable to find the right words. She was one of 6 million Jews murdered by the Nazis during World War II. She died in what we now call the
B **"Holocaust."** (The word means a great fire, often used to burn a sacrifice.) Her diary tells of how she and her family hid from the Nazis and tried to keep a little hope alive when much of the world seemed to be going mad.

A THINK IT THROUGH
In what ways is Anne Frank ordinary? In what ways is she special?

FOCUS
Read to find out how Hitler came to power.

Flight from Evil
30 Anne Frank was born in Germany, the country in which the Nazis came to power. Jews had lived in Germany for hundreds of years. Often they were victims of prejudice, much like that faced by some groups such as blacks in the United States.

The family of Otto Frank, Anne's father, had lived in Frankfurt, Germany, for a long time. About 30 thousand Jews lived there—5 percent of the city's people. Only Berlin, the capital, had more Jews than Frankfurt. There was anti-Jewish feeling in Anne's
40 hometown. For example, some restaurants refused to serve Jews. Yet compared with the rest of Germany,

B

Anne as a baby with her father, Otto, and her sister, Margot

COMPREHENSION

FOCUS SKILL: Patterns of Organization

Explain that this biography has two main **patterns of organization.** One pattern is main idea. The writer states the main idea, often in the first sentence, and then gives details to support the idea. In the other pattern, chronological order, events are organized in the order they happened. Explain that other organizational patterns are cause and effect, problem and solution, and compare and contrast.

For direct instruction on Patterns of Organization, see page T561.

A **THINK IT THROUGH** In what ways is Anne Frank ordinary? In what ways is she special? *(She has the ordinary problems of a typical 13-year-old, and her writing is also ordinary. She is special in that because of her diary, her name is known all over the world.)* **description**

B Ask: Where was Anne Frank born? *(in Frankfurt, Germany)* **details**

LITERATURE

FOCUS SKILL: Biography

Remind students that a **biography** is the story of a real person's life as told by someone else. Most biographies tell of important events in that person's life. Biographies are usually written in **chronological order,** or the order in which the events happened.

VOCABULARY

FOCUS SKILL: Context Clues

As students read this selection, remind them to use **context clues**—especially ones that provide definitions or opposite meanings—to figure out any unknown words.

A **ordinary** Students can use the context clues *no better than average* to figure out what *ordinary* means.

B **Holocaust** Students can use the definition in parentheses to understand what *Holocaust* means. Have them add the term to their vocabulary list.

FOR ENGLISH LEARNERS

Help students understand the following expressions and idioms:

Line 6: couldn't figure out the boys
Line 7: did not care for
Line 14: deeply moved
Line 27: tried to keep a little hope alive
Line 29: going mad

C Frankfurt was tolerant. Otto could recall no **anti-Semitic** (anti-Jewish) incidents when he was growing up. By the early 1930s, the city even had a Jewish mayor.

Otto's family did well in the retail department store business and he decided to make it his career too. In 1908, Otto dropped out of college and spent a year in New York, working in
50 Macy's department store. The parents of a friend he had met at school owned the store.

Like other young men his age, Otto served in the German army during World War I. He joined in 1915, became an officer, and won several medals. After the war, he went into business for himself.

A In 1925, Otto married Edith Hollander, whose family was also in business. Their first daughter, Margot, was born the next year. Anne was born in 1929.

60 In that year, the Great Depression began to spread through the United States and Europe. Stores closed, businesses failed, and many people lost their jobs. One out of every four persons in Frankfurt was unemployed. Those still working worried that they might be the next to become jobless.

Hard times made it easier for the Nazis and Adolf Hitler, their leader, to gain support. Many Germans were frightened. They were ready to believe anyone
70 who promised them a better and more secure life. Hitler told them that Germany didn't need freedom. It needed a leader to tell the country's people what to do—
C someone they should obey without question. He said he was that leader.

tolerant
(tŏl′ ər ənt)
adj. respectful of the beliefs or customs of others

Great Depression
period from 1929 to 1941 in which the U.S. economy failed and millions of people were out of work

secure
(sĭ kyŏŏr′)
adj. free from danger

410   Unit 12 Reader's Choice

Adolf Hitler, 1934

Hitler also played on German prejudices. He placed the blame for everything that had gone
80 wrong in their country on the Jews and on other people who were unpopular. These included gypsies, homosexuals, communists, and anyone
D who looked, thought, or acted differently from other Germans. Get rid of these "outsiders," he said, and
90 Germany's problems would go away. Soon, Hitler organized a movement headed by his own **Nazi Party**.

E **THINK IT THROUGH**
How did Hitler gain power in Germany?

FOCUS
Read to see why the German Jews became even more concerned.

The Nazis Take Control
In 1933, when Anne was four years old, the Nazis had almost complete power in Germany. The Franks watched with increasing alarm what the Nazis did. The Nazis quickly moved against their "enemies." When they found books with ideas they didn't like, they burned them. The Nazis also built **concentration camps**—large prisons—for those who opposed them. **D** At first, people sent to these camps simply lost their

from Anne Frank: Child of the Holocaust **411**

COMPREHENSION

C Explain that the Germans had lost World War I. Then ask what historic event made it easier for Hitler and the Nazis to take over and why. *(the Great Depression; many Germans were out of work and were frightened)* **cause and effect**

D Ask students to think of a term that means blaming one group or person for everything that goes wrong. *(scapegoating)* Ask who the scapegoats were for Hitler. *(Jews, gypsies, homosexuals, communists)* **clarifying**

E **THINK IT THROUGH** How did Hitler gain power in Germany? *(He promised the Germans a better life if they obeyed him without question. He also got them to believe that their problems were caused by the Jews and other "outsiders.")* **cause and effect**

LITERATURE

A Remind students that biographies are usually written in time, or chronological, order. Have them make a time line that shows the major events described in lines 46–59. *(1908: Otto Frank moves to New York and works at Macy's. 1915: Otto serves in the German army. 1925: Otto marries Edith Hollander. 1926: Margot Frank is born. 1929: Anne Frank is born.)* **chronological order**

VOCABULARY

C **anti-Semitic** Students can use the definition following this word to understand its meaning.

D **concentration camps** Ask students to think about how the meaning of *concentration* led to its use as a term. *(many people concentrated into small area)* Have students add the word to their list of terms.

FOR ENGLISH LEARNERS

Help students understand the following expressions and idioms:

Line 48: dropped out of college
Line 52: served in the German army
Line 54: won several medals
Line 55: went into business for himself
Line 74: obey without question
Line 76: played on German prejudices

100 freedom. Later, the concentration camps would become scenes of torture and mass killing.

torture
(tôr′ chər)
n. the causing of physical pain as punishment

E Jews got the worst treatment in Germany. They could no longer hold government jobs. All Jewish officials, like the mayor of Frankfurt, had to resign. Non-Jewish Germans were ordered not to go to Jewish doctors or hire Jewish lawyers. In the schools, Jewish students were segregated—put in separate classes. Jewish teachers were fired. Jews who 110 owned stores had to mark their windows with the word "Jew." Before long, the Nazis forced Jews to sell their businesses to non-Jews. These rules affected anyone who had even one Jewish grandparent.

REREAD
What is the main idea of this paragraph? What details support it?
F

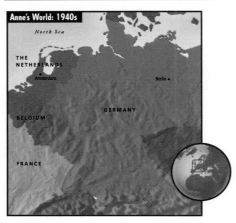

G Anne's World: 1940s

North Sea

THE NETHERLANDS

Amsterdam

Berlin

BELGIUM

GERMANY

FRANCE

412 Unit 12 Reader's Choice

Few Germans spoke out against these new rules. Many believed Hitler's lies about the Jews. Those who didn't were afraid of being sent to a concentration camp if they said what they thought. Even the Catholic and Protestant churches did little to stop the 120 Nazis.

F The Nazis used the Gestapo—their secret police—to scare people. The Gestapo was brutal and had spies everywhere. The Nazis **H** also frightened people with their **storm troopers**— party members who dressed like soldiers and acted like thugs. They began to beat Jews in the street. **G**

Gestapo
(gə stä′ pō)

Otto decided not to wait. He feared that conditions in Germany would get worse. Otto made up his mind to get his family out of the country. He sent Edith and 130 his daughters to live in the German city of Aachen, where his wife's family lived. Meanwhile, he got a job working for a company in Amsterdam, Holland, in the Netherlands, a country bordering Germany. About 90,000 Jews lived in Amsterdam. From there, Otto sent for his family.

Why did Otto Frank choose the Netherlands? It was close to home and, in many ways, like the area from which his family came. Jews had been treated fairly well there for many centuries, making Otto 140 think it would be a safe place. He could not have been more wrong.

I **THINK IT THROUGH**
Why didn't other Germans try to stop the Nazis?

COMPREHENSION

F **REREAD** What is the main idea of this paragraph? What details support it? *(Main idea: Jews got the worst treatment in Germany. Details: They couldn't hold government jobs, non-Jews couldn't go to Jewish doctors or lawyers, Jewish students were segregated, Jewish teachers were fired, Jewish store-owners had to mark their windows and eventually sell their businesses to non-Jews.)* **main idea and details**

G Ask: Which countries shown on the map surround Germany? *(the Netherlands, Belgium, and France)* **understanding visuals**

H **Reciprocal Teaching: Evaluating** This passage is a good one for you to model the Active Reading Strategy of evaluating.
Teacher Modeling You could say, *When I read this paragraph (lines 121–126), I can't believe*

how terrible this Gestapo was. They terrified everybody by using spies and by behaving like criminals. No wonder the Germans were so afraid of them. Why did they let the Gestapo get so powerful?

Student Modeling Then ask a student to read the following paragraph (lines 127–135) and evaluate Otto's decision to leave Germany. Based on the conditions discussed earlier, the student will probably say that leaving was a wise idea. **evaluating**

I **THINK IT THROUGH** Why didn't other Germans try to stop the Nazis? *(Many believed Hitler's lies; others were afraid of concentration camps, the Gestapo, and the storm troopers.)* **cause and effect**

VOCABULARY

E **segregated** Students can use the definition that follows the word to understand the meaning.

F **Gestapo** Tell students to notice that the definition of this word is set off by dashes. They should add the word to their list.

G **storm troopers** Students can use the definition that follows the word to understand the meaning.

FOR ENGLISH LEARNERS

Help students understand the following expressions and idioms:
Line 101: mass killing
Line 104: hold government jobs
Line 115: spoke out against
Line 125: party members who . . . acted like thugs
Line 128: made up his mind

FOCUS
Look for details that tell you more about what Anne was like.

Another Escape

Anne Frank grew up when terrible things were beginning to happen in the world. But her parents could still give her and Margot a loving and secure family life. Anne had good memories of her early years. For example, she could recall many of her parents' friends coming to visit on Sundays, and the wonderful smell of the coffee and cake that was served.

150 Anne was a slim girl with dark brown hair, intense dark eyes, and dimples. Visitors to the Frank home were likely to be greeted by the sight of her carrying her cat, Moortje. The cat's hind legs almost touched the floor as little Anne struggled to hold him.

Anne's sister, Margot, got better grades in school and was the more serious of the two. Anne called her "brainy." Margot was well-behaved and kept her clothes and other things neat. Anne was messier with her belongings. She also had high spirits. People

160 remembered her strong personality, which sometimes got her in trouble at school.

Margot was quiet and thoughtful, while Anne liked to say whatever was on her mind. This trait could be refreshing and honest, although at times some people found it thoughtless. Once, Anne told one of her parents' friends that his eyes were like a cat's. The friend found that very funny. But the other adults in the room considered it impolite for Anne to talk that way to an adult.

170 Anne liked attention, and she often got it by making people laugh. When she was only four years old, her mother wrote to a friend that Anne was like "a little comedian." Later, Anne loved to perform in school plays. She also enjoyed doing imitations— whether of a friend, a teacher, or even a cat.

By the time she was in grade school, Anne had many friends. Anne and her friends liked to play pingpong and a game similar to hopscotch. They also did handstands against the wall in a nearby 180 playground. Anne was a bit clumsy, though, and

LOOK CLOSELY What do these pictures reveal to you about Anne's personality?

COMPREHENSION

J In what ways was Margot Frank different from Anne? *(Margot got better grades, was more serious, and was neater than Anne. She was also quiet and thoughtful, while Anne was outspoken and said whatever was on her mind.)* **compare and contrast**

LITERATURE

B Point out that up to this time in the biography, the readers have been learning about the historical setting of Germany. This has helped put Anne's life in context. Now ask students what the biography is focusing on and why. *(Anne's childhood and her personality; readers need to learn about her as a person)* **biography**

C What did Anne do to get attention? *(Anne was like a little comedian. She loved to perform and enjoyed doing imitations of a friend, teacher, or even a cat.)* **character**

VOCABULARY

H **refreshing** Students can use context to figure out that *thoughtless* means the opposite of *refreshing and honest*. **context clue**

I **pingpong, hopscotch, handstands, playground** Point out these four compound words in two lines, all dealing with games and playing. Have students separate the compound words into their base words and explain their meanings. **compound words**

FOR ENGLISH LEARNERS

Help students understand the following expressions and idioms:

Line 152: likely to be greeted by the sight of her
Line 159: had high spirits
Line 174: doing imitations

sometimes fell over. No matter what Anne and her friends played, they usually went out for ice cream after the game.

J The mother of a friend of Anne's once said that, even when young, Anne seemed to "know who she was." She meant that Anne had a good sense of herself, that she was mature for her age. Yet Anne could also be childish. Sometimes she swung from one way of behaving to the other: an adult one minute, a 190 child the next.

Anne had strong opinions about the people she knew. She thought that some of the other students in her school were "absolute cuckoos," and that a few of her teachers were "freaks." Her math teacher thought that she talked too much in class. To punish her, he made her write a composition about why she couldn't be quiet. That didn't silence her, so he next told her to write about what her constant talking reminded him of: "quack, quack, 200 quack." She won him over by writing, instead, a funny poem about talking.

K | REREAD
What does this incident show about Anne?

At age 11, most girls her age were still playing children's games. Anne and her friends, however, were already "giggling over the boys," according to one girl who knew her. Anne was very aware of her effect on the boys around her. They constantly flirted with her.

As she approached her teenage years, Anne became very interested in how she looked. She and her friends 210 often read fashion magazines. They thought of her as "stylish."

One day, a girl who knew Anne was at the local dressmaker's shop with her mother. The dressmaker was in the fitting room with a customer. "It would

look better with larger shoulder pads," they heard the customer say behind the curtain, "and the hemline should be just a little higher, don't you think?" The girl was surprised when the curtains parted and out came Anne Frank. She was the person who seemed to 220 have known just what she wanted, sounding, for a moment, like an adult.

In ordinary times, Anne might have looked forward to being a teenager much like any other girl. But these were not ordinary times. Conditions kept getting worse in Germany throughout the 1930s, especially for the Jews. Before long, the Nazis were threatening to bring their system of hate, fear, and terror to other countries around the world.

L **THINK IT THROUGH**
In your own words, summarize the kind of childhood Anne had in ordinary times.

FOCUS
By the mid-1930s, the rights of Jews in Germany began to disappear. Find out the different ways in which conditions changed.

Life in Germany Grows Worse

K 230 In 1935, Germany took all political rights away from its Jewish citizens. It was as if they were no longer Germans, but foreigners in their own country. Jews could no longer marry non-Jews. Many Jews, fearing for their lives, left Germany. These people had to leave behind most of their property.

In 1938, all Jewish students were ordered out of German schools. At the end of that year, the Nazis staged mass arrests of Jews, sending 30,000 to concentration camps. They also encouraged mobs to

---

COMPREHENSION

K **REREAD** What does this incident show about Anne? *(She had a good sense of humor and won people over with it. She wasn't afraid to be herself.)*
characterization LITERATURE

L **THINK IT THROUGH** In your own words, summarize the kind of childhood Anne had in ordinary times. *(Anne's high spirits and strong personality often got her into trouble, both at home and at school. She talked a lot, liked attention, and loved to perform. She had lots of friends and had strong opinions about them. She had a good sense of who she was and was conscious of boys and fashion at an early age.)*
summarizing

VOCABULARY

J **mature** Have students notice the signal word that shows that *mature* means the opposite of *childish.* (yet)

K **citizens** Have students read the next sentence to see the contrasting clues. They should conclude that *citizens* are the opposite of *foreigners.*

FOR ENGLISH LEARNERS

Help students understand the following expressions and idioms:

Line 186: had a good sense of herself
Line 193: absolute cuckoos
Line 194: freaks
Line 200: won him over
Line 204: giggling over the boys
Line 207: flirted with her
Line 218: the curtains parted

attack Jews throughout the country—in
240　their homes, shops, and synagogues . One
hundred Jews were killed as the mobs left a
path of destruction—200 synagogues and
5,000 stores were destroyed. There was so
much broken glass afterwards on the streets that the
attack became known as "Crystal Night," although
the violence lasted several days.

synagogues
(sĭn' ə gŏgz')
n. places of
worship for Jews

The Nazis forced Jews to
wear a yellow Star of David
on the outside of their
250　clothing. In this way, Jews
could be easily recognized.
This meant that there was
almost no place in Germany
where Jews could be safe.

People all over the world
were horrified. There were
complaints to the German
government, but they did no
good. Many Jews remaining in

In 1941, Hitler's government forced
Jews to wear this image in public.

260　Germany now tried to get out. Two of Anne Frank's
aunts left for the United States. Anne's grandmother
left Aachen and went to Amsterdam to live with
Anne's family. By 1939, half the Jews who had lived
in Germany had left.

Most of the Jews still living in Germany could have
been saved, but many couldn't leave. They had
nowhere to go. Other countries, including the
Netherlands and the United States, only took in a
certain number of new people from other nations.
270　They might bend the rules a little for those who were
in danger, like the German Jews, but not much.

The countries that Jews wanted to move to said that
they were worried about not having enough jobs for
all the newcomers. Or they said they didn't have
enough housing—any number of reasons
were given. Often the reasons had more
to do with prejudice. Jews weren't wanted
because they were Jews. Anti-Semitism
was everywhere, not just in Germany.

REREAD
Why didn't the
countries take
more Jewish
newcomers?

280　Throughout the 1930s, the Nazis said that Germans
needed more "room to live." In 1939, when Anne
was 10, Hitler took direct action to obtain more land.
His armies invaded Poland. Great Britain and France
came to Poland's defense. When they declared war on
Germany, they officially began World War II.

At first, the war did not touch the Dutch, as the
people of the Netherlands were called. Until 1940, the
Netherlands seemed a safe place for Jews—compared
to much of the rest of Europe. There were 140,000
290　Jews living in the Netherlands. About 24,000 of them
had fled from Germany. There was anti-
Semitism, but the Franks encountered little
of it. That's why Anne could lead a fairly
normal life.

encountered
(ĕn koun' tərd)
faced

THINK IT THROUGH
Give details about daily life for Jews in Germany. Contrast this
with life for Jews in the Netherlands.

FOCUS
Find out how life got worse for Jews in the Netherlands.

Amsterdam Becomes Dangerous
On May 10, 1940, the hopes for a peaceful life in
their new country were dashed. Otto Frank was at his

COMPREHENSION

REREAD Why didn't the countries
take more Jewish newcomers?
*(Many of them said they were wor-
ried about job and housing short-
ages, but the underlying reason
was often anti-Semitism.)* **cause
and effect**

THINK IT THROUGH Give details
about daily life for Jews in
Germany. Contrast this with life
for Jews in the Netherlands.
*(Germany: In 1935, the Jews had
their political rights taken away;
they couldn't marry non-Jews; they
were attacked, killed, and sent to
concentration camps; they were
forced to wear a Star of David on
their clothing; most couldn't get
out of Germany. Netherlands: Until
1940, the Netherlands was a safe
place for the Jews. The Franks
encountered little anti-Semitism
and led a fairly normal life.)*
compare and contrast

LITERATURE

Make a time line that shows the
major events described in lines
229–264. *(1935: Germany takes
all political rights away from the
Jews. 1938: Jewish students are
forced out of German schools;
30,000 Jews are sent to concentration camps; Crystal Night occurs.
1939: Half of Germany's Jews have
left the country.)* **chronological
order**

VOCABULARY

Crystal Night Tell students to
look for clues within the sentence. Explain that sometimes a
sentence before or after the word
can also provide context clues. In
this case, *Crystal Night* became
known as the attack that left
behind so much shattered glass
from the Jewish stores and synagogues that were destroyed.

the Dutch Tell students that
context clues define the word
immediately after it is used.

FOR ENGLISH LEARNERS

Help students understand the following expressions and idioms:

Line 270: bend the rules
Line 282: took direct action
Line 284: declared war
Line 286: did not touch the Dutch
Line 295: hopes . . . were dashed

office that day and his face turned pale as he heard the report on the radio: the Germans had attacked the Netherlands. The Dutch fought back, but they were 300 quickly beaten. It was over in four days.

A deep shadow was suddenly cast over Anne's life—and over that of everyone she knew. The Germans used the Dutch Nazi party to help them rule the Netherlands. Gradually, the new government began to repeat what was happening in Germany.

Jews could not teach or work for the Dutch government. They couldn't go to public places like movies and libraries. Dutch Nazis began to attack Jews on the street. They also began to arrest some 310 Jews and send them to concentration camps. Soon the Nazis were regularly arresting large numbers of Jews on the street and taking them to prison.

Beginning in 1942, Jews, including children like Anne, had to wear a yellow Star of David on the left side of their coat. They had to wear the star even when they came to open their front door. When many non-Jews began to wear it in sympathy, the Germans arrested them. Dutch workers also protested the treatment of the Jews by 320 going out on strike. The Nazis broke the strike after a few days.

REREAD
How did the Dutch people try to fight back?

Jews weren't allowed to go anywhere with their non-Jewish Dutch friends. They also had a curfew: they had to be indoors by 8:00 at night.

It was hard enough being young and dealing with the usual criticism a child expects from her parents. Now Anne's mother and father had very real reasons to be concerned for her safety. One night, Anne was walking with a boy and came in a few minutes after 330 eight, making her father very angry. She wasn't used

German citizens salute a parade of German troops.

to such toughness from him, and he didn't like being so cross with her. But he knew she could have been arrested.

THINK IT THROUGH
Summarize how life changed for Jews in the Netherlands. In addition, describe how Anne's life changed.

FOCUS
Discover what Anne received that made her hardships a little easier to take.

A Wonderful Birthday Present

In the middle of this tense time, on June 12th, 1942, Anne turned 13. Her father's birthday present to her was a diary—a book with blank pages and a red-checkered hard cover. In it she could write about what happened in her life each day. She also could

---

COMPREHENSION

O **REREAD** How did the Dutch people try to fight back? *(They began wearing yellow stars in sympathy, and they went on strike to protest the Germans' treatment of the Jews.)* **clarifying**

P What does the image on page 421 show about the way German citizens felt about German troops? *(By saluting the troops, the German citizens show that they have respect and admiration for them.)* **understanding visuals**

Q **THINK IT THROUGH** Summarize how life changed for Jews in the Netherlands. In addition, describe how Anne's life changed. *(In 1940 the Germans attacked the Netherlands and began running it like they ran Germany. Again, Jews couldn't teach, hold government jobs, or go to public places; they were attacked, arrested, and sent to camps; they had to wear yellow stars; they had an 8:00 P.M. curfew.*

Anne's life became more restricted as her parents feared for her safety.) **summarizing**

VOCABULARY

N **curfew** Students can use the clue "they had to be indoors by 8:00 at night" to figure out what a *curfew* is.

FOR ENGLISH LEARNERS

Help students understand the following expressions and idioms:

Line 297: his face turned pale
Line 317: in sympathy
Line 320: going out on strike; broke the strike
Line 331: being so cross with her

record her thoughts and feelings about anything or
340 anybody.

R In her first entry in the diary, Anne gave the book a
name: "Kitty." She wrote that she and the diary
would be "pals." Anne felt that she needed a friend
with whom she could share her serious thoughts, and
the diary would be it. She couldn't really do that with
any of her family or friends. Kitty, unlike others in her
life, would always be patient and willing to listen.

It would have been hard for Anne to write only
about personal things in her diary. Too many horrible
350 events were happening in the outside world. The
Nazis were rounding up Jews as if they were animals.
One Dutch woman passing a home for Jewish
orphans said she saw "the Germans were loading the
children, who ranged in ages from babies to eight-
year-olds, on trucks. When they did not move fast
enough the Nazis picked them up, by an arm, a leg,
E the hair, and threw them into the trucks."

What were Jews like the Franks to do? Everyone
had to have an identification card. Besides, most
360 Dutch had blond hair and blue eyes. Jews, like Anne,
were likely to have dark hair and dark eyes. Their
appearance made them stand out.

As a result, many Jews went into hiding. They
found Dutch non-Jews who had attics, basements, or
extra rooms in which they could stay. The Dutch who
hid Jews faced arrest if they were found out.

No Place to Run

By the beginning of the summer of 1942, Anne's
parents were thinking of hiding themselves and their
children from the Nazis. They began to move some of
370 their belongings to the houses of non-Jewish friends,

who would keep them safe until after the war. On
July 5, Otto told Anne that they might have to hide.

That afternoon, the Franks sped up their plan.
Margot received a notice requiring that she report for
forced labor in Germany. The Nazis used many young
people, including Dutch non-Jews, to do work that
had been done by Germans now serving in the army.
If 16-year-old Margot didn't report, she would be
380 arrested. If she did go, the Germans would make her
a slave.

That settled it. Otto had already
picked out a hiding place. It was the
rooms used for storage, called the
O "**Annex**," above the office he managed.
He had talked to one of his workers, a
Dutch woman named | Miep Gies |, about
helping him and his family remain safe
there. She agreed to help. She told a few
other workers at the office who promised to keep the
390 Franks' hiding place a secret. They also would bring
the family food and anything else they needed until
the war ended.

> **REREAD**
> What event
> forces the Franks
> to go into
> hiding?

> **Miep Gies**
> (mēp gēs)

These are two pages from Anne's diary.

COMPREHENSION

R Think about Anne and what is
happening in her life. Why was a
diary a perfect birthday present
for her? *(Possible answer: She had
just turned 13. Given her inner
feelings, her outer circumstances,
and the fact that she loved to talk,
a diary was a perfect "friend," a
perfect place for her to write down
all the things she couldn't share
with anyone else.)* **drawing
conclusions**

S **REREAD** What event forces the
Franks to go into hiding? *(Margot
received a notice to report for
forced labor in Germany. If she
didn't go, she'd be arrested; if she
did, she'd be made a slave.)* **cause
and effect**

LITERATURE

E Point out that the writer included
a quote from an eyewitness.
What does this add to the biography? *(adds authenticity and
another viewpoint)* **biography**

VOCABULARY

O **Annex** Students can use context
to figure out that the *Annex* was
the name of the rooms used for
storage above Otto's office.
Annex can mean "an addition to
a building."

FOR ENGLISH LEARNERS

Help students understand the following expressions and idioms:

Line 351: rounding up
Line 362: stand out
Line 363: went into hiding
Line 366: if they were found out
Line 375: forced labor
Line 381: That settled it

The Franks were to be joined in their hiding place by another Jewish family, Mr. van Daan and his wife and son. Mr. van Daan worked with Otto Frank.

Margot was in the most danger, so she went to the hiding place immediately. Anne and her parents soon followed. (Anne's grandmother had died by this time.) The van Daans came a week later.

400 Anne did not have much time to get ready, and she couldn't carry many of her belongings to the Annex because it would look suspicious. She put just a few items in her school bag. The first thing she packed was her diary.

> **REREAD**
> Why do you think she packs the diary first?

T

It was a warm, rainy Monday morning, but Anne wore several layers of clothing to sneak clothes into the hideout without drawing attention.

410 Anne could not say goodbye to her friends because the family's secret might have gotten out. Once safe in the hiding place, Anne wrote a letter to one of her pals explaining what had happened, but it was never mailed.

Otto Frank said that he and his family were "disappearing." Anne thought of it as a 420 "vacation." Later, she would call it an "adventure." As Miep Gies saw it, "They had simply closed the door of their lives and vanished from Amsterdam."

This bookcase hid the entrance to the Annex.

424 Unit 12 Reader's Choice

Through Her Diary, Anne Lives On

Over the next two years, Anne's diary played a major part in her life. In it, she described what happened each day in the Annex. She poured out her feelings about life in a crowded, secret place. She described fears of being discovered. Often, Anne's writings were like any teenager's. Just as often, they were filled with wisdom.

It was Miep Gies who found the diary after the family's 1944 arrest. She saved it. "I was hoping she would still come back and that I would be able to give it to her," Miep once said. "I wanted to see her smile at me." Miep gave it to Anne's father. He was the only family member to survive the concentration camps.

The diary was first published as *Anne Frank: Diary of a Young Girl* in 1947. Because of Anne's diary, the world could view a time of great suffering through the eyes of one very real person. A play based on the diary, called *The Diary of Anne Frank*, was written in 1955. Read the diary or the play. Discover more about Anne Frank's amazing life.

U

THINK IT THROUGH

1. What conditions forced the Frank family to go into hiding?
2. Why do you think the author gives so many details about Anne's childhood?
3. Think about Anne's personality. How do you think she handled being in hiding? Support your opinion with details.
4. Imagine that you are Anne. How would you react to what is happening around you?

from Anne Frank: Child of the Holocaust **425**

COMPREHENSION

T **REREAD** Why do you think she packs the diary first? *(because it was a gift from her father, and because the diary had become the "friend" to whom she confided everything she thought and experienced)* **making inferences**

U **THINK IT THROUGH**

1. What conditions forced the Frank family to go into hiding? *(the Germans' terrible treatment of the Jews in the Netherlands, and the fact that Margot had received a notice to report for forced labor in Germany)* **cause and effect**

2. Why do you think the author gives so many details about Anne's childhood? *(Possible answers: to show what kind of person she was before the war; to show that she was no different from most other teenagers; to show how her life was changed by the war)* **author's purpose**

3. Think about Anne's personality. How do you think she handled being in hiding? Support your opinion with details. *(Accept any reasonable answers. Students may point out that Anne's humor and liveliness helped her cope while she was in hiding. Students may also say that her diary gave her a way to vent about the problems she encountered. Her energy must have made confinement very difficult.)* **making judgments**

4. Imagine that you are Anne. How would you react to what is happening around you? *(Students' responses will vary depending on their personalities and the extent of their knowledge of Anne's situation.)* **drawing conclusions**

Review the **Character Profiles** that students filled out while reading this biography.

VOCABULARY

FOR ENGLISH LEARNERS

Help students understand the following expressions and idioms:

Line 408: drawing attention
Line 411: secret might have gotten out

RETEACHING

If students need more help understanding **Context Clues,** use pages T608–T611.

Direct Instruction
for SkillBuilder Copymasters

---

1. COMPREHENSION

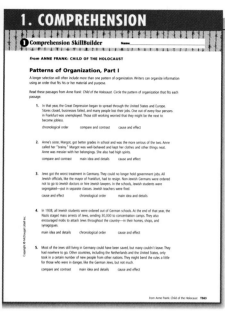

Patterns of Organization, Part I

Direct Instruction Remind students that there are different ways to organize information in any piece of writing. The way the ideas or facts are arranged is called the **pattern of organization.** Explain that, for any particular piece of writing and its special purpose, one pattern will work better than others, or two or three patterns may be needed.

Briefly discuss these four major patterns of organization, and ask students to suggest when they might use each of them in their writing:

• **Chronological order** The writer describes events in the order in which they happen or happened.

• **Main idea and details** All the sentences in a paragraph or a group of paragraphs relate to a single main idea. Every detail tells more about the main idea.

• **Cause and effect order** The writer describes an event (the cause) that brings about one or more events (the effect).

• **Compare and contrast** The writer organizes information point by point or subject by subject to discuss the similarities and differences of each.

> **Comprehension SkillBuilder Answer Key:**
> **1.** *cause and effect*
> **2.** *compare and contrast*
> **3.** *main idea and details*
> **4.** *chronological order*
> **5.** *main idea and details*

---

2. COMPREHENSION

Patterns of Organization, Part II

Direct Instruction Remind students that the way the ideas or facts are arranged in a piece of writing is called the **pattern of organization.** Tell them that the two patterns used most often are chronological (time) order and main idea and details. Have students describe each of these patterns.

> **Comprehension SkillBuilder Answer Key:**
> **1.** *main idea and details*
> **2.** *chronological order*
> **3.** *chronological order*
> **4.** *main idea and details*

3. VOCABULARY

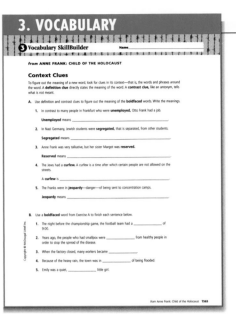

Context Clues

Direct Instruction Remind students that if they do not know the meaning of a new word, they should look for context clues. The context is the sentence or paragraph in which a word is found. Give students these hints on how to find the following types of context clues:

- **Definition clues:** Look for words and phrases such as *is, which is, who is, that is,* and *in other words.* Sometimes punctuation marks such as commas, dashes, and parentheses are used to signal definition clues. Example: The students <u>tallied</u>—counted—the votes.

- **Contrast clues:** Look for these key words: *although, but, however, yet, on the other hand, different from,* and *in contrast.* They signal that the writer is going to give a hint of the meaning of the new word by showing a contrast of things or ideas. A contrast clue helps the reader figure out what the word means by telling the opposite of the word. Example: Most of my relatives lived normal lives, while Aunt Nora, on the other hand, was quite <u>eccentric.</u>

Vocabulary SkillBuilder Answer Key:

A.
1. *not having a job*
2. *separated*
3. *not talkative*
4. *a time after which certain people are not allowed on the streets*
5. *danger*

B.
1. *curfew*
2. *segregated*
3. *unemployed*
4. *jeopardy*
5. *reserved*

4. WORDS TO KNOW

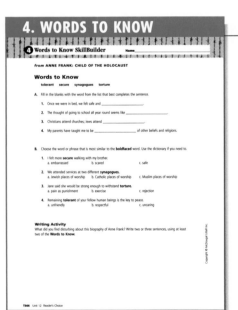

Words to Know

Direct Instruction As you introduce the **Words to Know,** point out how they are related to Latin and Greek words.

- **tolerant,** from the Latin *tolerāre,* "to bear"
- **secure,** from the Latin *sē-,* "without" + *cūra,* "care"
- **torture,** from the Latin *torquēre,* "to twist"

- **synagogue** + -s = *synagogues,* also spelled "synagog," from the Greek *sun-* "together" + *agein,* "to lead"

Writing Activity Have volunteers read their sentences aloud.

Words to Know SkillBuilder Answer Key:
A. 1. *secure* **2.** *torture* **3.** *synagogues* **4.** *tolerant*
B. 1. *c* **2.** *a* **3.** *a* **4.** *b*

5. SELECTION TEST

Selection Test Answer Key:
A. 1. *Germany* **2.** *Nazis* **3.** *Netherlands* **4.** *attention* **5.** *Margot*
   6. *thirteenth* **7.** *Kitty* **8.** *arrested* **9.** *Annex*
B. *Possible response: Crystal Night became known as the attack that left behind so much shattered glass from the Jewish-owned stores and synagogues that were destroyed.*

from **ANNE FRANK: CHILD OF THE HOLOCAUST**

Patterns of Organization, Part I

A longer selection will often include more than one pattern of organization. Writers can organize information using an order that fits his or her material and purpose.

Read these passages from *Anne Frank: Child of the Holocaust*. Circle the pattern of organization that fits each passage.

1. In that year, the Great Depression began to spread through the United States and Europe. Stores closed, businesses failed, and many people lost their jobs. One out of every four persons in Frankfurt was unemployed. Those still working worried that they might be the next to become jobless.

    chronological order   compare and contrast   cause and effect

2. Anne's sister, Margot, got better grades in school and was the more serious of the two. Anne called her "brainy." Margot was well-behaved and kept her clothes and other things neat. Anne was messier with her belongings. She also had high spirits.

    compare and contrast   main idea and details   cause and effect

3. Jews got the worst treatment in Germany. They could no longer hold government jobs. All Jewish officials, like the mayor of Frankfurt, had to resign. Non-Jewish Germans were ordered not to go to Jewish doctors or hire Jewish lawyers. In the schools, Jewish students were segregated—put in separate classes. Jewish teachers were fired.

    cause and effect   chronological order   main idea and details

4. In 1938, all Jewish students were ordered out of German schools. At the end of that year, the Nazis staged mass arrests of Jews, sending 30,000 to concentration camps. They also encouraged mobs to attack Jews throughout the country—in their homes, shops, and synagogues.

    main idea and details   chronological order   cause and effect

5. Most of the Jews still living in Germany could have been saved, but many couldn't leave. They had nowhere to go. Other countries, including the Netherlands and the United States, only took in a certain number of new people from other nations. They might bend the rules a little for those who were in danger, like the German Jews, but not much.

    compare and contrast   main idea and details   cause and effect

from **ANNE FRANK: CHILD OF THE HOLOCAUST**

Patterns of Organization, Part II

A single paragraph should follow a single **pattern of organization,** such as chronological order (also called *sequence*), or main idea and details. However, a longer piece of writing often combines several passages with different organizations.

Read these passages from *Anne Frank: Child of the Holocaust.* Tell how each is organized—by **chronological order** or by **main idea and details.**

1. Why would anyone want to read about the most private thoughts of a 13-year-old girl? That's what Anne Frank asked herself as she wrote in her dairy in the early 1940s. She was, after all, an ordinary 13-year-old. Her parents didn't seem to understand her. She often couldn't figure out the boys she knew. And she did not care for some of her teachers.

    This paragraph of the article is organized using _____.

2. In 1925, Otto married Edith Hollander, whose family was also in business. Their first daughter, Margot, was born the next year. Anne was born in 1929.

    This paragraph of the article is organized using _____.

3. Like other young men his age, Otto served in the German army during World War I. He joined in 1915, became an officer, and won several medals. After the war, he went into business for himself.

    This paragraph of the article is organized using _____.

4. By the time she was in grade school, Anne had many friends. Anne and her friends liked to play pingpong and a game similar to hopscotch. The also did handstands against the wall in a nearby playground.

    This paragraph of the article is organized using _____.

from ANNE FRANK: CHILD OF THE HOLOCAUST

Context Clues

To figure out the meaning of a new word, look for clues in its context—that is, the words and phrases around the word. A **definition clue** directly states the meaning of the word. A **contrast clue,** like an antonym, tells what is not meant.

A. Use definition and contrast clues to figure out the meaning of the **boldfaced** words. Write the meanings.

1. In contrast to many people in Frankfurt who were **unemployed,** Otto Frank had a job.

   Unemployed means _____.

2. In Nazi Germany, Jewish students were **segregated,** that is separated, from other students.

   Segregated means _____.

3. Anne Frank was very talkative, but her sister Margot was **reserved.**

   Reserved means _____.

4. The Jews had a **curfew.** A curfew is a time after which certain people are not allowed on the streets.

   A **curfew** is _____.

5. The Franks were in **jeopardy**—danger—of being sent to concentration camps.

   Jeopardy means _____.

B. Use a **boldfaced** word from Exercise A to finish each sentence below.

1. The night before the championship game, the football team had a _____ of 9:00.

2. Years ago, the people who had smallpox were _____ from healthy people in order to stop the spread of the disease.

3. When the factory closed, many workers became _____.

4. Because of the heavy rain, the town was in _____ of being flooded.

5. Emily was a quiet, _____ little girl.

from ANNE FRANK: CHILD OF THE HOLOCAUST

Words to Know

tolerant   secure   synagogues   torture

A. Fill in the blanks with the word from the list that best completes the sentence.

1. Once we were in bed, we felt safe and _____.

2. The thought of going to school all year round seems like _____.

3. Christians attend churches; Jews attend _____.

4. My parents have taught me to be _____ of other beliefs and religions.

B. Choose the word or phrase that is most similar to the **boldfaced** word. Use the dictionary if you need to.

1. I felt more **secure** walking with my brother.
   a. embarrassed   b. scared   c. safe

2. We attended services at two different **synagogues.**
   a. Jewish places of worship   b. Catholic places of worship   c. Muslim places of worship

3. Jane said she would be strong enough to withstand **torture.**
   a. pain as punishment   b. exercise   c. rejection

4. Remaining **tolerant** of your fellow human beings is the key to peace.
   a. unfriendly   b. respectful   c. uncaring

Writing Activity
What did you find disturbing about this biography of Anne Frank? Write two or three sentences, using at least two of the **Words to Know.**

from ANNE FRANK: CHILD OF THE HOLOCAUST

A. Complete the paragraph by filling in each blank with the appropriate word or phrase from the list.

arrested	Margot	Germany	Kitty	Netherlands
attention	Annex	Nazis	thirteenth	

Anne Frank was born in 1929 in the country of **(1)** _____. By the time Anne was four years old, the **(2)** _____ had gained almost complete power in her country. Anne's father, Otto, decided to move the family to the **(3)** _____ to keep them safe. Although terrible things were happening in the world, Anne's parents tried to give her a loving family life. As Anne grew up, she became a talkative, spirited girl who loved to get **(4)** _____. She was different from her sister, **(5)** _____, who was quieter and got better grades in school. On Anne's **(6)** _____ birthday, her father gave her a diary. Anne called it **(7)** "_____" and wrote all of her thoughts and ideas in it. A few weeks after Anne's birthday, her sister was ordered to report to Germany for forced labor. If she didn't go, she would be **(8)** _____. Once again the Franks were unsafe. They quickly went into hiding in the **(9)** _____ above Otto's office. They could only take a few things with them, but Anne was sure to take her diary. Two year after Anne's death, her father published her writing. Today the whole world knows the story of this "ordinary" girl.

B. In your own words, explain the meaning of the term "Crystal Night."

_____

_____

_____

Focus Skills

COMPREHENSION
Cause and Effect

LITERATURE
Figurative Language

VOCABULARY
Prefixes

SkillBuilder Copymasters

 Reading Comprehension:
1 Cause and Effect p. T583

 Literary Analysis:
2 Figurative Language p. T584

 Vocabulary:
3 Prefixes p. T585
4 Words to Know p. T586

Assessment

 5 Selection Test p. T587

Assessment Booklet
End-of-Year Skills Test Units 1–12

Readability Scores

DRP	LEXILE	DALE-CHALL
54	590	3.1

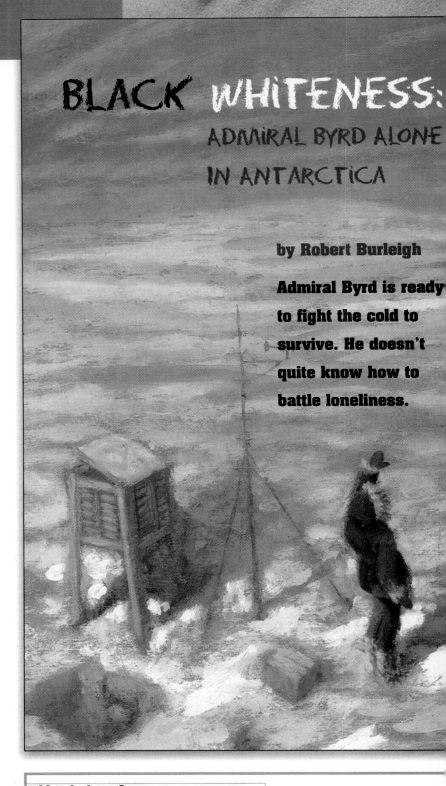

BLACK WHITENESS:
ADMIRAL BYRD ALONE IN ANTARCTICA

by Robert Burleigh

Admiral Byrd is ready to fight the cold to survive. He doesn't quite know how to battle loneliness.

Vocabulary Strategy: Preteaching

Prefixes Remind students that a **prefix** is a word part that can be added to the beginning of a word. Knowing the meanings of some common prefixes can help students understand unfamiliar words. Copy the chart on the next page on chart paper and have students add at least one more word to each line in the last column. Keep the chart on display as a reference during writing activities.

Connect to Your Life

What do you dislike the most about winter? How do you react to cold temperatures? The account you're about to read is set in a place of extremely low temperatures. Think about the coldest temperature you've ever been in. Tell a classmate and discuss your experiences.

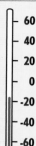

- 60
- 40
- 20
- 0
- -20
- -40
- -60

Key to the Account

Little was known about Antarctica until Admiral Richard Byrd went there. In 1928, Byrd flew to the South Pole. He was part of two major research trips, or *expeditions*. On the first trip, he helped to set up a science research base called Little America. This account deals with Byrd's second expedition, which lasted from 1933 to 1935. During this period, he spent one long winter doing research at a base called Advance Base. He was totally alone. In Antarctica, the winter season is from May to August.

Notice the unusual form of this account. It is presented in the form of stanzas, almost like a poem. The account also includes diary entries. They are based on Byrd's own writings.

Vocabulary Preview

Words to Know

aluminum	paralysis	circulation
cringe	nausea	

Black Whiteness: Admiral Byrd Alone in Antarctica **427**

Connect to Your Life

Do students know how cold temperatures get at the South Pole? Prepare them for reading this selection by having them begin a **K-W-L chart** on Antarctica. See page T664 for instructions and page T666 for copymaster.

Key to the Account

As students read this selection, have them think about why the author chose to write it in stanzas. Also have them think about why he included Admiral Byrd's diary entries.

Vocabulary Preview

Words to Know

aluminum *n.* silvery, lightweight, metallic element
cringe *v.* shrink back, as in fear
paralysis *n.* the loss of the power to move or feel
nausea *n.* sick feeling in the stomach
circulation *n.* the flow of blood through veins

 For direct instruction on Words to Know, see page T582.

Building Background

The continent of Antarctica, which surrounds the South Pole, is the coldest place on earth. On its "hottest" days Antarctica rarely reaches 32°F. Its coldest day, recorded in 1983, reached −128.6°. Between 1928 and 1957, American Admiral Richard Byrd (1888–1957) spent more time exploring Antarctica than any other person in the world. During his first expedition (1928–1930) Byrd established the base he called Little America. His second expedition (1933–1935) is the one described in "Black Whiteness" and in Byrd's own book, *Alone* (1938).

Prefix	Meaning	Examples
dis-	not; the absence of	dislike, disagreement, _____
in-	not; the opposite of	insensitive, inactive, _____
mid-	middle point or part of	midsummer, midnight, _____
mis-	badly; wrongly	misbehave, misunderstand, _____
re-	again; back	reheat, repay, _____
un-	not; the opposite of	unreal, uneven, _____

For more on Prefixes, see page T582.

FOCUS
Read to discover where Admiral Byrd lives at Advance Base, and what he does.

Antarctica. March 1934.
A man stands alone in the snow,
    watching a tractor disappear over the far horizon.

Wherever he turns now,
he sees the flat whiteness roll on forever to meet the
    sky;
he feels the things of the world "shrink away to
    nothing."

B   It is midafternoon,
10 but the sun to the south is already setting.
Night is coming on,
pressing down with its blue-black shadow.

Locations of Research Bases: 1930s

PACIFIC OCEAN

Little America
Advance Base

ANTARCTICA

INDIAN OCEAN

ATLANTIC OCEAN

428   Unit 12   Reader's Choice

He kneels and opens a small hatch.
Below, buried like a cave in the snow,
is the tiny shack where he will live alone for many
    months.
He puts his foot on the first rung of the ladder and
    lowers himself inside.

Admiral Richard Byrd, explorer, moves about his snug
20   house, "tidily built as a watch."
With four strides, he can cross the room:
past the bunk on a wall, a stove, shelves, hooks for
    clothes.

B   His narrow world is a dim one, too:
He has only a flashlight, a lantern, and a small gas
    lamp.
There are three thin windows in the roof;
the ceiling is made of aluminum
to reflect what little light there is.

> **aluminum**
> (ə lōō' mə nəm)
> *n.* silvery,
> lightweight
> metallic element

30 Outside the door is a kind of porch.
The ladder to the hatch rests on it.
Leading away are two long, low tunnels.
It is here that he stores his tons of fuel and food.
His toilet is a hole at the end of one of the tunnels,
    thirty-five feet away.

A The tunnels are dark as dungeons. But in the lantern light, they take on a breathless radiance. Icicles on the roof glisten like candelabra; the walls glow with a sharp, blue nakedness.

> **candelabra**
> (kăn' dl ä' brə)
> metal holder with
> arms for
> candlesticks

Black Whiteness: Admiral Byrd Alone in Antarctica   **429**

COMPREHENSION

FOCUS SKILL: Cause and Effect

Remind students that they can identify the **causes** and **effects** in this selection by asking themselves what happened and what caused it to happen.

 For direct instruction on Cause and Effect, see page T581.

A Say: Look at the map on page 428. What are the names of the two research bases in Antarctica? *(Little America and Advance Base)* **understanding visuals**

B Say: Line 24 calls Admiral Byrd's world a dim one. What detail gives you an idea of how dim it is? *(Possible answer: The ceiling is made of aluminum to reflect what little light there is.)* **details**

LITERATURE

FOCUS SKILL: Figurative Language

Remind students that authors use **figurative language** to help readers picture ordinary things in new ways. The main figures of speech are simile, metaphor, and personification. In a **simile,** the author compares two things using the word *like* or *as*. A **metaphor** is a comparison, too, but it doesn't use *like* or *as*. An author uses **personification** to make an animal or object seem human.

For direct instruction on Figurative Language, see page T581.

Use these questions to encourage literary analysis.

A Make sure students understand that the words on torn paper are taken from Admiral Byrd's diary and are his actual words. Ask why the writer might have included them. *(to add authenticity and to show Byrd's thinking)* Then ask what type of figurative language Byrd uses when describing the icicles. *(simile: icicles glisten like a candelabra)* **figurative language**

VOCABULARY

FOCUS SKILL: Prefixes

Remind students that knowing the meanings of different **prefixes** can help them understand unfamiliar words.

A **disappear** Students can use the meaning of the prefix *dis-* to help them figure out what this word means.

B **midafternoon** Students can use the meaning of the prefix *mid-* to help them figure out what this word means.

FOR ENGLISH LEARNERS

Help students understand the following expressions and idioms:

Line 3: the far horizon
Line 17: first rung of the ladder
Line 20: tidily built as a watch
Line 22: the bunk on a wall

Advance Base is the first inland base in
  Antarctica.
There are eight weather instruments,
  and each day Byrd must record the
40 information they give.
The instruments tell the wind's speed and direction.
They tell the temperature.
They tell the amount of moisture in the air.
Scientists around the world want to know these
  things.

But Admiral Byrd wants to know something else, too.
What is it like to live so completely alone?
In such intense cold and so much darkness?
Can any human being endure that?
50 Can he—Richard Byrd?

inland
(ĭn' lənd)
located some
distance within a
body of land

endure
(ĕn dŏŏr')
survive

C THINK IT THROUGH
What is Admiral Byrd doing at Advance Base? What does he
want to find out?

FOCUS
Read about the conditions under which Admiral Byrd lives.

He keeps a diary where, at the end of each day,
  he writes down his thoughts.
D Writing like this, he tells himself, is like "thinking out
  loud."

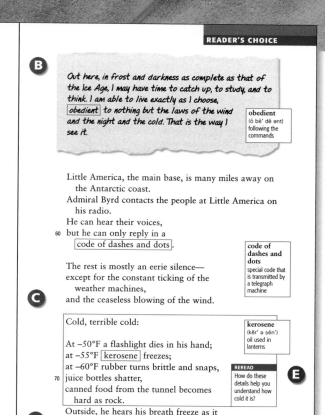

B
Out here, in frost and darkness as complete as that of
the Ice Age, I may have time to catch up, to study, and to
think. I am able to live exactly as I choose,
obedient to nothing but the laws of the wind
and the night and the cold. That is the way I
see it.

obedient
(ō bē' dē ənt)
following the
commands

Little America, the main base, is many miles away on
  the Antarctic coast.
Admiral Byrd contacts the people at Little America on
  his radio.
He can hear their voices,
60 but he can only reply in a
  code of dashes and dots.

The rest is mostly an eerie silence—
except for the constant ticking of the
  weather machines,
C and the ceaseless blowing of the wind.

**code of
dashes and
dots**
special code that
is transmitted by
a telegraph
machine

Cold, terrible cold:

At –50°F a flashlight dies in his hand;
at –55°F kerosene freezes;
at –60°F rubber turns brittle and snaps,
70 juice bottles shatter,
canned food from the tunnel becomes
  hard as rock.
D Outside, he hears his breath freeze as it
  floats away,
making a sound like firecrackers.

kerosene
(kĕr' ə sēn')
oil used in
lanterns

REREAD
How do these
details help you
understand how
cold it is?
E

COMPREHENSION	LITERATURE	VOCABULARY

COMPREHENSION

C THINK IT THROUGH What is
Admiral Byrd doing at Advance
Base? What does he want to find
out? *(He's recording scientific
information about the weather in
Antarctica. He wants to find out
what it's like to be alone in such
intense cold and darkness.)* **details**

D Besides using it as a place for
"thinking out loud," why else do
you think Admiral Byrd might
keep a diary? *(Possible answer: He
wants to record his thoughts, feelings, and actions so that in case
something happens to him, whoever finds his diary will know what
happened.)* **making inferences**

E REREAD How do these details
help you understand how cold it
is? *(Possible answer: The temperatures are below freezing. The
Admiral's supplies freeze, and
his food is as hard as rocks.)*
descriptive details LITERATURE

LITERATURE

B What does Admiral Byrd compare
the frost and darkness of
Antarctica to in his diary? Why?
*(the Ice Age, because he sees no
signs of civilization; it is only ice,
like the time before man came)*
figurative language

C What sense do the images in
this stanza appeal to? *(hearing)*
sensory imagery

D How does the author help you
hear the sound of Byrd's breath
freezing? *(He compares it in a simile to the sound of firecrackers.)*
figurative language

VOCABULARY

FOR ENGLISH LEARNERS

Help students understand the
following:

Line 62: eerie silence
Line 63: constant ticking of the
  weather machines
Line 65: ceaseless blowing of the
  wind

G

C

Sometimes the frozen breath hangs above his head
    like a small cloud;
if he breathes too deeply, his lungs burn
    with invisible fire.

80   There is also a terrible beauty:
afternoon skies that shatter "like broken goblets"
as tiny ice crystals fall across the face of the sun;
blood-red horizons, liquid twilights,
and pale green beams, called auroras,
that wind in great waves through the towering dark.

But it is April now,
and "each day more light is draining away."
Soon there will be no sun at all.
Days and days and days of total blackness.
90   The Antarctic night.

E

> With two weeks of daylight left, the sun was just a
> monstrous ball which could barely [hoist] itself
> free of the horizon. It would sink out of sight
> in the north not long after noon. I watched it
> go as one might watch a departing friend.

| hoist |
| raise |

F

F

Mornings are the worst.
The cold in the little room lies like a thick liquid.
This morning, in the shack, it is –40°F!
(He sleeps with the stove off and the door half open,
    in order to be safe from any possible fumes.)

432   Unit 12 Reader's Choice

COMPREHENSION

F Despite the bitter cold, why does Byrd sleep with his door half open? *(He wants to keep safe from any fumes that his tons of fuel might give off.)* **cause and effect**

G How does the illustration on page 433 help you picture conditions in Antarctica? *(Students may say that Byrd's parka, gloves, and goggles show how much protection he needs from the cold, ice, and snow. The snow swirling around him—and the fact that it almost obscures him—gives an idea of how windy and snowy it is.)* **understanding visuals**

LITERATURE

E Reread Byrd's journal entry. To what does he compare the sun? What figures of speech does he use? *(metaphor: the sun was a monstrous ball; personification: it could barely raise itself up and was like a departing friend)* **figurative language**

F How does the author help you understand what the cold is like in Byrd's room in the mornings? *(He uses a simile to compare the cold to a thick liquid that lies in the air.)* **figurative language**

VOCABULARY

C **invisible** Students can use the meaning of the prefix *in-* to help them figure out that this word means "not visible" or "not able to be seen."

FOR ENGLISH LEARNERS

Help students understand the following expression:

Line 80: terrible beauty

The slightest move sends blasts
of freezing air down his back or stomach.
The thought of his first foot on the floor
    makes him cringe .

cringe
(krĭnj)
v. shrink back, as
in fear

100 Ice coats the outside of the sleeping bag.
His clothes are so stiff
he must work them between his hands
    before putting them on.

He pokes with the flashlight
to find a pair of thin silk gloves.
Without the gloves,
the frozen metal of the lantern would
    tear skin off his fingers!

He strikes a match and touches it to the lantern's
110   wick.
The flame catches and goes out,
catches and goes out.
Then it wavers , steadies, thickens:
ah, light!

wavers
(wā′ vərz)
flutters

*It is a gloomy light, perhaps; things on the opposite
wall are scarcely touched by it. But to me the feeble
burning is a daily miracle.*

In this cruel world, even the
    simple is difficult.
G The snow is rough and
    brittle as white sandstone.
He cuts out blocks with a
120   saw,
then melts them in a bucket
    on the stove, slowly:
after several hours over the
    flame,
two gallons of snow make
    two quarts of water.

THINK IT THROUGH
H Summarize the problems Admiral Byrd faces.

FOCUS
An unexpected danger arises at the base. Read to find out
what happens.

Sometimes, as he opens the trapdoor,
the wind sweeps down
and sucks all the heat from the house.

130 At the close of each day, standing by the stove,
he bathes a third of his body.
I (Because warm air rises and cool air sinks,
it is often 20° colder at his feet!)

Finally, with all heat off,
he reads in the sleeping bed—until his hands are numb.

COMPREHENSION

H **THINK IT THROUGH** Summarize
the problems Admiral Byrd faces.
*(It is so cold and dark where he is
that he constantly has to protect
himself from getting hurt and/or
freezing to death.)* **summarizing**

I Why does Byrd only bathe a third
of his body? *(If he applied water
to the lower two-thirds of his body,
the water would freeze and burn
his skin.)* **making inferences**

LITERATURE

G What is the author comparing in
lines 117–118? What type of figurative language is he using?
*(He's comparing the snow to white
sandstone and is using a simile.)*
figurative language

VOCABULARY

FOR ENGLISH LEARNERS

Help students understand the following expressions and idioms:

Line 102: work them between his
hands
Line 111: catches and goes out
Line 113: wavers, steadies, thickens
Line 135: the sleeping bed

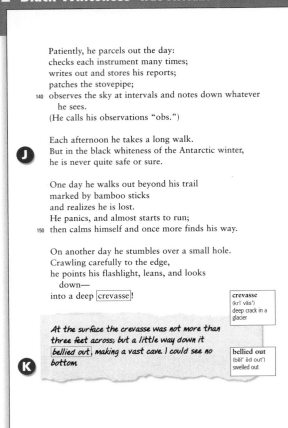

Patiently, he parcels out the day:
checks each instrument many times;
writes out and stores his reports;
patches the stovepipe;
140 observes the sky at intervals and notes down whatever
he sees.
(He calls his observations "obs.")

J Each afternoon he takes a long walk.
But in the black whiteness of the Antarctic winter,
he is never quite safe or sure.

One day he walks out beyond his trail
marked by bamboo sticks
and realizes he is lost.
He panics, and almost starts to run;
150 then calms himself and once more finds his way.

On another day he stumbles over a small hole.
Crawling carefully to the edge,
he points his flashlight, leans, and looks
down—
into a deep [crevasse]!

crevasse
(krĭ văs')
deep crack in a
glacier

At the surface the crevasse was not more than
three feet across; but a little way down it
[bellied out], making a vast cave. I could see no
bottom.

K

bellied out
(bĕl' ēd out')
swelled out

436 Unit 12 Reader's Choice

Blizzard.

Like an incoming tide, the snow rises:
over his ankles,
above his knees,
160 against his chest,
exploding into his eyes
"like millions of tiny pellets."

REREAD
What is
happening to
Byrd?

L

No night has ever seemed so dark.
The flashlight's beam blackens.
The trapdoor, weighted by the sudden snow, is stuck
tight.

Terrified, Byrd rips and claws at the hatch-edge.

D *You are reduced to a crawling thing on the*
margin of a [disintegrating] world.

disintegrating
(dĭs ĭn' tĭ grā' tĭng)
coming apart

The drift piles up around him.
The air comes at him in white rushes.
H 170 If he tries to stand,
the snow wall beats him back.

He stabs at the hatch with his shovel.
Again and again and again.
He pries open an inch, forces in his fingers,
hauls it up high and higher;
and, moaning, tumbles inside.

Black Whiteness: Admiral Byrd Alone in Antarctica 437

COMPREHENSION

J Why is Byrd never quite safe or sure? *(because one careless moment or false step could cause him to lose his life; he can't see well because of the dark)* **cause and effect**

K Ask students how they think they'd feel if they ran across this huge hole in the dark. *(Most would be very frightened.)* **connecting**

L **REREAD** What is happening to Byrd? *(He is caught outside in a blizzard, and is being hit by a "wave" of snow.)* **making inferences**

LITERATURE

H What type of figurative language is the author using in lines 170–171? What picture does this help you form in your mind? *(personification; Students may say that they picture the snow wall as a big bully that is standing over Byrd and waiting to knock him back down when he tries to stand up.)* **figurative language**

VOCABULARY

D **disintegrating** Students can use a dictionary, if necessary, and the meaning of the prefix *dis-* to help them figure out that *disintegrating* means "not coming together" or "falling apart."

FOR ENGLISH LEARNERS

Help students understand the following expressions and idioms:

Line 136: he parcels out the day
Line 139: patches the stovepipe
Line 164: flashlight's beam blackens

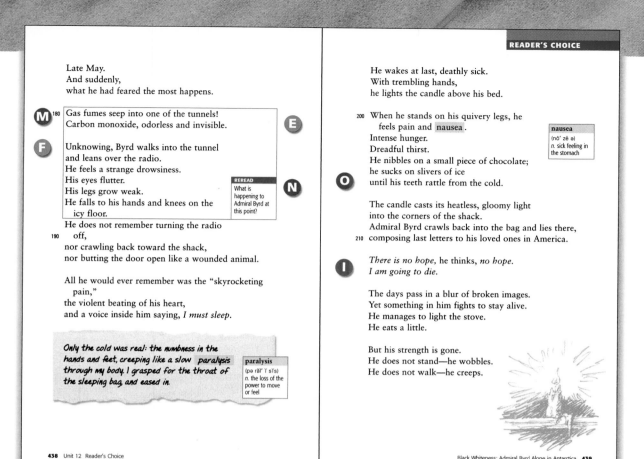

Late May.
And suddenly,
what he had feared the most happens.

M 180 Gas fumes seep into one of the tunnels!
Carbon monoxide, odorless and invisible.

F

Unknowing, Byrd walks into the tunnel
and leans over the radio.
He feels a strange drowsiness.
His eyes flutter.
His legs grow weak.
He falls to his hands and knees on the
icy floor.

190 He does not remember turning the radio
off,
nor crawling back toward the shack,
nor butting the door open like a wounded animal.

All he would ever remember was the "skyrocketing
pain,"
the violent beating of his heart,
and a voice inside him saying, *I must sleep.*

> Only the cold was real: the numbness in the
> hands and feet, creeping like a slow *paralysis*
> through my body. I grasped for the throat of
> the sleeping bag, and eased in.

paralysis
(pə răl' ĭ sĭs)
n. the loss of the
power to move
or feel

He wakes at last, deathly sick.
With trembling hands,
he lights the candle above his bed.

200 When he stands on his quivery legs, he
feels pain and nausea .
Intense hunger.
Dreadful thirst.
He nibbles on a small piece of chocolate;
he sucks on slivers of ice
until his teeth rattle from the cold.

E

nausea
(nô' zē ə)
n. sick feeling in
the stomach

O

The candle casts its heatless, gloomy light
into the corners of the shack.
Admiral Byrd crawls back into the bag and lies there,
210 composing last letters to his loved ones in America.

I

There is no hope, he thinks, *no hope.*
I am going to die.

The days pass in a blur of broken images.
Yet something in him fights to stay alive.
He manages to light the stove.
He eats a little.

But his strength is gone.
He does not stand—he wobbles.
He does not walk—he creeps.

REREAD
What is
happening to
Admiral Byrd at
this point?

N

COMPREHENSION

M **Reciprocal Teaching** To show students the Active Reading Strategy of visualizing, focus on lines 180–188.

Teacher Modeling You could say, *When I read lines 180–188, I picture Admiral Byrd slowly being overtaken by the powerful gas fumes. Lines 184–186 show how the gas fumes are affecting him physically. The first sign is "a strange drowsiness." Next his "eyes flutter" and his "legs grow weak." This description helps me to picture him weak and helpless as he falls to the icy ground.*

Student Modeling Have a volunteer read lines 197–206. Ask the student to demonstrate how to use visualizing to describe what is happening to Admiral Byrd. Remind the student to use examples from the passage in his or her description.

N **REREAD** What is happening to Admiral Byrd at this point? *(He is being overcome—poisoned—by carbon monoxide fumes.)* **cause and effect**

O What are the effects of carbon monoxide poisoning, as shown by Byrd's reactions? *(nausea, loss of consciousness, pain, paralysis)* **cause and effect**

LITERATURE

I Byrd tells himself he is going to die, yet he fights to stay alive. What does this tell you about him? *(Possible answers: He is physically stronger than he realizes; he is a survivor; he takes his mission very seriously and wants to see it through.)* **characterization**

VOCABULARY

E **carbon monoxide** Have students note the context clues that explain this "odorless and invisible" gas that can silently kill people who breathe it. Ask where one might come in contact with carbon monoxide. *(in car fumes and in homes, where it can build up from stoves and furnaces)* **context clues**

F **unknowing** Students can use the meaning of the prefix *un-* to help them figure out that this word means "not knowing" or "not aware."

FOR ENGLISH LEARNERS

Help students understand the following:
Line 192: butting the door open
Line 193: skyrocketing pain

Q

220 Getting fuel from the tunnel is a morning's work.
Climbing the ladder to go "topside,"
he stops to rest at every rung.

Outside or inside, day or night,
he is cold to his very bones.

Talking with Little America is harder, too.

He cranks the radio by hand.
"The room at –60°, sweat pouring down
   my chest."

cranks
(krăngks)
turns the handle
to create power

J
230 Should he say he is sick?
That he is going to die?
No, an attempt to rescue him would only doom the
   men.

P
*I had given a hard and fast order not to come for me
until a month after the sun returns.*

G
Do the people at Little America,
receiving his slow, misspelled replies,
know he is not well?

Noon. June 21:
the longest night of the Antarctic year.

COMPREHENSION

P Why doesn't Byrd tell Little America that he needs help? *(He had told them not to pick him up until a month after the sun returns. If they were to come any sooner than that, they would be putting their lives at risk.)* **cause and effect**

Q Which lines on pages 440 and 442 does the picture on page 441 help you "see"? *(lines 236–239)* **understanding visuals**

LITERATURE

J Explain the external and internal conflicts that Byrd is having at this point. *(external: fighting the cold and the carbon monoxide poisoning; internal: deciding whether or not to tell the rescue team that he's sick)* **conflict**

VOCABULARY

G **misspelled** Students can use the meaning of the prefix *mis-* to help them figure out that *misspelled* means "not spelled correctly."

FOR ENGLISH LEARNERS

Help students understand the following expressions and idioms:

Line 220: a morning's work
Line 224: cold to his very bones
Line 231: doom the men

Richard Byrd sits in the snow, staring out.
Darkness on three sides.
240 But in the north there is a faint dab of crimson on the
        distant horizon;
a thin pencil line of light,
like a secret message from the now-returning sun.
But beyond the weather records
(which he keeps up day after day)
he is too weak to write,
too despairing to see.

despairing
(dĭ spâr′ ĭng)
hopeless

In his struggle to stay alive,
all else falls away.
250 Uneaten food litters the floor.
Half-empty cans are flung out on the deck.
Frozen slop is dumped in the tunnels.
Spare parts are scattered about like ice chunks.
Books lie underneath their shelves,
their upthrust pages stiff as frozen sails.
A small mirror hangs on the wall.
He gazes into it.

He leans close, listens,
and thinks he hears a very tiny voice:
260 *Endure,* it says;
Live, it says.

THINK IT THROUGH
What has caused Admiral Byrd to become so weak?
How does he manage to stay alive?

FOCUS
Is there any chance for rescue? Read to find out what happens.

July is "born in cold."
(Twenty days will be colder than 60° below!)
Yet a message arrives from Little America:
A tractor team is coming—sooner than planned.
Is it possible?
A human face again?
A living voice?

Outside, the air rains with an unbelievable coldness.
270 Ice crystals
burn as they fall on his skin,
cling to his eyelashes,
sealing his eyes half shut.

My toes would turn cold and then dead. While I
danced up and down to restore the
circulation, my nose would freeze; by the
time I attended to that, my hand was frozen.

circulation
(sûr′ kyə lā′ shən)
n. the flow of
blood through
veins

Inside, "nothing is left for the ice to conquer":
It covers the floor;
it climbs up the walls;
it curves around the vent pipe;
it crawls across the ceiling.

COMPREHENSION

R **Reciprocal Teaching** To show students the Active Reading Strategy of predicting, focus on lines 258–261.

Teacher Modeling You could say: *The last four lines on page 442 make me think that Admiral Byrd will survive. Until now, he has inhaled deadly fumes and has become weaker, but he seems to have a strong will to survive. The lines say that Admiral Byrd "hears a very tiny voice" that says "endure," "live." This makes me think that Admiral Byrd has not given up hope and will survive.*

Student Modeling Have a volunteer read lines 260–278. Ask the student to demonstrate how to use predicting strategies to predict whether or not the tractor team will arrive on time to save Admiral Byrd. Remind him or her to use examples from the passage in his or her predictions.

S **THINK IT THROUGH** What has caused Admiral Byrd to become so weak? How does he manage to stay alive? *(The poison in his system, and the fact that he has barely eaten in days, have caused him to become weak. He stays alive through sheer force of will and the voice in his head that tells him to endure and live.)* **cause and effect**

LITERATURE

K What is the "faint dab of crimson on the distant horizon" and "a thin pencil line of light"? *(It is the sun beginning to rise.)* **figurative language**

L Reread the description of Byrd's shack on page 442. Name at least one example of a simile. *(Possible answers: Spare parts are scattered about like ice chunks and/or pages stiff as frozen sails.)* **figurative language**

VOCABULARY

H **uneaten** Students can use the meaning of the prefix *un-* to help them figure out that *uneaten* means "not eaten."

I **unbelievable** means "not to be believed" or "beyond belief."

FOR ENGLISH LEARNERS

Help students understand the following:

Line 245: keeps up
Line 249: all else falls away

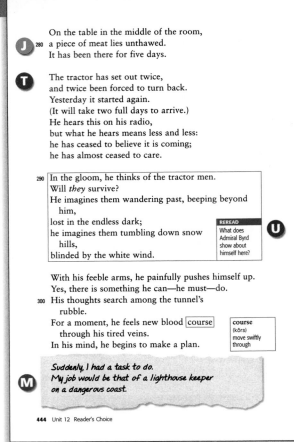

J 280 On the table in the middle of the room,
a piece of meat lies unthawed.
It has been there for five days.

T The tractor has set out twice,
and twice been forced to turn back.
Yesterday it started again.
(It will take two full days to arrive.)
He hears this on his radio,
but what he hears means less and less:
he has ceased to believe it is coming;
he has almost ceased to care.

290 In the gloom, he thinks of the tractor men.
Will *they* survive?
He imagines them wandering past, beeping beyond
him,
lost in the endless dark;
he imagines them tumbling down snow
hills,
blinded by the white wind.

REREAD
What does Admiral Byrd show about himself here?

U

With his feeble arms, he painfully pushes himself up.
Yes, there is something he can—he must—do.
300 His thoughts search among the tunnel's
rubble.
For a moment, he feels new blood course
through his tired veins.
In his mind, he begins to make a plan.

course
(kôrs)
move swiftly
through

*Suddenly, I had a task to do.
My job would be that of a lighthouse keeper
on a dangerous coast.*

M

444 Unit 12 Reader's Choice

August 10:
a night "black with threat."

Byrd stands by the open hatch,
hauling a T-shaped kite upward by a thin
string.
310 Around its long wire tail are wads of paper
and pieces of cloth.
He douses the kite's tail with gasoline,
and tries to light a match.
A dozen matches go out in his hand.

douses
(dou' sĭz)
wets thoroughly

REREAD
What is Admiral Byrd trying to do? Why?

V

K Finally, a violent uprush of light almost blinds him.
He jerks on the kite string.
The kite swoops into the air, caught on a wind gust,
flapping its spidery tail, blazing against the black.
320 It rises and rises, skates to a height of over a hundred
feet.

The sight of it swaying in the night sky delights him.
This beacon, he knows, can be seen for
miles and miles.

beacon
(bē' kən)
light

For five minutes the kite flames overhead.
Byrd squints. He blinks and peers northward.

L Against the backdrop of the horizon,
a single fingery beam moves up and down.
Afraid to believe it is true, he turns away,
shuts his two eyes tight and waits.
330 Then he turns and looks again.

Black Whiteness: Admiral Byrd Alone in Antarctica 445

COMPREHENSION

T What happens to the tractor the first two times it sets out? *(The tractor is forced to turn back.)* **details**

U REREAD What does Admiral Byrd show about himself here? *(In spite of the fact that he's almost given up, he still cares about the safety of the tractor men.)* **details**

V REREAD What is Admiral Byrd trying to do? Why? *(He's trying to set fire to his homemade kite so he can use it to show the tractor team where he is.)* **cause and effect**

LITERATURE

M In the journal entry, what does Admiral Byrd say his job will be? What does this mean? *(a lighthouse keeper on a dangerous coast; it means that he will guide or show the tractor team where he is.)* **figurative language**

VOCABULARY

J **unthawed** Students can use the meaning of the prefix un- to help them figure out that *unthawed* means "not thawed" or "frozen."

K **uprush** Have students separate this compound word into its parts to see that it means "a rushing upward." **compound words**

L **backdrop** Have students separate this compound word into its parts, *back* and *drop*. Explain that it means the same as "background." **compound words**

FOR ENGLISH LEARNERS

Help students understand the following expressions and idioms:

Line 282: set out
Line 288: ceased to believe
Line 306: a night "black with threat"
Line 314: go out in his hand
Line 326: Against the backdrop of the horizon

There it is, still poking at the dark!
Quickly, he lights a flare and ties it to a stick.
He holds the stick high, waving it wildly.
The flare makes "a huge blue hole in the night."

The light from the tractor grows and grows.
Treads crunch over the crusted snow.
Horns sound and the tractor stops.
Three fur-muffled figures leap out.

> **treads**
> (trĕdz)
> metal belts that
> work like wheels
> for tractors

340   Byrd wants to stay calm,
but his hands are shaking.
He wants to cry,
but he is too empty even to sob.

He tries to jest: "Come on below, boys,
I have bowls of hot soup waiting."

Then, following the men down the ladder,
he collapses on the porch.

M

Many weeks pass.
The men from Little America help
   Admiral Byrd regain his strength.
350   They chart the weather, cook, clean,
sleep on the floor.

> **REREAD**
> How has the
> base now
> changed?

W

N   *The darkness lifted from my heart, just as it presently
did from the Barrier.*

Black Whiteness: Admiral Byrd Alone in Antarctica   **447**

COMPREHENSION

W **REREAD** How has the base now changed? *(There are others there now, who have nursed Byrd back to health, have cleaned up the base, and are helping him with his work.)* **compare and contrast**

LITERATURE

N How does the simile in Byrd's journal entry help you understand the way he feels? *(Possible answer: For weeks it had been dark and lifeless outside, which was the way Byrd had been feeling inside. But in the same way that the sunlight had been returning, so did Byrd's health return and his spirits brighten.)* **figurative language**

VOCABULARY

M **regain** Students can use the meaning of the prefix *re-* to help them figure out that *regain* means "gain again" or "get back."

FOR ENGLISH LEARNERS

Help students understand the following:

Line 332: lights a flare
Line 338: fur-muffled figures
Line 343: tries to jest

Admiral Richard Byrd

The Granger Collection, New York.

At last, the Antarctic spring arrives
with a great blossoming of light.
One morning Admiral Byrd climbs
up the ladder and out the hatch.
He walks slowly across the snow,
to a small airplane waiting for him.
As the plane rises into the brightening air,
he looks down at the roof of his little house for the
360   final time.

Admiral Richard Byrd will return to Antarctica.
He will tell the people of the world more
        about this beautiful but harsh continent.

He will also write a book about his time alone.
He will talk about the cold and the fear and the
        courage.
But most of all he will tell about
"the sheer beauty and miracle of being alive."

"I live more simply now," he writes at the end of his
370   book,
"and with more peace."

THINK IT THROUGH

1. Why was Admiral Byrd able to survive such a
   terrible experience so long on his own? Explain.
2. In your opinion, was Admiral Byrd a hero? Give a
   reason for your answer.
3. What lessons might today's explorers learn from
   Admiral Byrd's experience? Use evidence from the
   account to support your response.

COMPREHENSION

THINK IT THROUGH

1. Why was Admiral Byrd able to survive such a terrible experience so
   long on his own? Explain. *(He survived because he was tough and
   had a strong will to live. He also felt
   that the work he was doing was
   very important.)* **cause and effect**

2. In your opinion, was Admiral Byrd
   a hero? Give a reason for your
   answer. *(Most students probably
   will say yes because he risked his life
   in order to help the world learn
   more about Antarctica. Others
   might think the experiment was not
   worth doing.)* **evaluating**

3. What lessons might today's explorers learn from Admiral Byrd's
   experience? Use evidence from
   the account to support your
   response. *(Possible answers: Being
   alone is a very big and difficult sacrifice. If people have to be alone or
   far away from others, they should
   make sure to have the best possible*

*supplies and communication equip-
ment. They also should know
enough about where they're going
to prepare in advance for every possible emergency.)* **making
inferences**

Have students complete the **K-W-L
chart** that they began before reading
this selection.

RETEACHING

If students need more help understanding **Cause and Effect,** use
pages T642–T646.

VOCABULARY

FOR ENGLISH LEARNERS

Help students understand the
following:

Line 353: a great blossoming of
          light
Line 368: sheer beauty

RETEACHING

If students need more help understanding **Prefixes,** use pages T612
and T613.

1. COMPREHENSION

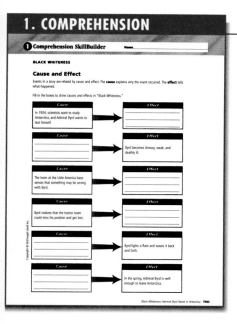

Cause and Effect

Direct Instruction Remind the students that events are joined by cause and effect. The **cause** is the first event, "why" something happens. The **effect** is the second event; it tells the result.

Read the sentence beginning "At –50°F. . ." on page 431. Ask: *When the temperature falls to 55 degrees below zero, what is the effect?*

(Kerosene freezes.) *If the effect is that juice bottles shatter and canned food is hard as a rock, what is the cause?* (The temperature falls to 60 degrees below zero.) Remind the students to ask "Why did this happen?" to find the cause. Tell them to ask "What is the result?" to find the effect.

Comprehension SkillBuilder Answer Key:

Effect: *Byrd is left alone for many months at a camp in Antarctica.*

Cause: *Byrd accidentally breathes carbon monoxide.*

Effect: *They send a message to Byrd that they are coming earlier than planned.*

Effect: *Byrd sets a kite on fire and sends it aloft.*

Cause: *Byrd sees a light in the distance.*

Cause: *The rescue team helps Byrd regain his strength.*

---

2. LITERATURE

Figurative Language

Direct Instruction Explain to the students that writers use **figurative language** to help readers see ordinary things in new ways. List and define the following types of figurative language:

- **metaphor:** One object or idea is compared to another; one thing is said to be the other.
- **simile:** Two things are compared using the word *like* or *as*.
- **personification:** Human or animal qualities or characteristics are given to an idea or nonliving thing.

Tell the students that "Black Whiteness" contains many examples of figurative language. Discuss each of the following examples: (1) Admiral Byrd's shack was *tidily built as a watch* (simile comparing shack to a watch); (2) He *butted the door open like a wounded animal* (simile comparing Byrd to a wounded animal); (3) *The sun was just a monstrous ball* (metaphor comparing the sun to a ball); (4) *Night is pressing down with its blue-black shadow* (personification: night engaging in human activity of pressing down).

Literary SkillBuilder Answer Key:

(Likenesses may vary.)

A.
1. *Byrd's breath is compared to a small cloud.*
   Both are visible in the air/puffy and white.
2. *The cold is compared to a thick liquid.*
   Both are thick/heavy and can be touched.
3. *The snow is compared to sandstone.*
   Both are hard/rough and brittle.
4. *The flare is compared to a huge blue hole.*
   The outline of the flare against the sky looks ragged, like a hole torn in cloth.
5. *July is born, just as animals and humans are born.*
6. *The kite skates, just as humans may skate.*

B. *Answers will vary. The verb in sentence 2 should describe a human activity, for example,* dance *or* skip.

---

3. VOCABULARY

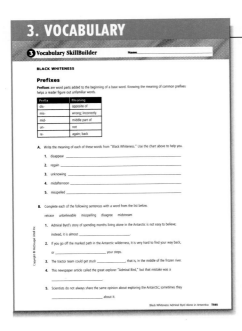

Prefixes

Direct Instruction Remind students that **prefixes** are word parts added at the beginning of a base word to change its meaning or to make a new word. State that *non-* and *pre-* are two very common prefixes. Have students identify their meanings. (*non-:* not or the opposite of; *pre-:* before.) Discuss the meanings of the following words: *prepay, preheat, prearrange, nonacceptance, nonworking, nonpayment.* Note how the prefix changes the meaning of the base word.

Vocabulary SkillBuilder Answer Key:

A.
1. *disappear: opposite of* appear/to leave or go away
2. *regain: to gain again/to get back*
3. *unknowing: not knowing*
4. *midafternoon: the middle part of the afternoon*
5. *misspelled: spelled incorrectly*

B.
1. *unbelievable*
2. *retrace*
3. *midstream*
4. *misspelling*
5. *disagree*

4. WORDS TO KNOW

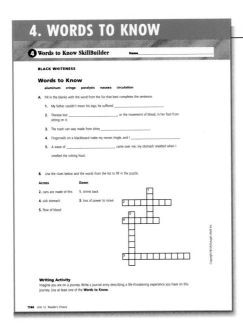

Words to Know

Direct Instruction As you introduce the **Words to Know,** here are some points you might want to cover. Help students to identify the parts of the vocabulary words. Stress the importance of finding the base of each word. Help students remove prefixes and suffixes first.
- **paralysis,** from the Greek *para-* + *lūein,* "to release"
- **nausea,** from the Greek *naus,* "ship"; point out that many people feel sick on board a ship.
- **circulate** – e + -ion = *circulation;* also defined as "passing of something, such as money or news, from place to place or person to person" and "number of copies of a publication."

Writing Activity Encourage students to be creative. Have volunteers read their creations aloud.

Words to Know SkillBuilder Answer Key:

A.
1. *paralysis*
2. *circulation*
3. *aluminum*
4. *cringe*
5. *nausea*

B.
1 **down:** *cringe*
2 **across:** *aluminum*
3 **down:** *paralysis*
4 **across:** *nausea*
5 **across:** *circulation*

5. SELECTION TEST

Selection Test Answer Key:
A. 1. *false* **2.** *true* **3.** *true* **4.** *false* **5.** *true* **6.** *true* **7.** *false* **8.** *true* **9.** *true*
B. *He learned to live more simply and with peace.*

BLACK WHITENESS

Cause and Effect

Events in a story are related by cause and effect. The **cause** explains why the event occurred. The **effect** tells what happened.

Fill in the boxes to show causes and effects in "Black Whiteness."

Cause
In 1934, scientists want to study Antarctica, and Admiral Byrd wants to test himself.

Effect
_____ _____ _____

Cause
_____ _____ _____

Effect
Byrd becomes drowsy, weak, and deathly ill.

Cause
The team at the Little America base senses that something may be wrong with Byrd.

Effect
_____ _____ _____

Cause
Byrd realizes that the tractor team could miss his position and get lost.

Effect
_____ _____ _____

Cause
_____ _____ _____

Effect
Byrd lights a flare and waves it back and forth.

Cause
_____ _____ _____

Effect
In the spring, Admiral Byrd is well enough to leave Antarctica.

BLACK WHITENESS

Figurative Language

Figurative language helps readers form vivid pictures in their minds. Both metaphors and similes compare things that seem different. **Similes** use *like* or *as* in the comparison; **metaphors** say that one thing is the other. **Personification** gives human qualities to ideas or nonliving things.

A. Answer each question about figurative language in "Black Whiteness."

   1. Outside, Admiral Byrd's breath hangs above his head like a small cloud.

      Byrd's breath is compared to _____.

      How are these two things alike? _____

   2. The cold in the little room lies like a thick liquid.

      The cold is compared to _____.

      How are these two things alike? _____

   3. The snow is rough and brittle as white sandstone.

      The snow is compared to _____.

      How are these two things alike? _____

   4. The flare makes a huge blue hole in the night.

      The flare is compared to _____.

      How are these two things alike? _____

   5. July is "born in cold."

      How is July made to seem alive? _____

   6. The kite skates to a height of over a hundred feet.

      How is the kite made to seem human? _____

B. Complete each sentence with your own figurative language.

   1. In the quiet cabin, the ticking of the clock sounded as loud as _____.

   2. Huge snowflakes _____ along the rooftop.

   3. During the Antarctic winter, the darkness is _____.

BLACK WHITENESS

Prefixes

Prefixes are word parts added to the beginning of a base word. Knowing the meaning of common prefixes helps a reader figure out unfamiliar words.

Prefix	Meaning
dis-	opposite of
mis-	wrong; incorrectly
mid-	middle part of
un-	not
re-	again; back

A. Write the meaning of each of these words from "Black Whiteness." Use the chart above to help you.

1. disappear _____

2. regain _____

3. unknowing _____

4. midafternoon _____

5. misspelled _____

B. Complete each of the following sentences with a word from the list below.

retrace   unbelievable   misspelling   disagree   midstream

1. Admiral Byrd's story of spending months living alone in the Antarctic is not easy to believe;

   instead, it is almost _____.

2. If you go off the marked path in the Antarctic wilderness, it is very hard to find your way back,

   or _____ your steps.

3. The tractor team could get stuck _____, that is, in the middle of the frozen river.

4. This newspaper article called the great explorer "Admiral Bird," but that mistake was a

   _____.

5. Scientists do not always share the same opinion about exploring the Antarctic; sometimes they

   _____ about it.

BLACK WHITENESS

Words to Know

aluminum   cringe   paralysis   nausea   circulation

A. Fill in the blanks with the word from the list that best completes the sentence.

1. My father couldn't move his legs; he suffered _____.

2. Therese lost _____, or the movement of blood, in her foot from sitting on it.

3. The trash can was made from shiny _____.

4. Fingernails on a blackboard make my nerves tingle, and I _____.

5. A wave of _____ came over me; my stomach revolted when I

    smelled the rotting food.

B. Use the clues below and the words from the list to fill in the puzzle.

Across

2. cans are made of this

4. sick stomach

5. flow of blood

Down

1. shrink back

3. loss of power to move

Writing Activity

Imagine you are on a journey. Write a journal entry describing a life-threatening experience you have on this journey. Use at least one of the **Words to Know.**

BLACK WHITENESS

A. Write **true** or **false** on the line next to each statement.

_____ **1.** This story takes place near the North Pole.

_____ **2.** Admiral Richard Byrd is in Antarctica to gather information about the weather.

_____ **3.** He keeps a diary, which he says is like "thinking out loud."

_____ **4.** In April, Byrd endures days and days of total sunlight.

_____ **5.** Byrd has to sleep with his door half open, so when he awakens, his room is −40°F.

_____ **6.** One day, Byrd gets carbon monoxide poisoning and gets deathly sick.

_____ **7.** He tells the men at Little America to come and rescue him.

_____ **8.** Little America sends Byrd a message that a tractor team will be coming soon.

_____ **9.** The tractor team arrives and stays with Byrd for several weeks.

B. In your own words, tell what Admiral Byrd learned from his experience in Antarctica (what he writes at the end of his book).

_____

_____

450

Student Resources

451

Active Reading Strategies

Good readers think while they read. Every so often they stop and check their understanding. They predict what might happen next. They question what they're reading. After they finish, they think about what they read. Each strategy below happens in a good reader's mind while he or she is reading.

> **CONNECT**
> Think about your own life when you read something. Think of something similar that you have gone through, seen, or heard.

> **VISUALIZE**
> Make a picture in your mind of what the text says. Imagine you are looking at what is described.

> **PREDICT**
> Try to guess what will happen next in the story or article. Then read on to find out if your guess was correct.

> **QUESTION**
> Let questions come to your mind when you read. If something doesn't make sense, don't pass it by. Ask or write a question to yourself. Look for answers as you read.

> **CLARIFY**
> Slow down and make sure you understand what you're reading. Reread something to make sure you understood what it meant. As you read farther, expect to understand or to find out more.
> These are ways you can clarify your understanding:
> • Sum up what happened in your own words, or summarize.
> • Identify the main idea of the paragraph, especially in nonfiction.
> • Make inferences about what the author meant but didn't say. Read between the lines and use your own experience to figure it out.

> **EVALUATE**
> Form opinions about what you read as you read it. Evaluate again after you read it.

The examples on the pages that follow show how each strategy works. The examples are from "Trombones and Colleges," by Walter Dean Myers. In this story, a boy brings home a bad report card. He has to decide whether to stay in hard classes or take easier ones.

> **CONNECT**
> Think about your own life when you read something. Think of something similar that you have gone through, seen, or heard.
>
> > "A little ability is better than none," I said. No one said anything so I figured it probably wasn't the right time to try to cheer Clyde up.
>
> **READER CONNECTS:** I know how the narrator feels. Sometimes I say the wrong thing and nobody laughs or says anything. Then I really feel stupid. I wish I could erase what I said.

> **VISUALIZE**
> Make a picture in your mind of what the text says. Imagine you are looking at what is described.
>
> > But everything else was either a C or a D except mathematics. His mathematics mark was a big red F that had been circled. I don't know why they had to circle the F when it was the only red mark on the card.
>
> **READER VISUALIZES:** In my mind I can see this report card. Everything is black except this big red F with a big red circle around it. It looks like nothing matters except that big old F—as if you wouldn't see it right away anyway.

PREDICT

Try to guess what will happen next in the story or article. Read on to find out if your guess was correct.

> "I got my report card today," Clyde said. His mother stopped taking the food out and turned toward us. Clyde pushed the report card about two inches toward her. She really didn't even have to look at the card to know that it was bad. She could have told that just by looking at Clyde. But she picked it up and looked at it a long time.

READER PREDICTS: I think she'll get mad at him. She might tell him that he's stupid or lazy and ground him until his grades get better.

> First she looked at one side and then the other and then back at the first side again. "What they say around the school?" she asked, still looking at the card. . . . "Well, what are you going to do, young man?"

READER CHECKS PREDICTION: Well, she didn't get mad after all; she just asked him what he was going to do.

QUESTION

Let questions come to your mind when you read. If something doesn't make sense, don't pass it by. Ask or write a question to yourself.

> "What are you going to do, Mr. Jones?"
> "I'm—I'm going to keep the academic course," Clyde said.
> "You think it's going to be any easier this time?" Mrs. Jones asked.
> "No."

READER QUESTIONS: Why does she ask him what he's going to do? I thought she'd tell him what to do. She didn't tell him to drop the course or to study harder. She just pointed out that it wasn't going to get any easier. I also wonder why he didn't go for the easier course and save himself some hard work. I'll look for answers as I read.

CLARIFY

Slow down and make sure you understand what you're reading. Reread something to make sure you understood what it meant. As you read farther, expect to understand or to find out more.

> And he says, 'Oh, that's a trombone I'm taking back to the pawn shop tomorrow." Well, I naturally ask him what he's doing with it in the first place, and he says he got carried away and bought it but he realized that we really didn't have the thirty-five dollars to spend on foolishness and so he'd take it back the next day. And all the time he's sitting there scratching his chin and rubbing his nose and trying to peek over at me to see how I felt about it. I just told him that I guess he knew what was best. Only the next day he forgot to take it back, and the next day he forgot to take it back, and finally I broke down and told him why didn't he keep it. He said he would if I thought he should.

READER CLARIFIES: I'm not sure I understand. Clyde's dad says he's going to take the trombone back because he shouldn't have bought it. He said he was going to return it, but he didn't. I guess he wants her to tell him to keep it. Then she tells him to keep it, and he acts like it was her decision. This way, I guess he won't feel guilty.

EVALUATE

Form opinions about what you read. Think about something as you read it and then again after you read it.

> For a minute there was a faraway look in her eyes, but then her face turned into a big smile. "You're just like your father, boy. That man would never give up on anything he really wanted. Did I ever tell you the time he was trying to learn to play the trombone?"

READER EVALUATES: I really like Clyde's mother. She didn't get mad at him about his report card. In fact, she's praising him for being brave enough to take the harder classes. She makes it sound like he's brave like his father. I admire her for this.

Fiction

A work of fiction is a story that the writer made up. It could be based on a real event, or it could be totally imagined. The **elements of fiction** are the most important parts of fiction. They are the **characters, setting, plot,** and **theme.** These elements make up the skeleton of the story.

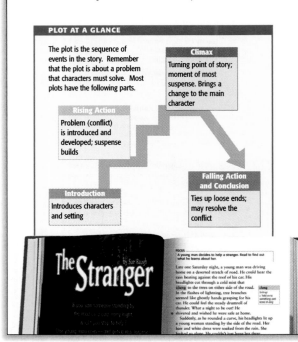

PLOT AT A GLANCE

The plot is the sequence of events in the story. Remember that the plot is about a problem that characters must solve. Most plots have the following parts.

Climax
Turning point of story; moment of most suspense. Brings a change to the main character

Rising Action
Problem (conflict) is introduced and developed; suspense builds

Falling Action and Conclusion
Ties up loose ends; may resolve the conflict

Introduction
Introduces characters and setting

TERMS IN FICTION

- **Characters:** the people or animals in the story
- **Setting:** where and when the story happens
- **Plot:** what happens. The plot grows around a problem, or conflict. The story is about how the characters deal with this problem.
- **Conflict:** the struggle between two forces. **External conflict** happens between a character and an animal, nature, or a person. **Internal conflict** happens in a character's mind, such as a hard choice or a guilty conscience.
- **Theme:** the message the writer wants to share with the reader
- **Narrator:** the voice telling the story to the reader
- **Point of view:** the way the narrator is telling the story
    First person point of view: The narrator is part of the story.
    Third person point of view: The narrator is not part of the story, but is reporting it.
- **Suspense:** the feeling of growing tension and excitement

TYPES OF FICTION

- **Short story:** a short work of fiction that can be read at one sitting. It has a few main characters and a single conflict.
- **Folk tale:** a story that was told over and over by word of mouth. The characters may be animals or people.
- **Historical fiction:** a story set in the past. It may refer to real people or events. The dialogue is usually made up.
- **Myth:** a very old story that was told by ancient people to explain the unknown. The characters often include gods or heroes.
- **Novel:** a long story that usually cannot be read at one sitting. A novel usually has many characters. The plot is complicated. A novel excerpt is one part of the novel.
- **Legend:** a story about a hero that has been told over and over. Most legends are based on a real person or event.
- **Horror story:** a short story that is meant to scare the reader

Literature Handbook **457**

Nonfiction

Nonfiction is writing about real people, places, and events. It is mostly based on facts.

NONFICTION AT A GLANCE

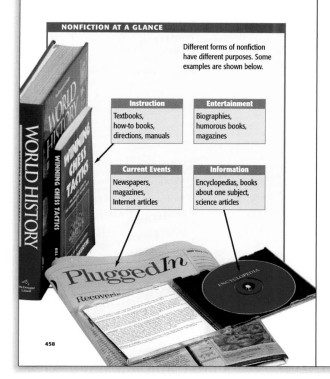

Different forms of nonfiction have different purposes. Some examples are shown below.

Instruction
Textbooks, how-to books, directions, manuals

Entertainment
Biographies, humorous books, magazines

Current Events
Newspapers, magazines, Internet articles

Information
Encyclopedias, books about one subject, science articles

458

TERMS IN NONFICTION

- **Facts:** statements that can be proved to be true
- **Opinions:** statements of personal belief that cannot be proved
- **Chronological order:** the order or sequence in which events happen in time
- **Cause and Effect:** The cause is the reason something happens. The effect is the result, or what happens due to the cause.
- **Visuals:** diagrams, maps, charts, photos, and pictures that are part of an article. They give facts by means of pictures and sketches, with just a few words.

TYPES OF NONFICTION

- **Biography:** a true story about someone's life, written by someone else. It can cover the whole life or just one part.
- **Autobiography:** the true story of a person's life, written by that person
- **Feature Article:** an article that gives facts about a current subject. It is often found in a newspaper or a magazine. Most include visuals.
- **Informative Article:** an article that gives facts about a subject. The article might be from an encyclopedia, textbook, or book.
- **Interview:** a conversation between two people. One asks the other questions. The answers are written in the form of an interview.
- **Essay:** a piece of writing about one subject. The writer might share an opinion or make a point.
- **True Account:** an article about a real event that is told as a story
- **Narrative Nonfiction:** an article about a real event told in chronological order. It is often historical.
- **Anecdote:** the true story of a small event, usually from the teller's life. An anecdote might be funny (to entertain) or might make a point.

Drama

A drama, or play, is a story that is meant to be acted out. Actors present the play onstage. They act out the story for an audience.

A DRAMA SCRIPT AT A GLANCE

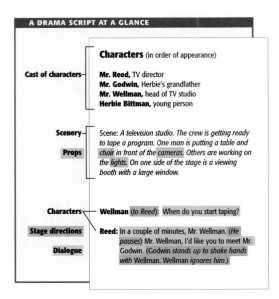

Cast of characters

Characters (in order of appearance)
Mr. Reed, TV director
Mr. Godwin, Herbie's grandfather
Mr. Wellman, head of TV studio
Herbie Bittman, young person

Scenery
Props

Scene: *A television studio. The crew is getting ready to tape a program. One man is putting a table and chair in front of the cameras. Others are working on the lights. On one side of the stage is a viewing booth with a large window.*

Characters
Stage directions
Dialogue

Wellman (*to Reed*): When do you start taping?

Reed: In a couple of minutes, Mr. Wellman. (*He pauses*) Mr. Wellman, I'd like you to meet Mr. Godwin. (Godwin *stands up to shake hands with* Wellman. Wellman *ignores him.*)

TERMS IN DRAMA

- **Stage:** the platform on which the actors perform
- **Script:** the written words for the play. This is the plan that everyone reads in order to perform the play.
- **Cast of Characters:** the list of people who play a part in the story
- **Dialogue:** the words the characters say
- **Stage Directions:** the directions to the actors and stage crew. These words tell how people should move and speak. They describe the scenery—the decoration on stage.
- **Acts and Scenes:** the parts of a play. These usually change when the time or the place changes.
- **Props:** the objects used on stage in the play, such as a telephone
- **Scenery:** the background art or structures on stage to help show the setting

A Stage

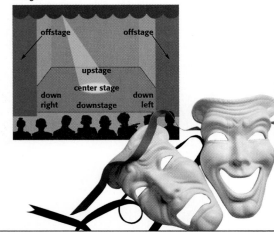

Poetry

Poetry is literature that uses a few words to tell about ideas, feelings, and images. The poet crafts the look of the poem and chooses words for their sound and meaning. Most poems are meant to be read aloud. Poems may or may not rhyme.

POETRY AT A GLANCE

Some People
By Rachel Field

Isn't it strange some people make — **line**
   You feel so tired inside, — **stanza**
Your thoughts begin to shrivel up
   Like leaves all brown and dried! — **rhyming words**

But when you're with some other ones,
   It's stranger still to find
Your thoughts as thick as fireflies — **simile**
   All shiny in your mind! — **visual imagery**

TERMS IN POETRY

- **Form:** the way a poem looks on the page; its shape
- **Lines:** Poets arrange words into lines. The lines may or may not be sentences.
- **Stanzas:** groups of lines in traditional poetry
- **Free verse:** poems that usually do not rhyme and have no fixed rhythm or pattern. They are written like conversation.
- **Rhyme:** sounds that are alike at the end of words, such as *make* and *rake*. Some poems have rhyming words at the end of lines. Some poems have rhymes in the middle of lines too.
- **Rhythm:** the beat of the poem. Patterns of strong (´) and weak (˘) syllables make up the beat.
- **Repetition:** the repeating of sounds, words, phrases, or lines in a poem
- **Imagery:** words and phrases that appeal to the five senses—sight, hearing, smell, taste, and touch. Poets often use imagery to create pictures, tastes, or feelings in the reader's mind. For example, "The smell of sizzling bacon filled the air."
- **Figurative language:** words and phrases that help readers picture things in new ways. For example, "Snow crystals displayed a rainbow of colors in the sun."
    - **Simile:** a comparison of two things using the words *like* or *as*. For example, "Confetti fell like rain."
    - **Metaphor:** a comparison of two things without the words *like* or *as*. For example, "His face is a puzzle."
    - **Personification:** a description of an animal or an object as if it were human or had human qualities. For example, "The dog smiled joyfully."
- **Speaker:** the voice that talks to the reader
- **Theme:** the message the poet gives the reader through the poem

A

advancing (ăd văn′ sĭng) *v.* moving forward
avanzando *v.* adelantando

affliction (ə flĭk′ shən) *n.* cause of pain
aflicción *s.* causa de dolor o pena

aggressive (ə grĕs′ ĭv) *adj.* forceful
enérgico *adj.* vigoroso

aluminum (ə lōō′ mə nəm) *n.* silvery, lightweight metallic element
aluminio *s.* metal de color y brillo parecidos a los de la plata, muy ligero

ambush (ăm′ bŏŏsh) *n.* hiding place for a surprise attack
emboscada *s.* lugar de escondite para un ataque sorpresivo

anchors (ăng′ kərz) *n.* heavy weights attached to a connecting rope that are used to keep ships in place
anclas *s.* pesas de hierro con ganchos que se atan a una cuerda para aferrar los barcos al fondo del mar

annoyed (ə noid′) *adj.* bothered
fastidiado *adj.* molestado

anxiously (ăngk′ shəs lē) *adv.* nervously
ansiosamente *adv.* de modo nervioso

apprentice (ə prĕn′ tĭs) *n.* one who is learning a job
aprendiz *s.* alguien que está aprendiendo un oficio o trabajo

approve (ə prōōv′) *v.* think to be right or good
aprobar *v.* considerar que algo es correcto o bien

astonishment (ə stŏn′ ĭsh mənt) *n.* amazement
asombro *s.* sorpresa

audition (ô dĭsh′ ən) *n.* performance to show a skill
audición *s.* actuación para demostrar una destreza

authorities (ə thôr′ ĭ tēz) *n.* persons who have power
autoridades *s.* personas que tienen el poder

B

barbarians (bär bâr′ ē ənz) *n.* brutal people
bárbaros *s.* personas fieras y crueles

barrels (băr′ əlz) *n.* large, round containers, usually made of wood
barriles *s.* grandes recipientes redondos, por lo común hechos de madera

bizarre (bĭ zär′) *adj.* strange
raro *adj.* extraño

boisterous (boi′ stər əs) *adj.* active and noisy
estrepitoso *adj.* alborotado y ruidoso

bristled (brĭs′ əld) *v.* stiffened; past tense of *bristle*
erizó *v.* se puso de punta; pasado de *bristle/erizar*

brutal (brōōt′ l) *adj.* extremely rough
brutal *adj.* extremadamente tosco; cruel

buckles (bŭk′ əlz) *v.* crumples
se desploma *v.* cae

bugles (byōō′ gəlz) *n.* horns that are shorter than a trumpet
corneta *n.* instrumento musical mas corto que una trompeta

bundled (bŭn′ dld) *adj.* wrapped up
arropado *adj.* envuelto

C

captive (kăp′ tĭv) *n.* prisoner
cautivo *s.* prisionero

cautious (kô′ shəs) *adj.* very careful
cauto *adj.* muy cuidadoso

cinders (sĭn′ dərz) *n.* ashes
carbonillas *s.* cenizas

circulation (sûr′ kyə lā′ shən) *n.* the flow of blood through veins
circulación *s.* flujo de sangre a través de las venas

clearing (klĭr′ ĭng) *n.* land from which trees have been removed
claro *s.* terreno al que se le han quitado los árboles

coarse (kôrs) *adj.* rough
burdo *adj.* tosco; áspero

coiled (koild) *adj.* wound into a series of rings
enroscado *adj.* enrollado

colonel (kûr' nəl) *n.* a military officer
coronel *s.* oficial militar

compassion (kəm păsh' ən) *n.* concern for the suffering of others
compasión *s.* preocupación por el sufrimiento de otros

compliment (kŏm' plə mənt) *n.* words of praise
halago *s.* palabras de elogio

comrades (kom' rădz') *n.* persons sharing an activity
camaradas *s.* personas que hacen una misma cosa

content (kən tĕnt') *adj.* satisfied
complacido *adj.* satisfecho

continent (kŏn' tə nənt) *n.* one of the seven large land areas on the earth
continente *s.* una de las siete grandes extensiones terrestres de la Tierra

contraption (kən trăp' shən) *n.* mechanical device
artefacto *s.* aparato mecánico

council (koun' səl) *n.* body of people elected to plan, discuss, or give advice
concilio *s.* quienes son elejidos para planear, discutir, o dar consejo

course (kôrs) *n.* route
curso *s.* ruta

coyotes (kī ō' tēz) *n.* small animals that are similar to wolves
coyotes *s.* pequeños animales que son parecidos a lobos

craft (krăft) *n.* ship
nave *s.* barco

cringe (krĭnj) *v.* shrink back, as in fear
menguarse *v.* encogerse, como de miedo

culture (kŭl' chər) *n.* the ideas, customs, and skills shared by a certain people
cultura *s.* ideas, costumbres y destrezas compartidas por un pueblo

cunning (kŭn' ĭng) *n.* skill in fooling others
artimaña *s.* habilidad para engañar

custom (kŭs' təm) *n.* something done regularly by a group
costumbre *s.* algo hecho con regularidad por un grupo de personas

D

dainty (dān' tē) *adj.* beautiful in a delicate way
exquisito *adj.* que tiene una gran belleza y delicadeza

daring (dâr' ĭng) *n.* boldness
arrojo *s.* atrevimiento

deceitful (dĭ sēt' fəl) *adj.* full of lies
engañoso *adj.* falso o lleno de mentiras

deck (dĕk) *n.* main level of the outside of a ship
cubierta *s.* nivel principal de la parte exterior de un barco

defy (dĭ fī') *v.* resist with boldness
desafiar *v.* atreverse; resistirse

descended (dĭ sĕn' dĭd) *v.* moved from a higher to a lower place; past tense of *descend*
descendió *v.* se rebajó a; pasado de *descend/descender*

determine (dĭ tûr' mĭn) *v.* decide
determinar *v.* decidir

determined (dĭ tûr' mĭnd) *adj.* not willing to change one's mind
resuelto *adj.* decidido firmemente

devastated (dĕv' ə stā' tĭd) *v.* destroyed; past tense of *devastate*
desoló *v.* destruyó; pasado de *devastate/desolar*

disgusted (dĭs gŭs' tĭd) *adj.* irritated and impatient
disgustado *adj.* fastidiado e impaciente

disputes (dĭ spyōōts') *n.* arguments
disputas *s.* discusiones

distracted (dĭ străk' tĭd) *adj.* not paying attention
distraído *adj.* no poniendo atencion

distress (dĭ strĕs') *n.* suffering
angustia *s.* sufrimiento o dolor

document (dŏk' yə mənt) *n.* official report
documento *s.* informe o escrito oficial

drifted (drĭf' tĭd) *v.* wandered; past tense of *drift*
deambuló *v.* vagó; pasado de *drift/deambular*

E

elegant (ĕl' ĭ gənt) *adj.* classy
elegante *adj.* refinado

emerged (ĭ mûrjd') *v.* came into view; past tense of *emerge*
emergió *v.* salió a la vista; pasado de *emerge/emerger*

employee (ĕm ploi' ē) *n.* person who works for pay
empleado *s.* alguien que recibe un pago por su trabajo

encouraged (ĕn kûr' ĭjd) *adj.* given a sense of hope
alentado *adj.* estimulado

entangled (ĕn tăng' gəld) *adj.* twisted together
embrollado *adj.* enredado

erupt (ĭ rŭpt') *v.* explode
hacer erupción *v.* explotar

essential (ĭ sĕn' shəl) *adj.* necessary
esencial *adj.* muy necesario

exhibited (ĭg zĭb' ĭ tĭd) *v.* presented for others to see; past tense of *exhibit*
exhibió *v.* presentó para que otros vean; pasado de *exhibit/exhibir*

F

fashioned (făsh' ənd) *v.* shaped or formed; past tense of *fashion*
moldeó *v.* formó o labró; pasado de *fashion/moldear*

fasts (făsts) *n.* periods of time without food
ayunos *s.* períodos de tiempo sin comer ningún alimento

fatal (fāt' l) *adj.* deadly
fatal *adj.* mortal

feuds (fyōōdz) *n.* bitter fights
enemistades *s.* luchas prolongadas

G

gladiators (glăd' ē ā' tərz) *n.* men who fought each other as a public show
gladiadores *s.* hombres que luchan entre sí en un espectáculo público

glaring (glâr' ĭng) *adj.* staring in anger
iracundo *adj.* que mira con rabia

H

handicaps (hăn' dē kăps') *n.* physical disabilities
discapacidades *s.* impedimentos físicos

harbor (här' bər) *n.* area of shelter where ships may anchor
puerto *s.* lugar donde anclan los barcos

heir (âr) *n.* one who gets a person's money or title after the person dies
heredero *s.* alguien que recibe dinero o títulos después de la muerte de otra persona

hilarity (hĭ lăr' ĭ tē) *n.* fun and laughter
hilaridad *s.* risa y animación

horizon (hə rī' zən) *n.* line where the earth seems to meet the sky
horizonte *s.* línea donde la tierra parece unirse con el cielo

huddled (hŭd' ld) *v.* crowded together; past tense of *huddle*
se acurrucó *v.* se apiñó; pasado de *huddle/acurrucarse*

I

idiotic (ĭd' ē ŏt' ĭk) *adj.* stupid
idiota *adj.* estupidez o torpeza

imbecile (ĭm' bə sĭl) *n.* silly or stupid person
imbécil *s.* persona tonta o estúpida

impostor (ĭm pŏs' tər) *n.* person who pretends to be someone else
impostor *s.* persona que se hace pasar por otra

inherit (ĭn hĕr′ ĭt) *v.* receive from one who has died
heredar *v.* recibir de alguien que ha muerto

instinctively (ĭn stĭngk′ tĭv lē) *adj.* by natural action; without thinking
instintivamente *adj.* de una manera que es natural o espontánea

J

jealousy (jĕl′ ə sē) *n.* fear of losing one's love to another person
celos *s.* temor a perder el amor de una persona a otra

M

menacingly (mĕn′ ĭ sĭng lē) *adv.* in a threatening way
amenazantemente *adv.* de un modo que amenaza o desafía

mimicking (mĭm′ ĭ kĭng) *n.* imitating
parodia *s.* imitación

mission (mĭsh′ ən) *n.* special duty
misión *s.* deber o tarea especial

mortal (môr′ tl) *adj.* extreme, almost threatening death
mortal *adj.* ser casi fatal o de muerte

motto (mŏt′ ō) *n.* sentence that expresses the group's goals
lema *s.* oración que expresa las metas de un grupo

N

nausea (nô′ zē ə) *n.* sick feeling in the stomach
náusea *s.* sensación de malestar en el estómago

navigator (năv′ ĭ gā′ tər) *n.* one who tells a pilot where to go
navegante *s.* quien le indica a un piloto en qué dirección ir

nonviolent (nŏn vī′ ə lənt) *adj.* not using force as a way of getting results
sin violencia *adj.* no emplear la fuerza como medio para obtener resultados

novice (nŏv′ ĭs) *n.* beginner
novato *s.* principiante

O

occurrence (ə kûr′ əns) *n.* event
occurrencia *s.* suceso

offended (ə fĕn′ dĭd) *v.* hurt; past tense of *offend*
ofendió *v.* lastimó; pasedo de *offend/ofender*

ominously (ŏm′ ə nəs lē) *adv.* in a threatening way
ominosamente *adv.* de modo amenazante

oppress (ə prĕs′) *v.* rule harshly
oprimir *v.* gobernar con tiranía

P

paralysis (pə răl′ ĭ sĭs) *n.* the loss of the power to move or feel
parálisis *s.* pérdida de la facultad para moverse o sentir

passes (păs′ ĭz) *n.* ways around, over, or through mountains
desfiladeros *s.* pasos estrechos entre montañas

plains (plānz) *n.* large, treeless area of land
planicies *s.* terreno extenso sin árboles

plantation (plăn tā′ shən) *n.* large farm in the South where workers raised crops
plantación *s.* granja grande del Sur donde los trabajadores sembraban

potential (pə tĕn′ shəl) *n.* ability
potencial *s.* habilidad

precisely (prĭ sīs′ lē) *adv.* exactly
precisamente *adv.* exactamente

prejudice (prĕj′ ə dĭs) *n.* unfair treatment, usually based on race or religion
prejuicio *s.* trato injusto por logeneral basado en raza o religión

procedure (prə sē′ jər) *n.* way of doing something
procedimiento *s.* forma de hacer algo

profile (prō′ fīl′) *n.* side view of a face
perfil *s.* vista lateral de un rostro

prospects (prŏs′ pĕkts′) *n.* people with possibilities
candidatos *s.* personas con buenas posibilidades

Q

quills (kwĭlz) *n.* sharp, hollow spines, like pointed needles
púas *s.* puntas agudas

R

radioactive (rā′ dē ō ăk′ tĭv) *adj.* containing particles of radiation
radioactivo *adj.* que contiene partículas de radiación

rails (rālz) *n.* two steel bars that form train tracks
rieles *s.* dos barras de acero que forman la carrilera del tren

reassuringly (rē′ ə shŏŏr′ ĭng lē) *adv.* in a way that makes one trust
alentadoramente *adv.* de un modo que brinda confianza o tranquilidad

reins (rānz) *n.* straps used to control a horse
riendas *s.* correas que se usan para controlar a un caballo

rejection (rĭ jĕk′ shən) *n.* act of being refused
repudio *s.* rechazo

reluctantly (rĭ lŭk′ tənt lē) *adv.* unwillingly
a regañadientes *adv.* de mala gana

required (rĭ kwīrd′) *adj.* needed
requerido *adj.* necesario

retreat (rĭ trēt′) *v.* withdraw from attack
replegarse *v.* retirarse de un ataque

revived (rĭ vīvd′) *v.* refreshed; past tense of *revive*
reavivó *v.* reanimó; pasado de *revive/reavivar*

routine (rōō tēn′) *adj.* regular
rutinario *adj.* regular

rumor (rōō′ mər) *n.* unproved information spread by word of mouth
rumor *s.* información no comprobada que va de boca en boca

S

sacred (sā′ krĭd) *adj.* holy
sagrado *adj.* bendito o divino

satellites (săt′ l īts′) *n.* man-made objects that orbit the earth
satétiles *s.* objetos lanzados para girar alrededor de la Tierra

savage (săv′ ĭj) *adj.* fiercely wild
salvaje *adj.* feroz

savage (săv′ ĭj) *n.* fierce, brutal person
salvaje *s.* persona feroz y brutal

scrolls (skrōlz) *n.* rolls of paper, usually with writing on them
volutas *s.* rollos de papel, por lo común con algo escrito

secondhand (sĕk′ ənd hănd′) *adj.* used; not new
de segunda mano *adj.* usado; que no es nuevo

secure (sĭ kyŏŏr′) *adj.* free from danger
salvo *adj.* libre de peligro

seized (sēzd) *v.* captured by force; past tense of *seize*
capturó *v.* tomó a la fuerza; pasado de *seize/capturar*

self-conscious (sĕlf′ kŏn′ shəs) *adj.* very aware of one's own actions and appearance
cohibido *adj.* que se refrena por temor a lo que otros piensen de sus acciones o apariencia

settlement (sĕt′ l mənt) *n.* small community
poblado *s.* pequeña comunidad

shimmering (shĭm′ ər ĭng) *adj.* shining with a flickering light
resplandeciente *adj.* que brilla tenuemente

spindly (spĭnd′ lē) *adj.* slender and long
larguirucho *adj.* alto y delgado

sprawled (sprôld) *v.* spread out; past tense of *sprawl*
se desparramó *v.* se extendió; pasado de *sprawl/desparramarse*

spunky (spŭng′ kē) *adj.* having spirit or courage
valeroso *adj.* que tiene ánimo o valor

stallion (stăl′ yən) *n.* adult male horse
semental *s.* caballo reproductor

stipulated (stĭp′ yə lā′ tĭd) *v.* ordered; past tense of *stipulate*
estipuló *v.* ordenó; pasado de *stipulate/estipular*

submitted (səb mĭt′ ĭd) *v.* presented for approval; past tense of *submit*
presentó *v.* entregó para aprobacion; pasado de *submit/presentar*

suspiciously (sə spĭsh′ əs lē) *adv.* without trust
suspicazmente *adv.* sin confianza; con dudas

swirling (swûr′ lĭng) *v.* moving with a twisting motion
revoleando *v.* dando vueltas; girando

synagogues (sĭn′ ə gŏgz′) *n.* places of worship for Jews
sinagogas *s.* lugares de oración para los judíos

system (sĭs′ təm) *n.* set way of doing things
sistema *s.* conjunto de métodos para hacer alguna cosa

T

tactics (tăk′ tĭks) *n.* methods used to get results
tácticas *s.* métodos utilizados para obtener resultados

terrapin (tĕr′ ə pĭn) *n.* turtle
terrapene *s.* tortuga

timber (tĭm′ bər) *n.* tree
maderamen *s.* tronco de árbol

tolerant (tŏl′ ər ənt) *adj.* respectful of the beliefs or customs of others
tolerante *adj.* respetuoso de las creencias o costumbres de otros

tomahawks (tŏm′ ə hôks′) *n.* lightweight axes used as tools or weapons
tomahawks *s.* hachas livianas utilizadas como herramienta o armas de guerra

topple (tŏp′ əl) *v.* push over
volcar *v.* caer

torpedo (tôr pē′ dō) *n.* cigar-shaped weapon that can explode
torpedo *s.* arma con forma de cigarro que puede explotar

torture (tôr′ chər) *n.* the causing of physical pain as punishment
tortura *s.* dolor físico como forma de castigo

turnover (tûrn′ ō′ vər) *n.* fruit-filled pastry
tarta *s.* pastelito relleno de fruta

U

uninhabited (ŭn′ ĭn hăb′ ĭ tĭd) *adj.* without people
deshabitado *adj.* sin habitantes

union (yōōn′ yən) *n.* organized group of workers
sindicato *s.* grupo organizado de trabajadores

V

vessel (vĕs′ əl) *n.* boat
embarcación *s.* barco

veterans (vĕt′ ər ənz) *n.* soldiers with long experience
veteranos *s.* soldados con mucha experiencia

vulture (vŭl′ chər) *n.* bird that eats dead things
buitre *s.* ave que se alimenta de cosas muertas

W

willful (wĭl′ fəl) *adj.* always wanting to get one's own way
voluntarioso *adj.* que quiere que las cosas siempre se hagan a su manera

wistful (wĭst′ fəl) *adj.* dreamy
melancólico *adj.* soñador

wits (wĭts) *n.* ability to think fast
agudeza *s.* habilidad para pensar rápidamente

Index of Authors and Titles

Acknowledgments

Literature

UNIT ONE

HarperCollins Publishers: *Cinder Edna* by Ellen Jackson, illustrated by Kevin O'Malley. Text copyright © 1994 by Ellen Jackson. Illustrations copyright © 1994 by Kevin O'Malley. Used by permission of HarperCollins Publishers.

Harcourt: "The No-Guitar Blues," from *Baseball in April and Other Stories* by Gary Soto. Copyright © 1990 by Gary Soto. Reprinted by permission of Harcourt.

UNIT TWO

Alfred A. Knopf Children's Books: "A Slave," from *Many Thousand Gone* by Virginia Hamilton. Copyright © 1993 by Virginia Hamilton. Reprinted by permission of Alfred A. Knopf Children's Books, a division of Random House, Inc.

Carolrhoda Books: *Wilma Mankiller* by Linda Lowery. Published by Carolrhoda Books, Inc., a division of the Lerner Publishing Group. Text copyright © 1996 by Linda Lowery. Used by permission of the publisher. All rights reserved.

J. Weston Walch, Publisher: "Cesar Chavez: Civil Rights Champion," from *16 Extraordinary Hispanic Americans* by Nancy Lobb. Copyright © 1995 by J. Weston Walch, Publisher. Used with permission of J. Weston Walch, Publisher. Further reproduction prohibited.

UNIT THREE

Viking Penguin: "Trombones and Colleges," from *Fast Sam, Cool Clyde, and Stuff* by Walter Dean Myers. Copyright © 1975 by Walter Dean Myers. Used by permission of Viking Penguin, an imprint of Penguin Putnam Books for Young Readers, a division of Penguin Putnam Inc.

Chronicle Books: "In a Neighborhood in Los Angeles," from *Body in Flames/Cuerpo en Llamas* by Francisco X. Alarcón. Copyright © 1990 by Francisco X. Alarcón. Reprinted by permission of Chronicle Books.

Marshall Cavendish: "Mudslinging," from *Mud Matters* by Jennifer Owings Dewey. Copyright © 1998 by Jennifer Owings Dewey. Reprinted by arrangement with Marshall Cavendish.

Jesse Stuart Foundation and Marian Reiner, Literary Agent: "Another April," from *Tales from the Plum Grove Hills* by Jesse Stuart. Copyright © 1942, 1946 by Jesse Stuart, copyright renewed by Jesse Stuart and the Jesse Stuart Foundation. Used by permission of the Jesse Stuart Foundation and Marian Reiner, Literary Agent.

Random House: "On Aging," from *And Still I Rise* by Maya Angelou. Copyright © 1978 by Maya Angelou. Reprinted by permission of Random House, Inc.

UNIT FOUR

Marjorie Murray: "The Telephone," from *The Haunting of Hathaway House* by John Murray. Reprinted by permission of Marjorie Murray.

Plays Magazine: "The Prince and the Pauper" by Mark Twain, adapted by Joellen Bland, *Plays* Magazine, April 2000, Vol. 59, No. 6. Copyright © 2000 Kalmbach Publishing Co. Reprinted by permission of Plays Magazine.

UNIT FIVE

Henry Holt and Company: "Dust of Snow" by Robert Frost, from *The Poetry of Robert Frost*, edited by Edward Connery Lathem. Copyright 1923, © 1969 by Henry Holt and Co., copyright 1951 by Robert Frost. Reprinted by permission of Henry Holt and Company, L.L.C.

Curtis Brown, Ltd.: "Elevator" by Lucille Clifton. Appears in *Home: A Collaboration of Thirty Distinguished Authors and Illustrators of Children's Books to Aid the Homeless*, edited by Michael Rosen. Published by HarperTrophy, a division of HarperCollins. Copyright © 1992 by Lucille Clifton. Reprinted by permission of Curtis Brown, Ltd.

"Graffiti" by Jane Yolen, published in *Sky Scrape/City Scape: Poems of City Life*, selected by Jane Yolen. Published by Wordsong/Boyds Mills Press. Copyright © 1996 by Jane Yolen. Reprinted by permission of Curtis Brown, Ltd.

HarperCollins Publishers: Excerpts from "Haiku" by Issa from *The Essential Haiku: Versions of Basho, Buson & Issa*, edited and with an introduction by Robert Hass. Introduction and selection copyright © 1994 by Robert Hass. Unless otherwise noted, all translations copyright © 1994 by Robert Hass. Reprinted by permission of HarperCollins Publishers, Inc.

Jesús Papoleto Meléndez: "Happy Thought," from *Street Poetry & Other Poems* by Jesús Papoleto Meléndez. Copyright © 1972 by Jesús Papoleto Meléndez. Reprinted by permission of the author.

Alfred A. Knopf: "Daybreak in Alabama," from *The Collected Poems of Langston Hughes*. Copyright © 1994 by the Estate of Langston Hughes. Reprinted by permission of Alfred A. Knopf, a division of Random House, Inc.

UNIT SIX

Dutton Children's Books: "High as Han Hsin," from *Shen of the Sea: Chinese Stories for Children* by Arthur Bowie Chrisman. Copyright © 1925 by E. P. Dutton, copyright renewed 1953 by Arthur Bowie Chrisman. Used by permission of Dutton Children's Books, a division of Penguin Putnam Inc.

Simon & Schuster Books for Young Readers: "For Want of a Horseshoe Nail," from *The Book of Virtues for Young People: A Treasury of Great Moral Stories*, edited by William J. Bennett. Copyright © 1997 by William J. Bennett. Reprinted with the permission of Simon & Schuster Books for Young Readers, an imprint of Simon & Schuster Children's Publishing Division.

"Crash Diet," from *It's Disgusting–And We Ate It!* by James Solheim. Text copyright © 1998 by James Solheim. Reprinted with the permission of Simon & Schuster Books for Young Readers, an imprint of Simon & Schuster Children's Publishing Division.

Multimedia Product Development: "Shot Down Behind Enemy Lines," from *Incredible True Adventures* by Don L. Wulffson. Copyright © 1986 by Don L. Wulffson. Reprinted by permission of Multimedia Product Development, Inc., Chicago, Illinois.

Hyperion Books for Children: *Fa Mulan* by Robert D. San Souci. Text copyright © 1998 by Robert D. San Souci. Reprinted by permission of Hyperion Books for Children.

UNIT SEVEN

Hugh B. Cave: "Two Were Left" by Hugh B. Cave. Copyright © 1942 by the Crowell Collier Publishing Co. Reprinted by permission of the author.

The Jewish Publication Society: *Terrible Things: An Allegory of the Holocaust* by Eve Bunting (Philadelphia: The Jewish Publication Society, 1989). Copyright © 1980, 1989 by Eve Bunting. Reprinted by permission of The Jewish Publication Society.

Scholastic: "Speech" by Parson Martin Niemöller, from *Bearing Witness: Stories of the Holocaust*, selected by Hazel Rochman and Darlene Z. McCampbell. Copyright © 1995 by Hazel Rochman and Darlene Z. McCampbell. Reprinted by permission of Scholastic Inc.

UNIT EIGHT

Curtis Brown, Ltd.: "Ships That Could Think," from *Great Mysteries of the Sea* by Edward F. Dolan, Jr. Copyright © 1984 by Edward F. Dolan, Jr. Reprinted by permission of Curtis Brown, Ltd.

HarperCollins Publishers: Excerpt from *Earthquakes* by Franklyn M. Branley. Text copyright © 1990 by Franklyn M. Branley. Used by permission of HarperCollins Publishers.

Diana Nightingale: "Sparky," from *Earl Nightingale's Greatest Discovery* by Earl Nightingale. Copyright © 1987 by Earl C. Nightingale. Reprinted by permission of Diana Nightingale.

DK Publishing: "The Roswell Incident," from *Invaders from Outer Space: Real-Life Stories of UFOs* by Philip Brooks. Copyright © 1999 by Dorling Kindersley Limited, London. Reprinted by permission of DK Publishing, Inc.

UNIT NINE

Curtis Brown, Ltd., and H. W. Wilson Company: "The Jade Stone" by Caryn Yacowitz, published by Holiday House. Adapted by Aaron Shepard, pp. 27–33, in *Stories on Stage: Scripts for Reader's Theater.* Copyright © 1992 by Caryn Yacowitz. Copyright © 1993 by Aaron Shepard. Reprinted by permission of Curtis Brown, Ltd. and the H. W. Wilson Company.

BOA Editions: "The Carver," from *Good Woman: Poems and a Memoir, 1969–1980* by Lucille Clifton. Copyright © 1986 by Lucille Clifton. Reprinted with the permission of BOA Editions, Ltd.

Westwood Creative Artists: "The Stolen Party" by Liliana Heker, which appeared in *Other Fires: Short Fiction by Latin American Women*, edited and translated by Alberto Manguel. Copyright © 1982 by Liliana Heker. Translation copyright © 1985 by Alberto Manguel. Reprinted by permission of Westwood Creative Artists Ltd.

Blackbirch Press: "Acceptance," from *Jane Goodall: Naturalist* by J. A. Senn. Copyright © 1993 by Blackbirch Press, Inc. Reprinted by permission.

James Haskins: "Growing Up in a World of Darkness," from *The Story of Stevie Wonder* by James Haskins. Copyright © 1976 by James Haskins. Reprinted by permission of the author.

UNIT TEN

Simon & Schuster Books for Young Readers: "Some People," from *The Pointed People: Verses & Silhouettes* by Rachel Field. Copyright 1924, 1930 by The Macmillan Company, copyright renewed © 1958 by Arthur S. Pederson. Reprinted with the permission of Simon & Schuster Books for Young Readers, an imprint of Simon & Schuster Children's Publishing Division.

HarperCollins Publishers: "Almost Human," from *Earth Lines: Poems for the Green Age* by Pat Moon. Copyright © 1991 by Pat Moon. Used by permission of HarperCollins Publishers.

"Point of View," from *Where the Sidewalk Ends* by Shel Silverstein. Copyright © 1974 by Evil Eye Music. Used by permission of HarperCollins Publishers.

"Nikki-Rosa," from *The Selected Poems of Nikki Giovanni* by Nikki Giovanni. Compilation copyright © 1996 by Nikki Giovanni. Reprinted by permission of HarperCollins Publishers.

UNIT ELEVEN

Sternig & Byrne Literary Agency: "The Invaders" by Jack Ritchie, first appeared in *Boy's Life* Magazine, March, 1978. Reprinted by permission of the Sternig & Byrne Literary Agency.

Perfection Learning Corporation: "Weapons of War," from *The American Revolution: Moments in History* by Shirley Jordan. Copyright © 1999 by Perfection Learning Corporation. Reprinted by permission of Perfection Learning Corporation.

Cynthia J. Nadelman: "The New Mother," from *They Knew Abe Lincoln: A Boy in Indiana* by Frances Cavanah. By permission of Cynthia Nadelman for the Estate of Frances Cavanah.

Doubleday: Excerpt from *California Gold Days* by Helen Bauer. Copyright © 1954 by Helen Bauer. Used by permission of Doubleday, a division of Random House, Inc.

Barbara S. Kouts, Literary Agent: "Rabbit Foot: A Story of the Peacemaker" by Joseph Bruchac, from *On the Wings of Peace*, edited by Sheila Hamanaka (Clarion Books, New York). Copyright © 1995 by Joseph Bruchac. Reprinted by permission of Barbara S. Kouts, Literary Agent.

UNIT TWELVE

Scholastic: Excerpt from *Hiroshima* by Laurence Yep. Copyright © 1995 by Laurence Yep. Reprinted by permission of Scholastic Inc.

Clarion Books/Houghton Mifflin Company: "Floating Lanterns XII" by Iri and Toshi Maruki, translated by Nancy Hunter with Yasuo Ishikawa, from *On the Wings of Peace*, edited by Sheila Hamanaka. Copyright © 1984 by Iri and Toshi Maruki. Text translation copyright © 1994 by Nancy Hunter. Compilation copyright © 1995 by Sheila Hamanaka. Reprinted by permission of Clarion Books/Houghton Mifflin Company. All rights reserved.

Blackbirch Press: Excerpt from *Anne Frank: Child of the Holocaust* by Gene Brown. Copyright © 1991 by Blackbirch Press, Inc. Reprinted by permission.

Atheneum Books for Young Readers: *Black Whiteness* by Robert Burleigh, illustrations by Walter Lyon Krudop. Text copyright © 1998 by Robert Burleigh. Illustrations copyright © 1998 by Walter Lyon Krudop. Reprinted with the permission of Atheneum Books for Young Readers, an imprint of Simon & Schuster Children's Publishing Division.

Art Credits

COVER

San Francisco Copyright © Corbis Images/PictureQuest; *door* Copyright © The Right Image/Stock Connection/PictureQuest; *dragon* Christie's Images/Superstock; *helicopter* AP/Wide World Photos; *memorial* Copyright © David Samuel Robbins/Corbis; *boy* Myrleen Ferguson Cate/PhotoEdit; *fan* Copyright © David Young-Wolff/Photoedit/PictureQuest; *lantern* Copyright © AFP/Corbis.

UNIT ONE

3 *top* Photo by Sharon Hoogstraten; **3** *center* Illustrations copyright © 1994 by Kevin O'Malley. Used with permission of HarperCollins Children's Books; **4** Photo by Sharon Hoogstraten; **6** Photo by Sharon Hoogstraten; **8** Photo by Sharon Hoogstraten; **9** Copyright © The Right Image/Stock Connection/PictureQuest; **10** Photo by Sharon Hoogstraten; **12** Photo by Sharon Hoogstraten; **14** Illustrations copyright © 1994 by Kevin O'Malley. Used with permission of HarperCollins Children's Books; **17** Illustrations copyright © 1994 by Kevin O'Malley. Used with permission of HarperCollins Children's Books; **20** Illustrations copyright © 1994 by Kevin O'Malley. Used with permission of HarperCollins Children's Books; **24** Illustrations copyright © 1994 by Kevin O'Malley. Used with permission of HarperCollins Children's Books; **26** Copyright © Yann Arthus-Bertrand/Corbis; **27** Myrleen Ferguson Cate/PhotoEdit; **29**

30 Copyright © Stockbyte; **30** Copyright © Yann Arthus-Bertrand/Corbis; **33** Copyright © Stockbyte; **36** Photo by Barbara Seiler.

UNIT TWO

39 Copyright © Form and Function, San Francisco; **40** *Into Bondage* (1936) Aaron Douglas. Oil on canvas 60 3/8" x 60 1/2". In the collection of the Corcoran Gallery of Art, Washington, DC. Museum Purchase and partial gift from Thurlow Evans Tibbs. The Evans-Tibbs Collection; **41, 43, 44, 47** detail of *Into Bondage* (1936) Aaron Douglas. Oil on canvas 60 3/8" x 60 1/2". In the collection of the Corcoran Gallery of Art, Washington, DC. Museum Purchase and partial gift from Thurlow Evans Tibbs. The Evans-Tibbs Collection; **48** Copyright © Peter Turnley/Corbis; **48** Copyright © Bettmann/Corbis; **49** Copyright © Charles Doswell/Stone; **50** Copyright © Corbis Images/PictureQuest; **51** Copyright © Charles Doswell/Stone; **57** Copyright © Kevin Fleming/Corbis; **58** Copyright © J. Pat Carter/Liaison Agency; **61** Copyright © Bettmann/Corbis; **61** Copyright © Stockbyte; **65** Copyright © Bettmann/Corbis; **65** AP/Wide World Photos; **68** Copyright © Bettmann/Corbis; **69** Digital Imagery copyright © 2001 PhotoDisc, Inc.; **69** AP/Wide World Photos; **72** Digital Imagery copyright © 2001 PhotoDisc, Inc.; **73** AP/Wide World Photos; **74** Copyright © Bettmann/Corbis; **77** Digital Imagery copyright © 2001 PhotoDisc, Inc.

UNIT THREE

79 Photo by Suzanne Page; **79** Copyright © Stephen Trimble; **80** Copyright © Bob Daemmrich/Stock, Boston/PictureQuest; **84** Digital Imagery copyright © 2001 PhotoDisc, Inc.; **88** Digital Imagery copyright © 2001 PhotoDisc, Inc.; **90** Digital Imagery copyright © 2001 PhotoDisc, Inc.; **93** Digital Imagery copyright © 2001 PhotoDisc, Inc.; **93** Copyright © Bachman/ Pictor; **94** Photo by Suzanne Page; **94** Photo by Suzanne Page; **94** Copyright © Stephen Trimble; **97** Photo by Suzanne Page; **98** Photo by Sharon Hoogstraten; **98** Copyright © Joel Dexter/Unicom Stock Photos; **98** Copyright © Pat O'Hara/Corbis; **98–99** Digital Imagery copyright © 2001 PhotoDisc, Inc.; **99** Copyright © Joe McDonald/Animals Animals; **100** Photo by Sharon Hoogstraten; **103** Digital Imagery copyright © 2001 PhotoDisc, Inc.; **105** Copyright © Pat O'Hara/Corbis; **105** Photo by Sharon Hoogstraten; **108** Copyright © Joe McDonald/Animals Animals; **113** Photo by Sharon Hoogstraten.

UNIT FOUR

116 Copyright © Storm Pirate Productions/Artville/PictureQuest; **116, 118, 120, 121, 122, 123, 124, 125, 127** Photo by Sharon Hoogstraten; **129, 131** Photofest; **131** Digital Imagery copyright © 2001 PhotoDisc, Inc.; **134** Photofest; **139** Giraudon/Art Resource, New York; **145** Photofest; **146** Photofest.

UNIT FIVE

159 Copyright © Laurance B. Aiuppy/Stock Connection/PictureQuest; **159** Photo by Sharon Hoogstraten; **160** Copyright © Form and Function, San Francisco; **161** Copyright © Wood River Gallery/PictureQuest; **162** Copyright © Michael Newman/PhotoEdit/PictureQuest; **164** Art by Ingrid Hess. Photo by Sharon Hoogstraten; **164** Photo by Sharon Hoogstraten; **166** Copyright © Caroline Wood/Stone; **166** Digital Imagery copyright © 2001 PhotoDisc, Inc.; **168** Copyright © Ron Chapple/FPG International/PictureQuest; **168** Digital Imagery copyright © 2001 PhotoDisc, Inc.; **168** Photo by Sharon Hoogstraten; **170** Copyright © Joe McDonald/Animals Animals; **171** Photo by Sharon Hoogstraten; **172, 173** Copyright © Laurance B. Aiuppy/Stock Connection/PictureQuest.

UNIT SIX

175 Copyright © David Young-Wolff/Photoedit/PictureQuest; **175** Copyright © Kit Houghton Photography/Corbis; **175** AP/Wide World Photos; **176** Digital Imagery copyright © 2001 PhotoDisc, Inc.; **177** from *Fun with Kites* by John and Kate Dyson. Published by Angus & Robertson, a division of HarperCollins UK. Illustration copyright © Brian Robins; **178** Copyright © Burke & Triolo/Artville/PictureQuest; **180** Copyright © Keren Su/Corbis; **184** Copyright © Stockbyte; **190** Copyright © Kit Houghton Photography/Corbis; **191** Copyright © Kit Houghton Photography/Corbis; **191** Copyright © Kit Houghton Photography/Corbis; **192** Digital Imagery copyright © 2001 PhotoDisc, Inc.; **193** Copyright © Gianni Dagli Orti/Corbis; **194** AP/Wide World Photos; **199** from *NAM: The Vietnam Experience 1965-1975*. Copyright © Orbis Books, London; **203** AP/Wide World Photos; **204** Copyright © David Young-Wolff/Photoedit/PictureQuest; **204** *Woman Sewing* (ca. 1790) Chinese. Watercolor. Victoria & Albert Museum, London/Art Resource, New York; **204–205** Copyright © The Board of Trustees of the Armouries; **207** Copyright © The Board of Trustees of the Armouries; **208** *Archer on Horse* (1290), Ch'ien Hsuan. Ink and color on paper. British Museum, London; **211** Copyright © David Young-Wolff/Photoedit/PictureQuest.

UNIT SEVEN

213 Copyright © Vince Streano/Stone; **216** Digital Imagery copyright © 2001 PhotoDisc, Inc.; **217** Copyright © Ken Cole/Animals Animals; **217** Copyright © Vince Streano/Stone; **220** Illustration by Ingrid Hess; **220** Copyright © Cheryl Graham/Stone; **230** Copyright © 1979 by Dover Publications, Inc.; **232** *bottom* Digital Imagery copyright © 2001 PhotoDisc, Inc.; **232** *left* Copyright © Form and Function, San Francisco; *top* Digital Imagery copyright © 2001

Vocabulary
Mini-Lessons

Using Context Clues

1 Explain to students that sometimes they can figure out the meaning of an unfamiliar word or term by thinking about the context, or the surrounding words of the sentence or passage.

2 Write the following paragraph on the board and read it aloud:

> There is a serious *scarcity* of books in our school. Many of the bookcases in our library are bare, forcing students to look elsewhere for print resources. School administrators plan to order more books. Until the books arrive, however, students will have to deal with the shortage.

3 Then model how to use context to figure out the meaning of *scarcity:*

MODEL

I'm not sure what scarcity *means. I can look for context clues in the sentence this word is in and in the surrounding sentences. The phrases "bookcases are bare," "plan to order more books," and "deal with the shortage" help me figure out that* scarcity *means "lack or shortage."*

4 Now write the following paragraph on the board and read it aloud. Have a volunteer underline the context clues that could be used to help determine the meaning of the word *drought.*

> No rain had fallen in the area for months. For miles around, the land was dry and cracked. Hot winds blew dust around the dying crops. Unfortunately, according to weather experts, the *drought* would continue for months.

Point out to students that in the example above, a type of clue known as **details from general context** helped them figure out the meaning of *drought.* Encourage students to use such clues throughout the year, along with other common types of context clues:

Definition and Restatement

The **epidermis**—that is, the outer layer of skin—protects the nerves and sensitive tissue below.

(The phrase introduced by *that is* helps define *epidermis* as "the outer layer of skin.")

Example

I am frightened of **arachnids,** such as spiders and scorpions.

(Spiders and scorpions are examples of arachnids.)

Comparison and Contrast

Like the overjoyed crowd in the audience, I was **ecstatic** when I heard he had won.

(The word *like* helps you understand that *overjoyed* has the same or nearly the same meaning as *ecstatic.*)

Here's How

See the next three pages for useful lessons on context clues that you can duplicate for students.

CONTEXT CLUES (EXAMPLE)

A good way to make sense of an unfamiliar word is to look at the **context:** the other words in the sentence and other sentences in the paragraph that might give clues to the meaning of the word. There are a number of ways you can use context clues to help you determine a word's meaning.

Sometimes a sentence will provide an **example** that will help you understand the meaning of the word. Examples are often signaled by words or phrases such as

like	for instance	this	such as	especially
these	for example	other	includes	

Here's How   Using Examples in Context to Figure Out an Unfamiliar Word

The governor asked that farmers make use of all *arable* land, such as corn and wheat fields.

1. Identify the unfamiliar word.

(I'm not sure what the word *arable* means.)

2. Read to see if there is a word that signals that an example may follow.

(I see the phrase *such as.* Those words could lead to an example.)

3. Find the example or examples.

(The phrase *corn and wheat fields* follows the phrase *such as.* These must be examples of arable land.)

4. Ask yourself how the example or examples relate to the unfamiliar word.

(Corn and wheat are crops.)

5. Use this information to figure out what the word means.

(Since the examples are fields of crops, *arable* land must be land on which crops are grown, and *arable* must mean "capable of growing crops.")

6. Now, look the unfamiliar word up in the dictionary and jot the word and definition down in your personal word list.

   arable *adj.* Fit for cultivation (planting and growing crops)

CONTEXT CLUES (COMPARISON OR CONTRAST)

A good way to make sense of an unfamiliar word is to look at the **context:** the other words in the sentence and other sentences in the paragraph that might give clues to the meaning of the word. There are a number of ways you can use context clues to help you determine a word's meaning.

Sometimes a sentence will provide a **comparison** or a **contrast** that will help you understand the meaning of the word. Certain words or phrases signal comparison or contrast.

Some Comparison Signals		**Some Contrast Signals**	
like	similar to	but	although
as	also	unlike	however
related	resembling	rather than	on the other hand

Here's How   Using Comparison or Contrast to Figure Out an Unfamiliar Word

Our small shop is nearly as *prosperous* as that fancy department store, although we made very little money when we first opened.

1. Identify the unfamiliar word.

    (I'm not sure what the word *prosperous* means.)

2. Read to see if there is a word or phrase that signals that a comparison or a contrast may follow.

    (I see the words *as* and *although. As* could signal a comparison, and *although* could signal a contrast.)

3. Identify the comparison or contrast.

    (The sentence compares the prosperous shop with a big, fancy store, while it also sets up a contrast, stating that the shop didn't make much money at first.)

4. Use this information to figure out what the unfamiliar word means.

    (The contrast to the way the shop used to be and the comparison to the department store suggest that the shop is doing well. *Prosperous* must mean "doing well.")

5. Find the word in the dictionary and record it in your personal word list.

    prosperous *adj.* Having success; well-off

6. A sentence may contain only comparison or only contrast as a context clue. You can still use the strategy above to find the meaning.

CONTEXT CLUES (RESTATEMENT)

A good way to make sense of an unfamiliar word is to look at the **context:** the other words in the sentence and other sentences in the paragraph that might give clues to the meaning of the word. There are a number of ways you can use context clues to help you determine a word's meaning.

Sometimes a writer will **restate** the meaning of a difficult word within a sentence, defining it for you. Restatements or definitions are often signaled by words or phrases such as

or	which is	that is
also called	also known as	in other words

Here's How   **Using Restatement in Context to Figure Out an Unfamiliar Word**

Our teacher received a small *stipend,* or payment, for giving travel lectures to local clubs.

1. Identify the unfamiliar word.

   (I'm not sure what the word *stipend* means.)

2. Read to see if there is a word that signals that a restatement may follow.

   (I see the word *or.* What follows may include a restatement or definition.)

3. Find the restated information.

   (The word *or* points to the word *payment.*)

4. Use this information to figure out what the unfamiliar word means.

   (Because the words *or payment* follow *stipend,* I think *stipend* must mean "payment.")

5. Now, look the unfamiliar word up in the dictionary and jot the word and definition down in your personal word list.

   stipend *n.* A regular payment, such as a salary or allowance

Word Parts: Prefixes, Suffixes, and Compound Words

VOCABULARY MINI-LESSON

1 Explain to students that sometimes they can figure out the meaning of an unfamiliar word by thinking about the meaning of the word parts it contains.

2 Write the word *depopulated* on the board and read it aloud. Model how to use the base word and affixes to figure out the meaning of the word.

You could say: I'm not sure what depopulated *means. I can try breaking the word into parts. I see the prefix* de-, *which means "opposite" and which I have seen in other words, such as* deactivate *and* defrost. *I see the base word* populate, *which means "to supply with people; to live in or inhabit." I also see the suffix* -ed, *which is used to form the past tense. By combining the meanings of these word parts, I can figure out that* depopulated *must mean the opposite of "supplied with people." Maybe it means "took people out of an area." When I look in the dictionary to see if I am right, I find that the definition is "having a greatly reduced number of people or animals, often because of disease, war, or forced relocation."*

3 Explain to students that they can also break down compound words, which are made up of two words put together. Tell students that they can sometimes tell the meaning of a compound word by looking at the meaning of each word part.

4 Write the word *arrowhead* on the board and read it aloud. Model how to break it into parts and figure out the meaning.

You could say: I've never seen the word arrowhead *before. I can try to figure out its meaning by breaking it into two words,* arrow *and* head. *I know that an arrow is a weapon that is shot out of a bow, and a head is often the top or most important part of something. I think an arrowhead must be the top or most important part of an arrow—the part that sticks into the target.*

5 Share with students the following lists of commonly used prefixes, suffixes, and compound words.

Prefixes	Suffixes	Compound Words
ab- (away or apart from)	*-like* (similar to)	beadwork
chron- (time)	*-ful* (full of, resembling)	headache
tri- (three)	*-less* (without)	field trip
hyper- (excessively)	*-er* (person who does)	daydream
inter- (among or between)	*-ery* (job or skill)	sandpaper
micro- (small)	*-ation* (action or process)	fishpond
tele- (far)	*-arium* (place for)	lightheaded
trans- (across, beyond, or through)	*-hood* (state or quality of)	skateboard
re- (again)	*-ate* (to make)	downturn

6 The following list provides additional words for you and your students to model. Have volunteers explain how to use word parts to figure out the meaning of each word.

abnormal	childlike	adulthood	scarecrow	hyperactive	chronology
planetarium	telemarketer	interconnect	schoolwork	machination	sweatshirt
microscope	rebroadcast	hailstorm	transaction	broadcast	

Here's How

See the next three pages for useful lessons on working with prefixes, suffixes, and compound words. You can duplicate these lessons for students.

PREFIXES

A **prefix** is a word part attached to the beginning of a base word or root. The meaning of a prefix combines with the meaning of the base word or root. For example, the prefix *in-* often means "not," as in *indirect,* which means "not direct."

Here's How Using Prefixes to Determine Word Meaning

1. When you first encounter an unfamiliar word, try to determine whether the word has a prefix.

    malnutrition

    (The base word seems to be *nutrition,* since it can stand on its own, so the prefix must be *mal-.* I also recognize the prefix from seeing it in other words.)

2. If you recognize the prefix from a word you know, make an educated guess about its meaning.

    (I know that *malfunction* is when something functions improperly, so maybe *mal-* has something to do with "improper" or "bad.")

    Based on what you know about the prefix and the base word or root, make a guess about the meaning of the entire word.

    (*Malnutrition* must mean "improper or bad nutrition.")

3. Look up the word's definition in the dictionary and compare it with your guess.

    malnutrition *n.* Poor nutrition because of an imbalanced diet or faulty digestion

    (*Malnutrition* does have to do with improper nutrition; my guess was correct.)

4. Look at other words in the dictionary with the same prefix. Look to see what they have in common.

    malefactor *n.* An evildoer

    malice *n.* The desire to harm others or see others suffer

    (Basically, the prefix *mal-* means "bad" or "evil.")

5. Look in the dictionary for more words with the same prefix. Make yourself familiar with their definitions.

    malnourish, maleficent, malignant, malicious

SUFFIXES

A **suffix** is a word part attached to the end of a base word or root. A suffix usually determines a word's part of speech. Familiarity with common suffixes can help you determine the meanings of some unfamiliar words.

Here's How Using Suffixes to Determine Meaning

1. When you first encounter an unfamiliar word, try to determine whether the word has a suffix.

    perishable

    (The base word seems to be *perish,* since it can stand on its own, so the suffix must be *-able.* I also recognize the suffix from seeing it in other words.)

2. If you recognize the suffix from a word you know, make an educated guess about its meaning.

    (I know that *inflatable* means "able to be inflated," so *-able* probably means "able to.")

    Based on what you know about the suffix and the base word, make a guess about the meaning of the entire word.

    (I know that *perish* means "to be destroyed," so *perishable* must mean "able to be destroyed.")

3. Look up the word's definition in the dictionary and compare it with your guess.

    perishable *adj.* Subject to decay, spoilage, or destruction, especially pertaining to food

    (*Perishable* does have to do with being destroyed or ruined, but it is usually specific to food; my guess was close.)

4. Try to think of other words with the same suffix. What do they have in common?

    movable, forgivable, edible, credible

    (Basically, the suffix *-able* or *-ible* means "able to be.")

COMPOUND WORDS

A **compound word** is a word made up of two words put together. The meanings of the two word parts combine to form a new meaning. Sometimes the meaning of a compound word is obvious when you look at the meaning of each word part. For example, the word *doghouse* is made up of the words *dog* and *house.* It simply means a small building where a dog can live. Other times, the meaning is not as clear, but it is usually still related to the meaning of the two word parts.

Here's How   Understanding Compound Words

1. When you see an unfamiliar compound word, look first for its two word parts.

downpour

(The word parts of *downpour* are *down* and *pour.*)

2. Look at the meanings of the two parts and think of how they might be related.

(*Downpour* probably has something to do with both *down* and *pour.* I know that *down* means "from a higher place to a lower place," and I know that to *pour* something means to make it flow or empty out. How are these two words connected? I've heard people say "It's pouring out" or "It's pouring down" when it rains, so maybe the word *downpour* is related to rain.)

3. Look up the word's definition in the dictionary and compare it with your guess.

downpour *n.* a severe rainstorm; a heavy fall of rain.

(My guess was correct.)

4. Some compound words have a meaning that doesn't make obvious sense. When you encounter such a word, break it into its word parts and see what sense you can make of it.

far-flung

(The word parts of *far-flung* are *far* and *flung.* Does it have something to do with throwing things?)

5. Look up the word's definition in the dictionary and compare it with your thoughts.

far-flung *adj.* Distant, wide-ranging, or widely distributed: *a far-flung family.*

(Although *far-flung* doesn't literally mean "thrown a long distance," it does mean "found over a wide area." I can imagine someone throwing a handful of seeds or rocks and watching them spread out as they fall, and the same idea could be used to describe things that aren't thrown. So there is at least a loose connection between *far-flung* and throwing something a long way.)

Word Parts: Roots

VOCABULARY MINI-LESSON

1 Explain to students that sometimes they can figure out the meaning of an unfamiliar word if they recognize its root from other, familiar words. You may want to explain that a **root** is a word part that contains the most important element of that word's meaning. A root must be combined with other word parts, such as prefixes or suffixes, to form a word.

2 Write the word *humidifier* on the board and read it aloud. Model how to use the root to help determine the word's meaning.

You could say: I've never seen the word humidifier *before. I've seen the root* humid *in other words, such as* humidity. *I know that* humidity *refers to how much water is in the air, so I think* humid *means "moisture" or "water." I've seen the word part* -ifier *in words such as* amplifier *and* purifier, *and I'm pretty sure it means "a person or machine that does something." Does* humidifier *mean "someone or something that adds water"? When I look up the word in the dictionary to confirm my guess, I see that it means "a device for increasing the amount of moisture in the air of an enclosed space, such as a room or greenhouse."*

3 Now write the following chart on the board:

Root	Meaning
arithm	number
aut	self
dict	speak
fin	end or limit
mim	imitate

Root	Meaning
mut	change
negat	deny
plac	please
poli	city

4 Have volunteers use the information in the chart as they try to define the words below. Make sure they explain the process they used to figure out the meaning of each word.

arithmetic   automated   automaton   dictator   diction   predict   finality
mimic   pantomime   immutable   mutation   negation   placid   metropolitan

5 As the year progresses, you may wish to review this strategy. The following chart provides you with additional words, roots, and meanings.

Root	Meaning	Examples
alter	other	alternate, alternative
cred	believe or trust	discredit, incredible
dent	tooth	dental, indent, trident
don	give	donor, donation
fac	make or do	factory, manufacture
ge	earth	geography, geocentric, geopolitical
log	word, speech, or idea	apology, monologue
ne	new	neon, neoclassical, neologism
phys	nature or growth	physician, physics
soph	wise	philosopher, sophomore
vis	see	visual, television, revise

Here's How

See the next page for useful lessons on using word roots to determine meaning. You can duplicate these lessons for students.

ROOTS

Many English words, especially long ones, can be broken into smaller parts. A **root** is the core of a word, or the part that contains the most important element of the word's meaning.

Many words in English have origins in other languages, particularly Greek and Latin. Knowing the meanings of Greek and Latin roots can help you to understand unfamiliar words.

Here's How Using Word Roots to Determine Meaning

1. When you first encounter an unfamiliar word, try to determine the word's root.

   ventilate

   (The root might be *vent* or *ate*. Since *ate* appears at the end of so many words, it is probably not part of the root. The root must be *vent*.)

2. If you recognize the root from a word you do know, make an educated guess about the word's meaning.

   (I know that a *vent* is an opening that air passes through, so maybe *ventilate* also has something to do with the movement of air.)

3. Look up the word's definition in the dictionary and compare it with your guess.

   ventilate *v.* To admit fresh air into (a mine, for example); to replace stale air

   (*Ventilate* does have to do with the movement of air; my guess was correct.)

4. Read the word's etymology at the end of the dictionary entry.

   [From Latin *ventilāre,* to fan, from *ventus,* wind.]

   (Basically, *vent* has to do with blowing air.)

5. Try to think of other words with the same root. (Hint: For words without prefixes, try looking at nearby words in the dictionary.)

   vent, ventilation, ventage, ventifact

Understanding Idioms

VOCABULARY MINI-LESSON

1 Tell students that an idiom is a phrase whose meaning is different from the meanings of its individual words put together. Explain to students that they can sometimes figure out the meaning of an unfamiliar idiom by thinking about its context, or the surrounding words of the sentence or passage.

2 Write the following sentences on the board and read them aloud:

> **Emily wasn't supposed to tell Fred that we're planning a surprise party for him, but she let the cat out of the bag. Now it won't be a surprise anymore.**

3 Then model how to use context to figure out the meaning of *let the cat out of the bag.*

MODEL
I've never seen the phrase let the cat out of the bag *before, and I have no idea what it means. To find out, I can look for context clues in the rest of the passage. Emily wasn't supposed to tell about the party; but then she did something, and now the party won't be a surprise. I think she must have told Fred the secret about the party. If I substitute* told a secret *for* let the cat out of the bag, *it makes sense in the passage. Therefore, I think that* let the cat out of the bag *means "tell a secret."*

4 The following boldface sentences contain commonly used idioms. Write these sentences on the chalkboard (but not the paraphrases given in parentheses). Ask students to read the sentences and use context clues to figure out the meanings of the idioms.

> **Can we *count on* you to help us with the cooking? Are you sure you will be there?** (Can we depend on, rely on, or trust you?)

> **Last night's math homework sure was *a tough nut to crack.* I spent an hour working hard on it before I got the answers.** (The homework was difficult and time-consuming.)

> ***"Hold your horses!"* Tammi said. "I'm not ready, so you'll have to wait!"** (Slow down! Be more patient!)

> **Ed didn't know whether the plans were *in cement* or whether he could make some changes.** (He didn't know if the plans were firmly set.)

5 As the year progresses, you may wish to review this strategy with the following list of idioms.

Idiom	Meaning
a bolt from the blue	a shocking, startling, unexpected event
give him (or her) the runaround	avoid a clear explanation
hit the books	study hard
ill at ease	uncomfortable
in a flash	very quickly
an iron hand	total control
just what the doctor ordered	precisely what is needed
knock our socks off	impress us, amaze us
knows his (or her) stuff	is an expert
make a bundle	earn a great deal of money
a mover and shaker	a powerful person
pull the wool over my eyes	fool me, deceive me
see red	become angry
the spitting image of	exactly like
top dollar	an extremely high price
What's eating you?	What's upsetting or bothering you?

Here's How
Duplicate the next page for a useful lesson on understanding idioms.

UNDERSTANDING IDIOMS

An **idiom** is a set phrase whose meaning is different from the literal meaning of its individual words. For example, the idiom *all fired up* has nothing to do with fires; it simply means "very angry or wildly excited."

Most idioms are so common that people use them without thinking about them. However, unfamiliar idioms can be very confusing. If you didn't know that *he sees the world through rose-colored glasses* really means "he has an unrealistically positive opinion of every situation" or "he is an optimist," you might wonder what the color of a person's glasses has to do with anything!

When you see an unfamiliar idiom, you can sometimes find clues in the idiom's context, or surrounding words and paragraphs.

Here's How Understanding Idioms

When Sandy saw the mess her little brothers had made in the kitchen, she knew they would all be *in hot water* with their mother. "Mom is going to be furious with us!" she said.

1. Identify the unfamiliar idiom.

   (I'm not sure what *in hot water* means. The first sentence mentions a kitchen, so does it have to do with cooking?)

2. Look for context clues, such as a restatement or explanation.

   (First, Sandy says that her little brothers have made a mess. Then there's the part about their mother and the hot water, and then Sandy says their mom will be very angry.)

3. Use this information to figure out what the idiom means.

   (If Sandy's brothers have done something to make their mom angry, they will probably get in trouble. Also, actually being in hot water would be awfully uncomfortable—maybe even dangerous. For these reasons, I think the expression *in hot water* means "in trouble.")

4. Some idioms appear in regular dictionaries under the definition of the phrase's main word. Look up this idiom in a regular dictionary or in a dictionary of idioms, under *hot* or *water.*

   hot water *n.* Trouble, difficulty, distress

5. If you can't find the idiom in a dictionary, ask a teacher, another adult, or a classmate what it means.

Using Words with Multiple Meanings

VOCABULARY MINI-LESSON

1 Explain to students that many words have more than one meaning. They can figure out the intended meaning of a word in a sentence by looking for clues in the context.

2 Write the following sentence on the board and read it aloud:

We didn't understand the *import* of her speech, but many of the other people in the audience grasped its meaning.

3 Then model how to use the context to figure out the meaning of the word *import:*

MODEL

I'm not sure which meaning of import *is being used in this sentence.* Import *can mean "something brought in from another country" and it can also mean "meaning or importance." I can look for context clues in the sentence. The phrases "didn't understand" and "grasped its meaning" help me figure out that, in this sentence,* import *means "meaning or importance."*

4 Now write the following sentence on the board and read it aloud. Have a volunteer underline the clues that help determine the meaning of the word *impression.*

With his helpful attitude and good manners, the student made an excellent *impression* on the new teacher.

5 If students are not familiar with a word or its multiple meanings, encourage them to look up the word in a dictionary. Sometimes dictionaries provide sample contexts to show the different meanings of a word. Tell students to compare the sample contexts and figure out the one that best fits the sentence. As the year progresses, you may wish to review these strategies.

The following chart provides you with additional words and some of their multiple meanings. Have students create sentences that demonstrate their understanding of the words' multiple meanings.

Word	Meanings	Word	Meanings
character	1. person in a story 2. personality 3. symbol or letter	key	1. lock opener 2. important element or point 3. musical pitch
store	1. a shop 2. a supply 3. put away for future use	seal	1. stamp 2. secure or close 3. aquatic animal
volume	1. one book in a series 2. quantity or amount 3. control for adjusting loudness	cast	1. actors in a play 2. dressing used to cover injury 3. throw something
watch	1. timepiece 2. observe 3. guard or sentry	aim	1. goal 2. direct toward a target 3. try
branch	1. limb of a tree 2. division of a business 3. area of specialized knowledge	project	1. task or undertaking 2. throw forward 3. cause images to appear on screen

Here's How

See the next page for a useful lesson on words with multiple meanings that you can duplicate for students.

WORDS WITH MULTIPLE MEANINGS

Because language constantly changes to meet the needs of those who use it, many words in English have more than one meaning. These multiple meanings may lead to confusion, causing readers to misinterpret a writer's message.

Here's How — **Selecting the Appropriate Meaning of a Word**

1. When you are not sure which definition of a word applies in a particular sentence, look for clues in the surrounding context.

   I stopped at the roadside stand and bought several bags of farm-fresh *produce*, including corn, tomatoes, and peppers.

   (I know that *produce* is a verb meaning "to bring about or create," but in this sentence the word seems to be used as a noun. Maybe *produce* can be a different part of speech and have another meaning.)

2. If the meaning you know does not make sense in the context of the sentence and you don't have enough clues to help you figure out the meaning, look up the word in a dictionary. Look for the definition that makes sense in the sentence.

   (I see that there are several meanings for the word *produce,* including "to create," "to show," and "farm products.")

3. Decide which dictionary definition works best in the sentence you are examining.

   (In this sentence, *produce* refers to the items purchased at a farm stand, so in this case, *produce* probably is a noun meaning "farm crops or products.")

Teaching Decoding Strategies

Teaching Decoding Strategies

By middle school, your students have had years of instruction in decoding strategies, primarily in phonics, structural analysis, and context clues. Readers are taught these strategies to help them determine the meanings of words unfamiliar in print but known as part of their receptive vocabulary or to determine the meaning of totally unfamiliar words.

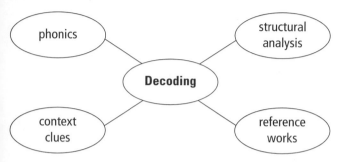

PHONICS

Phonics is a system of teaching the basic sound-letter relationships in the English language. Many early-grade educators believe phonics lays the foundation for young readers' understanding the relationship between spoken and written words. Instruction is usually coupled with decodable text so students can apply skills to predictable reading and develop automaticity—the ability to recognize words in text automatically and effortlessly. Good readers use phonics skills automatically in conjunction with other decoding strategies.

In the primary grades, phonics receives the main emphasis as a decoding strategy. The chart below shows when phonics instruction usually occurs.

Phonics	Grade where taught
consonants (initial, medial, final)	through first half grade 2
consonant digraphs (*sh, th,* etc.)	through first half grade 2
consonant clusters (*st, bl, br,* etc.)	through grade 2
short vowels	through grade 1
long vowels	through grade 2
r-controlled vowels (*er, ir, ar,* etc.)	through grade 2
diphthongs (*oi, oy,* etc.)	through grade 2
variant vowels (*ough, au, aw,* etc.)	through grade 2

As a result of phonics instruction, many young students can decode the vast majority of phonetically regular words they read. In the intermediate grades and beyond, the problem becomes how to decode irregular and multisyllabic words, which appear increasingly in reading materials.

STRUCTURAL ANALYSIS

Structural analysis is a strategy used to figure out the meaning of multisyllabic words. Students are taught to "chunk" words—that is, break words into recognizable parts based on syllabication rules or meaningful word parts.

Syllabication rules Instruction and practice in syllabication rules helps students break words into smaller parts and then use phonics skills to pronounce the word. The following pages contain lessons devoted to teaching students these high-utility syllabication skills.

Rule 1: When there are two consonants between two vowels, divide between the two consonants unless they are a blend or a digraph.

Rule 2: When there are three consonants between two vowels, divide between the blend or the digraph and the other consonant.

Rule 3: When there are two consonants between two vowels, divide between the consonants unless they are a blend or a digraph. The first syllable is a closed syllable, and the vowel sound is short.

Rule 4: Do not split common vowel clusters, such as long-vowel digraphs, *r*-controlled vowels, and diphthongs.

Rule 5: When you see a VCV pattern in the middle of a word, divide the word before or after the consonant. If you divide after the consonant, the first vowel sound is short. If you divide before the consonant, the vowel sound is long.

Rule 6: Always divide compound words between the individual words.

Rule 7: When a word includes an affix, divide between the base word and the affix (prefix or suffix).

When students use these syllabication rules to pronounce the word, they can match the word with a word already in their speaking vocabulary.

Meaningful word parts Another instructional strategy teaches students to look for meaningful word parts, beginning with the root or base word and moving on to prefixes and suffixes. Using knowledge of these parts, the reader assembles a meaning and attempts to match clues with words already in the speaking or receptive vocabulary. You can help your students use structural analysis by teaching the procedure outlined below.

Example Sentence and Procedure

His heart beat <u>thunderously</u>. There had been so many hope-filled moments before, all of them ending in bitter disappointment. (from *Zebra*)

1. Find the root or base word and recall its meaning. (thunder)

2. Find the prefix and/or suffix and recall its/their meaning(s). (-ous, -ly)

3. Use the knowledge clues to predict the word's meaning. (a sound like thunder)

4. Check the predicted meaning against the rest of the sentence. (His heartbeat sounded like thunder.)

5. Does the meaning make sense? (yes)

CONTEXT CLUES

Using context clues means using the knowledge provided by surrounding words and phrases to figure out the meanings of words. Students are taught to look for clues such as restatements, examples, comparisons, contrasts, definitions, and general description. In addition to context clues, readers often use other decoding strategies.

You can help your students use context clues by teaching the procedure beneath the sample sentence.

Example Sentence and Procedure

In 1917 the United States entered World War I as an active <u>combatant</u>. Like many socially prominent women, Eleanor [Roosevelt] threw herself into the war effort.

1. Look at the surrounding context for a description of the word or other clues.

2. Look at the word and apply other decoding strategies as necessary.

3. Use these clues to predict the word's pronunciation and meaning.

4. Check the predicted meaning against the rest of the sentence.

5. Does the meaning make sense?

QUICK DIAGNOSTIC TEST

Use the list below to determine how well your students read multisyllabic words. The lists are organized by syllabication rule. If your students are unable to read some or all of these words, teaching them high-utility syllabication rules may help improve their decoding skills. Use the lessons on the following pages to assist you.

(Rules 1, 3)	(Rule 5)
picture	model
happen	robot
feather	crazy
follow	never
usher	final

(Rule 2)	(Rule 6)
angler	whirlwind
merchant	grasshopper
tumbler	grapevine
children	wastebasket
purchase	earring

(Rule 4)	(Rule 7)
party	readjustment
poison	rebound
feature	childish
royal	unavoidable
chowder	unselfish

Syllabication

LESSON 1: Consonant Blends and Digraphs in Multisyllabic Words

This lesson will help students chunk, or syllabicate, multisyllabic words that contain consonant blends and digraphs. Your students most likely recognize blends and digraphs when they see them in print; however, they may have problems decoding multisyllabic words if they attempt to syllabicate between the two letters in the blend or digraph. If you think your students would benefit from a review of blends and digraphs, begin with Parts 1 and 2. If not, you may go directly to Parts 3 and 4.

PART 1: QUICK REVIEW OF CONSONANT BLENDS

Following are common consonant blends with examples of each. The two letters in each blend represent two sounds.

br	break, brand	sl	slick, slam
cr	crane, crack	ld	field, hold
dr	drive, drip	lk	milk
fr	free	lp	help
gr	green	lt	melt
pr	press	sc	scare
tr	true	sk	ski, risk
bl	blue	sm	smart
cl	clue, close	sn	snare, snack
fl	flame, flute	sp	spell, clasp
gl	glue, glide	st	state, twist
pl	please, plan	sw	switch, sway

DIRECT INSTRUCTION

To help your students focus on consonant blends, write the following sentences on the board.

1. Brown bears slide on the frost.
2. The grand prize was a silk scarf.
3. Flutes fly in blue skies.
4. Sly smelt swim in swift surf.

Ask a student to read aloud the first sentence. Call attention to the words *brown, slide,* and *frost.*

You could say: What two letters do you see at the beginning of *brown? (br)* at the beginning of *slide? (sl)* at the beginning and end of *frost? (fr, st)* These are called consonant blends. The consonant blends are made up of two consonant letters and stand for two sounds. You will always say both sounds when you sound out a word.

Follow the same procedure with the remaining sentences.

Answers: #2: grand (*gr*), prize (*pr*), silk (*lk*), scarf (*sc*); #3: Flutes (*fl*), fly (*fl*), blue (*bl*), skies (*sk*); #4: Sly (*sl*), smelt (*sm, lt*), swim (*sw*), swift (*sw*)

PART 2: QUICK REVIEW OF CONSONANT DIGRAPHS

Following are consonant digraphs and examples of each. The two letters in each digraph represent one sound.

ch	cheat, check, touch
sh	shine, fish, push
th(voiced)	that, the, this
th(voiceless)	think, teeth, thumb, thank
wh(hw blend)	where, whoops, when, white, wheel

DIRECT INSTRUCTION

Write these sentences on the board.

1. How much fish does a whale eat?
2. She will think the thing is cheap.
3. When will you change and wash the sheets?
4. Do white hens have teeth?

Ask a student to read aloud the first sentence.

You could say: What two letters do you see at the end of *much? (ch)* at the end of *fish? (sh)* at the beginning of *whale? (wh)* The consonant digraphs are made up of two consonant letters but represent only one sound. You will say only one sound when you sound out a word.

Follow the same procedure with the remaining sentences.

Answers: #2: She (*sh*), think (*th*), the (*th*), thing (*th*), cheap (*ch*); #3: When (*wh*), change (*ch*), wash (*sh*), the (*th*), sheets (*sh*); #4: white (*wh*), teeth (*th*)

PART 3: SYLLABICATION STRATEGY: CONSONANT BLENDS AND DIGRAPHS

In the following lesson, students will use their knowledge of consonant blends and digraphs to syllabicate words. You may find it helpful to review the most basic syllabication rule: *Each syllable has one and only one vowel sound.*

DIRECT INSTRUCTION

Write Rule 1 and the example words on the chalkboard. Remind students that *V* stands for *vowel* and *C* stands for *consonant*. Ask a student to give examples of vowel and consonant letters.

> **Rule 1: VCCV**
> **When there are two consonants between two vowels, divide between the two consonants unless they are a blend or a digraph.**
>
> **picture   happen   abrupt   feather**

Have a student read Rule 1. Ask a student to explain the rule in his or her own words and then to read the first word.

You could say: Find the VCCV pattern in the word *picture. (ictu)* **Do you see a blend or digraph?** (*no*) **Where would you divide this word according to Rule 1?** (*between the* c *and the* t) **Look at each syllable. Pronounce the word. Do you recognize the word?**

Repeat the process with the remaining words.

Answers: hap/pen, a/brupt, feath/er

Write Rule 2 and the example words on the board.

> **Rule 2: VCCCV**
> **When there are three consonants between two vowels, divide between the blend or the digraph and the other consonant.**
>
> **angler   merchant   tumbler   children**

Have a student read Rule 2. Ask a student to explain the rule in his or her own words and then to read the first word.

You could say: Find the VCCCV pattern in the word *angler. (angle)* **Do you see a blend or digraph?** (*yes*) **Where would you divide this word according to Rule 2?** (*between the* n *and the* gl) **Look at each syllable. Pronounce the word. Do you recognize the word?**

Repeat the process with the remaining words.

Answers: mer/chant, tum/bler, chil/dren

PART 4: STRATEGY PRACTICE

Write the following words on the board. Have students divide the words according to the two rules, identify the rules, and pronounce the words.

Practice applying Rule 1

	Answers		Answers
scatter	scat/ter	whether	wheth/er
garden	gar/den	zipper	zip/per
crafty	craft/y	fashion	fash/ion
scarlet	scar/let	forget	for/get
traffic	traf/fic	respect	re/spect

Practice applying Rule 2

	Answers		Answers
hungry	hun/gry	nothing	noth/ing
concrete	con/crete	purchase	pur/chase
hundred	hun/dred	address	ad/dress
worship	wor/ship	supply	sup/ply
handsome	hand/some	employ	em/ploy

Cumulative practice

	Answers		Answers
written	writ/ten	toddler	tod/dler
constant	con/stant	lather	lath/er
secret	se/cret	sandal	san/dal
surplus	sur/plus	merchant	mer/chant
kindling	kin/dling	silver	sil/ver

LESSON 2: **Short Vowels in Multisyllabic Words**

When your students have trouble figuring out words unfamiliar in print, they are most likely having problems decoding the letters that stand for the vowel sounds in the words. Usually this is because the relationship between vowel sounds and letters that represent them isn't as predictable as the relationship between consonant sounds and the letters that represent them.

This lesson will help your students syllabicate words that contain short vowels. If you think your students would benefit from a review of short vowels, you may begin with Part 1. If not, you may skip directly to Parts 2 and 3.

PART 1: QUICK REVIEW OF SHORT VOWELS

Of the vowel sounds in English, the short vowels have the most predictable relationship between the sounds and the letters that represent them.

DIRECT INSTRUCTION

To help students focus on short vowels, write the list below on the board.

at	end	in	on	up
bat	bend	fin	odd	cup
and	vest	lick	mop	duck
fad	tell	drip	trot	lump

Have a student read the first column of words.

You could say: What vowel sound do you hear in each of these words? (/ă/ *or short* a) **What letter represents that sound in each of these words?** *(the letter* a)

Follow the same procedure with the remaining lists.

Answers: column 2: /ĕ/ or short e; column 3: /ĭ/ or short i; column 4: /ŏ/ or short o; column 5: /ŭ/ or short u

PART 2: SYLLABICATION STRATEGY: SHORT VOWELS

Use the following syllabication strategy to help your students figure out some of the vowel sounds in multisyllabic words. You will note that Rule 3 expands upon Rule 1 introduced in Lesson 1.

DIRECT INSTRUCTION

Write Rule 3 and the example words on the board. Remind students that *V* stands for *vowel* and *C* stands for *consonant*.

> **Rule 3: VCCV**
> **When there are two consonants between two vowels, divide between the consonants unless they are a blend or a digraph. The first syllable is a closed syllable, and the vowel sound is short.**
>
> | | | | |
> |---|---|---|---|
> | butter | lather | follow | usher |
> | summer | traffic | tender | invent |

Have a student read Rule 3 and explain the rule in his or her own words.

Have a student read the first word.

You could say: Find the VCCV pattern in the first word. *(utte)* **Do you see a blend or a digraph?** *(no)* **Where would you divide this word according to Rule 3?** *(between the two* t's) **What vowel sound do you hear in the first syllable?** *(short)* **Look at each syllable and pronounce the word. Do you recognize the word?**

Repeat this process with the remaining words.

Answers: but/ter, lath/er, fol/low, ush/er, sum/mer, traf/fic, ten/der, in/vent

PART 3: STRATEGY PRACTICE

Write the following on the board. Have students divide the words according to the rule and pronounce the words.

	Answers		Answers
under	un/der	billow	bil/low
bother	both/er	enter	en/ter
bottom	bot/tom	number	num/ber
rather	rath/er	object	ob/ject
practice	prac/tice	dipper	dip/per
snapper	snap/per	silver	sil/ver
after	af/ter	grammar	gram/mar
cashew	cash/ew	sudden	sud/den
pulpit	pul/pit	vintage	vin/tage
pencil	pen/cil	member	mem/ber

LESSON 3: Vowel Clusters in Multisyllabic Words

This lesson will show students how to chunk, or syllabicate, multisyllabic words that contain vowel clusters: long-vowel digraphs, *r*-controlled vowels, and diphthongs. If your students aren't aware of vowel clusters, they might syllabicate between the two vowels in a cluster. In that case, they will syllabicate incorrectly and mispronounce the word when they attempt to sound it out. If you think your students would benefit from a review of vowel clusters, begin with Parts 1–3. If not, skip to Parts 4 and 5.

PART 1: QUICK REVIEW OF LONG–VOWEL DIGRAPHS

In long-vowel digraphs, two letters represent one vowel sound.

DIRECT INSTRUCTION

Write the list below on the board.

cream	play	boat
beast	gray	coal
bean	paint	goat
green	aim	row
peel	stain	slow

Have a student read the first column of words.

You could say: What vowel sound do you hear in each of these words? *(long e)* **What letters stand for the long e sound in** *beast?* *(ea)* **What letters stand for the long e sound in** *green?* *(ee)* **These are called long-vowel digraphs. A digraph is made up of two letters that stand for one sound.**

Follow the same procedure with the remaining lists.

Answers: column 2: long *a, ay* in *gray, ai* in *paint;* column 3: long *o, oa* in *boat, ow* in *slow*

PART 2: QUICK REVIEW OF *R*-CONTROLLED VOWELS

In an *r*-controlled vowel, the vowel sound is influenced by the *r* that follows it.

DIRECT INSTRUCTION

Write the list below on the board.

fern	car	born
dirt	star	cord
fur	arm	sort
her	yarn	more
birth	farm	horn

Have a student read the first column of words.

You could say: These words all have the "er" sound. What letters stand for the "er" sound in *fur? (ur)* **in** *her? (er)* **in** *birth? (ir)* **These are called *r*-controlled vowels. An *r*-controlled vowel is made up of a vowel and the letter *r*. In words with *r*-controlled vowels, the vowel sounds are influenced by the *r* that follows them.**

Follow the same procedure with the remaining columns.

Answers: column 2: All words have the "ar" sound; letters are *ar;* column 3: All words have the "or" sound; letters are *or.*

PART 3: QUICK REVIEW OF DIPHTHONGS

DIRECT INSTRUCTION

To help students focus on diphthongs, write this list on the board.

oil	ouch
boil	cloud
boy	how
spoil	scout
toy	towel

Have a student read the first column of words.

You could say: These words all have the "oi" sound. What letters stand for the "oi" sound in *boil? (oi)* **in** *boy? (oy)* **These are called diphthongs. A diphthong is made up of two letters that stand for two vowel sounds.**

Follow the same procedure with the remaining column.

Answers: column 2: All words have the "ow" sound; letters are *ou* or *ow.*

PART 4: SYLLABICATION STRATEGY: VOWEL CLUSTERS

Use the following syllabication strategy to help your students syllabicate words that contain vowel clusters.

DIRECT INSTRUCTION

Write Rule 4 and the example words on the board or use the copymaster on page 49.

> **Rule 4:**
> **Do not split common vowel clusters, such as long-vowel digraphs, r-controlled vowels, and diphthongs.**
>
> party   poison   feature   royal   chowder   garden

Have a student read Rule 4. Have a student explain the rule in his or her own words.

Have a student read the first word.

You could say: Do you see a vowel cluster in this word? (*yes*) If you do, what is the cluster? (*ar*) Where would you avoid dividing this word, according to Rule 4? (*between the* a *and* r) Where do you think you should divide the word? (*after the cluster, between the* r *and* t) Look at each syllable and pronounce the word. Do you recognize the word?

Repeat this process with the remaining words. In the cases of *poison, feature,* and *royal,* students will be asked to syllabicate words for which they haven't learned all of the syllabication rules. Encourage them to try out what they know and attempt a pronunciation based on what they've learned so far.

Answers:

poison: *oi*; avoid dividing within cluster; divide after cluster.

royal: *oy*; avoid dividing within cluster; divide after cluster.

feature: *ea*; avoid dividing within cluster; divide after cluster.

chowder: *ow*; avoid dividing within cluster; divide after cluster.

garden: *ar*; avoid dividing within cluster; divide after cluster.

PART 5: STRATEGY PRACTICE

Write the following on the board. Have students divide the words according to the rules they know, and pronounce the words.

	Answers		Answers
carton	car/ton	peanut	pea/nut
powder	pow/der	council	coun/cil
circus	cir/cus	purpose	pur/pose
mountain	moun/tain	moisture	mois/ture
maintain	main/tain	voyage	voy/age
fertile	fer/tile	mayor	may/or
darling	dar/ling	freedom	free/dom
coward	cow/ard	tailor	tai/lor
hornet	hor/net	eager	ea/ger
barter	bar/ter	order	or/der

LESSON 4: Short and Long Vowels in Multisyllabic Words

This lesson will help your students develop flexibility in applying syllabication strategies as they attempt to decode multisyllabic words.

PART 1: QUICK REVIEW

If you have skipped over Lessons 1–3, you may want to preview this lesson to be sure your students are prepared for a more complicated syllabication strategy.

PART 2: SYLLABICATION STRATEGY: IS THE VOWEL SOUND LONG OR SHORT?

Use the following syllabication strategy to help your students decide whether a vowel letter stands for a long or short vowel sound.

DIRECT INSTRUCTION

Write Rule 5 and the example words on the board. Remind students that *V* stands for *vowel* and *C* stands for *consonant*.

Rule 5: VCV

When you see a VCV pattern in the middle of a word, divide the word before or after the consonant. If you divide after the consonant, the first vowel sound is short. If you divide before the consonant, the vowel sound is long.

   model   robot   crazy   never

Have a student read Rule 5 and explain the rule in his or her own words.

Ask a student to read the first word.

You could say: Find the VCV pattern in the first word. (*ode***) Where should you first divide the word? (***after the*** d, *the first consonant*) What happens to the vowel sound in the first syllable? (***The vowel sound is short.***) Say the word. Do you recognize it? (***yes***) When the consonant is part of the first syllable, the first syllable is said to be closed.**

Ask a student to read the second word.

You could say: Find the VCV pattern in the second word. (*obo***) Where should you first divide the word? (***after the*** b, *the first consonant*) What happens to the vowel sound in the first syllable? (***The vowel sound is short.***) Say the word. Do you recognize it? (***no***)**

Try the second part of the rule. Where should you divide the word? (*before the consonant***) What happens to the vowel sound in the first syllable? (***The vowel sound is long.***) Say the word. Do you recognize it? (***yes***) When the consonant is part of the second syllable, the first syllable is said to be open.**

Repeat this process with the remaining words.

Answers: crazy: *azy*; divide after the *z*, the first consonant; vowel is short; no, do not recognize the word; divide before the *z*; vowel is long; yes, recognize the word.

never: *eve*; divide after the *v*; vowel is short; yes, recognize the word.

PART 3: STRATEGY PRACTICE

Write the following words on the board. Have students divide the words and pronounce the words.

	Answers		Answers
legal	le/gal	final	fi/nal
gravel	grav/el	prefix	pre/fix
basic	ba/sic	level	lev/el
driven	driv/en	moment	mo/ment
minus	mi/nus	paper	pa/per
panic	pan/ic	soda	so/da
spider	spi/der	devil	dev/il
honor	hon/or	tiny	ti/ny
seven	sev/en		

LESSON 5: Compound Words

When students encounter multisyllabic words, they often don't try the obvious—looking for words or word parts they already know within the longer words. Lessons 5 and 6 will help students develop this skill.

PART 1: SYLLABICATION STRATEGY: COMPOUND WORDS

Use the following syllabication strategy to help your students determine where to divide a compound word.

DIRECT INSTRUCTION

Write Rule 6 and the example words on the board.

> **Rule 6:**
>
> **Divide compound words between the individual words.**
>
> | | | |
> |---|---|---|
> | grapevine | lifeguard | whirlwind |
> | butterfly | grasshopper | |

Have a student read Rule 6. Ask a student to explain the rule in his or her own words.

You could say: When you see a multisyllabic word, stop and see if it is made up of one or more words that you already know.

Have a student read the first word.

You could say: How many words do you see in the first word? *(two)* **Where should you divide the word?** (*between* grape *and* vine)

Repeat the process with the remaining words in the first row.

Answers: life/guard, whirl/wind

Have a student read the first word in the second row.

You could say: How many words do you see in the word? *(two)* **Where should you divide the word?** (*between* butter *and* fly) **Where else should you divide the word?** (*between the two t's*) **How do you know?** (*Rule 1 says to divide two consonants between vowels.*)

Repeat the process with the remaining word. *(grass/hop/per)*

PART 2: STRATEGY PRACTICE

Write the following words on the board. Have students divide the words, identify the rule(s) they used, and pronounce the words.

	Answers		Answers
shipwreck	ship/wreck	buttermilk	but/ter/milk
postcard	post/card	notebook	note/book
screwdriver	screw/dri/ver	volleyball	vol/ley/ball
oatmeal	oat/meal	washcloth	wash/cloth
windmill	wind/mill	wastebasket	waste/bas/ket
dragonfly	drag/on/fly	peppermint	pep/per/mint
pancake	pan/cake	hardware	hard/ware
earthquake	earth/quake	handlebar	han/dle/bar
pigtail	pig/tail	earring	ear/ring
wristwatch	wrist/ watch	weekend	week/end

LESSON 6: Affixes

This lesson will give students help in dividing multisyllabic words that contain one or more affixes. These are the kinds of words that give students the most problems because they tend to be long and can look overwhelming. If you think your students would benefit from practice with identifying prefixes and suffixes, start with Parts 1 and 2. If not, go directly to Parts 3 and 4.

PART 1: QUICK REVIEW OF PREFIXES

Recognizing prefixes in multisyllabic words can help your students chunk words into manageable parts. You may use the following list of common prefixes and their meanings to expand upon the lesson described below.

auto-	self	by-	near, aside
mis-	bad	under-	below
pre-	before	un-	not
re-	again	de-	from, down
with-	back, away	dis-	opposite
bi-	two	uni-	one
on-	on	be-	make
tri-	three		

DIRECT INSTRUCTION

Write the following prefixes and their meanings on the board.

> **auto- self   bi- two   un- not**

You could say: The word part on the left side of each pair is called a prefix. Prefixes can be added to roots or to base words to change the meanings of the words. Think of a word that begins with auto-.

Write the word on the board.

Follow the same procedure with the remaining prefixes. If you wish, include additional prefixes. Save the words and use them for syllabication practice later.

Possible answers: *auto- (autobiography); bi- (bicycle, bilingual); un- (unhappy, unlikely)*

PART 2: QUICK REVIEW OF SUFFIXES

Recognizing suffixes in multisyllabic words can help your students chunk words into manageable parts. You may use the following list of common suffixes and their meanings to expand upon the lesson described below.

-ness	state or quality of	-less	without
-like	resembling	-ship	state or quality of
-ish	relating to	-ful	full of
-ways	manner	-er	one who
-ly	like, resembling	-ous	full of
-ion	state or quality of	-ment	action or process

DIRECT INSTRUCTION

Write the following suffixes and their meanings on the board.

> **-ness   state or quality of   -ly   resembling**
> **-ful   full of**

You could say: The word part on the left side of each pair is called a suffix. When a suffix is added to a base word, it often changes the part of speech of the base word. Think of a word that ends with -ness.

Write the word on the board.

Follow the same procedure with the remaining suffixes. If you wish, include additional suffixes. Save the words and use them for syllabication practice later.

Possible answers: *-ness (happiness, sadness); -ly (quickly, lively); -ful (thankful, eventful)*

PART 3: SYLLABICATION STRATEGY: AFFIXES

Use the following syllabication strategy to help your students determine where to divide words that contain affixes.

DIRECT INSTRUCTION

Write Rule 7 and the examples on the board.

> **Rule 7:**
>
> **When a word includes an affix, divide between the base word and the affix (prefix or suffix).**
>
> | | | |
> |---|---|---|
> | rebound | restless | unavoidable |
> | preschool | childish | readjustment |
> | disprove | joyous | unselfish |

Ask a student to read Rule 7 and to explain the rule in his or her own words.

Have a student read the first word in column 1.

You could say: What prefix do you see in *rebound*? (*re-*) **Where should you divide** *rebound* **according to Rule 7?** (*re/bound*) Continue with the remaining words in column 1. In each case, have students apply the rule, divide the word, pronounce the word, and then see if they recognize it.

Answers: pre/school, dis/prove

Have a student read the first word in column 2.

What suffix do you see in *restless*? (*-less*) **Where should you divide** *restless*? (*rest/less*) Continue with the remaining words in column 2. In each case, have students apply the rule, divide the word, pronounce the word, and then see if they recognize it.

Answers: child/ish, joy/ous

Have a student read the first word in column 3.

What affixes do you see in this word? (*un-, -able*) **Where should you divide the word?** (*un/avoid/able*) Continue with the remaining words in column 3. In each case, have students apply the rule, divide the word, pronounce it, and then see if they recognize it. Point out to students that they can use other rules to further divide *unavoidable* as follows: un/a/void/a/ble.

Answers: re/ad/just/ment, un/self/ish

To extend this lesson, have students analyze each word to see if they should apply additional syllabication rules.

PART 4: STRATEGY PRACTICE

Write the following words on the board. Have students divide the words, identify the rule(s) they use, and pronounce the words.

	Answers
uniform	u/ni/form
fairly	fair/ly
beautiful	beau/ti/ful
unlikely	un/like/ly
recall	re/call
misfit	mis/fit
rigorous	rig/or/ous
hopelessness	hope/less/ness
childlike	child/like
unwind	un/wind
selfish	self/ish
opinion	o/pin/ion
hardship	hard/ship
sticker	stick/er
sideways	side/ways
department	de/part/ment
disbelieve	dis/be/lieve
withstand	with/stand
become	be/come
refreshment	re/fresh/ment

Comprehension
Mini-Lessons
with Graphic Organizers

Main Idea and Supporting Details

COMPREHENSION MINI-LESSON

1 For students who have trouble grasping the main idea of a paragraph or passage, discuss these points.

- The main idea is the most important idea a writer makes in a paragraph or passage.
- The writer may state the main idea in a sentence. This sentence can appear at the beginning, middle, or end of a paragraph or passage.
- Sometimes the writer implies the main idea. The reader must then figure it out by thinking about the details and stating it in his or her own words.

2 Duplicate the following paragraph. A master is provided on page T637. Have students follow along as you read it aloud, using it to model **stated main idea.**

> **Every year teens spend billions of dollars. In 1999 American teens spent $153 billion! According to one research company, the average teenager spends about $35 every time he or she goes to the mall. Experts expect more sales as the population of teens increases by 4 million by the year 2010.**

You could say: *Writers often put the main idea in the first sentence.* Every year teens spend billions of dollars *seems like the main idea. The second and third sentences tell how teenagers spend billions of dollars each year. The last sentence makes an additional point about teenage spending. Each sentence gives a detail that supports the first sentence. It is, therefore, logical to conclude that the first sentence is the main idea.*

3 Duplicate the following paragraph. A master is provided on page T637. Have students follow along as you read it aloud, using it to model **implied main idea.**

> **Ballooning got its start in 1783 when two ballooning pioneers launched a duck, a sheep, and a rooster in the first historic balloon flight. Since then, many people have ballooned successfully across lakes, channels, and even oceans. Ballooning has become so popular that people now compete for the world record in time and distance.**

You could say: *Let's look at the first sentence for the main idea. It tells me something about the history of ballooning. The second sentence tells me how the popularity of ballooning has grown. The third sentence gives me an additional detail about ballooning. In this case the writer chose not to state the main idea. I'll have to figure it out by looking at all the details. Each sentence gives a detail about the history of ballooning. Therefore, the implied main idea is* ballooning throughout history.

4 Duplicate the following paragraphs and read them aloud. A master is provided on page T638.

> **Have you ever seen a flying saucer? Every year hundreds of people report seeing UFOs, or unidentified flying objects. Most UFOs turn out to be ordinary things. Some are weather balloons. Others are planes. Still others are shooting stars. Some people make fake pictures of UFOs to get attention.**
>
> **Most scientists don't think aliens have visited Earth. So far, we have not found intelligent life in space. Also, the distance from Earth to other planets is huge. It would be very hard for aliens to come here.**

5 Duplicate and distribute the Main Idea Web on the next page. Correct responses are shown in the Answer Key on page T682.

6 Make additional copies of the Main Idea Web and have them available for students to use when necessary throughout the year.

Main Idea Web

Detail:

Detail:

Main Idea:

Detail:

Detail:

Main Idea

Every year teens spend billions of dollars. In 1999 American teens spent $153 billion! According to one research company, the average teenager spends about $35 every time he or she goes to the mall. Experts expect more sales as the population of teens increases by 4 million by the year 2010.

Ballooning got its start in 1783 when two ballooning pioneers launched a duck, a sheep, and a rooster in the first historic balloon flight. Since then, many people have ballooned successfully across lakes, channels, and even oceans. Ballooning has become so popular that people now compete for the world record in time and distance.

Main Idea

Have you ever seen a flying saucer? Every year hundreds of people report seeing UFOs, or unidentified flying objects. Most UFOs turn out to be ordinary things. Some are weather balloons. Others are planes. Still others are shooting stars. Some people make fake pictures of UFOs to get attention.

Most scientists don't think aliens have visited Earth. So far, we have not found intelligent life in space. Also, the distance from Earth to other planets is huge. It would be very hard for aliens to come here.

Sequence

COMPREHENSION MINI-LESSON

1 Ask students if they have ever told a friend a story with events that weren't in the exact order in which they occurred. If details were out of order, the friend could ask questions to clarify the sequence. Explain that it is important to keep track of the sequence of events in a story in order to understand the meaning of the story and the way the plot moves forward. The following points will be useful to students who need more help.

- Sequence is the order in which events happen. *Sequence* refers to the chronological order in a story or piece of nonfiction. It may also refer to steps in a process or in a set of directions.

- Writers sometimes use words such as *first, next, after, before, then,* and *later* to connect ideas and indicate the order in which events occur.

- Words, phrases, or dates that tell when something is happening can also help readers figure out the sequence of events.

- A paragraph or story may begin by telling about an event that happens in the present. Other sentences may tell about events that happened in the past, leading up to the present.

- When events are not clearly laid out, it may help the reader to visualize in his or her mind how the events happened.

2 Duplicate the following paragraph. A master is provided on page T641. Have students follow along as you read it aloud, using it to model **sequence**.

> **I discovered the best recipe for a strawberry milk shake. First you gather all the ingredients: vanilla ice cream, fresh strawberries, 1 cup of skim milk, 2 tablespoons of cream cheese, and granola or your favorite topping. Then you mix all the ingredients, except the granola, in a blender for one to two minutes. Once you pour the milk shake into a tall glass, sprinkle the granola on top and the shake is ready to serve.**

You could say: *The first sentence tells me something about a recipe for a strawberry milk shake. Chances are that the first sentence is not the first step in the sequence. The second sentence gives me a list of ingredients to gather. The third and fourth sentences give me additional steps in the recipe. So if I were to list the order of steps in the recipe I would say that first you gather the ingredients. Then you blend the ingredients. Next, you pour the milk shake into a glass and add the topping; and finally you serve the milk shake.*

3 Duplicate the following paragraph. A master is provided on page T641. Have students follow along as you read it aloud.

> **My babysitting days are over! Yesterday afternoon, I got an emergency call from the Smiths asking if I could take care of the twins for a few hours. After dinner, I walked over to the Smiths'. As soon as Mr. and Mrs. Smith left, the twins started to run around the house, playing hide and seek. While I was frantically searching for the twins, the doorbell rang and a pizza delivery boy appeared at the door. As soon as I saw the order slip, I knew the troublemakers who had called for pizza. As I walked towards the twins' room, the fire alarm went off in the kitchen. With all the commotion, I had forgotten to turn off the stove and had burnt the popcorn. By midnight the twins finally fell asleep.**

4 Duplicate and distribute the Sequence/Flow Chart on the next page. Work with students to fill in the first event. Then have them complete the chart. Tell students to highlight any words or phrases that helped them determine the order of events. Ask volunteers to share how they mapped out the events of the paragraph. Possible responses are shown in the Answer Key on page T682.

5 Make additional copies of the chart on page T640 and have them available for students to use throughout the year.

Name _____   **Date** _____

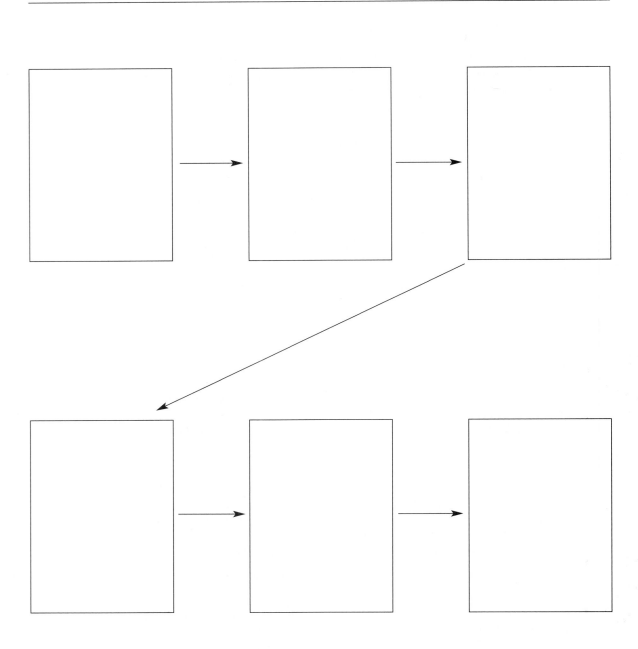

Sequence

I discovered the best recipe for a strawberry milk shake. First you gather all the ingredients: vanilla ice cream, fresh strawberries, 1 cup of skim milk, 2 tablespoons of cream cheese, and granola or your favorite topping. Then you mix all the ingredients, except the granola, in a blender for one to two minutes. Once you pour the milk shake into a tall glass, sprinkle the granola on top and the shake is ready to serve.

My babysitting days are over! Yesterday afternoon, I got an emergency call from the Smiths asking if I could take care of the twins for a few hours. After dinner, I walked over to the Smiths'. As soon as Mr. and Mrs. Smith left, the twins started to run around the house, playing hide and seek. While I was frantically searching for the twins, the doorbell rang and a pizza delivery boy appeared at the door. As soon as I saw the order slip, I knew the troublemakers who had called for pizza. As I walked towards the twins' room, the fire alarm went off in the kitchen. With all the commotion, I had forgotten to turn off the stove and had burnt the popcorn. By midnight the twins finally fell asleep.

Cause and Effect

1 Write the following sentence on the board and read it aloud.

Travis felt sick because he ate eight slices of pizza.

Ask students which event caused the other event to happen. *(Travis ate eight slices of pizza, which caused him to feel sick.)* Discuss the following points:

- A **cause** is an action or event that makes something else happen.
- An **effect** is what happens because of a certain action or event.
- Writers use clue words or phrases *(because, since, as a result)* to indicate causes and effects. However, clue words alone do not automatically indicate a cause-effect relationship. One event must make another event happen.
- A single cause can result in more than one effect. *(Because Travis ate eight slices of pizza, he felt sick and went to the school nurse's office.)* Also, several causes can lead to a single effect. *(Since you are a talented artist and have some free time this weekend, you should help us paint a mural.)*
- Sometimes a series of events are linked in a cause-and-effect chain in which one event causes another, which in turn causes another, and so on. *(Because I didn't listen to the weather report, I didn't bring an umbrella with me. As a result, I got soaked when the rain started.)*

Watch out for events that happen in sequence. Just because one event follows another doesn't mean the first event caused the second one: *Just as we got ready to go to the beach, it started to rain.* (The rain was not a result of our getting ready to go to the beach.)

2 Duplicate the following paragraph. A master is provided on page T646. Ask students to follow along as you read it aloud, using it to model **cause-effect.**

> **Amanda worked hard to make this year's talent show a success. Because she put up so many posters, just about everyone in the area knew about the show. Lots of people bought tickets. More people attended than ever before, which meant that the show raised more money for charity than ever before.**

You could say: The first sentence tells what happened. The second sentence has a signal word, because, *that may indicate a cause-effect relationship. If you look at sentences three and four, it is logical to say that Amanda's hard work also caused people to buy tickets and attend the show. These sentences show how one cause can result in more than one effect. Now look at the last sentence. It is an example of a cause-and-effect chain in which the first event (hard work) caused another event (more people attending), which in turn caused another event (more money being raised).*

3 Duplicate the following paragraph. A master is provided on page T646. Have students follow along as you read it aloud.

> **Last year, my mom decided that our family should learn more about nature. For this reason, we went on a camping trip—and had an awful time! We didn't have the right kinds of tents and other supplies for the cool, damp weather at the campsite. As a result, we decided to do more research before planning this year's vacation.**

4 Duplicate and distribute the Cause-and-Effect Chart on the next page. Work with students to fill in the first cause-and-effect relationship. Possible responses are shown in the Answer Key on page T682.

5 Make copies of the additional Cause-and-Effect Charts on pages T644–T645 and have them available at appropriate times.

Cause-and-Effect Chart

Name _____ **Date** _____

Cause	→	Effect(s)

Name _____ **Date** _____

Single Cause with Multiple Effects

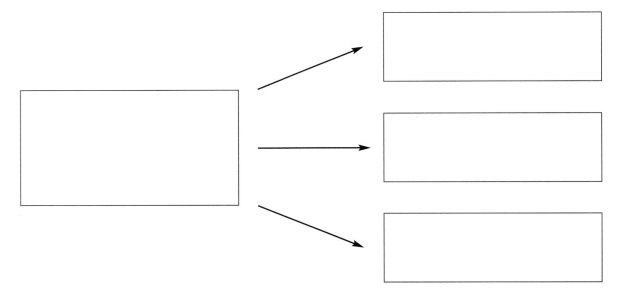

Multiple Causes with Single Effect

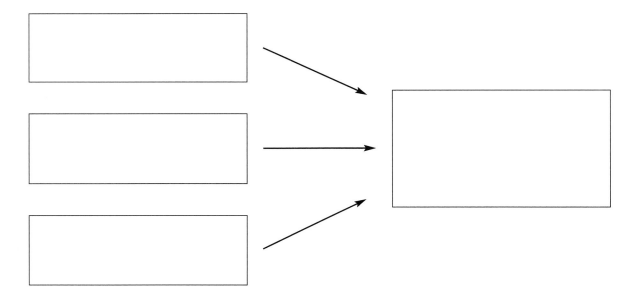

Cause-and-Effect Chain

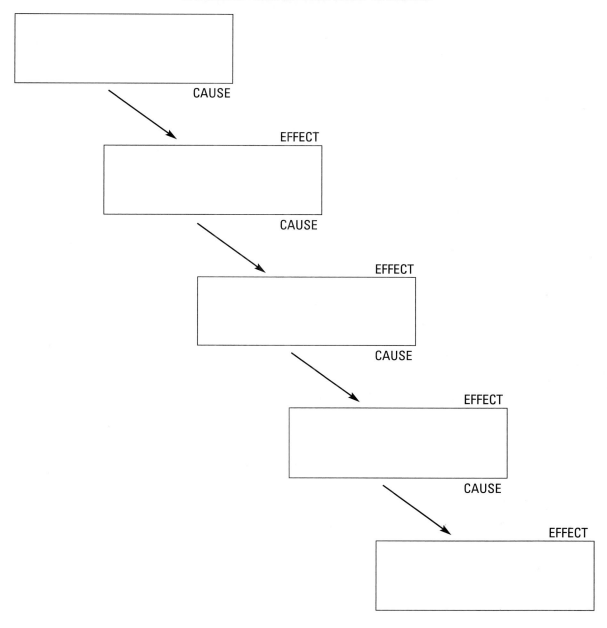

CAUSE

EFFECT

CAUSE

EFFECT

CAUSE

EFFECT

CAUSE

EFFECT

Cause and Effect

Amanda worked hard to make this year's talent show a success. Because she put up so many posters, just about everyone in the area knew about the show. Lots of people bought tickets. More people attended than ever before, which meant that the show raised more money for charity than ever before.

Last year, my mom decided that our family should learn more about nature. For this reason, we went on a camping trip—and had an awful time! We didn't have the right kinds of tents and other supplies for the cool, damp weather at the campsite. As a result, we decided to do more research before planning this year's vacation.

Comparison and Contrast

COMPREHENSION MINI-LESSON

1 The following points will be helpful to students who have trouble understanding the terms *compare* and *contrast*.

- **Comparing** is thinking about the ways in which two or more people or two or more things are alike. *(Edgar Allan Poe and Agatha Christie wrote mysteries.)* Writers sometimes use words such as *both, same, alike, like, also, similarly,* and *too* to make comparisons. *(Both Edgar Allan Poe and Agatha Christie wrote mysteries.)*

- **Contrasting** is thinking about ways in which two or more people or two or more things are different. *(Mike likes to read mysteries. Manuel likes to read science fiction.)* Writers sometimes use words or phrases such as *unlike, but, while, although, instead, yet, even though, however,* and *on the other hand* to indicate contrasts. *(Mike likes to read mysteries, while Manuel likes to read science fiction.)*

- Sometimes there are no signal words. Readers must figure out what the writer is comparing and contrasting from the details given.

2 Duplicate the following paragraph. A master is provided on page T649. Have students follow along as you read it aloud, using it to model **comparison and contrast.**

> **Ulysses S. Grant and Robert E. Lee were both Civil War generals. Both were leaders. Both were smart. Also, both badly wanted to win. However, Grant took more risks. Lee was a more cautious general.**

You could say: *The first sentence tells me that two people—Ulysses S. Grant and Robert E. Lee—are being compared. The first four sentences contain the word* both, *which signals ways in which Grant and Lee were alike. The fifth sentence contains the word* however, *which signals a difference between Grant and Lee. Therefore, Grant and Lee were alike in that they were both intelligent and were both determined to win the war. The difference is that Grant took risks while Lee was more cautious.*

3 For reference, write on the board the signal words and phrases listed in the second bulleted item above. Then duplicate the following paragraph and read it aloud. A master is provided on page T649.

> **Some people like watching movies at home. I prefer going to a movie theater. Television and movie screens can show the same movie. However, a theater screen is much bigger. The sound is better. Movies seem more real there. It's also fun to share the feelings of a big crowd. People who see movies at home miss out on all these things.**

4 Duplicate and distribute the Venn Diagram on the next page. Have students fill in the diagram, using information in the paragraph along with what they already know about television and movie theaters to compare and contrast the two.

5 Have volunteers share the information in their diagrams by first describing the similarities between television and movie theaters and then describing their differences. Possible responses are shown in the Answer Key on page T683.

6 Make additional copies of the diagram on page T648 and have them available for students to use at appropriate times during the year.

Venn Diagram

Name _____ **Date** _____

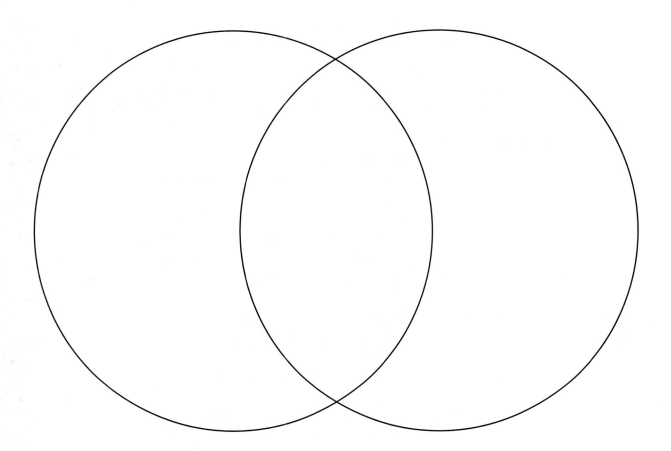

Compare and Contrast

Ulysses S. Grant and Robert E. Lee were both Civil War generals. Both were leaders. Both were smart. Also, both badly wanted to win. However, Grant took more risks. Lee was a more cautious general.

Contrast

Some people like watching movies at home. I prefer going to a movie theater. Television and movie screens can show the same movie. However, a theater screen is much bigger. The sound is better. Movies seem more real there. It's also fun to share the feelings of a big crowd. People who see movies at home miss out on all these things.

Making Inferences

COMPREHENSION MINI-LESSON

1 Present students with the following situation:

You look out the window of a high-rise building. You see people carrying umbrellas and cars running their windshield wipers. What inference can you make? (Students will most likely say that it's raining.) For students who need more help making inferences, discuss the following points.

- It is not possible for writers to include every detail about what is happening in a work of literature.
- Often writers purposely choose to hint at details rather than state them; this can add meaning and suspense for the reader.
- Inferences are logical guesses based on clues in the text and on the reader's own knowledge and common sense.
- To make inferences, readers must: look for details that the writer provides about character, setting, and events; think about what they already know about a topic; and connect the story to their own personal experiences.

2 Duplicate the following paragraph. A master is provided on page T652. Ask students to follow along as you read it aloud, using it to model the skill **making inferences.**

> **Donna paced up and down the room. When she heard footsteps outside, she ran to the window and looked outside. As her eyes searched up and down the street, her hopeful smile faded. She turned away from the window, glanced at her watch, and heaved a big sigh.**

You could say: In the first sentence, I learn that Donna is pacing up and down a room. From her movements, I can infer that she is nervous or impatient about something. The second sentence tells me that Donna is probably waiting for someone because she looks out the window when she hears footsteps outside. In the third sentence, I learn that the person she is expecting has not arrived. Donna's smile fades as she scans the street. In the fourth sentence, Donna's sigh suggests that she is disappointed or sad. The glance at her watch tells me that the person she is waiting for is late.

3 Duplicate the following passage. A master is provided on page T652. Have students follow along as you read it aloud.

> **Donna walked over to the kitchen phone and dialed a number. As she held the receiver to her ear, she drummed her fingers on the counter. She slammed the phone down when no one answered. With a sudden gesture, she picked up a magazine and leafed quickly through its pages. Then, just as quickly, she threw the magazine down on the table in front of her. She sat stiffly in her chair, her feet tapping rapidly. Finally, the sound of running footsteps pounding up the steps made Donna sit up. She grabbed her jacket and ran out the door.**

4 Duplicate and distribute the Inferences Chart on the next page. Work with students to fill in the first row. Then have them add to the chart any other inferences they make about the passage. Sample responses are shown in the Answer Key on page T683.

Inference Chart

Name _____ **Date** _____

Selection Information	+	My Opinion/ What I Know	=	My Inference/ My Judgment
	+		=	
	+		=	
	+		=	
	+		=	

Making Inferences

Donna paced up and down the room. When she heard footsteps outside, she ran to the window and looked outside. As her eyes searched up and down the street, her hopeful smile faded. She turned away from the window, glanced at her watch, and heaved a big sigh.

Donna walked over to the kitchen phone and dialed a number. As she held the receiver to her ear, she drummed her fingers on the counter. She slammed the phone down when no one answered. With a sudden gesture, she picked up a magazine and leafed quickly through its pages. Then, just as quickly, she threw the magazine down on the table in front of her. She sat stiffly in her chair, her feet tapping rapidly. Finally, the sound of running footsteps pounding up the steps made Donna sit up. She grabbed her jacket and ran out the door.

Predicting

COMPREHENSION MINI-LESSON

1 To introduce the concept of predicting, ask students to make a guess about what they will study in their next class based on what they already know. Use the following points to explain how the strategy applies to reading a story.

- When you **predict,** you try to figure out what will happen next based upon what has already happened.
- To make a **prediction,** you must combine clues in a story with your own knowledge and experience to make a reasonable guess.
- Good readers make and revise predictions about characters, setting, and plot as they read. Sometimes, they don't even realize they're doing it.
- Sometimes you must first make a guess or inference about what is happening before you can predict what will happen next. *(Chan read his book as he walked down the street. A sleeping dog lay in his path.)* You might infer that Chan isn't looking where he is going. Since a sleeping dog lies in his path, you could then use the inference to predict that Chan is going to trip over it.

2 Duplicate the following paragraph. A master is provided on page T655. Have students follow along as you read it aloud, using it to model the skill of **predicting.**

> **Rachel walked into her room, sat down at her desk, and opened up her math book.**

You could say: *The first sentence tells me that Rachel is at home and sitting at her desk. Since she opens her math book, I think that Rachel is preparing to do some homework. I'll read further to see if my prediction is right.*

> **As she worked on some word problems, she felt her eyelids become heavy and she had trouble keeping her eyes open.**

You could say: *The second sentence tells me that Rachel is working on word problems. However, the description of her heavy eyelids suggests that she is very sleepy. Since she is having trouble keeping her eyes open, I predict that Rachel will fall asleep.*

> **With an effort, Rachel shook her head and sat up straighter. She had to be ready for the big math test tomorrow. Even as she told herself this, however, her head sank until it was resting on her arm, and she fell fast asleep.**

You could say: *My predictions were right. On the basis of the fact that Rachel isn't going to be prepared for the math test, I can also predict that she won't do very well on it.*

3 Duplicate the following passage. A master is provided on page T655. Instruct students to follow along as you read it aloud. Afterwards, students should be ready to infer what has happened and to predict what will happen next.

> **Marcus grabbed the leash off the hook and whistled for his dog. "Come on, Max," Marcus said, attaching the leash to the dog's collar. "Let's go to the park."**
> **The park was full of people. Marcus led Max to a quiet area away from the crowds. He unleashed the dog and let Max roam freely on the grass.**
> **Marcus watched the dog, but after a while his mind began to wander. Then with a start, Marcus remembered the dog. He looked all around, but Max was nowhere in sight. As he neared the picnic area, Marcus heard loud, angry voices. Suddenly, Max appeared with a couple of hamburgers in his mouth. Marcus leashed his dog and made him drop the burgers. Marcus was holding the pieces of meat when the angry picnickers caught sight of him.**

4 Duplicate and distribute the Predicting Chart on the next page. Have students work in pairs to complete the chart. Possible responses are shown in the Answer Key on page T683.

Predicting Chart

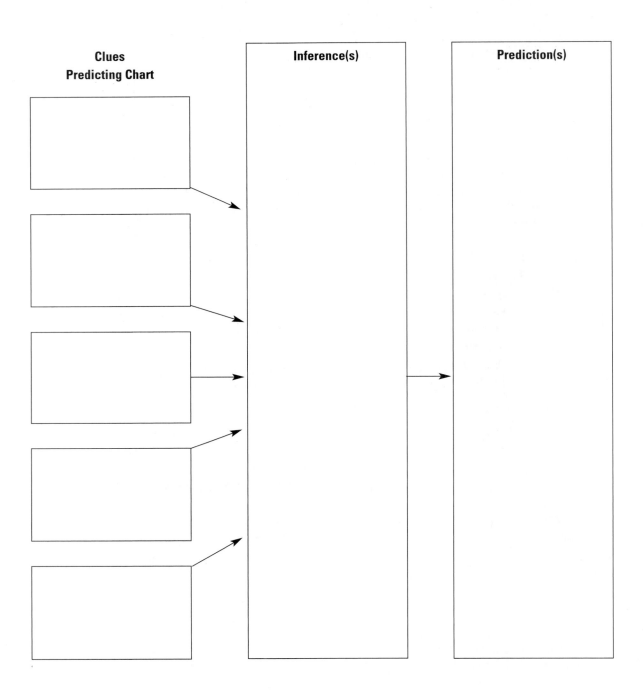

Clues
Predicting Chart

Inference(s)

Prediction(s)

Predicting

Rachel walked into her room, sat down at her desk, and opened up her math book.

As she worked on some word problems, she felt her eyelids become heavy and she had trouble keeping her eyes open.

With an effort, Rachel shook her head and sat up straighter. She had to be ready for the big math test tomorrow. Even as she told herself this, however, her head sank until it was resting on her arm, and she fell fast asleep.

Marcus grabbed the leash off the hook and whistled for his dog. "Come on, Max," Marcus said, attaching the leash to the dog's collar. "Let's go to the park."

The park was full of people. Marcus led Max to a quiet area away from the crowds. He unleashed the dog and let Max roam freely on the grass.

Marcus watched the dog, but after a while his mind began to wander. Then with a start, Marcus remembered the dog. He looked all around, but Max was nowhere in sight. As he neared the picnic area, Marcus heard loud, angry voices. Suddenly, Max appeared with a couple of hamburgers in his mouth. Marcus leashed his dog and made him drop the burgers. Marcus was holding the pieces of meat when the angry picnickers caught sight of him.

Fact and Opinion

COMPREHENSION MINI-LESSON

1 Use examples from textbooks, newspapers, magazines, and pamphlets as you discuss the following points about distinguishing fact and opinion:

- A **fact** is a statement that can be proved or disproved through observation, experience, and research. A fact may include supporting evidence, such as statistics or quotations from a recognized expert.

- An **opinion** is a statement that tells what a writer thinks, believes, or feels about a subject. It cannot be proved true or false.

- A writer may use words and phrases such as the following to signal an opinion: *according to, I think, in my opinion, perhaps, seem, should, bad, good, the best, the worst, terrible*. A writer may also use words that appeal to the reader's emotions.

- Sometimes a writer will use one or more facts to support an opinion.

- A single statement can contain both a fact and an opinion.

- A statement that you agree with is not necessarily a fact.

2 Duplicate the following paragraph. A master is provided on page T658. Have students follow along as you read it aloud, using it to model the skill of **distinguishing between fact and opinion.**

> **Every student should take a computer class. Computers are used in more and more jobs. Some students don't have computers at home. Also, computers are fun. I think everyone should use them.**

You could say: First I look for numbers, statistics, or quotations from experts. If I don't find any, there's a good chance that the statements are the writer's opinion.

Next I look for words that might signal opinions. The first sentence contains the signal word should. *This word tells me that the first sentence is an opinion. The second and third sentences do not contain any signal words, but I know that these statements are true. The fourth sentence does not contain any signal words that would tell me it is an opinion. However, it is not a statement that could be proved true or false. Some people think computers are fun; others don't like them. The last sentence contains the words* I think *and* should. *These words signal an opinion.*

3 For reference, write on the board the signal words and phrases listed in the third bulleted item above. Then duplicate the following paragraph and read it aloud. A master is provided on page T658.

> **Volunteer work is the best. I have been a volunteer at an animal shelter for six months. It is great! I walk the dogs and answer the phones. Many hospitals, shelters, and soup kitchens use volunteers. Everyone should be a volunteer.**

4 Duplicate and distribute the Two-Column Chart on the next page and ask students to use it to list the facts and opinions in the paragraph. Suggest that they highlight any signal words that helped them distinguish between the two types of statements.

5 Have volunteers share their completed charts, explaining why they listed each statement where they did. Correct responses are shown in the Answer Key on page T684.

6 Make additional copies of the chart on page T657 and have them available for students to use at appropriate times during the year.

Two Column Chart

Name _____ **Date** _____

<table>
<tr><td></td><td></td></tr>
<tr><td></td><td></td></tr>
</table>

Fact and Opinion

Every student should take a computer class. Computers are used in more and more jobs. Some students don't have computers at home. Also, computers are fun. I think everyone should use them.

Volunteer work is the best. I have been a volunteer at an animal shelter for six months. It is great! I walk the dogs and answer the phones. Many hospitals, shelters, and soup kitchens use volunteers. Everyone should be a volunteer.

Narrative Elements

COMPREHENSION MINI-LESSON

1 Duplicate the following passage. A master is provided on page T661. Have students follow along as you read it aloud.

> Last Friday night I had a scary experience. I was baby-sitting the two Guterson kids while their parents were at the movies. The kids were asleep in bed, and I was looking forward to a peaceful evening. Then I heard it—a *thud, thud, thud* on the door to the basement. Someone or something was trying to get out.
>
> I walked quietly over to the basement door. What should I do? Call the police? Go to a neighbor's house? Open the door?
>
> "Maybe it's nothing," I told myself. "Maybe it was just the wind, or I was imagining things."
>
> *Thud, thud, thud.* The door shook a little on its hinges.

Ask students when and where this story takes place. *(at a neighbor's house last Friday)* Have them tell whom the story is about. *(a babysitter, two kids named Guterson, the kids' parents, and someone or something in the basement)* Ask them what the story problem is. *(The person or animal in the basement is trying to get out!)*

2 Discuss with students the following elements of a narrative:

- The **setting** is when and where a story takes place. It is important for two reasons. First, it helps the reader visualize the story where it occurs. Also, a setting creates a context for the events that take place. For example, if you are reading a story that takes place at the North Pole, you would know that the characters are very unlikely to face a heat wave. Or, if you are reading a story that takes place in prehistoric times, you would not expect any of the characters to be talking on the telephone.

- **Characters** are the people in a story. The main character is the person who the story is mostly about. One of the reasons good stories are effective is that the characters seem real or interesting, so that the reader cares about what happens to them. Remind students that the characters in a story can also be animals or imaginary creatures.

- The **plot** is the series of events that happen in a story. Most stories have a problem, or **conflict,** that the main character must try to resolve. The **resolution** is the solution to the problem. In general, plot is driven by conflict. In other words, the events in a story generally revolve around the conflict, and the events that occur either contribute to the problem or contribute to the solution of the problem.

3 Continue the story by duplicating the following passage and reading it aloud. A master is provided on page T662.

> "Who's there?" I asked, my voice shaking a bit. "What do you want?"
>
> Then the door opened—the front door, not the basement door. Mr. and Mrs. Guterson walked in.
>
> "What a great movie!" Mrs. Guterson said. "You've just got to see—hey, what's wrong?"
>
> "The basement," I mumbled. "There's something . . ."
>
> *Thud, thud, thud.*
>
> "Oh, that's just Sarah," Mrs. Guterson said. She opened the basement door. An orange-and-black cat slipped through, gave me a furious look, and ran upstairs.
>
> "You weren't scared, were you?" said Mr. Guterson.
>
> "No, of course not," I answered.

4 Duplicate and distribute the Story Map on page T660. Work with students to fill in the setting and characters. Then have them complete the plot portion of the map. Possible responses are shown in the Answer Key on page T684.

5 Make additional copies of the Story Map and have them available for students to use at appropriate times during the year.

Story Map

Name _____ Date _____

Setting

Characters

Plot

    Problem:

    Events:

    1

    2

    3

    4

    Resolution:

Narrative Elements

Last Friday night I had a scary experience. I was baby-sitting the two Guterson kids while their parents were at the movies. The kids were asleep in bed, and I was looking forward to a peaceful evening. Then I heard it—a *thud, thud, thud* on the door to the basement. Someone or something was trying to get out.

I walked quietly over to the basement door. What should I do? Call the police? Go to a neighbor's house? Open the door?

"Maybe it's nothing," I told myself. "Maybe it was just the wind, or I was imagining things."

Thud, thud, thud. The door shook a little on its hinges.

"Who's there?" I asked, my voice shaking a bit. "What do you want?"

Then the door opened—the front door, not the basement door. Mr. and Mrs. Guterson walked in.

"What a great movie!" Mrs. Guterson said. "You've just got to see—hey, what's wrong?"

"The basement," I mumbled. "There's something . . ."

Thud, thud, thud.

"Oh, that's just Sarah," Mrs. Guterson said. She opened the basement door. An orange-and-black cat slipped through, gave me a furious look, and ran upstairs.

"You weren't scared, were you?" said Mr. Guterson.

"No, of course not," I answered.

Additional Graphic Organizers

How to Use Additional Graphic Organizers

On the following pages you will find additional graphic organizers that can be used in a number of different situations to help students comprehend and monitor what they read. Consult the chart below to decide how and when to use each graphic organizer.

Graphic Organizer	Purpose	When and How to Use
K-W-L Chart (page T666)	To help students comprehend a nonfiction selection	*Before Reading:* 1. Identify the topic for students. 2. Have students write what they already **know** about it in the *K* column. 3. Have them write what they **want** to find out in the *W* column. *During Reading:* 4. Have students record what they **learn** in the *L* column.
Q & A Notetaking Chart (page T667)	To help students memorize key facts in a nonfiction selection	*During Reading:* 1. Tell students that as they read, they should turn each heading or main idea into a question and write it in column 1. *After Reading:* 2. Have students answer the questions they wrote without opening their books. 3. Have students reread the selection to find answers to any questions they could not answer.
Concept Web (page T668)	To guide students to think of related words or concepts	*Before Reading:* Have students form small groups. List key concepts or vocabulary words on the board. Ask students to discuss meanings and to fill out a web for each concept or word by writing it in the center of the web and then writing related terms in the circles around the center.
Reflection Chart (page T669)	To help students stop and think about key points or events	*During Reading:* 1. Ask students to note important or interesting passages in the left column. 2. Have them record in the right column their thoughts about each passage noted.
Event Log (page T670)	To help students keep track of story events	*During Reading:* 1. Have students list each event as they read about it. *After Reading:* 2. Students should use the list to give an oral retelling or summary of the selection.

Graphic Organizer	Purpose	When and How to Use
Story Frames (page T671)	To help students summarize story events	*After Reading:* 1. Ask students to draw sketches of key events in the selection. 2. Have them use the sketches to retell the selection orally.
Plot Diagram (page T672)	To help students classify events as being part of the introduction, rising action, climax, or falling action and conclusion	*After Reading:* 1. Review the terms *introduction, rising action, climax,* and *falling action and conclusion* with students. 2. Encourage students to use the diagram to list the events that form each of these plot phases.
Character Profile Chart (page T673)	To help students identify character attributes	*During or After Reading:* Have students write the character's name at the center and then, in the surrounding boxes, list qualities and the behaviors that exemplify those qualities.
New Word Diagram (page T674)	To help students understand new vocabulary they encounter	*During or After Reading:* 1. Have students write a new word in the box at the top of the diagram. 2. Encourage them to think of—or look in the dictionary for—synonyms and antonyms of the word and record them in the appropriate boxes. 3. Ask students to think of real people or characters they've read about whom they associate with the concept of the word. They can then add the names to the diagram.
Reading Log (page T681)	To encourage students to keep track of what they read	*After Reading:* Have students record on this form each selection they read during the year. Review the form periodically with students.

K-W-L Chart

Name _____   Date _____

Topic: _____

K What I Know	W What I Want to Find Out	L What I Learn

Q & A Notetaking Chart

Name _____ **Date** _____

Turn the Heading or Main Idea of Each Passage into a Question	Write a Detailed Answer Here
1.	
2.	
3.	
4.	
5.	
6.	
7.	

Concept Web

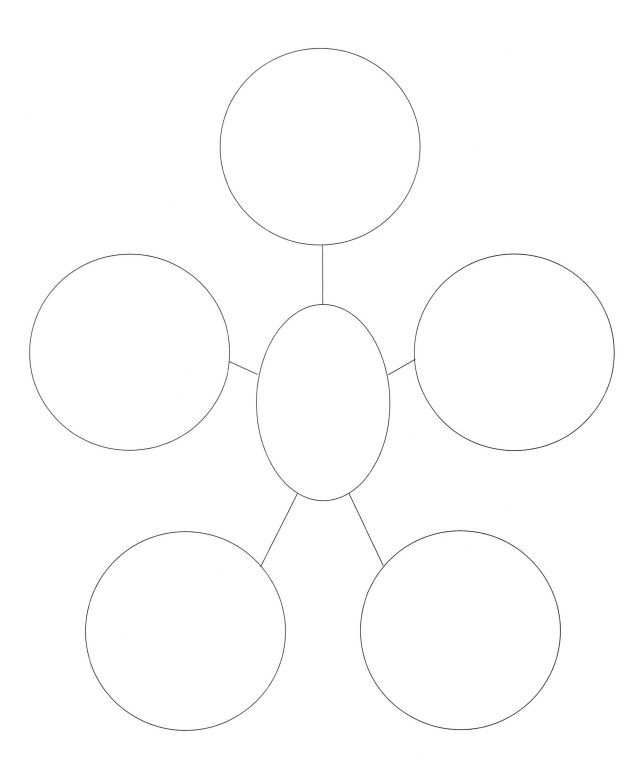

Reflection Chart

Quotation or Paraphrase from Text (include page number)	Thoughts About It

Event Log

Event 1

Event 2

Event 3

Event 4

Event 5

Event 6

Event 7

Event 8

Event 9

Event 10

Story Frames

Name _____ **Date** _____

Plot Diagram

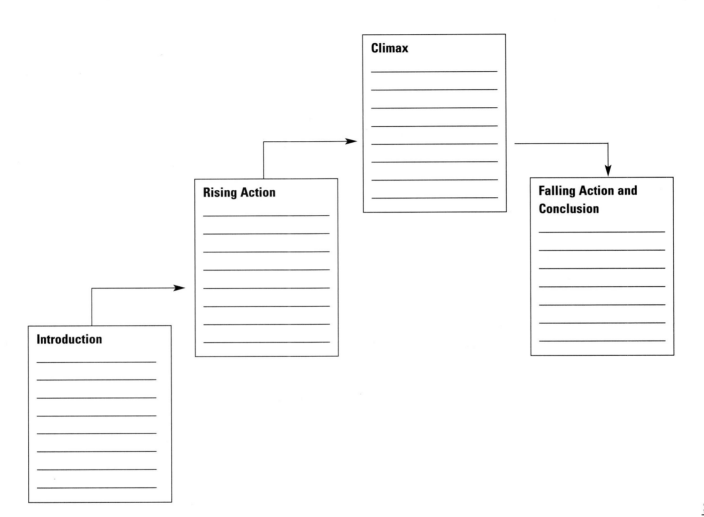

Climax
_____
_____
_____
_____
_____
_____

Rising Action
_____
_____
_____
_____
_____
_____
_____

Falling Action and Conclusion
_____
_____
_____
_____
_____
_____

Introduction
_____
_____
_____
_____
_____
_____
_____

Character Profile Chart

Name ______________________ **Date** ______________

Quality: ______________
Example: ______________

Quality: ______________
Example: ______________

Quality: ______________
Example: ______________

____
Character's Name

Quality: ______________
Example: ______________

Quality: ______________
Example: ______________

Quality: ______________
Example: ______________

New Word Diagram

Word:

Synonyms:

Antonyms:

People or Characters I Associate with the Word:

Independent Reading

HELPING STUDENTS TO BECOME INDEPENDENT READERS

- Become an avid reader and show students your love of reading. Become familiar with popular books and magazines. Share information with students—they will appreciate it.

- Provide students with the opportunity to visit the school library on a regular basis.

- Build a classroom library. If possible, provide a wide range of reading materials so that students are exposed to diverse topics and genres. Respect students' reading choices. Struggling readers need first to view themselves as readers.

- Have each student keep a Reading Log. As the list grows, students will be encouraged to read more.

- Encourage students to keep a reading journal. Tell students to write down their thoughts every time they read. Prepare a list of questions for them to think about as they read. Be sure to emphasize that grammar, spelling, and length are not important in their journal.

- Encourage students to read to a younger sibling, a friend, or a parent.

- Read aloud to your students and hook them on some authors and genres they might not have tackled themselves. For most material, students' listening comprehension is more advanced than their comprehension of written material. Listening helps them develop the thinking skills needed to understand complex text.

- Provide opportunities for readers to reflect on what they have read. These can involve group or class discussion and writing in journals and logs.

WHEN IS A GOOD TIME FOR STUDENTS TO DO INDEPENDENT READING?

Have students read daily. Allow time for sustained silent reading. Set aside classroom time for students to read self-selected materials. Students who read independently become better readers and are more likely to choose to read if they can pursue ideas they find interesting.

BOOKS FOR INDEPENDENT READING LEVEL III

BOOK	ANNOTATION
Joyful Noise: Poems for Two Voices Fleischman, Paul; 1988 44 pp. Mean DRP: N/A	Poems about insects
American Sports Poems Knudson, R. R., & Swenson, May; 1988 226 pp. Mean DRP: N/A	An anthology of sports poems
My Own True Name Mora, Pat; 2000 81 pp. Mean DRP: N/A	A collection of poems about growing up Mexican-American in the Southwest
Falling Up Silverstein, Shel; 1996 176 pp. Mean DRP: N/A	An anthology of humorous poems
A Fire in My Hands Soto, Gary; 1990 63 pp. Mean DRP: N/A	Gary Soto's personal poems about growing up in California in the '60s
Neighborhood Odes Soto, Gary; 1992 70 pp. Mean DRP: N/A	Poems in praise of growing up in a Latino neighborhood
It Came from Ohio!: My Life as a Writer Stine, R. L.; 1997 140 pp. Mean DRP: 50	Nonfiction: R. L. Stine, author of the Goosebumps and Fear Street series, tells about his childhood in Ohio.
*A Wrinkle in Time** L'Engle, Madeleine; 1962 211 pp. Mean DRP: 51	Meg and her little brother, Charles, travel through time in search of their father, a prisoner on an alien planet.
My Life with Chimpanzees Goodall, Jane; 1988 123 pp. Mean DRP: 52	Nonfiction: Jane Goodall studies wild chimpanzees in Africa.
*Number the Stars** Lowry, Lois; 1989 137 pp. Mean DRP: 52	Annemarie, a Dutch girl, and Ellen, a Jewish girl, are best friends. Annemarie tries to save Ellen from the Nazis.

BOOK	ANNOTATION
The Story of Harriet Tubman, Conductor of the Underground Railroad McMullan, Kate; 1991 108 pp. Mean DRP: 52	Nonfiction: The story of Harriet Tubman, an escaped slave who led over 300 slaves to freedom
Marco Polo: His Notebook Roth, Susan L.; 1990 30 pp. Mean DRP: 52	Nonfiction: The journal of 17-year-old Marco Polo as he begins an incredible adventure in 1271
Taking Sides* Soto, Gary; 1991 138 pp. Mean DRP: 52	Fourteen-year-old Lincoln Mendoza's loyalties are divided when his new suburban basketball team plays against his old team from the barrio.
Marching to Freedom: The Story of Martin Luther King Jr. Milton, Joyce; 1987 92 pp. Mean DRP: 53	Nonfiction: A biography of Martin Luther King, Jr.
Island of the Blue Dolphins* O'Dell, Scott; 1960 189 pp. Mean DRP: 53	Karana, an Indian girl, lives alone on an island for 18 years.
Woodsong Paulsen, Gary; 1990 132 pp. Mean DRP: 53	Nonfiction: Author Gary Paulsen tells about his life and adventures with his sled dogs.
The Bronze Bow Speare, Elizabeth George; 1961 254 pp. Mean DRP: 53	Daniel's parents are killed, and all he can think about is revenge. Something happens to change his mind.
Roll of Thunder, Hear My Cry* Taylor, Mildred D.; 1976 276 pp. Mean DRP: 53	Cassie Logan, a young black girl, struggles to remain proud and independent during the Depression in Mississippi.
Dicey's Song Voigt, Cynthia; 1982 196 pp. Mean DRP: 53	Dicey Tillerman brings her brothers and sister to live with their eccentric grandmother.
The Education of Little Tree Carter, Forrest; 1976 216 pp. Mean DRP: 54	Forrest Carter remembers living with his Cherokee grandparents during the 1930s.

BOOK	ANNOTATION
Memories of Anne Frank: Reflections of a Childhood Friend Gold, Alison Leslie; 1997 135 pp. Mean DRP: 54	Nonfiction: Hannah Goslar, Anne Frank's close friend and classmate in Amsterdam, shares her memories of Anne before the war separated them.
The Lion, the Witch, and the Wardrobe Lewis, C. S.; 1950 186 pp. Mean DRP: 54	Peter, Edmund, Suzy, and Lucy magically pass through a wardrobe into the land of Narnia.
The Story of Nin: The Chimp Who Learned Language Michel, Anna; 1980 59 pp. Mean DRP: 54	Nonfiction: The story of Nin, a chimpanzee who was raised like a human baby
Your Two Brains Stafford, Patricia; 1986 75 pp. Mean DRP: 54	Nonfiction: Informational book about the function of the left and right sides of the brain
Stuart Little White, E. B.; 1945 131 pp. Mean DRP: 54	A humorous story about Stuart, second son of the Littles, who is only 2 inches tall and a mouse!
I'm Nobody! Who Are You? Barth, Edna; 1971 128 pp. Mean DRP: 55	Nonfiction: The life and times of the famous poet Emily Dickinson
My Life as an Astronaut Bean, Alan; 1988 105 pp. Mean DRP: 55	Nonfiction: Alan Bean tells how he came to be an astronaut and what it felt like being part of the Apollo crew.
*Johnny Tremain** Forbes, Esther; 1943 256 pp. Mean DRP: 55	In 1773, Johny Tremain, a young apprentice silversmith, becomes involved in the American Revolution.
Lost Star: The Story of Amelia Earhart Lauber, Patricia; 1988 106 pp. Mean DRP: 55	Nonfiction: The story of Amelia Earhart, the first woman to fly solo across the Atlantic Ocean
Baseball in April and Other Stories Soto, Gary; 1990 137 pp. Mean DRP: 55	Eleven short stories about life in California's Central Valley
Call It Courage Sperry, Armstrong; 1963 92 pp. Mean DRP: 55	Ten-year-old Mafatu fears the sea but sets out to sea in a canoe to prove he is not a coward.

BOOK	ANNOTATION
Pride of Puerto Rico: The Life of Roberto Clemente Walker, Paul Robert; 1988 157 pp. Mean DRP: 55	Nonfiction: A biography of baseball legend Roberto Clemente
Anne Frank: Child of the Holocaust Brown, Gene; 1991 64 pp. Mean DRP: 56	Nonfiction: The story of Anne Frank, a 13-year-old girl who kept a diary while she was hiding from the Nazis
The Midwife's Apprentice Cushman, Karen; 1995 122 pp. Mean DRP: 56	A homeless girl in 14th-century England is taken in by a midwife named Jane, who makes her her apprentice.
Boy: Tales of Childhood Dahl, Roald; 1984 176 pp. Mean DRP: 56	Nonfiction: Roald Dahl recalls his boyhood in England, summers in Norway, and the "Great Mouse Plot" of 1924.
Nelson Mandela Falstein, Mark; 1994 73 pp. Mean DRP 56	Nonfiction: The story of Nelson Mandela's fight against apartheid
Frozen Man Getz, David; 1994 68 pp. Mean DRP: 56	Nonfiction: Scientists use clues to recreate the death and life of a man who died more than 5,000 years ago.
Great Lives: Human Rights Jacobs, William Jay; 1990 278 pp. Mean DRP: 56	Nonfiction: A portrayal of 29 people who contributed to the struggle for human rights in the United States
The Giver* Lowry, Lois; 1993 180 pp. Mean DRP: 56	Jonas discovers the truth about his "perfect" society when he is chosen to become a "receiver of memories."
How Do We Dream? and Other Questions About Your Body Myers, Jack; 1992 60 pp. Mean DRP: 56	Nonfiction: Scientists answer questions about the human body.
Satchel Paige: All-Time Baseball Great Rubin, Robert; 1974 157 pp. Mean DRP: 56	Nonfiction: The life and career of one of baseball's greatest pitchers, Leroy "Satchel" Paige

BOOK	ANNOTATION
Knots in My Yo-Yo String: The Autobiography of a Kid Spinelli, Jerry; 1998 148 pp. Mean DRP: 56	Nonfiction: The creator of Maniac Magee recalls his childhood.
Journey to Topaz Uchida, Yoshiko; 1971 149 pp. Mean DRP: 56	Nonfiction: When Pearl Harbor is bombed, Yuki's life suddenly changes.
Earthquake!: San Francisco, 1906 Wilson, Kate; 1993 62 pp. Mean DRP: 56	People unite to survive when a terrible earthquake devastates San Francisco in 1906.
Arctic Explorer: The Story of Matthew Henson Ferris, Jeri; 1989 80 pp. Mean DRP: 57	Nonfiction: The story of Matthew Henson, a black explorer who reached the North Pole alongside Robert Peary in April 1909
Seeing Earth from Space Lauber, Patricia; 1990 80 pp. Mean DRP: 57	Nonfiction: A look at photographs taken from space
Michael Jordan Lovitt, Chip; 1995 186 pp. Mean DRP: 57	Nonfiction: The life and career of one of basketball's greatest legends

*Available in a Literature Connections volume from McDougal Littell

Reading Log

Name _____ **Date** _____

Title/Author	Genre	Date Finished	Reactions

Comprehension Mini-Lessons Answer Key

Main Idea and Details

Main Idea	Details
Paragraph 1: Every year hundreds of people report seeing UFOs, or unidentified flying objects.	• Have you ever seen a flying saucer? • Most UFOs turn out to be ordinary things. • Some are weather balloons. • Others are planes. • Still others are shooting stars. • Some people make fake pictures of UFOs to get attention.
Paragraph 2: Most scientists don't think aliens have visited Earth.	• So far, we have not found intelligent life in space. • Also, the distance from Earth to other planets is huge. • It would be very hard for aliens to come here.

Sequence

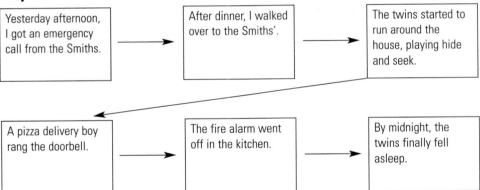

Yesterday afternoon, I got an emergency call from the Smiths.	→ After dinner, I walked over to the Smiths'.	→ The twins started to run around the house, playing hide and seek.
A pizza delivery boy rang the doorbell.	→ The fire alarm went off in the kitchen.	→ By midnight, the twins finally fell asleep.

Cause and Effect

Cause	→	Effect(s)
The narrator's mother decided the family should learn about nature.	→	The family went on a camping trip. They had an awful time.
The family brought the wrong kinds of camping supplies.	→	The family will do more research when planning the next vacation.

Comparison and Contrast

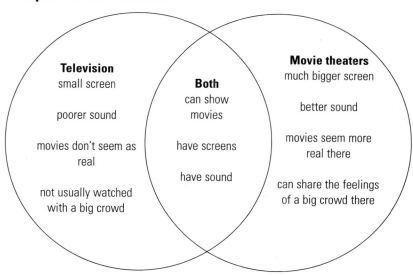

Television
small screen

poorer sound

movies don't seem as real

not usually watched with a big crowd

Both
can show movies

have screens

have sound

Movie theaters
much bigger screen

better sound

movies seem more real there

can share the feelings of a big crowd there

Making Inferences

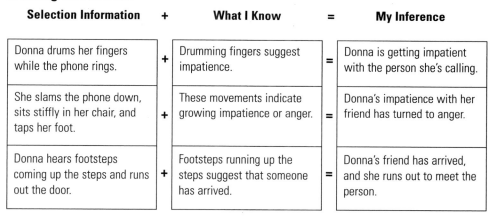

Selection Information	+	What I Know	=	My Inference
Donna drums her fingers while the phone rings.	+	Drumming fingers suggest impatience.	=	Donna is getting impatient with the person she's calling.
She slams the phone down, sits stiffly in her chair, and taps her foot.	+	These movements indicate growing impatience or anger.	=	Donna's impatience with her friend has turned to anger.
Donna hears footsteps coming up the steps and runs out the door.	+	Footsteps running up the steps suggest that someone has arrived.	=	Donna's friend has arrived, and she runs out to meet the person.

Predicting

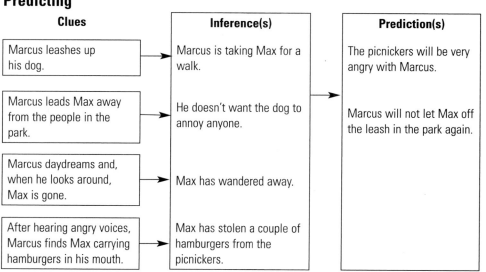

Clues	Inference(s)	Prediction(s)
Marcus leashes up his dog.	Marcus is taking Max for a walk.	The picnickers will be very angry with Marcus.
Marcus leads Max away from the people in the park.	He doesn't want the dog to annoy anyone.	Marcus will not let Max off the leash in the park again.
Marcus daydreams and, when he looks around, Max is gone.	Max has wandered away.	
After hearing angry voices, Marcus finds Max carrying hamburgers in his mouth.	Max has stolen a couple of hamburgers from the picnickers.	

Fact and Opinion

Fact	Opinion
• I have been a volunteer at an animal shelter for six months. • I walk the dogs and answer the phones. • Many hospitals, shelters, and soup kitchens use volunteers.	• Volunteer work is the best. • It is great! • Everyone should be a volunteer.

Narrative Elements

Setting at the Gutersons' house last Friday night	**Characters** the narrator, the two Guterson kids, their parents, and possibly someone or something in the basement

---

Plot

Problem: The narrator is baby-sitting when he or she hears noises at the basement door. Who or what is trying to get in the house?

Events:

   1. The narrator walks to the door and hears the noises again.

   2. The narrator asks who is there.

   3. The parents get home. The narrator tries to explain what is wrong.

Resolution: Mrs. Guterson opens the basement door to let the cat out.

Skills Index

*Numbers in **boldface** refer to SkillBuilder worksheets.*

Comprehension Skills

Anticipatory guide, T401
Argument, T328, T329, T330, **T331, T334**
Author's perspective, T84, T86, T361, T362, **T363, T366**
Author's purpose, T131, T132, **T133, T136,** T301, T402, T405, **T406, T409,** T458, **T460, T462,** T541, T558, T560
Bias, **T363, T366**
Building background, T13, T27, T41, T57, T69, T83, T95, T111, T131, T159, T173, T199, T203, T207, T215, T229, T245, T255, T285, T297, T311, T327, T373, T387, T401, T415, T432, T437, T442, T447, T457, T469, T481, T497, T505, T533, T551, T569
Cause and effect, T16, T42, T44, T45, **T47, T49,** T59, T71, T73, T85, T86, T178, T179, T181, T184, T187, T199, T231, T232, T233, T235, T272, T273, T298, T301, **T302, T304,** T328, T341, T342, T351, T352, T376, T391, T392, T402, T403, T404, T405, **T406, T408,** T443, T448, T459, T485, T488, T539, T553, T554, T557, T559, T560, **T561, T563,** T570, T572, T574, T575, T576, T577, T578, T580, **T581, T583**
Character, T17
Chronological order, T58, T59, T60, **T61, T63,** T71, T96, T97, T98, T99, **T100, T102,** T470, **T473, T476,** T552, T553, T557, **T561, T563**
Clarifying, T14, T16, T163, T164, T175, T183, T185, T234, T313, T330, T553, T558
Compare and contrast, T15, T16, T28, T29, T30, T31, T32, **T33, T35,** T84, T143, T145, T147, T148, T179, T184, T207, T233, T299, T301, T328, T342, T375, T377, T378, T418, T433, T470, T472, **T473, T475,** T508, T509, T521, T534, T537, T540, T541, **T542, T544,** T555, T557, **T561, T563,** T579
Conclusions, drawing, T60, T74, T85, T126, T132, T145, T146, T147, T148, T163, T164, T235, T259, T286, T314, T315, T328, T330, **T331, T333,** T361, T362, T378, T389, T392, T418, T420, T498, T499, T541, T559, T560

Connecting, T13, T27, T41, T56, T69, T83, T95, T111, T124, T130, T141, T159, T173, T198, T202, T206, T210, T214, T219, T229, T244, T255, T269, T285, T297, T311, T327, T339, T350, T360, T373, T387, T401, T415, T419, T432, T437, T442, T447, T469, T481, T497, T505, T519, T533, T551, T569, T574
Contrast. *See* Compare and contrast.
Description, T471, T552
Details, T17, T30, T32, T43, T44, T70, T72, T73, T74, **T75, T78,** T84, T96, T97, T98, T99, T112, T113, T114, T115, T132, T142, T143, T146, T148, T149, **T151,** T186, T187, T256, T257, T272, **T290,** T340, T341, T342, **T343, T345,** T352, T389, T390, T403, T448, T470, T485, T487, **T489,** T509, T520, T536, T537, T552, T554, **T561, T563,** T570, T571, T578
Evaluating, T30, T32, T273, T312, T313, T315, **T316, T318,** T351, T352, **T353, T355,** T362, T554, T580
Evidence, T328, T329, T330, **T331, T334**
Fact and opinion, T84, T85, T86, **T87, T89,** T361, T362, **T363, T365,** T405
Fluency. *See* Reading fluency.
Inferences, making, T17, T31, T32, T59, T60, T71, T99, T112, T114, T115, **T116, T118,** T126, T132, T144, T145, T148, T160, T161, T162, T163, T164, **T165, T167,** T175, T176, T177, T178, T179, T180, T182, T183, T184, T185, T199, T207, T211, T220, T234, T235, T246, T258, T273, T286, T299, T314, T374, T375, T377, T378, T388, T390, T391, T404, T405, T416, T417, T421, T448, T459, T472, T483, T484, T485, T486, T487, T488, T507, T509, T520, T521, **T522, T524,** T535, T539, T541, T560, T571, T573, T574, T580
Judgments, making, T70, T72, T73, T74, **T75, T77,** T85, T97, T114, T258, T287, T290, T388, T392, **T393, T395,** T421, T486, T509, T541, T560
K-W-L chart, T533, T541, T580
Main idea, T58, T340, T341, T342, **T343, T345,** T405, T416, T420, **T422, T424,** T470, **T473, T476,** T482, T483, **T489, T491,** T506, T509, **T510, T512,** T554, **T561, T563**

Opinion. *See* Fact and opinion.

Oral interpretation, T484

Organization, T470, **T473, T476,** T552, **T561, T563, T564.** *See also* Cause and effect; Chronological order; Compare and contrast; Details; Main idea.

Outcome, T416

Paraphrasing, T231, T235

Predicting, T43, T113, T161, T162, T178, T180, T186, T187, T258, T270, T271, T286, T287, **T288, T290,** T329, T374, T376, T378, **T379, T381,** T459, T498

Problem and solution, T162, T230, T231, T234, T259, T270, T271, T272, **T274, T276,** T416, T417, T419, T421, **T422, T425,** T472, T534, T536, T537

Questioning, T362. *See also* SQ3R.

Reading fluency, **T25, T107, T195, T267, T281, T295, T323, T413, T429, T517, T549**

Reading for details, **T100, T103**

Recall, T186

Recording. *See* SQ3R.

Reviewing. *See* SQ3R.

Sequence, T174, T176, T180, T182, T183, **T188, T190,** T230, T235, **T236, T238,** T471, T498, **T500, T501**

Signal words, T58, T174

SQ3R, **T100, T103**

Summarizing, T16, T98, T131, T132, **T133, T135,** T211, T234, T245, T246, **T247, T249,** T287, T290, T329, T471, T538, T556, T558, T573

Supporting details. *See* Details.

Surveying. *See* SQ3R.

Text structure, T340, **T343, T346**

Topic sentence, T506, **T510, T512**

Visualizing, T14, **T18, T20,** T144, T176, T256, T257, T259, **T260, T262,** T470

Visuals, understanding, T71, T471, T506, T507, **T510, T513,** T540, T554, T558, T570, T572, T576

Literature Skills

Acrostic, T134, T138

Alliteration, T125, T126

Ballad, T496, T497

Biographical essay, T351

Biography, T84, T85, T86, **T87, T90,** T551, T555, T559

Character, T15, T30, T32, **T33,** T159, T163, T177, T233, T271, T288, T482, T485, T488, T498, T499, T555. *See also* Motive.

Characterization, T28, T29, T30, **T33, T36,** T112, T113, T125, T126, T146, T178, T483, T556, T575

Character profile, T60, T551

Climax, T17, T18, **T21,** T174, T186, **T188, T191,** T270, T273, **T274, T277,** T488

Conclusion, **T18**

Conflict, T42, **T47, T50,** T74, T176, T181, T374, T376, **T379, T382,** T392, T534, T576. *See also* Internal conflict.

Descriptive details, T31, T256, T257, T258, T259, **T260, T263,** T471, T508, T552

Dialogue, T159, T178, T180, **T393, T396**

Dramatic form, T159, T160, **T165, T168.** *See also* Dialogue; Scenes; Stage directions.

End rhyme, T199

Essay, T351, **T353, T356.** *See also* Biographical essay.

External conflict. *See* Conflict.

Fairy tales, modern, T27, T29

Falling action, **T18,** T187, **T188, T191**

Figurative language, T299, T570, T571, T572, T573, T574, T577, T578, T579, **T581, T584.** *See also* Imagery; Metaphor; Personification; Simile.

First-person point of view. *See* Point of view.

Folk tale, T229

Foreshadowing, T234, T235

Form, poetic, T203, **T204, T205**

Free verse, T147, T220, T448, **T449, T450**

Haiku, T206, T207, **T208, T209**

Historical fiction, T245, T246, **T247, T250,** T482, T484, **T489, T492,** T536

Historical writing, nonfiction, T470

Humor, T175, T232, T443

Imagery, T126, T207, T215, **T216, T217,** T571

Informative nonfiction, T70, T328, T361, T402, T470, T506. *See also* Historical writing, nonfiction.

Internal conflict. T44, T45, T374, **T379, T382,** T418. *See also* Conflict.

Introduction, **T18, T188, T191**

Communications

Modeling

Assessment

Acknowledgments

Marshall Cavendish: Excerpt from "Mudslinging," from *Mud Matters* by Jennifer Owings Dewey. Copyright © 1998 by Jennifer Owings Dewey. Reprinted by arrangement with Marshall Cavendish.

Jesse Stuart Foundation and Marian Reiner, Literary Agent: Excerpt from "Another April," from *Tales from the Plum Grove Hills* by Jesse Stuart. Copyright © 1942, 1946 by Jesse Stuart, copyright renewed by Jesse Stuart and the Jesse Stuart Foundation. Used by permission of the Jesse Stuart Foundation and Marian Reiner, Literary Agent.

Hugh B. Cave: Excerpt from "Two Were Left" by Hugh B. Cave. Copyright © 1942 by the Crowell Collier Publishing Co. Reprinted by permission of the author.

Blackbirch Press: Excerpt from *Anne Frank: Child of the Holocaust* by Gene Brown. Copyright © 1991 by Blackbirch Press, Inc. Reprinted by permission.